COALITIONS BETWEEN TERRORIST ORGANIZATIONS

REVOLUTIONARIES, NATIONALISTS AND ISLAMISTS

Ely Karmon

MARTINUS NIJHOFF PUBLISHERS
Leiden / Boston

A C.I.P. Catalogue record for this book is available from the Library of Congress.

Printed on acid-free paper.

ISBN 90-04-14358-0
© 2005 by Koninklijke Brill NV, Leiden, The Netherlands.
Koninklijke Brill NV incorporates the imprints Brill Academic Publishers,
Martinus Nijhoff Publishers and VSP.

http://www.brill.nl

Printed and bound in the Netherlands

CONTENTS

In memory of my father

ACKNOWLEDGMENTS

It was many years after achieving three undergraduate degrees that I returned to academia and without the forceful encouragement of Dalia Hochberg, who urged me to embark on a doctorate at Haifa University, neither my academic career nor this book would have materialized. Dr. Uzi Arad, director of the Institute for Policy and Strategy at The Interdisciplinary Center, Herzliya, advised me to focus my research on the field of terrorism. He could not have realized then how important and strategic the issue of terrorism would become during the troubled 1990s. Prof. Ariel Merari of Tel Aviv University, the internationally acclaimed scholar of terrorism, gave me valuable advice as I took my first steps towards the thesis.

My thesis director, Prof. Zeev Maoz, then head of the Political Science Department at Haifa University, not only provided invaluable advice on the theoretical aspects of political science and personal support in a new and complex field but also opened for me the gates of the academia at Haifa University for which I am immensely grateful to him.

I would like to thank Haifa University, and especially the Political Science Department and the library staff of the university for their support during this research. The university also helped to finance my field trip to Europe for the research of archives in France and Italy.

Two individuals greatly helped in my difficult quest for primary data relating to terrorist organizations: Judge Severino Santiapichi of Italy, who presided over three of Italian premier Aldo Moro's assassination trials, granted me access the archives of the Rome Corte d'Assise and enabled me to study the invaluable juridical material on the Italian Red Brigades; Xavier Raufer, director of studies at the Institut de Criminologie, Université de Paris II, opened his personal archive, mainly on French and Belgian but also other European groups. My friend Reuven Paz, director of the Project for the Research of Islamist Movements (PRISM) at The Global Research in International Affairs (GLORIA) Center, The Interdisciplinary Center (IDC), Herzliya offered written articles, translated primary Arabic documents and engaged in personal discussions which enhanced my understanding of the ideology and strategy of Islamist organizations.

My warm academic home for the last seven years, the International Policy Institute for Counter-Terrorism (ICT) at IDC, under the leadership of its director Dr. Boaz Ganor, helped finance the translation of the book from Hebrew to English and thus brought about its publication.

Many thanks go to Yaffa Murciano for the professional translation that gave life to a quite dry text and to Juliet Landau-Pope who edited the manuscript into its present elegant form and gave me good advice for improving it.

Finally I must thank to my loving wife Aurelia and daughters Daniela and Maya who for five years supported my work on the book and missed a lot of the attention they deserved.

PREFACE

This book is based on a doctoral thesis submitted to the Department of Political Science at Haifa University, Israel. The theoretical framework describes conditions that favor the formation of coalitions between international terrorist organizations, and how they function within the changing international system. These theories are tested against empirical data on actual cooperation between European and Palestinian terrorist organizations from 1968 to 1990, and cooperation between European left-wing terrorist organizations (the phenomenon known as Euro-terrorism) from 1984 to 1988. These findings form the basis of a broader theory concerning cooperation and coalitions between organizations involved in international terrorism.

During the period under review, the international system was characterized by the existence of two polarized blocs, the Western democratic camp led by the US, and the Communist one led by the Soviet Union. While the relations between the blocs improved significantly since the mid-1980s, the respective political and military opposing alliances, namely the North Atlantic Treaty Organization (NATO) and the Warsaw Pact, still shaped their relations. Positioned between these forces were the majority of the so-called Third World countries, some of which achieved independence as late as the 1960s.

These specific international conditions influenced the strategies of various terrorist organizations, including their propensity to ally to other groups. Their behavior stemmed in great measure from their analysis of the interplay between the superpowers and their allies, major influential regional events and the changes in ideological or operational conditions.

The crumbling of the Soviet empire, the demise of the communist regimes in Eastern Europe and the disappearance of the Warsaw Pact at the beginning of the 1990s brought to an end the Cold War and the perceived military threat to the West. The victory of the broad US-led coalition in the first Gulf War against Iraq, the subsequent involvement of US military forces in Iraq, Somalia and the Balkans (following the dismantling of the former Yugoslavia), definitely signed the disappearance of the bi-polar system and the emergence of the US as the unique superpower.

In the terrorist arena major changes also occurred in the 1990s. Radical leftist and rightist groups and organizations still active by the end of the 1980s were either completely dismantled by the relentless activity of law enforcement agencies in Europe or renounced the armed struggle in light of the demise of Marxist-Leninist ideology and strategy. The nationalist organizations, with the Palestine Liberation Organization (PLO) in the forefront, followed by the Irish Republican Army and to a lesser degree the Basque Euzkadi ta Askatasuna (ETA), understood that survival in the new international environment would

depend on more than fighting; therefore they turned to the political and diplomatic process.

In parallel, new types of terrorist organizations developed and flourished.
Radical Islamist groups had been active since the beginning of the 1980s under
the influence of the 1979 Khomeini-led revolution in Iran, challenging the very
stability of Arab and Muslim countries but presenting an increasing threat to the
US itself, mainly by their presence in the Middle East, Central and South East
Asia. Radical Sunni Islamist groups, many identified as part of a global network
commonly known as al-Qaeda, became powerful new players, virtually the only
ones openly engaged in international terror.

It is important therefore to verify whether the new terrorist players driven, at
least theoretically, by religious motivation, will imitate the behavior of the
ideological or nationalist organizations. Will the new international circumstances
have a diverse effect on them? Do previous theories concerning cooperation and
coalitions between organizations apply to the new reality? A final chapter, in fact
more of an afterword on coalitions of the Islamist movement attempts to check
the theory which was developed and tested by this author on specific nationalist
and revolutionary organizations.

A clear lack of historical perspective, the vast number and diversity of Islamist
groups and movements involved, scarcity of reliable written sources, and the very
mystery that still surrounds the leadership and organizational framework of the al-
Qaeda network make it difficult to arrive at decisive conclusions. The task of this
author and others will remain, therefore, to continue the monitoring and analysis
of radical Islamist organizations in order to seek an answer to the viability and
effectiveness of the coalition of these radical religious/political movements and
the possibility for new kind of alliances, between them and anti-globalization or
ideologically driven groups.

ABOUT THE AUTHOR

Ely Karmon is a senior research scholar at the International Policy Institute for Counter-Terrorism (ICT), an internationally renowned think tank based at the Interdisciplinary Center (IDC) in Herzliya, Israel. He lectures on terrorism and guerrilla warfare at the IDC.

He holds a B.A. in English and French Culture from the Hebrew University in Jerusalem, a *licence* in international relations from the Institut d'Etudes Politiques and a *licence* in Bantu languages from the Ecole de Langues Orientales, in Paris. He took both his M.A and Ph.D. at the Department of Political Science at Haifa University.

In 2003, Dr. Karmon lectured on international terrorism in the Department of Political Science at Bar-Ilan University, Israel. In 2002, he was the Herbert and Shari Rosen visiting fellow at The Washington Institute. From 1992 to 2000, he lectured on international terrorism and European right-wing radical organizations in the Department of Political Science at Haifa University.

Dr. Karmon is an advisor to the Israeli Ministry of Defense and a member of the UN Interregional Crime and Justice Research Institute's (UNICRI) International Permanent Observatory on Security Measures during Major Events. He is also involved in several NATO workshops on terrorism. Previously, he served as advisor to the Anti-Semitism Monitoring Forum of the Israeli Government Secretariat.

Dr. Karmon has written extensively on international terrorism, WMD terrorism, the Israeli-Palestinian conflict, state-sponsored terrorism, and terrorism in Turkey. His last publication was 'Fight on All Fronts?: Hizballah, the War on Terror, and the War in Iraq,' a *Policy Focus* paper published by The Washington Institute for Near East Policy in December 2003.

INTRODUCTION

In the 1970s and 1980s many researchers emphasized the importance of international terror as a weapon in the struggle between the two ideologically opposed blocs. Some even defined this period as the Age of Terrorism.[1] Palestinian organizations evidently played an increasing role in international terror after the Six Day War of 1967, exerting a direct influence on other terrorist organizations, some of whose members trained in Palestinian camps.[2] The participation of German terrorists in operations carried out by the Popular Front for the Liberation of Palestine (PFLP), such as the hijacking of planes in European skies, and attacks on strategic targets such as OPEC headquarters in Vienna, as well as the emergence of 'Carlos' (Ilich Ramirez Sanchez) as a master of international terror, intensified fears in the mid-1970s that terrorist organizations were forming networks that threatened Western democratic states. The fact that most terrorist organizations belonged to the revolutionary left and had affiliations with the USSR or its satellites in the communist bloc or the Third World gave rise to theories of a Soviet-led international conspiracy against the West.

Bowyer Bell claimed that 'even if there is not a specific organizational structure for world revolution, the conviction of the committed is that there is a world revolutionary society, perhaps organized by national parties, perhaps in ideological disarray, but nevertheless real'.[3] International solidarity, he held, existed on an ideological level between revolutionary groups in Africa and the Middle East, Western Europe and Latin America. He described the leader of the PFLP, George Habbash, as an 'Arab Marxist-Leninist' who, as such, 'would anticipate continued fraternal intercontinental cooperation with his ideological allies'.[4] In a similar vein, Mansbach, Fergusson and Lampert, writing about non-state actors, and more specifically about international revolutionary and guerrilla movements, claimed that 'functional linkages create transnational perceptions of mutual interest and lead to regularized communication among status groups across state frontiers'.[5]

Indeed, many researchers pointed to financial and technical assistance as proof of growing links between national and international terrorist groups. Examples of

---

[1] Yonah Alexander and M. John Gleason (eds.), *Behavioural and Quantitative Perspectives on Terrorism* (New York: Pergamon Press, 1981), p. xiii.
[2] See Paul Wilkinson and A.M. Stewart (eds.), *Contemporary Research on Terrorism* (Aberdeen: The University Press, 1987), p. xvi.
[3] J. Bowyer Bell, 'Contemporary Revolutionary Organizations', in R. Keohane and J. S. Nye (eds.), *Transnational Relations and World Politics* (Cambridge, MA: Harvard University Press, 1972), p. 156.
[4] Ibid., p. 163.
[5] R.W. Mansbach, Y.H. Fergusson, and D.E. Lampert, *The Web of World Politics. Non-state Actors in the Global System* (Englewood Cliffs, NJ: Prentice-Hall, 1976), p. 45.

such collaboration were the Palestinian training camps in Jordan and Lebanon where West European, African and Latin American terrorists trained, or ties between the Irish Republican Army (IRA) and the Basque and Breton separatists.

At the end of the 1980s, revolutionary left-wing terror activities in Western Europe were almost entirely eradicated. Palestinian terrorism was reduced to sporadic activity of small organizations. At the international level Palestinian terrorists carried out isolated acts as their sponsor states (Libya, Iraq, Syria and lately Iran) became increasingly deterred by the prospect of direct confrontation with the West, particularly the US.

Various events in the early 1990s – the 1991 Gulf War and its aftermath, the disintegration of the USSR and Yugoslavia, the increase in radical right-wing terrorist activity in Europe and the US, the suicide bomb attacks on the Israeli embassy and the Jewish community center (AMIA) in Buenos Aires (1992 and 1994, respectively), the bombing of the World Trade Center in New York (1993) and of the federal building in Oklahoma City (1995) – once again reminded the world of the dangers of terrorism.

At the beginning of the twenty-first century Palestinian organizations have been superseded by militant Islamist organizations, whose activities extend beyond the Middle East or Islamic countries, to include countries with Muslim minorities. Once again, there is talk of an international conspiracy against the West, and particularly against the US, this time by Islamist organizations against moderate regimes in their lands. Palestinian camps in southern Lebanon have been supplanted by Hizballah camps in the Lebanese Bekaa Valley, which trained Turkish, Kurdish, and Algerian terrorists, this time under the tutelage of Iran. The last years of the millennium saw the emergence of a new terrorist Islamist network, led by Osama bin Laden, a wealthy Saudi businessman.

In an article on academic research on terrorism, Crenshaw pointed out that 'what made the phenomenon of terrorism noteworthy in the 1970s was its internationalization…There appeared to be a growing collaboration among groups based in different countries…Interest in terrorism as an international problem was heightened in the 1980s by the prominence accorded to "state-sponsored" terrorism, usually defined as proxy or surrogate warfare'.[6] Crenshaw continued:

> The claim that terrorism is not only an international phenomenon but a new form of warfare is often made. If terrorism is a form of international warfare, it should be analysed as a result of underlying changes in the international system, particularly differential growth in national power. Yet studies of international terrorism are rarely linked to the literature on international politics.[7]

---

[6] Martha Crenshaw, 'Current Research on Terrorism: The Academic Perspective', *Studies in Conflict and Terrorism*, Vol. 15 (1992), pp. 3-11.

[7] Ibid., p. 4.

Crenshaw subsequently proposed trying 'to link the two levels of analysis – the group and society – in national and international settings'.[8]

Surveying studies on European terrorism, Pluchinsky advocated comparative research on Fighting Communist Organizations (FCOs) for fear that at some point in the future they would join forces with the communist old guard in the CIS and Eastern Europe.[9] He suggested a similar approach to Middle Eastern terrorist activity in Europe (to which very little systematic research had been devoted), including examination of their infrastructure and the assistance received by these organizations since their emergence in 1968.

There is clearly a paucity of research on the subject of cooperation and coalitions between terrorist organizations. Most studies are limited to factual descriptions based on information relating to the trial of individuals involved in international acts of terror. Case studies of specific terrorist organizations include only brief discussions of international cooperation by these organizations. Many questions raised in the early 1970s therefore remain unanswered. In view of the fact that international terrorism is obviously here to stay, at least in the foreseeable future, it is imperative to find answers to these questions: Did cooperation between international terrorist organizations in the 1970s and 1980s lead to the creation of working coalitions between organizations from different countries? Is a formal coalition between actors other than sovereign states feasible in the first place? Which domestic and international factors encourage the establishment of coalitions between terrorist organizations? Is ideology the main force behind the establishment and operation of a coalition, or do political and material interests override ideological ones? How do coalitions work within the changing scene of international politics? Is an alliance between terrorist organizations comparable to an alliance between states? For example, does such a coalition include superpowers and satellite organizations, and what kind of reciprocity or dependency exists between the two?

I.   OUTLINE OF THE STUDY

Within this book two chapters deal with theoretical aspects, seven chapters analyze empirical data concerning the terrorist organizations under scrutiny from the late 1960s to 1990. The final chapter examines a new phenomenon, the radical Islamist organizations.

---

[8]   Ibid., p. 9.
[9]   A. Dennis Pluchinsky, 'Academic Research on European Terrorist Developments: Pleas from a Government Terrorism Analyst', *Studies in Conflict and Terrorism*, Vol. 15 (1992), p. 17.

Chapter 1 presents the theoretical framework and research paradigm. Chapter 2 defines the operative variables and introduces the research hypotheses. Chapters 3-9 analyze empirical data under three sub-headings:

(a) Cooperation between various European radical left-wing, right-wing and nationalistic organizations and the main Palestinian terrorist organizations.
(b) Cooperation from the point of view of the Palestinian organizations.
(c) Cooperation between the European Fighting Communist Organizations (FCOs).

Chapter 10 tests the hypotheses against the empirical data to determine if they can support an original and more comprehensive theory.

Chapter 11 updates the theoretical findings with regard to the emerging coalition of Islamist organizations known as the al-Qaeda or Osama bin Laden's network and groups during the 1990s until the major terrorist attacks of 11 September 2001 (9/11).

II.   DEFINING TERMS

1.   Terrorism

During the period under review the definition of terrorism was a subject of sharp contention, mainly between Western democratic states, on the one hand, and Communist bloc and Third World countries, on the other. With the end of the Cold War, controversy on this sensitive political subject seems to have subsided. In reality, the dispute has continued between states traditionally affected by terrorism, namely the democracies, and those newly affected ones, such as Russia, and developing countries, where most of the terrorist organizations and groups are active.

This debate also encompasses the academy. In their exhaustive handbook on terrorism, Schmid and Jongman registered more than a hundred definitions![10] Most liberal or conservative scholars in the West define all acts perpetrated against states as terrorist acts. Those with leftist leanings, however, define only those acts perpetrated by a colonialist state as terrorist acts, while acts perpetrated by 'national liberation movements' are considered legitimate. PLO chairman Yasser Arafat expressed this distinction in his famous speech to the UN General

---

[10] A.P. Schmid, A.J. Jongman, et. al., *Political Terrorism: A New Guide to Actors, Authors, Concepts, Data-bases, Theories, and Literature* (2nd edn.) (Amsterdam: SWIDOC and New Brunswick, NJ Transaction Books, 1988), pp. 1-30.

Assembly in 1974: 'Those who fight for their country's freedom, those who fight occupation, oppression or colonialism, should not be defined as terrorists.'[11]

Discussion on the definition of terrorism has recently resurfaced, even between researchers belonging to the same ideological camp and within law enforcement agencies of the same country.[12] Various American institutions, such as the FBI, the State Department and the Defense Department have adopted different definitions.[13] Since there is no consensus, this study resorts to definitions used by leading scholars.

Laqueur defined terrorism as 'an act of violence or a threat of violence committed in order to gain concessions from a primary target as distinguished from an immediate target'.[14] Stohl defined it as 'the purposeful act or the threat of the act of violence to create fear and/or compliant behaviour in a victim and/or audience of the act or threat'.[15] Crenshaw, in my opinion, felicitously combined these two definitions: 'In focusing on terrorism directed against governments, we are considering the premeditated use or threat of symbolic, low-level violence by conspiratorial organizations for purposes of political change. Terrorist violence communicates a political message. Its ends go beyond damaging an enemy's material resources. The victims or objects of terrorist attacks represent an audience from whom terrorists seek a reaction.'[16]

Crenshaw's definition constitutes a satisfactory point of departure for this research, with the addition of two qualifications:

(1) The political change to which the terrorist aspires is a radical one.
(2) The audience at which the terrorist act is aimed includes not only victims (primary or immediate, according to Laqueur's definition), but also sympathizers and potential allies whom the terrorist organization wishes to enlist in its struggle.

---

[11] Yehuda Lukacs (ed.), *The Israeli-Palestinian Conflict: A Documentary Record* (Cambridge: Cambridge University Press, 1992), pp. 317-32.

[12] The subject of definition is treated extensively in: Rosalyn Higgins and Maurice Flory (eds.), *Terrorism and International Law* (London: Routledge, 1997); Boaz Ganor, *Defining Terrorism: Is One Man's Terrorist Another Man's Freedom Fighter?* The Interdisciplinary Center, Herzliya, ICT Papers, Vol. 4, August 1998. Ganor's definition states that 'terrorism is the intentional use of, or threat to use violence against civilians or against civilian targets, in order to attain political aims'; Alex Obote-Odora, 'Defining International Terrorism,' *E Law – Murdoch University Electronic Journal of Law*, Vol. 6, No 1 (1999) <http://www.murdoch.edu.au/elaw/issues/v6n1/obote-odora61_ notes.html>.

[13] See Bruce Hoffman, *Inside Terrorism* (New York: Columbia University Press, 1998), p. 38. Hoffman devotes his first chapter (pp. 13-44) to the definition of terrorism.

[14] Walter Laqueur, *Terrorism* (London: Weidenfeld and Nicolson, 1977), p. 145.

[15] Michael Stohl (ed.), *The Politics of Terrorism* (3rd edn.) (New York: Marcel Dekker, 1988), p. 3.

[16] Martha Crenshaw, *Terrorism and International Cooperation* (Boulder, CO: Westview Press, 1989), p. 113.

2.   International terrorism

The international community remains divided on the question in spite of continuous efforts by some countries such as Russia and France to advance UN resolutions relating to terrorism.

Obote-Odora, analyzing the search of a definition at the UN observed that the problem of definition is political rather than legal: 'Consequently, questions relating to definition of terrorism is (sic) best solved when addressed by political and legal committees of the United Nations ... because causes of terrorism are usually political. Thus, a purely legal approach may not necessarily address the political dimension of international terrorism.'[17]

A number of researchers differentiate between two types of terrorism:

(1) International terrorism – terrorism sponsored by a state but perpetrated beyond the frontiers of that state.

(2) Transnational terrorism – terrorism perpetrated by groups or individuals against targets associated with foreign countries beyond their countries of origin.

Wilkinson explained how political terrorism turns into international terrorism:

> International terrorism in its most obvious manifestations is a terrorist attack carried out across international frontiers, or against a foreign target in the terrorist's state of origin. Yet in reality international dimensions often take a more indirect form: a terrorist group may seek foreign cash, weapons, political support or other resources. Or its members and leaders may occasionally find safe havens abroad or establish ad hoc cooperation with friendly foreign states and terrorist groups.[18]

Wilkinson rejected a distinction between 'transnational' and 'international' terrorism. In his opinion, the term 'international' was never restricted to intergovernmental relations, but also reflected cultural, economic and other activities involving citizens and institutions of different countries. Adopting Wilkinson's approach, which also implies the possibility of alliances between terrorist organizations, the term 'international terrorism' refers in this study to any terrorist activity within an international context.

---

[17]   Obote-Odora, 'Defining International Terrorism', p. 13.
[18]   Paul Wilkinson, *Terrorism and the Liberal State* (2nd edn.) (London: Macmillan, 1986), pp. 181-82.

3. Coalitions

In previous studies, an alliance was defined as a formal agreement between two or more states for the purposes of cooperation on national defense issues,[19] or as a formal or informal settlement for the purposes of cooperation between two or more sovereign states on defense issues.[20] The term 'coalition' was used mainly in the context of domestic policy, such as coalitions between political parties. Riker was one of the first to use it in the field of international relations.[21] The term 'coalition' will be used in this study since terrorist organizations do not have the kind of formal agreements that governments do. 'Coalition' is defined as ideological, material and operational cooperation between two or more terrorist organizations directed against a common enemy which may be a state targeted by one of the member organizations or a rival ideological bloc.

4. The typology of political terrorism

The classification of terrorist organizations into categories is no less controversial. Typologies are useful inasmuch as they establish correlations between, and rules for, various types of social phenomena.[22] This study uses the association of an organization with a category as an independent variable for examining its behavior in forming coalitions with other organizations. The most comprehensive survey of the typologies of terrorist organizations was proposed by Fleming, Stohl and Schmid.[23] They stressed the difficulties of discerning similarities or differences between the various categories, claiming that many typologies provided only partial descriptions of modern terrorism.[24]

---

[19] See Ole Holsti, Terrence Hopmann and John Sullivan, *Unity and Disintegration in International Alliances* (New York: University Press of America, 1985), p. 4.

[20] See Stephen Walt, *The Origins of Alliances* (Ithaca and London: Cornell University Press, 1987), p. 1.

[21] See William H. Riker, *The Theory of Political Coalitions* (4th edn.) (New Haven and London: Yale University Press, 1968).

[22] According to Fattah, the typology of terrorism is essential for differentiating between the various organizations, sorting them into categories, and understanding their motivations and the influences at work on them. See A. Ezzat Fattah, 'Terrorist Activities and Terrorist Targets: A Tentative Typology', in Alexander and Gleason (eds.), *Behavioural and Quantitative Perspectives on Terrorism* (New York: Pergamon Press, 1981), p. 11.

[23] Peter Fleming, Michael Stohl and Alex Schmid, 'The Theoretical Utility of Typologies of Terrorism: Lessons and Opportunities', in Stohl (ed.) *The Politics of Terrorism*, pp. 153-96.

[24] While the typologies proposed by Fleming, Stohl and Schmid are satisfactory they are too broad. It is necessary, therefore, to define sub-types too. Examples would be Marxist-Leninist, anarcho-communist, Maoist, or Trotskyist on the radical left, and neo-Nazis, 'Third Way movements' etc., on the radical right. Obviously, these sub-types must meet the general definition of a terrorist organization, and the reasons for including an organization in one or other category must be specified. Some of the organizations classified as territorial, separatist or nationalist could equally well be classified as ideological (the radical right or left) or religious (Catholic, Protestant, Jewish, Sikh, etc.).

III.   RESEARCH ON TERRORISM AND COALITIONS

From the early 1970s to the mid-1980s there was a steady proliferation of books, articles and studies on the subject of terrorism. This profusion was largely due to the fact that the subject of terrorism straddled various disciplines: political science and international relations, psychology and sociology, criminology and law, policing techniques and technology.[25]

In the mid-1980s, with the decline in terrorist activity of revolutionary European and South American terrorist organizations, there was a parallel waning of interest in the subject on the part of researchers and journalists. On the other hand, the revolution in Iran and the rise of Shi'ite terrorism in Lebanon and its international repercussions awakened a keen interest in militant Islamist groups and movements, with a correspondingly high production of books and studies on the subject of what is commonly called Islamic 'fundamentalism' (or Islamism).[26] However, little serious research on Islamist terrorism has been published.[27]

The massive terrorist attacks at the beginning of the 1990s in New York, Buenos Aires and Oklahoma City, culminating with the sarin gas attack in the Tokyo underground in March 1995, gave rise to fear of a new kind of terrorism, commonly called 'Weapons of Mass Destruction (WMD) terrorism.' This generated a wave of articles and books, mostly by American researchers, on the threat of chemical, biological and nuclear terrorism.[28]

---

[25]   Schmid and Jongman provide a systematic bibliography on the subject (about 6000 entries). See Schmid, Jongman et al., *Political Terrorism*, pp. 237-445.

[26]   For a discussion on the definitions of Islamic fundamentalism and Islamism see Martin Kramer, 'Fundamentalist Islam at Large: The Drive for Power', *Middle East Quarterly*, Vol. 3, No. 2, June 1996 and Ali Abootalebi, 'Islam, Islamists, And Democracy,' *MERIA Journal*, Vol. 3, No. 1, (1998). For a comprehensive exploration of fundamentalist ideology and activity, see Emmanuel Sivan, *Radical Islam: Medieval Theory and Modern Politics* (New Haven, CT: Yale University Press, 1985); Nazih Ayubi, *Political Islam: Religion and Politics in the Arab World* (London: Routledge, 1991); Hrair R. Dekmejian, *Islam in Revolution: Fundamentalism in the Arab World* (New York: Syracuse University Press, 1985); John L. Esposito, *The Islamic Threat: Myth or Reality?* (New York: Oxford University Press, 1992).

[27]   On this subject, see A. Nizar Hamzeh, 'Islamism in Lebanon: A Guide', *MERIA Journal*, Vol. 1, No. 3 (1997); Ely Karmon, 'Why Tehran Starts and Stops Terrorism', *Middle East Quarterly*, Vol. 5, No. 4, December 1998; Ely Karmon, 'The Demise of Radical Islam in Turkey', <http://www.ict.org.il/articles/radical-islam-turkey.htm> in Barry Rubin, *Revolutionaries and Reformers: Contemporary Islamic Movements in the Middle East* (State University of New York Press and the Begin-Sadat Center for Strategic Studies, Bar Ilan University) (forthcoming); Barry Rubin, 'Islamic Radicalism In The Middle East: A Survey and Balance Sheet', *MERIA Journal*, Vol. 2, No. 1 (1998); David Zeidan, 'Radical Islam in Egypt: A Comparison of Two Groups', *MERIA Journal*, Vol. 3, No. 3 (1999).

[28]   On this vast subject see, for example: Paul Leventhal and Yonah Alexander (eds.), *Nuclear Terrorism: Defining the Threat* (Washington, DC: Pergamon-Brassey's, 1986); Ron Purver, *Chemical And Biological Terrorism: The Threat According To The Open Literature*, Canadian Security Intelligence Service documents, June 1995, <http://www.csis-scrs.gc.ca/eng/miscdocs/

The literature surveyed below covers three fields: theories on terrorism; literature relating to specific organizations; and theories on alliances and coalitions.

1. Theories on terrorism

There are various schools of thought regarding the phenomenon of terrorism. Among the most comprehensive works on theories of terrorism are: Kegley's anthology, which devotes a special section to the reasons for terrorism; Schmid and Jongman's guide to political terrorism; Stohl's anthology, or the more recent one by Crenshaw.[29] Other researchers who discuss theories of terrorism include Wilkinson and Laqueur. The latter is also one of the most-frequently quoted authors in the professional literature.[30]

Schmid argued that theories of terrorism were derived from research conducted in the 1970s and the beginning of the 1980s. He argued that from the mid-1980s on, there was no significant development in this field.[31] Indeed, throughout the last fifteen years there has been little serious theoretical research on terrorism. Hoffman, in his comprehensive book on terrorism, focused on trends in terrorism rather than conceptual reinterpretation.[32] Charters argued that scientists had not yet managed to prove why terrorism existed, or why certain individuals or groups

---

tabintre.html>; David E. Kaplan and Andrew Marshall, *The Cult at the End of the World: The Incredible Story of Aum* (London: Hutchinson, 1996); Richard Falkenrath, Robert Newman and Bradley Thayer, *America's Achilles' Heel*, (Cambridge, MA: The MIT Press, 1998); D.W. Brackett, *Holy Terror: Armageddon in Tokyo* (New York and Tokyo: Weatherhill, 1996); Walter Laqueur, *The New Terrorism: Fanaticism and the Arms of Mass Destruction* (New York and Oxford: Oxford University Press, 1999); W. Seth Carus, *Bioterrorism and Biocrimes: The Illicit Use of Biological Agents in the 20th Century* (Washington DC: Center for Counterproliferation Research, National Defense University, 1999).

29 Charles W. Kegley (ed.), *International Terrorism: Characteristics, Causes, Controls* (New York: St. Martin's Press, 1990); Schmid, Jongman, et al., *Political Terrorism*; Stohl (ed.), *The Politics of Terrorism*; Martha Crenshaw (ed.), *Terrorism in Context* (State College PA: Penn State University Press, 1995).

30 Paul Wilkinson, *Political Terrorism* (2nd edn.) (London: Macmillan, 1976); *Terrorism and the Liberal State*; Crenshaw, *Terrorism and International Cooperation*; Martha Crenshaw, 'Is International Terrorism Primarily State-Sponsored?, in Kegley, *International Terrorism*, pp. 163-69; Martha Crenshaw, 'The Causes of Terrorism', in Kegley (ed.), *International Terrorism*, pp. 113-26; Martha Crenshaw 'The Logic of Terrorism: Terrorist Behaviour as a Product of Strategic Choice', in Walter Reich (ed.), *Origins of Terrorism: Psychologies, Ideologies, Theologies, States of Mind* (Cambridge: Cambridge University Press, 1990), pp. 7-24; Walter Laqueur, *The Age of Terrorism* (Boston, MA: Little, Brown & Co., 1987).

31 According to Schmid, 'the term "theory" is taken more in the sense of current thinking and interpretations than in terms of formal propositions that have been rationalized and tested empirically'. See Schmid, Jongman et al., *Political Terrorism*, p. 62.

32 See Hoffman, *Inside Terrorism*, p. 7.

opted for terrorism when the oppression they suffered or their grievances against the state were negligible.[33]

Kegley differentiated between two conflicting schools of thought: those who favor the theory of root causes, and those who reject it, view terrorism as a campaign of violence waged outside the framework of the standard rules of war.[34] Those who believe in root causes claim that terrorism is the result of political or economic oppression. Therefore, terrorists frequently experience feelings of hopelessness, despair, and paranoia. According to Moorhead Kennedy, 'a constellation of factors, such as colonialism, ethnic division, and political oppression, are conducive to terrorism'.[35] Rubenstein saw terrorism as a specific social phenomenon, with detectable origins and predictable goals. In his opinion, the real causes of terrorism are situational: 'the constellation of economic, political, and psychological factors that have the effect, in a particular society, of inciting young people to engage in conspiratorial violence.'[36]

Critics of the theory of root causes, such as Decter, claimed that, 'rather than being the result of poverty and oppression, [terrorism] is the consequence of a decision by unprincipled actors operating outside the norms of conventional behaviour who rationalize the killing of innocent people'.[37] According to this theory, terrorists are motivated by political opportunism rather than ideals.

Similarly, Hamilton regarded the causes of terrorism as 'obscure': 'It has risen among rich and poor, oppressive and relatively unoppressive societies. It has been used to promote causes with no popular support as well as causes endorsed by a large majority. And it has emerged to fight against the overwhelming forces of foreign invaders and has been used, by other invaders, as an extension of inter-state war.'[38]

Crenshaw also rejected the theory of root causes:

The group chooses terrorism as one of several alternatives, after examining its effectiveness as a way of achieving its political goals. Since terrorism is not the only way of achieving radical goals, we may wonder what influences the choice of terrorism as opposed to other options. One of the claims of terrorist organizations is that they chose this method as a last resort, when all other options have failed.

---

[33] David Charters, 'Terrorism: A Survey of Recent Literature', Review essay in *Conflict Quarterly* (1987), p. 66.
[34] Kegley (ed.), *International Terrorism*, pp. 97-100.
[35] Cited in Kegley (ed.), *International Terrorism*, p. 98.
[36] See Richard Rubenstein, *Alchemists of Revolution* (London: I.B. Tauris., 1987), p. 83.
[37] Cited by Kegley (ed.), *International Terrorism*, p. 141, from Moshe Decter, 'Terrorism: The Fallacy of "Root Causes"', *Midstream* 33 (1987).
[38] Cited in Schmid, Jongman et al., *Political Terrorism*, p. 67.

According to Crenshaw, this helps explain the use of terror by the Palestinians after Israel defeated the Arab armies in the Six Day War.[39]

Small organizations may adopt violence in order to compensate for their numerical weakness – a weakness that sometimes originates from lack of public support for their ideological tenets (as in the case of the Red Army Faction – RAF – in West Germany), or their inability to recruit members due to internal organizational problems. Sometimes the political situation may be conducive to terrorism, as when the regime is suddenly weakened (the IRA began its anti-British operations during the First World War), or the international climate may favor terrorism (international antagonism toward the South African regime encouraged terrorist activities by black liberation movements). In the final analysis, a strategic decision is adopted, according to Crenshaw, after the pros and cons of terrorist policy have been weighed up.[40]

The price of terrorism is undoubtedly high. As an internal strategy, it always invites a punitive reaction on the part of the government. A further cost could be the loss of popular support for the cause, although this is less likely to occur within ethnically divided societies such as Spain or Ireland. Some terrorists are also likely to become disaffected when they realize that their organization is, in fact, removed from its declared ideology, which postulates popular participation in the liberation struggle.

As for the rewards of terrorism these include: the possibility of preparing the ground for a true revolution and a broad-based popular uprising by undermining governmental authority and demoralizing the administrative cadres. Terrorism has the benefit of placing the initiative in the hands of the terrorist organization and granting it a prime role in inciting popular resistance through personal example. As Crenshaw pointed out, radical elements which opt for terrorism may make erroneous judgments concerning the alternatives open to them, or the consequences of their activities. Nevertheless, they base their choice on a logical decision-making process. She defined this approach as a 'collectively rational strategic choice'.[41]

Kegley discussed whether international terrorism was the result of internal or external factors.

Those persuaded that internal factors are powerful emphasize the domestic sources of terrorist activity – the personal, societal, cultural, and governmental variables nested within nations that may prompt terrorist activities. Those emphasizing external sources stress the attributes of the international system that influence terrorists'

---

[39] Crenshaw, 'The Logic of Terrorism', pp. 20-24.
[40] Ibid.
[41] Ibid., p. 20.

decisions, such as the foreign policies of other states and the global circumstances in general that create a conducive environment for terrorist activity.[42]

The most radical theory concerning external sources is the conspiracy theory or network theory, which explains all international terrorism in terms of a single external influence. 'Some analysts are drawn hastily to the reassuringly simple theory that international terrorism is the product of a conspiracy orchestrated by state sponsors, who are alleged to direct and manage terrorism worldwide through an elaborate network of terrorist organizations.'[43] Sterling and Cline and Alexander advocated belief in a Soviet conspiracy, while Chomsky and Herman blamed the 'American conspiracy' for all the world's ills, including terrorism.[44]

Wilkinson pointed out the need to identify the political motivation of terrorists, and how these relate to their ideology, the surrounding regimes, prevailing conflicts, and political and strategic conditions. According to him, most attempts by social scientists to find a theory of terrorism suffered from a serious drawback: the failure to recognize the power of ideologies and beliefs as the driving force behind revolutionary movements and their role in fostering hatred and violence.[45]

2.   Literature on specific organizations

Although there are many studies of terrorist organizations on the radical left, there are only a few on terrorist organizations on the radical right. Published research on the radical right in Europe deals mainly with Nazism and fascism, or with non-violent movements and parties which are associated with the neo-Nazi or neo-fascist far right, and the 'New Right' that emerged after the Second World War. Each country has its own literature relating to organizations active in that country, which for the most part, have not been translated into other languages.

While thousands of books and articles on terrorist organizations have been published most are journalistic and sensationalist, focusing on the operational and more spectacular aspects of terrorism. These are useful mainly for their factual information about terrorist events or organizations.

In recent years, several accounts by former or arrested terrorists have been published. An increasing amount of historical and original documents relating

---

[42]   Kegley (ed.), *International Terrorism*, p. 97.
[43]   Ibid., p. 98.
[44]   See Claire Sterling, *The Terror Network: The Secret War of International Terrorism* (New York: Holt, Rinehart and Winston, 1981); Ray Cline and Yonah Alexander, *The Soviet Connection* (New York: Crane Russak, 1984); Noam Chomsky and Edward Herman, *The Washington Connection and Third World Fascism* (Boston, MA: South End Press, 1979).
[45]   See Paul Wilkinson, 'The Sources of Terrorism: Terrorists' Ideologies and Beliefs', in Kegley (ed.), *International Terrorism*, pp. 139-142.

to terrorist organizations (manifestos, flyers and even whole books), unavailable to most researchers until three to four years ago, has been published on the Internet.[46]

---

[46] The following publications are recommended: On Fatah, Ehud Ya'ari, *Fatah* (Tel Aviv: A. Levine-Epstein, 1970), (Hebrew); and Abu-Iyad, *Lelo Moledet. Sihot 'im Erik Rulo* [Stateless: Conversations with Eric Rouleau] (Jerusalem: Mifras Publications, 1983); [Abu-Iyad is the *nom de guerre* of Salah Khalaf, deputy chairman of Fatah]; On the development of international terrorism by the main Palestinian organizations, see Ariel Merari and Elad Shlomi, *Paha' Hul: Teror Palestinai be-Hutz la-Aretz* [Palestinian Terror Abroad] (Tel Aviv: United Kibbutz and Jaffee Center for Strategic Studies publication, 1986); on the PLO, Helena Cobban, *The Palestinian Liberation Organization. People, Power and Politics* (Cambridge: Cambridge University Press, 1984); Arieh Yodfat and Yuval Arnon-Ohanna, *PLO. Strategy and Politics* (London: Croom Helm, 1981). From the second half of the 1980s on few studies on Palestinian organizations were published. However, some need to be mentioned: Barry Rubin, *Revolution until Victory? The Politics and History of the PLO* (Cambridge, Mass.: Harvard University Press, 1994); Harold M. Cubert, *The PFLP's Changing Role in the Middle East* (London: Frank Cass, 1997). The most comprehensive (953 pages) work on PLO's armed struggle is without doubt Yazid Sayigh's *Armed Struggle and the Search for State: The Palestinian National Movement, 1949-1993* (New York: Oxford University Press, 1997).
     On German terrorism see, Jillian Becker, *Hitler's Children* (London: Granada Publishing, 1978); Stefan Aust, *The Baader-Meinhof Group: The Inside Story of a Phenomenon* (London: Bodley Head, 1987); Anne Steiner and Loïc Debray, *La Fraction Armée Rouge. Guérilla urbaine en Europe occidentale* (Paris: Méridiens Klincksieck, 1987) and some of Hans Josef Horchem's articles cited in the bibliography. Two autobiographical works by German terrorists on the radical left draw a realistic picture of left-wing terrorist organizations in Germany: Michael Baumann, *Terror or Love? 'Bommi' Baumann's Own Story of His Life as a West German Urban Guerrilla* (New York: Grove Press 1979); Jean Bougereau, 'An Interview with Hans Joachim Klein', in Jean Bougereau, *The German Guerrilla: Terror, Reaction and Resistance* (Orkney: Cienfuegos Press, 1981) pp. 7-66.
     Italy, apparently, is the country with the largest number of publications on terrorist organizations operating within its borders. Hundreds of studies, articles and books were written in Italian, mostly on organizations on the radical left, and a few on organizations on the extreme right. Among the best are: Alessandro Silj, *'Mai più senza fucile!'. Alle origini dei NAP e delle BR* (Firenze: Vallecchi Editore, 1977); Donatella della Porta (ed.), *Terrorismi in Italia* (Bologna: Società Editrice il Mulino, 1984) and *Il Terrorismo di Sinistra* (Bologna: Società Editrice il Mulino, 1990); Raimondo Catanzaro (ed.), *The Red Brigades and Left-Wing Terrorism in Italy* (London: Pinter, 1991). Ferraresi's studies on the radical right are well-known in the field, after the pioneering work of Galli: Franco Ferraresi (ed.), *La Destra Radicale* (Milano: Feltrinelli, 1984); Giorgio Galli, *La Crisi Italiana e la Destra InterNazionale* (Torino: Arnaldo Mondadori Editore, 1977). Some key terrorists in Italy have published their memoirs: Renato Curcio, *A viso aperto. Intervista di Mario Scialoja* (4th edn.) (Milano: Oscar Mondadori, 2000); Alberto Franceschini, P. Buffa, F. Giustolisi, *Mara, Renato e io. Storia dei fondatori delle Br* (4th edn.) (Milano: Oscar Mondadori, 2000); Mario Moretti, *Brigatte Rosse. Una storia italiana. Intervista di Carla Mosca e Rossana Rossanda* (Milano: Edizione Anabasi, 1994).
     Other than journalistic accounts, little has been written about terrorist organizations in France. The most important study is Michael Dartnell, *Action directe: Ultra-leftist terrorism in France, 1979-1987*, (London: Frank Cass, 1995).
     For full texts produced by various terrorist organizations see: Walter Laqueur and Yonah Alexander (eds.), *The Terrorism Reader* (2nd edn.) (New York: Nal Penguin Inc., 1987); Yonah Alexander and A. Dennis Pluchinsky (eds.), *Europe's Red Terrorists: The Fighting Communist Organizations* (London: Frank Cass, 1992).

In conclusion, while the literature on terrorism is extremely prolific and diverse, there is an appreciable shortfall in the theoretical field, a field that has barely evolved since the late 1970s. This shortfall is particularly acute with respect to the international systemic aspects of global terror, and the integration of research at the group and society level with research at the national and international level, as Crenshaw so rightly pointed out. The imbalance between studies into revolutionary left-wing organizations as opposed to radical right-wing organizations should also be noted. The lack of interest in radical right-wing organizations has been felt more acutely in recent years, as scholars and policymakers have been increasingly caught off their guard by the rise of right-wing terrorist groups, particularly in Western Europe and the US.

3.   Theories on alliances and coalitions

Most of the relevant literature, written in the 1950s and 1960s, was based on the balance of power theory, as developed by Morgenthau, Liska, and Rothstein.[47] According to a study conducted by Ward, based mainly on American sources, about 270 books and articles were written on the dynamics of alliances, but only a small part of this research was cumulative.[48]

According to Morgenthau,

> Alliances are a necessary function of the balance of power operating within a multiple-state system. Nations competing with each other have three choices in order to maintain and improve their relative power positions. They can increase their own power, they can add to their own power the power of other nations, or they can withhold the power of other nations from the adversary. When they make the first choice, they embark upon an armaments race. When they choose the second and third alternatives, they pursue a policy of alliances.[49]

Morgenthau adds:

Many terrorist organizations themselves published manifestos, declarations, and documents. For the German RAF see: *Rote Armee Fraktion, Widerstand heisst angriff! Enklarungen, redebeitrage, flugblatter und briefe. 1977-1988* (Amsterdam: Bibliotheek voor ontspanning en ontwikkeling, 1988). In Spain, eighteen volumes of ETA documents were published in *Documentos de ETA* (San Sebastian: Editorial Hordago, 1984).

The PLO has published important texts and resolutions in its Journal of Palestine Studies (JPS).

47   See Hans Morgenthau, *Politics Among Nations* (New York: Alfred Knopf, 1959); George Liska, *Nations in Alliance: The Limits of Interdependence* (Baltimore: John Hopkins Press, 1962); Robert Rothstein, *Alliances and Small Powers* (New York: Columbia University Press, 1968).

48   Cited in Walt, *The Origins of Alliances*, p. 6.

49   J. Hans Morgenthau, 'Alliances', in J. Friedman, C. Bladen and S. Rosen (eds.), *Alliances in International Politics* (Boston, MA: Allyn and Bacon, 1970), p. 80.

The opposition of two alliances, one or both pursuing imperialistic goals and defending the independence of their members against the imperialistic aspirations of the other coalition, is the most frequent configuration within a balance of power system.[50]

According to Liska,

States enter into alliances with one another in order to supplement each other's capability. Put negatively, an alliance is a means of reducing the impact of antagonistic power, perceived as pressure, which threatens one's independence. The object is to check or divert pressure with counterpressure, applied at the point of the adversary's initiative or at his weakest point.[51]

Walt pointed out that one of the shortcomings of this traditional viewpoint is the lack of a methodical test for the general assumptions.[52] He also noted that balance of power theories were rejected by quantitative researchers such as Healey and Stein, who claimed that European alliances of the period they researched (1870-81) were inspired more by the wish to 'jump on the bandwagon' of the strongest power than to counterbalance it.[53]

Another group of researchers approached the subject from a sociometric perspective, examining the similarity and dissimilarity between nations as a basis for their tendency to enter into alliances (affiliation theories). Holsti classified Guetzkow and Osgood in this group.[54] The basic assumption of these theories is that nations choose their allies selectively, preferring partners with common institutions, cultural and intellectual values and economic interests.

Riker's original theory on political coalitions, based on the 'theory of games' was critical of the balance of power theory.[55] According to Riker, international players are motivated exclusively by the desire for victory and maximization of their part in the spoil. He suggested

---

[50]   Ibid., pp. 87 88.
[51]   See George Liska, 'Alliances and Realliances', in Friedman, Bladen and Rosen, *Alliances in International Politics*, p. 109.
[52]   See Walt, *The Origins of Alliances*, pp. 7-8.
[53]   See Brian Healey and Arthur Stein, 'The Balance of Power in International History: Theory and Reality', *Journal of Conflict Resolution* Vol. 17, No. 1 (1973).
[54]   Holsti, Hopmann and Sullivan, *Unity and Disintegration in International Alliances*, pp. 12, 265. Harold Guetzkow, 'Isolation and Collaboration: A Partial Theory of International Relations', *Journal of Conflict Resolution*, Vol. 17, No. 1 (1973); Robert E. Osgood, *Alliances and American Foreign Policy* (Baltimore: John Hopkins Press, 1968).
[55]   H. William Riker, *The Theory of Political Coalitions* (4th edn.) (New Haven, CT and London: Yale University Press, 1968).

Players will form that grouping which is the smallest winning coalition, that contains just enough power to gain the decision, but no more than is necessary for the purpose...This is attributed to a desire on the part of the potential winners not to spread the winnings out among superfluous partners – the fewer the actors who must be rewarded, the greater the payoff to those who are rewarded.[56]

Walt pointed out that 'Riker's prediction that the players will seek a minimum winning coalition implies that states will join the weaker side'.[57] Unfortunately, however, the theory of games fails to relate at all to the perceptions, feelings, ideologies or geographies of the states in question.

Russett also saw serious limitations in Riker's theory.[58] First, he claimed, it is impossible to reach a solution when there are more than a few isolated players. Second, the theory offers no indication as to how to calculate the relative importance of the different states in order to ascertain the likelihood of the formation of a minimum winning coalition in *international* politics (Russett's emphasis). Holsti shared Walt and Russett's criticism.

Walt himself tried to improve the balance of power theory by claiming that 'states ally to balance against threats rather than against power alone,' where the level of threat is influenced by geographical closeness, aggressive capabilities, and overt intentions.[59] Since the balance of power theory is in essence a theory that relates to the behavior of superpowers, Walt wondered about the priorities of smaller nations in choosing their allies. Do these countries, too, attempt to form a balance of power, and if so against whom? His answer was that in a state of anarchy, states enter into alliances in order to protect themselves, and that their behavior is determined by the perceived threats, and the power of the other countries is only one, albeit important, factor in their calculations.[60]

In practice, even before Walt, many researchers emphasized external threats as an important or even major factor in the formation of alliances. Liska, for example, claimed that external threats, more than national strength or weakness, were the primary source of alliances.[61] A number of researchers, such as Holsti, Wolfers, and Sheriff, claimed that an alliance depends on the strength of the external threat: the weaker the threat, the weaker the alliance.[62]

---

[56] Riker, as cited by Walt, *The Origins of Alliances*, p. 240.
[57] Ibid., p. 10.
[58] See Bruce Russett, 'Components of an Operational Theory of International Alliance Formation', in Friedman, Bladen and Rosen, *Alliances in International Politics*, p. 240.
[59] Walt, *The Origins of Alliances*, p. 5.
[60] Ibid., p. viii.
[61] Cited in Holsti, Hopmann and Sullivan, *Unity and Disintegration in International Alliances*, p. 5.
[62] Ibid., pp. 126, 245.

Two publications have compiled important research in this field: Friedman, Bladen and Rosen's book, *Alliances in International Politics*, and Holsti, Hopmann and Sullivan's book, *Unity and Disintegration in International Alliances*. The former is a rich collection of articles by the most prominent researchers of the different schools. The latter provides a concise and systematic presentation of a wide range of theories and hypotheses in an attempt to identify points of compatibility or incompatibility between them.[63] This prepared the ground for an empirical study that they themselves conducted.[64] The most vital finding of these empirical researches is that the general theories on alliances have limited validity.[65] Sullivan used independent variables that are standard in the literature on alliances (such as ideology, political stability, geographical dispersion, size of state, objectives, and international conflict) in a study of 130 alliances in the period 1815-1939 and consistently found low correlations. The evaluation of the three researchers *vis-à-vis* the three main schools (affiliation theories, balance of power theories, and minimum-winning-coalition theories) is that none provide a complete or satisfactory answer to all the problems surrounding the subject of alliances.[66]

The only researcher to combine the various theories, in particular those on the role of transnational actors in the international arena, and to use them to study coalitions between terrorist organizations, was Oots.[67] Oots examined the correlation between the size of the organizations or coalitions and the practical consequences of their terrorist acts, based on an analysis of coalitions between various organizations. Unfortunately, Oots' study, which is simply quantitative and narrow in focus, contains a number of methodological flaws: basic errors in identifying the various Palestinian terrorist organizations, unclear definitions of the term 'international coalition' and research population, and reliance on a small number of events.[68]

---

[63] This is a joint work although the introduction explains how the seven chapters and three appendices were divided between the three researchers. Since the name of the author does not appear at the beginning of each chapter, they are not entered separately in the bibliography of this volume. However, in the body of the research, each of the authors is quoted in connection with the chapter he wrote.

[64] Holsti, Hopmann and Sullivan, *Unity and Disintegration in International Alliances*, p. 2.

[65] Ibid., p. 219.

[66] Ibid.

[67] See Kent Lane Oots, *A Political Organisation Approach to Transnational Terrorism* (New York: Greenwood Press, 1986).

[68] For example, Oots examines the 'coalition' between Fatah and Black September although Black September was a terrorist arm of Fatah itself, and the 'coalition' between the PFLP and the Muhammad Budyah Commando, which is simply a pseudonym for one of the PFLP cells in Europe.

CHAPTER 1
THEORETICAL FRAMEWORK AND RESEARCH PARADIGM

I. THEORETICAL FRAMEWORK

Given that existing theories relate only to coalitions between states, and fail to provide satisfactory answers to questions regarding alliances, the choice of framework is difficult. Walt's 'balance of threat theory', which accounts for international developments during the fifteen years following the emergence of the balance of power theories, is the most suitable point of departure.

Walt saw his theory as a refinement of the balance of power theory.

> Whereas balance of power theory predicts that states will react to imbalances of power, balance of threat theory predicts that when there is an imbalance of threat (i.e., when one state or coalition appears especially dangerous), states will form alliances or increase their internal efforts in order to reduce their vulnerability.[1]

According to Hopmann, many researchers hold that alliances are usually formed in response to an external threat.[2] The internal cohesion of the alliance depends to a large extent on the intensity and duration of the threat. It follows that one of the main reasons for the collapse of an alliance is the mitigation or evaporation of the threat that was the reason for the alliance in the first place. Hopmann points out that this hypothesis has been extensively tested, not only for states but also for social groups. Hopmann himself tested the hypothesis at the international level of analysis, and more specifically found a positive correlation between the level of consensus and solidarity within NATO and the communist bloc, on the one hand, and the level of conflict and threat that existed between the two, on the other.[3]

Many researchers focus exclusively on alliances between great powers. Walt explains why his research focuses on the Middle East:

> Because most propositions about alliance formation (or international relations theory in general, for that matter) have been derived from the history of the European great power system, it is especially appropriate to examine their utility in predicting the behaviour of states that are neither European nor great powers.[4]

---

[1] See Stephen Walt, *The Origins of Alliances* (Ithaca and London: Cornell University Press, 1987), p. 263.
[2] Holsti, Hopmann and Sullivan, *Unity and Disintegration in International Alliances*, p. 88.
[3] Ibid., p. 143.
[4] Walt, *The Origins of Alliances*, p. 13.

Almost all studies on the subject of alliances and coalitions relate to sovereign states, rather than to international actors such as terrorist organizations. Singer, who analyzed the problem of levels of analysis in international relations, emphasized that researchers in the West, and certainly in the English-speaking world, saw the state as the traditional focus of their interest.[5]

Can terrorist organizations also be considered international actors capable of realizing one of the most important functions of states – namely, the establishment of international coalitions?[6] The question of the international status of revolutionary, guerrilla, and terrorist organizations became a burning issue in the 1960s, when anti-colonialist liberation movements proliferated and achieved independence and political recognition. A number of researchers subsequently addressed this issue.

Keohane and Nye were among the first to emphasize the importance of non-state actors, or 'transnational actors' as they called them, such as business enterprises, international organizations, trade unions, and revolutionary organizations, including terrorist organizations.[7] They claimed that these actors have 'developed autonomous foreign policies that may deliberately oppose or impinge on state politics'.[8] 'Winning may be costly, even for governments. Transnational relations may help to increase these costs and thus increase the constraints on state autonomy.'[9] Transnational relations may also encourage alliances and agreements between the actors themselves and between them and governments. As Keohane and Nye put it: 'Coalitions between revolutionary groups … strengthen their legitimacy in their struggles against governments.'[10]

Keohane and Nye used the term 'world politics' as a broader concept that includes transnational actors: 'The world politics paradigm attempts to transcend the "level-of-analysis problem" both by broadening the conception of actors to include transnational actors and by conceptually breaking down the "hard shell" of the nation-state.'[11] The main feature of world politics is agreement between various autonomous, or semi-autonomous actors.

Bowyer Bell, author of the chapter on revolutionary organizations in Keohane and Nye's book, stated:

---

[5]   J. David Singer, 'The Level-of-Analysis Problem in International Relations', in Klaus Knorr and Sidney Verba (eds.), *The International System. Theoretical Essays* (Princeton: Princeton University Press, 1967), p. 82.

[6]   According to Holsti's characterization of an alliance or coalition, as cited in Walt, *The Origins of Alliances*, p. 1.

[7]   Keohane and Nye (eds.), *Transnational Relations and World Politics*.

[8]   Ibid., p. xvii.

[9]   Ibid., p. 372.

[10] Ibid., p. 373.

[11] Ibid., p. 380.

During the past century, revolutionary organizations have, in the name of mankind, sought the violent transformation of the existing international framework. Their aim has been the liberation of nations submerged by fate or repressed by coercion and the destruction of the entire nation-state system, considered a passing phase of history. Even those revolutionary organizations dedicated to a specific national struggle have tended to see the triumph of their cause as a step toward a conflict-free world society in which the basic aspirations of all will have been achieved... In the last decade, with fewer countries to liberate from a foreign oppressor and more to be liberated from domestic regimes supported by worldwide imperialism, the universal ideological context of the revolutionary struggle has become more pronounced. Today most, but by no means all, revolutionary movements proclaim an allegiance to world revolution... Such organizations may have deep sympathies, even specific alliances, with fellow national revolutionary organizations or legitimate governments, but they are often comparable, if not parallel, to normal international arrangements.[12]

Mansbach, Fergusson and Lampert delivered a similar message: 'The far-reaching changes that have taken place in the global system since 1945 challenge not only the concept of sovereignty but also the adequacy of regarding the nation-state as the sole actor in world politics.'[13] In their evaluation:

As nuclear and conventional warfare have become more expensive to contemplate and less effective, new means of gaining influence, including guerrilla warfare, political terrorism, economic boycott, and political propaganda, have become more common, thereby permitting actors lacking the traditional instruments of power to exercise considerable influence and enjoy considerable autonomy.[14]

Mansbach, Fergusson and Lampert reviewed the activity of international actors ('non-state actors') in the Middle East, Western Europe and Latin America. They found that interstate non-governmental actors were no less autonomous than states – a phenomenon they termed 'the democratization of global politics'.[15]

Bertelsen went further by calling some of these actors 'non-state nations' (NSNs), including in this category entities that operate in a manner similar to nation states but are not recognized as such. According to her 'all the non-state nations described [in her book] have deep historical roots and have endured substantial periods of dispersion and suppression. Many have been directly

---

[12] Bowyer Bell, *Contemporary Revolutionary Organizations*, p. 153.
[13] Mansbach, Fergusson and Lampert, *The Web of World Politics*, p. 25.
[14] Ibid., p. 35.
[15] Ibid., p. 276.

encouraged in their resurgence by a twentieth century trend of championing the right to national self-determination.'[16]

The aforementioned researchers saw revolutionary and nationalist terrorist organizations as actors wielding influence within the international context, with the Palestinian organizations heading the list. So much so, that Mansbach, Fergusson, Lampert and Bertelsen devoted entire chapters of their books to a study of Palestinian organizations from this perspective. Mansbach, Fergusson and Lampert stressed that the Palestinian guerrilla organizations had regular army units, conducted negotiations for formal agreements with Arab states, and even jeopardized diplomatic understandings between the super powers.[17]

In the late 1970s, therefore, the theoretical tools that proved that revolutionary, national liberation, guerrilla, and terrorist organizations were autonomous international actors were finally perfected. Some researchers preferred to define these organizations as transnational actors. These transnational actors are characterized by their ability to develop an autonomous or even independent foreign policy, to confront sovereign nations and governments, exacting a high price in the process, and in certain cases, to achieve national independence on a par with that of legitimate governments.

These characteristics were evident among the Palestinian organizations, particularly the larger ones. Fatah, the organization that embraces most Palestinian militants and controls the PLO, excelled itself in this respect. Shortly after Arafat's election as chairman of the organization in February 1969, the PLO was recognized by Arab states as the sole legitimate representative of the Palestinian people, with a status equal to that of member states of the Arab League. In 1975, India became the first non-Arab state to confer full diplomatic recognition on the PLO; other states swiftly followed suit. In October 1974, Arafat was virtually accepted as a head of state when he addressed the UN General Assembly.

Fatah/PLO, and to a lesser extent other organizations such as the PFLP and the Democratic Front for the Liberation of Palestine (DFLP), not content with mere recognition as equal international actors, set about developing their own military forces. The PLO military arm – the Palestinian Liberation Army – was effectively incorporated into the various Arab armies as Palestinian units. Fatah's own units, comparable in size to battalions and brigades, succeeded in gaining control of territory in southern Lebanon, turning them into an extraterritorial zone known as 'Fatahland'. Other organizations also set up military units, albeit smaller ones, but still large enough to constitute a threat to nations such as Jordan (see the events of

---

[16] Judy S. Bertelsen, 'The Palestinian Arabs', in Judy S. Bertelsen (ed.), *Non-state Nations in International Politics. Comparative System Analysis* (New York: Praeger Publishers, 1977), p. 245.

[17] See Mansbach, Fergusson and Lampert, *The Web of World Politics*, p. 27.

September 1970) or Lebanon (particular after the outbreak of civil war). In 1981 Israel was constrained to reach a cease-fire agreement with Palestinian forces bombarding northern Israel from South Lebanon and ultimately launched a sweeping military strike against their presence in Lebanon in June 1982.

During periods of military and political stagnation, Palestinian organizations again resorted to terror against Arab governments (e.g. the 1971 assassination of Jordanian prime minister Wasfi at-Tal by Black September, and the 1969 attack by the PFLP on the Saudi oil pipeline 'Tapline', for example), against Israel and against Western states whom they considered Israel's allies. According to Bowyer Bell, the very fact that the PFLP tried to undermine a number of legitimate Arab regimes testifies to its significance as an international actor.

The use of terror provided Palestinian terrorist organizations with a bargaining tool for obtaining concessions from foreign governments. In 1973, for example, Fatah/PLO reached an agreement with the Italian government whereby it would refrain from terrorist activity in Italy in exchange for freedom of political action on its territory. In a similar move, Turkey agreed to the establishment of a PLO office in Ankara after Fatah/PLO mediated in the release of hostages seized by PFLP terrorists at the Egyptian embassy in Ankara in 1978.

German left-wing terrorist organizations attacked American targets in West Germany for many years, and in the late 1970s and early 1980s directly threatened NATO commanders in Europe. In a number of cases, German terrorists took part in extremely complex international terrorist operations (such as the seizure of the OPEC headquarters in Vienna in 1975 and the hijacking of the Air France plane to Entebbe in June 1976). While Italian left-wing terrorist organizations were far less involved with international terror as such, they occasionally attacked sensitive American targets (the kidnapping of Gen. Dozier in December 1981 and the assassination of Leamon Hunt in February 1984) in an attempt to sabotage the pro-American policy of the Italian government. At the time of the kidnapping of Gen. Dozier, the Red Brigades conducted negotiations with the Bulgarian intelligence services on the possibility of intelligence/propaganda cooperation between the two.[18]

During the 1970s and 1980s researchers addressed the as yet theoretical problem of the use of non-conventional weapons (chemical, biological and nuclear) by terrorist organizations. The attack perpetrated by members of the radical Japanese Buddhist sect, Aum Shinrikyo, in the spring of 1995, when toxic gas sarin was released in the Tokyo subway, demonstrated for the first time the destructive potential inherent in terrorist weapons of this kind. The fact that the sect used

---

[18] Gen. James Lee Dozier was deputy chief commander of the NATO ground forces in Southern Europe. Leamon Hunt, an American, was director-general of the Multinational Force of Observation in Sinai (MFO), with headquarters in Rome.

such lethal weapons against Japanese targets in Japan itself does not detract from the seriousness of the crime, especially in view of the copycat syndrome in the world of terror and the existence of the sect's many branches worldwide (Russia, Germany, the US and Sri Lanka). No doubt international developments over the last decade, widespread instability in many parts of the world, and the real danger of the proliferation of non-conventional weapons among terrorist or criminal elements, have enhanced the global bargaining power of the latter.

Terrorist organizations, like states, occasionally developed special departments for handling international relations with other organizations and states. Some clearly defined the organizational institutions responsible for devising and handling their foreign policy. Thus the head of the Basque Fatherland and Liberty (Euzkadi ta Askatasuna – ETA) 'foreign affairs directorate' conducted international relations on behalf of the organization from Brussels, where he lived. The German Revolutionary Cells had its 'international section' responsible for handling international contacts and planning joint operations with the PFLP. The PFLP itself had a 'foreign relations branch', which masterminded, *inter alia*, terrorist attacks abroad. The Red Brigades handled international ties through its executive committee, or rather through the head of the organization himself and one or two of his aides.

In view of the above, European and Palestinian terrorist organizations most definitely fit Keohane and Nye's definition of 'transnational actors' as 'significant actors, whose characteristics include autonomy, the control of substantial resources relevant to a given issue area, and participation in political relationships across state lines'.[19]

II.   RESEARCH PARADIGM

The purpose of this study is to establish the causes and conditions for the formation of coalitions between terrorist organizations of the 'transnational actor' kind, as defined above, and to examine the practical parameters of cooperation arising from the coalition of two or more organizations. As stated above, Walt's balance of threat theory, which has been endorsed by a number of leading researchers, most recently by Holsti, Hopmann and Sullivan in their comprehensive empirical research, has served as an important tool. This book attempts to adapt this tool to the specific area of terrorist organizations, or transnational actors, in an effort to find a theoretical framework that matches their particular characteristics.

---

[19]   Keohane and Nye (eds.), *Transnational Relations and World Politics*, p. 380.

The basic premise of this research is that terrorist organizations are eager to form coalitions with other organizations when they feel threatened by internal, regional and international political and strategic conditions and events, other states, or super powers.

The choice of the balance of threat theory as the basis for this research into the behavior of terrorist organizations in forming coalitions does not imply the indiscriminate use of techniques or tools used by Walt in his research. Terrorist organizations, despite being significant transnational actors, obviously brook no comparison with sovereign, independent states in terms of freedom of action, available human and material resources, and ability to influence international developments

Research on alliances between states is irrelevant in the case of terrorist organizations, which consistently avoid formal agreements, and are careful to hide basic understandings with other organizations from their enemies, from the public at large, and even from their own members.[20] As shown below, only in isolated cases did organizations publish joint declarations or manifestos, and even these can hardly be defined as formal or informal agreements. Thus, rather than the term 'alliance' this study uses the term 'coalition' to describe understandings and cooperation between organizations.[21]

Presumably, one of the reasons for secrecy among terrorist organizations is the clandestine nature of their activities. These organizations must maintain maximum secrecy in order to neutralize the superior offensive and defensive capacities of their perceived enemy. In some cases, the reason for secrecy may stem from political interests, the need to keep options open in a changing reality, or the wish to avoid being perceived as allies of other radical and violent organizations.

According to Bowyer Bell, contacts between a legitimate sovereign state and a revolutionary movement are exceptional.[22] Nevertheless, he considers transnational relations of this kind the lifeblood of revolutionary movements, since very few can operate in total isolation or without a host state which offers them sanctuary. When revolutionaries are based in the territory of an ally, complications and conflict are inevitable, since the partners in such an alliance are not only unequal, but also have different priorities.

---

[20] Holsti, Hopmann and Sullivan examined formal alliances between various countries. Their research related to the NATO alliance, the Warsaw Pact, bilateral pacts within the communist bloc after the Second World War, as well as formal alliances established between various countries in the period between 1815 and 1939. Walt, for his part, studied not only formal but also informal alliances in the Middle East, such as the unwritten strategic agreements between the US and Israel.

[21] The *New Webster's Dictionary and Thesaurus* (Danbury, CT: Lexicon Publications, 1992) defines a coalition as 'a temporary union of political parties for some common aim.'

[22] Bowyer Bell, *Contemporary Revolutionary Organizations*, pp. 165-6.

Although the sole aim of this research is to examine coalitions between terrorist organizations, it should be noted that Palestinian terrorist organizations have
formed coalitions with states in the Middle East, and even with the super powers.
The Palestinian organizations that sought sanctuary within Israel's Arab
neighbors, and sometimes even further afield, reached agreements with these
countries regarding their status within the host country, the degree of political and
military freedom allowed them in their struggle against Israel, the amount of
economic and military assistance they would receive, etc.

The stronger the Palestinian organizations became militarily and politically,
the broader the scope of the international agreements of which they were part.
Thus, the Cairo agreement signed in November 1969 and mediated by Egypt,
regulated PLO relations with Lebanon and the Palestinian military presence in
southern Lebanon; the Hussein-Arafat agreement of February 1985 was drawn up
in an attempt to formally establish political and territorial relations between
Jordan and the PLO.

The European nationalist organizations, ETA and the IRA, occasionally entered agreements with the governments of Spain and Britain – usually cease-fire
agreements or preliminary political negotiations. Radical left-wing terrorist
organizations in Europe were far more isolated politically than the Palestinian
organizations, or even the European nationalist organizations. This was because
states, which may have identified with their struggle, were wary of troubles in the
relations with the legitimate governments if ties of this kind were discovered.
After the unification of Germany, the presence of RAF members in East Germany
seemed to indicate the existence of agreements between the communist government of East Germany and the West German terrorist organization. There is,
however, no legal proof so far, that the two colluded in the terrorist acts perpetrated in West Germany in the 1970s and 1980s.

Contacts and agreements between terrorist organizations and states suspected
of supporting international terror constitute a major aspect of research into
international terror. However, it is not within the scope of this work to approach
this subject either from a theoretical or empirical perspective.

The balance of power theory, like Walt's balance of threat theory, examines
two alternatives in choosing an ally: balancing (allying *against* a stronger party)
and 'bandwagoning' (allying *with* the stronger party). Walt himself found that
'bandwagoning' is far less common than balancing in coalitions between states,
and is almost always the option of particularly weak and isolated states.[23]

Wilkinson claimed that terrorist organizations divide the world into the Mani-
chean concept of friend or foe ('either with us or against us').[24] A neutral position

---

[23]   Walt, *The Origins of Alliances*, p. 263.
[24]   Wilkinson, *Terrorism and the Liberal State*, p. 194.

is untenable. Therefore, instead of resorting to negotiations, diplomacy and concessions, terrorists view their struggle in zero-sum terms: they will wage war until the bitter end.

As Steiner and Debray pointed out, in a war between revolutionaries and imperialism, the possibility of negotiation does not exist.[25] The RAF made no attempt whatsoever to 'reform' the enemy: for it, the only solution was to annihilate it. The principal ideological document of the RAF, 'The Concept of the Urban Guerrilla', opens with a quotation from Mao Tse Tung: 'To be attacked by the enemy is desirable... In my opinion, the fact that we are not attacked indicates that we are collaborating with the enemy. To be attacked by the enemy signifies that we have established clear demarcation lines between it and us.'[26] Negri, an ideologue of the Italian radical left, claimed that no dialogue, compromise or contact whatsoever was possible with 'the representatives of the capitalist system'.[27] A PFLP document from 1969 argued that all the problems of the Palestinian people were due to Israel and the US, and that under no circumstances could either of these countries become allies of the Palestinians.[28]

The chances of a terrorist organizations bandwagoning with a strong and threatening enemy are minimal, since this contradict their very *raison-d'être*. Therefore, the basic premise that terrorist organizations always aspire to form a coalition *against*, rather than with, a stronger state/power, seems far more tenable. Nonetheless, it is not uncommon for one of the Palestinian terrorist organizations, including Fatah and the PFLP, for reasons of survival, the need for sanctuary, or regional considerations, to jump on the bandwagon of the stronger adversary (whether Syria, Iraq, Egypt or even Jordan, which is sometimes considered the Palestinians' archenemy). Indeed, some small organizations, like the Fatah-Revolutionary Council led by Sabri al-Banna (Abu Nidal), turned 'bandwagoning' into an art.[29]

There is a need to define the type of threat that creates the desire for a coalition, and the immediacy of this threat. Walt lists four factors which, in his opinion, are critical in evaluating the nature or immediacy of a threat:[30]

---

[25] Steiner and Debray, *La Fraction Armée Rouge*, p. 205.

[26] Quoted from the French version, in Xavier Raufer and François Haut, 'RAF – Une organisation zéro traces', *Notes et Etudes*, No. 5 (1988), p. 54.

[27] Cited in Richard Drake, 'The Red Brigades and the Italian Political Tradition', in Yonah Alexander and Kenneth Myers (eds.), *Terrorism in Europe* (London: Croom Helm, 1982), pp. 102-140, p. 113.

[28] See document entitled 'Political and Organizational Strategy', cited in Carré, *L'Idéologie palestinienne de résistance. Analyse de textes: 1964-1970* (Paris: Armand Colin, 1972), p. 82.

[29] The topic of ties between terrorist organizations and hostile states, where yesterday's friend can swiftly turn into today's foe, is a research topic in its own right.

[30] Walt, *The Origins of Alliances*, pp. 22-6.

(1) *Aggregate power:* 'All else being equal, the greater a state's total resources
     (e.g. population, industrial and military capability, and technological prow-
     ess), the greater a potential threat it can pose to others.'[31]

(2) *Geographic proximity:* 'Because the ability to project power declines with
     distance, states that are nearby pose a greater threat than those that are far
     away. Other things being equal, therefore, states are more likely to make
     their alliance choices in response to nearby powers than in response to those
     that are distant.'[32]

(3) *Offensive power:* 'All else being equal, states with large offensive capabili-
     ties are more likely to provoke an alliance than are those that are incapable
     of attacking because of geography, military posture, or something else.'[33]

(4) *Aggressive intentions:* 'States that are viewed as aggressive are likely to
     provoke others to balance against them... Indeed, even states with rather
     modest capabilities may prompt others to balance if they are perceived as
     especially aggressive.'[34]

The terrorist organization's starting point is fundamentally different from that of a
sovereign state. The very fact that it resorts to terror is because of its undeniable
position of inferiority. Even when armed struggle erupts, the aggressive intentions
and cumulative offensive power of the oppressive regime constitute a real and
immediate threat. The issue of geographical proximity is not relevant in cases of
internal revolutionary struggles, separatist struggles or national liberation
struggles. It is relevant only with respect to struggles against colonial or imperialist states that are remote from their colonies.

Despite their obvious inferiority *vis-à-vis* the institutionalized enemy, the
organizations themselves generally indulge in hyperbole when describing their
ability to overcome the enormous obstacles in their path, and to awaken and lead
the masses to a glorious victory. Wright points out that the success of the revolutionary forces in Cuba and the publication of Che Guevara's *The Guerrilla War*
contributed significantly to a feeling of revolutionary euphoria that maintained
that victory was possible even under the most adverse conditions, even though no
empirical proof existed of the revolution's success in the urban environment.[35]
Optimism and faith, whether subjective feelings or based on a profound conviction of the justice of one's cause, are necessary for an organization to recruit new

---

[31]   Ibid., p. 22.
[32]   Ibid., p. 23.
[33]   Ibid., p. 24.
[34]   Ibid., p. 35.
[35]   Joanne Wright, *Terrorist Propaganda. The Red Army Faction and the Provisional IRA, 1968-86*
       (London: Macmillan, 1991), p. 45.

members, maintain morale, and persuade the enemy and the public at large of its ability to defeat the enemy, and lead the nation to victory.

This tendency toward demonization of the enemy on the one hand, and self-glorification, on the other, renders even more difficult the task of understanding how terrorist organizations realistically evaluate the need for coalitions.

The main question is, therefore: What causes a terrorist organization to decide that a threat is so serious as to necessitate a coalition with another organization(s)? All agree that the strategic decision to form a coalition is an important and, under certain conditions, even critical decision for any international actor.

Crenshaw claimed that an organization decides to use terror according to its assessment of the effectiveness of this strategy to help achieve its aims.[36] This theory is corroborated by the documents of various terrorist organizations, as shown below. Indeed, this trend is clear in the establishment of the Red Brigades' 'Strategic Leadership', which was responsible, among other things, for adopting and publicizing important strategic decisions.

If the choice of terror is a deliberate and considered choice, adopted after serious examination of available data and a rational evaluation of the situation, the decision to form or join a coalition is undoubtedly the result of a similar process of deliberation, which takes into account the balance of power between the organization and its opponents. A major way a terrorist organization can tip the balance in its favor is through the acquisition of new resources, such as an alliance with a wealthier revolutionary organization or a friendly government.

According to Crenshaw, terrorist organizations 'arrive at collective judgments about the relative effectiveness of the different strategies on the basis of observation and experience, as much as on the basis of abstract strategic conceptions derived from ideological assumptions'.[37] The strategy may change in accordance with changing conditions. Similarly, Wilkinson showed how factors such as ideology, the prevailing regime, conflicts and certain strategic and tactical conditions, may affect the political motivations of terrorist organizations.[38]

This study evaluates the causes and conditions governing the formation of a coalition between terrorist organizations, and how such a coalition works in practice. To this end, it uses independent variables at three levels of analysis:

(1) The *international* level (global and regional),
(2) The *organizational* level,
(3) The *decision-maker* level.

---

[36] Crenshaw, *The Logic of Terrorism*, pp. 7-20.
[37] Ibid., p. 8.
[38] Wilkinson, *The Sources of Terrorism*, pp. 139-40.

Table 1 describes the independent variables at the various levels of analysis.

Table 1: Independent variables influencing coalitions between terrorist organizations

Variable	Description
(1) *Variables at the international system level*	
- Bipolarity	Tension within the bipolar system encourages the formation of coalitions.
- New revolutionary foci	Rifts between great powers sharing the same ideology and the emergence of new revolutionary foci encourage the formation of coalitions.
- War and tension	Regional wars and tensions are perceived as a threat and encourage the formation of alliances.
- International security/military cooperation	International security/military cooperation against terrorist organizations encourages the formation of coalitions.
(2) *Variables at the organization level*	
- *Ideology*	Coalitions exist when organizations share a common ideological base.
- The radical left or right	Revolutionary organizations of the radical left or right that place strategic emphasis on the struggle against the régime in their country tend to avoid coalitions.
- Anarcho-communism and anarchism	The special nature of anarchist organizations makes them more likely to enter coalitions.
- Nationalism	Because the goal of nationalist movements is independence, they are less likely to set up coalitions.
- *Structural characteristics*	
- Non-state nations (NSN)	NSN organizations are affected by considerations relating to international policy.
- The 'strong' versus the 'weak' partner	In a coalition between a 'strong' partner (the patron) and a 'weak' one (the client), the weaker partner is not significantly dependent on the stronger one.
- Geographical distance	Coalitions are usually bilateral. Where more than two organizations are involved, geographical proximity and a common goal are essential.
(3) *Variables at the decision-maker level*	
- Antisemitic preconceptions	The antisemitic and racist attitudes of leaders of terrorist organizations affect their decision to cooperate against Israel and/or Jews.

The independent variables relate to *global factors* such as bipolar tensions and the emergence of new revolutionary foci, as well as *regional factors*, such as regional wars or conflicts, or military/security cooperation against terrorist organizations. At the *organizational level*, it assesses how ideology and structural characteristics (size of organization, geographical proximity between them) affect the formation and operation of a coalition. At the *decision-maker level*, it narrows the focus to a single aspect, namely how antisemitic preconceptions among leaders of European terrorist organizations influenced their decision to form a coalition with Palestinian terrorist organizations. This limitation will be explained later. The operative definitions of the independent variables will be specified during the presentation of each group of variables.

In order to evaluate whether two or more organizations have reached a degree of cooperation that may be defined as a coalition, and to measure the extent of this cooperation, dependent variables that reflect the concrete expression of this cooperation will be used: the level of ideological cooperation, logistic cooperation (material assistance), and operational cooperation. A description of the dependent variables is provided after the section on independent variables, and is relevant to the description of the research methodology.

CHAPTER 2
VARIABLES AND RESEARCH HYPOTHESES

This chapter examines a number of hypotheses regarding the behavior of terrorist organizations in the process of forming coalitions. The hypotheses are tested in subsequent chapters by case studies of various organizations with different ideological, geographical and structural backgrounds. This chapter also outlines the research methodology and sources. The period under review can be divided into three main sub-periods:

1968-80: This period began with the student uprising in Europe and ended with Ronald Reagan's inauguration as president of the US. Among significant events during this period were: the Vietnam War (1968-72), the aftermath of the Six Day War (1967-72), and the events and consequences of the Yom Kippur War (1973-75), President Sadat's visit to Israel and the Camp David accords (1977-80).

1981-84: Reagan's first term of office was marked by a hard-line policy towards the communist bloc and international terror. The period included the Lebanese War and its immediate aftermath (1982-84).

1985-90: This period covers Reagan's second term in office, the first years of George Bush's presidency, and the Gulf Crisis in late 1990. Significant events during this period were: progress in Reagan's 'Star Wars' program (Strategic Defense Initiative – SDI) and the stationing of American cruise missiles in Western Europe. During the second half of this period, the effects of Mikhail Gorbachev's policy of *glasnost* were felt, with the enfeeblement and ultimate dissolution of the communist bloc. After their eviction from Lebanon, Palestinian organizations embarked on the intricate path of peace negotiations with Israel. It was a period of division and weakness in the Arab world, set against the background of the Iraq-Iran War.

I.   THE INFLUENCE OF INTERNATIONAL AND REGIONAL VARIABLES

Terrorist organizations fit Liska's definition of domestic factions aligning with outside (regional and international) actors in their internal struggle against governing factions in their own country. Therefore, reference must be made to international and regional factors, to domestic and foreign policy in countries where the terrorist organizations operated and to the implications for the coalition strategy of these organizations.

Hypothesis 1: Tension within the bipolar system heightens the terrorist organizations' sense of vulnerability vis-à-vis the superpowers, and encourages them to cooperate and form coalitions.

The international system after the Second World War was characterized by hostility between two main ideological blocs headed by the US and the USSR, respectively. The alliances that formed around these two superpowers dominated international politics, so much so that for many years the system was defined as essentially bipolar.[1] The level of tension between the two blocs vacillated but dropped significantly towards the mid-1950s. The end of the 1950s witnessed a growing ideological and strategic rift between the two most important allies within the communist bloc – the USSR and the Peoples Republic of China.[2]

This bipolarity evidently influenced the behavior of all international actors, from the great powers to small states.[3] The concept of bipolarity in international politics was interpreted in different ways by various terrorist organizations. Many saw it as a conflict between the Western imperialist bloc under the leadership of the US, and the 'anti-oppression' bloc, which included countries that had liberated themselves from the yoke of colonialism, liberation movements and revolutionary movements throughout the Western world. The USSR was perceived as an imperialist power that dominated the communist bloc and as a rival, or sometimes a partner, of the Western imperialist camp. From the early 1980s, however, attitudes towards the USSR changed; some terrorist organizations began to consider it a potential ally. The Palestinian organizations, for their part, were mostly affected by the Middle Eastern policies of the superpowers, and their struggle for hegemony in the region. Throughout the period in question they saw the US as their arch-enemy and as Israel's main ally.

The behavior of terrorist organizations, it should be stressed, is not governed by the same criteria as that of states. For example, it was actually during periods of rapprochement between the two blocs that terrorist organizations were most active, particularly against the US. They never, however, targeted the USSR, except for occasional verbal attacks by some of the organizations. Interestingly, revolutionary anti-communist movements on the far right were sometimes also hostile to the US.

---

[1]   The term 'bipolar system' was usually used with reference to the conflict between the Western 'imperialist' camp and the 'anti-imperialist' camp ('progressive' states, such as Vietnam, Algeria, Cuba, etc., national liberation movements and Western revolutionary movements). Occasionally, it was used to designate the 'classical' bipolar tension between the Western and communist blocs. Throughout this book, the particular context in which the term is being used will be specified.

[2]   For a description of the period, see Holsti, Hopmann and Sullivan, *Unity and Disintegration in International Alliances*, pp. 89-92.

[3]   Hopmann, for example, saw a clear correlation between the degree of cooperation among NATO states or Warsaw Pact states, on the one hand, and the level of conflict or polarity between these two alliances, on the other. Ibid., p. 143.

During the détente period, revolutionary left-wing organizations and some nationalist movements believed the West was undergoing a serious political, economic and structural crisis, driving it to adopt a more aggressive posture. They perceived the world as on the threshold of war, a war contrived by the forces of imperialism against 'the world proletariat and the forces of progress and liberation in the developing countries'. This evaluation was based on an analysis of economic, technological and social developments in the West, particularly in the US, after 1968, the year of worldwide student unrest. Tensions within the bipolar system were especially apparent after Ronald Reagan was elected president of the US in 1980. His hard-line policy towards the USSR and the communist bloc was accompanied by hawkish intransigence towards international terror and Latin American guerrilla organizations.

When discussing bipolar tension, it is important to determine which particular events were perceived as especially threatening by the terrorist organizations. Did tension between the Western and communist blocs enhance interest in coalitions? Did changes in the bipolar system affect their coalition strategy?

Hypothesis 2: Rifts between ideologically-similar powers and the emergence of new revolutionary and ideological foci create a new type of solidarity, and encourage the formation of coalitions between terrorist organizations which support one of the new ideologies.

Attitudes towards international alliances changed with the onset of détente, the rise in the number and strength of non-aligned states and growing rifts within the ideological blocs.[4] The rift between China and the USSR influenced the strategy of the international revolutionary movement.[5] The traditional Soviet line, which advocated the gradual development of an alliance between communist parties and the national bourgeoisie against imperialism, clashed with the historical experience of Maoism, which saw the peasants as the new revolutionary force, emphasized the importance of the Third World and perceived imperialism as a 'paper tiger'. Maoism had a profound effect on Third World revolutionary movements, and on radical groups in industrialized countries. At the same time, the Sino-Soviet struggle for hegemony left its mark on the international communist movement, and

---

[4]   According to Lall, in a bipolar system, the leaders of alliances were keen to recruit as many allies as possible, regardless of their military significance. Holsti, on the other hand, believed that in a bipolar context, alliances tended to be closed systems which small states found hard to leave. Liska pointed out as early as in 1968 that the weaker the bipolar system, the narrower the gap becomes between aligned and non-aligned states. Wallace, on the other hand, believed that a climate of international instability actively encouraged the formation of alliances as a way of trying to change the status quo. Ibid., pp. 250-53.

[5]   Angelo Ventura, 'Il problema delle origini del terrorismo di sinistra', in Donatella della Porta (ed.), *Terrorismi in Italia* (Bologna: Società Editrice il Mulino, 1984), p. 81.

led to a dramatic change of strategy. China provided political and material support to radical tendencies, and upheld as models the armed struggles in Vietnam, Latin America and the Middle East.

The Tricontinental Conference, which took place in January 1966 in the Cuban capital of Havana, gave birth to a new revolutionary credo in the anti-imperialist cause, one no longer based on antiquated Marxist and Leninist doctrines, but on the new doctrines of Mao, Gen. Giap and the strategy of Che Guevara.[6] As a result, revolutionaries worldwide came to espouse a similar ideology and to venerate the same heroes.

Was this new solidarity translated into the formation of new coalitions? Did terrorist organizations feel a commitment towards other movements (such as Palestinian organizations), which were considered an integral major part of the revolutionary Third World? Was this commitment expressed through practical cooperation and alliances? Were alliances with Third World movements given preference over alliances with organizations in the developed world? Was the international activity of the Palestinian organizations themselves dictated by their sense of solidarity with the 'anti-imperialist camp'?

Hypothesis 3: Regional wars and crises that are perceived as threats to terrorist organizations or their ideological allies encourage them to form a common front against the mutual enemy, or in order to help an organization that is under attack in another region.

War threatens the sovereignty and territorial integrity of a state, and the territorial achievements of a liberation or revolutionary organization, as well as the human and material resources at their disposal. On occasion, war can lead to the total destruction of a country or organization. It has been suggested that alliances between states serve not only to promote cooperation, but also, and primarily, to preserve, enhance or create positions of strength in the face of war, or to propose diplomatic measures designed to prevent war.[7] During times of significant threats, such as during major wars, nations aspire towards contractual commitments of the highest possible order.[8]

According to Liska, conflicts on the global, regional and domestic level sway states to form alliances. 'A regional system consists of states which are parties to

---

[6]   See J. Bowyer Bell, 'Contemporary Revolutionary Organizations', in R. Keohane and J. S. Nye (eds.), *Transnational Relations and World Politics* (Cambridge, MA: Harvard University Press, 1972), pp. 156-7.

[7]   See Julian R. Friedman, 'Alliance in International Politics' in J. Friedman, C. Bladen and S. Rosen (eds.), *Alliances in International Politics* (Boston, MA: Allyn and Bacon, 1970), p. 10.

[8]   See Sullivan in Holsti, Hopmann and Sullivan, *Unity and Disintegration in International Alliances*, p. 83.

local conflicts that determine alignments within and beyond the region.' A regional system can then comprise outside powers that are 'present' as allies on a local issue. '[T]he domestic system is defined by parties to internal conflicts – domestic factions and outside forces capable of influencing local events. The domestic system is fully part of the international system when two or more factions are aligned with outside actors in ways which relate internal and external conflicts.' In such a system, the competing groups will seek to neutralize the opposed group by countervailing alignments.[9]

Between the 1960s and 1980s revolutionary terrorist organizations and revolutionary nationalist organizations believed that Western imperialism was pushing the world to the brink of a third world war. Regional measures adopted by the West in response to global tensions or regional disputes were consistently interpreted by terrorist organizations as part of a plot to control global resources, and to crush the liberation and revolutionary movements. In the same vein, any serious conflict or concentration of military forces, let alone small-scale armed struggle or dispute in the Middle East, Central America or South East Asia, were seen as paving the way towards a definitive strike against 'the forces of progress and revolution', and therefore as a direct threat not only to the local or regional forces involved in the dispute, but also to all forces belonging to this camp.

This is what Rote Armee Fraktion (RAF) leader Horst Mahler meant when he declared that his organization was participating in a war to end all wars, a war rendered all the more savage by the ruthlessness of exploitative classes in suppressing any challenge to its supremacy. This war was not perceived as a war between nations, but a class war that would embrace all nations, and transcend all social, cultural and religious barriers.[10]

Was this view translated into assistance to terrorist organizations considered at risk due to regional disputes or war? Were some regions or disputes considered more dangerous than others to the revolutionary camp, and if so, why? Did the geographical location of a country, or its direct or indirect participation in more distant disputes, have an effect on a terrorist organization's decision to join a coalition with other organizations?

If Hypothesis 3 is correct, terrorist organizations sometimes participate in regional disputes in order to help terrorist organizations in other locations. This support may be provided in the local country of the terrorist organization, or in the region where the dispute occurs.

---

[9] See George Liska, 'Alliances and Realliances', in Friedman, Bladen and Rosen, *Alliances in International Politics*, pp. 105-106.

[10] See notes Horst Mahler prepared for his trial, published *in CONTROinformazione*, Nos. 1-2, February-March (1974), pp. 26-29.

Hypothesis 4: International and regional cooperation between security forces against terrorist organizations encourages the latter to form coalitions.

On a day-to-day basis, terrorist organizations have to grapple less with the 'forces of imperialism' or regional conflicts, than with local police and security forces. The fiercer or longer the armed struggle, the greater the confrontation between the protagonists, until gradually the security forces invariably become the main target of terrorist operations. Indeed, there is a direct correlation between the security forces' success in catching terrorists, and the strategic primacy of goals such as the release of imprisoned comrades, improvements in prison conditions, and attempts to influence the outcome of trials.

The rapid spread of Middle Eastern terrorism to Europe has intensified the need for international cooperation between the police and security services of the various countries concerned. The emerging legal problems call for a degree of legislative and constitutional coordination, resulting in new international conventions designed to cope with international terror. New patterns of international terror, in particular plane hijacking and kidnappings in remote, unstable countries such as Lebanon, have driven a number of countries to establish special anti-terrorist squads.

The need for international cooperation against terror has grown in direct proportion to the degree of international cooperation between the terrorist organizations themselves. International anti-terror cooperation received an added impetus in the mid-1970s when a number of particularly daring operations were perpetrated by terrorists from various countries. The PFLP operations masterminded by the notorious 'Carlos' (Ilich Ramirez Sanchez) were particularly significant in this regard.

The counter-terrorist tactics of the security establishments were not seen by the terrorist organizations as defensive or deterrent in nature, but rather as part of an imperialist plot to eradicate any form of revolutionary resistance wherever their supremacy was challenged. In practice, the terrorists regarded this security cooperation as a direct military threat of the kind described by Walt in his theory on the origins of alliances.[11]

Did this focus on the struggle against local security forces rather than the pursuit of declared strategic goals encourage the formation of alliances? Did terrorist organizations seek out allies to help them in this struggle, either directly or indirectly, through undermining the common enemy in some other area? In other words, did international cooperation against terror intensify or weaken the tendency to form coalitions with other organizations?

---

[11]   See Stephen Walt, *The Origins of Alliances* (Ithaca and London: Cornell University Press, 1987), p. 35.

II.   THE INFLUENCE OF VARIABLES AT THE ORGANIZATIONAL LEVEL

1.   Ideological factors

Hypothesis 5: A coalition between two terrorist organizations exists only when there is some shared ideological base between the two.

The role of ideology in the establishment of coalitions has always been considered an important, albeit problematic, factor. On the face of it, ideological conformity or similarity would naturally lead to the formation of alliances. Morgenthau, however, refuted the possibility of a purely ideological alliance:

> It is unable to determine policies or guide actions and misleads by presenting the appearance of political solidarity where there is none. The ideological factor, when it is superimposed upon an actual community of interests, can lend strength to the alliance by marshaling moral convictions and emotional preferences to its support.[12]

Walt pointed out that most of the realistic school of researchers played down the importance of ideology in the choice of ally.[13]

While certain researchers, influenced by Arendt's analysis of totalitarianism, saw terrorism as an essentially ideological phenomenon, Wievorka pointed out that each terrorist act had an ideological component, however minor, which might be explicit (as in the case of the radical left), or implicit (as in the case of the radical right, which tends towards greater secrecy).[14] Wilkinson challenged existing rationales of terrorism, suggesting that the behavior of terrorists is best understood as a product of ideological fervor, the same fervor that spurs them on towards tactical successes, particularly publicity on behalf of their organization.[15]

Wright, like Crenshaw, claimed that terror was a strategy, not an ideology, the proof being that it was used by both the radical left and the radical right, and

---

[12]   See Hans Morgenthau, *Politics Among Nations* (New York: Alfred Knopf, 1959), p. 83.
[13]   See Walt, *The Origins of Alliances*, p. 33. Walt referred, *inter alia*, to Sullivan's quantitative study in this field. Sullivan claimed that ideology has an influence on relationships between states. According to him, a shared ideology leads to greater commitment, such as the establishment of a military alliance rather than a simple non-aggression pact which is usual among states with different ideologies. Once an alliance is already established, however, ideological differences have a minimal impact. See Holsti, Hopmann and Sullivan, *Unity and Disintegration in International Alliances*, pp. 61-64.
[14]   See Michel Wievorka, *The Making of Terrorism* (Chicago: The University of Chicago Press, 1993), pp. 10, 34.
[15]   See Wilkinson, 'The Sources of Terrorism: Terrorists' Ideologies and Beliefs', in Kegley (ed.), *International Terrorism*, p. 141.

political and non-political actors. Nevertheless, ideology determines the goals for which terror is used. Therefore, it is important to assess the ideological goals of most members of terrorist organizations. These ideological goals will be determined mainly by the environment in which a terrorist organization operates.[16]

Terrorist organizations themselves see ideology as critical for the success of their activities. Even small anarchist organizations have tried to build some ideological base, however rudimentary. Ideology determined the organization's ultimate objective, its enemy, and its strategic goals. Within every revolutionary organization, there is an ongoing struggle over the nature of its ideology. When ideological differences occur, such a struggle may lead to splits within the organization. Finally, ideology determines not only the organization's foes, but also its actual and potential friends, and the broader ideological camp to which it belongs.

It is also necessary to determine how ideology affected an organization's decision to form a coalition, and to what extent it serves as a cohesive force during cooperation with other partners. Are ideological factors the sole determinants, or are other interests at stake? Is a coalition at all possible between organizations with radically different ideologies?

Hypothesis 6: Anarchist or anarcho-communist movements have a greater tendency to enter coalitions with other organizations.

The terrorist organizations in this study can be divided into four main ideological groups:[17] anarchist or nihilist organizations; radical left-wing organizations; radical right-wing organizations; and organizations with a religious or cultural ideology, expressed either as nationalism or separatism, depending on the territorial orientation.

The modern anarchist organizations exhibited a hodgepodge of anarchist and socialist concepts, advocated revolutionary violence for its own sake, and aimed to topple capitalist regimes without offering any alternative agenda. They emulated the nineteenth century model of anarchist revolutionaries. They were loosely organized into small, unstable frameworks, with no hierarchy or institutionalized leadership.

The revolutionary left-wing organizations were divided over ideological issues such as the timing of the proletarian uprising against the bourgeois, capitalist state, and the use of terror as a weapon in the revolutionary struggle.[18]

---

[16]   See Wright, *Terrorist Propaganda. The Red Army Faction and the Provisional IRA, 1968-86* (London: Macmillan, 1991), p. xi.
[17]   See also Peter Fleming, Michael Stohl and Alex Schmid, 'The Theoretical Utility of Typologies of Terrorism: Lessons and Opportunities', in Stohl (ed.) *The Politics of Terrorism.*
[18]   See Paul Wilkinson, *Political Terrorism* (2nd edn.) (London: Macmillan, 1976), p. 112.

Trotskyist organizations, as 'good Bolsheviks' were familiar with Marxist texts and knew that the time was not yet ripe for armed revolutionary struggle. Moreover, they believed that the revolutionary vanguard had to keep its distance from the lumpenproletariat. The only Trotskyist organization to choose terror as a weapon in the political struggle was the Argentinean Ejercito Revolucionario del Pueblo (ERP).

Anti-Soviet Maoist organizations, on the other hand, engaged in clandestine operations to complement the movement's legal activities.[19] Although Maoist organizations skirted the threshold of terrorism, they were usually reluctant to cross it. This explains why future leaders of the BR left the ranks of the Maoist Partito Communista d'Italia – Marxista-Leninista (PCd'L-ml) in order to step up the violent struggle in the factories of Milan. It also explains why the leaders of the French Maoist organization, La Gauche Prolétarienne (Proletarian Left), decided to disband the organization in 1973 rather than adopt the PLO-style terrorism urged by some North African members of the organization.

Only organizations regarded as anarcho-communist embraced terror wholeheartedly. Like other revolutionary left-wing movements, they dreamt of a classless and stateless society, free of poverty, inequality and war. Such a society could be attained, they believed, by a working-class uprising. Their strategy was based on the notion of a violent vanguard, responsible for perpetrating symbolic acts of violence as a means of inciting the masses to rebel. Anarcho-communist organizations, however, lacked the advantages of nationalist organizations, namely broad-based internal coalitions, wealthy sponsors, a climate of deep social unrest, and popular support for their goal.[20]

According to Walt, 'ideological solidarity is less important than [significant] external threats as a cause of alliances'.[21] He argued that 'conflicts between communist regimes have been among the world's most virulent quarrels' and that 'unity of leftist forces … is probably more apparent than real'.[22] Walt also pointed out that in centralized movements such as the Marxist-Leninist ones, the likelihood of conflict among members is increased.[23] Walt's theories apply equally to states and radical right-wing movements, where conflicts usually occurred over leadership issues. (Who would lead the alliance/movement, thereby threatening the autonomy of the other states/members?) Since the leader's authority was based on the interpretation of a common ideology, ideological conflicts were widespread.

On the face of it, common enemies, similar aspirations, and ideological and strategic solidarity would seem to favor coalitions between revolutionary left-wing

---

[19] See Ventura, 'Il problema delle origini del terrorismo di sinistra', pp. 106-10.

[20] On this subject, see the chapter on anarcho-communism in E. Richard Rubenstein, *Alchemists of Revolution* (London: I.B. Tauris, 1987), pp. 87-107.

[21] See Walt, *The Origins of Alliances*, p. 266.

[22] Ibid., p. 280.

[23] Ibid., pp. 35-36.

movements, including anarcho-communists. One might have expected the formation of alliances to be a natural response to the vulnerability of these organizations *vis-à-vis* the perceived threat of Western imperialism. Reality proved rather more complex. The revolutionary movements accepted Marxism as their basic tenet, but combined or influenced by other ideologies. Some organizations emphasized elements of Leninist dogma, while others embraced elements of Trotskyism. The modernists were influenced by Maoism and Vietnamese and Cuban strategy, and particularly by the revolutionary neo-Marxists, such as Marcuse and Negri. Thus, despite shared aspirations and goals, fierce antagonism emerged between and within the organizations over ideological and strategic issues.

The ideological strength of terrorist organizations influenced their willingness to seek a coalition outside the narrow confines of the camp to which it belonged. Anarcho-communist organizations shared a number of characteristics that encouraged the formation of coalitions: a more fluid and decentralized ideological base; the absence of a hierarchical leadership or internal discipline to ensure adherence to a strict ideology; and the fact that, generally speaking, they were small and vulnerable. Affiliation with a larger camp intensified their sense of belonging, internal cohesion, and self-confidence.

Hypothesis 7: Radical left-wing or right-wing revolutionary organizations which give strategic priority to the struggle against the régime in a bid to seize power in their country, tend not to enter coalitions with other organizations.

If an organization is united around a single and immediate goal, such as seizing power in the country where it operates, is it less likely to enter a coalition with other organizations?

Hypothesis 8: Nationalist organizations, whose main goal is the attainment of independence for the minority they represent, are less likely to set up coalitions with other organizations.

Bowyer Bell pointed out that

> the theory of national liberation in Latin America, under whatever guise, resembles that of nineteenth century nationalism: Once the nation-state is 'liberated' all problems will disappear in the new revolutionary society. There exists an unarticulated, fraternal society of revolutionaries, bound as it has been for generations by similar aspirations, often joint exile, and a common heritage of political action.[24]

---

[24]   Bowyer Bell, *Contemporary Revolutionary Organizations*, pp. 160-161.

Che Guevara was the first to attempt to transcend the appeal of party politics and the magic of nationalism, by attempting to ignite 'two or three new Vietnams' in the battle against American imperialism through his naïve strategy of fraternity and goodwill. Despite his efforts, isolated Latin American attempts to set up international brigades along the lines of the Spanish international brigades of the 1930s, failed. Bowyer Bell claimed that 'most revolutionary organizations fighting for national liberation have been exclusive, fearful of contaminating the purity of their cause by 'internationalizing' their armed struggle.[25] This would seem to apply equally to the European national liberation organizations, such as the Basque ETA and the Irish IRA, whose urban terrorism never even approached Latin American-style guerrilla warfare. The main goal of these organizations was territorial independence – in the case of ETA, through separatism, and in the case of the IRA through national integration in the Republic of Ireland. The narrow ideological basis in both cases – the Basque language in the case of ETA, and Catholicism in the case of the IRA – and the lack of a common ideological or political heritage, curtailed the possibility of alliances based on ethnic solidarity with other peoples or nations.

Although both ETA and IRA (especially the former) tried to broaden their popular appeal by borrowing from radical left-wing revolutionary ideologies, their main ideological goal did not change. Indeed, the acquired ideology served the organization's internal goals more than its international struggle against a remote and rather abstract enemy.

The history of the Palestinian terrorist organizations seems to refute Hypothesis 8. As many researchers point out, they played a major role in the expansion of international terror.[26] They helped terrorist organizations worldwide, and promoted credibility of the 'international conspiracy' theory among some researchers, and in the mass media and public opinion.[27]

The issue was rendered more complex by the disproportionate number of Palestinian organizations involved in international terrorism. Some, such as Ahmed Jibril's PFLP-General Command and Sabri al-Banna's Fatah-Revolutionary Council, were even involved in international state terror. This study is limited to the two major Palestinian organizations, Fatah and the PFLP. These organizations shared a common goal: the liberation of the land of Palestine and the independence of the Palestinian people. The PFLP also incorporated elements of pan-Arabism and Marxism into its national liberation ideology. Both movements may be defined as revolutionary national liberation movements,

---

[25] Ibid., p. 161.

[26] See Wilkinson, *The Sources of Terrorism*, Martha Crenshaw, 'The Causes of Terrorism' in Charles W. Kegley (ed.), *International Terrorism: Characteristics, Causes, Controls* (New York: St. Martin's Press, 1990).

[27] See Claire Sterling, *The Terror Network*, and Y. Alexander and J. Sinai, *Terrorism: The PLO Connection* (New York: Crane and Russack, 1989).

comparable to similar organizations operating in Africa and Asia after the Second World War. Of course, both were somewhat maverick organizations that do not fit into traditional categories. Their conduct will be examined in light of the Hypotheses 6, 7 and 8. However, the main discussion on the Palestinian organizations will be found in the following section.

2.   Structural factors

Hypothesis 9: Organizations that are non-state nations (NSNs) tend to operate as independent political entities, primarily taking into consideration their international policy interests when setting up coalitions.

Of all the organizations studied in this book, only the Palestinian organizations had sufficient military might, economic resources, popular support and international recognition to be defined unquestioningly according to Bertelsen's classification as 'non-state nations' (NSN).[28] The IRA came close to being defined as such, more so since the onset of peace negotiations in Northern Ireland. Nevertheless, it never managed to recruit military units of any significance, and despite its great popularity with the Catholic population of Northern Ireland, the Sinn Fein, its political arm, failed to win any of the free elections there.

The size and strength of a state influence its policies towards coalition-formation.[29] Most terrorist organizations operating on the international arena are far inferior to the states they target in terms of resources and legitimacy. Does the size and power of a terrorist organization affect its behavior as far as coalitions are concerned?

Macintyre argued that national liberation movements, like states, could not disregard the international or regional systems in which they operate.[30]

> National liberation movements cannot hope to secure international support for their cause without compensatory losses in freedom to pursue the goals of the revolutionary military struggle... A national liberation movement which seeks to maximize international support must of tactical necessity moderate its freedom to pursue strategic goals. Ideally, planning should seek to maximize both alternatives (i.e., international support and organizational freedom) within the framework of the revolutionary struggle.

---

[28]   See Bertelsen, 'The Palestinian Arabs'.
[29]   Morgenthau argued that weak states seek strong partners, while Liska pointed out that weak nations seek an alliance with geographically distant states. Waltz saw the economic decline of a state as a reason for seeking strong allies. Cited in Holsti, Hopmann and Sullivan, *Unity and Disintegration in International Alliances*, p. 13.
[30]   See Ronald R. Macintyre, 'The Palestine Liberation Organization. Tactics, Strategies and Options towards the Geneva Peace Conference', *JPS*, Vol. 4, No. 4, 1975, pp. 67-70.

As the Palestinian organizations gradually evolved into NSNs, their policy on international terror evolved accordingly. Political considerations, international developments in the region, and ties with Arab or sponsor states were factors influencing their decision to resort to international terror. However, cooperation with terrorist organizations in Europe was not compatible with the Palestinian goal of obtaining recognition and support for their rights and demands from European states. Did the Palestinian organizations take such considerations into account, and if so, how did they maneuver in order to further their political goals?

Hypothesis 10: In a coalition between a strong organization (the patron) and a weak one (the client), the smaller organization is not significantly dependent on the larger one, and retains freedom to make its own decisions.

Walt focused particularly on the impact of foreign aid and 'transnational' penetration (defined as one state's manipulation of another's domestic system). He found that 'neither foreign aid nor penetration has proven to be of much use as an explanation of alliance formation'. On the contrary, 'the modest independent impact of aid and penetration is revealed by the fact that even extremely vulnerable and dependent clients have retained considerable freedom of action'.[31]

The differences in available resources between terrorist organizations raise similar queries: which partner has a greater say in determining the goals of the coalition and the relationships within it? Can the large organization influence or even impose policy on strategic issues? Does dependency exist in a coalition between a large, established organization and a small, vulnerable one? Who stands to gain from such a relationship – the patron or the client?

Hypothesis 11: Coalitions between terrorist organizations are usually bilateral. A coalition between more than two terrorist organizations is viable only when they are geographically close and share a common ideology and strategic goal.

Hopmann examined the two premises that the more parties to the alliance, and the greater their geographical distribution, the less effective the alliance. He found that fewer parties to an alliance made for a more enduring alliance, but was unable to reach an unequivocal conclusion regarding the second premise.[32]

The fact that the Palestinian terrorist organizations had ties with organizations that were situated far from the Middle East proves that geographical distance did

---

[31] See Walt, *The Origins of Alliances*, p. 268.
[32] See Holsti, Hopmann and Sullivan, *Unity and Disintegration in International Alliances*, pp. 57, 69-73.

not prevent coalition formation between terrorist organizations. Willingness to form a coalition with a distant organization was based on worldwide ideological solidarity, as described above.

Revolutionary solidarity alone cannot resolve the specific domestic and regional problems a terrorist organization encounters in its day-to-day struggle. Although bilateral cooperation can help solve specific problems and alleviate isolation in the face of a common enemy, a broader coalition is liable to be fraught with problems. If, for example, the parties to the coalition are widely dispersed, each has to contend with its own local problems. In such a case, a request for help may be rejected if the partners do not consider the local problem serious enough to warrant their intervention. Also, the more members there are, the harder it will be to reach a joint decision regarding goals and strategy, due to the multiplicity of views and interests. Each organization will try to exploit the others, promote its own interests, and present demands that are irrelevant to the other participants.

Hypothesis 11 suggests that the formation of a coalition or broad front of terrorist organizations on an international scale was extremely difficult when the organizations did not share a geographic or strategic affinity.

III.   THE INFLUENCE OF VARIABLES AT THE DECISION-MAKER
        LEVEL

Hypothesis 12: The personal experiences of revolutionary leaders and their racist and antisemitic preconceptions influence decisions to join a coalition against Israel and/or Jews.

In non-rational models of international relations an individual faced with a choice regarding an international event responds in terms of non-logical influences – influences unconnected with the event, of which he is unaware and which he would not consider legitimate if he were aware of. In rational models the individual bases his response upon 'a cool and clearheaded means-ends calculations' and chooses 'from the universe of possible responses' the alternative that is most likely to maximize his goals.[33]

The rational approach supports Crenshaw's theory that terrorist organizations make decisions based on a deliberate consideration of final goals, available means, and a cost-benefit assessment of the chosen strategy. This aspect was discussed in the section dealing with other independent variables.

---

[33] See Sidney Verba, 'Assumptions of Rationality and Non-Rationality in Models of the International System', in Klaus Knorr, and Sidney Verba (eds.), *The International System. Theoretical Essays* (Princeton: Princeton University Press, 1967), pp. 106-107.

Non-rational pressures and influences may stem from a leader's personal background, family and environment, the opinions and beliefs assimilated while studying, or the impact of a charismatic or dominant figure within the organization itself.[34]

In order to investigate coalitions between European and Palestinian terrorist organizations operating against Israeli and Jewish targets, this study examines at least one type of non-rational influence, namely antisemitism. Did antisemitic preconceptions influence the leaders of European terrorist organizations to cooperate with Palestinian organizations, despite their knowledge that Palestinian terrorists targeted Israeli civilians and Jews throughout the world, sometimes on a scale opposed by the European organizations? Does antisemitism explain why some European activists themselves participated in attacks against Israelis and Jews? Some even published leaflets or documents justifying antisemitic terrorism.[35]

The link between antisemitic preconceptions and the infiltration of antisemitic ideology into some European revolutionary left-wing organizations, pushing them in the direction of anti-Jewish terrorism, has been virtually ignored to date.

Although antisemitism is generally associated with radical right-wing ideology, it has, in the guise of anti-Zionism, often penetrated the ranks of the radical left too. This occurs despite the fact that the radical left distinguishes between anti-Zionism and antisemitism, in which Zionism is associated with Israeli aggression, Israel's colonialist occupation of Palestine, and its affiliation with Western imperialism. Thus it is clear that anti-Zionism has often become a surrogate for antisemitism. Antisemitism and anti-Zionism both claim that, unlike other nations, the Jews do not have the right to exist as a free and independent nation.[36]

Wistrich pointed out that in the late 1960s the PLO understood the propaganda value of demonizing Israel and exploiting anti-Nazi feeling in Europe for its own ends.[37] In addressing the West, therefore, it began to draw parallels between the plight of the Palestinians in the Middle East and the plight of Jews under Hitler. The Palestinians, like the Jews, were depicted as a defenseless and stateless

---

[34] Some researchers attempted a study of the personality development of leaders of the BR and the RAF in this light. For the BR see in particular, A. Silj, *Mai più senza fucile*. Some of the research conducted by German scholars to unravel the roots of the German terrorist organization related to such aspects. See *Analysen zum Terrorismum* (1981).

[35] Becker even titled her book on the RAF 'Hitler's Children', *inter alia* because of the antisemitism she found among some of them. See Jillian Becker, *Hitler's Children* (London: Granada Publishing, 1978).

[36] Wistrich argued that there was a basic link between classical antisemitism and contemporary anti-Zionism. See Robert Wistrich, 'Anti-Zionism as an Expression of Antisemitism in Recent Years', in Yehuda Bauer (ed.), *Present-Day Antisemitism* (Jerusalem: The Vidal Sassoon International Center for the Study of Antisemitism, Hebrew University of Jerusalem, 1988), p. 177.

[37] Ibid., pp. 180-183.

nation of refugees, deprived of independence and human dignity. This propaganda was especially effective after the Six Day War. The PLO even began to adopt 'Zionist' terminology, stressing the aspirations of the Palestinian people to return to the historical homeland. The propaganda claimed that the extermination and deportation of Jews from Europe had led to the even greater 'crime' of Zionism – the expulsion of Palestinians by Jews and Israelis. By exploiting Europeans guilt, the West was morally obliged to support the Palestinians.

The success of PLO propaganda efforts was particularly evident after the Lebanese War of 1982, when anti-Zionism began to insinuate itself into the cultural code of many left-wing circles. The left began to equate Zionism with Nazism, the Third Reich with Israel, and the Wehrmacht with the Israeli Defense Forces (IDF), while repudiating antisemitism, in theory at least, as a reactionary doctrine. Curtis saw the crux of this neo-antisemitism in the political denunciation of Israeli policies in Lebanon in 1982, when Israel was accused of launching a 'holocaust' and 'final solution' against the Palestinians and the Star of David was equated with the swastika.[38]

Volkov believed that anti-Zionism became more rampant, and more antisemitic in character, when Third World ideology – with its repudiation of the colonialist aspects of Zionism, due to ignorance or Soviet propaganda, and its solidarity with the Arabs – began to make inroads into European left-wing culture.[39] Consequently, a left-wing activist who denounced colonialism, capitalism and militarism had no choice but to denounce Zionism. Indeed, anti-Zionism became a yardstick of loyalty to the movement, particularly where Jewish activists were concerned. In their case, anti-Zionism became the absolute proof of their devotion to the cause.

One of the most obvious indications that antisemitism infiltrated the radical left was its acceptance of Holocaust denial theories. Such theories aimed, among other things, to delegitimize the State of Israel, whose *raison-d'être* was to serve as a refuge for Holocaust survivors. Other than Holocaust researchers themselves, few experts knew that some of the most vociferous Holocaust deniers, such as Paul Rassinier and Pierre Guillaume, belonged to the French radical left.[40]

---

[38]   See Michael Curtis, 'The Baffling Observer', in Bauer (ed.), *Present-Day Antisemitism*, p. 227.

[39]   See Shulamit Volkov, 'Western Antisemitism Today – An Evaluation', in Bauer (ed.), *Present-Day Antisemitism*, p. 73.

[40]   Rassinier was a pacifist, and from 1922, a communist activist. In 1934, he joined the French Socialist Party. After the Second World War, he left the party and published articles in anarchist periodicals. See Limor Yagil, *Holocaust Denial in France* (Tel Aviv: Tel Aviv University, The Project for the Study of Antisemitism, 1994), p. 31. Pierre Guillaume ran a Trotskyist publishing company in Paris in the 1960s. After 1978, he joined a left-wing group affiliated with the periodical *La Guerre Sociale*, which published articles by Holocaust deniers. See Yagil, *Holocaust Denial in France*, pp. 65-66.

It is debatable whether the issue of antisemitism within terrorist organizations belongs more to the organizational level, or to the decision-maker level. In this book it shall be discussed at both the organizational level, in terms of ideological influences, and at the decision-maker level, in terms of personal influences.

The immediate implication of Hypothesis 12 is that cooperation between European terrorist organizations and Palestinian organizations was triggered, at least in part, by non-rational considerations. In broader terms, more research is clearly required into how non-rational considerations influence the behavior of terrorist leaders, in general.

IV.   DEPENDENT VARIABLES

As previously stated, no formal agreements have been found between terrorist organizations cited in this study or others. As a rule, any information on cooperation between organizations is fragmentary, vague, and sometimes even tendentious. It was therefore necessary to find indices that would permit both a qualitative and quantitative analysis of cooperation between terrorist organizations. Concrete expressions of cooperation between terrorist organizations can be divided into three categories:

(1) *Ideological cooperation* is the lowest level, involving a verbal commitment and expressions of solidarity. Nevertheless, it has moral and even practical implications, since it bears the seeds for cooperation of a more concrete nature. Ideological cooperation is expressed through: the publication of documents and leaflets that express support for the organization's outlook and goals; a declaration of identical ideological and operational goals; and assuming responsibility for terrorist acts in the name of 'martyrs' of the other organization.

(2) *Logistical cooperation* between terrorist organizations is quite widespread. Once again, however, the degree of cooperation depends on the degree of intimacy between the organizations and the willingness of one organization to take risks on the other's behalf. Logistical cooperation is expressed through: the provision of propaganda resources (printing presses, distribution of propaganda abroad, etc.); forged documents, operation manuals, and financial assistance; and weapons and ammunition.

(3) *Operational cooperation*, the highest level, is somewhat akin to the military assistance allied states offer each other in times of war. Here, the commitment may actually entail physical or political danger, in the form of reprisals by the injured party (the government). Operational cooperation is expressed through: provision of military training in the organization's camps; provision of tactical

information, safe houses, and escape routes; attacking the other organization's targets; a coordinated terrorist strategy; physical participation in the terrorist acts of the other organization; the attempted or actual release of jailed members of the other organization and/or provision of a safe house for fugitives; the planning and perpetration of joint terror attacks.

The lowest level of cooperation – ideological cooperation – does not qualify as a coalition relationship. For the purposes of this study, only logistical cooperation involving a significant and consistent transfer of resources, or important operational cooperation may be considered a coalition relationship. The term 'significant transfer of resources' refers to assistance provided in an area vital to the organization's terrorist activities, and 'consistent' means that such resources were provided for at least a year. Operational cooperation may be considered a coalition relationship when it contributed qualitatively to the organization's ability to carry out strategic terror operations.

V.   RESEARCH METHODOLOGY

This study is based on Holsti, Hopmann and Sullivan's 'integrated approach' to research strategy.[41] This includes: comparative studies at several levels of analysis; the formulation and testing of hypotheses; the creation of a broad range of indices for key concepts; and special attention to conditions that may affect the validity of the main theories. In terms of theory, this study navigates uncharted territory, with few points of reference or comparison to provide bearings. However, as illustrated in Chapter 1, Walt's balance of threat theory presents the most suitable point of departure.

In order to provide the best conditions for formulating a theory in this new field two major areas of international terrorism were selected: Europe and the Middle East. Similarly, a broad spectrum of leading international terrorist organizations was studied over an extended period of time. These organizations were measured at all four levels of analysis that are standard in international relations: the structural level, the regional level, the individual-actor level, and the decision-maker level.

Qualitative analysis was conducted separately for each terrorist organization, in the context of the ideological group to which it belonged. Radical left-wing, radical right-wing and nationalistic organizations were studied in terms of coalitions with Palestinian terrorist organizations. Radical left-wing organizations were also studied in terms of coalitions with like organizations (Euro-terrorism).

---

[41]   See Holsti, Hopmann and Sullivan, *Unity and Disintegration in International Alliances*, pp. 219, 226.

The research hypotheses were tested against the coalition behavior of each organization/ideological group.

The activities of each organization are described over three periods of time (1968-80, 1981-84, and 1985-90). These activities were examined in terms of the independent variables at all levels of analysis throughout the periods in question. The nature and strength of the coalition was measured by indices at the ideological, logistic, and operational levels. The qualitative analysis quotes liberally from documents, personal testimonies and available literature.

Although the book was intended to include a quantitative analysis, this proved virtually impossible due to objective difficulties: the small number of concrete cases of cooperation between terrorist organizations (about a hundred in all); the lack of accurate indices; and the absence of hard data concerning the true commitment of the parties to the coalition.[42]

1.   Research population

In order to research cooperation between Palestinian terrorist organizations and European terrorist organizations (radical left-wing, radical right-wing, and nationalistic), this study focused on organizations that were particularly active and influential.

ETA was chosen as representative of the nationalist organizations. As for cooperation among European radical left-wing terrorist organizations, this study concerns only four out of the seven Fighting Communist Organizations' (FCOs) which were active in Europe from 1984-88.[43] The remaining three – the Spanish First of October Anti-Fascist Resistance Group (Grupo Revolucionario Antifascista Primero de Octubre – GRAPO), the Greek 17 November (Epanastatiki Organosi 17 Noemvri – N 17), and the Portuguese Popular Forces-25 April (Forces Populares 25 de Abril – FP-25) – were excluded because their influence was marginal, and because there is very little documentary or research material about them.

The research focuses on Fatah and the PFLP, the two largest Palestinian organizations operating during the period in question. Since Fatah controlled the PLO and determined PLO policy, the terms 'Fatah' and 'PLO' will be used

---

[42]   Holsti pointed out that researchers into alliances between states have relatively few case studies on which to base their studies (about 130 for the entire period from 1815-1939). This places some perspective on the shortage of case studies on coalitions between terrorist organizations during the short period covered by this research. See Holsti, Hopmann and Sullivan, *Unity and Disintegration in International Alliances*, p. 41. Crenshaw claimed that since there is no universally accepted definition of a terrorist act it is questionable whether most of the cases cited in existing databases are, in fact, terrorist acts. See Martha Crenshaw, 'Current Research on Terrorism: The Academic Perspective', *Studies in Conflict and Terrorism*, Vol. 5 (1992), p. 6.

[43]   See Yonah Alexander and A. Dennis Pluchinsky (eds.), *Europe's Red Terrorists: The Fighting Communist Organizations* (London: Frank Cass, 1992), p. 16.

interchangeably when quoting from documents or data which, in fact, expressed the Fatah position on relevant issues.[44]

Radical left-wing and right-wing organizations were selected in those countries where such organizations were extremely active. One drawback was the relatively short life-span of some revolutionary European organizations, due to internal difficulties or clampdowns by the security forces. Therefore, the comparative analysis by period is incomplete. Below is a breakdown of these organizations by country:

Germany: *Radical left-wing organizations:* The Red Army Faction (Rote Armee Fraktion – RAF), which is also discussed in the context of Euro-terrorism; the Second of June Movement (Bewegung 2 Juni – M2J), which merged with the RAF in 1980; and the Revolutionary Cells (Revolutionare Zellen – RZ).

Italy: *Radical left-wing organization:* Red Brigades (Brigate Rosse – BR), which is also discussed in the context of Euro-terrorism.[45]

Radical right-wing organizations: New Order (Ordine Nuovo – ON); National Vanguard (Avanguardia Nazionale – AN); Third Position (Terza Posizione – TP), and Armed Revolutionary Cells (Nuclei Armati Rivoluzionari – NAR).

France: *Radical left-wing organization:* Direct Action (Action Directe – AD) which is also discussed in the context of Euro-terrorism.

Belgium: *The radical left-wing organization:* Combatant Communist Cells (Cellules Communistes Combatantes – CCC), which is discussed only in the context of Euro-terrorism.

Spain: *Nationalist organization:* Basque Fatherland and Liberty (Euzkadi ta Askatasuna – ETA).

Islamist organizations: The World Islamic Front for the Struggle Against Jews and Crusaders (WIF) and affiliated groups and organizations.

---

[44] Yasser Arafat headed both organizations concurrently.

[45] According to della Porta, the BR was the largest terrorist organization operating in Italy during the period in question. Prima Linea (Front Line – PL), the second largest organization, operated for only 6 months. By 1983, the BR had carried out 645 operations in 40 provinces, and was responsible for 68% of all deaths, while the PL carried out 258 operations in 19 provinces. During the same period, there were about 23 organizations operating under 125 different names. See Donatella della Porta, *Il Terrorismo di Sinistra* (Bologna: Società Editrice il Mulino, 1990), p. 92.

2. Sources

The main difficulty in researching terrorist organizations is the scarcity of reliable and independent sources and the clandestine nature of the organizations themselves.[46] Therefore, an eclectic range of sources were used:

(1) Original texts published by the terrorist organizations themselves (ideological documents, leaflets, official communiqués, etc.), and the memoirs of some leading terrorists. Note that very few ideological documents were published by the radical right-wing organizations. A detailed list of original documents appears in the bibliography.[47]

(2) Legal documents relating to the trials of members of various terrorist organizations in Europe, particularly Italy and France.

(3) Published research on the subject.

(4) Chronologies of terrorist acts.[48]

The original research for this study was updated on the basis of a few new books, but mostly on a profusion of older documents and recent (often auto-critical) analysis of past events by the protagonists themselves, as recently published on the Internet. The Italian and German left-wing organizations and their ideological supporters are especially prolific in this field.[49]

---

[46] As remarked by Ferraresi while writing about the right-wing groups. See Franco Ferraresi 'Da Evola a Freda. La dottrina della destra radicale fino al 1977', in Franco Ferraresi (ed.), *La Destra Radicale* (Milano: Feltrinelli, 1984), p. 54.

[47] Note in this context the contribution of Alexander and Pluchinsky in publishing a collection of texts and announcements by organizations defined as Euro-terrorists. See Alexander and Pluchinsky (eds.), *Europe's Red Terrorists*.

[48] See detailed list of studies in the bibliography. Since no single chronology covered all the organizations, this study referred to a number of sources: Edward Mickolus' database, ITERATE III, a chronology of international terrorist acts for the years 1968-90, published also in book form: Edward Mickolus, *Transnational Terrorism: A Chronology of Events, 1968-1979* (London: Aldwych Press, 1980) and *International Terrorism in the 1980s. A Chronology of Events* (Ames: Iowa State University Press, 1989); chronologies of international terrorist acts for the years 1984-89, published by the Terrorist Research Project, University of Tel Aviv's Jaffee Center for Strategic Studies; chronologies listing the activities of the German RAF (1967-87), the French AD (1969-87) and the Spanish ETA (1968-87), published in *Notes et Etudes* by the University of Paris Criminology Institute; fragmentary chronologies encountered in various books and studies.

[49] An important source on left-wing revolutionary organizations worldwide is the Canadian *Arm.The.Spirit* website, which gathers in the framework of The ETEXT Archives, documents from the Autonome Forum, an anti-imperialist collective. See <http://www.etext.org/Politics/Arm.The.Spirit>.

A comprehensive bibliography on terrorist organizations active since the 1990s can be found in the US Air University's Library Publications on 'Terrorist and Insurgent Organizations', updated to July 2000. See <http://www.au.af.mil/au/au/bibs/tergps/tgitl.htm#per>.

Since this study is based on long original texts and documents in five languages, only a small proportion of the quotations were translated literally by the author. In most cases, they were paraphrased as accurately as possible.

Wievorka pointed out that most radical left-wing terrorist organizations published texts and communiqués in which they explain and take responsibility for their actions.[50] Nevertheless, no in-depth research and analysis of such documents and texts was conducted prior to the mid-1980s, despite the fact that some of these organizations, notably the BR and RAF, made a point of publicizing their ideological documents.[51]

A.   Italy

Italy had by far the richest primary material, although most of it related to radical left-wing organizations. This study draw on most of the files on the trials of members of radical left-wing organizations in Italy between 1978-84, including documents pertaining to the Italian judiciary and Ministry of the Interior. All quotations from the legal material bear the name of the witness (member of the organization) and the reference number of the deposition.[52]

The Italian radical left-wing organizations published numerous manifestos, books, strategic decisions, leaflets, etc., some of which stretch to hundreds of pages. Here too, tracing the material proved no easy matter. Even the National Library in Rome had not yet obtained these publications. Many of the ideological documents (including BR publications) were collected personally by the author. Today, it is possible to access these documents on the Internet.[53] The archives of *La Repubblica*, one of Italy's leading newspapers, were amply used.

---

[50] See Michel Wievorka, 'Les maoistes français et l'hypothese terroriste', *Esprit*, No. 94. Oct.-Nov. (1984), pp. 133-45.

[51] Della Porta based some of her research in *Terrorismo di Sinistra* on an analysis of texts published by the terrorist organizations. Steiner and Debray did something similar with respect to the RAF in *La Fraction Armée Rouge*. See Anne Steiner and Loïc Debray, *La Fraction Armée Rouge. Guérilla urbaine en Europe occidentale* (Paris: Méridiens Klincksieck, 1987). Pluchinsky rightly emphasized the importance of analyzing terrorist propaganda. Pluchinsky cited, by way of example, one of the best studies in this field, namely Wright's book *Terrorist Propaganda* on RAF and IRA propaganda. See Dennis A. Pluchinsky (eds.), 'Western Europe's Red Terrorists: The Fighting Communist Organisations', in Alexander and Pluchinsky, *Europe's Red Terrorists*, p. 17.

[52] The juridical documents of various Italian courts to which I had access were obtained due to the invaluable support of Judge Severino Santiapichi, who presided over some of the trials against the BR militants.

[53] For the Italian left-wing organizations, there are several important sources, representing the various factions and doctrines, including those of the opposition or the establishment. See for instance the 'Bibliografia sui Conflitti Sociali, la Violenza Politica e le Istituzioni dello Stato' on the site dedicated to the infamous assassination of the late Italian prime minister Aldo Moro, *Moro punto Doc*, at <http://www.apolis.com/moro/index1.htm>; or the bibliography of BR documents published electronically by the Centro di Documentazione 'Fausto e Jaio' del centro sociale Leoncavallo at <http://www.ecn.org/leoncavallo/cdoc/br/index.htm>; Misteri d'Italia, is a

There are far fewer sources relating to the radical right.[54] Evola's book, and a number of pamphlets and articles written by activists of a lesser stature, represent the sum total of ideological material produced by the radical right. As stated, unlike the radical left, the radical right rarely bothered to justify or explain its actions through written statements.[55]

B.   France

In France, AD was active for a much shorter period (1979-87), and accomplished far less than its Italian counterparts. Its ideological output was particularly meager. Almost all its ideological documents, legal material relating to investigations into the organization's activities, and journalistic material, including the organization's own organ, were found in the archives of the Institute of Criminology at the University of Paris. Today, the views of imprisoned AD leaders are published on the Internet and the Paris Institute of Criminology has published most of its archives electronically.[56]

In June 1992, the author conducted personal interviews with Xavier Raufer, one of the few French researchers into terrorism, and (off the record) with two attorneys of the Attorney General's Office in Paris, responsible for conducting investigations into terrorist activities. Although these interviews did not contribute much in the way of new material, they clarified and confirmed a number of points relating in particular to AD's international ties.[57]

C.   Belgium

The CCC existed for little more than a year, and was, by any standard, a transitory and rather inconsequential phenomenon on the European revolutionary

---

historical-journalistic archive of modern Italian history at <http://www.misteriditalia.it/terrorismo/brigate-rosse/index.html>.

54   When Ferraresi edited the first serious study on the Italian radical right in 1984, he drew attention to the lack of scientific studies and autobiographical documentary material, as opposed to the abundance of journalistic accounts of terrorist acts.

55   The Misteri d'Italia site has also a section concerning right-wing terrorism: <http://www.misteriditalia.com/lestragi/index.html> and <http://www.misteriditalia.com/estremadestra/annisettan>. The radical right-wing literature can be found at its main publishing company, Edizioni di Ar at <http://www.libreriaar.it/catalogoconnote.htm>.

56   For AD documents and their bulletin *Front*, see the site of the imprisoned leaders at: <http://www.crosswinds.net/~actiondirecte> and more documents at *La Page d'information sur Action Directe* at <http://www.geocities.com/CapitolHill/Congress/6781/index.html>. The archives of the Institute of Criminology and its publication *Notes and Etudes* are at <http://www.u-paris2.fr/mcc/html/ archives/ne/ index.html>.

57   The interviews confirmed that some of the information on the AD published by French journalists was based on official material and could be verified. See Alain Hamon and Jean-Charles Marchand, *Action Directe. Du terrorisme français a l'euroterrorisme* (Paris: Editions du Seuil, 1986), and Roland Jacquard, *La longue traque d'Action Directe* (Paris: Albin Michel, 1987).

scene. To its credit, it published detailed communiqués in its mouthpiece, *Ligne Rouge*, after each terrorist act.

D.   Germany

RAF documents were published in two collections, one covering the period 1970-77, and the other 1977-87. Although a collection of documents of the M2J also exists, it could not be traced at the time.[58] The German radical leftist organizations have since published many documents on the Internet.[59]

E.   Spain

ETA published all its literature in a series running to eighteen volumes, published by a San Sebastian publishing house, which was closed several years ago. Typically, the material cannot be found in any of the large libraries of Europe, and even the National Library of Madrid has only two volumes of the collection. In the absence of primary material, the study relies on fragments of texts cited in books, most of them unrelated to international issues.[60]

F.   Palestinian organizations

Two main sources of primary material were used:

(1)   Between 1968 and 1996 the *Journal of Palestine Studies* published a large number of documents by the PLO and other Palestinian terrorist organizations, as well as interviews with the leaders of these organizations; and

---

[58]   See *Bewegung Zwei Juni. Der Blues-Gesammelte Texte* (1983), 2 vols.

[59]   Many RAF, RZ and B2J documents, as well as chronologies about their activities, can be found at the radical leftist website *Nadir* at <http://www.nadir.org/nadir/archiv/Politische Stroemungen>. A comprehensive bibliography about the RAF can be found at another leftist site, *Rote Hilfe* from Gottingen, at <http://rafinfo.virtualave.net/quellen.shtml>. Even amazon.com sells now the texts of the main German terrorist organization: *Rote Armee Fraktion. Texte Und Materialien Zur Geschichte Der RAF*.

[60]   See Bereciartu Gurutz Jauregui, (2nd edn.), *Ideologia e estrategia de ETA. Analisis de su evolucion entre 1959 y 1968* (Madrid: Siglo XXI de Espana Editores, 1985) and Pedro Ibarra Guell, *La evolucion strategica de ETA* (Donostia: Kriselu, 1987), who researched the ideology and strategy of ETA over the years, and *Il Bollettino*, Nos. 37-38, Sept. (1989), pp. 35-55. A good bibliography on ETA can be found at the Air University Library at <http://www.au.af.mil/au/aul/bibs/tergps/tgeta.htm#int>. The *Euskal Herria* Journal: *Basque Country Journal* is the mouthpiece for ETA and therefore offers historical documents and articles about the more updated activities of the Basque organization at <http://www.contrast.org/mirrors/ehj/index.html>.

(2) Translations of Arabic newspapers and broadcasts by Palestinian organizations by the IDF Intelligence Branch, housed at Tel Aviv University's Dayan Center for Middle Eastern and African Studies.

Collected texts published by specific authors were also consulted.[61] Merari and Elad's book (1986) was useful in providing a chronological analysis of Palestinian international terror until 1985. For the years 1984-89, this book relies heavily on the Jaffee Center for Strategic Studies' annual publication, *InTer*. The Palestinian organizations active in the 1970s and 1980s are not well represented on the Internet. Some newer texts of the PFLP can be found on semi-official sites.[62]

G.   Islamist organizations

Most of the texts, manifestos and even videos of these organizations appear on the Internet and will be cited in Chapter 11.

---

[61]   See, in particular, Yehuda Lukacs (ed.), *The Israeli-Palestinian Conflict: A Documentary Record* (Cambridge: Cambridge University Press, 1992); and Khadder and Naim Bichara (eds.), *Testi della revoluzione Palestinese. 1968-1975* (Verona: Bertoni Editore, 1975).

[62]   See, for example, the site *Welcome to Democratic Palestine* at <http://members.tripod.com/~ freepalestine/home.html>. Journal of Palestine Studies (JPS) from 1995 on, including a few articles on-line, can be found at <http://www.ipsjps.org/jps/online.html>.

CHAPTER 3
GERMANY – RADICAL LEFT-WING ORGANIZATIONS

I.   HISTORICAL BACKGROUND

The narrowing of class differences in post-Second World War Germany was reflected in the policy of the two large parties, the Christian Democratic Union (Christlich Demokratischen Union Deutschlands – CDU) and the Social Democratic Party (Sozialdemokratische Partei Deutschlands – SPD). From 1966-69, the SPD paved the way for the Great Coalition with the CDU – the only way, in their opinion, to enhance the respectability of the 'Red party' in the eyes of the bourgeoisie, and to conduct an effective policy towards East Germany. These developments led many young Germans to seek more radical movements.[1] The youth branch of the SPD, the Young Socialists (Jungsozialisten – JUSOS), and its student organization, the Organization of German Socialist Students (Sozialisticher Deutscher Studentenbund – SDS), demanded a return to pure Marxism. In the latter 1960s, this opposition evolved into a broader protest movement, known as the Extraparliamentary Opposition (Ausserparlamentarische Opposition – APO) and spearheaded by the SDS.[2]

Radical students staged political and ideological battles against the reactionary party line and against the universities. In the late 1960s and early 1970s, left-wing students stepped up the campaign against pedagogical methods and outmoded infrastructures.[3] The Free University of Berlin became the center of the protest movement and SDS leader Rudi Dutschke advocated terrorist tactics as a way of preparing Germany for revolution. He accepted Marcuse's views that students, as an oppressed marginal group, could act as a catalyst for social revolution. From early 1966 German cities, particularly Berlin, witnessed violent demonstrations by radical students and unemployed and working-class youth. Most of these demonstrations revolved around the Vietnam War and the Springer Press, the German press empire which supported conservative views and attacked leftist circles.

On 2 June 1967, during a protest in Berlin against the visit of the Iranian shah, a student was shot dead by a police officer. This incident sparked further violent demonstrations. A year later, on 11 April 1968, Dutschke was shot and seriously

---

[1]   See Alfred Grosser, *L'Allemagne de notre temps (1945-1970)* (Paris: Fayard, 1970), pp. 266-73.

[2]   See Corrado and Evans, 'Ethnic and Ideological Terrorism in Western Europe,' in Michael Stohl (ed.), *The Politics of Terrorism* (3rd edn.) (New York: Marcel Dekker, 1988), pp. 417-41.

[3]   See F.T. Gregory Winn, 'Terrorism, Alienation, and German Society', in Yonah Alexander and M. John Gleason (eds.), *Behavioral and Quantitative Perspectives on Terrorism* (New York: Pergamon Press, 1981), pp. 256-82 and Grosser, *L'Allemagne de notre temps*, p. 450.

wounded in Berlin by a radical right-wing activist, triggering further violence. These two events likely encouraged dozens, if not hundreds, of youngsters to support terrorism.[4]

The radical left-wing camp in Germany comprised three main terrorist organizations: the Red Army Faction (Rote Armee Fraktion – RAF), the Second of June Movement (Bewegung 2 Juni – M2J) and the Revolutionary Cells (Revolutionare Zellen – RZ).

II.   TYPOLOGICAL DEFINITION

The RAF clearly leaned towards anarchism, as shown by its emphasis on the concept of freedom, the rejection of stages in achieving its goal, its anti-hierarchical structure, and its refusal of 'democratic centralism', so dear to Marxism-Leninism. Steiner and Debray labeled the RAF a Marxist organization since it championed the main goals of historical materialism.[5] However, the liberal use of Marxist terminology was intended mainly to win political support, and to appease the more dogmatic elements among its radical left-wing sympathizers. Even Wright argued that RAF ideology comprised certain Marxist-Leninist influences.[6] Closer adherence to such ideas would clearly have resulted in greater success. Wright, and Raufer and Haut emphasized the influence of the Third World, and Wright of the revolutionary models of Mao, Che Guevara and Marighella, on RAF ideology.[7]

The M2J was a confirmed anarchist organization, according to Steiner and Debray, with no Marxist pretensions.[8] It did not publish any significant ideological documents. Most of its activists came from anarchist circles. Later, by joining the RAF, they helped strengthen the latter's anarchist base.

The RZ were described by Raufer and Haut as a loose federation of revolutionary, albeit not Marxist-Leninist, cells.[9] Hans Joachim Klein, one of the main RZ activists and the product of a small anarchist group (Federation of the New Left – FNL), described the organization as the antithesis of the Leninist principles

---

4   See the testimony of Baumann in Michael Baumann, *Terror or Love? 'Bommi' Baumann's Own Story of His Life as a West German Urban Guerrilla* (New York: Grove Press 1979) *Terror or Love?*, pp. 22-40.

5   Steiner and Loïc Debray, *La Fraction Armée Rouge. Guérilla urbaine en Europe occidentale* (Paris: Méridiens Klincksieck, 1987), pp. 110-122.

6   See Joanne Wright, *Terrorist Propaganda. The Red Army Faction and the Provisional IRA, 1968-86* (London: Macmillan, 1991), p. 43.

7   See Xavier Raufer and François Haut, 'RAF – Une organisation zéro traces', *Notes et Etudes*, No. 5 (1988), p. 7; Wright, *Terrorist Propaganda*, p. 41.

8   Steiner and Debray, *La Fraction Armée Rouge*, p. 118.

9   Raufer and Haut, *RAF – Une organisation zéro traces*, p. 21.

of the German student movement, which after a brief meteoric rise, was plagued by dogmatism and factionalism.[10]

In conclusion, the RAF may be typified as an anarcho-communist organization, with a particularly strong anarchist bias. The two other organizations, M2J and RZ, may be classified as anarchist organizations with radical left-wing tendencies. The activities of these three organizations during the periods under review can be summarized as follows:[11]

(1) 1968-80: During this period, the RAF emerged (1968-71), carried out its first major offensive (1972). After a brief hiatus (1973-74), a second generation of RAF activists launched a second offensive (1975-77) that ended in ignominious defeat.

The M2J was set up in 1971. Some of its members were former RAF members, and some of its activities were coordinated with the RAF. 1974 and 1975 were peak periods of activity for the M2J, which disbanded in 1980.

The RZ, which was established in 1973, kept a low profile until 1976 when it began to attack American targets in Germany. The RZ had an international division which was extremely active from 1974-76 and cooperated closely with the PFLP.

(2) 1981-84: During this period the third generation of RAF activists were busy reorganizing and most of their terrorist attacks were unsuccessful. The RZ also kept a low profile.

(3) 1985-90: During 1985 and 1986, the RAF was involved in Euro-terrorism. Two further political assassinations were carried out in 1989 and 1990, but these effectively marked the end of German radical left-wing terror. The RZ was also active in 1985-86 against German and American targets. From 1987 it became less active, despite the fact that most of its members avoided detection.

III.   THE RISE AND FALL OF TWO 'GENERATIONS' OF TERRORISTS (1970-80)

1.   The RAF

On 2 April 1968 the RAF carried out its first serious operation. Two students, Andreas Baader and Gudrun Ensslin, planted bombs in two Frankfurt department

---

[10] See Bougereau, 'An Interview with Hans Joachim Klein', in Jean Bougereau, *The German Guerrilla: Terror, Reaction and Resistance* (Orkney: Cienfuegos Press, 1981), p. 16.
[11] For a good short history of the German leftist terrorist organizations see *Armed Struggle In Germany* (undated), at <http://www.burn.ucsd.edu/~ats/MH/armed_groups.html>.

stores. They were promptly arrested and brought to trial. Among their supporters were Horst Mahler, who acted as their attorney, and Ulrike Meinhof, a journalist for the fashionable left-wing magazine *konkret*.

In November 1968, after the Supreme Court sentenced them to jail for arson, the two RAF activists skipped bail and escaped to France. Some of those who participated in demonstrations for their release decided to set up terrorist groups on a regional basis. On their return to Germany, Baader was arrested but Meinhof and others managed to secure his release in May 1970. Chased by the security authorities, the group had no choice but to go underground.

In early 1970 the entire faction (Baader, Meinhof, Ensslin, Mahler and another four or five individuals) left Germany in two groups for Lebanon and Jordan to train in Fatah camps.[12] According to a late testimony, Baader and Meinhof also contacted the PFLP and DFLP during a 'reconnaissance trip' to Beirut in 1969.[13] Before the events of September 1970 in Jordan, the group returned to West Germany where it began its terrorist activities in earnest.[14] The group subsequently adopted the name Red Army Faction after the Japanese Red Army.

Back in Germany, the Baader-Meinhof Gang, as it became known, carried out a series of bank raids. From September to October 1971 it undertook no less than three such raids. However, the police subsequently arrested five RAF activists, including Horst Mahler. During shoot-outs with the police, a number of RAF members and a police officer were killed.

The first major RAF offensive took place in May 1972. Between 4 and 11 May it bombed several targets: the American military headquarters in Frankfurt and Heidelberg, police headquarters in Augsberg and Munich, the Springer Press building in Hamburg, and the car belonging to a judge who was handling the case of a RAF member.

The organization, however, had little time to reap the benefits of its operational success. In June 1972, its entire leadership – Baader, Meinhof, Ensslin and Meins – were arrested. During 1973, the jailed leadership campaigned exclusively for improved prison conditions, twice embarking on a hunger strike to this end.

It took a few years for the RAF to recover. In April 1975 a RAF commando occupied the German embassy in Stockholm. The West German government,

---

[12] See H.J. Horchem, 'Terrorism in Germany: 1985', in Paul Wilkinson and A.M. Stewart (eds.), *Contemporary Research on Terrorism* (Aberdeen: The University Press, 1987), pp. 151-52; and Jillian Becker, *Hitler's Children* (London: Granada Publishing, 1978), pp. 219-220.

[13] See Bassam Abu-Sharif and Uzi Mahnaimi, *Tried by Fire. The Searing True Story of Two Men at the Heart of the Struggle between the Arabs and the Jews* (London: Warner Books, 1995), pp. 66-67.

[14] In September 1970 King Hussein of Jordan repressed an attempt by Palestinian organizations to take control of the kingdom by force. Most of their militants were either killed or expelled to Lebanon or other countries. These events were called 'Black September' and led to a new wave of Palestinian international terrorism.

however, refused to accede to the terrorists' demands for the release of their imprisoned comrades. The issue was resolved when a Swedish police unit stormed the embassy building. In July the RAF again raided a number of banks; this effectively marked the end of its second offensive. Meanwhile, the M2J also launched a series of large-scale attacks, *inter alia*, as an expression of solidarity with jailed RAF members.

The third and most serious RAF offensive took place in 1977; its main objective was to secure the release of its jailed leaders, who had been sentenced on 28 April to life imprisonment.[15] On 5 September the RAF kidnapped former Nazi Hanns-Martin Schleyer, president of the Federation of German Industry, in Cologne. The West German government, however, rejected the kidnappers' demands. On 13 October Palestinian terrorists hijacked a Lufthansa plane to Mogadishu (Somalia) demanding, *inter alia*, the release of the jailed RAF leaders. The successful action of the West German anti-terror squad against the hijackers put paid to any hope of liberating the RAF leadership. Baader, Ensslin and Jan-Carl Raspe subsequently committed suicide in prison. Meinhof had already committed suicide in 1976 in her prison cell. Official commissions of inquiry ruled out accusations by leftist circles that the prisoners had been murdered by the authorities.

In 1978-80 the German authorities continued to track down other members of the organization, and many 'second-generation' activists were arrested or killed while resisting arrest. The RAF was not heard of again until June 1979 when an attempt to blow up the car of Gen. Alexander Haig, commander of NATO forces in Europe, failed. Plans to bomb American bases came to light when the organizers were killed in a road accident. According to a later document, the Haig communiqué contained the first hint of a significant change in perception that would subsequently harden into a strategic shift: 'the front is moving nearer to the centre, it is coming closer to the metropoles'. It was therefore seen as the first step towards the Euro-terrorism strategy.[16]

2. The M2J

The M2J evolved along similar lines to the RAF. It was the offshoot of a small anarchist group – the Hash Rebels – which mixed in the same circles as the RAF in

---

[15] On 7 April the organization murdered the chief federal prosecutor, Siegfried Buback. On 30 July Jurgen Ponto, chairman of the Dresdener Bank, was murdered in his home. According to an unofficial history of RAF, Buback's assassination opened the 'German Autumn' campaign and marked a shift to a strategy of eliminating key members of the state apparatus and the business elite, culminating with the kidnapping and assassination of Hanns-Martin Schleyer. See *A Brief History of the Red Army Faction*, Spring 1994, p. 3, at <http://www.etext.org/Politics/Arm.The. Spirit/Guerrilla/Europe/Red.Army.Faction/history.of.the.raf>.

[16] Ibid., p. 4.

West Berlin. The Hash Rebels were active from the spring of 1968 to 1970, particularly on issues relating to the Vietnam War. The Blues, a splinter group of the Hash Rebels, sent some of its members to train in 'Palestine'.[17] On their return, they called for immediate armed action, but since not all members of the Blues agreed with this, the 'Middle East contingent' formed a group known as the Tupamaros West Berlin (TW).[18] The latter's first action was in 1969, when it attempted to bomb a Berlin synagogue on the anniversary of Kristallnacht. Subsequent targets included: the judges and prosecutors in the trials of radical leftists, 'America House', the American Officers Club and the office of the Israeli airline El Al. A further split occurred when some members chose to go underground. Many others turned to heavy drugs and joined sects such as Hare Krishna.

In early 1970, a number of anarchists from the groups listed above, including Michael Baumann, Thomas Weisbecker and George Von Rauch, set up a clandestine group, the Second of June Movement (M2J). The M2J carried out its first serious operation in February 1972, when it blew up the British Military Yacht Club in Kladow. Around this time, the M2J lost two of its main activists, namely Von Rauch and Weisbecker, who were shot during confrontations with the police.

There were structural and ideological differences between the RAF and M2J. The RAF was more disciplined and used firearms right from the start, while the M2J initially used only bombs and Molotov cocktails. It was after serious crackdowns against M2J activists that the movement accepted RAF criticism, and decided to go underground. The Kronzberg quarter of West Berlin – with its sympathetic working-class population, particularly Turkish immigrants – proved ideal for this purpose. The M2J advocated a militant solution to industrial disputes, support of large-scale guerrilla activities, solidarity with immigrants, and ties with immigrants organizations.[19]

After the death of its two main activists, however, the movement split into two groups: those who favored Robin Hood-type bank raids, the proceeds of which were distributed among the poor, and those who advocated 'tougher' action, such as attacks on American firms or police cars. In late 1972, the hard core apparently got the upper hand. In November 1974 an M2J commando killed the president of the Supreme Court in West Berlin.[20] Thus, its first real foray into the world of terror was an act of solidarity with its sister organization – the RAF.

---

[17] The German activists probably considered the Palestinian camps in Jordan 'Palestine'.

[18] 'Tupamaros' (from Tupac Amaru, last member of the Inca royal family, murdered by the Spanish in 1571) was the name of the National Liberation Movement (Movimento de Liberacion National – MLN), a guerrilla organization formed in Uruguay in 1965 and very successful in its struggle against the regime at the end of the 1960s. See Train, Brian R., 'The Terror War', 1993, <http://www.islandnet.com/~citizenx/TWbody.html>.

[19] See Baumann, *Terror or Love?*, pp. 86-87.

[20] The attack was carried out the day after RAF leader Holger Meins died in jail following a hunger strike.

In February 1975 the M2J kidnapped Peter Lorenz, the CDU candidate for the Berlin mayoralty – the first act of its kind in the Federal Republic. The kidnappers' demands were granted: five jailed M2J and RAF members were released and permitted to leave for South Yemen. RAF leader Horst Mahler was offered his freedom but desisted.[21] In June 1980 the M2J disbanded and merged with the RAF, a clear indication of its organizational and ideological disarray.

3.   The RZ

The RZ first appeared on 16 November 1973 when it attacked the West Berlin offices of ITT to draw attention to the participation of this multinational corporation in Pinochet's military putsch in Chile. The RZ was apparently headed by Wilfried Böse, who also helped set up Red Aid to assist jailed members of the RAF and other German terrorist organizations.

Unlike the RAF, the RZ was not an underground organization; it engaged in legal activities among radical left-wing groups (ecological or otherwise), only occasionally sallying forth into the realm of terror. The RZ had 'anti-authoritarian structures and a decentralized decision-making process for choosing targets'. No less important than terrorist 'direct actions' were 'handing out flyers or leaflets, going to demonstrations, having sit-ins, publishing newspapers, educating people, squatting houses, or organizing strikes'.[22] The RZ operated through small, self-contained cells, with no central command, rendering their discovery and arrest virtually impossible. Members felt it important to retain ties with the 'anti-dogmatic left' and to combine the armed struggle with local political campaigns.[23]

According to a recent 'history' of the organization, the first issue of its journal, *Revolutionarer Zorn* (Revolutionary Rage), 'the RZ subdivided their actions into three main categories: 1) anti-imperialist actions, 2) actions against the branches, establishments, and accomplices of Zionism in the FRG [West Germany], and 3) actions supporting the struggles of workers, wimmin (sic!) and youth, and attacking and punishing their enemies'.[24]

In contrast to events in 1976, most RZ operations were restricted to minor acts of sabotage, arson and small-scale bombings.[25] Their first serious terrorist attack

---

[21]   Mahler later dissociated himself from the armed struggle and opposed terrorism.

[22]   Cited from *A Herstory* [sic] *of The Revolutionary Cells And Rote Zora – Armed Resistance in West Germany*, p. 3, written by a 'West German comrade' in 1988 and published in December 1993 by Arm.The.Spirit. It is more a history of Rote Zora, the female branch of the RZ. See <http://www.etext.org/Politics/Arm.The.Spirit/Guerrilla/Europe/Rote.Zora/mini-herstory.1988>.

[23]   See Steiner and Debray, *La Fraction Armée Rouge*, pp. 163-166 and Raufer and Haut, *RAF – Une organisation zéro traces*, p. 21.

[24]   See *A Herstory Of The Revolutionary Cells And Rote Zora*, pp. 1-2.

[25]   For example, planting a bomb in the Chilean consulate in West Berlin in June 1974.

was the bombing of the American military headquarters in Frankfurt on 1 June 1976. This coincided with the fourth anniversary of the imprisonment of the RAF leaders and was portrayed as a continuation of their struggle (Meinhof had committed suicide in prison about a month earlier). The RZ continued with these 'propaganda of the deed' attacks against American military installations, branches of the ITT corporation, and nuclear power stations sites. Only in 1978 were human targets selected in the course of two operations; victims were shot in the legs, evidently in imitation of Red Brigade tactics during the same period.

Despite differences in their modus operandi, the RZ regarded the RAF as its role model. The RAF, however, saw the refusal of the RZ to go underground as a sign of vacillation and perhaps even of evasion.[26]

In 1974-76, some RZ activists were evidently involved in operations of the PFLP – Wadi' Haddad Faction. This blatantly contradicted the declared RZ policy of limiting its activities to local political struggles. According to Hans Joachim Klein, a former RZ militant, the group responsible for cooperation with the PFLP-Wadi' Haddad Faction was, in fact, an international division of the RZ, acting independently of its parent organization in Germany.[27]

4. Cooperation with Palestinian organizations

Research into cooperation between German and Palestinian terrorist organizations encountered various difficulties: arrested leaders of the organizations did not cooperate with the authorities during interrogation; some information came from former terrorists, who were reluctant to divulge details about other comrades;[28] unlike in Italy, no relevant data emerged during the trials; the German terrorist organizations published few ideological documents up to 1972; and finally, only the RZ published details of its political and strategic positions through an official organ.

Another difficulty was posed by the non-hierarchical and fluid structure of the anarchistic terrorist organizations in Germany.[29] Researchers subsequently attrib-

---

26 In an open letter to 'all members of RAF' in early 1977, members of the RZ announced 'that the RZ and other groups owed their existence to the RAF'. In the same letter, they expressed their wish to reach a strategic dialogue with the RAF while preserving their autonomy. According to Steiner and Debray RZ activists did not succeed in reaching a strategic understanding with the second generation of RAF activists (who in mid-1977 were about to launch a new offensive), mainly due to different attitudes to underground activity. See Steiner and Debray, *La Fraction Armée Rouge*, pp. 164-165.

27 See Bougereau, *An Interview with Hans Joachim Klein*, p. 52.

28 Among those former terrorists were Michael 'Bommi' Baumann, Hans Joachim Klein and Peter Hoffman.

29 It was difficult to classify the activities of the TW – the first serious terrorist organization operating in The Federal Republic. Michael ('Bommi') Baumann, one of its leaders and virtually

uted terrorist acts to one organization, when they were actually perpetrated by another. Furthermore, although the RZ apparently had the closest operational ties with Palestinian organizations, there is little documentary evidence to this effect.[30]

A.   The establishment and development of ties

Very little is known of the way initial ties were established between German terrorists and the Palestinian terrorist organizations. It is clear, however, that a significant number of Germans found their way into Palestinian training camps as early as 1969-70, some via underground channels. This probably came about for two main reasons: firstly, West Germany at that time had the highest concentration of Palestinian students and workers in Europe, thanks to the availability of government stipends for Arab students. Fatah managed to infiltrate and dominate the Palestinian student organization (General Union of Palestinian Students – GUPS), which enabled it to establish ties with local student and radical left-wing organizations.[31] Secondly, German terrorist organizations were active in areas with a high concentration of Muslim – mainly Turkish – immigrants, who also provided links with Middle Eastern terrorist organizations.[32]

German terrorists who trained in Palestinian camps maintained ties with Palestinian organizations, coordinated the training of other groups, and helped German terrorists escape to the Middle East. An interesting phenomenon, unique to German terrorism, concerned the personal relationships that evolved between female members of the German terrorist organizations and individual Palestinian terrorists. It is also noteworthy that German terrorist organizations had a higher percentage of female members than similar organizations in other countries.

Some accounts claimed that ties with the Palestinian organizations were orchestrated by the East German intelligence services, which also facilitated the training of German terrorists in Palestinian camps. According to one testimony, ties with the East German intelligence services were established in Berlin before and after the arrest of Baader.[33] It could be argued that such complex mediation

---

the only good source of information on this organization, described it as the precursor of the M2J. This book considered only the ideological/organizational impact of TW on the leaders of M2J, while drawing a line between the operational activities of the two organizations. See Baumann, *Terror or Love?*, pp. 59-73.

30   Most of the information is based on Hans Joachim Klein's testimony.

31   See Ehud Ya'ari, *Fatah* (Tel Aviv: A. Levine-Epstein, 1970), (Hebrew), pp. 21, 47. Hani al-Hasan, one of the ideologues of Fatah, was enrolled at a German university and played a leading role in expanding union activity among the Palestinians in West Germany. See Yazid Sayigh, *Armed Struggle and the Search for State: The Palestinian National Movement, 1949-1993* (New York: Oxford University Press, 1997), p. 87.

32   See Baumann's testimony, *Terror or Love?*, pp. 86-87.

33   See the testimony of Fioroni, of the Italian Red Brigades (MI), p. 22.

was unlikely and unnecessary, especially since the Palestinian terrorist organizations had already established an active infrastructure in West Germany.

There is no evidence of any agreements or general understandings between German and Palestinian organizations. Although Klein does mention 'senior-level' contacts between the M2J and the PFLP to this end, and between the RZ and the PFLP, such contacts appear to have been inconsequential.[34]

B.   Summary of cooperation in this period

The RAF was the only organization to express solidarity with the Palestinian organizations in writing, at least in the years 1971-72. In one document, it even supported Black September's murder of Israeli athletes at the Munich Olympics, an act that met with mixed reactions in radical left-wing circles in Europe and in Germany itself. In the years 1973-80, such expressions of solidarity dwindled.[35]

The M2J and RZ published fewer communiqués or leaflets, and these appeared only in radical publications with a limited circulation. The near total absence of written expressions of solidarity with the Palestinians is conspicuous, especially in the case of the RZ whose members actively participated in a number of major PFLP operations. The RZ never made any attempt to explain to its followers or to the public at large the rationale for such cooperation.

As for logistical aid between the RAF and Palestinians, only isolated cases have been reported. Although other cases may have occurred, mutual aid on a significant scale was unlikely.[36] Klein claimed that the RZ depended on the PFLP for financial aid and weapons but no details were published on the subject.[37] Little was known about the exact relationship between the RZ and its international division (which, according to Klein, was effectively an operational branch of the PFLP) until the 1990s.

The main type of cooperation between the RAF/RZ and Palestinian terrorist organizations, in particular the PFLP, was operational. Such cooperation was particularly strong from 1970-73 in the case of the RAF,[38] and from 1975-76 in

---

[34] The M2J contacted the PFLP in connection with their plan to kidnap the Pope. RZ contacted the PFLP in connection with 'a large-scale international terrorist operation' to be perpetrated by members of the RZ. See Bougereau, *An Interview with Hans Joachim Klein*, pp. 30, 46.

[35] See 'The Black September Operation in Munich: The strategy of the anti-imperialist struggle', published in late 1972, in *Texte der RAF*, pp 411-447.

[36] One of the few known cases was the purchase by RAF leader Meinhof of 35 revolvers from an Arab, probably provided by Fatah, later used by the RAF. See *Frankfurter Algemeine Zeitung*, 20 April 1971.

[37] See Bougereau, *An Interview with Hans Joachim Klein*, pp. 31, 46.

[38] After Baader's release from prison, in May 1970 about 15 RAF members, including their leaders, fled to Jordan, where they trained for about two months in a Fatah camp. It is not clear if Palestinian agents provided the fugitives with documents or facilitated their escape in other ways.

the cases of both the RAF and RZ.[39] Many German terrorists participated in PFLP operations, particularly against Israeli targets, but also against 'imperialist' targets such as the OPEC headquarters in Vienna.[40] Palestinian assistance to German

The Black September cell that attacked the residence of the Saudi ambassador in Khartoum in March 1973 and held three Western diplomats hostage demanded, *inter alia*, the release of the imprisoned members of the Baader-Meinhof gang in Germany. Their demand was turned down because the West German ambassador was not present at the event. See Edward Mickolus' database, ITERATE III, a chronology of international terrorist acts for the years 1968-90, published also in book form: Edward Mickolus, *Transnational Terrorism: A Chronology of Events, 1968-1979* (London: Aldwych Press, 1980), pp. 375-378.

[39] Four M2J members and one RAF member, released by the German authorities in response to the demand by the kidnappers of Peter Lorenz in late February 1975, fled to South Yemen where they trained in a PFLP camp. Several other RAF members were being trained in the same camp, including Siegfried Haag, leader of the RAF in the mid-1970s. Most of the M2J members who trained there later assumed an active role in the RAF. See Becker, *Hitler's Children*, pp. 379-89 and *Ma'ariv*, 17 January 1977.

In late January 1975 a PFLP cell comprising three Palestinians and two Germans, Brigitte Schultz and Thomas Reuter, was caught in Nairobi (Kenya), where it had attempted to attack an El Al plane. The five were brought to Israel in a secret operation, and sentenced to long prison terms. The Germans were RAF members who had trained in South Yemen.

On 25 May 1976 a suitcase of explosives, which a German terrorist, Bernard Hausmann, tried to smuggle into Israel, exploded at Ben Gurion airport. Hausmann may have been unaware of the contents.

On 13 October 1977 a Lufthansa plane was hijacked in Majorca by a cell of the 'Organization of the Struggle against World Imperialism', a pseudonym for the PLFP. The organization demanded, *inter alia*, the release 'of all German political prisoners' and published statements in support of Hanns Martin Schleyer's RAF kidnappers. The RAF also issued a communiqué supporting this action and reiterating the demands. The West German Information Ministry pointed out that the announcement by the Arab 'Halimah commando' had been typed on the same typewriter as the announcement by the 'Siegfried Hausner commando' claiming responsibility for the kidnapping of Schleyer. See Dennis Pluchinsky, 'An Organizational and Operational Analysis of Germany's Red Army Faction Terrorist Group (1972-1991)' in Alexander and Pluchinsky (eds.), *European Terrorism. Today and Tomorrow.* (Washington: Brassey's, 1992), pp. 62-63.

In the 1990s Monika Haas, a former terrorist, was tried in Germany not only for helping to kidnap Schleyer but also aiding the hijacking of the Lufthansa plane by smuggling weapons onto Majorca in a child's pram. See *Reuters*, 18 January 1996.

[40] RZ leader Wilfred Böse helped Black September to prepare the kidnapping of the Israeli athletes at the Munich Olympics. See Bougereau, *An Interview with Hans Joachim Klein*, p. 44. Together with another German he was also involved in two Carlos-assisted PFLP attempts to attack an El Al plane at Orly airport near Paris on 13 and 19 January 1975, respectively. They apparently hired a car and were responsible for gathering the operational information.

About six RZ members participated in the Carlos-led PFLP operation to seize OPEC headquarters in Vienna on 21 December 1975. Four helped in the logistic/intelligence preparations leading up to the operation, while Hans Joachim Klein and Gabriella Krocher-Tiedemann helped the cell that actually kidnapped the participants at the OPEC conference. Klein was the only terrorist to be seriously wounded during the operation.

Several RZ members of the 'national branch' trained at a PFLP camp in 1976. See Bougereau, *An Interview with Hans Joachim Klein*, p. 46.

On 27 June 1976 a cell of the PLFP-Wadi' Haddad Faction hijacked an Air-France plane to Entebbe airport in Uganda, demanding the release of over 50 terrorists: Palestinians imprisoned in Israel, German terrorists imprisoned in Germany, a German RAF terrorist imprisoned in

terrorists usually took the form of providing safe havens and training. Evidently the training had a dual function: to prepare German terrorists to strike out on their own (some of those involved in the 1975 attack on the German embassy in Stockholm had trained in South Yemen), and also to prepare them for tasks within the PFLP itself.

On the face of it, there was no operational cooperation between the M2J and the Palestinian terrorist organizations. In the few cases where M2J activists did cooperate with Palestinian organizations, it is hard to ascertain whether they did so as individuals or as representatives of their organization.[41] For example, M2J members who were released from jail in February 1975 after the kidnapping of the German politician Peter Lorenz, joined their RAF comrades in a PFLP camp in South Yemen. Was this due to an independent agreement between the PFLP and the M2J, or to an agreement between the PFLP and the RAF, which wished to recruit M2J members to its ranks?[42] In his interview, Klein claimed that the M2J abandoned its plan to kidnap the Pope in Rome due to opposition by Wadi' Haddad.[43] This implies that some cooperation between the two organizations existed, at least at the planning level.

The characteristics of cooperation for this period may be summarized as follows:

(1) From 1968-77, Palestinian organizations allowed German terrorists from all the organizations to train in their camps in Jordan (at least up till 1970 when the crisis with the Jordanian authorities erupted), Lebanon, and particularly South Yemen, where the PFLP operated freely.

(2) Palestinian organizations felt a deep commitment towards their German comrades; kidnappings and hijackings were conducted in an attempt to pressure the West German authorities to release jailed terrorists.[44]

Switzerland, and two German RAF terrorists who had been caught in Nairobi several months earlier (the operation was called 'Remember the Kenyan betrayal'). The cell was led by Wilfred Böse and another RZ terrorist, Brigitte Kuhlmann, was one of its members. Most of the terrorists, including the Germans, were killed when the IDF stormed Entebbe airport.

Klein disclosed a plan to murder two leaders of the Jewish community in Germany, Galinski of Berlin, and Lipinski of Frankfurt. A letter on the subject sent by Klein to the weekly *Der Spiegel* torpedoed the plan.

[41] Becker cited the case of an M2J activist who learnt how to make bombs from an Arab comrade, member of the PFLP. See Becker, *Hitler's Children*, p. 265.

[42] One of the released terrorists, Gabriele Krocher-Tidermann, participated in the January 1976 raid on the OPEC headquarters in Vienna as a member of a PFLP cell. It is not clear if this was M2J's 'contribution' to the operation, or she was acting on behalf of the RZ, which played a major role in the German side of the Vienna operation.

[43] See Bougereau, *An Interview with Hans Joachim Klein*, p. 30.

[44] The last RAF official statement ended with the following tribute to the Palestinians: 'We will never forget the comrades of the Popular Front for the Liberation of Palestine (PFLP) who lost their lives

(3) A relatively large number of Germans worked for Palestinian terrorist organizations, in particular the PFLP, and even participated in dangerous and large-scale operations which caused (or could have caused) many casualties, despite the fact that this violated principles they themselves defended when operating on German soil. Most of these terrorists came from the RZ, and only a minority from the RAF. However, it is hard to ascertain whether they worked as a distinct organizational unit, or as individuals who were recruited by the Palestinian organizations for personal, ideological or mercenary reasons.

C. The reasons for cooperation between the German and Palestinian organizations

As noted above, Tupamaros West Berlin (the precursor of the M2J) was set up by a group of left-wing anarchists who, after training in 'Palestine' in 1969, returned to Germany eager, to launch an armed struggle.[45] Most of their attacks were directed at the government, in particular the judiciary.

In the course of 1968, Palestine also became the symbol of the Third World struggle. It therefore seemed natural for TW leaders to attack American, Israeli and Jewish targets.

The RAF underwent a similar process. As noted above, the Fatah camps provided a haven for gang members who wished to escape prison and flee Germany. However, the RAF's sojourn in the Fatah camp in Jordan in the summer of 1970 was not successful. The training did not take into account topological differences (desert conditions as opposed to urban conditions), organizational and political factors, or the psychological idiosyncrasies of the German group leaders.[46]

Despite these difficulties, it was no doubt their experience in the Palestinian training camp that launched the organization on its terrorist career. It provided the young German terrorists the impetus to go underground in Germany, to organize and perpetrate a series of bank raids and to launch their first terrorist offensive in May 1972.

Criticism leveled at RAF members by German left-wing radicals, and possibly also by their Palestinian mentors, rendered the need for a 'doctrine' or ideological and strategic justification of their activities all the more imperative. It is not, therefore, surprising that four ideological texts were published before the May

---

in the fall of 1977 in an act of internationalist solidarity, seeking to liberate the political prisoners'. See *Statement of the RAF (the 1998 disbanding of the Rote Army Faction)*, March 1998, p. 14, at <http://www.baader-meinhof.com/students/resources/communique/engrafend.html>.

45   Baumann, *Terror or Love?*, pp. 59-61.

46   According to Hoffman's testimony in *Der Spiegel*, Baader was described by the Palestinians as a coward, and Meinhof as extremely unsure of herself.

1972 offensive. These were: 'The Concept of the Urban Guerrilla', 'On the Armed Struggle in Western Europe', 'The Anti-Imperialist Struggle', and the 'Urban Guerrilla and Class Warfare'.

'The Concept of the Urban Guerrilla' (April 1971), considered the RAF's major ideological document,[47] was largely a defense of anarchism, violence and terrorism under the guise of promoting the armed struggle.

According to the RAF, West Germany played a major role in Western imperialism, not only in economic terms, but also in terms of its increasing political clout on both the domestic and foreign fronts. Its policy of courting the East opened up new markets and contributed to the balance of power and alliance between America and the USSR, an alliance which gave the US a free hand in its aggression against the Third World. Under the guise of military and economic aid, the West German government was effectively participating in America's wars, and profiting from its exploitation of the Third World.[48]

In the German student revolution of the 1960s, claimed the document, students realized that the national struggle in Germany should be combined with the international struggle against global imperialism. The student movement gained its sense of self-worth not from progress in class warfare in Germany, but rather from its sense of belonging to an international movement, the feeling that it was confronting the same class enemies as the Vietcong, the same 'paper tigers'. Protests against American intervention in Vietnam should be accompanied by attacks against American warplanes, and denunciation of the German military should be combined with attacks against NATO air bases. In conclusion, the RAF was careful to emphasize the international context of its revolutionary struggle in the metropolis.[49]

'Urban Guerrilla and Class Warfare' (April 1972) was a general critique of West German economic and social policies at home and abroad, which it accused of serving the interests of multinational corporations and imperialists. The national struggle could not be separated from the international struggle. Only an armed struggle on a united front could overturn the balance of power and loosen the hold of imperialism. Although a section of the document discussed the need for solidarity, it was phrased in the most general terms, without any reference to specific organizations or movements.[50]

---

[47] This book uses the French translation published in *Notes et Etudes*, No. 5 (1988), pp. 54-67. Most researchers believe that the document was written by Meinhof, the most intellectual RAF leader.

[48] Ibid., pp. 57-58.

[49] Ibid., pp. 58-60. 'Metropolis' is a key concept in the terminology of European radical left-wing terrorist organizations. It designates both imperialist countries and the large cities where the urban guerrilla warfare is waged.

[50] See 'Urban Guerrilla and Class Warfare' (Rote Armee Fraktion: Stadtguerilla und Klassenkampf – rafzeitung 1972), *texte der RAF*, pp. 368-410).

In May 1972, the RAF began to implement its terror strategy by attacking German police targets, a judge involved in RAF trials, a building of the Springer Press, and US military headquarters in Heidelberg.

D.   International and regional factors

Surprisingly, 'The Concept of the Urban Guerrilla' hardly alluded to the struggle of Palestinian organizations or the Middle East situation. It mentioned that certain left-wing circles took credit for arranging the training of RAF members in Palestinian camps in the Middle East. It also blamed left-wing intellectuals for expressing their internationalism by awarding grades to various Palestinian organizations. The revolutionary struggle in Palestine was mentioned in the same context as those taking place in Russia, China, Cuba, Algeria and Vietnam. While alluding to their trip to the Middle East there is no reference to a coalition between the RAF and Palestinian terrorist organizations. There are probably two reasons for this omission:

(1) Personal antagonism between RAF trainees in Palestinian camps in Jordan and their Palestinian instructors, perhaps due to the inappropriate nature of the training.

(2) The predicament of Palestinian organizations after their expulsion from Jordan in September 1970. During 1971 most Fatah and PFLP attacks were directed against Jordanian targets, and it was only at the end of that year that Black September emerged on the international terror scene.[51] 'The Concept of the Urban Guerrilla' was published in April 1972, when the Palestinian terrorist organizations were licking their wounds and could no longer serve as an immediate role model. Hence, the only reference to solidarity with the Palestinians was in a leaflet circulated in connection with the attack on the Springer newspaper chain in May 1972.[52]

---

[51] Its first attack was the assassination of Wasfi at-Tal, the Jordanian prime minister, in Cairo on 28 November 1971.

[52] The leaflet assuming responsibility for the attack against Springer on 19 May 1972 claimed that the operation was intended to put an end to incitement by the Springer newspapers against the Third World liberation movements, 'and in particular against the Arab peoples who are fighting for the liberation of Palestine'. Springer publications were ordered 'to cease their propaganda and support of Zionism and the imperialist policies of the ruling class in Israel'. See *Texte der RAF*, p. 451.

E.   The impact of Black September

The clearest expression of solidarity with the Palestinian organizations came in the wake of the Black September massacre of Israeli athletes at the Munich Olympics in September 1972. In a speech by Horst Mahler at his trial on 9 October 1972, and in an unusually long ideological document devoted to this topic, the RAF defended the location of the attack, 'the vanguard of European imperialism, and the heirs to Nazi Germany with its policy of Jewish genocide'.[53]

According to this document, the Black September operation had brought the regional conflict between Israel (the imperialist metropolis) and the Palestinians to center stage, and forced Germany to show its true colors as an imperialist state fighting freedom movements in the Third World. Chancellor Brandt was accused of leading the 'criminal attack' against the Palestinian commandos in Furstengeldbruch airport, and providing weapons to West German imperialists in an American NATO base.

The RAF admired the 'tough stance' of the Black September commandos during the Munich attack. Like Black September, the RAF claimed that imperialist forces were incarcerating and torturing Palestinian, Turkish and Iranian comrades in their countries, trying anti-imperialist left-wing radicals in the German courts, and slaughtering Black September Palestinian freedom fighters. The peoples of the Third World, as the spearhead of the anti-imperialist revolution, represented the one true hope of the revolutionaries in the metropolis. The self-appointed mission of the RAF, therefore, was to act as a bridge between freedom fighters in the Third World and their counterparts in the metropolis.

Most of the RAF leaders had been jailed by June 1972, but their morale was boosted on learning that the Black September terrorists had demanded their release. Interestingly, in February 1972 Black September carried out several attacks in Germany or relating to Germany.[54] RAF leaders may well have believed that their Palestinian comrades would succeed in securing their release by means of a hijacking operation.[55] Indeed, a Black September cell which

---

[53] The document entitled 'The "Black September" operation in Munich, the Strategy of the Anti-Imperialist Struggle' was supposedly written by Horst Mahler, who was imprisoned in June 1972. Some of the main themes in this ideological document figured in the speech Mahler delivered at his trial in September 1972. See also *CONTROinformazione*, Nos. 1-2, Feb.-Mar. 1974, pp. 26-29.

[54] These attacks were: sabotaging a generator plant and an oil pipeline near Hamburg; the assassination in Cologne of five Jordanians, accused of collaborating with Israel; and the hijacking of a Lufthansa plane from New Delhi to Athens.

[55] On 29 October 1972, another Lufthansa plane flying from Damascus to Munich was hijacked. The hijackers demanded and secured the release of three members of Black September who were imprisoned in Germany after the Munich massacre.

occupied the home of the Saudi ambassador in Khartoum in March 1973 did demand the release of RAF leaders.[56]

F.   Other factors

Even if the RAF had planned to cooperate with Palestinian organizations, it was prevented from doing so by the arrest of its leaders in 1973-74. This brought the organization to a complete standstill. In late 1974, the M2J burst on to the scene but it mainly targeted judicial officials involved in the trials of members of the RAF and the M2J. The abduction of Peter Lorenz by the M2J in February 1975 achieved its goal – the release of jailed members. However, a very complex RAF operation – in which the staff of the German embassy in Stockholm in April 1975 were taken hostage – was less successful. It ended in a high number of casualties, and the remaining activists were arrested.

The RAF did not fare much better in the years 1976 and 1977. In June 1976 Meinhof committed suicide in prison. The German authorities were doubtless less inclined to release other leaders following a series of murders of senior government officials and leading industrialists. After disbanding in 1998, the RAF described 1975-77 as a phase 'during which it did everything possible to liberate its prisoners from jail'. After the kidnapping of Schleyer, '[w]hen it became clear that the state was prepared to abandon [him], the RAF gave its approval for a civilian airliner to be hijacked in a guerrilla action as part of its own offensive'.[57]

Nevertheless, the years 1975-77 were the most fertile as far as cooperation between German and Palestinian organizations (in particular the PFLP) was concerned. There was greater readiness on the part of the Palestinian organizations to enlist members of the RAF, the M2J and the RZ in their training camps in Lebanon, and particularly South Yemen. More German terrorists participated in major PFLP operations or operations masterminded by Carlos himself on behalf of the PFLP (the seizure of OPEC headquarters, the attempted bombing of an El Al plane in Paris, the attempted hijacking of an El Al plane in Nairobi, and the hijacking of an Air France plane to Entebbe). It was the failed hijacking of a Lufthansa plane to Mogadishu that effectively put paid to this operational cooperation.

It is hard to determine which global or regional factors, if any, influenced the decision of RAF activists to cooperate in attacks that generally ran counter to the organization's philosophy and even strategy (the hijacking of civilian planes, for example). If the tardy admission by the RAF that it approved the hijacking of a civilian airliner in a joint operation with the PFLP is taken as genuine, it seems

---

[56]   The terrorist activity of Black September, a secret offshoot of Fatah, ceased in 1974.
[57]   See *Statement of the RAF*, pp. 2-3.

that as a last resort in order to liberate its leaders, the organization was ready to overcome its own constraints.[58]

The plight of the Palestinians in Lebanon during the civil war that ravaged the country from April 1975 aroused the sympathy of German revolutionary organizations. Their members became increasingly eager to help the Palestinians, directly or indirectly. Some, no doubt, felt an obligation to repay their Palestinian comrades for the shelter and help they themselves had received in times of trouble.

G.   The international counter-terrorist cooperation

In an interview published in the German weekly *Der Spiegel* of 20 January 1975, jailed RAF leaders labeled West Germany a repressive state that was an integral part of the imperialist system. Nonetheless, they claimed that the proletarian counter-force could develop within an international context, through cooperation with other oppressed peoples. Although the leaders were aware of their isolation, even within German left-wing circles, they felt that other international terrorist organizations were sympathetic to their cause.

A document entitled 'The Other Process' (late April 1976), argued that West Germany had become a model of counter-insurgency.[59] In Germany, it stated, internal security was integrated with external security. In a US-West German joint venture, the West Germany police apparatus had been incorporated into NATO. The perceived aims were to develop a military-intelligence network, a global war machine under Pentagon supervision operating through mobile commando forces, a united police force in the various German states (*Länder*) with expanded powers, and state-of-the-art computer technology.

Another RAF document of the period argued that 'occupied' Germany (the territory occupied by the US army) was being used as a base for the expansion of American aggression against the Third World and anti-imperialist national movements.[60] It also alleged that agents had been dispatched from the American intelligence base in the Federal Republic to the Middle East, Africa and South East Asia, and that the I.G. Farben company served as the headquarters of American activity in the Middle East and East Asia.

The views expressed in these documents were those of jailed RAF leaders. It is doubtful how much control these individuals exercised over activists who joined the Palestinian organizations in the Middle East, usually in remote countries such as South Yemen. The new motif that dominated the short texts of the period was the

---

[58]   Ibid.
[59]   See *Texte der RAF*, pp. 27-34.
[60]   See 'Defense and Vietnam' (4 May 1976), ibid., pp. 476-83.

growing role of the West German police and intelligence services, and international security cooperation under the American umbrella. Indeed, RAF leaders may well have correctly assessed the capabilities of the international security and government agencies, as reflected in the Israeli rescue operation in Entebbe in June 1976, and the German GSG-9 operation in Mogadishu in October 1977. On 28 September 1977 West Germany signed the Council of Europe Convention for a joint counter-insurgency strategy that specified that fugitive terrorists should be extradited, or tried in the country where they were hiding.

IV.   THE THIRD GENERATION OF RAF LEADERS (1981-84)

Despite the *débâcles* of 1980, the extensive arrest of activists, and the RAF-M2J merger due to strategic failure, 1981 was one of the most prolific years for the terrorist organizations, a year in which they attacked against American and German targets in the Federal Republic. Although some of these attacks were carried out by autonomous elements, the major ones were carried out by the RAF. These included the attempted assassination of Gen. Kroesen, commander of American ground forces in Europe.[61]

Once again, however, this wave of terrorism was followed by the discovery and neutralization of the organization's core members. In November 1982 the new RAF leaders, Brigitte Monhaupt, Adelheid Schulz and Christian Klar, were arrested. The police later unearthed about fifteen arms caches containing weapons, ammunition and money looted from banks. After the arrest of its leaders in 1982, the organization went into hibernation. In 1983 it carried out only two operations. This lull in activity continued until the autumn of 1984, when a series of bank raids indicated that logistic and financial preparations were under way by new members of the organization. In the course of the year these activists went underground and a new wave of attacks was launched in December 1984 (See Chapter 6).

The only significant operation of the RZ during this period was the assassination of the minister of economic affairs of the state of Hesse, Heinz-Herbert Karry, on 11 May 1981.[62]

---

[61]   The attacks included the bombing of an American military train carrying soldiers to West Berlin, the time bomb discovered near the American military headquarters in Weisbaden, and the bomb planted in the American Ramstein air-base, in which 17 soldiers and senior American officers were injured. The RPG-7 assault rockets aimed at Gen. Kroesen were fired by Brigitte Monhaupt, who had been trained in South Yemen. See Pluchinsky, *An Organizational and Operational Analysis of Germany's Red Army Faction*, p. 65.

[62]   The organization argued *post facto* that the attack was designed to injure the minister, not kill him. In June 1984, the organization blew up an oil pipe that served NATO forces in West Germany.

1.   Cooperation with Palestinian organizations

There were no real expressions of solidarity with the Palestinians and no evidence of logistical or operational cooperation between the RAF/RZ and Palestinian organizations during this period. There are some indications, however, that German terrorists fled to Lebanon and joined PFLP camps. Most of these terrorists, however, were female, and it is unclear whether they were representing their organizations, or motivated by mere personal reasons.[63] Similarly, the few leaflets that were published by German organizations in the wake of attacks were short, and gave no explanation of the ideological or strategic background to their operations.

In May 1982 the RAF published its first strategic document after ten years of silence – 'Guerrilla, Resistance and Anti-Imperialist Front'.[64] The book specified the main goal of the RAF as the development of a new stage of revolutionary strategy in the metropolis, in which the struggle of the revolutionary front would complement the struggle of freedom fighters in Asia, Africa and Latin America. Although revolutionary movements in the metropolis were operating within their own particular historical and social context, they were perceived as sharing the same goals as Third World peoples. Therefore, the document argued, the struggle should be waged on a common front, albeit in different contexts. In practice, developments in Western Europe were to play a major role in the confrontation with imperialism.

This document mentioned the Middle East as a region of vital strategic/military and economic importance (as a supplier of oil) for the forces of imperialism but omitted any reference to the Palestinian organizations. Similarly, two leaflets that were circulated after attacks against German and American targets, and a series of letters written by jailed RAF leader Christian Klar, praised the anti-imperialist struggle of the Lebanese people and the Arab masses, but made no mention at all of the Palestinians.[65]

---

[63] Thus, for example, Suzanne Albrecht, who took part in several important terrorist attacks, escaped in 1980 to Lebanon. Frederika Krabbe escaped to Baghdad in 1980 where she lived with her boyfriend, a member of the 15 May Faction.

[64] See the French version, 'Guérila, résistance et front anti-impérialiste', *Notes et Etudes*, No. 5 (1988), pp. 69-80.

[65] The RAF leaflet published after its bombing of the Honeywell Bull building in Düsseldorf (20 November 1983) claimed that despite military escalation aimed at eradicating the Palestinian and Lebanese revolutionary movement in Lebanon, the Lebanese people was renewing the armed struggle and the US and NATO could no longer rely on Israel, their representative in the area.

The RAF leaflet taking responsibility for the bombing of the Deutsche Bank (June 1984) equated racism in Israel with racism in South Africa and mentioned Israel's role within imperialist war on socialist states and liberation movements. There was no mention of Palestinian organizations.

As for the RZ, after its mouthpiece *Revolutionarer Zorn* (Revolutionary Anger) ceased publication in January 1981, it published only four ideological texts.[66] None referred to the issue of Palestine or the Palestinian organizations. (Only one document discussed international issues and this is analyzed below).

2. International and regional factors

The RZ and M2J both attacked US and NATO targets from the mid-1970s on. The RAF itself resumed attacks against US targets towards the late 1970s. According to Pilat, such activity was sporadic, albeit significant, up to the early 1980s, when these movements began to protest the stationing of US ballistic missiles in Europe.[67]

The popular protest movement emerged in Europe when NATO announced plans in December 1979 to modernize its nuclear capability. Following the decision of the Reagan administration in August 1981 to manufacture and store neutron bombs in the US, protestors subsequently joined forces with the European nuclear disarmament movement. This led to the formation in 1981 of a broad coalition across Western Europe of pacifists, ecologists, feminists, socialists, social democrats and left-wing radicals.

The RAF renewed a terror campaign against US and NATO military installations and personnel in late 1981. In its final document, the RAF explained again the change in strategy: 'From the 1970s to the 1980s, the RAF had gambled everything and suffered a huge defeat', exposing the limitations of the former urban guerrilla concept. Therefore, the 'RAF wanted new ties and a basis for a joint struggle with radical segments of the resistance movements which had arisen in the late 1970s' and 'sought to attack … the militarization policies of the NATO states … the war against the Soviet Union and, at the same time, warlike interventions against liberation movements and revolutions, like in Nicaragua'.[68]

A series of letters sent from jail by RAF leader Christian Klar (April, June 1984) referred to Israel as capable of using its nuclear force against the Arab masses. In order to highlight Middle Eastern pressure against American imperialist activities in the area, Klar mentioned the 300 coffins dispatched from Beirut to the US. The reference was to the attack that the Hizballah perpetrated against the American Marines base in Beirut, on 23 October 1983. According to Klar, the Hizballah action had a proletarian dimension that had a bearing on the entire strategy of the revolutionary movement. None of the three letters mentioned the Palestinians.

[66] These texts were: 'Action against the expansion of the Frankfurt airport route' (August 1983), an assessment of the 'Peace Movement' (December 1983), a paper on the 35-hour work week (March 1984), and an interview with *Rote Zora*, RZ women's branch (June 1984).

[67] See J. F. Pilat, 'Research Note: European Terrorism and the Euromissiles,' *Terrorism*, Vol. 7, No 1 (1984), pp. 65-6.

[68] See *Statement of the RAF*, p. 4.

This shift in RAF strategy was also triggered by its assessment that Third World freedom movements, traditionally considered spearheads of the revolutionary struggle, had lost their dynamism and motivation of the 1960s and early 1970s. A document of June 1980, announcing the M2J merger with the RAF, argued that the struggle between imperialist and revolutionary forces would ultimately be resolved in the metropolis because successful Third World freedom movements would inevitably become part of the East/West conflict, thereby becoming vulnerable to economic or military pressure on the part of imperialist powers.

This argument formed the main thesis of the document entitled 'Guerrilla, Resistance and Anti-Imperialist Front' (May 1982). One chapter opened with the assertion that 'developments in Western Europe have become the cornerstone of global confrontation'.[69] The document also claimed that many of the freedom movements had evolved into states and those which had not evolved were, in the course of the struggle, behaving almost as sovereign states. The newly liberated states thus enjoyed new political power and were allowed a certain degree of flexibility within the framework of international organizations. This was regarded as a logical process, an expression both of their newly acquired power, and of their former vulnerability, which was forcing them to work within the state system, as dictated by the rules of imperialism. This was an allusion to the PLO, which had acquired extra-territorial status in Southern Lebanon and was attempting to participate in political negotiations, as indicated by the 1981 cease-fire with Israel (prior to the IDF attack in June 1982).[70]

Christian Klar, a jailed RAF leader, explained in more detail how international developments from the late 1970s affected the doctrine and strategy of the German radical left.[71] According to his account, the revolutionary process erupted in the early 1960s due to the 'encirclement of the towns by the villages', the confrontation between North and South, and the Vietnam War, which proved that it was possible to triumph over imperialism.

Until the late 1970s national freedom struggles had provided the main impetus for the revolutionary process in the metropolis. Negative developments in Vietnam after the victory over the US, and in the liberated countries, said Klar, led to disillusion in left-wing circles, which began to emphasize the centrality of Western Europe in the global revolutionary process, and of the metropolis in the confrontation with imperialism.

---

[69] See *Notes et Etudes*, No. 5 (1988), pp. 77-78.
[70] This can be seen as recognition of the PLO's status as an NSN.
[71] His views appeared in a letter dated 9 June 1984, published in *L'internationale*, No. 10/11 (Sept.-Oct. 1984), p. 8.

The RZ were far more skeptical of the peace movement in Western Europe, describing it as a bourgeois attempt to spread fear of nuclear war and global destruction, in order to deflect attention from the true socio-economic causes of the crisis in the capitalist world. The movement, it claimed, was effectively cooperating with capitalist régimes, and thereby hindering radical left-wing organizations.[72]

In a similar vein, the RZ interpreted the stationing of missiles as an expression of weakness on the part of US imperialism, which hoped to neutralize the Eastern bloc, clearing the field for intervention in conventional wars (such as the war in Central America and the most recent war in the Middle East).[73] The RZ dismissed the USSR as economically incapable of continuing with its revolutionary goals or helping Third World countries and freedom movements, such as those in Nicaragua. West Germany, on the other hand, was described as a rising economic and political power, the second most powerful member of NATO, and the spearhead of imperialism. Thus, alongside the US, Britain, France and Japan, West Germany had become a key actor within the imperialist system. This gloomy assessment largely explains the relative lull in RZ terrorist activity.

V.   THE PERIOD OF EURO-TERRORISM AND THE DECLINE OF THE GERMAN TERRORIST ORGANIZATIONS (1985-90)

From December 1984 to the end of 1986 the RAF focused on a Euro-terrorist strategy, trying to set up a West European Guerrilla Front. During 1987 the organization lay low. It was only in September 1988 that the RAF struck again – this time with the attempted assassination of the German deputy finance minister. This effectively marked the end of the period of Euro-terrorism (see Chapter 6).[74]

The RZ carried out several terrorist operations in 1985-87, mainly targeting German industry or government ministries, particularly those dealing with foreign immigrants. In three separate incidents, NATO oil lines in Germany were blown up. In another three incidents, South African targets, including the South African

---

[72]   After a long period of silence, the organization presented its views on the subject in a document published in December 1983. See the text as published in *L'internationale*, Nos. 5, 6, and 7 (Dec. 1983-May 1984) under the title 'The RZ answers the movement: a wrong policy does not become any more right by becoming more radical'.

[73]   This was the period of active American involvement in Lebanon following the IDF incursion into that country and the arrival of American and French peacekeeping forces.

[74]   Until the end of the period the organization carried out only two major terrorist attacks. On 30 November 1989, after a lull of 14 months, Alfred Herrhausen, manager of the Deutsche Bank, was murdered, and on 27 July 1990 an attempt was made on the life of Hans Neusel, the secretary of state responsible for internal security in the Ministry of the Interior.

legation in Bonn, were chosen. RZ terrorist activity continued sporadically into the late 1980s.

Throughout this period, logistical or operational cooperation between German and Palestinian terrorist organizations was virtually non-existent. The RAF was preoccupied with solidarity with European terrorist organizations, while the RZ focused on domestic problems, and occasionally on symbolic targets connected with NATO or South Africa.

The RAF did, however, express ideological solidarity with Palestinian organizations. For example, the German groups which claimed responsibility for the five attacks carried out in 1986, 1988 and 1989, were called after Palestinian terrorists who died during attacks against Israel.[75]

1.   Reasons for the lack of cooperation between 1981-90

As noted above, 1980 marked a turning point in RAF strategy. Henceforth, emphasis was placed on the perceived American threat and the major role played by NATO and West Germany in spreading international tension. This strategy was reflected in its terrorist activity in 1981, followed by two years of unsuccessful operations and repeated crackdowns by the authorities. After a surprise recovery in late 1984, it focused on setting up the West European Guerrilla Front to combat American imperialism and the European political/security establishment. Throughout this period of Euro-terrorism, issues such as the struggle of Third World national freedom movements, including the Palestinians, were marginalized.

In 1980-81, the international terrorist activities of the main Palestinian organizations (Fatah and the PFLP) declined dramatically. Terrorist attacks were

---

[75]   On 24 July 1986 a RAF group calling itself the 'Shaaban Atlouf' group (after a Palestinian terrorist of that name who was killed in Israel in 1986) planted a bomb in the Laser Technology Laboratory in Aachen. On 16 November 1986 a RAF group calling itself the 'Hind Alma' group (supposedly after one of the three Arabs involved in the hijacking of the Lufthansa plane to Mogadishu in October 1977) planted a bomb near the IBM building in Heidelberg.

On 21 December 1986 a RAF group known as the 'Mustafa Aktes Celal Fighting Cell' attacked the Friedrich Ebert Foundation building of the German Social-Democratic Party. In a letter claiming responsibility for the attack, Mustafa Celal was described as a Kurdish fighter of the PKK, who fought in Lebanon in 1982 alongside the Palestinians against the Zionists and was killed in Paris on 25 December 1985.

The group, which on 20 September 1988 set out to assassinate Hans Tietmeyer, state secretary in the Finance Ministry, called itself the 'Khaled Akel' commando. Akel, who was a member of Ahmed Jibril's PLFP-General Command, was killed on 27 November 1987 when terrorists tried to infiltrate northern Israel using gliders.

On 10 December 1989 a unit named after Shaaban Atlouf and Connie Wissmann tried to bomb the offices of Bayer AG in Manneim. This was the second time in three years that a group was named after Atlouf. Wissmann, a member of an autonomous German group, was killed during a demonstration in Göttingen in November 1989.

perpetrated by small splinter groups, such as the Fatah-Revolutionary Command, led by Sabri El-Bana (Abu Nidal) and the small offshoots of the Wadi' Haddad faction, which had split from the PFLP in 1976.[76]

The military strength of the PLO, under Fatah's leadership, grew in south Lebanon. It used guerrilla warfare and even conventional artillery against the Israeli Defense Forces (IDF), until it reached a cease-fire agreement with Israel in July 1981. In June 1982, however, IDF forces entered Lebanon to destroy the Palestinians' military hold there. They managed to reach Beirut and to surround Palestinian forces in the Lebanese capital. Ironically, just when the Palestinians were more vulnerable, the enfeebled RAF was unable to assist. The RAF leadership later admitted its weakness:

> In 1982, when the Israelis invaded Lebanon in order to suppress the Palestinian revolution there, we were not in a position to help, either here [in Germany] or there, in the bombed [sic] camps of Sabra and Shattila… Even though they used the Rhein Main air base as a maintenance base [for their bombers], we were not in a position to intervene in any practical way.[77]

After Palestinian forces withdrew from Lebanon and dispersed throughout the Arab world in 1983-84, the operational capabilities of the major Palestinian organizations declined even further. Meanwhile, Shi'a organizations in Lebanon soon erupted on to the international terror scene, filling the vacuum left by the Palestinian organizations.

The RAF followed these developments with interest, even claiming that its 1984-85 offensive was designed, *inter alia*, 'to show the pigs [the imperialists] what would happen if they stepped up [military action] in Beirut and El Salvador'.[78] On the other hand, after Hizballah hijacked a TWA plane (14 June 1985), the RAF admitted that it knew little about Shi'ite movements except that they were foiling imperialist plans and proving that American imperialism was merely a strategic 'paper tiger'. Although the RAF did not share the objectives of the militant Islamist movements, it respected the autonomy of the Arab revolutionary movement.

The interest of the jailed RAF leaders in the Palestinian problem resurfaced in 1988 after the outbreak of the intifada in December 1987. They saw the Palestinian insurrection as a landmark in the struggle of national freedom movements and

---

[76] These were the 15 May Faction, under Muhammad Hussein Al-'Umri (Abu Ibrahim) and the PFLP-Special Commando Faction, headed by Salim Abu Salem (Abu Muhammad).

[77] Quoted from *Zusammen Kampfen*, No. 5 (Jan. 1986) in Jillian Becker, *Terrorism in West Germany. The Struggle for What?* (London: Institute for the Study of Terrorism, 1988), p. 68.

[78] Quoted from *Zusammen Kampfen*, No. 4 (Sept. 1985) in Becker, *Terrorism in West Germany*, pp. 63, 66.

an integral part of the struggle of radical movements in the metropolis too.[79] However, apart from isolated incidents in 1988 and 1989, the RAF effectively abandoned armed struggle. Only later did the RAF recognize the mistakes of that period. These developments, like 'the Intifada in Palestine – were the beginning of a new process in which in many countries of all over the world an organization from below was added to the liberation struggles'.[80]

At the end of the 1980s, the PLO tried to achieve a political breakthrough that would put it on a par with Arab countries in negotiations with Israel. This was achieved at the Madrid conference in October 1991. Thus, by the end of the decade, both the main Palestinian organization and the top German terrorist organization, the RAF, had abandoned international terror as a means of achieving their political goals.

VI.   ANALYSIS OF THE RESEARCH ASSUMPTIONS

In the major RAF document, 'The Concept of the Urban Guerrilla', European guerrilla movements were portrayed as weak and ineffective in the face of the imperialist threat. The US, together with its ally West Germany, was accused of conducting a policy of aggression towards the Third World. This would naturally lead to a savage war and global exploitation, unless the process was halted by a resurgence of the revolution in the West. Apart from general references to proletarian internationalism, the need to combine national and international struggles and to build a common strategy for the international communist movement through the deployment of the urban guerrilla, the document did not mention the need for coalitions with other organizations.

The document entitled 'The Black September Operation in Munich, the Strategy of the Anti-Imperialist Struggle' went into greater detail on the subject of imperialist aggression, with specific reference to the traumatic experience of the Vietnam War. It stated that imperialism had not only managed to resolve not only its own internal contradictions, but also those that existed between it and the developing nations.[81] For the first time, solidarity, even if dangerous, was mentioned as an integral part of the revolutionary reality. This contrasted sharply with the more 'opportunistic' approach of the German Left.[82] The situation was

---

[79]   Quoted from a document prepared by Eva Haule in April-June 1988, to be read at the Stammheim trial (Sept. 1987-May 1988). See *Il Bollettino*, No. 36 (1989), p. 22.

[80]   See document 'RAF: We must seek what is new', pp. 4-5, as published by the Hamburg *Konkret* in August 1992 and republished as FBIS document JPRS-TOT-92-040-L on 17 November 1992.

[81]   See *Texte der RAF*, p. 421.

[82]   Ibid., p. 425. There is an allusion here to the risk taken by the members of Black September in the Munich attack, during which they demanded the release of the RAF leaders.

regarded as 'ripe' for launching an anti-imperialist struggle in the metropolis, and the task was to create 'a bridge between the struggle to free the Third World nations and the struggle for freedom in the metropolis'.[83]

The M2J, however, rejected the RAF position on the centrality of the Third World liberation movements. The M2J saw itself as participating in a global revolutionary offensive conducted by guerrilla organizations in the metropolis. The document which announced its merger with the RAF in June 1980 stated that in the new reality of emasculated national liberation movements, it was up to revolutionary movements in Western Europe to take up the fight against imperialism.

In 1982, after sustaining a number of failures, the RAF once again emphasized the aggressive nature of imperialism in the document entitled 'Guerrilla, Resistance and Anti-Imperialist Front'. Imperialism, it stated, concentrated its power through the instruments of state, the combined instruments of US satellite states, and renewed military might. To combat this, it was necessary to create a united anti-imperialist front. It was clear, however, since the initiation of an internal dialogue within the revolutionary movement in 1979 that constraints still existed within and between the various anti-imperialist groups. Only coordinated action through parallel struggles in different regions could achieve this objective.

In conclusion, the RAF, more than any other German terrorist organization, felt threatened by American imperialism, the West German regime – which it frequently described as fascist – and supranational bodies such as NATO and the European Union. Given this perceived vulnerability, it felt the need to join forces with external allies of the revolutionary camp.

1.   Influence of the variables at the international and regional level

The RAF saw the international system as a bipolar confrontation between the forces of imperialism, on the one hand, and Third World forces, on the other. Within this scenario, the USSR and the communist bloc hardly existed. None of the RAF's ideological/strategic documents during the first 10-12 years of its existence contained any reference to them. In 'The Concept of the Urban Guerrilla' there is only a passing reference to the precarious alliance between imperialism and the USSR.[84]

In the late 1970s and early 1980s, as noted above, the Third World lost some of its significance for the RAF. In the document 'Guerrilla, Resistance and Anti-

---

[83]   The Third World was the vanguard of the anti-imperialist revolution, and the struggle in the metropolis was 'the international brigades' contribution to the freedom struggles of [the Vietcong], Palestine, Lebanon, Angola, Mozambique and Turkey'. Ibid., pp. 432, 436.

[84]   See *Notes et Etudes*, No. 5 (1988), p. 8.

Imperialist Front', however, a new attitude can be detected towards the USSR.[85] The USSR was portrayed as a superpower on a par with the US, one of the reasons for the tension between East and West, North and South, a tension which threatened world stability. Imperialist forces, aware that any slight shift in the delicate balance of power could trigger a final crisis, were planning to attack on all fronts, including on the East-West front.

The restructuring of the imperialist system as a result of international developments, the RAF claimed, had led to the emergence of a new imperialist focus – West Europe and NATO – a focus in which West Germany played a major role.[86] It was, therefore, essential to set up a united revolutionary counter-force within the imperialist center itself. As the RAF became increasingly convinced of this position, it moved steadily in the direction of Euro-terrorism, through the establishment of the West European Anti-Imperialist Guerrilla Front. Within this strategic framework, the RAF attitude towards the USSR also changed.

In the late 1980s, the RAF appeared to again reassess changes in the international system. According to the organization's leaders, or more specifically, the remnants of its jailed leadership, imperialism lacked an overall plan. It therefore had to find new ways of reasserting its control at all levels through the establishment of the European Union (EU) and within each country – in order to stamp out internal conflicts and revolutionary struggles alike.[87] Therefore, each battle by revolutionaries worldwide was actually a fight against the entire imperialist system. The only way to halt the imperialist machinery was through the strategic unity of exploited nations. The bipolar international system was still characterized by imperialist aggression against the Third World. The USSR and the Soviet bloc were portrayed similarly as victims of imperialist aggression, particularly during the period of Euro-terrorism.

The Sino-Soviet split no doubt contributed to the RAF view of the Third World as the main stage of the struggle against global imperialism. Mao Tse Tung's theory of imperialism as a 'paper tiger' encouraged the organization to continue its struggle, despite weakness and failure. The M2J and RZ, on the other hand, underplayed the role of the Third World, although according to Steiner and Debray, M2J texts also testify to Maoist influences.[88]

From an international perspective, West Germany, as the epitome of local capitalism and the lackey of world imperialism, was considered the main enemy throughout the period.[89] In the early 1970s, West Germany was portrayed as a

---

[85] Ibid., p. 73.
[86] Ibid., pp. 76-78.
[87] See Eva Hanle's declaration in *Il Bollettino*, No. 36 (May 1989), pp. 21-25.
[88] See Steiner and Debray, *La Fraction Armée Rouge*, p. 160.
[89] See Wright, *Terrorist Propaganda*, pp. 39, 80-81.

vital US ally in its war against Vietnam (by providing a take-off and maintenance base for American bombers) and against the peoples of the Third World. By the late 1970s it had become the main ally of NATO, allowing nuclear missiles to be stationed within its territory.

The Middle East was not considered of major importance to RAF strategy. Rather, it represented yet another area in which the struggle between imperialist forces and national liberation movements was being enacted. The RAF never identified with the Palestinian movements in the same way that it identified with the struggle of the Vietnamese people, for example.[90] Naturally, once the Vietnamese struggle was dropped from the international agenda, the Palestinian struggle took its place in RAF sympathies but never to the same degree.[91]

One of the reasons for the relative lack of interest in the Middle East was undoubtedly the limited interest shown by the West German government towards the region. Unlike Britain and France, Germany never played an active part in Middle East politics, or mediated in the Israeli-Arab conflict. The German organizations were angered mainly by what they considered West German intervention in the region, particularly the provision of logistical assistance to US forces en route to the Middle East.

Regional wars and tensions, therefore, had a bearing on expressions and acts of solidarity. Of course the event that had the greatest impact on all three German terrorist organizations was the Vietnam War. They responded by attacking American targets in Germany or German institutions which they perceived as collaborating with the American war effort. Events in the Middle East – the struggle of the Palestinians after the Jordanian crackdown in September 1970, the civil war in Lebanon, and Israeli war against the Palestinians in Lebanon in 1982-84 – also left their mark. It is ironic, however, that other than during the initial stages of the civil war in Lebanon (1975-76), the German terrorist organizations, particularly the RAF, were in the midst of crisis just when the Palestinians needed them most.

Finally, international tension in Western Europe following the stationing of American nuclear missiles there, led to a radical turnabout in RAF strategy and influenced its decision to enter into an alliance with other revolutionary forces in Western Europe.

Throughout the 1970s only one document explicitly cited close cooperation in the field of counter-insurgency in the imperialist camp as a major factor in

---

[90] According to Hans Joachim Klein, the Vietnamese problem had ceased to be merely an international problem. It had turned into an internal German problem. See Bougereau, *An Interview with Hans Joachim Klein*, pp. 12-14.

[91] The only time that RAF documents discussed the Middle East in any depth was in connection with the Black September attack at the Munich Olympics. However, as soon as more urgent issues began to surface, the Middle East was once again relegated to the sidelines.

cementing solidarity in the revolutionary camp.[92] Most other texts allude to this cooperation as part of imperialist efforts (via its military/security/police apparatus) to control the peoples of the Third World and the revolutionary organizations in the metropolis. This was to become a dominant theme during and even after the period of Euro-terrorism.[93]

In conclusion, all four independent variables at the international level affected the RAF, and to a far lesser extent, the M2J and the RZ.

The RAF felt threatened, to a certain degree, throughout the period in question by the superior forces of Western imperialism. At times, it believed a world war was about to erupt due to tension within the bipolar system. However, bipolarity in 1970-78 was evidently different from bipolarity in 1979-88. From the RAF point of view, the international system was divided during the first period between the Western imperialist camp, and the Third World and Western revolutionary camp. As noted above, the USSR was hardly mentioned. During the second period, the main actors were perceived along more traditional lines as the Western imperialist camp and the communist revolutionary camp (with an unwritten pact between the revolutionary movement in the West and the Soviet-led communist bloc).

At the end of the 1980s, with the inauguration of the New World Order in which the US remained the sole superpower, the situation was reassessed. In view of the growing isolation and decline of revolutionary worldwide, the RAF reached the only logical conclusion – abandonment of the armed struggle.

Unlike the RAF, the M2J and RZ both focused their anti-imperialist struggle on the domestic front, and did not believe in the existence of a significant Third World revolutionary camp. Any solidarity felt towards this camp was inspired by the enormous psychological impact of the Vietnam War, as noted above. Members of the M2J, whose strategic perspective changed towards the end of the 1970s, did not attempt to change their organization's strategy. They simply joined the ranks of the RAF.

The RZ continued to focus on domestic issues until the late 1980s. Reservations regarding the peace movement's struggle (1980-86) against NATO's growing strength and the stationing of nuclear warheads in West Europe, effectively destroyed any residual influence it had among German radical left-wing circles, until it gradually ceased to exist as a terrorist organization of any significance.

---

[92] See 'The Other Process, Late April 1976' in *Texte der RAF*, pp. 27-34.

[93] Witness, for example, RAF's attempted assassination of the German secretary of state in the Ministry of the Interior, Hans Neusel, on 27 July 1990, as the leader of the war against the liberation movements, and as a senior member of the 'Trevi group' – the West European anti-terror think-tank.

2. Influence of the variables at the organizational level

A. Ideology as a cohesive force?

The main ideological inspiration for RAF activities in the 1970s was the role of the Third World liberation movements ('Tricont', in the organization's jargon) in the struggle against imperialism. It followed that the function of revolutionary movements in the West was to help this struggle. Ulrike Meinhof expressed this idea in a letter to the Labor Party in the Peoples' Republic of North Korea:

> [We] think that the organization of armed operations in the big cities in the Federal Republic is the right way to support the liberation movements in Africa, Asia, and Latin America, the correct contribution of West German and West Berlin communists to the strategy of the international socialist movement in splitting the powers of imperialism by attacking them from all sides.[94]

Wright, in quoting Meinhof's letter, claimed that the RAF expected anti-fascists to identify with these goals.[95] Similarly, RAF support of the Palestinian struggle and the Black September operation at the Munich Olympics was based on its perception of this struggle as part of the global war against imperialism, colonialism and fascism.

The ideological and strategic change of emphasis in the late 1970s and early 1980s from the Third World struggle to the revolutionary struggle in the metropolitan centers, turned unity and solidarity among West European organizations into an issue of top priority. The Third World struggle had lost much of its momentum and became of marginal interest. Indeed, it reemerged as an important issue after the RAF defeat, as a result of certain regional developments (the intifada in the West Bank and Gaza, struggles in Kurdistan and Central America). Certainly, as far as the RAF was concerned, its sense of solidarity with its revolutionary counterparts was based on a shared ideological platform.

The M2J and RZ, on the other hand, did not share this wholehearted support for Third World movements. They chose to wage their anti-imperialist struggle at home, or to support social and popular causes (the status of working class women and youngsters, the immigrant problem, the housing shortage, etc.). The M2J operated primarily in West Berlin – its main power base – unlike the RAF, which had branches in other regions of the Federal Republic. Nonetheless, M2J members, and particularly those of the RZ, actively participated in the Palestinian struggle – particularly the PFLP.

---

94   Wright, *Terrorist Propaganda*, p. 104.
95   Ibid.

An explanation for this can be found in the anarchic character of these two organizations, as reflected in the lack of a defined or solid ideology, lack of a strong central leadership, and the high degree of mobility from one organization to the other. All this made it easy for a foreign organization to recruit members of these groups into their ranks, despite the fact that they espoused different goals and methods. Thus, for example, while the RZ apologized for the assassination of a German minister in 1978, under the pretext that it had simply intended to injure, not kill him, senior RZ members, such as Wilfred Böse, participated in operations (such as the attacks on the El Al planes in Paris and Entebbe) that could have caused hundreds of casualties.

An important RZ document from 1989 pointed to the ideological weakness of the cells participating in the pro-Palestinian operations:

> We would like to see groups from the old RZ take a critical look at their past... [W]e have some difficulties with some RZ actions from the past, especially with the involvement in the hijacking to Entebbe. Of course, those days are now past, when hijackings were an instrument of the militant Left, so we needn't fear a re-peat. Still one has to wonder why the only mention of this event in the book *200 Years RZ* is a tribute to those RZ'ers (sic) who died in action. As far as we know, no RZ text exists which takes a critical look at this action.[96]

The operational cooperation with the PFLP in the mid-1970s continued to hound the RZ and its impact on the organization's unity only became clear at the beginning of the 1990s. Internal conflicts were first discussed in the paper entitled 'Gerd Albartus Is Dead', published in December 1991, which sparked a fierce debate among the various RZ cells. Albartus, a RZ militant, was accused of 'treason' by members of the internationalist faction during a visit to Lebanon in 1987 and was 'executed' by Carlos. According to various documents dealing with this strange affair, one part of the RZ movement evidently broke off contacts with the Palestinian resistance following the joint attack by Palestinian, Latin American, and German commandos on the OPEC conference in Vienna in December 1975 and the June 1976 hijacking of an Air France flight to Entebbe, claimed by the 'International Section' of the RZ. A small number of RZ activists maintained contacts with the PFLP. But the RZ in Germany made a clear break with this tradition and no connection whatsoever between the two factions remained.[97]

---

96 Cited from *200 Years Is Not Enough: Revolutionary Cells In The Post-Fordist Era*, November 1989, p. 15, published by Arm.The.Spirit at <http://www.etext.org/Politics/Arm.The.Spirit/ Guerrilla/Europe/Revolutionary.Cells/rz-fordism>.

97 For a discussion on this subject, see *Brief History and Critique of the RZ and Rote Zora*, pp. 2-3, text written in September 2000 by the Dia-Gruppe of Berlin and translated by Arm The Spirit from Interim, No. 499 at <http://burn.ucsd.edu/archives/ats-l/2001.03/msg00028.html>, and *Armed Struggle In Germany*, p. 12.

However, despite criticism of the coalition with the PFLP, some cells could not renounce the concept of international revolutionary solidarity.

Anyone who is in solidarity with the struggles in the Three Continents must be on the same side of the barricade as those forces which are resisting the destructive imperialist violence and its open and hidden forms of economic, military, and psychological war which is being waged against the peoples of the Three Continents. Solidarity always implies critical solidarity... [W]e also feel that hijacking planes is problematical – its' important to keep in mind the existing conditions of the Palestinian people. In short: life under Israeli occupation or as refugees, the experience of massacres (in Palestine and Lebanon), and even genocide (Jordan 1970)... The Palestinian resistance found itself in a state of war with Israel... The hijacking of the plane departing from Israel and the taking of hostages was designed to put pressure on the Israeli government.[98]

It seemed as if RZ militants still believed that '[t]hose that can work together and work in coalitions and mixed groups will be victorious'.[99]

B.   Antisemitism and anti-Zionism lead to anti-Jewish terrorism

Another explanation for this collaboration relates to the infiltration of anti-Zionist dogma into the ideology of German revolutionary organizations, particularly the RAF. In many cases this anti-Zionism was merely a front for deep-rooted antisemitism – leaders of the organizations themselves often found it hard to distinguish between anti-Zionist ideology and antisemitic sentiment.

Although RAF leaders did not deny the existence of the Holocaust, they accused Israel and Zionism of imitating the worst features of Nazism in an attempt to portray them not only as the lackeys of imperialism, but also as enemies of the Third World peoples, particularly the Palestinians.

The clearest expression of this ideological distortion can be found in documents relating to the Black September operation at the Munich Olympics. Horst Mahler, for example, argued that while the German proletariat had failed to destroy fascism and prevent the murder of six million Jews, it was this same fascist policy that had inspired reactionary Zionist ideology. 'Macabre as it may seem, Zionism has become the heir of German fascism, by cruelly ousting the

---

[98]   Quoted from *Revolutionary Cell Communiqué – Tendency For The International Social Revolution*, May 1992, pp. 1-2, at <http://www.etext.org/Politics/Arm.The.Spirit/Guerrilla/Europe/Revolutionary.Cells/rz-tisr.may-1992>.

[99]   Quoted from another undated RZ document of the same period. See *Statement Concerning The Attack On The Refugee Administration Centre In Boblingen*, p. 5 at <http://www.etext.org/Politics/Arm.The.Spirit/Guerrilla/Europe/Revolutionary.Cells/rz-bobl>.

Palestinian people from its land, where it has been living for thousands of years.'[100] Therefore, he called on the German proletariat to recognize its responsibility for the fate of the Palestinian people and insisted that any guilt feelings it might harbor towards the Jews should not blind it to the evils of 'Zionist fascist aggression'. It is perhaps not surprising, therefore, that years later Mahler joined the far wing and became a militant Holocaust denier.[101]

The document entitled 'The Black September Operation in Munich, the Strategy of the Anti-Imperialist Struggle' described Israeli policy as a 'Nazi fascist policy ... aiming for the annihilation of the Palestinian people'.[102] The action taken by Israeli defense minister Moshe Dayan in response to the hijacking of the Sabena plane to Tel Aviv (8 May 1972) was described as 'treacherous and criminal' towards the hijackers.[103] Although the document admitted that antisemitism (and the Second World War) discredited German fascism and the German ruling classes, it added that the Black September terrorist operation at Munich was an anti-fascist act because 'it was meant to wipe out the memory ... of the 1936 [Berlin] Olympics, Auschwitz, and Kristallnacht'. Similarly, Israel was blamed for the death of the athletes, just as the Nazis were blamed for the death of the Jews.[104]

Despite such views, the RAF leaders were quick to deny accusations of antisemitism. In 'The Concept of the Urban Guerrilla' they declared that their morale had not been affected by German media efforts to describe them as carriers of the 'antisemitism syndrome'.[105] In the late 1960s members of left-wing movements even tended to label themselves as 'the Jews of today'. By drawing parallels between themselves and the victims of Nazism, they tried to emphasize their role as victims of the new 'fascist regime'.[106]

A similar atmosphere prevailed in the M2J. As stated above, this movement evolved out of a smaller, anarchist movement, the Tupamaros-West Berlin (TW). In November 1969, the TW attempted unsuccessfully to blow up the main synagogue in West Berlin. It is symbolic that this attack, carried out by German terrorists as a token of solidarity with the Palestinians, took place on the anniver-

---

[100] See quotation from his speech shortly before his trial in *CONTROinformazione*, Nos. 1-2 (February-March 1974), p. 26.

[101] Only lately, in March 2001, Mahler published on the Internet a fiercely antisemitic article, *Discovery of God instead of Jewish Hatred*, which was due to be presented to the Conference of Revisionist Historians in Beirut, Lebanon on 3 April 2001 (meeting prohibited by the Lebanese government). See the article in German Lecture Series on the Final Solution of the Jewish Question at <http://www.regmeister.net/h_mahler.htm>.

[102] See *Texte der RAF*, pp. 422, 455.

[103] Ibid., p. 441.

[104] Ibid., pp. 433-444.

[105] See quotation in *Notes et Etudes*, No. 5 (May 1988), p. 63.

[106] See Becker, *Hitler's Children*, p. 69.

sary of Kristallnacht. The TW claimed responsibility for the attack in a leaflet entitled 'Peace and Napalm', emphasizing that the act was perpetrated by the Left as 'a demonstration of international solidarity'. The members of TW claimed that the events of Kristallnacht were being reenacted daily by the Zionists in the occupied territories, in refugee camps, and in Israeli jails.

In conclusion, the three German organizations shared some ideological commitments with the Palestinian organizations. This ideological identification was strongest on the part of the RAF which saw the Third World and the Palestinian people as spearheads of a global anti-imperialist struggle.

Two ideological factors were key in the decision of the German terrorists to cooperate with or even join Palestinian terrorist organizations: their anarchist, or in the case of the RAF, anarcho-communist make-up, and the infiltration of antisemitic ideology into the organization's doctrine.

The coalition between the Palestinian and German organizations involved a strong and weak partner. Throughout most of its existence, the RAF admired the Palestinian revolutionary organizations and their dominant role in the anti-imperialistic struggle. This admiration found clearest expression in the document published after the Black September attack at the Munich Olympics.

Palestinian organizations, in particular the PFLP, were the main sources of assistance for German terrorist organizations. This assistance took two vital forms: training in guerrilla tactics and warfare, and the provision of sanctuary in times of danger. The German terrorists tried to reciprocate through actively participating in PFLP-sponsored international terror operations and by encouraging West German and West European radical left-wing circles to support the Palestinian cause.

Did the participation of the German organizations in PFLP operations which contradicted their ideological, strategic, and operational principles indicate a total dependence on their Palestinian mentors and sponsors? According to Klein, the RZ 'international division,' at least, was financially dependent on the PFLP, which paid its members' salaries.

It is intriguing that German terrorist organizations barely participated in operations against Israeli targets within the Federal Republic itself. The three German terrorist organizations, on the other hand, frequently attacked American targets, and the RAF and RZ attacked Turkish, Chilean and South African targets within the Federal Republic. Moreover, neither the RAF nor the RZ published any justification of PFLP international terror, besides the infamous attack at the Munich Olympics.

Therefore, on the basis of the available information, it is impossible to determine with any degree of certainty the extent to which the German terrorist organizations were dependent on their Palestinian counterparts, particularly during the period in which their coalition was most active (1975-77). It seems that the recruitment of German terrorists in the PFLP was mainly on an individual basis. In some cases, the recruits were more akin to mercenaries, albeit 'ideological' ones. This was facilitated by the tradition of close ties between the Germans and sympathy of the German organizations for the Palestinian cause.

3.   Influence of the variables at the decision-making level

Traditional antisemitic ideology may have inspired the anti-Zionist slogans of the German left-wing revolutionary organizations; some of their leaders undoubtedly harbored antisemitic sentiments. Becker described an incident in which Ralf Reinders, an M2J leader, wanted to blow up the 'Jewish Center' in Berlin, which the Nazis had already attempt to destroy in the past, in order 'to get rid of that thing with its Jewish associations, which has been there since the Nazi period'.[107]

Hans-Joachim Klein decided to abandon the RZ when he realized that his comrades were behaving like the Nazis in Auschwitz by separating the Jewish passengers from the non-Jewish ones after the hijacking of the Air France plane to Entebbe. Klein also condemned the RZ plot to assassinate Galinski, leader of the German Jewish community, and exposed the plot.[108]

Klein expressed the view that the two German terrorists who had participated in the Entebbe operation were more antisemitic than Wadi' Haddad, leader of the PFLP operational division, for planning to assassinate the famous Nazi hunter, Simon Wiesenthal. Even the notorious Carlos opposed this operation on the grounds that Wiesenthal was an anti-Nazi.[109]

The RZ rejected Klein's accusations of antisemitism. A communiqué concerning Klein's disengagement from the RZ addressed the leftist circles in Germany supporting Klein:

> You easily believe the horror story of Hans Joachim Klein instead of reflecting on Galinski's role in the crimes of Zionism, for the cruelties of Israel's imperialistic army, you don't reflect on the propaganda work and material support of this guy, you don't see him as anything other than 'a leader of the Jewish community', and you don't reflect about what to do against this fact, and what could be done in a country like ours... You avoid this political discussion and get exited about the maintained (antisemitism?) fascism of the RZ and the men behind them.

---

[107] See Becker, *Hitler's Children*, pp. 299-300.
[108] See Bougereau, *An Interview with Hans Joachim Klein*, p. 31.
[109] Ibid., pp. 43, 47. Antisemitism among the German terrorists was reportedly so deeply entrenched that they could not bear to hear anyone whistling the theme tune of the film 'Exodus'. In contrast, the Palestinians were far more tolerant.

The men behind RZ are no others than the PFLP.[110]

It seems that the anarchist character of the RZ, and the anarchist backgrounds and deeply entrenched antisemitic feelings of members of all three German terrorist organizations, explain their readiness to join the Palestinian organizations, either as volunteers or recruits. They justified their position as contribution to the war against imperialism, colonialism, and fascism.

VII. SUMMARY

Did a coalition effectively exist between the three radical left-wing revolutionary organizations and the Palestinian terrorist organizations? Evidence suggests that conditions for such a coalition did exist, with certain distinguishing features.

(1) At all three levels of cooperation (ideological, logistical, and operational), the RAF met all the conditions, and attained the highest degree.

(2) Cooperation, particularly operational, only existed between the RZ and Palestinian terrorist organizations during the initial period.

(3) Ideologically, there were points of conflict between the two. The RZ, for example, did not recognize the centrality of Third World freedom movements and did not endorse international terror. It is not clear to what extent M2J cooperated with the PFLP, and whether it did so as an independent organization, or under the aegis of the RAF, its 'sister organization'.

(4) Operational cooperation extended over a relatively lengthy period, between 1970-77, peaking in the years 1975-76.

(5) Practical, and sometimes even ideological cooperation, was influenced by: the operational state of the organizations; major international events that had a bearing on one of the parties concerned; and shifts in strategic perspectives during each period.

---

[110] Cited from *The Dogs Are Barking And The Caravan Moves On – The Revolutionary Cells Respond To Hans Joachim Klein*, 24 May 1977, p. 2. The document is published on Arm.The.Spirit website at <http://www.etext.org/Politics/Arm.The.Spirit/Guerrilla/Europe/Revolutionary.Cells/rz-klein>. In the same document the Zionists are accused, together with 'the cops, the justice system … and the CIA' of attempting, albeit unsuccessfully, to destroy 'the guerrilla in Germany'.

CHAPTER 4
ITALY – THE RED BRIGADES

I.   HISTORICAL BACKGROUND

Many researchers have stressed the role of violence and terrorism in the Italian political tradition, from the struggle for independence (1815-70), through Italian anarchism in the last quarter of the nineteenth century, to the struggle between Left and Right in Italy after the First World War.[1] Fascist terror was widespread during the years 1919-26, when paramilitary gangs eliminated political opponents through arson, kidnappings, murder and intimidation. Mussolini's downfall led to the rise of the partisan movement, most of whose members were communists. The partisans used terrorist techniques against the fascists and their Nazi German supporters.

Italy's integration in the West, its recovery after the war, and the 'economic miracle' of 1958-63, which turned it into the seventh greatest industrial power in the West, were largely due to the dominant role of the Italian Christian Democratic Party (Democrazia Christiana – DC) in Italian political life from 1945 on. However, the Christian Democrats were unable to cope with the swift socio-economic transformations that the country underwent during that period.[2]

Rapid economic and cultural changes, coupled with mass internal migration from the backward rural areas in the south to the industrialized urban north, took their toll on socio-cultural traditions and the local administrative infrastructure, which in any case was suffering from the mismanagement and corruption of the DC.[3]

The Italian Communist Party (Partito Comunista Italiano – PCI) was instrumental in the struggle against the Nazis at the end of the Second World War and the liberation of Italy from the fascist yoke. Several years after the war, the PCI became the second largest party in the country. The PCI succeeded in carrying the idea of socialist revolution to broad sections of the public through its press, the parliament, the trade unions, and its hold on many local councils and municipalities. Indeed, it became the largest communist party in the West. But as it grew, its

---

[1]   Richard Drake, 'Contemporary Terrorism and the Intellectuals: the Case of Italy', in Wilkinson and Stewart, *Contemporary Research on Terrorism*; Giorgio Galli, *La Crisi Italiana e la Destra InterNazionale*; Marco Rimanelli, 'Italian Terrorism and Society, 1940s – 1980s: Roots, Ideologies, Evolution, and International Connections', *Terrorism*, Vol. 12 (1989), pp. 249-96.

[2]   See Rimanelli, 'Italian Terrorism and Society', p. 253.

[3]   See Drake, 'Contemporary Terrorism and the Intellectuals: the Case of Italy', p. 133.

ideology changed. In the early 1960s, it declared it would maintain the multiparty system in parliament and in 1968, for first time, publicly criticized the Soviet Communist Party for invading Czechoslovakia.[4]

However, the PCI played a major role in the proliferation of radical left-wing groups because it was unable to resolve the internal contradiction between its support of the democratic values of freedom and parliamentarism, and its adherence to the ideological principles of democratic centralism and the revolutionary path. This contradiction caused confusion among some of its more dogmatic, revolutionary and pro-Stalinist members. Many switched allegiance to the Maoist groups that proliferated after the split between the USSR and communist China, or joined what was known as the 'extra-parliamentary left', a loose assortment of violent organizations and terrorist groups.

1.   The birth of the Red Brigades

The radical student movement, which developed in the university towns of Trento and Milan, initially demanded improvements in study and living conditions. It later claimed radical changes in the curriculum. This movement comprised both students with a communist background and former members of Catholic organizations with a left-wing bias.

The birth of the BR owed a great deal to three Maoist students from Trento University: Renato Curcio, Mara Cagol and Alberto Franceschini. In the autumn of 1968, after completing their studies, the three moved to the industrial city of Milan. There, they set up an Urban Political Collective (Colletivo Politico Metropolitano – CPM) in order to maintain ties with the autonomous workers groups (which had splintered from the official trade unions dominated by the communists, socialists and neo-fascists). This collective later metamorphosed into the Proletarian Left (Sinistra Proletaria – SP). Its aim was not so much to obtain economic benefits for workers, but rather to denounce capitalist exploitation of the working class, and to create propaganda that would prepare the masses for violent and systematic opposition to the bourgeois order. The organization claimed responsibility for a number of attacks against trade union representatives and factory managers.[5]

On 9 April 1969 the police opened fire against farm workers during a demonstration in southern Italy, killing two of them. This was followed by a number of bomb attacks in train stations and markets in Padua, Milan, Rome, and Torino.

---

[4]   See Robert C. Meade, *Red Brigades: The Story of Italian Terrorism* (London: Macmillan, 1990), p. 27.

[5]   For a detailed description of how the BR came into being, see Alessandro Silj, *'Mai più senza fucile!'. Alle origini dei NAP e delle BR* (Firenze: Vallechi Editore, 1977).

Rumors circulated in July of a possible right-wing coup by neo-fascist organizations. On 12 December 1969 a number of bombs were planted in Rome and Milan. This opened what became to be known as the far right's 'strategy of tension', which was to culminate with a bomb attack on an Italicus train in August 1974.

The SP meanwhile continued to rally together groups which supported the use of violence against the far right. Up to 1971 the legal and underground branches of the organization operated in tandem. The organization, identified as the Red Brigades (Brigate Rosse – BR) for the first time in September 1970, defined itself as an 'armed propaganda' organization acting in accordance with a revolutionary strategy against those who threatened the interests and unity of the working class. The organization quickly went underground, from where it led its armed struggle against 'the political-democratic system of bourgeois society.'[6]

II.   TYPOLOGICAL DEFINITION

Of all the terrorist organizations discussed in this book, the BR maintained the most consistent ideology, as reflected in the many texts published by the organization and its splinter groups throughout its lengthy existence. The leaders of the BR always saw themselves as the standard-bearers of Marxism-Leninism in its purest form. According to Ventura, the Italian revolutionary left developed in the 1960s out of the dramatic break between the PCI's reformist policy and Marxist-Leninist revolutionary ideology, which helped shape the mentality of party activists and the Italian intelligentsia.[7]

According to Ventura, the extra-parliamentary far left in Italy embraced two trends: Marxism-Leninism in the narrow sense of the word, and workers' autonomy (Autonomia Operaia – AO). The basic difference between these two trends lay in the different emphases they placed on 'party' and 'class', on the 'organized, aware avant-garde' and the 'spontaneity of the masses'. For the Marxist-Leninists, who clung to the doctrine advocated by Lenin in 'What to Do?', the party clearly came first. The advocates of AO, however, interpreted Marx and Lenin differently. Although they were aware of the importance of the party as an essential stage in the revolutionary process, they stressed the importance of political organization and political awareness among the 'maturing' working class, thereby reversing the Leninist relationship between party and

---

[6]   Ibid., p. 82.
[7]   See Angelo Ventura, 'Il problema delle origini del terrorismo di sinistra', in Donatella della Porta (ed.), *Terrorismi in Italia* (Bologna: Società Editrice il Mulino, 1984), pp. 106-10.

class. The BR saw themselves as offshoots of the AO movement, not so much a party as an 'armed avant-garde' working within the proletariat in order to establish a party.[8]

Of all European terrorist organizations, the BR maintained the strongest Marxist-Leninist base; at the same, it was imbued with the ideology of the New Left and neo-Marxism. Events, in the final analysis, strengthened its anarchist orientation, so that it almost qualifies as an anarcho-communist organization.

III.   1970-80: THE ADVENT AND HEYDAY OF THE BR[9]

1.   'Armed propaganda' (1970-74)

At the beginning of this period, the BR focused its activities on the large northern industrial cities of Milan and Torino and apparently identified with the interests of trade unions and a broader political movement. Indeed, the organization was simply an extremist faction of a larger, fragmented, protest movement. It operated mainly in factories, where social disparities were more evident and labor disputes more acute. From 1970-71 its campaign was directed mainly against the far right but it gradually started to provide armed assistance to trade unionists.

From September 1971 the BR's program of armed struggle moved from the tactical to the strategic. From initial acts of sabotage against cars and factory equipment, it gradually began to undertake break-ins into trade union headquarters and the offices of industrialists. 1972 marked a turning point: it was the first time the BR actually attacked a human target, in the person of a factory foreman who was kidnapped briefly.

---

[8]   The Italian radical left had a number of prestigious ideologues, who were accepted by the intelligentsia and left-wing student activists. One of the most influential was Prof. Antonio Negri of the University of Padua. Despite his arrest, his direct and practical implication in terrorist events was never proved. However, his books and articles had great influence on the leaders of the BR and other terrorist organizations. According to Drake, Negri justified terrorist violence by depicting shooting, sabotage, strikes, subversive and even criminal behavior as legitimate tools for the 'de-structuralization' of the capitalist economy. See Drake, 'Contemporary Terrorism and the Intellectuals: the Case of Italy', pp. 135-6.

[9]   Caselli and Della Porta, who researched Italian radical left-wing terrorism up to 1982, divided BR activity into four periods: 1970-74: 'armed propaganda'; 1974-76: 'striking at the heart of the State'; 1977-78: 'the strategy of liquidation'; 1979-82: 'the strategy of survival' in the form of military clashes with the state. The last period was marked by great schisms, defections and expulsions from the organization. From a broader historical perspective, the fourth period could be considered 1979-80, because from 1980 on, each urban division (*colonna*) of the organization began working autonomously. See G. C. Caselli and Donatella Della Porta, 'La storia delle Brigate rosse: strutture organizzative e strategie d'azione', in Donatella Della Porta, (ed.) *Terrorismi in Italia*, p. 155.

2. 'Striking at the heart of the state' (1974-76)

This period began with the kidnapping of a district magistrate, an operation that earned the organization national notoriety and extended its sphere of influence to Rome, Genoa and the Venice region.

In late 1974 the BR set up a Strategic Directorate (Direzione Strategica – DS) in order to determine ideology and strategy, and enforce regulations. The DS elected an executive committee to run the organization's day-to-day activities. The organization itself was divided horizontally into urban/regional divisions (*colonne*), and vertically into 'fronts' (*fronti*), responsible for coordinating activity at a functional level (logistics, workers', and counter-revolution).[10] In practice, the clandestine nature of the organization and the high degree of compartmentalization within and between the divisions swiftly turned it into a hierarchical and bureaucratic structure in which most decisions were taken by the executive committee.[11]

In April 1975 the BR published its first document, described as the Resolution of the Strategic Directorate (Risoluzione della Direzione Strategica – RDS). This defined the immediate strategic goal of the BR as a concentrated strike against the heart of the state, and its intermediate goal as the state's political disintegration. The state, in general, was described as 'an imperialist collection of multinational corporations' (Stato Imperialista delle Multinazionali – SIM), as a kind of giant bank serving large, imperialist, multinational concerns. Italy, which was perceived as aspiring to the status of SIM based on the American and German model, was no exception.[12]

During this period, attacks were directed against political targets (members of the DC party), and 'militarism' supplanted 'populism' (popular struggles). The BR's main target was the security forces (which had made considerable inroads in its war against terror), the police and the legal authorities. June 1974 marked the BR's first murderous attack when two activists of the neo-fascist party, the Italian Social Movement (Movimento Sociale Italiano – MSI), were killed in Padua.

Due to heavy crackdowns by the security forces and the consequent need for greater secrecy, the BR moved further away from its natural social base, gradually abandoning its activities among the masses and the workers. In late 1976, a number of its founders, including Curcio and Franceschini, were arrested. Mara Cagol was killed while resisting arrest, leaving only about ten leading activists at large. Despite this crisis, the security forces were unable to destroy the organization completely.

---

[10] See Mario Moretti, *Brigatte Rosse. Una storia italiana Intervista di Carla Mosca e Rossana Rossanda* (Milano: Edizione Anabasi, 1994), p. 58.
[11] See Caselli and Della Porta, 'La storia delle Brigate rosse', pp. 173-4.
[12] See *RDS*, April 1975.

From this point on, the liberation of prisoners became one of the main strategic goals of the organization.[13]

3.   'The Strategy of Liquidation' (1977-78)[14]

During this period, terrorist activity in Italy expanded so rapidly that it overtook all other West European countries. In April 1977 the BR declared that since a working-class avant-garde already existed, the time had come to set up the Communist Combatant Party (Partito Comunista Combattente – PCC) to guide the working-class.[15] In practice, the BR failed to set up the PCC but did manage to consolidate its position and gain new ground.

From 1977 on, terrorist attacks were carried out almost daily, usually in the form of 'campaigns' devoted to specific themes. A significant number of attacks targeted the security services (police and Carabinieri), magistrates and prison wardens. The idea was to bring about the 'collapse of the system' and intimidate judges and jury into adjourning or even closing cases against BR leaders.

These developments must be viewed against the broader context of the political protest movement that emerged in 1977. This was a response to a number of proposed university reforms, perceived as attempts to neutralize the achievements of the 1968 movement.[16] After several months of intense activity, the protest movement entered a period of crisis in 1978; it subsequently split into two branches, one violent and one more moderate. The violent branch, which became known as Organized Autonomy (Autonomia Organizzata – AO), engaged in violent skirmishes not only with the security forces, but also with its adversaries within the movement itself. The moderate wing died a natural death.

The BR managed to enlist new recruits from the Workers' Autonomy (Autonomia Operaia – AO), part of which had gone underground. The second wave of terrorists, who took over from the imprisoned leadership, comprised younger activists, more students and fewer workers. The influx of new blood and the growth of its violent arm convinced the BR leaders, as well as a number of observers, that the transition from armed propaganda to a general civil war was imminent.

The fierce terrorist offensive, which began in 1977, reached its peak in early 1978 with the kidnapping and murder of former prime minister Aldo Moro in

---

[13]   Moretti later claimed that this was due to the mass arrests at the time, which reversed the proportion between the militants in prison – the majority – and those free. See Moretti, *Brigatte Rosse. Una storia italiana*, p. 82.

[14]   This section is based on Caselli and Della Porta, 'La storia delle Brigate rosse', pp. 184-201, and Meade, *Red Brigades*, pp. 82-97.

[15]   See *Portare l'attaco allo SIM. 1977.*

[16]   The movement included some social aspects too: proletarian youth clubs, anti-drug patrols in the slums, committees against electricity and transport price hikes, and feminist groups.

March-May 1978.[17] The BR leadership and sympathizers perceived Moro's abduction as a perfect action 'from a technical-military standpoint'. Politicians and the public, on the other hand, saw it as a serious blow to the régime and as the most serious challenge facing the country since the end of the Second World War. The RDS of February 1978, attached to Statement No. 4 which was published during the operation, described its political objectives. Moro, the architect of the 'historic compromise' between the PCI and the ruling DC, was accused of trying to enslave the working class to the SIM with the help of communist revisionists.

4.   'The struggle for survival' (1979-80)

Although the kidnapping of Aldo Moro was the crowning glory of the BR's terrorist campaign, it also marked the beginning of its decline. Firstly, politicians and the security forces resolved to wage an out-and-out war against the perceived threat to the stability of the regime. Secondly, the BR decision to murder a popular leader, against the better judgment of a large sector of the radical left, led to the resignation of two BR leaders who had taken part in the operation. The executive committee was accused of moving away from the working class and abandoning the proletarian front. By the end of the year, even the imprisoned leaders Curcio and Franceschini were accusing the external leadership under Moretti of bureaucratic and militaristic aberrations.[18]

With the disappearance of the protest movement and the diffuse terrorism of 1977, hope of a large-scale guerrilla offensive also evaporated. Although the BR was left with a pool of young, highly motivated activists, it lacked a solid political program. As noted, Patrizio Peci's disclosure of the organization's structure and goals, and the subsequent wave of arrests in 1980 marked the beginning of the end, despite the organization's impressive record of murder attacks.[19]

5.   Cooperation with Palestinian organizations

In the early 1980s numerous references appeared in the local and foreign press, as well as in professional studies, of BR cooperation with Palestinian terrorist organizations. Most of the data published on this subject was based on repetitive

---

[17]   The number of casualties tripled from 1976-77, although there was a slight drop in the number of fatalities. On the other hand, the number of murder attacks rose from four in 1977 to 28 in 1978. See Della Porta, *Il Terrorismo di Sinistra*, 236-7.

[18]   The imprisoned leaders were even prepared to support the establishment of autonomous groups and *colonne*, such as the 'Walter Alasia' *colonna* in Milan, which rebelled in 1980, and demanded the resignation of Moretti.

[19]   Peci, head of the Genoa *colonna*, was the first arrested leader to cooperate with the security authorities. See Della Porta, *Terrorismi in Italia*, pp. 201-5 and Della Porta, *Il Terrorismo di Sinistra*, p. 237.

statements by dozens of leaders and hundreds of activists during interrogations or trials. However, a careful comparison of this data with legal sources shows that most of them recycled the same information, giving the (erroneous) impression of an overwhelming stock of evidence indicating cooperation between the BR and Palestinian organizations.

The main problem that emerges from legal evidence is that the small circle of informed leaders (e.g. Moretti, Giovanni Senzani, Barbara Balserani) refused to cooperate with their interrogators.[20] Again, although some members were aware of some facts, in most cases this concerned the 'logistical' aspect of cooperation, rather than the political/strategic dialogue between the two parties. All other BR members were privy to only isolated scraps of information, invariably based on rumors circulating between activists. Thus, after sorting and comparing the voluminous material, the picture that emerges is somewhat fragmentary, and fails to provide an authoritative explanation of the main issues, as detailed below. Neither the published debates of the first trial relating to the assassination of Moro, which included a chapter on the BR's international relations, nor later testimonies of BR leaders contribute to or change even slightly the thesis presented in this book.[21]

Furthermore, no single document published by the BR deals exclusively with this issue. Since no written documents concerning contacts with the Palestinians were found after the arrests of leaders or discovery of safe houses, it appears that such communication was conducted verbally.[22] Research on this subject is therefore based mainly on textual analysis of strategic decisions, statements published during attacks, or articles by the BR referring to cooperation or solidarity with foreign terrorist organizations or by other organizations.[23]

A.   The establishment and development of ties

According to Curcio, contacts with the Palestinians during his leadership of the BR took the form of 'political propaganda'; documents of the PFLP and of the

---

[20] Only in 1994 was a book of interviews with Moretti published. It contained a very small section on the BR's international ties and only three short pages on ties with the PLO. See Moretti, *Brigatte Rosse. Una storia italiana*, pp. 188-91.

[21] See *I collegamenti internazionali delle Br*, pp. 976-1001, at <http://www.apolis.com/moro/processi/moroprimo/47.html>.

[22] There is probably only one published document on a political and strategic dialogue between two terrorist organizations – the meeting that took place between the BR and the RAF in January 1988. See the Chapter 6.

[23] The quantity and quality of legal and documentary material available for the research on the BR is particularly rich. Unfortunately, due to logistical and time constraints during the work in the Italian courts, it was not always possible to link the citations to the exact juridical document, but the list of these documents is presented in the bibliography.

Democratic Front for the Liberation of Palestine (DFLP led by Nayef Hawatmeh) were disseminated inside the organization.[24] More serious contacts between the BR and the PLO were established immediately after the kidnapping of Aldo Moro, in the spring of 1978.[25] The initiative came from the Palestinians through a Paris-based organization that offered international assistance to guerrilla movements worldwide. Italian revolutionaries in exile who belonged to this organization (comrades of Moretti, the BR leader at the time) made the link. Moretti himself established initial contact in France.[26]

The PLO approach surprised the BR leadership because it seemed to run counter to Arafat's attempts to woo West European countries, and his unofficial meetings with Moro himself. Indeed, evidence suggests that Arafat asked the BR, at least publicly, to free the Italian politician.[27] As the Palestinian representative explained in talks with Moretti, the initiative for contacts came from a particular faction within the PLO that was opposed to abandoning the armed struggle against Israel. This faction was interested in setting up a militant anti-Israel front with the help of the BR and RAF, which were supposed to carry out attacks against 'Zionists' in their countries. The French organization, for its part, asked Moretti to step up support for the Palestinian national liberation struggle. A meeting was arranged between Moretti and 'the Palestinian minister of the interior' (later identified as Salah Khalaf/Abu Iyyad), who introduced himself as leader of a Marxist faction that sought to extend its influence within the PLO through alliances with European guerrilla organizations. In a subsequent meeting between Moretti and Abu Iyyad, the following terms of cooperation were drawn up with Arafat's approval:[28]

---

[24] See Renato Curcio, *A viso aperto. Intervista di Mario Scialoja* (4th edn.) (Milano: Oscar Mondadori, 2000), p. 143.

[25] There are a relatively large number of testimonies on ties between the BR and the PLO/Fatah (Savasta, Peci, Galetta, etc.), but the most detailed is Savasta's (Documents 1, 4, and 5, which serve as the basis of this chapter).

[26] Among the Italian expatriates who formed the clandestine group called the Super-Clan, were Corrado Simioni, Duccio Berio and Vanni Mulinaris, the founders in Paris of the language school Hyperion, considered to be an international basis for the traffic of weapons to revolutionary movements. Curcio claimed that the real channel for these encounters was different, but he did not specify it. See Curcio, *A viso aperto*, pp. 65-8, 143 and Moretti, *Brigatte Rosse. Una storia italiana*, p. 15.

[27] See Commissione Parlamentare sul Caso Moro, *Processo Moro I grado* (The Italian Parliamentary Commission, The first Moro trial), at <http://www.apolis.com/moro/commissioni/moro/mag/67.htm>, pp. 134-5.

[28] This was evidently a verbal agreement, which has been divided into sections for the purpose of this research. According to Savasta, there was no internal BR document on ties with the Palestinians.

(1) The PLO would deliver weapons to the BR.
(2) BR members would be allowed to train in Palestinian camps in the Middle East.
(3) The PLO would offer assistance to BR fugitives.
(4) The BR would store weapons in Italy for use by the PLO.
(5) The BR would participate in attacks against Israeli individuals in Italy.[29]

B.   Ideological cooperation

Although the Palestinian terrorist organizations had reached the apex of their activity and international influence, they were hardly mentioned in BR publications. Occasional references to the struggle of the Palestinian people against imperialism and Zionism were framed in general terms. It is strange, to say the least, that the Palestinian issue was glossed over in BR publications, only featuring as a main theme for the first time in the RDS of 1978. A study of the semi-official BR bulletin *CONTROinformazione* shows that the Middle East was of absolutely no interest to the mouthpiece of the main Italian terrorist organization during the ten years of its existence until December 1981.[30] The June-July 1982 edition carried, for the first time, an article on the Israeli-Palestinian conflict – an anti-Israeli article inspired by the Israel incursion into southern Lebanon.[31]

C.   Logistical cooperation

The volumes of depositions and confessions by BR members reveal only four confirmed cases of assistance granted by Palestinian organizations to the BR and other Italian terrorist organizations.[32] This assistance took the form of two particularly large arms consignments by Fatah to the BR in 1978-79, and two other arms consignments by the PFLP to small Italian terrorist organizations,

---

[29] The conclusions of the Italian Parliamentary Commission concord with the description on the subject found in this chapter. See *Processo Moro I grado*, pp. 131-5. Moretti, unlike others, argued that the Palestinians never asked the BR to carry out attacks against Israelis, and that the PLO was only interested in strengthening the BR! He also played down the importance of the arms deal. See Moretti, *Brigatte Rosse. Una storia italiana*, p. 189.

[30] On the other hand, it regularly reviewed the RAF struggle in Germany or the IRA struggle in Ireland. Over the years, articles also appeared on Chile (1973-74), Brazil (1978), and Argentina (1979). Mostly, however, the journal focused on internal issues (factory workers), and ideological issues.

[31] See 'Pax Sionista' in *CONTROinformazione*, Nos. 24-25, June-July 1982.

[32] Alfredo Buonavita, who headed the BR logistics division until the mid-1970s, testified that up to 1973, the BR had no difficulties in obtaining weapons. From 1973, they began to purchase weapons on the Italian black market. As head of weapons procurement up to 1975, Buonavita knew the BR had not received weapons from any other organization during that period.

through Maurizio Follini, an arms dealer who also belonged to one of these organizations.

There was a basic difference between the PLO shipments and the PFLP shipments orchestrated by Follini. The former were part of a broader agreement between the BR and PLO/Fatah. In addition to items for the IRA and ETA, about a quarter of the consignment was set aside for the PLO's own use on Italian soil at some future date. The consignments consisted of light weapons, anti-aircraft missiles, RPG bazookas, and large amounts of explosives and grenades.[33] The consignments orchestrated by Follini, on the other hand, were apparently a personal initiative. Follini, an enigmatic personality, was suspected of being a Soviet agent. It is not clear why Follini stipulated that the weapons be divided between the smaller organizations only – not among the larger ones, such as the BR.[34] Be this as it may, the BR and the Prima Linea (PL) organization managed to purchase some of Follini's automatic weapons.[35]

D.   Operational cooperation

Some of the weapons delivered by Follini to the Italian organizations in 1978, and about a quarter of the weapons sent by Moretti to northern Italy in July 1979, were designed for use by PLO/Fatah and possibly also PFLP in Italy or elsewhere in Western Europe.[36] These weapons, which were stored in arms caches, in safe houses or in the mountains of Sardinia, were apparently seized by the authorities

---

[33] The following is a list of weapons that appears in the indictment of examining magistrate Carlo Mastelloni: 70 Sterling submachine guns, five bazookas, ten S-A missiles, a large number of MK2 grenades, several kilograms of plastic explosives, FAL rifles, thousands of bullets, (9, 7.62, 38S) and spare weapon parts. According to the Venice charge sheet, some of the weapons were originally sold to Libya and Tunisia, the French missiles were sold to Lebanon, and the RPG-7's were manufactured by Fatah. See *Sentenza Ordinanza del Giudice Istruttore presso il Tribunale Civile e Penale di Venezia Carlo Mastelloni contro Alunni Corrado + 77, No. 298/81 AGI.*

[34] See legal testimonies of Marco Donat-Cattin and Anna Maria Granata, as cited in *Ministero dell'Interno. Dipartamento della Pubblica Sicurezza. Raporti Internazionali dei gruppi terroristici italiani di sinistra* (undated), pp. 60-66. These testimonies are also amply cited in the report of the Italian Parliamentary Commission on the Moro affair.

[35] According to Pietro Mutti's testimony, the delivery included three Kalashnikov storm rifles, 20 hand grenades, two FAL machine guns, three revolvers, a sniper rifle, 30 kilograms of explosives, and about 10,000 detonators. Ibid., pp. 78-80.

[36] For the Follini case, see Azzaroni's testimony to the examining magistrate, ibid., pp. 67-77. In the summer of 1979, Follini delivered another arms consignment, again to be distributed among smaller terrorist organizations (CoCoRi – Comitati combattenti rivoluzionari, and the PL). The weapons were delivered in Italy itself and belonged to the PLO. Follini tried to send two more consignments in 1978-79, but the first sank and Bulgarian border police seized the second. See the legal testimony of Mutti, *Ministero dell'Interno*, pp. 78-80. For Moretti, see legal testimony of Galletta, Savasta and Peci and Moretti, *Brigatte Rosse. Una storia italiana*, pp. 187-90.

before the Palestinians managed to use them, as corroborated by the legal evidence and by Moretti in his book.[37]

Carlo Brogi, a BR member working as an Alitalia air steward, served as Moretti's interpreter in his encounters with the PLO. He testified in court that after meeting with members of the PLO, Moretti asked him to deliver explosives to Tel Aviv for the Palestinians to use there. Brogi refused, saying that he would never get through security control at Israel's Ben Gurion airport.[38]

E.   Summary of cooperation for this period

Ideological, logistical, and operational cooperation between the BR and Palestinian organizations evidently began at some point in the summer of 1978, and reached a peak in 1978 and 1979. This cooperation amounted to no more than four or five arms consignments from Fatah and the PFLP to the BR and several other small Italian terrorist organizations. In return, the BR, and possibly other organizations too, agreed to store weapons in Italy for the Palestinians to use at some future date.[39] The BR neither carried out, nor intended to carry out attacks on behalf of the PLO/Fatah against Israeli targets. Apparently the BR was not operationally involved in Palestinian activities in Italy.[40]

---

[37]   A strange incident occurred in this context: In 1979 three Italian members of Autonomy in Rome and one Arab member of the PFLP in Perugia were implicated in the smuggling to a Lebanese ship anchored in the port of Ortona of two Soviet anti-aircraft SA-7 missiles. The affair ended when the Italian police seized the missiles. In a letter to the Italian government, the PFLP argued that the missiles were owned by the organization, and were not intended for use in Italy. A statement by the 'autonomous workers committees' declaring solidarity with those sentenced in the Ortona affair and with the international campaign for the rights of the Palestinian people was published. See 'L'Internazionalismo proletario non e reato' in *CONTROinformazione*, July 1983.

[38]   See his deposition in *Corte d'Assise di Roma. Pres. Sergio Sarichilli, Filiberto Pagano. 13.10.89 (3/83RPG, 995/81 RGI)*, p. 175.

[39]   According to one testimony, the weapons which Folini delivered to the Italians in the summer of 1979 came from an Italian depot which the PLO was anxious to dispose of after it had promised the Italian government that it would desist from carrying out attacks on Italian soil. See Mutti's testimony.

[40]   In September 1972, two Italians were arrested and accused of helping to collect information for Black September in preparation for its attack on the Trieste oil containers on 4 August 1972. Ludovico Codella, one of those arrested, was tried in 1977, but the source does not specify the outcome of the trial. In any case, Codella belonged to a legal leftist Italian party, the PDUP, and not to a terrorist organization. See Edward Mickolus, *Transnational Terrorism: A Chronology of Events, 1968-1979* (London: Aldwych Press, 1980), p. 335.

        According to the weekly *Europeo* of 25 January 1982, the police, while searching a BR safe house in Torino in 1975, found a document indicating some kind of operational connection between the BR, the PFLP and the RAF. There is no reliable corroboration of this piece of information.

        In April 1978, 24 people connected with the international terrorist ring which planned to kill the participants in the peace negotiations between Israel and Egypt, were arrested in Egypt. According to the Egyptian authorities, the head of the group was a Palestinian who apparently

The agreement between the PLO and the BR relating to the delivery of weapons was apparently fully implemented, although the weapons were seized before the PLO managed to make use of them. The BR never had the opportunity to avail itself of the PLO offer to help BR fugitives; most BR fugitives fled to France, famous for its tradition of granting political asylum to refugees.

The proposal to train BR members in Palestinian camps also foundered. The PLO was unable to guarantee safe passage for prospective trainees and insisted on secrecy under all circumstances. The BR, for its part, realized that training in Palestinian camps would turn its members into 'military activists' before their political training was complete. This contradicted BR policy regarding the nature of its cadres.[41]

The BR attitude towards PLO demands to attack Israelis in Italy was ambiguous, to say the least. Although BR leader, Moretti, agreed in principle to carry out such attacks, they never actually did so. In at least one case they did carry out some intelligence work on behalf of Fatah.[42] Savasta, in his testimony, solved this seeming contradiction: such an operation, he stated, could not be carried out unless backed by a clearly defined political program. An international operation of this kind was justified only if it influenced the balance of power within the state. An attack against the infrastructure of another country, which bore no relationship to the BR's internal political program, was simply an 'outmoded form of proletarian internationalism'. Therefore, the organization dismissed the project.[43]

Peci was even more forthright: 'What concerned us was class war in Italy, not war against the Israelis. In other words, we were not interested in serving as a military arm of the PLO. We believe that we can be useful to each other, but we are not prepared to do their work for them.' According to Peci, the BR clarified its position in talks with the PLO.[44]

---

belonged to the 'Black June' organization (alias Abu Nidal organization), and had ties with an Italian called Sergio Mantovani in Zurich, and a West German called Vera Marte Gunter. The Egyptian authorities alleged that the group was connected with the Italian BR. No legal or other source corroborating this allegation was found. See Mickolus, *Transnational Terrorism: A Chronology of Events*, p. 784.

[41] According to Raufer, the members of the BR were not professional terrorists. The vast majority had no experience with arms prior to their recruitment, and training was usually given only before the operation itself. Raufer brings the 1992 testimony of a divisional head, the only senior member of the organization's Golden Age to remain at large, who declared that BR members never received training in the camps of a foreign organization. See Xavier Raufer, 'The Red Brigades: Farewell to Arms', *Studies in Conflict and Terrorism*, Vol. 16 (1993), pp. 315-25.

[42] See Savasta's testimony, Document 4/27.

[43] Moretti himself claimed that they were not asked to carry out attacks. His testimony contradicts most of the legal sources.

[44] See Peci's testimony, *Ministero dell'Interno*, p. 27.

According to the examining magistrate for the prosecution in Venice, who investigated Arafat's complicity in the delivery of weapons, Moretti was keen for joint BR-PLO statements to be published during the attacks. Anxious not to damage relations with Italy and other friendly European states, the Palestinians, however, turned down this request.

Savasta summarized the principles of international cooperation between the two organizations as mutual aid between guerrilla organizations eager to undermine imperialist hold on the countries of the Mediterranean. Although the BR did not actually attack Israeli targets, it did maintain contact with the PLO, and received weapons from them. The PLO therefore constituted a political embarrassment to the Italian government. Moretti's book confirms this interpretation.

Savasta blames the severance of ties with the PLO in late 1979-early 1980 on a simple technical hitch – Moretti lost the telephone number of the Paris agency which linked him with the PLO. The ties never got off the ground, said Savasta, because of the BR's inability to propose a consistent political program to the PLO, and its lukewarm contribution to the international revolutionary movement as a whole. Although, in theory, the BR considered the issue of operational cooperation with the PLO, they conducted little debate on the subject. In practice, they attacked only Italian targets. Unlike the RAF, they never attacked NATO or American targets. Indeed, the possibility of attacking NATO or American targets in Italy only arose during the kidnapping of Gen. Dozier in December 1981.

F.   The reasons for cooperation between Italian and Palestinian organizations

As noted above, throughout the period under review the BR focused on internal issues, although their choice of targets, strategy, and modus operandi underwent several changes. BR publications confirm that attacks against foreign targets were given very low priority by the organization.[45] Thus, the lack of ties between the BR and the PLO until 1978 can be explained in terms of the organization's exclusive focus on internal issues, and its strategic assessment that war against the SIM and imperialism, in general, should be waged primarily on Italian soil.

According to Valerio Morucci, a BR leader who was implicated in Moro's kidnapping, it was the latter event that brought about a change in policy. Although there had never been any technical obstacles to the establishment of such ties, the BR leadership had always resisted ideological concessions. The BR's immediate goal, as formulated by its leaders, was to consolidate and expand. Only

---

[45]   The Italian terrorist organizations carried out a total of five attacks against diplomatic representations in the 1970-83 period (out of a total of 621 attacks against people). The years or the targets of the attacks were not specified. See Della Porta, *Il Terrorismo di Sinistra*, pp. 211-13.

then could it turn its mind to international cooperation and revolution. After the RAF kidnapping of Schleyer (see Chapter 3), the BR kidnapping of Moro reinforced its own sense of power. The self-styled leader of the revolutionary movement in Europe, it decided to renew ties with the RAF and establish contact with the PLO. Given Arafat's condemnation of the Moro kidnapping, the BR was particularly appreciative of the Palestinian desire for cooperation.[46]

According to the PLO representatives in Paris, the BR was courted by PLO factions who opposed the PLO mainline policy of rapprochement with the West and abandonment of the armed struggle, and by 'Marxist circles' within the PLO who felt that cooperation with the BR would strengthen their hand. This tallied with Savasta's account of the PLO decision to woo the BR, which stresses the fact that the BR success in the Moro operation enhanced its prestige in the eyes of the PLO leaders. According to Peci, the PLO was motivated by its wish to weaken Italy and helped all revolutionary movements in return for alliances when necessary.

Interestingly, top BR militants were unable to give a satisfactory reason as to why their leaders agreed to cooperate with the PLO when they seemed to have little to gain from such cooperation, apart from the weapons they received for a period of eighteen months.[47] This agreement is even more surprising in view of the fact that the BR at that time was stronger than ever, having succeeded in throwing the entire Italian political arena into disarray. Since the BR negotiators, Moretti and Balserani, refused to cooperate with the magistrates, this riddle has never been solved. An attempt is made here to solve it through a comparative analysis of two important texts: the RDS of April 1975, regarded as BR's basic strategic manifesto, and the RDS of February 1978, which was attached to the statement relating to Moro's kidnapping.

The RDS of April 1975 proposed the following theory concerning international issues: the US was perceived as the archenemy of all nations and governments, the center of global imperialism. Economically, politically, and militarily, European countries promoted imperialism and the world balance was determined in Europe. Italy was not only an integral part of US-led global imperialism, but also played a key role within it, since the crisis-ridden Italian government was largely dominated by the PCI, which had become a powerful

---

[46] On this subject, see Maurizio's interview in the German weekly *Der Spiegel* of 28 July 1986. Maurizio belonged to the group that kidnapped Moro, and in that period was close to Moretti. He left the BR due to his opposition to Moro's assassination.

[47] According to Moretti himself, the BR had no real difficulty acquiring weapons, either on the black market or from old communist partisans. He referred however to the 'political relationship' with the Palestinians in contrast to the traffic of arms of other organizations. See Moretti, *Brigatte Rosse. Una storia italiana*, p. 60.

force within social-imperialism. Therefore, Italy served as a good starting point for the revolution that would destroy European imperialism.

On the global level, imperialism was in the throes of a serious crisis, economically, politically and militarily. The crisis was due to three factors: states fighting for liberation and communism; Soviet social-imperialism which was interested in controlling strategic areas, vital raw materials, and new markets for its goods; and the struggle of the proletariat and the establishment of proletarian guerrillas in metropolitan industrial centers. The counter-revolution would erupt most forcefully in Italy, the weak link in the 'Western democratic chain'. Therefore, the Italian proletariat had to take on not only the enemy from within, but also the entire economic, political, and military apparatus of imperialism. The territory of Italy constituted the operative front for the Italian guerrilla. The immediate goal of the guerrilla was to strike at the heart of the Italian state. It is worth noting that the RDS of April 1975 carried no calls for international solidarity, and made no reference to the Palestinian people or organizations.

The RDS of February 1978 reiterated the 1975 assessment but saw deterioration in the international scene: the worsening crisis in global imperialism appeared to be bringing the world to the brink of war. The document identified the first stage in this process of imperial expansion as the partial skirmishes in the Middle East and Africa through a 'third party'. From a historical perspective, the only possible response for the proletariat was a frontal and definitive clash with the forces of imperialism; the only possible tactic was class war in the imperialist metropolis, or an imperialist Third World War. Under such circumstances, guerrilla warfare in the metropolis supplanted the strategy of a Third World uprising. In this strategic document, two new major themes appeared for the first time: the existence of a counter-insurgency pact between imperialist nations and the need for a new kind of aggressive proletarian internationalism and for the political integration of all European communist organizations.[48]

Five sections of the document were devoted to the issue of a counter-insurgency cooperation pact between imperialist forces.[49] According to the BR, such pacts aimed at improving the response of states to the revolutionary initia-

---

[48]   The quantitative breakdown of the text is equally interesting: About 23% of the RDS of 1975 is devoted to international issues, compared to about 33% of the RDS of 1978 (of which about 22% focused on imperialist attempts to oppress the revolutionary communist forces).

[49]   For example, in May 1977 a London conference of nine ministers of the interior of the EC countries expressed rising concern over developments in Italy. In 1977, after the kidnapping of Schleyer by the RAF, the hijacking of a Lufthansa plane from Mogadishu by the 'Halima Commando', and the subsequent 'massacre' of 18 October, the political-military apparatus of European nations rallied round the German 'senior echelons'. The 'massacre' is a reference to the suicide of RAF leaders in Stammheim jail, following the failure of the Mogadishu hijacking operation on 18 October 1977, which aimed, *inter alia*, to achieve the release of the imprisoned RAF leaders.

tive, and at uniting anti-guerrilla forces at the highest possible level. In two cases (Entebbe and Mogadishu) joint anti-terror operations had been carried out across national borders. This was indicative of the international character adopted by class war and reflected the imperialist determination to shore up the weaker links in the chain [Italy, *inter alia*] through direct intervention. The EC's counter-insurgency program and plans for international police cooperation were not simple bureaucratic measures but rather new facts whose importance should not be downplayed, since they altered the conditions of war.

In the section of the RDS dealing with the need for a new kind of proletarian internationalism, the guerrilla was defined as a metropolitan front in the international struggle against imperialism. The RAF in West Germany, the Armed Cells for Popular Autonomy (Noyaux Armés pour l'Autonomie Populaire – NAPAP) in France, and the secessionist movements (ETA, IRA) were fighting the same enemy – the imperialist bourgeoisie. Therefore, it was necessary to encourage 'operational cooperation' [sic], mutual aid, and solidarity, as far as possible.

The BR had underestimated the importance of this issue for far too long, the document claimed. The limitations of the choice of the 'national' character of the guerrilla organization had become intolerable. The increased strength of the guerrilla movement, intensification of the class war throughout Europe, and information arriving from the most progressive part of the international proletariat forced the BR to adopt a new mission: to continue every possible initiative for the political integration of communist forces and anti-imperialist organizations in Europe. 'Breaking the isolation', and creating the conditions for a broader-based cooperation, would soon constitute the test of the maturity attained by the European organizations (inverted commas in source).

In practice, after the Stammheim and Mogadishu massacres, all the fighting avant-gardes of Europe had finally realized the importance of the continental dimension in the revolutionary class war, said the RDS. This was reflected not only in expressing solidarity, or demonstrations of aversion to the West German government's 'final solution' ... but rather in calls for an aggressive response.[50] On 18 October it finally transpired that a new kind of aggressive proletarian internationalism had matured in the consciousness of the fighting avant-gardes. Finally, proletarian internationalism implied not only a theoretical declaration, but also a practical stand alongside all those fighting against imperialism, in particular the heroic Palestinian people in the Middle East. This phrase ended BR's strategic resolution.

---

[50] The reference here is to all acts of violence and attacks against West German targets throughout Western Europe carried out after 18 October by organizations and individuals belonging to the far left following the suicide of the RAF leadership.

6.   International and regional factors

The BR described the international arena as a struggle between the imperialist bloc led by the US and the social-imperialist bloc led by the USSR, with the revolutionary and anti-imperialist forces in the middle. Nevertheless, throughout the period, the US was defined as the main enemy. Almost all the texts refer to crisis, tension, the imminence of war etc. Only the RDS of February 1978 featured the idea that tension between the two blocs could lead to 'an inevitable and direct clash' between the US and the USSR. The BR saw the first signs of such a process in regional disputes in the Middle East and Africa, which served the bloc struggle through proxy wars.

According to this view, the clash between revolutionary and imperialist forces also worsened during this period. The RDS of 1978 emphasized that the aggressive stance of the Italian DC towards the proletariat was a result of US and West German aggression, and pressure exerted by these countries through international imperialist mechanisms (NATO, the IMF and the EC). Since this pressure was directed against the entire revolutionary movement in Europe through the national governments, the need for active solidarity and a united front was self-evident.

It seems therefore that the major factor influencing the BR decision to cooperate with the Palestinians was fear of international and regional cooperation between European police, security and intelligence services, with US assistance. The BR fear of a successful strike against their leaders, despite, or perhaps because they were at the apex of their career a few days before Moro's kidnapping, is evident in their recurring reference to the RAF leadership imprisoned in Stammheim.[51]

According to the testimony of the 'repentant' Alfredo Buonavita, the last pages of the RDS of February 1978 (describing the need for international solidarity) were added by the BR external leadership to the text that was originally prepared by the imprisoned leadership. Only the active leaders were aware of international developments, and could relate to them intelligently. If this argument is valid, it is understandable that these leaders were afraid that they too might end their lives in jail, and therefore felt a need for allies. The BR leader, Moretti, also alluded *post factum* to this when he said: 'Although in 1978 we appeared strong, we understood [after Moro's assassination] that the guerrilla period was over, and that the real war

---

[51]   The statement of 14 February 1978 taking responsibility for the murder of Judge P. Palma stated that the murder of the RAF leadership was no random occurrence, but rather a strategic choice adopted by imperialism against revolutionary forces throughout the world.

The second statement taking responsibility for the kidnapping of Moro, distributed on 25 March 1978, had a section on 'imperialist terrorism' which again referred to the role of the united police forces in Europe and the assistance that the British SAS (Special Air Service), the German BKA (BundesKriminalAmt) and the Israeli secret services were offering the weaker links of the imperialist chain in order to massacre the militants of the IRA, RAF, the Palestinian people and the communist guerrillas of Latin America.

was about to begin – a war that would lead to tragedy.'[52] At the same time, he stressed that the RDS of 1978 was very important in the eyes of BR militants because it presented the liberation of imprisoned comrades as one of the main strategic tasks of the organization. Moretti himself stated that the leaders bore in mind what happened to the RAF at Stammheim after the hijacking to Mogadishu.[53]

The last question that requires clarification is why the BR selected the Palestinians as their coalition partners, and why they placed such strong and unexpected emphasis in the RDS of 1978 on the Palestinian problem and the struggle of 'the heroic Palestinian people'. At the time the RAF was in a desperate situation, after the unsuccessful kidnapping of Schleyer, the disappearance of all the original leadership, and the clampdown against the organization in the course of 1978. The so-called 'socialist' secessionist organizations, namely the IRA and ETA, were not considered true partners, and the French organization NAPAP also lacked the ability and status to assist the BR. Thus, the Palestinians were a natural choice, partly *faute de mieux*. They already controlled part of southern Lebanon and Beirut, possessed important material resources and were in a position to help revolutionary movements, as proved in the hijacking of the Lufthansa plane and the request to release the imprisoned RAF leaders. Despite the failure of the Mogadishu operation, the Palestinian organizations were doubtless considered by the European revolutionaries as courageous 'heroes' who might be prepared to help the BR leadership.

The need for such assistance arose in late 1977-early 1978 after the decline in the struggle by the violent faction of Autonomia, the failure of efforts to suspend or adjourn the trial of the organization's historical leaders, and the demise of the RAF leaders in Stammheim prison. After the assassination of Moro, the BR leadership rightly predicted that their clash with the regime would be to the finish and that their chances of survival were slim. In spite of official declarations of support published by the imprisoned leaders, they recognized that the BR could hardly handle huge political consequences of the kidnapping.[54] As one of these leaders remarked: 'I have the impression that the comrades have in their hands an atomic bomb, which they handle as a firecracker.'[55]

---

[52] See Moretti, *Brigatte Rosse. Una storia italiana*, p. 176.

[53] Ibid., pp. 111-12, 155.

[54] Years later Curcio described his feelings during this tense period. Aware of what happened at Stammheim the imprisoned leaders even feared for their lives, and tried to remain outside the decision circle. Unable to continue the confrontation with the Italian state at such a high level of conflict the assassination of Moro was seen by most of them as the end of the BR. See Curcio, *A viso aperto*, pp. 150-61.

[55] See Alberto Franceschini and Giustolisi P. F. Buffa, *Mara, Renato e io. Storia dei fondadori delle Br* (4th edn.) (Milano: Oscar Mondadori, 2000), pp. 152-63, 198. Franceschini described too, in crude terms, the fear felt by the imprisoned leaders when Moro's corpse was found in an abandoned car in Rome.

IV.   1981-84: MILITARY FAILURE, SCHISMS, AND IDEOLOGICAL
       QUESTS

The kidnapping of Judge d'Urso in December 1980 was the last action carried out
by the BR as a united organization. That same month, the imprisoned BR
leadership published a long ideological document entitled 'The Bee and the
Communist'. It was followed by 20 major propositions that provided the ideological basis of a new BR faction, the Guerrilla Party of the Metropolitan
Proletariat (Partito-Guerriglia del Proletariato Metropolitano – P-GPM) led by
Giovanni Senzani.

      In April 1981 the Naples *colonna* of the BR kidnapped one of the leading
local politicians of the DC, later released with the help of the local Mafia for a
high ransom. This operation revamped the rift between the Naples and Rome
divisions and other factions of the organization. In the summer of that year the P-
GPM was born.[56]

      On 17 December 1981 BR terrorists kidnapped Gen. James Dozier, the high-
est-ranking American NATO officer in Italy, from his apartment in Verona. The
abduction, the first such operation against a foreign citizen, was perpetrated by
the Venice division of the Red Brigades for the Construction of the Communist
Combatant Party (Brigate Rosse per la Costruzione del Partito Comunista
Combattente – BR-PCC) led by Antonio Savasta. According to his testimony, the
BR-PCC launched an anti-NATO campaign in order to enhance its international
influence. The operation was described as an effort on the part of the BR-PCC to
enlist support for the new 'peace movement'.[57] Italian security forces freed Dozier
in January 1982.

      One of the BR's aims during this difficult period was to regain control of
smaller factions that had splintered from the organization. Another goal was to
preserve its organizational identity and attract media attention. To this end, it
placed more emphasis on the technical success of its attacks than on their political
impact. For the same reason, it tended to target people more often than property.

      There were two reasons for the crisis and failures that characterized the period
1981-84: isolation from the BR's working-class base and from public opinion,
and the 1981 *pentiti* legislation which encouraged defection and enhanced the

---

[56]   In December 1981 two conflicting documents were published: 'Crisis, War and Proletarian
        Internationalism' (300 pages) by the P-GMP, and 'Two years of Political Struggle' (184 pages)
        by the rival Red Brigades for the Construction of the Communist Combatant Party (Brigate
        Rosse per la Costruzione del Partito Comunista Combattente – BR-PCC). The latter document
        was attached to statement No. 2 in which the BR claimed responsibility for the kidnapping of
        Gen. Dozier.

[57]   See Caselli and Della Porta, *La storia delle Brigate rosse*, p. 212.

powers of the security forces.[58] Like other clandestine organizations, the BR became less concerned with political propaganda, and focused increasingly on its confrontation with the security forces.[59]

In April 1984 four imprisoned leaders of the BR – Curcio, Moretti, Ianelli and Bertolucci – published an 'open letter' in which they rejected the armed struggle as pointless: 'The international conditions that made this struggle possible no longer exist', they stated.[60] The main reason, however, for the failure of the revolutionary ideologues to carry out their political program or to appeal to the working class was misconception of the latter's impending impoverishment. In fact, the socio-economic conditions of all Italians in post-industrial society improved far beyond expectations.

1. Cooperation with Palestinian organizations

A. Continuation of contacts between the BR and the Palestinians

Savasta claimed that the BR executive raised the issue of international ties again in January-February 1981; Moretti sought to renew ties with the French organization that had initiated his contacts with the PLO, but was unable to retrieve the Paris contact telephone number.[61] Consequently, the link between the BR executive and Paris was severed. After Moretti was imprisoned in April 1981, Senzani, head of the 'prison front', was responsible for maintaining ties with the Paris 'coordinating agency'.

Due to Senzani's refusal to cooperate with the authorities after his arrest in January 1982, we must rely on secondary sources for information regarding BR-Palestinian ties.[62] Senzani, like Moretti, established international ties with European organizations (ETA, IRA, RAF), 'revolutionary' African and Asiatic states (probably Angola and Cambodia) and the PLO, through French intermediaries. Under Senzani, ties with the PLO were less important than they had been under Moretti, especially since Senzani represented only one faction of the

---

[58] In 1982 alone 915 activists of various terrorist organizations were arrested, and 1523 BR members were already imprisoned. See Xavier Raufer, *La Storia poco conosciuta delle Brigate Rosse (1980-1987)* (Institut de Criminologie de Paris: Seminario di Ricerca sulla Violenza Politique, 1987), pp. 23-4.

[59] In this context, see Caselli and Della Porta, *La storia delle Brigate rosse*, pp. 213, 216, and Raufer, *La Storia poco conosciuta delle Brigate Rosse*, pp. 13, 19.

[60] Cited in Raufer, *La Storia poco conosciuta delle Brigate Rosse*, p. 49.

[61] The number was not written down for security reasons. An appeal to the 'prison front' *colonne* and to two people who knew the number was abortive.

[62] The main testimony was delivered by Robert Buzzati, who was not directly involved in contacts outside Italy, but heard about them from Senzani and others. See his testimony in the Rome court (RGI 995/81, and RPG 3/83).

organization, which had already split into two major factions and a number of autonomous *colonne*.

Senzani apparently traveled twice to Paris to meet with the PLO representative, known as Al.[63] After these meetings, Senzani informed his comrades that they had a good chance of obtaining weapons of different kinds, including Kalashnikovs and bazookas. There was talk of more weapons consignments by sea, although no actual agreement was reached on this issue.[64]

Upon Senzani's arrest in early 1982 ties were once again severed. Throughout the remainder of the period, the Palestinians were preoccupied with their own problems (the Israeli incursion into southern Lebanon and the evacuation of PLO and other forces from southern Lebanon and the Beirut area) to even consider ties with other organizations.

B.   Ideological cooperation

As stated above, it was only in 1981 that the BR, through its mouthpiece *CON-TROinformazione*, began to show an interest in the Middle East and the Palestinian issue. This interest is also reflected in ideological documents published by various BR factions.[65] Between 1981 and 1984 the Palestinian issue

---

[63] According to the Venice charge sheet in the Padua court, the French security service confirmed the existence of a Fatah representative in Paris in 1978-79 known as Al Mubassem Nazi, who held a Tunisian passport. This again illustrates the monumental ignorance of the BR leaders regarding the Arabs. Incapable of remembering his full name, they labored under the impression that Al was his real name!

[64] Judge Ferdinando Imposimato, who in his capacity as chief justice interrogated a large number of BR prisoners, later claimed that a document was found in Senzani's safe house entitled 'The Foreign Colonna and its Function'. The document stated that a strategic agreement was drawn up in 1979 between the Euro-terrorists and the Middle Eastern terrorists, whereby the Europeans gave their support to the Palestinian 'Rejection Front' and attacked Arafat's moderate line. See 'Terrorismo Internazionale', *La Repubblica* (1989), p. 156.

   This statement was strange, given that all the testimonies indicated that the 1979 agreement was drawn up between Moretti and Fatah with the approval of none other than Arafat himself and that Fatah at that time spearheaded the 'Resistance Front' against Egypt and the peace process with Israel. Senzani was not involved in this stage of the negotiations. Apparently Imposimato was misled by the reference to 'Marxist elements' within the PLO, when in fact it was Abu Iyyad, Arafat's right-hand man. Once again, ignorance of the Palestinian setup is evident.

[65] In November 1981 a group of prisoners from Trani prison, the self-styled '16 March ideological group', published a strategic document entitled 'Down with Imperialist War, up with Revolutionary War and 'militant internationalism'. The document accused Israel of being the spearhead of all Mediterranean states to participate in the Reagan administration's program of aggression. It considered 'the militant avant-gardes of the heroic Palestinian people ... the prime factor in internationalist solidarity with the BR'. See 'Contro la guerra imperialista, intensificare la guerra rivoluzionaria, sviluppare l'internazionalismo combattente', *CONTROinformazione*, No. 22, February 1982.

   In December 1981 the 'Palmi prison brigade' comprising the BR founders, published a strategic document which defined Israel as a sub-imperialist state, emphasized the centrality of the

occupied a far more central place in the BR's strategic and ideological thinking. This was partly due to increasing Israeli military intervention in Lebanon which was perceived not only as an attempt to oppress the legitimate struggle of the Palestinian people, but also as part of an American-led imperialist plot to seize control of the Middle East. West European nations such as Italy and Israel were perceived as aiding and abetting the US to this end.

C.   Logistical cooperation

The only available information concerning logistical cooperation is the transfer of remote control detonators in November 1981 to the Rome *colonna* under Senzani. The period of large weapons consignments and complex logistical operations, characteristic of the late 1970s, was over. French militants, who may have belonged to the AD, delivered the few weapons provided by the Palestinians during this period.[66]

D.   Operational cooperation

Sometime in 1981 (the date was unspecified in the documentation), Claudio Seghetti, a member of the Rome section of the BR, was arrested. A slip of paper was found in his pocket, containing the addresses of the Israeli ambassador and military attaché in Rome. The note was written in English, a language with which Seghetti was unfamiliar.[67] Antonio Savasta also testified that the BR had begun to conduct 'investigations' into the Israeli military attaché in Rome.

Palestinian avant-garde, and considered all means justified in the struggle against Zionism. See 'Crisi, guerra e internazionalismo proletaria', ibid.

CONTROinformazione published an articled called 'Pax Sionista,' which attacked the Israel role in the Lebanese War, and used antisemitic undertones when it attacked Jewish communities throughout the world for their support to the Israeli policy. See *CONTROinformazione*, Nos. 24-25, July-August 1982.

An ideological document put out by a faction of the First Line (Prima Linea – PL) severely censured the Israeli action in Lebanon and the 'political holocaust' against the Palestinian fighters, and expressed solidarity with the struggle of the Palestinian people. This document was also the first ideological document to refer to the importance of the radical Islamic movement. See 'Intelligenza collectiva e comando del capitale' in *CONTROinformazione*, July 1983.

66   Paul Bandit, apparently an AD militant, delivered the remote control detonators. Although the 'prison front' planned to attack the DC headquarters and the Rome Law Courts with bazookas, these belonged to an old 1979 consignment, which had been kept for PLO use in caves on the island of Sardinia, and were removed without the Palestinians' permission. According to Senzani, the PLO was delighted with the kidnapping of Gen. Dozier and was convinced that it symbolized the BR rapprochement to the Soviet bloc. See R. Buzzati's testimony.

67   See Padua court records, *Tribunale di Padova, Uff. Istr. GI Palombarini. Sentenza-Ordinanza n. 183/79 AGI del 4/9/81 contro Del Alisa + 138 (Autonomia Operaia)*, which cite the prosecution's cross-examination of the BR international ties in Venice.

On 15 February 1984 Leamon Hunt, chief of the Multinational Force and Observer Group (MFO) (sent to Sinai after the Camp David accords), was assassinated in Rome. The BR-PCC claimed responsibility for the attack and published a leaflet explaining why they had chosen Hunt as a target. The Lebanese Revolutionary Armed Forces (Fractions Armées Révolutionnaires Libanaises – FARL), however, also took responsibility for the attack They placed a telephone call in Beirut in which they linked it to another FARL attack, namely the assassination of the American military attaché in Paris, Charles Ray, on 18 January 1982.[68]

In August 1984 Abdallah Mohd al-Mansour was arrested at the north Italian border carrying 8 kilos of explosives, and in December 1984 Josephine Abdou was arrested at Rome Fiumicino airport. Both belonged to the FARL and had been in Rome on the day Hunt was killed. These events led to the arrest of George Ibrahim Abdallah, the FARL leader, who was staying in Lyons, France, and was responsible for several attacks in France, including some against Israeli targets. Information provided by Judge Priore showed that Abdallah had contacts with the BR and had even trained with the BR in 1979.[69] In November 1987 BR member Rosa Fresa Lambetti was also arrested for conspiring to murder Hunt.

Given the significance of Hunt's murder, it is important to clarify whether, in fact, the attack represented a step towards solidarity with Palestinian organizations. True, the Italian leaflet claiming responsibility for the attack referred to the massacres of Tel al-Zaatar, and Sabra and Shattila, condemned the Camp David accords, Zionism as well as American imperialism. However, most of the document emphasized European, especially Italian intervention and the NATO role in the Middle East. This was defined in the broader context of an American imperialist offensive in the region, in response to the Soviet invasion of Afghanistan and revolutionary developments in Iran. There was a general call for international solidarity with the proletariat and progressive nations throughout the world, but communists worldwide were asked to build a new Communist International, based strictly on Marxist-Leninist principles. The document ended with general slogans calling on the proletariat to unite in the struggle against imperialism, and demanded the withdrawal of Italian forces from the Middle East and the Italian withdrawal from NATO, without any reference to either the

---

[68] This small organization was composed mainly of Lebanese Christians from a clan from the village of Koubeyat, which fought 'against imperialism and for the Palestinian cause'. Note that the organization's leader, George Ibrahim Abdallah, had previously been a senior member of the PFLP operational branch. See also A.P. Schmid, A.J. Jongman, et. al., *Political Terrorism: A New Guide to Actors, Authors, Concepts, Data-bases, Theories, and Literature* (2nd edn.) (Amsterdam: SWIDOC and New Brunswick, NJ Transaction Books, 1988), p. 547.

[69] See *Corriere della Sera*, 16 September 1986.

Palestinian or Lebanese people. Although the attack against Hunt in February 1984 symbolized a new stage in the BR's involvement with Middle East affairs, the BR related to the Palestinian problem only in the most general of terms.

In operative terms, there is still no clear-cut answer to the question of who actually killed Hunt. Some researchers believe that FARL terrorists carried out the operation while the BR simply provided a political/ideological cover and logistical assistance. Although Abdou, a FARL leader, was accused of organizing the attack, the Italian courts, were unable to prove her involvement, and ultimately reduced the charge to that of smuggling explosives. In any case, the BR role in this incident was bound up with its struggle against American and NATO intervention in the Mediterranean and the Middle East, and Italy's role therein, as indicated by the slogans scattered throughout the leaflet.

2.   International and regional factors

The BR tendency to determine its revolutionary strategy in terms of international conditions, as indicated in the RDS of February 1978, found concrete expression with the 1981 kidnapping of Gen. Dozier, the first operation against a foreign national on Italian soil. The conclusion of the 1980 document 'The Bee and the Communist', had called on the BR to attack NATO and its special anti-guerrilla units, extricate Italy from the imperialist network, bring Italy round to a position of non-alignment, and develop proletarian internationalism.

The document clarifying the strategy behind the kidnapping of Gen. Dozier and the ideological reasons for alliances with revolutionary forces and other terrorist organizations was published in November 1981.[70] According to the BR-PCC, the historical process that would lead towards a third world war had been set in motion, and Europe was at the heart of this process. They saw the election of President Reagan and the continuation of the veteran Soviet leadership as a desire on the part of the two superpowers to tighten their hold on their respective areas of control. West European countries, which were showing increasing signs of independence, and some 'sub-imperialist' nations, primarily Israel, supported this trend, in particular in the Mediterranean region. Europe was effectively regarded as the third imperialist power.

According to the BR-PCC, the Mediterranean region was important to the two superpowers politically, militarily and economically. American interest in the region was regarded as twofold: to renew its military superiority in the area via NATO, and to counteract Soviet expansionism, as recently witnessed in North

---

[70] The document was written by the '16 March ideological group' which included imprisoned members of the BR-PCC faction, and which carried out the kidnapping. Quotations from the document have been freely rendered by the author.

Africa, the Horn of Africa, and Angola. The centerpiece of Reagan's strategy was the redeployment of ballistic missiles in Italy, West Germany, and Britain. This strategy was implemented by means of NATO, through the establishment of military units in all NATO countries, in case a Middle East offensive became necessary.

The document asserted that revolutionary movements had to work together with all democratic movements opposed to imperialism, and all movements and organizations which were in conflict with American imperialism, 'first and foremost the fighting vanguards of the heroic Palestinian people. The Palestinians were important in terms of their historical experience and their protracted struggle against American imperialism (and Zionism)' (parentheses in source). In particular, 'the Palestinian problem is a fundamental contributory factor to the undermining of the Middle East and indeed of Europe in general. In this context, it is essential to support all offshoots of the Palestinian movement, irrespective of their ideology'. In conclusion, the party's internationalist line advocated unity with all anti-imperialist movements and *alliances* with all anti-imperialist states in a situation of *true and effective* non-alignment (emphases in source).

Even the *movimentisti* faction, the P-GPM led by Senzani, emphasized the importance of international factors in determining overall strategy, although its analysis differed from that of the BR-PCC. In December 1981 the group of detainees known as the 'Palmi prison brigade', authors of 'The Bee and the Communist', wrote another document entitled 'Crisis, War and Proletarian Internationalism'. However, this document put much greater emphasis on the economic causes of the imperialist historical crisis.

Neither faction fully accomplished its strategic goals in the short term. Although the BR-PCC kidnapped Gen. Dozier a month after publishing its document, it regarded his release as a serious setback. The P-GPM also suffered several knocks in the course of 1982, from which it never recovered. The BR-PCC on the other hand, was back in operation by the end of 1983. It orchestrated or helped orchestrate the murder of Hunt in early 1984, and tried to implement its new strategy of Euro-terrorism in 1984-88. In the process, it had to contend with further splits.

V.   1985-90: THE DUAL PATH – INNER STRUGGLE VERSUS THE EUROPEAN FRONT

From March 1984 the fragmentation within the BR-PCC continued, now between the majority faction known as the First Position (Prima Posizione), which retained the organization's name, and the minority faction, or Second Position (Seconda Posizione). The differences between the two factions became known after publication of a long tract entitled 'An Important Political Struggle is being Waged within the Revolutionary Italian Avant-garde'.[71]

The majority faction, the BR-PCC, remained faithful to the original ideology of the organization. Priority was given to armed military operations and to the strategy of 'long-term civil war' led by the communist avant-garde, on the assumption that the masses were not yet mature enough to take revolutionary initiatives. Ideologically, the faction was close to other European terrorist organizations and revolutionary movements outside Europe that had declared war on NATO and American imperialism. It was a 'militaristic' faction, which attacked the 'idealism' of the right (P-GPM) and the 'impatience' of the left (the Second Position).[72]

From 1986 the Second Position called itself the Red Brigades – Union of Combatant Communists (Brigate Rosse – Unione dei Comunisti Combattenti – BR-UCC), and advocated strategic ties with all social classes interested in the revolutionary struggle. According to members of this faction, the first task of the true revolutionary was to carry out the revolution in his or her country, and thereby further the cause of proletarian internationalism. Solidarity with Marxist-Leninist liberation movements was to be preferred.[73]

After 1985 some Italian revolutionaries exiled in France began to return to Italy, exploiting the fact that the police and security forces were preoccupied with fighting the Mafia and organized crime.[74] Once again terrorist attacks increased, in particular robberies, which were always a useful way of obtaining funds. In one of the attacks, a senior Italian economist was killed.

Meanwhile, a number of top BR militants (from both factions) were arrested. Politically, attempts were made to penetrate the ranks of the pacifist and ecological protest movements. During 1986 a number of 'non-repentant' terrorists returned, and further ideological clarifications took place between the two factions, accompanied by the publication of voluminous documents.

In February 1986 the BR-PCC was responsible for murdering the former mayor of Florence, Lando Conti, and for the attempted murder of Prime Minister Craxi's advisor. In March 1987 Gen. Giorgieri was murdered in Rome by the BR-UCC. This was followed by publication of a document entitled 'How to Get Out of the Emergency Situation', the last ideological text before the arrest of the faction's Strategic Directorate in June 1987.

---

[71] The rift occurred in December 1984, but only became officially known in March 1985, when the new organ, *Il Bollettino*, published the text. See also *Ligne Rouge*, No. 16, October 1985.

[72] See Raufer, *La Storia poco conosciuta delle Brigate Rosse*, pp. 35-37.

[73] According to Raufer, members of the faction were a new generation of BR, dogmatic Stalinists under Balserani's leadership. See Raufer, *La Storia poco conosciuta delle Brigate Rosse*, p. 37.

[74] Ibid., p. 38.

In October 1987 some of the BR-PCC's 'toughest' leaders, including Balser-ani, published a document in which they admitted that 'political and social changes in Italy and, in particular, developments in international relations, invalidated our revolutionary project and strategy'. On 16 April 1988 the assassi-nation of the Italian senator Rufillini marked the end of the BR-PCC's terrorist career for that decade.[75]

1.   Cooperation with Palestinian organizations

During this period there was no logistical or operational cooperation between either of the two BR factions, on the one hand, and Palestinian organizations, on the other. Ideological cooperation or solidarity found its clearest expression during the assassination of Conti in February 1986. The leaflet claiming responsi-bility for the murder described the Italian minister of defense, Spadolini, as a 'Zionist pig', who encouraged weapons exports to Israeli Zionists, and as an avid supporter of American policy in the Mediterranean. The organization called for war against NATO and for all guerrilla movements in Europe and the Middle East to unite in an armed struggle against imperialism.[76]

From the cessation of terrorist activity in 1988 until the end of the decade, many declarations of support for the struggle of the Palestinian people, and later of the intifada, appeared in *Il Bollettino* and *CONTROinformazione Internazion-ale*.[77]

2.   International and regional factors

The BR-PCC's international strategic positions were described in the RDS No. 20 of March 1985, which emphasized the European revolutionary front, and the struggle against NATO.[78] The document mentioned problems arising from growing Italian involvement in the Mediterranean and the Middle East. Italy's consistently pro-Arab policy clashed with the US-Israel axis. The Italian govern-ment was responsible for several independent initiatives in the international arena,

---

[75]   Ibid., p. 49.

[76]   According to Della Porta, the attack was meant to protest Spadolini's pro-Israel policy. The Conti family owned a radar factory. Conti was former mayor of Florence and a close friend of Defense Minister Spadolini, leader of the Republican Party (PRI), who was considered the most pro-American and pro-Israeli Italian politician at the time. See Della Porta, *Il Terrorismo di Sinistra*, p. 261.

[77]   Six such declarations were published in 1988, five declarations or sympathetic articles in 1989, and a special edition of *CONTROinformazione* carrying an interview with George Habash on the intifada, in November 1990.

[78]   The document was left at the murder scenes of the DC Professor of Economics, Enzio Tarantelli (27 March 1985) and of the former mayor of Florence, Laudo Conti (10 February 1986).

including a meeting between Prime Minister Craxi, Foreign Minister Andreotti and PLO Chairman Yasser Arafat. According to the document, Spadolini's appointment as defense minister, with American backing, ensured that Western interests would be better served. Interestingly, the RDS did not refer to Middle Eastern affairs in any depth; nor did it mention the Palestinian people. Anti-Zionist references emphasis appeared only in February 1986, in a leaflet claiming responsibility for Conti's murder.[79] This apparent lack of interest was probably due to the focus of BR factions on the internal debate and the BR-PCC's policy of rapprochement with the European anti-imperialist front.

Important evidence indicates that at some point after the outbreak of the intifada in December 1987, the BR-PCC leadership considered forming an alliance with Palestinian organizations. Its aim was to fight the 'united front' policy of Western Europe and NATO, in particular in the Middle East. Its point of departure was that both European and Palestinian revolutionary organizations aimed to strike a blow at imperialism, whatever its guise. This position was presented at a meeting with RAF representatives in an attempt to draft a cooperation agreement with the RAF. Indeed, Western European intervention in the Middle East against the Lebanese and Palestinian peoples was mentioned in the declaration of a partnership between the RAF and the BR in September 1988.[80]

In the course of 1988, the BR-PCC reviewed its policy in favor of the Palestinian struggle and in firm opposition to elements in the PLO who were prepared to join in the negotiation process with Israel. One of the statements asserted, 'Palestine in flames is the symbol of long-term struggle, and invokes the practical implications of internationalism'.[81] Italian policy in the region, even when it supported the negotiation process, was perceived as pro-American, pro-Zionist, and opposed to Palestinian interests.[82] Due to the arrest of the BR-PCC leaders in September of that year, and the subsequent end of terrorist activity, the agreement with the RAF and the putative coalition with the Palestinians were never implemented.

VI.   ANALYSIS OF RESEARCH ASSUMPTIONS

The BR documents clearly indicate that most of the time the BR felt threatened by the national bourgeoisie, the Italian security forces, the broader front of US-led

---

[79]   See note 77.

[80]   See Yonah Alexander and A. Dennis Pluchinsky (eds.), *Europe's Red Terrorists: The Fighting Communist Organizations* (London: Frank Cass, 1992), p. 229.

[81]   Note that *Il Bollettino* of September 1988 carried four statements of various groups affiliated with the BR-PCC in support of the Palestinian struggle.

[82]   See *Il Bollettino*, No. 34, September 1988, p. 23.

imperialism, and governmental and 'anti-revolutionary' forces in Western Europe, the Mediterranean or the Middle East. It therefore seemed natural to turn to other revolutionary organizations in Europe and worldwide for support and assistance.

1.   Influence of the variables at the international and regional level

It is difficult to assess whether tension within the bipolar system deepened the BR's sense of its own vulnerability and encouraged it to cooperate with other organizations due to the BR's ambivalence towards the communist bloc. The USSR and its satellites were perceived as a social-imperialist bloc, competing with Western imperialism for control of strategic geographical regions, commercial markets and raw materials. Nevertheless, throughout the period in question, Western imperialism was considered the real enemy of the revolutionary forces and the proletariat worldwide. Differences of opinion emerged between the various factions, particularly between the PCC and the UCC, concerning the dangers of social-imperialism. The more leftist faction (the UCC) saw the USSR as the most serious threat to the unity of the revolutionary camp and to revolutionary ideology, since it forced revolutionaries to serve the interests of Soviet foreign policy. However, it was the PCC position that won out in most debates, and which influenced the Euro-terrorist strategy of the BR in the mid-1980s.

Until 1975 the BR focused inwards. Its activities were limited to campaigns in factories, the battle against the ruling bourgeoisie and the 'quisling' trade unions, and clashes with right-wing opponents on the streets. It was only in April 1975 that the organization first presented a strategic analysis of the international situation. According to this, the imperialist crisis was due to three contradictions: between imperialism on the one hand, and communism and national liberation struggles on the other; between Western imperialism and Soviet social-imperialism; and between imperialism and the fighting revolutionary guerrillas in metropolitan centers.

In the RDS of April 1975, the BR leadership upheld communist China's belief in a worldwide trend towards revolution (in the wake of the revolutionary victories in Vietnam, Cambodia, and Portugal). Italy, regarded as the weak link in the imperialist chain, was considered fertile ground for revolution. This explains why the BR directed its attacks against domestic targets in 1975-78 and showed little interest in international affairs.

The RDS of February 1978 stated that the period of 'armed peace', during which the guerrillas had focused mainly on armed propaganda, was over, and that the period of 'war' [sic] had begun in earnest. During this period, imperialism gave priority to class oppression, while the revolutionary forces gave priority to revolutionary civil war.

According to the document, the Italian forces of oppression, as recipients of assistance from other nations within the imperialist chain, were the obvious targets for the revolutionary struggle. To this end, it was necessary to cooperate with other revolutionary forces in a similar position. This explains the call for solidarity with the RAF and, in particular, with the Palestinians. But evidently, more was required. It was necessary to 'initiate new techniques to destroy the forces of imperialism, and break them down politically and militarily'. The kidnapping of Moro was one such technique, aimed at undermining the new political system that had evolved after the 'unholy alliance' between the DC and the PCI.

According to the document published by the BR-PCC in late 1981, the Reagan administration and Western Europe chose to strengthen NATO as the main weapon in the 'war between Western and Eastern imperialism', and the Middle East as their immediate scene of action (the attack against Libya in the Gulf of Sirte). Therefore obstruction of NATO and Italian involvement in the Middle East (Lebanon, Malta, and Sinai) became a BR strategic goal.[83] This was translated into the kidnapping of Gen. Dozier, an operation that closely followed the publication of the aforementioned document. Leaflet No. 1, claiming responsibility for the kidnapping of the general emphasized the need to close ranks and cooperate with the Palestinian and progressive Lebanese forces in the Middle East. (This was also the case with the murder of Hunt in February 1984).

Clearly, the PCC and UCC differed on this issue.[84] Since, according to the UCC, the failure of the guerrilla movement stemmed from its alienation from the working class, it decided to focus its efforts once again on internal and social issues. In March 1987, following the murder of an Italian air force general, the UCC appeared to have changed its positions and drawn somewhat closer to the strategy of Euro-terrorism. The subsequent crackdown on the UCC by the security forces completely paralyzed it.

Between 1984-88, the PCC faithfully continued the strategy of the European revolutionary front, with an occasional sidelong glance at Middle Eastern and Palestinian affairs. Changes in the Middle East, the burgeoning peace process, the PLO role within it, and the outbreak of the intifada, once again stirred PCC interest in the Middle East, especially after the disintegration of the communist bloc.

The evolution of the BR's international strategy over the three periods corroborates several of the research assumptions (see Chapter 2).

Tension within the bipolar system (whether it was social-imperialism or the revolutionary forces versus Western imperialism), intensified the BR's sense of vulnerability, and encouraged it to seek alliances (Hypothesis 1).

---

[83]   See 'Contro la guerra imperialista, intensificare la guerra rivoluzionaria.
[84]   See 'Crisi, guerra e internazionalismo proletario.'

Regional wars or conflicts, such as the Lebanese War or the American offensive against Libya in the Gulf of Sirte, encouraged the BR to seek regional allies in an attempt to enhance its position in the struggle against the state (Italian intervention in the Middle East, for example) or a rival power (American imperialism, the occupying Zionists, etc.) (Hypothesis 3).

Counter-insurgency cooperation between security forces at the international or regional level encouraged the BR to seek alliances and coalitions with other terrorist organizations (Hypothesis 4). This was particularly noticeable in 1978-79 and during the implementation of Reagan's international counter-insurgency policy on a worldwide and European scale.

The assumption that rifts between great powers sharing the same ideology (the USSR and the People's Republic of China) and the emergence of new revolutionary foci (the guerrillas in Latin America) encouraged the formation of coalitions was not borne out in the case of the BR (Hypothesis 2). There are a number of reasons for this. If there was any Chinese influence on the BR, it was the attempt by Chinese students during the Cultural Revolution to draw closer to the workers, a trend that the BR tried to emulate;[85] inasmuch as Chinese ideology still had an effect on the revolutionary forces before its capitulation to the American administration in the mid-1970s, it convinced the BR leadership that the world in general, and Italy in particular, were approaching the revolutionary stage. Therefore, unlike the RAF, the BR focused its struggle in Italy, the weak link in the imperialist chain, not on the Third World.[86]

2.   Influence of the variables at the organizational level

A.   Ideology as a cohesive force?

Among the hypotheses of this research, it was argued that a common ideological basis between two terrorist organizations encourages the formation of an alliance between them (Hypothesis 5). The common ideology that led the BR to express solidarity with seemingly different revolutionary forces, such as the RAF, the IRA, Fatah or, from the early 1980s, militant Islamic movements, was proletarian internationalism, in the broadest sense of the term, namely solidarity with all revolutionary forces which opposed Western imperialism, particularly the US. This belief was expressed most clearly in the RDS of April 1978.

---

[85]   See Mario Capanna, *Formidabili quegli anni* (Milano: Rizzoli, 1988), pp. 47-57.
[86]   Moreover, the three founders of the BR – Curcio, Cagol, and Franceschini – began their political career as members of the pro-Chinese Italian Marxist-Leninist Communist Party (PCd'l-ml). Soon disenchanted with the ineffectiveness and elitism of the party leaders, they abandoned it in order to set up the CPM, the nucleus of the future BR.

According to Savasta, the theory of proletarian internationalism accounted for a similar interpretation of international events by the PLO and the BR. Hence, the generous donation of weapons by the PLO to the BR. Proletarian internationalism, however, did not eliminate the strategic and tactical differences of opinion with other organizations and movements that embraced the same ideology. On the contrary, differences between organizations that are very close ideologically can actually hinder rapprochement and practical cooperation. As far as BR-Palestinian relations were concerned, it is clear that solidarity was determined by the role of Palestinian organizations in the struggle against imperialism in the Middle East and the Mediterranean. As stated, however, proletarian internationalism did not automatically entail close operational cooperation. As Savasta explained, the BR turned down the Palestinians' request to attack Israelis in Italy, on the grounds that such an operation would not effect the balance of power within Italy. Operational cooperation which held no practical strategic goal for the organization concerned was condemned by the BR as 'proletarian internationalism of the most outmoded kind'.[87]

What finally influenced the BR decision to cooperate with a Palestinian organization was not the latter's ideological platform but rather its practical contribution to the cause of 'proletarian internationalism'. In this context, it is noteworthy that none of the BR publications referred to a specific Palestinian organization by name, but only to the Palestinian people or the Palestinians in general (unlike the IRA, ETA, etc., which were mentioned by name). Savasta also pointed out that the BR chose to establish ties with the PLO rather than with the PFLP, which was ideologically closer to the BR. This was because the BR saw ties with Arafat as part of a broader strategic process that included attacking Israel, 'the gendarme of imperialism' in the Mediterranean, and helping the Palestinian people to obtain autonomy (sic). Michele Galati, in his legal deposition, declared that from a strategic and ideological viewpoint, the Marxist-Leninist PFLP was far closer to the BR. Nonetheless, the BR had no illusions that any form of cooperation, in particular any material assistance, was possible without the express authorization of the PLO leaders.[88]

According to the BR-PCC, anyone who believed that politics stemmed from ideology 'was totally mistaken'.[89] Therefore, after analyzing the centrality of the Palestinians in the anti-imperialist and anti-American struggle, it concluded that all streams of the Palestinian movement, irrespective of ideological affiliation, deserved its support. The BR-PCC, although supported all struggles against the

---

[87] See Savasta's Deposition 5/23.
[88] See *Ministero dell'Interno*, p. 152.
[89] See 'Contro la guerra imperialista, intensificare la guerra rivoluzionaria,' p. 8.

twin evils of colonialism and Zionism, it also held that initiatives that objectively weakened these struggles must be condemned.[90]

The BR-UCC, on the other hand, did not completely rule out the possibility of tactical alliances, but opposed cooperation with non-Marxist-Leninist liberation movements. Although it never abandoned the idea of the proletarian international, it believed that many years of hard work were necessary before this could come about. The alternative was a half-baked 'spontaneous' movement that did not espouse true Marxism-Leninism.

The hypothesis that organizations whose revolutionary social ideology stressed the seizure of power in their countries are reluctant to enter coalitions with other organizations is true in the case of the BR, as witnessed by the BR's policies until 1978, and as expressed in the RDS of 1975 (Hypothesis 7). Factions like the UCC, which later decided to focus on internal affairs, almost completely abandoned the international arena, making do with vague ideological declarations of solidarity with other struggles. Proletarian internationalism was to be postponed to some time in the future on the grounds that this was the only way to preserve the true spirit of Marxism-Leninism.

Note that most radical left-wing organizations in Europe were small, anarcho-communist organizations. The BR, on the other hand, was a large organization, particularly up to 1982-83, when many of its activists were arrested. The BR ideology and strategy always comprised nihilistic or anarchistic elements, particularly its idea of the armed party which demanded the systematic destruction of society, without proposing any alternative in its place.[91]

These anarchist tendencies found more concrete expression once the organization abandoned the working-class struggle to focus mainly on the struggle against security forces (Hypothesis 6). To this end, it did not hesitate to use criminal elements (even exploiting the good services of the Mafia in the Cirillo affair), or to take revenge on 'informers' or their relatives, such as Peci's brother. Although it is impossible to prove that this was the reason behind its willingness to strengthen ties with other organizations, there is no doubt that the somewhat anarchical atmosphere of the times (1970-82) helped it to seriously consider similar organizations, such as the RAF or AD, as potential allies.

---

[90]   Interestingly, this statement was made in the context of what attitude to adopt towards the Kurdish Nationalist Movement, whose struggle for autonomy was regarded as 'objectively' weakening the struggle of the Iranian Islamic régime against American imperialism!

[91]   Ventura emphasized that in most European countries, terrorist organizations comprised a small group of marginal fanatics. The armed struggle in Italy, on the other hand, drew thousands of activists, a broad stratum of collaborators and sympathizers, and won the 'understanding' and sympathetic neutrality of a number of intellectual circles. See Ventura, 'Il problema delle origini del terrorismo di sinistra,' pp. 114-15.

3.   Influence of variables at the decision-maker level

Hypothesis 12 suggested that the antisemitic and racist attitudes of leaders of terrorist organizations affect their decision to cooperate against Israel and/or Jews. BR documents, however, were devoid of antisemitic undertones; the organization and all its splinter groups attacked Israel and Zionism on a political level only. The only antisemitic publications, including some that supported Holocaust denial, belonged to autonomous or Maoist groups close to BR ideology.[92] In all BR publications and leaflets studied, only one article showed antisemitic undertones.[93] It is therefore very unlikely that antisemitism played any part in the pro-Palestinian or anti-Israeli position of the various BR factions. Likewise, none of the testimonies or depositions indicates that any of the organization's leaders entertained antisemitic views.

Unlike the RAF, the BR was an important organization of European stature. It was, in effect, the number one revolutionary organization in Europe. And yet, it could not compare to Palestinian organizations, in particular Fatah, in terms of resources and influence. The BR's awareness of its inferiority *vis-à-vis* the PLO may well have accounted for its reluctance to form a coalition with an organization that had attained the status of a 'non-state nation'.

As far back as the early 1970s, when RAF members were known to have established ties with Palestinian organizations, BR leaders believed that the unequal power of the two organizations would work against the RAF, and lead to its domination by the stronger Palestinian organizations.[94] Therefore, when the PLO first approached BR leaders, the latter were at first suspicious, especially since Arafat at the time was keen to court the Western Europe states, as witnessed by his unofficial meeting with Aldo Moro, the Italian prime minister.

Nonetheless, the BR agreed to cooperate with the PLO/Fatah and its leader Moretti even agreed, in principle, to carry out attacks against Israeli targets on Italian soil. This commitment was never fulfilled, despite the fact that the PLO honored its own commitment to provide the BR with large stocks of weapons. This demonstrates that in an alliance between a stronger and weaker party, the weaker party is not necessarily dependent on the stronger one, and retains the option of taking its own, independent decisions (Hypothesis 10). As Savasta attempted to explain to the examining magistrate: since the PLO represented a people fighting against imperialism, the power struggle was equal, and no single

---

92   See, for example, the booklet entitled 'Israele, il sionismo, gli ebrei' published by Gruppo Comunista Internazionalista Autonomo, 1984, Milan, which expressed support for the views of the Holocaust denier Paul Rassinier.

93   See note 65.

94   See Buonavita's testimony, *Ministero dell'Interno*, p. 4.

party was in a position to manipulate or exploit the other.[95] Peci described how the BR leaders informed the Palestinians in no uncertain terms that they had no intention of becoming their military arm in Italy.[96] The PLO leaders, for their part, understood the position of the Italians, and agreed to provide the promised weapons nevertheless.

VII.   SUMMARY

The cooperation agreement between the BR and PLO/Fatah lasted eighteen months to two years (1978-79). Agreement was reached in an institutionalized manner, as befitted an established, hierarchical organization such as the BR. It is not clear if the decision to establish ties was taken by the leaders alone, or whether it was discussed by the executive, and formally endorsed by the leadership; some internal debate, albeit minimal, did appear to have taken place concerning the strategic and political repercussions of cooperation with a Palestinian organization. What is clear is that only very few BR members were aware of the agreement. Both parties were very sensitive to secrecy. It was this cloak of secrecy that subsequently enabled Arafat to deny any connection with the BR.

Due to the limited scope of cooperation between the two organizations, and the failure to honor important commitments (in particular on the Italian side), the agreement can hardly be defined as a coalition.

---

[95]   See Savasta's Deposition 1/129.
[96]   See Peci's Deposition, *Ministero dell'Interno*, p. 273.

CHAPTER 5
FRANCE – *ACTION DIRECTE*

I.   HISTORICAL BACKGROUND

France, unlike West Germany and Italy, did not witness domestic terrorism until the late 1970s, despite widespread workers' strikes, the student riots of May 1968, a particularly brutal police force, and one of the world's most conservative communist parties. Even the radical Maoist Proletarian Left (Gauche Prolétari-enne – GP), with its program of violence (kidnappings and bombings) failed to evolve into the equivalent of either the RAF or BR. This may have been because the events of May 1968 were not perceived by the French public as a reaction to fascism, but rather as the natural outcome of a long democratic tradition.[1]

The French student protest movement emerged in late 1967 at the University of Nanterre. It grew out of a general sense of dissatisfaction with living conditions on campus and the strict discipline that was enforced there. What brought matters to a head, however, was the introduction of undercover police agents on campus by the authorities. Although some anarchist and Trotskyist elements joined the movement, most of its members were unaffiliated. On the contrary, they were as wary of fly-by-night groups as they were of the fossilized French Communist Party (Parti Communiste Français – PCF).

The riots soon spread to the Latin quarter of Paris and the Sorbonne. Harsh anti-riot measures by the police caused the protests to escalate, as an increasing number of students joined the protest movement. The regime of Gen. Charles de Gaulle was initially unable to find a suitable response to this pre-revolutionary situation. However, after enlisting the support of the military command in Germany, and of the middle classes in France, de Gaulle's comeback led to new economic and political measures that broke the strike and the protest movement.

Unlike Germany and Italy, the French terrorist movement was not born of the student revolt of 1967-68. The only serious radical organization, Action Directe (AD), began to operate in 1978-80 during a period of transition. The imminent collapse of the presidency of Giscard d'Estaing (an uncharismatic technocrat) ushered in hopes of a change of government after twelve years of Gaullist rule. François Mitterand's rise to power in 1981 in a socialist coalition with the PCF raised the expectations of the New Left while sowing anxiety in right-wing circles. The French government, which in the 1970s had had to contend with

---

[1]   See Peter Fritsche, 'Terrorism in the Federal Republic of Germany and Italy: Legacy of the 68 Movement or "Burden of Fascism"?', *Terrorism and Political Violence*, Vol. 1, No. 4 (1989), p. 479.

imported terror only (particularly from the Middle East), was taken unawares. Not only was domestic terrorism hitherto unknown, but France had actually provided a refuge for political fugitives, including West German and Italian terrorists.

The AD was founded in early 1978 by a group of young people experienced in revolutionary or armed activity. It recruited members from other defunct organizations such as the Proletarian Left – New Popular Resistance (Gauche Prolétarienne – Nouvelle Résistance Populaire – GN-NRP), the Internationalist Revolutionary Action Groups (Groupes d'Action Révolutionnaire Internationaliste – GARI), the Armed Cells for Popular Autonomy (Noyaux Armés pour l'Autonomie Populaire – NAPAP), and the International Brigades (Brigades Internationales – BI), as well as the autonomy movements.

The anarchist organization GARI was set up in 1974 by Jean-François Rouillan near Toulouse, on the Spanish border, in order to undermine Franco's dictatorship in Spain. The GP and NAPAP were both short-lived organizations that did not engage in any serious terrorist activity. The BI, which was only active from 1974-76, murdered foreign – particularly South American – diplomats in France who were involved in anti-guerrilla activity back home. Some of the top AD activists – including Rouillan's girlfriend, Nathalie Ménigon – were drawn from the ranks of the autonomy movements.[2]

II.   TYPOLOGICAL DEFINITION

If any terrorist organization deserves the title of anarcho-communist, it is the AD. As stated, its leader and some of its founders were key actors in the anarchist movement GARI. One of the organization's principal activists was the anarchist Max Frérot, who not only had contacts with the underworld, but carried out lone attacks when other organization members were imprisoned.[3]

The organization's name – Action Directe – was derived from the term coined in 1887 by the French anarchist Fernand Pelloutier. He advocated gaining control over the trade unions (direct action) rather than the use of terror which, he claimed, simply discredited the movement. It was thus that French anarcho-

---

[2]   See also the AD document, *Short Collective Biography of Action Directe Prisoners* by Joëlle Aubron (jailed AD militant), July 1996 at <http://www.tao.ca/~solidarity/texts/ad/collbio.html>.

[3]   Aubron wrote about Rouillan: He 'joined the anarcho-communist movement, notably the Autonomous Libertarian Groups (Groupes Autonomes Libertaires – it is important to note that in Europe the word 'libertarian' is not associated solely with anarcho-capitalism as in the US, but also with left-wing anarchism and anti-authoritarianism)'. Menigon joined the autonomous communist group 'Camarades' (Comrades), which called for anti-capitalist and anti-imperialist social revolt and lent its support to the Italian guerilla movement. Ibid. See also Jean-Francois Gayraud, 'Histoire politique d'une Organisation Communiste Combatante', *Notes et Etudes*, No. 7/8 (Oct. 1988), p. 21.

syndicalism – a doctrine that refrained from systematic violence, but did not totally rule out revolutionary violence – was born. The element of anarchism was evident in the AD's first ideological document, which analyzed the political/economic reality in Marxist-Leninist terms.[4] In it, the AD proposed the establishment of 'workers committees' (*conseils ouvriers*) that would 'combine Marxist analysis with anarchist practice'.[5] During its relatively short existence (early 1978 to February 1987), the AD underwent several transformations, revised its ideology and targets, and divided into splinter groups. The radical changes in strategy form natural divisions between the various periods.

III.   THE ANARCHIST PERIOD (1978-80)

The AD chose a symbolic date – 1 May 1979 – to carry out its first attack, against the headquarters of the Association of French Industrialists. Subsequent attacks were directed at institutions that the AD held responsible for growing unemployment, inflation and housing shortages (the Inland Revenue, the Ministry of Labor, the Department of Social Security, etc.), at 'the forces of oppression' (police and law courts), or at symbols of the consumer society (selling luxury goods shops). Armed robbery to 'finance the revolution' was also a frequent tactic (nine robberies were staged within two years).[6]

During this period, the AD consisted of a loose cluster of small groups which tried to appeal to politically aware, unemployed youngsters who belonged to the autonomy movement and were not averse to violence.[7] This is borne out by the names of the AD cells: the Committee for the Liquidation or Deterrence of Computers (CLODO), Angry Lambs, Young Mole, etc. At this early stage, their activities were directed against property, rather than live targets. Statements and leaflets were typically laconic and to the point. According to one AD militant: 'In 1980, even though the autonomist group that [she] was a part of participated in AD actions and lent our logistical support, its members were not members of Action Directe'.[8]

Right from the start, the AD was interested only in those international issues that had a bearing on the plight of African immigrants in France. In March 1980 the AD planted a bomb near the offices of the Direction de la Surveillance du

---

[4]   *Pour un projet communiste*, Action Directe, March 1982.

[5]   Ibid., p. 11.

[6]   See *Short Collective Biography of Action Directe Prisoners*.

[7]   See Michael Dartnell, *Action Directe: Ultra-leftist Terrorism in France, 1979-1987*, (London: Frank Cass, 1995), p. 458.

[8]   See Aubron's description of her status in the AD, in *Short Collective Biography of Action Directe Prisoners*.

Territoire (Directorate of Territorial Security – DST), the French Security Service in Paris. The leaflet deposited at the scene bore the following message: 'After Kolwezi, Gafsa and Djibouti, regards from Barbès'. This reflects the perceived link between French policy in Zaïre and Djibouti (where there was a large French marine base) and the situation of the Arab and African immigrants living in the run-down Barbès-Rochechouart quarter of Paris.[9]

Three days later, the French Ministry of Cooperation was attacked 'for its neo-colonialist' activity in Chad and the Central African Republic. According to the AD, global armed action against 'slave trader countries' was not only justified, but was actually regarded as a revolutionary obligation. 'The struggle against French imperialist policy in Africa is part of the struggle against state institutions in general.'[10]

April 1980 saw the arrest of AD members and the confiscation of weapons and about 1600 kg. of explosives. Rouillan and his girlfriend Nathalie Ménigon, both of whom were arrested in September 1980, accepted responsibility for all AD operations. Prior to their arrest, they had apparently been willing to develop ties with foreign terrorist organizations, as demonstrated by the trap laid for them by the police: a meeting with the notorious international terrorist 'Carlos' to plan the blowing up of the Aswan Dam in Egypt. Following the incarceration of most of its members, the AD lay low until mid-1981, when the newly elected socialist president, François Mitterand, granted an amnesty for the imprisoned terrorists.

IV.   RESTRUCTURING, PRO-PALESTINIAN ACTIVITY, AND SCHISM (1981-82)

1.   Restructuring

The amnesty and the inauguration of the new socialist government in France did little to dampen the revolutionary fervor of AD members, most of whom lived in Parisian slums alongside squatters and North African and Turkish immigrants (some of whom joined the restructured organization). During 1981 and early 1982, AD members restricted their activities to armed robberies in order to fund future operations, while continuing the ideological debates that had begun in prison. The first real attacks following their release took place in November 1981.[11]

---

[9]   Ibid., p. 459.
[10] Ibid., p. 460.
[11] On 23 November 1981, four bombs were planted near prestigious stores in Paris in time for the pre-Christmas shopping rush, and on 13 February 1982 the AD carried out its first murder, that of a Lebanese painter suspected of being a police agent.

Gayraud claimed that, in view of the naïveté that had led to their wholesale arrest, AD leaders were forced to do some serious thinking.[12] They concluded that the struggle could only be continued by basing activities on the models of the German and Italian FCOs and Marxist-Leninist ideology. In the summer of 1981 their journal *Rebelles* (Rebels) carried vitriolic diatribes against the social democratic government and called for armed struggle against the bourgeoisie.

The period ended in March 1982 when the AD published its first ideological document entitled 'For a Communist Project'. According to Gayraud, this was supposed to provide an intellectual front for the organization's former illegal activities.[13] This, in turn, would facilitate its metamorphosis into a full-time, disciplined, clandestine organization that was 'going international'. In April of that year, the AD published a second ideological document, entitled 'On American Imperialism', which clearly mirrored a change in strategy.[14]

'For a Communist Project' devoted two chapters to organizational issues. It proposed that 'workers committees' (soviets) would bring the struggle to the factories and inner city areas. The third chapter described the three main areas of involvement (*axes d'intervention*) in which capitalist reorganization was to take part: imperialism and immigration, unemployment and economic growth, and housing.

The chapter on imperialism argued that the French colonial past had evolved into a neo-colonialism based on technological superiority and deliberate suppression of indigenous culture among the oppressed nations of the Third World. French imperialism, however, was regarded as subordinate to the US and its institutions of control (the IMF, the World Bank). Although French imperialists were regarded as wielding power over the Third World, they were themselves subject to the dictates of the EC and American multinational corporations.

The document went on to describe how imperialism, already weakened in the jungles of Vietnam, was further winded by the oil crisis of the mid-1970s. The election of President Reagan (the 'cowboy' president) in the US ushered in a new international economic order, characterized by a tougher policy toward the Third World and the fledgling Fourth World (including the world's poorest nations), and by renewed arrogance in North-South relations.

The chapter ended with a call for a united struggle against all forms of imperialism – American, French and Soviet. The document pointed out that although Soviet imperialism was usually overlooked, it played a key role within oppressor-oppressed relationships on a global plane, just like American imperialism. For example, the USSR used the same techniques as the US to control COMECON,

---

12 See Gayraud, 'Histoire politique d'une Organisation Communiste Combatante,' p. 22.
13 Ibid.
14 See *Pour un projet communiste*, Action Directe, March 1982 and *Sur l'imperialisme Americain*, Action Directe, April 1982.

the economic organization of the communist countries. It did not balk at direct or indirect military intervention (like in Poland and Afghanistan) and had recently even appeared ready to join forces with the US against Third World countries. In short, the document concluded, there was no such thing as 'good' imperialism. Imperialism, whatever its guise, had to be destroyed by the international proletariat.

The second ideological text, focusing on American imperialism, was published in May 1982 before the Versailles Conference of industrialized nations. The conference was described as paving the way for the establishment of 'a new international economic order' under America, with the participation of France. The document provided a chronological breakdown of European and Japanese imperialism, following the oil crisis of the late 1970s. It concluded that what kept imperialism alive was not power per se, but the ability to maintain a leading edge in the consumer and high-tech industries. It was therefore essential that revolutionary organizations outline a correct interpretation of international events in order to formulate a new strategy predicated on the loyalty of all sections of the revolutionary movement.

According to Dartnell, these two ideological documents, the culmination of a long radicalization process, were instrumental in changing the orientation of the AD terrorist strategy.[15] AD offensives between 1982-86 were subsequently directed against targets identified with American, French, Israeli and South African imperialism (commercial companies, diplomatic representations, etc.).[16]

2.   Cooperation with the Palestinian organizations

Researchers and security forces regarded AD as one of the organizations most closely identified with the Palestinian struggle and accused it of actively assisting in terrorist attacks against Israeli and Jewish targets. In August 1982 it was outlawed for having carried out a number of 'anti-Zionist' operations, including the attack against a Jewish restaurant in Paris.[17] Nevertheless, there is little concrete evidence of contacts between the AD and Palestinian organizations. Hamon and Marchand, who had access to police sources, pointed out that police reports were both confusing and unconvincing.[18] These reports mentioned contacts in Grenoble between

---

[15] See Dartnell, *Action Directe: Ultra-leftist Terrorism in France*, p. 468.

[16] See Gayraud, 'Histoire politique d'une Organisation Communiste Combatante,' p. 23.

[17] The attack against the Goldenberg restaurant was carried out on 9 August 1982, and the organization was banned on the 18th of that month. The AD denied responsibility for the attack. It later transpired that the Fatah-Revolutionary Command (Abu Nidal's organization) was behind this attack. See also Ariel Merari and Elad Shlomi, *Paha' Hul: Teror Palestinai be-Hutz la-Aretz* [Palestinian Terror Abroad] (Tel Aviv: United Kibbutz and Jaffee Center for Strategic Studies publication, 1986), p. 177.

[18] See Alain Hamon and Jean-Charles Marchand, *Action Directe. Du terrorisme français a l'euroterrorisme* (Paris: Editions du Seuil, 1986), p. 163.

anarchists who sympathized with the AD and representatives of the PLO office in France. However, most of the testimonies and circumstantial evidence of contacts with Middle Eastern terrorist organizations related to the Lebanese Armed Revolutionary Fractions (Fractions Armées Révolutionnaires Libanaises – FARL).[19]

As noted below, the exact nature of these ties remains unclear. Indeed, until the last in a series of arrests of AD activists in 1986-87, the French police appeared to be groping in the dark. The fact that AD leaders refused to cooperate with their interrogators did not help matters. Their main motive was reluctance to be identified with foreign terrorist organizations that had staged major attacks within French territory. To this day, the AD continues to preach armed struggle against the French regime and against global imperialism.

A.   Ideological cooperation

The AD 'anti-Zionist' attacks began on 31 March 1982. Interestingly, there is no trace of any published expressions of solidarity with the Palestinians prior to this date. Neither of the two ideological documents published during this period mentioned the Palestinian question.[20] Even later, there were few manifestations of ideological solidarity with the Palestinians, other than some leaflets left at the sites of the 'anti-Zionist' attacks.[21] The same was true of *L'internationale*, the monthly associated with the AD, which survived until early 1985. On the other hand, Frédéric Oriach, sentenced to five years imprisonment for his role in the AD terrorist attacks of August 1982, continued to publish pro-Palestinian materials from prison. He was assisted by the Frédéric Oriach Liberation Collective (CLFO), set up immediately after his arrest, the journal *Solidarité anti-impérialiste*, and the private radio station Radio Mouvance.[22]

B.   Logistical cooperation

None of the available data – including interviews with members of the attorney-general's office in Paris – indicate the existence of logistical cooperation between

---

[19] Information on FARL and its connections with the PFLP can be found in Chapter 4. See the description of the kidnapping of Leamon Hunt by the BR-PCC in February 1984.

[20] Even stranger was the fact that the FARL claimed responsibility for the first attack against the Israeli Ministry of Defense delegation in Paris, while the AD denied any involvement with it. A week later, the weapon used in the attack was found in an arms cache belonging to AD activist J. Aubron. Several months later, the organization accepted full responsibility for the attack.

[21] On 3 April 1981 FARL terrorists killed Yaacov Bar Siman-Tov, an Israeli diplomat, in Paris. According to a press report, AD activists in the Parisian quarter *La Goutte d'Or* distributed leaflets in which FARL took responsibility for the attack. See *Le Matin*, 16 April 1982.

[22] These, however, were affiliated with an independent group headed by Oriach, and were not directly connected with the AD.

the AD and Palestinian organizations, or even with the FARL, with which it identified ideologically. Most AD weapons were purchased from members of the underworld, or were stolen from French military warehouses.[23] Some weapons, especially explosives, were provided by European organizations (see Chapter 6). Likewise, money and documents were either stolen or donated by European organizations. There is no evidence that the AD allowed its safe houses to be used either by Palestinian or Lebanese terrorists in France. In any case, the FARL had its own network of hideouts, which it used to store weapons or as operational head-quarters. These apartments were discovered after the arrest of its leader, Georges Ibrahim Abdallah.

C.   Operational cooperation

During 1982 the AD carried out eight attacks against Israeli or Jewish targets in Paris. Apart from the first attack, all were carried out in the space of a month, from 19 July to 19 August, during the height of the Lebanese War.[24] All followed a similar modus operandi: automatic fire aimed at specific buildings or bomb attacks. The targets were property rather than people. The only exception, at least as far as timing went, was the shooting at the office of the Israeli Defense Ministry delegation on 31 March 1984. The AD was also suspected of involve-ment in the murder of Israeli diplomat Yaakov Bar Siman-Tov on 3 April 1982. In both cases, the FARL claimed responsibility while the AD denied any in-volvement. Only later did it transpire beyond any reasonable doubt that the AD was responsible for the attack on the office of the Israeli Defense Ministry but not for the murder.

The AD also carried out five armed robberies in 1982. About two weeks be-fore the shooting of the Israeli Defense Ministry delegation, a Lebanese police informer was murdered, the AD first killing. Four more attacks were carried out in 1982, two against French targets, and two in Paris against the Bank of America and the American School, in May and June 1982 respectively.

---

[23]   See Xavier Raufer, 'Que nous aprennent les archives du 'Groupe Olivier' d'Action Directe?', *Notes et Etudes de l'Institut de Criminologie de Paris*, No. 7/8 (Oct. 1988), p. 30. Raufer focused mainly on André Olivier's 'national' faction.

[24]   31 March: The Israeli Defense Ministry delegation building was shot at; 19 July: A bomb was set off in the 'Leumi Bank' building; 19 July: A bomb detonated in a building housing an im-port/export company with connections with Israel; 1 August: 'The Marcel Rayman fighting unit' opened fire at a parked car belonging to an Israel Embassy security guard (the car was empty); 7 August: 'The Marcel Rayman fighting unit' bombed the 'Discount Bank' building; 7 August: 'The Marcel Rayman fighting unit' bombed a store owned by the NEMOR company, with Israeli connections; 11 August: 'The Lahouari Benchalal Fighting Unit' bombed the Meyer Bank and the CITRUS building; 19 August: 'The Red Panther Unit/Dir Yassin Brigade' bombed the of-fices of the far right journal *Minute*, accused of supporting Israel in the Lebanese War.

3.   Splits within the organization

In order to better understand the motivation of its leaders, it is necessary to describe the various factions that made up the AD. As noted, the AD was a small organization loosely embracing the vestiges of several smaller organizations (the NAPAP, BI, GARI) and various anarchist and autonomous elements.[25] The first schism dated back to 1981, when jailed AD members Rouillan and André Olivier were amnestied by Mitterrand. According to Rouillan, unable to agree on ideological issues, each tried to strengthen his own base (Paris and Lyons, respectively). According to Raufer, the true reason for the split within the AD was the rivalry between the two 'tribal chieftains', Rouillan headed the faction that later became known as 'the international faction' while Oliver headed the so-called 'national faction'.[26]

Most of Rouillan's attacks were directed against international targets and he developed ties with foreign organizations. Raufer, however, argues that there was no essential difference between the two factions since, of the list of proposed targets found in Olivier's possession, 36% were military or NATO targets, too high a percentage for a faction described as 'national'.[27] Note that the list included 24 'Zionist' targets and 30 American ones. In practice, however, the 'national' faction, operating from Lyons, carried out very few operations against foreign targets. An exception was its attack on the Israeli Bank Leumi on 13 April 1985. Typically, the leaflet announcing the attack consisted of a mere five lines.

The AD offensive against Israeli and Jewish targets led to a further schism. During a stormy discussion that took place on 1 August 1982, a number of AD militants accused Rouillan of 'authoritarian and bureaucratic behavior, designed to encourage all units to adopt an aggressive and elitist strategy'. This group favored proletarization, rather than internationalization of the struggle, and split from the AD to form the Revolutionary Collective of 1 August, led by Eric Moreau. This faction was also 'national' in scope and according to Gayraud, was absorbed by the Lyons group when Moreau had to flee France after a shoot-out with the police.[28]

---

[25] According to Raufer, there were, all in all, about 250 activists involved in terrorist attacks, operating intermittently over a period of about 20 years in the various organizations, many of them switching between the organizations. See Raufer, *Que nous aprennent les archives du 'Groupe Olivier'*, pp. 33-4.

[26] Ibid.

[27] Ibid.

[28] See Gayraud, 'Histoire politique d'une Organisation Communiste Combatante', p. 25.

Finally, there was the matter of Frédéric Oriach's status within the AD. Oriach was an unusually intelligent man, who had been active in Maoist groups, had visited Vietnam and been involved with Palestine support committees from the age of 14.[29] As stated, Oriach was arrested in October 1982 and charged with possessing a document claiming responsibility for the AD attacks of the summer of 1982, and about 40 files with information on proposed attacks against Israeli and Jewish targets, including four that were actually implemented in August of that year.[30] Oriach denied any personal involvement in the attacks, arguing that the documents were merely background material for an article on Zionist infiltration into France! Oriach subsequently argued in his writings that he had never belonged to the AD, and was even opposed to it on ideological grounds. Although he blamed the AD for failing to corroborate this, he never actually condemned the revolutionary path itself. Indeed, he claimed to support the AD actions out of a sense of revolutionary solidarity.[31] Oriach was also accused of orchestrating ties between the AD and FARL. It is noteworthy that during the kidnapping of the French diplomat Giles Peyrolles in Beirut in 1985, the FARL requested the release of Oriach, rather than Rouillan or other AD militants.[32] In conclusion, Oriach and his followers were the only ones to express active solidarity with the Palestinian cause.

Some researchers believed, along with the French courts, that Frédéric Oriach was actively involved in AD operations.[33] However, his ideological influence on the AD, particularly his support for the Palestinians and Lebanese, was far more significant. For example, it is interesting that the AD backed down from its pro-Palestinian position after Oriach's arrest and his denial of any connection with the organization. In view of his ideological influence, Oriach's writings could shed light on the AD 'anti-Zionist' policy, at least until his imprisonment. Oriach's prolific pro-Palestinian and anti-Zionist activity, both within prison and after his release, are not relevant for this study, since by then he had obviously severed all ties with the AD.

---

[29] Oriach belonged to NAPAP, and also apparently to BI. In 1978 he was arrested for possessing arms, and sentenced to seven years imprisonment. Two comrades who were arrested with him were carrying weapons that were later identified as having been used in BI attacks against South American diplomats. See Oriach's confession in *Libération*, 8 January 1977.

[30] The files were prepared on 15 June 1982, about a month before the first anti-Israeli attack. See *Le Monde*, 17 June 1983.

[31] See Oriach's letter of 21 June 1984 to *L'internationale*.

[32] See Roland Jacquard, *La longue traque d'Action Directe* (Paris: Albin Michel, 1987), p. 232.

[33] According to certain sources, Oriach mediated between French and Middle East terrorist organizations. Note in this context that immediately after his release in 1986, Oriach travelled to Damascus for several weeks. See Hamon and Marchand, *Action Directe. Du terrorisme français a l'euroterrorisme*, p. 101.

4.   Influence of the variables at the international and regional level

As already noted, the AD documents of March and April 1982 omitted any reference to the Palestinian question. Why then did the anti-Israeli attacks begin as early as March, accounting for two thirds of all attacks perpetrated by the organization in 1982?

In the author's opinion, the first attack (31 March 1982) was coordinated, or at least based on some kind of understanding, with the FARL. This assessment is supported by a number of factors: the attack took place just before the FARL attack against an Israeli diplomat (3 April 1982); the FARL claimed ultimate responsibility for the attack and the AD denied any involvement in it for several months;[34] and the timing of the attack was more consistent with the FARL agenda.[35]

The seven attacks carried out between July-August were almost certainly sparked by the war in Lebanon. The leaflet circulated after the AD attacked the car used by an Israeli embassy security guard stated: 'AD's Jewish fighters formally announce that they will not tolerate the holocaust of the Palestinians by the Israeli forces ... and will not permit the destruction of the Palestinian people in the ghetto of West Beirut'. The organization, it continued, undertook 'to fight to the bitter end against the Saudi princes and Zionist aggressors, the gendarmes of American imperialism'.[36] The leaflet was signed 'The Marcel Rayman Fighting Unit'.[37] In light of the AD attitude towards Jews and Israel, their use of the term 'Jewish fighters' and reference to Marcel Rayman (a Jewish partisan) appear particularly cynical.

The leaflet circulated after the bombing of the building that housed both Banque Meyer and the Citrus Marketing Company condemned the Israeli invasion of Lebanon, declared solidarity with the Third World, and demanded the immediate and unconditional withdrawal of 'Israeli fascists' from Lebanon. The AD threatened to murder the 'financiers and propagandists of Zionism' if the Palestinians were driven out of Beirut.[38] The explosion near the building of the extreme

---

[34] According to *Libération* of 21 December 1984, a Turkish left-wing organization calling itself the Marxist-Leninist Brigades for Armed Propaganda also claimed responsibility for the attack. There is no proof that the FARL did in fact claim responsibility in Beirut for that attack.

[35] The FARL, which launched its terrorist campaign against American targets in France in November 1981 (the attempt to murder the acting US ambassador), continued with the murder of the American military attaché on 18 January 1982, the killing of an Israeli diplomat in early April, and an attempted murder of another American diplomat on 21 August 1982. The FARL's last attack, on 17 September 1982, was to blow up a car of the Israeli Embassy in Paris.

[36] See *Quotidien de Paris*, 3 July 1982.

[37] Marcel Rayman was a Jew who led a group of communist partisans in France against the Nazis. He was caught and executed in February 1944 together with 20 other communist activists.

[38] See Dartnell, *Action Directe: Ultra-leftist Terrorism in France*, p. 468.

right-wing weekly *Minute* was described as a response 'to the pro-Israel position the paper took on Middle Eastern affairs'.[39]

In a press interview, Rouillan, leader of the 'international faction' of the AD, claimed responsibility on behalf of the organization for three attacks.[40] These attacks were 'a totally normal response to the situation in Lebanon', a question of international solidarity.[41] On the other hand, Rouillan emphatically denied AD logistical or operational participation in the murderous attack against the Goldenberg kosher restaurant in Paris. A day after the interview, the French government decided to outlaw the AD.

In October 1982 the AD published a document entitled, '82, From the Versailles Summit to Lebanon'. This explained, for the first time, its policy during this period, in response to the 'tendentious' publications following Oriach's arrest. The AD denied any involvement in those terrorist attacks involving fatalities, or any connection with the FARL. According to the document, a significant event cast its shadow over all national political dealings in June 1982: Reagan's visit to Europe and the Versailles G-7 summit. The purpose of the summit, it claimed, was to strengthen the imperialist NATO pact and conduct negotiations in preparation for a tactical 'nuclear war' in Europe, the manufacture of a French neutron bomb and assistance to nations involved in peripheral disputes, such as the Falkland Islands. This period also marked the beginning of the Israeli incursion into Lebanon.

Since, the document claimed, American imperialism (as symbolized by Reagan) was threatening a 'selective holocaust', it was imperative not to give way to a sense of defeat, but to continue the fight. For this reason the AD had decided to launch a limited campaign against American and Israeli objectives. The large-scale attacks that had taken place in Paris, it claimed, had been planned and carried out by pressure groups and the secret services. These attacks, the documents explained, were reminiscent of similar attacks in Italy (Bologna) and West Germany (Munich), and had been used by the minister of the interior as a pretext for rounding up activists, although he knew full well who the true culprits were.

A special chapter of the document discussed the situation in Lebanon. According to the AD, the Lebanese War was part of a larger war proliferating throughout the Middle East. The popular forces were being subjected to terrible atrocities, similar to the Sabra and Shattila massacres, by American, European and Zionist imperialists in a so-called attempt to 'restore order'. The document condemned French support of Lebanese 'sectarianism' and the inadequacy of the UNIFIL

---

[39]   See *Quotidien de Paris*, 20 August 1982.
[40]   The attacks against the car of a member of the Israeli Embassy staff, the Discount Bank building, and a Jewish store. See *Libération*, 18 August 1982.
[41]   See also *Quotidien de Paris*, 18 August 1982.

forces in southern Lebanon. To solve the Israeli-Palestinian problem it advocated a class war that would topple the local oligarchies and the lackeys of imperialism.

The document ended with a diatribe against the French security forces and a warning of the dangers of European counter-insurgency collaboration which, it claimed, was part of imperialist preparations for a total global war. In order to be a revolutionary in such times, it was necessary to establish *strategic lines that would link up the various struggles*. Thus the struggle *should only be maintained if international* (emphasis in source).

Rouillan tried to justify AD activities against foreign targets. In a press interview, he mentioned that the AD had come a long way since 1979, when it had focused on social objectives and occupied squats for immigrants. In view of new developments engineered by imperialist forces, including a curtailment of French freedom of action, the AD was forced, he argued, to substitute global targets for domestic ones.[42] The danger of a nuclear war was imminent now that the imperialist war against the Third World had returned to the metropolis, after having butchered entire populations. Rouillan described his persecution by the security forces but denied any ties with important Palestinian militants.[43]

The most convincing and detailed explanation for the AD anti-Zionist attacks appears in the document found in Oriach's possession at the time of his arrest. This document, written in September 1982 was entitled 'Palestine Will Live, Palestine Will Conquer!'.

For years now, Oriach declared, the Palestinian people had been fighting not only the encirclement strategy in which Israel played a major part, but also a growing tide of European conspiracy and collusion. The actions carried out in July 1982 against Zionist targets in Paris were intended to show that the AD was not simply paying lip-service to the idea of solidarity, but wished to actively participate in the struggle of the Palestinian people.

On the eve of 20 July 1982 two attacks took place within a few hours of each other, earning a large share of media attention. Oriach discussed the advantage of carrying out a number of small, simultaneous operations rather than a single large

---

[42]   See *Le Matin*, 15 October 1982.

[43]   Aubron described in 1996 the reasons for the attacks on Israeli targets: 'On the last day of the [G-7] summit, June 6th, Israel attacked Lebanon. One of the lines of imperialist redeployment was thus illustrated in the most concrete way possible. There followed the invasion of Lebanon by Israeli troops, with all that followed for the Lebanese and Palestinian people. This led to AD reorienting itself towards new targets, claiming responsibility for the machinegunning of the car of the Israeli embassy's chief of security and a number of actions against Israeli companies. After a massacre-attack against a Jewish restaurant (Goldenberg) on Rosiers Street in Paris, the powers that be orchestrated a counter-revolutionary propaganda campaign throughout the media.' In an interview with the newspaper Libération, Jean-Marc defended the machine-gunning of the chief of security and condemned the massacre attacks. See *Short Collective Biography of Action Directe Prisoners*.

one. Logistical problems, however, made the first option impracticable. The choice of economic targets, he claimed, was to protest the presence of Israeli capital in France. The leaflet accompanying the attack on Bank Leumi drew a parallel with the struggle of French partisans during the Second World War. It implied that just as the AD militants would not hesitate to fight the Nazis, they should not hesitate to join the struggle of the Palestinians, who had been fighting for years for 'mankind and for freedom'.

The second attack, targeting the GANCO Corporation, was signed by The Red Panthers. Although there was apparently no accompanying leaflet, the timing and choice of target spoke for themselves, according to Oriach. The use of pseudonyms was calculated to throw the police off the scent. Since a full coalition of all the various fighting units was not as yet feasible, the uniting factor was the common target – the imperialist enemy – provided care was taken not to harm the civilian population.[44]

Leaflets claiming responsibility for AD attacks on a car belonging to an Israel Embassy security guard and the Discount Bank building were signed 'Marcel Rayman, Jewish fighter member of the Manuchian Partisan Unit'.[45] According to Oriach, however, Rayman was first and foremost a communist, not a Jew. Again, he compared the attack to the partisans' struggle against the Nazis, adding that this operation showed that revolutionary praxis surmounted differences of origin, belief or tongue.

> Our fear of being accused of antisemitism must not lead us to make any concessions in our confrontation with Zionism. Every operation we undertake is a declaration of our resolve to fight alongside the Palestinian people: Their victory is our victory.[46]

France, continued Oriach, was a haven for Zionist capital, equipment and services, and through them, their American and European sponsors. Therefore it was the duty of the revolutionary to take the necessary risks and chose the right targets. The basic condition for revolutionary success was the choice of suitable targets, not the loss of human life.

The Frédéric Oriach Liberation Collective, which published the aforementioned document in June 1984, further illuminated the objectives of the attacks. In its introductory article, Israel was portrayed as cynically exploiting the massacre launched by the Western imperialists against the Jews in order to justify its own

---

[44] This was a warning not to carry out large-scale attacks of the kind being perpetrated by Arab organizations at the time, in order not to trigger negative public opinion.

[45] Manuchian was another partisan, of Armenian extraction, mentioned in AD leaflets of the period.

[46] See 'Frederic Oriach – militant anti-sioniste pro-palestinien – Le sens d'un combat,' *Collectif 'Liberation de F. Oriach'*, June 1984.

legitimacy. Zionism, it claimed, was not confined to Israel, but had evolved into a financial, political and ideological force, bent on disseminating the idea of white supremacy and imperialist ascendancy throughout the world.[47]

For the past 40 years, the collective claimed, the Palestinian people had fought for land and freedom and its struggle was an example for all oppressed people. Therefore, the Palestinian struggle had, of necessity, an international dimension, especially since the Palestinian people had always helped liberation struggles. Palestine existed not only in the Middle East, but throughout the world. It existed in France, where their immigrant brothers were victims of racist hatred.

In a press conference, Oriach stressed the importance of the Palestinian issue for the Arab workers in France, a realization he had come to during his work on 'the Palestine committees'.[48] When a major sector of the proletariat gave priority to the anti-imperialist struggle, it was possible to link the class struggle in the metropolis (such as that of the immigrant Arab workers in France) to liberation struggles in oppressed countries (the Palestinians). In a political statement, Oriach again emphasized that a large percentage of the proletariat in France were Arabs or Muslims who identified with the Palestinians.[49] The statement portrayed the 'Palestinian geopolitical area' as 'the key to the turbulent Middle East, determining the balance of the entire Mediterranean area, in which French imperialism plays a major role'.

Later on, Oriach held French imperialism accountable for the massacres of Sabra and Shattila, through French assistance to 'the Zionists' and its willingness to join forces with American imperialists against Lebanese revolutionary forces. At the same time, French imperialism was held responsible for the oppression of Arab immigrants at home. In order to enlist the proletariat in the struggle against the French imperialist state, it was deemed essential for the immigrants to adopt the Palestinian and Lebanese struggle against American and French imperialism as their own. In conclusion, solidarity could be achieved by focusing the struggle (propaganda and recruitment) against *French imperialism* (emphasis in the original).[50]

Some months later, the focus on the Palestinian and Lebanese issue among Oriach's group subsided. Henceforth, the AD was to concentrate its offensive wholly against NATO and French imperialism.

---

[47] Ibid.

[48] See *Libération*, 13 June 1983.

[49] The document was published together with another prisoner, Marina da Silva, on 21 November 1983.

[50] Quoted from the journal *Solidarité anti-impérialiste*, 1 October 1983, a publication whose views matched those of the Oriach group. This edition focused on French military intervention in Chad and Lebanon.

V.   ANALYSIS OF RESEARCH ASSUMPTIONS

In 1982 when the AD began to attack American and Israeli targets, the organiza-tion's leadership believed that imperialism was gearing up for an all-out offensive against revolutionary forces worldwide. The G-7 at Versailles in May 1982, attended by President Reagan, was seen as a turning point in imperialist policy. This called for renewed strategic planning on the part of AD leaders, as reflected in the document published shortly before the Versailles summit. In this document, imperialism was portrayed as wracked by internal contradictions, desperate to reassert a hegemony that had been challenged by the developing nations.

1.   Influence of the variables at the international system level

As stated, the AD published very little documentation, especially compared to the BR. Typically, from 1982 on, most attacks were not even accompanied by leaflets. A more detailed explanation was published subsequently in the document entitled '82, From the Versailles Summit to Lebanon' (October 1982) and in another document written by AD militants from prison in 1993.[51] The first document ascribed international tension to Reagan's resolve to strengthen the imperialist NATO pact against the forces of revolution, and his preparations for 'a tactical nuclear war'. The imperialist war, however, had also penetrated the metropolises of the developed nations, threatening the proletariat there with 'a selective holocaust'.

The AD attitude toward bipolarity within the international system was particu-larly interesting. In the document 'For a Communist Project', the AD portrayed Soviet imperialism as an important factor in the global ruler/ruled hierarchy. In a retrospective analysis of attacks of 1982, written by imprisoned AD activists in November 1993, the USSR and Eastern Europe, together with the liberation movements, were portrayed as the enemies of American imperialism. A change in attitude toward the USSR and the communist bloc occurred in 1984 and was reflected in the AD Euro-terrorist strategy. During the pro-Palestinian period, bipolar tension related exclusively to the conflict between Western imperialism on the one hand, and Third World liberation movements and revolutionary forces in the West, on the other.

Of all the regional wars that influenced the AD decision to act on behalf of the Palestinians, the Lebanese War was by far the most important. This was analyzed on several levels: as a victory for the Falangist far right in Lebanon, aided by

---

[51]   See 'Unité des révolutionnaires en Europe de l'Ouest,' *Cahier Front*, No. 2, 16 Nov. 1993, pp. 32-61.

Israel, imperialism and the oligarchic Arab regimes;[52] as part of a more general war in the Middle East, namely 'the situation in Kabul, Asmara, and Khorramshar';[53] as a diversionary tactic on the part of the Israelis, who were anxious to prevent the Israel-Palestine conflict turning in a class war; and as an opportunity for France to play out its role as an imperialist and neo-colonialist power, by directly or indirectly (through joining the UN forces) restoring order to Lebanon (including its alleged share in the Israeli massacre of Palestinian and Lebanese civilians).

The document discussed at length international cooperation between the security forces in the West. The AD was convinced that the major attacks in France against Jewish targets, or in Western Germany and Italy against civilian populations (such as the attack at Bologna train station or the Munich 'Oktoberfest') were part of a conspiracy devised by the secret services. The reinforcement and modernization of police systems were perceived as part of a pan-European counter-insurgency plan in which Western Germany played a leading role. To this end, France had set up new elite units and had trained 'super-spies' to murder the leaders of the revolutionary movement. To counteract this trend, it was necessary for all revolutionary forces to launch a joint international offensive against imperialism.

The Sino-Soviet rift did not particularly affect AD leaders, despite the Maoist indoctrination some had received in the ranks of the GP and the NAPAP, because their main activities occurred many years after China had made peace with the US and the West. The neo-colonial image associated with French foreign policy, particularly in Africa and the Middle East, the AD's physical proximity to Arab and Muslim immigrants in the Parisian slums, and the fact that several AD activists were of Algerian origin, encouraged sympathy and identification with the Palestinian problem.

2.   Influence of the variables at the organizational level

A.   Ideology as a cohesive force?

AD ideology was difficult to describe since the organization only published two documents, of which only about 15 pages were devoted to international issues. Gayraud pointed out, scathingly, that the quantitative weakness of AD's ideological output was paralleled only by its intellectual weakness![54] At best, its ideology

---

52   Interestingly, Syria is not mentioned in this document, perhaps because of FARL's pro-Syrian stand, and Oriach's support of the Syrian regime.

53   The leaflet thus included a reference to the Soviet invasion of Afghanistan, the revolt of the Eritreans against the Ethiopian regime, and the Iraqi-Iranian battle over Khorramshar.

54   See Gayraud, 'Histoire politique d'une Organisation Communiste Combatante,' p. 23.

was viewed as a feeble reworking of Leninist themes. At worst, the AD made do, as Oriach himself pointed out, with dictionary translations of RAF and BR texts. Despite the fact that AD leaders admired the revolutionary organizations in Italy (in particular the BR) and West Germany (especially the RAF), and even copied some of their documents, the terms 'proletarian internationalism' was conspicuously absent from their writings during this period. It is similarly absent from Oriach's writings, although Oriach at least saw the Palestinian struggle in an international context.

Oriach probably influenced the AD pro-Palestinian policy directly; a link can definitely be identified between the revolutionary internationalism he preached and AD's choice of anti-Israeli and anti-Zionist targets. One may wonder at the low priority given to American targets prior to Reagan's arrival in France (two, versus eight 'Zionist' targets hit) some two months after publication of the important document, 'On American Imperialism'. There are several reasons for the AD predilection for Israeli and Jewish targets in the summer of 1982, unlike all other European terrorist organizations of that period:

(1) A desire to jump on the propaganda bandwagon provided by the Lebanese War. The Lebanese War was perceived as the first operative decision to emerge from the Versailles summit, coordinated between American, European, and Zionist imperialism. AD leaders were presumably aware of the impact of the media of the 'Peace for Galilee' operation, and tried to derive some propaganda advantage from it, as testified by Oriach.
(2) The need to enlist the support of North African and Muslim immigrants through identification with the Palestinian struggle.[55]
(3) The antisemitic aspects of AD ideology and actions. It is hard to distinguish between the ideological influences that penetrated AD 'dogma' and the antisemitic backgrounds of its leaders and many of its militants.

AD documents or communiqués avoided direct antisemitic statements; such sentiment was usually expressed by way of allusion. Any mention of the Holocaust invariably referred to the 'holocaust' of the Palestinians, not that of the Jewish people. Zionists were repeatedly portrayed as Nazis or fascists: the murdered Israeli diplomat was described as 'an agent of the Israeli Gestapo who

---

[55] For instance, on 16 September 1983, a demonstration took place in Paris to commemorate the anniversary of the Sabra and Shattila massacres. The organizers of the demonstration, supporters of Oriach, complained on the pages of *Solidarité anti-impérialiste* of 1 October 1983 of the poor turnout of French workers and immigrants. However, while admitting that they were unable to recruit more than a handful of French activists in order to 'meet our anti-imperialist obligations', they called for a more intensive propaganda effort in order to persuade immigrant workers to overcome their fears of government oppression, and take part in pro-Palestinian activities.

was executed in France for having shot Palestinian children in the West Bank';[56] a leaflet taking responsibility for the shooting at the Israeli Defense Ministry delegation building stated that the AD would not tolerate the 'holocaust of the Palestinian people by the Israeli forces in the ghetto of West Beirut'; sprayed on the wall of the Banque Meyer building was the following message: 'The Israeli fascists will not give up ... we will kill the financiers and disseminators of Zionism'.[57]

AD leaders, however, were careful to deny any antisemitic motivation in their attacks and disclaimed responsibility for large-scale attacks against Jewish targets.[58] Indeed, how could they be antisemitic, they claimed, if two of their attacks (on 1 and 7 August 1982) had been carried out by the Marcel Rayman Fighting Unit, a unit of 'Jewish fighters?' Despite the fact that the AD had already published a special document on the subject, it still felt the need to justify its actions.[59] In November 1982, a communiqué was dispatched by the Marcel Rayman Fighting Unit to the AFP in which the 'Jewish fighters' blamed Israel for 'collaborating with the military fascist juntas of South America'.[60] The authors claimed that although they 'were members of the Jewish people, they were neither observant Jews nor nationalist Jews, but were rather allied with the anti-capitalist struggle'. As Jews they 'were incensed by the fact that some of those who had themselves suffered the atrocities of the Nazi or Stalinist era should support racism and justify the racist laws in the occupied territories'. As Jews, however, they were not prepared to condone the parallel drawn between anti-Zionism and antisemitism.

In actual fact, the AD had no 'Jewish fighters unit'. The only identified Jewish AD militant, Michel Azeroual, was opposed to attacking Jewish targets. He later abandoned the organization, together with Eric Moreau, to set up the '1 August Revolutionary Collective'. According to recent research, two brothers of Jewish origin, Claude and Nicolas Halfen, were behind the Marcel Rayman Fighting Unit.[61]

The groups that supported and rallied round Oriach were far more outspoken. The CLFO argued that Zionism would not limit itself geographically to the

---

[56] See interview with three AD activists on the radio station Gilda, as quoted in Hamon and Marchand, *Action Directe. Du terrorisme français a l'euroterrorisme*, p. 70. The Israeli diplomat was murdered by the FARL.

[57] Ibid., p. 74.

[58] See Rouillan's interview to *Le Matin*, 15 October 1982.

[59] See *Action Directe 82, du sommet de Versailles au Liban, Octobre 1982*.

[60] See Hamon and Marchand, *Action Directe. Du terrorisme français a l'euroterrorisme*, pp. 98-9.

[61] See Yair Auron, *We Are All German Jews. Jewish Radicals in France During the Sixties and Seventies* (Tel Aviv: Am Oved Publishers, 1999), in Hebrew, pp. 163-7. The names of these two militants were mentioned in the data examined by the author of this book, but their Jewish identity was not mentioned.

colonial State of Israel.[62] The Zionist movement was regarded as a financial, political and ideological force that disseminated the idea of white superiority throughout the world. Zionism justified its own barbarity by invoking the crimes perpetrated by the Nazis against the Jews... Ironically, the racism condemned by these Zionist propagandists was the same racism experienced by the immigrant workers in France.[63] On 1 October 1983 the newspaper, *Solidarité anti-impérialiste* accused the Zionist lobby in France of being responsible for Oriach's conviction, and the French minister of justice of heading three large Zionist organizations. Another article argued that as many people were killed in the Lebanese War as in the Commune of Paris in 1871.

These factors indicate that antisemitism had filtered through the ranks of the organization, providing an additional reason for anti-Israeli attitudes on the part of AD leaders. It would seem, however, that a subsequent change of strategy within the AD, and Oriach's waning influence on Rouillan's 'international faction', dampened AD motivation either to carry out anti-Israeli attacks or seek Palestinian allies.

Although antisemitism was more deeply entrenched in Olivier's 'national faction', it was hardly ever expressed in attacks against foreign targets. The only anti-Israeli attack it carried out (against Bank Leumi) was not the result of any strategic or ideological thinking.[64] The accompanying leaflet, signed by the 'Commando Sana Mheidli', protested 'the oppression of the Lebanese and Palestinian peoples by the Zionists, courtesy of the UN forces'. The leaflet also protested the 'racist policy of the National Immigration Office'.[65]

The wholesale adoption of anti-Zionist ideology in its most antisemitic form fostered a feeling of identification with the Palestinian struggle, as reflected in the perpetration of anti-Zionist attacks as part of the AD international struggle. A comparison of AD's position *vis-à-vis* that of the BR yields a fundamental difference: the BR refused to attack Israeli targets in Italy when asked to do so by the top PLO cadres, although they considered Israel a strategic enemy in the Mediterranean region. Such action did not conform with their strategic goals, as

---

[62] See *Frederic Oriach – militant anti-sioniste pro-palestinien – Le sens d'un combat.*

[63] This is an allusion to the League against Racism and Antisemitism (LICRA), most of whose members were Jewish.

[64] Note, nonetheless, that when Olivier was arrested, a long list of Israeli and Jewish targets was found in his possession. The list, which was examined in the archives of the Paris Institut de Criminologie, contained only addresses and phone numbers of the potential targets.

[65] The suicide attack carried out by Sana Mheidli, a young Lebanese woman, against an IDF convoy in Lebanon, may have had such an impact on the faction's leaders that they felt the need to identify with her by attacking an Israeli target. On the same day, a similar attack was launched against the Paris building of the French immigration authority (DNI). The leaflet that accompanied this attack carried the following anti-racist slogan: 'Do not touch my friend, the immigrant worker from Chad, Palestine, Lebanon, etc'.

Savasta pointed out; in addition the BR leadership had not adopted the antisemitic undertones of anti-Zionist ideology.

The AD had no clearly defined political or social ideology and despite its slogans, was not active among the working classes. Consequently, most of its operations during this period were directed either against international targets or against targets connected with the North African immigrants. The North African immigrants provided an important infrastructure for the AD and, according to its neo-Marxist ideologues, were a major 'revolutionary subject' within the French proletariat. Since the Arab immigrants naturally identified with the Palestinian struggle, it was important for the AD to prove that it was ready and able to struggle for the same objectives.

As a small organization with anarchist features, it was easy for AD to adopt an active program of solidarity with the Palestinians without having to prepare its militants in advance through profound ideological argumentation. It was just as easy for it to drop the anti-Israeli offensive when negative public opinion and crackdowns by the security authorities made this expedient.

Despite its focus on American imperialism, the anti-Zionist attacks of the AD also indicated the cynical use of an event that had enraged public opinion and radical left-wing circles throughout Europe – the Israeli invasion of Lebanon. As stated above, that it was relatively easy for an anarchist organization to form a coalition when its immediate interests were at stake, without needing to justify its decision on ideological or strategic grounds. The sudden cessation of its anti-Zionist strategy, accompanied by mumbled explanations to the media, without any internal debate, was likewise in keeping with anarchist behavior.

Since mutual assistance between the AD and the Palestinian organizations has not been proved, the issue of the dependence of a weaker organization on a larger one is irrelevant. Both the decision to attack Israeli and Jewish targets, and the decision to cease the anti-Zionist offensive were based on internal considerations alone.

3.   Influence of the variables at the decision-maker level

The AD leader Jean-Marc Rouillan was only 18 years old when he joined a Spanish terrorist anarchist organization. The anarchist influence (ostentatious acts such as 'propaganda of the deed', identification with the oppressed of the earth, etc.) was evident throughout his career.[66] He decided to reside among the North African immigrant squatters, thereby fostering a 'brotherhood of fighters' with his

---

[66] According to Segaller, he expressed his identification with the Palestinians through winding a *kafiyyah* round his neck. See Stephen Segaller, *Invisible Armies. Terrorism into the 1990s* (1st American edn.) (New York: Harcourt Brace Jovanovich, 1987), p. 42.

Algerian comrades.[67] Rouillan's interest in the immigrants and their support of him were probably instrumental in shaping his pro-Palestinian stand. He evidently believed that such a stand would instill a revolutionary fervor in the Muslim and Arab immigrants. 'Proletarian internationalism', on which he had been nurtured since his youth, would be a constant factor in his life. Rouillan constantly pursued international objectives. It is not surprising, therefore, that he became the leader of the 'international faction'.

André Olivier, leader of the so-called 'national faction', was a lesser known personality. He was never interviewed and, unlike Rouillan, left no published documents. He has been portrayed as an uncompromising and authoritarian figure, 'the chieftain of a small tribe', who ruled his faction (comprising a mere 30 individuals) through intimidation and even violence. The group portrait that emerges from Max Frérot's lengthy confession is that of a faction lacking any definitive ideology. Its actions were evidently prompted by the whims of its leader, who enjoyed sole discretion in the choice of target.[68] The anarchist character of the faction is further corroborated by the ratio between its armed robberies and its political attacks (33:12). Olivier's cultural background appears far too parochial to prepare him for action at an international level.

It is also significant that Oliver was a rabid antisemite. Frérot related how Olivier ranted against 'les sales Juifs' ('dirty Jews'). The fact that the antisemite Frérot was cultivated as one of the organization's chief activists was in itself an indication of Olivier's antisemitic leanings. However, these sentiments were rarely translated into action. Despite the long list of Israeli/Jewish targets found in Olivier's possessions, the faction carried out only one anti-Israeli attack (in 1985, apparently by Frérot himself). Frérot emerged as a vacuous, cowardly and selfish thug, with connections to the underworld – the total opposite of an ideal revolutionary. His devotion to the AD was solely a function of his blind admiration for its authoritarian leader and a strong desire for action.[69]

Frérot's brand of antisemitism was not only deeply entrenched but apparently knew no bounds. For example, in order to 'atone' for his shameful behavior towards his comrades in the organization, Frérot asked Olivier for permission to 'blow himself up together with the Jewish scum in the attack against the Bank

---

[67] Mohand Hamami and Lehouari Benchellal were the principal Algerian militants. After Benchellal was killed in a shoot-out with the police, he was regarded as a martyr.

[68] Frérot was the 'chief terrorist' of the 'national' faction. A personal letter to Olivier, the AD leader (29 closely-written pages) shed light on the relationship between members of the organization, the leader, and Frérot himself.

[69] Of all the activists in Olivier's group, most is known about Max Frérot, Olivier's 'chief operator'. This was due to a long confession he wrote to Olivier, which was published by the Paris newspaper, *Libération*.

Leumi, as an act of human dignity'.[70] During his second trial in October 1992, he ranted against the 'Jewish lobby' for ruling France since 1981 via the socialists. He also accused the 'Jewish leadership' of the GP and Benny Lévy of destroying the organization, and pronounced the 'god of the Jews a wicked God'.[71] He dismissed his lawyer for being a Jew and nicknamed the president of the court 'Chief Rabbi Columbus'.[72]

Although Frérot accused his father and brothers of being fascists, he was a true racist. He described how in meetings with black activists from the Antilles, he felt a sense of superiority akin to that of a 'white leader' toward a primitive black tribe. Possibly, the only thing that may have prevented Frérot from carrying out more anti-Israeli or anti-Jewish attacks was the fact that Olivier focused on French targets, mainly robberies, to keep his small faction afloat.

Oriach's antisemitism, on the other hand, was more intellectual, masked as ideological. He criticized the Marcel Rayman Unit for naming itself after a Jewish partisan, arguing that for the true revolutionary, background, religion, or language were irrelevant. Although denying the Jewish right to national self-determination, Oriach defended the right of all other peoples, particularly the Palestinians. Concern that their anti-Zionism might be misconstrued as antisemitism should not deter them from action, he added.[73]

The CLFO published another booklet in Oriach's defense in May 1985. In it, Oriach declared that 'Jerusalem should be purged of Zionists, who should be repatriated to … Paris and Washington'.[74] Drawing yet another parallel between Nazism and Zionism, he accused Israel of running 'concentration camps'. Oriach also accused the French minister of justice, Roger Badinter, of Jewish origin, of being 'a hypocrite, who hid behind the tragic mask of victim, in typical Zionist fashion'.[75]

In addition, Oriach ranted against his Jewish comrades, accusing former Maoist leaders Serge July, Geismar, Gluksman, and Benny Lévy of spearheading Zionism and reactionary ideas, and of bringing about the collapse of the communist movement at a time when he, Oriach, had persisted in the struggle. Not

---

[70] See Frérot letter to Olivier.
[71] See *Le Monde*, 13-14. October 1982.
[72] See *Quotidien de Paris*, 15 October 1992.
[73] See the document entitled, *Palestine vivra, Palestine vaincra!*
[74] The booklet, entitled 'Palestine our Struggle', contains a number of texts written by Oriach, particularly during his stay in jail. The text referred to here is 'The People's War is Alive' of 27 February 1985.
[75] The booklet entitled 'A Chosen People, a Chosen Nation' was published on 20 February 1985. One of the most antisemitic texts was illustrated by a photograph of the French president Mitter- and near a synagogue, over which a large Star of David loomed.

surprisingly, three of the four people he specified were Jews.[76] In the same context, Oriach praised the Black September organization for 'having placed the question of internationalism in its true perspective in Munich 1972'. The above quotations provided sufficient insight into the background that turned Oriach into a sworn anti-Zionist activist.

VI.   SUMMARY

The relationship between the AD and Palestinian organizations is not easy to define. On the one hand, the AD openly carried out attacks against Israeli and Jewish targets, and one of its major periods of terrorist activity was motivated by unqualified solidarity with the Palestinian struggle. On the other hand, there is no proof of any important contacts with Fatah, PFLP or any other terrorist organiza- tions. The one exception was the circumstantial evidence concerning the relationship with the FARL, the radical Lebanese revolutionary organization, but this was only on an ideological and personal level.[77] Interestingly, although all the anti-Zionist attacks were purportedly carried out in solidarity with the Palestinian people, they coincided with the Israeli invasion of Lebanon, when the FARL was busy attacking Israeli and American targets. It is possible that the FARL was acting as an arm of the PFLP, especially since FARL leader Georges Ibrahim Abdallah was a member of the PFLP.

Another feature peculiar to AD was Oriach's overwhelming influence on the organization's anti-Israeli and antisemitic policy; when he broke with the AD, the latter abandoned its emphasis on the Palestinian issue as a major strategic goal. (This decision was also influenced by public opinion and crackdowns by the security forces).

The AD anti-Zionism was probably an integral part of its strategy, not merely an expression of solidarity in the period under discussion. The factors that support this opinion are: the AD social entrenchment among Arab and Muslim immi- grants, some of whom belonged to the AD; the strategic perception of French imperialism as victimizing these immigrants in France and attacking their countries of origin (Algeria, and in a broader sense, Lebanon too); and last but not least, the rabid antisemitism of AD leaders, both on an ideological and personal level.

---

[76] Cited from *Libération*, 18 June 1983. The reference was to the voluntary disbandment of the GP, in 1973, following the leaders' decision to stop the possible transformation of their organization into a terrorist group under the influence of Palestinian terrorism.

[77] This data and assessments matches the information received from the office of the French attorney-general.

CHAPTER 6
EURO-TERRORISM (1984-88)

I.   HISTORICAL BACKGROUND

The term 'Euro-terrorism' first appeared in the American press in the first half of 1985 to describe attacks against NATO targets or the arms industry in the West. Dennis Pluchinsky, the main source for the background to this chapter, described Euro-terrorism as an anti-imperialist front set up to coordinate the 'fighting communist organizations' (FCOs) throughout Western Europe, particularly against the political/military infrastructure of NATO. He defined the FCOs as small, highly dangerous, urban terror organizations, ruled by Marxist-Leninist ideology. These organizations also represented a significant security threat to US diplomatic, military and economic interests in Western Europe.[1]

During the 1980s the FCOs twice tried to set up regional alliances in order to coordinate targets. In 1985 the RAF and AD established the Anti-Imperialist West European Guerrilla Front, but this failed to attract other FCOs. In 1988, after the AD was neutralized in France, the RAF and BR-PCC tried to form a second anti-imperialist front. This, too, failed because other organizations were reluctant to join and the BR itself was immobilized by the arrests of late 1988. This was the last attempt of the European FCOs to coordinate activities on a regional level.[2]

Cordes argued that the transition from local organization to membership of a West European Guerrilla Front was more indicative of a pervasive mood swing than a radical change in policy. European organizations which participated in this process were always, to some extent, anti-imperialist and anti-American, and some had already attacked US targets. The formal coalition of the RAF and AD in January 1985 did not prevent either of them from continuing to act on a national level. Cordes also pointed out that the unification of revolutionary organizations was meant to thwart the unification of West European countries, regarded as yet another step towards 'imperialist hegemony'.[3]

---

[1]   See Dennis A. Pluchinsky, 'Western Europe's Red Terrorists: The Fighting Communist Organizations', in Yonah Alexander and A. Dennis Pluchinsky (eds.), *Europe's Red Terrorists: The Fighting Communist Organizations* (London: Frank Cass, 1992), p. 28.

[2]   Ibid., p. 293.

[3]   See B. Cordes, 'Euroterrorists Talk about Themselves: A Look at the Literature', in Paul Wilkinson and A.M. Stewart, (eds.) *Contemporary Research on Terrorism* (Aberdeen: The University Press, 1987), pp. 329-30.

Euro-terrorism certainly reflected a change of strategy by European left-wing revolutionary organizations. The small anarcho-communist organizations, such as the RAF and AD, changed their perception of the Third World as the center of revolutionary power; the ideologically sounder ones, such as the BR, abandoned the domestic struggle somewhat in favor of internationalism. This change, however, was gradual – taking four to five years. This chapter examines the processes of coordination that took place between the FCOs from 1984-88. It identifies the factors that contributed to changing priorities of the European revolutionary organizations towards NATO and EC targets, and explains why the West European Guerrilla Front ultimately failed. This chapter relates only to those FCOs that were most active in setting up the front, as indicated by their ideological documents, namely the AD, the BR-PCC, the RAF and the Belgian Combatant Communist Cells (Cellules Communistes Combattantes – CCC).[4]

II.   THE RED ARMY FACTION[5]

Chapter 3 discussed the influence of international and regional factors on the activities of third generation RAF militants. It pointed out that by 1979, when the RAF attempted to assassinate Gen. Haig, commander of NATO forces in Europe, there were already signs of a change in the RAF strategy.[6] This coincided with the decision by NATO members to approve the deployment of American nuclear missiles on their territories – a decision which led to the development of a significant anti-war movement in Western Europe. New themes appeared in statements published after the two most significant anti-American attacks of 1981: the car bomb at the Ramstein airbase, and the attempted murder of Gen. Frederick Kroesen in Heidelberg. (Kroesen was commander of US forces in Europe, accused of coordinating counter-insurgency operations in Western Europe.) Both operations, which took place after two years of low-profile terrorist

---

[4]   Pluchinsky divided the FCOs into three groups: the anti-imperialist group: the RAF, AD (international faction) and BR-PCC; the Marxists-Leninist group: the GRAPO, CCC, BR-UCC, and AD (national faction); the neutral organizations such as 17-N, FP-25, and DEV-SOL. According to Pluchinsky, GRAPO was extremely critical of the front set up by the RAF and AD, and in March 1987 published a long document called 'Texts for the discussion of the West European movement,' in which it expressed its reservations. See Pluchinsky, *Western Europe's Red Terrorists*, pp. 43-44. There are serious reservations about Pluchinsky including the Turkish DEV SOL in the category of FCOs, because of the different political/social conditions in Turkey. Also, defining the AD national faction as a Marxist organization seems rather strange, considering its ideological poverty.

[5]   See also Chapter 3 and, more specifically, the section on the period of Euro-terrorism and the decline of the German terrorist organizations (1985-90).

[6]   See notes 15 and 16 in Chapter 3.

activity, indicated that American targets in Western Europe had become priorities. The communiqué accompanying the attempted attack on Kroesen developed this theme: 'The imperialist war of destruction is now returning from the Third World to Europe, from whence it began... West Europe is no longer the hinterland from where imperialism is waging war ... [it] has become part of the worldwide front line'.[7] The statement referred for the first time to the West European revolutionary front.

The real ideological and strategic shift, however, found expression in the document entitled 'Guerrilla, Resistance and the Anti-Imperialist Front' (May 1982).[8] Within the new international context, it claimed the revolutionary front in the center [metropolis] belonged to the struggles within Asia, Africa and Latin America. It was from Western Europe, the new springboard of global conflict, that imperialist forces drew their military power in an attempt to put pressure on socialist countries and quash liberation struggles. West Germany, which had succeeded in suppressing its revolutionary movements in the late 1970s and had since evolved into a leading European power, currently aspired to lead an international offensive in the context of a united Western Europe. Unity in the revolutionary camp was therefore essential to counteract the unity of the imperialist camp.

On the national level, the RAF aimed to strike at the heart of German society, thereby turning the West European Guerrilla Front and the United German Revolutionary Front into a reality.

The RAF leaders, however, were unable to implement this strategy. In November 1982, RAF leaders Brigitte Mohnhaupt and Christian Klar were arrested, delaying the reorganization of the commando units by about two years. The first indication that reorganization was imminent occurred in July 1984, during the police search of a RAF safe house. This led to the discovery of a draft proposal for a joint RAF-AD declaration of intent to set up an anti-imperialist guerrilla front in Western Europe.[9]

Despite their incarceration, Mohnhaupt and Klar continued to play active parts in the formation of this front. Letters sent by Klar from prison in mid-1984 and the communiqué of the jailed RAF hunger-strikers highlight two central issues: the need to coordinate the campaign of jailed revolutionaries, especially in Western Europe, against the anti-revolutionary forces and against NATO; and the

---

[7]   See *A Brief History of the Red Army Fraction*, Spring 1994, p. 4, at <http://www.etext.org/Politics/Arm.The.Spirit/Guerrilla/Europe/Red.Army.Fraction/history.of.the.raf>.

[8]   See the document in *Notes et Etudes*, No. 5 (May 1988), pp. 70-80.

[9]   The RAF militants interviewed in June 1985 in *Zusammen Kampfen* claimed that the security personnel only found a paper on talks between activists, not a strategic decision. This confirms that the strategic decision was only adopted after serious internal debate within the two organizations. The interview was quoted in *Ligne Rouge*, No. 15 (July 1985), pp. 8-16.

importance of the new anti-imperialist front as a means, *inter alia*, of alleviating imperialist pressure against the new Third World countries, and against the socialist states in the East and the Warsaw Pact.[10]

In an attempt to demonstrate the operational ability of the front, the RAF detonated a car bomb in the NATO Officers' Academy in Oberammergau. The accompanying communiqué warned the West German government that it 'would be defeated by the joint struggle of the prisoners and the West European guerrillas, and the imminent establishment of a West European revolutionary front', details of which would shortly be published.[11]

1.   The West European Revolutionary Guerrilla Front

The first joint manifesto by two European terrorist organizations – the RAF and AD – was published on 15 January 1985, in both French and German, and was titled 'For the Unity of West European Revolutionaries'. The manifesto opened with a somewhat formal declaration concerning the need for a new revolutionary strategy in the imperialist centers. As a condition for this quantum leap, it was necessary to consolidate the international organization of the proletarian struggle in the metropolis, and its political/military nucleus, namely the West European guerrilla. Given the unified strategy of imperialists, the West European communist guerrillas needed to discuss ways of uniting, as part of the global war between the international proletariat and the imperialist bourgeoisie.

Imperialist strategy, at this stage, was perceived as attempting to assemble its forces into a homogeneous system, namely NATO, while broadening its scope of war as a solution to its own general crisis. This strategy included: a military campaign against the victorious nations of Asia, Africa and Latin America and practical moves towards an offensive against the socialist states in the East. European nations were being enlisted to help the US war machine. Concrete expression of this could be found in the deployment of nuclear missiles in European countries, the resuscitation of the West European Union (WEU), the establishment of a rapid intervention force in France, and greater cooperation in arms production. On the domestic, level NATO was promoting a joint policy against revolutionary forces in order to prevent them from forming a united front.

---

[10]   See Klar's letters in *L'internationale*, No. 10, Sept.-Oct. 1984. For the text of the 4 December 1984 manifesto, see Alexander and Pluchinsky (eds.), *Europe's Red Terrorists*, pp. 59-64.

[11]   According to Pluchinsky, who quotes the manifesto of 18 December 1984, this was clearly an allusion to the joint statement that the RAF and AD were about to publish. See Dennis Pluchinsky, 'An Organizational and Operational Analysis of Germany's Red Army Faction Terrorist Group (1972-1991)' in Yonah Alexander and Dennis Pluchinsky (eds.), *European Terrorism. Today and Tomorrow*. (Washington: Brassey's, 1992), p. 66.

In contrast to their ideological debates, the RAF and AD declared that the proletariat and the oppressed nations should emphasize the political dimension of the anti-imperialist struggle – a struggle in which the proletariat of Western Europe had a decisive role to play. The proletariat strategy included attacks against NATO targets, similar to those carried out in Portugal, Belgium, Spain, Greece, France and West Germany. Italy was conspicuously absent from countries associated with revolutionary recruitment and the anti-imperialist struggle.

From 11 December 1984 to late February 1985, RAF fighting units carried out 39 attacks to launch the new strategy and enlist sympathizers. These units carried out most of the minor operations (arson or non-lethal bombings). The commando units, made up of underground activists, carried out the more complex and dangerous attacks.

The beginning of a more serious offensive was marked by the murder of Ernst Zimmerman, chairperson of the Association of German Weapons, Aeronautical, and Space Industries. This was carried out on 1 February 1985 by the Patsy O'Hara Commando Unit.[12] A few days earlier, the AD had killed Gen. René Audran, the first attack after its alliance with the RAF. RAF leaders portrayed these two operations as the first steps towards a strategy that aimed to unite all revolutionaries in Western Europe.[13]

Another major issue was cooperation and coordination between European police and security services regarding counter-insurgency. RAF leaders referred to Reagan's counter-terrorist policy, and to the statement of US Secretary of State Shultz that defined Western Europe, the Middle East and Latin America as the three main fronts in the war against terror. They also claimed that after the parallel actions of the RAF, the AD and the Portuguese Popular Forces-25 April (Forces Populares 25 de Abril – FP-25), Shultz was pressuring European governments to intervene directly in the war against the West European guerrillas.

On 8 August 1985 a car bomb was exploded at the US airbase in Rhein Main near Frankfurt by the George Jackson commandos of the RAF and AD.[14] It was the first and only joint action of the RAF and AD. According to the leaflet that took responsibility for the operation, the base was serving as a springboard for war against the Third World, a hive of espionage, and a gateway for war against the socialist states. At this juncture, the RAF and AD urged the revolutionary

---

[12] O'Hara was a member of the Irish National Liberation Army (INLA), who died in 1981 during a hunger strike in Northern Ireland. This was the first time that a RAF commando was named after a terrorist who did not belong to the organization. As such, it symbolized the inauguration of the European revolutionary front with the AD.

[13] See the interview with the RAF leaders published in June 1985 by *Zusammen Kampfen*, and reprinted in *Ligne Rouge* of July 1985.

[14] George Jackson, a member of the black activist group Soledad Brothers, was killed in August 1971 while attempting to escape from prison in California.

movement in Western Europe to proceed to a new stage of dialogue and reorganization. Every anti-imperialist strategic offensive, they asserted, changed the balance of power in favor of the revolution and contributed to the collapse of the imperialist system.[15]

The fighting units carried out about 20 more operations in 1985, and eleven in 1986, while the commando units carried out two large-scale operations in each of those years.[16] The two major operations of 1986 were the murders of industrialist Karl-Heinz Beckurts and policy-maker Gerold Von Braunmuehl.[17] The murder of Braunmuehl, a deputy minister and political-director of the German Ministry of Foreign Affairs, was the first attack against a senior government official, and the first to be perpetrated in the West German capital. Braunmuehl was accused of being instrumental in drawing up European policy, and in setting up, coordinating and strengthening imperialist supranational organizations. In the communiqué accompanying his murder, the RAF repeated its call for the establishment of a revolutionary front in Western Europe. 'Organizing a revolutionary front means planning an attack. Ideological nuances or revolutionary models are irrelevant'.[18] According to the statement, the imperialist system was in the throes of a grave crisis following US fiascos in Nicaragua, Angola and Lebanon. The US air strike on Libya (following terrorist attacks on US targets in West Germany) and the Middle East political process, were viewed by the RAF as part of the global war against the revolutionary fighters, on a level with counter-insurgency cooperation by the secret services, police and armed forces in Western Europe. The US attack on Libya was important in that it set the confrontation with international liberation struggles on a military footing.

Throughout 1987 and most of 1988, RAF commandos and the smaller fighting units virtually ceased to operate. The organization's mouthpiece, the *Zusammen Kampfen*, also closed around that time.

In February 1987 the leaders of the AD's international faction, Jean-Marc Rouillan and Natalie Ménigon, were arrested in France. On 27 November of that year, the arrest of Max Frérot, operational leader of the AD's national faction, and the last to remain at large, signaled the end of this period of Euro-terrorism. After his arrest, Rouillan declared that the RAF was about to launch a new offensive, but history proved otherwise.

---

[15] See also Pluchinsky, *An Organizational and Operational Analysis of Germany's Red Army Faction*, p. 68.

[16] These figures were taken from Becker's chronologies. See Jillian Becker, *Terrorism in West Germany. The Struggle for What?* (London: Institute for the Study of Terrorism, 1988).

[17] Beckurts was a board member of the Siemens company and president of the West German Association of Industrialists and the Atomic Energy Work Group; he was accused of representing the most reactionary sectors of the German industrial/military complex.

[18] Quoted from the French text in *Notes et Etudes*, No. 5 (May 1988), pp. 85-89.

Raufer and Haut ascribed the operational paralysis of the RAF to a combination of factors: tactically, the RAF leaders, who never fully trusted their French comrades, were anxious to reassess the situation in view of the damage caused by the arrest of the AD leaders; strategically, the West European Front comprised the RAF and AD only. Following the arrest of the AD leaders, the RAF needed to seek a new strategic direction.[19]

Indeed, the final issue of *Zusammen Kampfen* (March 1988), carried a long article, entitled 'From Defense to Offense – the Struggle against Imperialism's Contemporary Strategic Plans'. The RAF, it asserted, was to forge an alliance with the Italian BR-PCC. In September 1988, it sent a joint proposal in German and Italian, together with a statement on the attempted murder of Hans Tietmeyer, to several newspapers – a clear sign that the BR-PCC had replaced the defunct AD within the Anti-Imperialist Guerrilla Front.[20]

The establishment of a coalition between the RAF and BR was a long and arduous process. Efforts by the RAF to enlist the BR in the anti-imperialist front had begun in 1985.[21] BR records of a meeting between the two organizations in January 1988 suggest that serious talks took place between their representatives in the course of 1987.[22] The dialogue between the RAF and the BR-PCC highlighted a conflict of interests between the two parties, as well as several differences of opinion on regional and international issues.

The RAF favored action against industrial reorganization. It cited as examples its attacks against Beckurts and Braunmuehl, and cooperation with the AD in this field, including the AD attack against the president of the Renault company. The BR on the other hand, believed that industrial reorganization had already run its course in most West European countries. It believed that the strategic struggle (symbolic attacks) should focus on European unification. The front should attack the policy behind the economy, rather than the economy itself. Thus, the main targets should be the politicians, rather than industrialists. The murder of Braunmuehl, was consistent with this view.

On regional issues, the BR wished to focus on the situation in the Middle East and the Persian Gulf, and explore an alliance with Palestinian organizations. The

---

[19] See Raufer and Haut, *RAF – Une organisation zéro traces*, p. 42.

[20] On 20 September 1988, the RAF Haled Aqar commando unit attempted to kill Hans Tietmeyer, state secretary of the West German Finance Ministry.

[21] A number of articles by BR militants, some of whom were jailed, were published in *Zusammen Kampfen* No. 6 (May 1986). Beckurts was murdered in July 1986 by the 'Mara Cagol commando.' Mara Cagol, the wife of jailed BR leader Curcio, was herself a leader of the organization. She was killed in 1975 while evading arrest in Italy. The assassination of Beckurts by the 'Mara Cagol commando' was probably the RAF way of trying to persuade the BR to change its mind about joining the anti-imperialist front.

[22] The document summarizing the meeting was discovered when the Italian police searched a BR-PCC safe house in June 1988. The document was first published in the German *Terrorismus*, No. 2, February 1990.

RAF, meanwhile, preferred to establish new guerrilla movements in Norway, Sweden and Holland.[23]

Finally, there was disagreement regarding Soviet foreign policy. The RAF believed that the Soviet decision to cut off aid to liberation movements was motivated by a desire to defuse international tension; the BR believed that it stemmed from internal, objective difficulties.

Despite the apparent intractability of both sides during negotiations, an agreement was finally reached and a joint manifesto was published in September 1988. This stated that differences in the historical background and perspectives of organizations should not obstruct the unification of the various struggles. It emphasized the need to overcome dogmatism among the fighting forces and the revolutionary movement of Western Europe. Despite this magnanimous declaration, the BR positions prevailed:

(1)   Western Europe, as the intersection of three axes (state and society, North and South, and East and West), was portrayed as the main theatre of conflict between the international proletariat and the imperialistic bourgeoisie. As the political power of the US waned, Western Europe was perceived as playing an increasing part in the anti-revolutionary imperialist struggle – on economic, military, political and diplomatic fronts.

(2)   Of all conflict zones in the Third World, only the Middle East was singled out specifically; West Europe was condemned for oppressing the Palestinian and Lebanese peoples.

Despite these auspicious beginnings, the establishment of a united West European revolutionary front was stillborn, due to the arrest in Rome on 7 September 1988 of the entire operational leadership of the BR-PCC. This effectively disrupted the second attempt to set up a Euro-terrorist (RAF – BR-PCC) coalition.

In 1989 the imprisoned RAF leaders staged a hunger strike and proposed to start discussions on a new orientation for the revolutionary struggle. During this period, radical changes such as the collapse of communist East Germany (GDR) and the 'imminent collapse of the socialist system of states' convinced the external leadership to revise its strategy. In April 1992 the RAF announced that it 'unilaterally called off the campaign of assassinations of the political and economic apparatus as a first step towards a negotiated settlement with the state'.[24]

---

[23]   It is not clear why the RAF chose Scandinavia in particular.

[24]   See 'RAF: We must seek what is new', *Konkret* (August 1992), pp. 6-7, and A Brief History of the Red Army Fraction, Spring 1994, p. 1 at <http://www.etext.org/Politics/Arm.The.Spirit/ Guerrilla/Europe/Red.Army.Faction/history.of.the.raf>.

III.   THE ACTION DIRECTE

The AD was a relatively new organization when it allied with the RAF. Contacts between the two organizations apparently began at some point in 1982 or 1983, engineered by Jean Asselmyer, a senior activist in French radical left-wing circles.[25] For many years Asselmyer was considered the RAF representative in France, working tirelessly for the release of RAF prisoners. He was the founder of *L'internationale*, the AD publication which also reproduced texts by other terrorist organizations, and a fervent advocate of a joint front with the RAF.[26]

In the autumn of 1982, following a series of attacks against Jewish targets, including the bloodiest one against the Goldberg restaurant in Paris, the French government outlawed the AD. Although Rouillan (leader of the AD international faction) claimed responsibility for most of these attacks, it later transpired that the Palestinians had attacked the restaurant.

Differences of opinion concerning strategy and targets culminated in the formation of a splinter group, the 'First of August Revolutionary Collective', which advocated participation in struggles in factories and working class neighborhoods. Although the collective believed the AD was sincere in attacking 'Zionist' targets, it felt that this strategy was politically misguided and prejudiced the cause of communism. The group disbanded after a number of its members were arrested in September and October of that year.

Meanwhile, Olivier's national faction continued to act independently of the international faction. (Personal rivalry between Rouillan and Olivier precluded political activity.)

In October 1982 Oriach was arrested and charged with planning anti-Israeli and anti-Jewish attacks. The ideological and personal differences between the two groups intensified as his supporters campaigned separately to free him. This development considerably diminished the faction's interest in the Palestinian issue. In November, after the arrest of more AD militants, and the discovery of a large stock of weapons and documents, distrust and suspicion intensified among the remaining members.

In effect, it was Rouillan's international faction that continued the struggle on an international level and joined the West European Revolutionary Front. In 1983 it launched a campaign on behalf of imprisoned comrades, protesting their prison conditions. The special group which was set up for this purpose, Active Defense

---

[25] Asselmyer, born in Alsace, was active in West German leftist circles in 1967, and published revolutionary newspapers in support of terrorist and guerrilla organizations.

[26] On this topic see Gayraud, 'Histoire politique d'une Organisation Communiste Combatante,' pp. 134-37, and Alain Hamon and Jean-Charles Marchand, *Action Directe. Du terrorisme français a l'euroterrorisme* (Paris: Editions du Seuil, 1986), p. 47.

(Défense Active – DA), grew close to similar groups in Europe, particularly in Belgium, Germany and Spain.

During 1983 a number of journals promoting world revolution and international cooperation appeared. These included: *L'internationale*, the AD's unofficial organ; *Subversion*, published from prison by Oriach; *Solidarité anti-impérialiste*, *Combattre pour le communisme*, and *Correspondances internationals*, which published RAF and BR texts in French. These publications raised awareness of international problems, in particular of revolutionary campaigns in West Germany, Italy and Spain.[27]

On the operational level, the AD renewed activities in August, exactly a year after its previous campaign against 'Zionist' targets.[28] The last attack of 1983, in November, targeted the headquarters of the Adventist Church in Paris, to protest the support by the French Church of Western nuclear deterrents. The brief memorandum accompanying the attack warned 'supporters of the crusades to desist!' and denounced the deployment of Pershing and other cruise missiles on French soil. This marked the first occasion that slogans of the European Revolutionary Front appeared in AD leaflets.

AD militants also took part in five armed robberies in and around Paris. These were followed by a shoot-out with the police in May 1983 in which two police officers were killed and a third injured. AD leaders were subsequently forced to leave the capital and went into hiding in Belgium.

During police raids against AD activists, Italian terrorists were found to be heavily involved with the organization. They belonged to the Organized Communists for the Proletarian Liberation (Comunisti Organizzati per la Liberazione Proletaria – COLP), a small group that split from Prima Linea, the second largest Italian terrorist organization.[29] The connection between COLP and AD was maintained by Régis Schleicher, Rouillan's right-hand man, and one of the 'professional' terrorists

---

[27]   See Stephen Segaller, *Invisible Armies. Terrorism into the 1990s* (1st American edn.) (New York: Harcourt Brace Jovanovich, 1987), pp. 50-51, and Roland Jacquard, *La longue traque d'Action Directe* (Paris: Albin Michel, 1987), p. 109.

[28]   On 28 August 1983 the AD blew up the Ministry of Defense headquarters and French Socialist Party headquarters. AD leaflets demanded the withdrawal of French forces from Chad and the release of revolutionary prisoners irrespective of nationality. Similar demands were included in the leaflets accompanying the bombing of French naval headquarters on 26 September 1983, and that of a military club on 29 September 1983.

[29]   Ciro-Rizzato, a COLP member who joined an AD cell, was killed during an armed robbery of a Parisian bank in October 1983. An AD 'unit' bearing his name attacked three targets during 1984. At least three other COLP members worked for the AD: Franco Fiorina, Vincenzo Spano and Gloria Argano. Two of them took part in the shoot-out of May 1983 in which two French police officers were killed. Fiorina, according to the testimony of a COLP member interrogated in Italy, supplied some of the weapons used by the AD in its attacks. Spano was arrested in February 1984 in France. Weapons and documents belonging to the AD were found in his apartment. See Jacquard, *La longue traque d'Action Directe*, pp. 90-98.

of the AD.[30] 1983 was therefore described by Segaller as AD's 'Italian period,' although ties with the Italian revolutionaries had began in 1980.[31]

1.   The idea of the 'international anti-imperialist front'

The strategic evolution of a formal alliance between the AD and RAF in January 1985 can be followed by studying *L'internationale*. The editorial of its first issue, entitled 'The Destruction of the War Party', warned against the aggressive tendencies of capitalist agents (US-controlled multinational corporations, NATO), which could easily spark war, despite protests by pacifist circles. According to the article, imperialist France, for its part, the world's third largest arms manufacturer, never ceased to fight in Africa and Chad, and was currently embroiled in Lebanon against the Palestinian and Lebanese people.

Proletarians and progressive intellectuals understood that the collapse of imperialism could be brought about only through support of liberation movements (witness the Algerian and Vietnamese fighters). Such support, however, was not enough to establish the direct connection between proletarian struggles in the metropolis and in the periphery.[32] The RAF contributed to the revolutionary movement by recognizing that proletarian internationalism should strike at the heart of the imperialist metropolis. Internationalism was not restricted to solidarity with liberation movements, but included solidarity between communist groups on the periphery and revolutionary groups in the metropolis (The attempt of PFLP commandos to obtain the release of RAF members by hijacking a Lufthansa plane to Mogadishu was cited as an example).[33]

According to the RAF, the fall of the Shah in Iran and the Soviet invasion of Afghanistan triggered a new shift in US strategy – the reorganization of the imperialist military system through the establishment of a 'swift intervention force' and the development of new military technologies. This facilitated the deployment of NATO forces in regional disputes (Chad, the Falkland Islands and Lebanon). The election of President Reagan had led to the expansion of strategic arms and the proposed 'Star War' program in March 1983. The US, for its part, was seeking the reinforcement of the nuclear missile system in Europe, and the deployment of cruise missiles that could target the USSR. Thus, NATO was preparing itself for war. France had played its part in this trend through developing

---

[30]   Note the COLP attack against a synagogue in Milan in September 1982, possibly in solidarity with the AD attacks of that period.

[31]   See Segaller, *Invisible Armies*, pp. 50-51.

[32]   Two major articles, 'This is internationalism' and 'Against the imperialist war, Waging the class war', developed this ideological line.

[33]   This theme appeared in the BR RDS of February 1978.

its own 'swift intervention force' and preserving a military presence in Africa, the Mediterranean and the Indian Ocean.

The editorial also claimed that the notion of a Soviet threat was mere propaganda to pave the way for a war that would grant NATO free rein against the USSR. The Pentagon, it argued, ruled over a worldwide network of bases, while 90% of Soviet bases were situated within the narrow confines of Warsaw Pact countries. In order to prevent a general war in US satellite states, with the danger of nuclear escalation in Europe and the Middle East, it was essential not only to support the pacifist resistance movement, but to direct it against the true decision-making centers: NATO, the Pentagon and the secret services.[34]

At the same time, the AD published a text entitled 'Revolutionary Assignment, the International Struggle'. Given the capitalist crisis and the imminence of war, claimed the document, it was essential to establish an international organization of the proletariat in Western Europe. In practice, this meant working in each country on the basis of its special conditions, in order to further promote an international proletarian consciousness and create structured information and dialogue networks.[35]

According to this document, the previous stage of the development of revolutionary movements in Europe was limited by two factors:[36]

(1) The tendency to develop the revolutionary movement on a national basis and then 'mechanically apply the national experience to the international scene'. This was the BR case in Italy. The perception of the imperialist system as a chain of strong and weak links failed to take into account its attempts to concentrate forces in international areas where its interests were in danger.

(2) The tendency towards a general, static and theoretical unification only, based on an erroneous analysis of the confrontation between the bourgeoisie and the proletariat on a global level. Thus for example, in Western Europe, limited attempts to support the proletarian struggles had been restricted to those of the Third World.[37] L'internationale sought to organize the international struggle from a global strategic perspective of opposing forces, and to regenerate a militant communist focus in Western Europe, irrespective of current differences that arose from different national conditions.[38]

---

[34] The second issue of L'internationale (December 1983) focused even more on the 'the anti-imperialist front'. It reported the activities of German organizations (RZ and Rote Zora), the attack on NATO bunkers in Holland, and operations against military installations in the US. The purpose of these articles was to revive the 'Heidelberg spirit', as the paper called it, in memory of the first time the RAF bombed an US base in West Germany in May 1972.
[35] The article appeared in L'internationale, No. 4, Feb. 1984.
[36] Ibid.
[37] This argument was critical of RAF attitudes in the 1970s.
[38] The text appeared in an editorial in issue No. 5, March 1984. This issue also contained theoretical texts of the BR-PCC and the German RZ. Issue No. 6, April 1984, was dedicated to

2.   Implementation of the 'global anti-imperialist front' strategy

After this consolidation, the AD was ready to launch a new campaign against NATO, the French arms industries, and the WEU. In 1984 it carried out seven bomb attacks: three in July, two in August, and another two in October.[39] A clear shift in the AD strategic orientation from late January to early July 1984 was reflected by the leaflets accompanying the attacks.

The first operation, against the Atlantic Institute in Paris, was depicted as a turning point in AD political/military offensive. The success or failure of imperialist plans depended on the ability of the progressive elements in the proletariat to unite.[40] The Atlantic Institute was portrayed as a NATO propaganda tool, and as a major link with the countries of Western Europe.[41] Another leaflet acknowledged that each organization had to fight in the area it excelled in, but should identify with the struggles of proletariats in other areas.[42] The main aim was 'the destruction of NATO and the imperialist program'.[43] The purpose of the two October attacks was described as renewal of the offensive.[44] Indeed, the united offensive had resumed in early 1985.

3.   The West European Revolutionary Guerrilla Front

The AD was first to fulfill its commitment to the West European Guerrilla Front. On 25 January 1985, Gen. Audran, director of international relations in the French Ministry of Defense, was assassinated. This was the first political killing carried out by the AD.[45] The leaflet accompanying the attack was bilingual (French and German) and signed by the Elizabeth Van-Dyke Commandos, after

---

the AD and included a chronology of attacks perpetrated by the organization, in which for the first time certain attacks were confirmed as AD operations.

[39]   The Ciro Rizzato Unit and the Benchellal Lehouari Unit carried out the attacks.

[40]   The attack was carried out on 12 July 1984 and was reported in *L'internationale* under the rubric 'Anti-imperialist global front'.

[41]   The institute dealt with high-priority issues for NATO and Europe, such as industrial reorganization, the deployment of missiles, and European political and military unification under the aegis of NATO.

[42]   The leaflet referred to two attacks, namely against the computer department of the Ministry of Defense and a department of the Ministry of Industry responsible for operating oil pipes for NATO allies.

[43]   The slogans of the two attacks carried out in August 1984 are similar to those of the leaflets of July 1984. One attack was carried out against the building of the European Space Agency and another, which failed against the building of the WEU.

[44]   The attacks were against Dassault, manufacturers of aircraft and missiles, and Hispano-Bugatti, manufacturers of spare parts for NATO planes.

[45]   The killing of the police agent of Lebanese extraction in 1982 might also be considered a political murder.

the RAF member who was killed in Nuremberg in a clash with the German police. The AD argued that Audran played a major military and economic role in the imperialist strategy to unify the countries of Europe under NATO supervision. Emphasis was placed on the Paris-Bonn political/military axis, which combined French nuclear power with West German military, financial and economic might and turned it into the 'vanguard of the struggle against the international proletariat'. The revolutionaries, stated the leaflet, had 'to establish a political/military front in Western Europe as part of the global war between the international proletariat and the imperialist bourgeoisie'.

The AD offensive continued with a series of bombings. Attacks against the IMF and the World Bank were linked to the G-7 summit due to take place in Bonn to discuss 'the re-organization and concentration of the political, economic and military initiatives of the imperialist centers, and the strengthening of the preventive counter-revolution'.[46]

Gen. Blandin was targeted for his role in implementing many of the French Ministry of Defense's reorganization projects and for the industrial and military integration of France into NATO. This operation, albeit abortive, represented a step forward for the AD in the campaign that had begun in July 1984. It is particularly interesting that the terrorist unit responsible for the attack was named after Antonio Lo Muscio, of the Armed Proletarian Nuclei (Nuclei Armati Proletari – NAP), an Italian organization which merged in 1976 with the BR. This might indicate that the AD was considering entering into a dialogue with the BR-PCC.[47]

The last attack in the series, against a US military base near Frankfurt, was carried out in conjunction with the RAF. It was the first time that the AD operated outside France.[48] The leaflet was signed by both the AD and RAF on behalf of the George Jackson Commandos. It presented the attack as a response to a new imperialist offensive, 'the struggle against international terror'. President Reagan's speech to the European Parliament in which he supported 'a Europe stretching from Lisbon to Moscow' was interpreted as an attempt to intervene in Soviet affairs, and was compared to the retaliatory operations against Nicaragua and Lebanon.

The AD international faction rounded off the year with four attacks against targets associated with French commercial interests in South Africa, against a

---

[46] An allusion to the attacks against the buildings of the IMF and the World Bank on 27 April 1985; against TRT and SAT Communications, which worked for the Ministry of Defense and NATO, on 30 April 1985; a combined AD-RAF car bomb attack against an US army base in Rhein Main in West Germany on 8 August 1985; the attempted murder of the general supervisor of armed forces, Gen. Henri Blandin on 26 June 1985.

[47] After this attack, the AD no longer called its units after Ciro Rizzato and Benchellal Lehouari, perhaps in order to demonstrate a broader international solidarity.

[48] This attack was the most lethal as far as the AD was concerned. The car bomb that exploded in the US military base near Frankfurt caused two deaths and about 20 casualties. It is not clear exactly what role the AD played in the attack.

background of violent protests by blacks in South Africa.[49] Leaflets accompanying these attacks also referred to the wretched situation of immigrant workers in France, but did not mention either NATO or issues relating to the West European Guerrilla Front.

In February 1986 *Zusammen Kampfen* published an interview with anonymous AD militants in order to summarize the year that had elapsed since the publication of the joint RAF-AD statement.[50] The AD activists described the Paris-Bonn axis as a lever for the unification of Western Europe under a global US strategy that included the deployment of nuclear missiles in Europe and MX missiles in the US, and the development of the SDI program. France, although not officially a member of NATO, played a major role in this strategy, particularly in relation to the Eureka space technology development program, closely related to the SDI program. France was willing to join the new NATO strategy that called for an offensive against the Warsaw Pact countries and promised to replace the US forces in Europe in case they were embroiled in Third World conflicts. The AD militants were diffident when questioned about the unity of the revolutionary movement. Strangely, there was no mention of joint activity with the RAF despite the fact that only a year had elapsed since the establishment of the strategic alliance between the two organizations. The subject, raised only in a question by the newspaper's correspondent, was left unanswered.

In April and July 1986 the AD attempted to murder Guy Brana, deputy president of the Association of French Industrialists, and exploded bombs in front of the headquarters of the Organization for Economic Cooperation and Development in Paris. The most significant operation carried out by the AD international faction was the murder of Renault president G. Besse on 17 November 1986.

The only attack in this period that did not appear to conform to AD strategy was the bombing of Interpol headquarters. The AD subsequently published a statement announcing that the reorganization of the private and public sectors was in fact preparation for an imperialist war, as demonstrated by the G-7 Tokyo summit, which had been accompanied by an intensive war against 'terror', culminating in the bombing of Libya.[51] Interpol, as a branch of NATO headed by an American president and English director-general, was viewed as coordinating the oppression of revolutionary movements.[52]

The AD published its last significant document shortly before the arrest of its two historical leaders, Rouillan and Ménigon. The document claimed that the

---

[49]   All the attacks were carried out on 4 September 1985.
[50]   For the English version of the interview, see Alexander and Pluchinsky (eds.), *Europe's Red Terrorists*, pp. 142-46.
[51]   The attack was carried out on 16 May 1986 and 'Communiqué No. 2' was published on 29 May.
[52]   See Dartnell, *Action Directe*, pp. 474-46.

attacks against Besse, Brana, Interpol and the airbase in Frankfurt marked the end of the second stage in the revolutionary offensive, namely the reconstruction of the working class in Western Europe as part of an internationalist process.[53] This stage had been ended by the emergence of new conditions, the heightened contradictions between the classes and the savage suppression of RAF and AD terror. The AD hoped to use the student demonstrations and railworker strikes of 1986-87 as a catalyst for revolutionary activity. By murdering the president of Renault, the AD had tried to prove its involvement in the workers' movement. Nonetheless, the AD never had the chance to proceed to the next stage of its new strategy.[54]

IV. THE RED BRIGADES

1. Historical RAF-BR ties

The violence and propaganda of German revolutionary students had a strong impact on Italian students who were already in a state of revolt in the late 1960s. According to Capana, this was because the German students were the first to lead a revolutionary movement in a progressive industrialized country.[55] According to Ventura, some of the founders of the BR, including Curcio, held a three-day conference in Paris with Andreas Baader, leader of the RAF, in the early months of 1970 to organize terrorist activity.[56] Franceschini, Curcio's comrade-in-arms, claimed that from 1970 on, the RAF and M2J militants came to the BR. They met with the Germans in the apartments of 'legal' militants to discuss previous operations and exchange false documents. This relationship with RAF disintegrated after 1972 because the Germans were mainly interested in global matters and the Third World. Relations with the M2J continued because of the mutual interest in the issues of squatting, foreign immigrants (Turks and Italians in Germany) and even operational experience.[57] These contacts evidently found no concrete expression until the second half of the 1970s. Buonavita believes that before 1974, the BR preferred to establish ties with the RZ and M2J, since their political line was closer to the BR.[58] The RAF not only supported the Third World

---

[53] The document, 26 pages long and untitled, was circulated on 11 February 1987.
[54] Dartnell, *Action*, pp. 427-28.
[55] See Mario Capanna, *Formidabili quegli anni* (Milano: Rizzoli, 1988), p. 51.
[56] See Angelo Ventura, 'Il problema delle origini del terrorismo di sinistra', in Donatella della Porta (ed.), *Terrorismi in Italia* (Bologna: Società Editrice il Mulino, 1984), p. 91.
[57] According to Franceschini, the M2J discussed with the BR the modus operandi for the kidnapping of Peter Lorenz in Berlin. See Alberto Franceschini and Giustolisi P. F. Buffa, *Mara, Renato e io. Storia dei fondatori delle Br* (4th edn.) (Milano: Oscar Mondadori, 2000).
[58] See Buonavita's testimony, Corte d'Assise di Roma. 32/81 R.G. Agostini. Sergio Luigi + 70, p. 4.

liberation movements, it maintained ties with the Palestinian *fedayeen* – a policy considered rash by the historical BR leadership. It was another Italian terrorist organization, Workers' Power (Potere Operaio – PO) that cooperated with the RAF and offered it logistical assistance during this period.[59]

Moretti's decision to branch out into the international arena and strengthen the BR links with other revolutionary organizations in 1977-79 led to the reestablishment of ties with the RAF.[60] After lengthy debates, the two parties concluded that differences between the historical, political, and social backgrounds of their two countries and organizations ruled out a common strategy. However, according to Moretti, the BR occasionally supplied forged documents and financial assistance to the RAF. According to Morucci, the RAF saw the US as the main obstacle to the political evolution of the German people. According to the BR, this indicated that the RAF harbored German national sentiment.[61] In sum, the BR leadership was convinced that the ideological approach of the RAF ran counter to true revolutionary development. Consequently, the two organizations drew apart.

Links resumed after the BR success in kidnapping Moro, the RAF abortive kidnapping of Schleyer and the suicide of most of its jailed members. Morucci testified that until this point, a kind of rivalry existed between the two organizations. Each sought to strengthen its image and sphere of influence in the European arena. Indeed, the kidnapping of Schleyer infuriated Moretti, who feared it would steal the limelight from the Moro operation, which was already in the planning stage.

Savasta presented a more complex picture of RAF-BR relations.[62] He claimed that occasional meetings took place in 1980-81 between representatives of the two organizations but as Moretti was wary of the Soviet influence on the RAF and its alienation from the political/social reality, no agreement was reached. The BR leaders could hardly fail to notice how the move towards greater rapprochement between West Germany and the communist bloc was swiftly followed by the arrest of RAF activists, indicating their probable betrayal by the Soviets to the West German authorities.[63]

---

[59] See Fiorini's testimony, *Ministero dell'Interno. Dipartamento della Pubblica Sicurezza. Raporti internazionali dei gruppi terroristici italiani di sinistra* (undated), pp. 16-18.

[60] Moretti himself testified that ties with the RAF resumed in the summer of 1978. See Moretti, *Brigatte Rosse*, pp. 186-88.

[61] Becker, *Terrorism in West Germany*, pp. 77-78.

[62] See Savasta's testimony, *Ministero dell'Interno*, p. 100, and Procura della Reppublica di Venezia – PM Gabriele Ferrari. Requisitoria del 18/7/83 nel p.p. 179/82 contro Alunni Corrado + 122 (BR). Requisitoria finale, Documents 1/19, 5/9.

[63] Another leader, Senzani, considered the recommendation to join forces with the RAF, as proposed in the leaflet accompanying the kidnapping of Gen. Dozier, as tantamount to unification with the Soviet bloc, given the RAF's pro-Soviet stance. Senzani strongly opposed this move, as reflected in the leaflet put out by the Venice cell.

2.   Ties with French organizations

Until the establishment of the AD there were no terrorist organizations in France of the caliber of the BR or RAF. In the first half of the 1970s, the French Proletarian Left (Gauche Prolétarienne – GP) established ties with the Italian terrorist organizations PL and BR. In the second half of the 1970s, the NAPAP, another small and operationally insignificant organization, became active in France.[64] Donat-Cattin described the French organizations predating the AD as weak groups which admired the Italians because they believed that they had reached the stage of civil war.[65]

The most significant form of cooperation mentioned by BR militants was the help offered by French terrorist Paul [Bandit] to Senzani's 'Prison Front'. Bandit provided training in the assembling of missiles received from the Palestinians, the launch of bazooka attacks, and detonating of remote-control bombs.[66] Although there was some question as to whether Bandit represented the AD in these transactions, he clearly had extensive military experience.[67] In the main, the assistance offered by the French organizations to their Italian counterparts involved smuggling fugitive members into France and helping them to integrate into French society. Indeed, France became a major refuge for Italian terrorists and revolutionaries, some of whom subsequently became active within AD, as described above.

3.   The idea of the West European Anti-Imperialist Guerrilla Front

The first reference to political integration of European FCOs appeared in the RDS of February 1978, which called for 'a constructive debate between the various organizations, a search for tactical and strategic programs in areas where it was possible to unite the various revolutionary initiatives into reference points for the entire proletariat in the European continent'.[68] Some researchers saw the 20

---

[64] This organization's main ties were with the PL in 1979-80, whom it even provided with explosives. See Fernando della Corte's testimony, *Ministero dell'Interno*, p. 176.

[65] See Donat-Cattin's testimony, p. 40 (unidentified juridical source).

[66] See testimonies of Gino Aldi, *Ministero dell'Interno*, pp. 81-90, and Michele Buzzati, p. 129. The surname 'Bandit' appears in an article by Judge Imposimato, called 'Strategies and Ties between European and Middle East Terrorists', p. 154. According to this, Bandit was a member of the AD.

[67] According to Hamon and Marchand, Paul's real name was Jean-Louis Baudet. He was arrested in France at the behest of the Italian authorities, but claimed that in fact he had been sent by the French authorities to help persuade the French terrorists (not AD militants) to lay down their arms. He was sentenced to four years' imprisonment in France. See Hamon and Marchand, *Action Directe*, pp. 160-61

[68] See *Risoluzione della Direzione Strategica*, February 1978 as translated by this author.

propositions of 'The Bee and the Communist', drawn up by the jailed BR leaders in December 1980, as a blueprint for the European FCOs.[69] Proposition No. 19 of this text declared war on NATO and on the special anti-guerrilla forces; Proposition No. 20 demanded Italy's dissociation from the imperialist chain, cooperation with all nations on an equal basis, and the development of proletarian anti-nationalism.

The first contribution to this new struggle was the kidnapping of US Gen. Dozier, a senior commander of NATO forces in Europe. The leaflet circulated after the kidnapping called for further attacks against NATO and similar targets, under the leadership of the RAF and BR, and called for 'a new proletarian internationalism' and 'closer ties with other European revolutionary forces'. In a document explaining the kidnapping, the BR-PCC portrayed NATO as the main imperialist tool in ruling Western Europe, the Mediterranean and the Middle East.[70] This document stressed that the enemy in the mid-term was the one representing the most dangerous tendency, namely US imperialism. It was therefore impossible to completely rule out tactical reliance on forces associated with the USSR and the socialist camp. Obviously, this choice would be made in full awareness of the growing role of social-imperialism and from a position of total political and organizational autonomy.

The anti-NATO and anti-US emphasis was a logical consequence of the analysis of BR-PCC leaders of the international situation: growing tendency to war fostered mainly by the Reagan administration, unjustified aggression towards the 'progressive' nations of the Mediterranean and the Middle East (the attack against Libya in the Sirte Gulf), and counter-insurgency coordination between imperialist states.

According to this text, the RAF was the key to the establishment of proletarian internationalism in Europe. Its experience in attacks against NATO officials was an important asset in the fight against the common enemy, namely, the military and political apparatus of US imperialism. The document cited various obstacles to a full understanding such as RAF criticism of BR parochialism, the belief that each organization had to fight its own enemy in its own country. The BR did not reject this criticism outright, but claimed that its actions – intensification of the anti-imperialist and anti-NATO campaign – would prove its case. The document also called for the adoption of the slogan of the leaflet accompanying the RAF attack against the NATO base in Ramstein: 'A war to end the imperialist war, by attacking the strategic centers of the war, and the heart of the American war

---

69   See for example Pluchinsky, *Western Europe's Red Terrorists*, p. 26.

70   See 'Contro la guerra imperialista, intensificare la guerra rivoluzionaria, sviluppare l'internazionalismo combattente', Gruppo di elaborazione '16 Marzo', Nov. 1981, in *CONTRO-informazione*, No. 22, Feb. 1982, and an analysis thereof in the chapter on the BR.

machine.' It appealed to all FCOs 'to commit themselves to immediate participation in the war against NATO'.

The P-GPM faction of the Red Brigade, which included some of the BR founding members, and signed its documents 'Brigata di Palmi', also devoted an entire section of an underground document published in December 1981 to the issue of NATO.[71] This document defined the Atlantic Pact as 'an integrative transnational mechanism for an internal and external counterrevolution', an aggressive and threatening force unleashed against the European proletariat. However, unlike the BR-PCC, the document did not explicitly demand the integration of revolutionary forces into a front with common strategic goals. Nonetheless, a special chapter in the above document was devoted to internationalist unification with the RAF. It looked up to the RAF as the forebear of the urban guerrilla movement in Europe, and admired it for having adopted an internationalist language from the outset. It likewise applauded the RAF offensive against US imperialism (citing attacks against Gen. Kroesen, the Ramstein military base, and the US headquarters in Heidelberg).

The document also pointed to friction between the two organizations. For the RAF, the main contradiction was that between US-led imperialism and the Third World, and this dictated its political/military strategy. Until recently, the RAF had claimed that the urban guerrilla and the struggle of the masses were subordinated to the struggle of the Third World. The BR, on the other hand, maintained that the struggle should be waged 'from the centre to the periphery'.

The BR-PCC also criticized the RAF for disregarding the role of Soviet social-imperialism and for applying the term imperialism exclusively to the US. Members of the RAF, they pointed out with blatant sarcasm, 'were quite capable of believing that US imperialism was licking the wounds inflicted on it by the struggling nations … with social-imperialism's kind assistance'. The overall conclusion was that in order to establish an internationalist union, a strategic debate with the RAF was essential in order to examine all possible levels of political and military integration.

Two months after the authorities freed Gen. Dozier, the BR-PCC announced 'a strategic withdrawal … to give the vanguard time to prepare its next offensive in a close dialectic tie with the masses'.[72] The tactical fiasco of the Dozier operation enhanced existing divisions. As noted, 1982-83 was a fairly quiet period, both on the operational and on the ideological fronts.

---

[71] See 'Crisi, guerra e internazionalismo proletario', Brigata di Palmi, Dec. 1981. in *CONTROinformazione*, No. 22, Feb. 1982 and an analysis thereof in the chapter on the BR.

[72] Quoted from Xavier Raufer, *La Storia poco conosciuta delle Brigate Rosse (1980-1987)* (Institut de Criminologie de Paris: Seminario di Ricerca sulla Violenza Politique, 1987), p. 25.

The murder of Hunt in 1984, which was specifically connected to developments in the Middle East, merely represented an isolated departure from BR's anti-NATO strategy. However, the leaflet accompanying this murder did refer to the Italian role in NATO, the deployment of nuclear missiles in Sicily, and the presence of the Italian forces in Lebanon as lackeys of US imperialism.

Chapter 4 of this book described the divisions within the BR towards the end of 1984; the larger militant faction, the BR-PCC, identified with European terrorist organizations that prioritized the anti-imperialist and anti-NATO struggle, while the BR-UCC focused on domestic issues. This coincided with a growing rapprochement between the RAF and AD, culminating in the joint manifesto of January 1985 on the establishment of the West European Anti-Imperialist Guerrilla Front.[73]

The RDS No. 20, the last strategic resolution of the BR-PCC, published in March 1985, emphasized the economic integration and interdependency of the imperialist nations.[74] The alliance of imperialist forces made it imperative to strengthen the anti-imperialist front so as to prevent the enemy from focusing on one area of conflict, such as: the US attempt to isolate the revolution in Nicaragua. *For internationalism to be meaningful, the revolution had first to be carried out within the (nation) state*, while still taking into account international developments (emphasis in source). The RDS ended with a description of the increasing likelihood of an imperialist war. The defeat of the proletarian dictatorship in the USSR and China proved that the communists had failed in their task to set up a united, international, proletarian movement. The struggle against Western imperialism was common to all revolutionary forces irrespective of their strategic goals, be these national liberation or the seizure of political control through the proletariat.

The BR-PCC saw itself as part of the anti-imperialist front, as illustrated by its political platform and its tactical achievements (the kidnappings of Gen. Dozier and Hunt). These anti-NATO actions were not undertaken in support of national liberation wars, but *were regarded as part of the basic platform of the revolutionary process in Italy*. For these reasons, the BR activities were *linked to those of all the other revolutionary forces* (emphasis in source).

A BR-UCC leaflet of a later period also referred to international issues, such as Reagan's SDI program, increases in war budgets, involvement in the conflicts of other nations and peoples (Nicaragua, Salvador, Palestine, Lebanon, etc.) and Spadolini's role in bringing Italian defense policy into line with that of the US

---

[73] The Italian translation of the manifesto was distributed in Venice on 5 March 1985.

[74] On 27 March, the BR-PCC murdered the professor of economics, member of the DC, Enzio Tarantelli in Rome. The RDS No. 20, together with the leaflet taking responsibility for the murder, were found next to his body.

and NATO.[75] Nonetheless, the BR-UCC continued to focus on internal issues and on activity among Italian workers. Rather than demanding the establishment of a united European front, it called for the collapse of the Craxi government and the continuation of the armed socialist struggle.

A year later, a short BR-PCC leaflet presented a radically new position.[76] US imperialism, it stated, had succeeded in whittling away the power of the Soviet bloc and winning over newly emerging countries – the sequel of national liberation struggles – to the Western camp. Imperialism had exchanged bombs in the Middle East for political negotiations. This marked a new stage, one in which political and diplomatic initiatives would pave the way for a global pro-Western strategy. The Italian government was perceived as working in full coordination with this war strategy, as well as playing an active role of its own.

As a result, solidarity was no longer enough for revolutionaries. Therefore the BR-PCC sought to strengthen the anti-imperialist front, and draw up a concrete policy that could be implemented under suitable conditions. In other words, it was proposing a policy of true alliances to be established with revolutionary forces whose goals and criteria differed from its own. Political unification within this alliance should spring from the struggle against the common enemy.

Guerrilla activities in Europe were directed against the same goals, and shared a common aim: to strike against US imperialism and NATO. These goals had much in common with the struggle of progressive nations in the Mediterranean and Middle East. The RAF and AD struggle to promote the anti-imperialist front was an important political goal which the BR sought to emulate.

On 16 April 1988 the BR-PCC murdered the Italian senator Roberto Ruffilini in what would be its last terrorist attack, and after the arrest of most of its leaders it ceased to act as an organization.

The BR-UCC published a document entitled 'How to Get Out of the Emergency Situation', which ended with a call for Italian withdrawal from NATO and the abandonment of its role as watchdog of the Mediterranean. The leaflet accompanying the murder of the Gen. Giorgieri, unlike other BR-UCC documents, emphasized international issues.[77]

Reagan's policy was portrayed as attempting to defeat the USSR through the arms race in space and escalating the 'diplomacy of guns' (bombings over Libya). This aggressive policy was apparently endorsed by European countries, including

---

[75] The leaflet was distributed on 21 February 1986, after attempted murder of Da Empoli, the prime minister's advisor on economic affairs.

[76] The leaflet was published on 14 February 1987, following an armed robbery in Rome by the BR-PCC 'to fund the revolution'.

[77] On 20 March 1987, less than a month after the robbery carried out by the BR-PCC, the BR-UCC murdered Lucio Giorgieri, director of arms procurements for the Italian Air Force. Several days later, the BR-UCC published a 14-page communiqué, followed by this ideological document.

Italy, keen to improve its autonomous imperialist status in the Mediterranean, as well as to maintain its position within the Atlantic bloc. The BR-UCC heavily condemned Defense Minister Spadolini's pro-US policy. It also derided Prime Minister Craxi's so-called 'independent stance' during the Signorella incident, when Italian military forces resisted the US attempt to abduct the Palestinian terrorist leader Abu Abbas at the end of the Achilles Lauro affair.[78]

In light of the above, it was necessary to establish unity from below and base the national policy on these issues. The document, accordingly, made no reference to either a European revolutionary or anti-imperialist front nor to other campaigns against NATO or US targets in Europe. These were the last documents published by the BR-UCC before it was eliminated by the security forces.

V.   THE BELGIAN COMBATANT COMMUNIST CELLS

1.   Historical background

Belgium, unlike its neighbors, was not noted for revolutionary or radical politics. Even when terrorism flourished in other European countries, particularly in Germany, it appeared to bypass Belgium. It should be noted that a number of institutions perceived by radical left-wing terrorist organizations as representing the 'transnational leadership of world imperialism' – namely the NATO headquarters and organizations affiliated with the EC – were located in Belgium.

Belgium in the early 1980s was ravaged by political conflict – due to an economic crisis that led to growing unemployment and cuts in government subsidies to industry and the social services. From 1983, the center-right coalition government was severely criticized for its economic austerity program and permitting the deployment of US cruise missiles in Belgium.[79]

There was increasing evidence from the 1980s that a number of radical left-wing activists, including Pierre Carette, had established ties with AD militants. Carette who maintained ties with AD and BR activists hiding in Paris, and was considered a supporter of the RAF in Belgium ran a printing press in Brussels called Documentation Communiste (DOCOM), which printed the texts of European terrorist organizations.[80]

---

[78] The Abu Abbas-led Palestinian faction was responsible for the hijacking in October 1985 of the Italian cruise ship Achille Lauro. This took place a few days after Israeli warplanes attacked the Tunis headquarters of PLO. The US citizen Leon Klinghoffer, an elderly wheelchair-bound New Yorker, was killed and thrown overboard from the ship.

[79] See Philip Jenkins, 'Strategy of Tension: The Belgian Terrorist Crisis, 1982-1986', *Terrorism*, Vol. 13, (1990), pp. 301-2.

[80] Apparently, the FARL leaflet that claimed responsibility for the murder of Israeli diplomat Bar Siman-Tov in 1982, was printed by DOCOM.

After a number of AD leaders fled to Belgium in 1982, police began to suspect that they had established a base and infrastructure there.[81] In March 1984, following an abortive attempt by Belgian police to arrest the AD leaders in Brussels and the theft of large quantities of explosives from Belgian quarries, Carette and some of his consorts were forced to go underground and formed the Combatant Communist Cells (Cellules Communistes Combattantes – CCC).[82] According to the testimony of CCC members, the organization evolved into a fully-fledged political movement in late 1982.[83]

In September 1983 a new publication, called *Ligne Rouge*, appeared in Brussels, to promote the views of the collective of the same name set up by Carette. The journal appeared concurrently with *L'internationale* and a number of other revolutionary publications that circulated in France at the time.[84] While *Ligne Rouge* did not publish any AD documents, it served as a platform for Oriach's manifestos from jail. This fact corroborated claims by CCC and AD leaders alike that there was no connection between the two organizations.

2.   Terrorist activity (October 1984-December 1985)

The first terrorist campaign by the CCC, involving 12 attacks, began on 2 October 1984 and ended in January 1985.[85] The timing of the attacks coincided with the deployment of US missiles in Belgium. The campaign was described as 'the first anti-imperialist offensive' and the targets reportedly influenced by political goals, namely economic sectors affiliated with the war machine (the arms industry), political forces ruling the bourgeois state (the coalition parties), and the ruling military-imperialistic system (NATO installations).[86] Two attacks in May 1985 also protested against government economic policy.[87]

---

[81]   They fled after the AD was outlawed. At the same time, Ménigon was wounded in a car accident. Pierre Carette was also in the car.

[82]   See the survey by the GIA (the Belgian 'Anti-terrorist interdisciplinary group'), *Cellules Communistes Combattantes, Comment tombe une organisation bavarde. Notes et Etudes*, No. 11/12, (Aug.-Oct. 1989), pp. 11-17.

[83]   See Alexander and Pluchinsky (eds.), *Europe's Red Terrorists*, p. 161.

[84]   *Ligne Rouge* published 18 issues until December 1985. Its final (19th) issue came out in December 1986. The first CCC manifestos were published in issue No. 9, Oct. 1984.

[85]   A political and strategic explanation for all its attacks can be found in the CCC communiqué, 'Concrete Answers to Concrete Questions' quoted in Alexander and Pluchinsky (eds.), *Europe's Red Terrorists*, pp. 155-56.

[86]   The following targets were attacked: the buildings of the Litton, MAN, and Honeywell corporations, the airbase in Bierset, the pumping stations of the oil pipe serving NATO installations, and the NATO Shape Support Group building.

[87]   The first attack on 1 May 1985, targeted the Belgian Association of Industrialists. As a result of the explosion, two fire-fighters were killed, the only fatalities in all CCC attacks. On 6 May, a

The second campaign, the self-styled 'Karl Marx offensive,' comprised seven operations between October and December of 1985. This also protested against austerity measures before the general elections, and encouraged the establishment of a broader revolutionary front. Targets included regional electricity companies, banks, income tax offices, and companies that were being restructured within a European context. Even before this campaign had run its course, the CCC launched its third and last campaign (the 'Pierre Akkerman offensive') to combat 'bourgeois militarism and petty bourgeois pacifism'. The sudden switch in goals was occasioned by demonstrations against the deployment of American missiles and Reagan's visit to Belgium – developments which demanded new strategic targets.

From October to December 1985, the CCC carried out five attacks against the arms industries, a NATO pipeline, and a pacifist target (the car belonging to the leader of the Belgian peace movement). The CCC final operation – the twin attacks against the Versailles (France) and Peteghem (Belgium) pipelines serving NATO – was defined as an 'international operation', for which the CCC claimed joint responsibility together with 'a group of French revolutionaries'. On 16 December 1985 the arrest of four of its key militants marked the end of the CCC's short-lived career.[88]

It is noteworthy that all CCC attacks involved the use of explosives, such as car bombs, TNT bombs or briefcases containing explosives. Unlike other terrorist organizations, CCC tactics eschewed shooting operations, and avoided the loss of human life.[89]

3.   The CCC attitude towards the West European Guerrilla Front

The first and third campaigns, and 17 out of a total of 26 attacks, were directed against US and NATO targets, indicating an international bias. Even the statement accompanying the attack against the Litton Corporation (2 October 1984) justified the attack in global terms, namely the growing threat of war as reflected in the deployment of Cruise and Pershing missiles in Europe, the breakdown of East-West negotiations, the increase in military conflicts associated with imperialist Europe, and last but not least, the arms race.[90] In another leaflet, the CCC

---

bomb was set off in the headquarters of the Belgian gendarmerie in order to 'punish' it for the death of the two fire-fighters.

[88] In an interview that appeared in *Il Bollettino*, Oct. 1991, p. 20, the four admitted from jail that they alone constituted the political expression of the organization.

[89] The document 'Concrete Answers to Concrete Questions' stated explicitly that the group decided that the first offensive would not include 'the execution of the enemy's leaders'. Following two deaths in May 1985 the CCC expressed their regret. The incident was described at every opportunity as a base attempt by the authorities to cause casualties, in order to incriminate members of the organization! See Alexander and Pluchinsky (eds.), *Europe's Red Terrorists*, p. 159.

[90] See *Ligne Rouge*, No. 9 (Oct. 1984), pp. 3-4.

castigated NATO for its war mongering, but blamed the USSR for the arms race.[91] The fact that the USSR was not actively advocating a global war policy could not disguise its capitalist character – which had long since been responsible for its exclusion from the world communist revolution. The USSR remained the second, objective enemy of the European proletariat. The pacifist movement was also accused of contributing to the likelihood of war by failing to prevent the deployment of US missiles in Europe.

In its last leaflet, the CCC related, for the first time, to the question of international solidarity in response to frequent allegations that it was the Belgian branch of the AD. The CCC asserted its complete independence from the AD, pointing out that had political or organizational unity with the AD been feasible, it would have happened long ago.[92] The CCC took also the liberty of criticizing some AD activities, although, it hastened to add, such criticism was rooted in a basic sense of solidarity. As the leaflet stated: 'Political unity cannot be achieved through the use of explosives or other military acts'. The CCC, for its part, openly admitted that it was inferior to the BR, that it did not really qualify as a FCO, and had no pretensions to lead the proletarian struggle.

The CCC attitude to inter-organizational cooperation was also evident when it drew parallels between its own operations against the Litton, M.A.N. and Honeywell companies, and those undertaken by Direct Action in Canada, and the RZ in Mayence and Düsseldorf against the same corporations.[93] The CCC saw these attacks as a response to the internationalization of global oppression and the increasingly homogeneous nature of social contradictions on an international level. According to the leaflet, 'a breathe of hope was blowing, albeit sporadically, through the center of imperialism, but this did not imply the existence of objective political unity between all streams'. In the same vein, the CCC accepted the BR-PCC view that it was necessary to develop the objective unity of the world proletariat and build a communist international based strictly on Marxist-Leninist principles.

A communiqué of October 1984 condemned the massive deployment of police against Belgian revolutionaries, and criticized the minister of justice for exploiting the attack against the synagogue in Brussels's Rue Régence in order to step up its counter-insurgency program. The organization justified the 'attack by the Palestinian opposition against Zionist imperialism', since the synagogue was regarded as a breeding ground for the police and 'the Zionist security services'.[94]

---

[91]   Ibid., p. 6. The leaflet refers to the attack on the MAN company on 2 October 1984.
[92]   Ibid., p. 8.
[93]   Ibid., p. 9. The attack in Canada was carried out in December, and those in Germany in September and November 1983.
[94]   Apparently, this was a reference to the attack on the Brussels synagogue perpetrated by the Abu-Nidal group on 19 September 1982. The Belgian police reaction was perceived by the CCC as

In May 1985 the CCC protested against social and economic conditions in Belgium. In late April, it published two documents, both of which related, albeit cursorily, to the issue of relations with other revolutionary organizations. The document entitled 'Concrete Answers,' indicated that the CCC had conducted serious discussions with other foreign groups and organizations, and reached a basic agreement on limited cooperation regarding logistical issues.[95] As part of this agreement, various international revolutionary organizations carried out a joint operation – the theft of 815 kg. of explosives which were divided up among them. All the explosives used by the CCC in its first anti-imperialist offensive came from this source. The authors of the document expressed the hope of carrying out similar operations in the future.

The third [Pierre Akkerman] offensive, portrayed as a sequel to the first anti-imperialist campaign of October 1984, was described as part of the struggle against 'bourgeois militarism and petty-bourgeois pacifism'.[96] Although four out of the five attacks were directed against 'bourgeois militarism', and although the single attack against a pacifist target was merely symbolic (the burning of pacifist leader Galaud's car), the texts published at the time accused the pacifist move-ment of harming the working class and the anti-war movement of the masses.[97] The leaflets blamed the pacifists for their law-abidingness, their stupidity, and their nationalism, and even went so far as to equate pacifism with bourgeois militarism. Galaud, the leader of the pacifist movement, was personally accused of treachery and described as an agent of social democracy.[98]

The CCC documents linked the last three attacks (late November to early December 1985) to the Geneva summit between Reagan and Gorbachev. The summit aim, they claimed, was to prepare for war, much like the Munich summit of September 1938.[99] The last operation of the Pierre Akkerman campaign was designed to promote proletarian internationalism and embraced, for the first time, open cooperation with a group of revolutionaries in France.[100] The leaflet accom-panying the joint attack alleged that international action was necessary to counteract one of the most deplorable aspects of pacifism, namely nationalism. The revolutionary movement itself had initially been beset by national rivalry, and the workers' struggle had developed along different lines in each European

---

modeled on the special methods used by West Germany and Italy in their war against revolution-ary organizations.

[95]   Alexander and Pluchinsky (eds.), *Europe's Red Terrorists*, p. 161.

[96]   Pierre Akkerman was a Belgian communist who died while fighting in the 'international brigades' alongside the republican forces during the Spanish Civil War.

[97]   The targets were the army PR centre, Motorola, the Bank of America, and the NATO oil pipes.

[98]   See *Ligne Rouge*, No. 17 (Nov. 1985), p. 10.

[99]   See *Ligne Rouge*, No. 18 (Dec. 1985), p. 7.

[100]   Ibid., pp. 10-11. From the 'Communiqué on actions by the CCC and a group of international communists against the NATO oil pipeline in Belgium and France.'

nation. Thus, it was currently in the throes of a political, ideological and strategic crisis. The only way forward was through joint action. The joint offensive was based on a common goal: to conduct a class war in every place in order to further the revolutionary movement. The possibility of the CCC or any other organization operating beyond national borders was never discussed. The joint actions that were perpetrated in Belgium and France were the first of their kind. According to the CCC, the reasons for this development were clear: given the increasing economic interdependence between all countries worldwide, no single nation could be isolated from the imperialist network; the struggle for communism called for a new relationship between nations in the spirit of proletarian internationalism; it was necessary to combat concepts such as 'socialism in one country' in light of the tragic reversion to capitalist method of production in the USSR and China; and after the failure of the Geneva summit, it was clear that the two superpowers were preparing public opinion for war.

The document ended with a call for unity beyond borders. For the communists, it stated, there was only one border – between the world of the oppressors and that of the oppressed. For the first time, slogans such as 'world-wide consolidation of FCOs' and 'long live proletarian internationalism' appeared. The leaflet was signed by the CCC and an anonymous group of French communists. Presumably, the CCC intended to develop the idea of internationalism, and this operation was meant to be the first of a series, but the incarceration of all its members a few days later put paid to these plans. Years after the arrest of CCC activists, relations with the French group, identified as the Front Revolutionnaire d'Action Proletarienne (FRAP), were clarified. The merger of the CCC was described as a 'maneuver by the powers ... to depoliticize the struggle of the CCC'. The CCC distanced themselves several times from the FRAP and denied the existence of a front. It was portrayed as a satellite of the AD, intended to give the illusion that a West European Guerrilla Front existed, but the CCC in Belgium (and GRAPO in Spain) had refused to join.[101]

VI.   ANALYSIS OF RESEARCH ASSUMPTIONS

The documentation cited in this chapter clearly indicated that the RAF, BR, AD and CCC all perceived a threat by the mighty 'imperialist war machine' and therefore advocated, or at least aspired to some form of cooperation with similar

---

[101] The CCC published already in 1990 a document on this subject, 'Le 'FRAP', provocation et repentir'. See *Interview With The CCC Prisoners Collective*, published by the Anarchist Black Cross in Gent, Belgium, June 1998 at <http://www.etext.org/Politics/Arm.The.Spirit/Guerrilla/ Europe/CCC/ccc.prisoners.interview.june-1998>, p. 6.

organizations. The texts also show that this perception grew stronger from the early 1980s, as US campaigns against terrorism worldwide intensified, as the USSR and the communist bloc in general grew economically weaker, and as the national liberation movements of the Third World increasingly turned to the capitalist world for economic aid or political support.

Although European terrorist organizations continued to argue that the imperialist camp was growing weaker from one crisis to the next, there was growing concern that these crises would lead to a world war, perhaps even a nuclear war in Europe. In the final analysis, these organizations were aware of the weakness of the 'revolutionary communist camp', and tried hard to shore it up through common fronts, international solidarity or abstract proletarian internationalism.

A distinction should be drawn, however, between the RAF and BR, two sizeable organizations, which had existed long before the advent of Euro-terrorism, and the AD or CCC, two small, short-lived organizations. In practice, only two bilateral coalitions were set up: the first, between the RAF and AD, for a period of two to three years; and the second, between the RAF and BR, which turned out to be stillborn. The CCC flirted with all three organizations, never actually decided whether to join any of them. Therefore, analysis of the research assumptions will relate exclusively to these two sets of coalitions, and will discuss the CCC separately.

1.   Influence of the variables at the international and regional level

A.   The RAF-AD

Both the RAF and AD viewed the international system as bipolar, and US imperialism and NATO as aggressive forces that constantly threatened the global balance of power. The RAF had discussed global polarity in Western Europe as opposed to the polarity between imperialism and the Third World as early as May 1982, in its document, 'Guerrilla, Resistance and the Anti-Imperialist Front'. Klar argued that NATO and Western Europe feared the influence of the socialist countries on local public opinion, despite the supposedly anti-communist stance the regimes were trying to impose from above and were therefore considering a military assault on the Warsaw Pact countries. The front was thus intended to foil imperialist designs against the socialist countries.[102]

The AD position was very close to that of the RAF. Articles in the first issue of *L'internationale* argued that the US and its allies were far stronger than the USSR, and that talk of a Soviet threat was merely a foil for NATO's military

---

[102] His views were expressed in a letter published in *L'internationale*, No. 10, Sep.-Oct. 1984.

build-up. In a joint statement on the establishment of a guerrilla front, the similarities of the two organizations once again came to light in their condemnation of NATO and Western Europe for advocating an offensive against the socialist states in the East. Tension between West and East therefore demanded that all revolutionary organizations in Western Europe unite. The only joint attack (against the Rhein Main base near Frankfurt) was described, *inter alia*, as a reaction to Reagan's policy against the USSR.

The RAF and AD understood that the Peoples Republic of China and the Third World national liberation movements had lost much of their influence and had even defected to the 'enemy camp' when faced with growing economic problems at home. Raufer pointed out that from 1982, all 'Maoist' reservations within the AD regarding the USSR and the Eastern bloc had disappeared: the 'three worlds' of Maoist theory were no longer relevant, only the two camps of the 'imperialist bourgeoisie and the international proletariat'.[103] This assessment found concrete expression in a strategic move towards solidarity with other European organizations.

Neither of the two organizations, in particular the RAF, completely abandoned the Third World, although it appeared low on their list of strategic priorities. Whenever a new focus of anti-imperialist activity arose, they would express solidarity with it, or even claim that their operations were designed to help it. This was the case with Central America (of great concern to the Reagan administration at the time), the Persian Gulf, Iran, and, in particular, Libya.[104]

Regional tension, and in particular the perceived consolidation of the Bonn-Paris axis, helped cement the RAF-AD coalition.[105] This axis combined the French nuclear force with German economic, financial, and military might and altogether enhanced the offensive capability of the imperialists. RAF militants declared that to attack the Paris-Bonn axis was to attack 'the heart of the imperialist program in Europe' and to affirm the strategic unity of revolutionaries in Western Europe.[106]

Tensions in other regions caused, according to the RAF and AD, by the power-seeking tendencies of US or West European imperialism – such as US

---

[103] See *Notes et Etudes*, No. 7/8 (Oct.-Dec. 1988), p. 98.

[104] The confrontation between the West and Iran was due to the latter's support of international terror attacks. The US military strike against Libya was equated with the imperialist suppression of the European revolutionary movements.

[105] Indeed, a major theme of the AD leaflet explaining the murder of Gen. Audran, its first attack as part of the RAF coalition, was the strengthening of the Bonn-Paris axis. This theme was also emphasized in an interview given by AD militants to *Zusammen Kampfen* in February 1986. For the text of the interview, see Alexander and Pluchinsky (eds.), *Europe's Red Terrorists*, pp. 142-6.

[106] Quoted from an interview to *Zusammen Kampfen*, June 1985, which appeared in *Ligne Rouge*, No. 15 (July 1985).

involvement in El Salvador, Angola or Lebanon – also necessitated unity among the revolutionary ranks. In an interview to *Zusammen Kampfen*, members of the two organizations argued that the joint operations of summer of 1985 were designed 'to show the pigs what would happen if they overstepped the mark in Beirut or El Salvador'.[107]

International and regional cooperation between the police and security services increased pressure on European terrorist organizations, in particular the RAF. An interview to *Zusammen Kampfen* in June 1985 stressed the Reagan administration's counter-terrorist policy and the declarations of Secretary of State Shultz of war against international terror and guerrilla movements.[108] In a statement on the murder of Braunmuehl, a comparison was even drawn between this anti-terror policy and military action against Libya in 1986. The AD frequently stated that the French 'swift intervention force' was designed to put down Third World revolutionary movements. It went so far as to attack Interpol headquarters in Paris, describing this as a new stage in its strategy.

Both organizations were also very concerned by their countries' role in the international arena. The RAF saw West Germany as the backbone of NATO, as the most faithful servant of US interests in Europe, and as an imperialist power in its own right.[109] Dartnell argued that the change that took place in the AD strategy and its abandonment of pro-Third World populist ideology was mainly due to concern at French rapprochement to NATO.[110] Indeed, this theme was taken up in most AD communiqués of the period. Despite French exclusion from NATO's united command, it was seen as playing an aggressive role in the formulation of imperialist strategy.

B.   The RAF-BR

Until the kidnapping of Gen. Dozier in December 1981, the BR saw Soviet 'social-imperialism' and its Italian lackey, the PCI, as almost on a par with US imperialism, although its main target of attack was the 'revisionist' PCI. An analysis of texts published by the various BR factions after 1981 attest to a lively internal debate on the status of the USSR within the global anti-imperialist struggle. On the whole, the P GPM and BR-UCC continued to oppose any ideological or strategic compromise with Soviet social-imperialism.

---

[107] The quotation appeared in the edition of 5 January 1986. See Becker, *Terrorism in West Germany*, p. 66.

[108] See article by US Secretary of State George Shultz, 'New Realities and New Ways of Thinking', *Foreign Affairs*, No. 3. (1985), pp. 705-21.

[109] The statement on the murder of Beckurts emphasized his role on the board of Siemens, the third largest nuclear energy concern in the world.

[110] See Dartnell, *Action directe*, p. 472.

The BR-PCC, the main stream of the organization, on the other hand, gradually came to regard US imperialism/NATO as their prime enemy and began to entertain the possibility of tactical reliance on the USSR or forces identified with it. This change in outlook was influenced by international developments following Reagan's election and RAF actions against US and NATO bases in the summer of 1981, which left a strong impression on the BR-PCC leaders. The RDS No. 20 of March 1985, circulated together with the joint AD/RAF statement, argued again that Western imperialism was the main enemy, and condemned the approach that advocated equidistance from the two blocs. In a similar vein, the BR-PCC communiqué accompanying the postal van robbery in Rome on 14 February 1987 spoke of imperialist ambitions to dismantle the Soviet bloc. Talks in early 1988 regarding a possible alliance with the RAF showed up minor differences between the RAF and BR interpretations of change in Soviet policy towards Third World liberation movements. In an attempt to bridge this difference, the status of the USSR within Western imperialism was omitted from the joint RAF-BR statement of September 1988.

For some time, the BR had criticized the RAF focus on aid to Third World liberation movements. This issue was evidently not raised in talks between the two organizations in January 1988, and was mentioned in only the most cursory fashion in the joint statement of September.

If the RAF and AD saw cooperation within NATO and the EC as the main cause for concern, the BR-PCC was far more preoccupied by Italian activities within the Mediterranean and the Middle East. Indeed, the subject of the Middle East and the Mediterranean appear in all BR documents. It follows that the BR showed a steady interest in the situation of the Palestinians, particularly after the 1982 Lebanon War. In talks with the RAF in January 1988, BR representatives spoke explicitly of their intention to form an alliance with 'the Palestinian revolutionary forces' in the Middle East. The reaction of RAF representatives was interesting: they approved the Palestinians' position which alleged that while they were attacking Israeli targets in West Europe, they also needed to maintain political relations with these countries, and therefore an alliance with them was out of question.

Surprisingly, the BR-PCC, unlike the RAF and AD, hardly mentioned the danger of international counter-insurgency cooperation, a departure from the position expressed in the RDS of February 1978. There is no satisfactory explanation for this, since BR leaders were highly aware of the counter-terrorist policy publicized by the Reagan administration and the governments of Western Europe. This omission is all the more puzzling in view of the fact that Italian terrorist organizations had themselves suffered serious blows at the hands of the security authorities, at home and abroad, especially after the French government changed its policy towards Italian exiles with a terrorist past.

C.   The CCC

Unlike the RAF and BR, and despite its admiration of the former, the CCC was consistently anti-Soviet. In one of its first leaflets, it declared that the prime war-mongering role of the US should not obscure the fact that the USSR was still the second objective enemy of the European proletariat. The summit between Reagan and Gorbachev in late 1985 was compared to the 1938 Munich summit, designed to prepare public opinion for the next war. The CCC's last attack, the only one carried out jointly with the 'French revolutionaries', was meant to initiate 'a new stage of proletarian internationalism', and represented a response to the failure of the Geneva summit.

In all the documents referring to attacks against NATO or Belgian army bases, the main theme was the prevention of war between the two superpowers. Ironically, the most vitriolic of its diatribes were directed at the peace movement, portrayed as nationalist and petty-bourgeois. The CCC was probably the only revolutionary European organization to attack, albeit symbolically, a leader of the anti-war movement. This may be viewed as yet another sign of the CCC anti-Soviet position, since the pacifist movement, fostered by local communist parties, was perceived as serving Soviet interests. According to Bernard Francq, the CCC saw the pacifist movement as alien to the working-class movement, and detracting from the main issue, namely the link between the capitalist crisis and war.[111]

Despite the fact that about a third of its attacks targeted NATO, none of the lengthy CCC texts referred to international issues, probably because the CCC saw the willingness of the Belgian government to pander to NATO and US aggression. The CCC believed that although Belgium was the center of the imperialist metropolis, it had been bypassed by the anti-imperialist struggle. Therefore, it aimed to launch 'a historic armed struggle' in Belgium; national objectives would be tackled after its initial anti-NATO onslaught.[112]

VII.   SUMMARY

European terrorist organizations reached mutual understandings and even formed coalitions when their perceptions of the nature and structure of the imperialist system coincided. The coalition only became possible when both parties saw the international system as a bipolar struggle between Western imperialism led by the US, united within NATO, and the socialist camp led by the USSR, which was

---

[111] See Bernard Francq, 'Les Cellules Communistes Combattantes: les deux figures d'une inversion,' *Sociologie du travail*, No. 4 (1986), pp. 459-83.

[112] Ibid., p. 470.

trying to assist progressive forces and liberation movements worldwide. Terrorist organizations stressed the need for unity in the struggle against the Western camp, which was always portrayed as repressive, domineering and aggressive. The only real coalition formed during this period, namely that between the RAF and AD, emerged because the two organizations shared this perception. The AD attitude towards the USSR and the communist bloc changed within a short period of time, from March 1982 (which marked the publication of its first document, 'For a Communist Project') to early 1984, when political analyses published in *L'internationale* increasingly identified with the RAF position. It was the anarchist nature of the AD and the lack of ideological coherence among its leaders that made this change possible.

The difference in outlook between the RAF and the BR on this major issue was one of the main reasons why the coalition to which the organizations aspired during the early 1980s never got off the ground. The gradual move of the BR-PCC towards the RAF positions, enabled them to reach an understanding and publish a joint statement towards the end of 1987. By then, however, the security forces had dismantled both organizations.

The CCC clung staunchly to its anti-Soviet position, and was the most extreme in its condemnation of the Belgian and West European pacifist movements. A strategic agreement with the RAF or AD was therefore ruled out, although a limited form of logistical cooperation existed between them.

Due to the classical perception of bipolarity (between the imperialist West and the communist East), the idea of the centrality of the Third World was abandoned. The RAF, which more than any other organization acclaimed the centrality of the Third World in the anti-imperialist struggle, had understood by the late 1970s that liberation movements it previously admired had been defeated by events. The advance of new revolutionary foci, such as the guerrillas in Central America and the Palestinian intifada were viewed as limited regional events rather than as part of the Third World anti-imperialist struggle.

One new focus of revolutionary activists, however, had an impact on the European terrorist organizations: the Khomeini revolution in Iran and the emergence of radical Islamic terrorist organizations. European organizations initially failed to grasp the significance of this phenomenon, so alien to their own culture. Nonetheless, they appreciated the contribution of the Iranian revolution to the general struggle against Western imperialism. If European terrorist organizations had not been paralyzed in the late 1980s, they might have reached greater understanding and cooperation with this new revolutionary camp, as implied by their publications from the late 1980s to present day.

Regional tension to some extent affected the willingness of organizations to enter into coalitions. The coalition between the RAF and AD, for example, was facilitated, *inter alia*, by the assessment that the Bonn-Paris axis was an important factor in the strengthening of Western imperialism. The understanding between the BR-PCC and RAF emerged slowly because they differed in their perceptions of the importance of regional disputes in the Middle East and the Mediterranean versus tension in Central America or Northern Europe.

1. Influence of variables at the organizational level

A. The RAF-AD

It is clear that the RAF and AD were ideologically quite similar. Both viewed Western Europe as the main arena of imperialism because of its military and economic might, its growing political unity within NATO and the EC, and its unqualified support of the Reagan administration. Both viewed the USSR and the communist bloc as a positive factor within the international system. Furthermore, both supported national liberation and anti-imperialist movements operating in the Third World.

This similarity between the organizations probably stemmed from the fact that the AD leaders had accepted RAF propositions about a year after publication of the document 'Guerrilla, Resistance and Anti-Imperialist Front'. In its second issue of December 1983, *L'internationale*, had praised RAF activity against US military staff in 1972 and hailed the 'Heidelberg spirit'. The same issue featured letters written by jailed RAF leader Klar. The attacks perpetrated by the AD in 1984 were influenced by this new strategy, and an ideological understanding with the RAF was reached even before publication of the joint statement of January 1985, as confirmed by the draft statement found in Germany in July 1984. The tendency towards coordination and cooperation continued into the first half of 1985, reaching its peak in July of that year during the joint attack against the Rhein Main base.

By January-February 1986, however, a certain chill had set in between the two organizations: interviewed by *Zusammen Kampfen*, neither AD nor RAF militants spoke during this period of an alliance between the two organizations, but in more general terms of the revolutionary front, despite being questioned directly on this subject. The RAF communiqués during attacks against Beckurts and Braunmuehl of that year also failed to mention the RAF-AD alliance. At the same time, AD terrorist activity declined considerably during 1986 (a total of four attacks) and the choice of symbolic targets no longer coincided.

Two events had a major influence on the relationship between the terrorist organizations and the supporters of the RAF within European left-wing movements. The first was the murder of an American soldier during preparations for the attack against the Rhein Main base, so that his identity card could be used to smuggle a car bomb into the base. The murder produced an outcry in left-wing circles in West Germany and Europe. The RAF published a special document to justify its action while apologizing for the way the matter had been handled. Much later, the RAF recognized that the action itself, and more so the killing of the soldier 'were big mistakes for the further development of the revolutionary struggle and for anchoring in society'.[113]

The second event was a conference in Frankfurt between 31 January and 4 February 1986 on the subject of 'Anti-Imperialist and Anti-Capitalist Resistance in Western Europe'. This was organized by legal supporters of the RAF and German autonomous elements in order to strengthen public support for the RAF anti-NATO strategy among the far left in particular. Representatives of fifteen – mainly European – countries took part in the conference, including representatives from the US, Turkey, Sri Lanka and the Middle East. Despite the general resolution adopted at the conference, calling for action against NATO, the war alliance and joint counter-insurgency and anti-terrorist activities, the conference failed to rally round the participant organizations. The RAF was attacked by various German organizations as well as by European terrorist organizations, such as the CCC and GRAPO.[114] The AD did not participate in the Frankfurt conference.

Although AD texts made no reference to the controversy that developed around these two events, there is no doubt that it encouraged AD leaders, who had portrayed the Rhein Main attack as a joint AD-RAF venture, to distance themselves from their German colleagues.

Throughout 1986 the AD placed increasing emphasis on internal problems and the workers' struggle against French capitalism. In November, the AD published a long ideological document after murdering the president of the Renault company. According to this document, recent attacks symbolized the completion of the second offensive of the guerrilla and revolutionary movement.[115] The attack against the Renault leader was designed 'to brutally implant the power of the working class into the heart of [Capitalist] strategy ... and create the awareness required for the development of a proletarian policy'. The years 1986-88, when France was led by a right-wing government under a socialist president (the cohabitation period), were marked by nationwide strikes of railway workers and large student demonstrations, which AD hoped to exploit.

Years later the imprisoned AD leaders continued to publish propaganda. Analyzing the history of the AD in 1993, their publication, *Cahier Front*, stressed the positive aspects of the alliance with RAF during the years 1983-85 and even

---

[113] See *RAF: We Must Seek What is New*, p. 4
[114] See also *Notes et Etudes*, No. 5 (May 1988), p. 14.
[115] The document (untitled) was published on 11 February 1987. Some paraphrased quotations are taken from Dartnell, *Action directe*, pp. 476-78.

claimed that the strategic path of ten years ago was still valid. However, it gave no explanation to the dissolution of the short-lived coalition with the German comrades.[116]

The volatile, anarchistic nature of the AD certainly helped to win its leaders round to the positions of the stronger, more inflexible and more active RAF, especially after the 1982 offensive against Israeli and Jewish targets had triggered strong internal opposition, and isolated it from supporters in French left-wing circles. The change was further facilitated by international developments and the anti-US and anti-NATO climate that prevailed in Western Europe at the time.

Other variables relate to the size, success and character of the organization and how these influenced the decision to enter a coalition. The picture is fairly clear as far as the RAF and AD are concerned. The RAF suffered serious setbacks after 1981, when some of its leaders were arrested, and others fled to East Germany (as was discovered a decade later) or France. In 1984, when it recovered, the RAF was compelled, for pragmatic as well as ideological reasons, to find an ally in Western Europe in order to assert its legitimacy.

The AD underwent a similar process during its early period. Its first terror campaign in 1979 was characterized by amateurism and ideological confusion, culminating in the arrest of its leadership. Although the second campaign, in the summer of 1982, was technically superior, it divided the organization on ideological grounds, and provoked vehement criticism among radical left-wing circles and the general public. When the organization was banned, its leadership sought a new strategy in order to survive and attract new members. The strategy of the Anti-Imperialist West European Guerrilla Front was a pragmatic and timely solution, especially in light of international developments. The alliance with the 'legendary' RAF enhanced its status at home and abroad, raised the morale of its members, and turned it into enemy number one of the French regime.

Although both organizations were numerically small, the RAF was still far superior in terms of human resources, 'battle tradition' and operational experience. The AD leaders themselves perceived the RAF as the more experienced and stronger partner. Several researchers emphasized the fact that the RAF felt a certain distrust and contempt towards the AD, due to the latter's instability and inexperience. Despite its obvious inferiority and wholesale acceptance of RAF strategy, the AD perceived no dependency whatsoever towards its senior partner. Within 18 months of coordinated RAF-AD activity, the AD leaders evidently decided that the partnership no longer suited their interests, but without explicitly declaring their intention.

---

[116] See the article 'Unite des revolutionnaires en Europe de l'Ouest', in *Cahier Front*, No. 2 (16 Nov. 1993), p. 50. Neither did the RAF gave an explanation on this event in its various documents published during the 1990s.

B.   The RAF-BR

An ideological rapprochement between the RAF and the BR was discernible from the early 1980s. The RAF, disenchanted with developments in the Third World at the end of the previous decade, developed the thesis of the centrality of the revolutionary struggle in the industrialized countries of Western Europe. The Italian organizations, particularly the BR-PCC, began to downplay the importance of the revolutionary effort in the homeland, while stressing the importance of the international revolutionary struggle, especially within Western Europe.

This tendency reached its apex in the mid-1980s. The BR-PCC not only began to support the international struggle, thereby isolating itself from the local working class, but gradually adopted the RAF-AD position on the international arena of struggle, as explained above. This process evidently coincided with its dwindling membership and its metamorphosis into a typical anarcho-communist organization.

The gradual rapprochement between the RAF and BR-PCC was influenced by a number of factors: failures and delays at times when an operational break-through or significant ideological change seemed imminent due to crackdowns by the security services; splits within the BR that forced the leadership to remain sensitive to the feelings of rank-and-file militants and sympathizers, publishing lengthy explanations of its ideological shifts. The final bone of contention between the BR-PCC and the RAF, namely the strategy towards the USSR and primary targets in Western Europe, was resolved after keen and lengthy discussions between the two parties.[117] Just as they reached an understanding, however, they were effectively immobilized by the security services.

The different attitudes of the two BR factions towards the domestic political/social struggle and the international struggle against world imperialism was reflected in their alliance strategies. The BR-PCC, which favored the internationalist approach, aspired from the start towards a coalition with similar revolutionary forces in Western Europe and the Mediterranean, even if it failed to realize this ambition for reasons specified above. The presence of a large number of wanted Italian terrorists in France may have strengthened BR-PCC ties with French, German and Spanish terrorists and anarcho-communists operating in Paris at the time.

The BR-UCC, on the other hand, focused on the internal struggle and paid only lip-service to the principle of proletarian internationalism. It never failed to find reasons for preserving the purity of the Marxist-Leninist doctrine and for avoiding its commitments to revolutionaries in other countries. Thus, the question

---

[117] This occasionally found expression in the synchronization of attacks carried out by the two factions, indicating secret competition for the support of radical left-wing circles in Italy.

of an alliance with the RAF, AD or indeed any other organization never arose. This supports the hypothesis that revolutionary organizations which focus on the internal struggle to seize power are less likely to form coalitions with other organizations (Hypothesis 7).

There is no evidence regarding the influence of the size of the organization on the relationship between the RAF and the BR-PCC during the period of Euro-terrorism. On the other hand, significant data exists concerning the attitude of BR leaders to this subject in the years 1970-80. In his description of the ambivalent relationship between the BR and RAF, Morucci stressed, beyond ideological differences, BR leader Moretti feared that a significant operational success by the RAF (the kidnapping of Schleyer) could transform it into a leading revolutionary organization that would compete with the BR in the European arena.[118] Another senior BR activist, Buonavitta, testified that the BR leadership considered close cooperation between the RAF and Palestinian organizations in the mid-1970s risky, wary that the weaker organization [the RAF] might be dominated by the stronger one [the Palestinians].

Several BR leaders admitted concern that the RAF was too close to the USSR, and may even have been run by the intelligence services of the Eastern bloc. This fear was echoed in BR documents, and for a long time this was one of the main reasons for the BR's reluctance to cooperate with the RAF. Since, however, the coalition between the BR-PCC and the RAF never got off the ground, there is no way of assessing how the differences in size and character of the organizations affected the relationship between them.

C.   The CCC

The CCC consistently adhered to Marxism-Leninism and supported the BR-PCC and GRAPO as representatives of 'true' Marxist-Leninist theory. The CCC leader, Carette, actively campaigned for the release of RAF prisoners, but opposed the RAF ideological tenets. This opposition intensified until the CCC, at the international conference of February 1986, publicly rejected the RAF in favor of rival left-wing German organizations, such as Proletarian Action and other autonomous groups. In fact, CCC criticism of the RAF tended towards the general and vague. It accused the RAF of being ignorant of revolutionary theory, of relying to much on action, and of failing to analyze the socio-economic conditions of modern West German society and class relationships at the time. The RAF was also severely censured for murdering of the American soldier in its operation against the Rhein Main base.[119] The CCC never got a chance to clarify

---

[118] See Becker, *Terrorism in West Germany*, pp. 75-78.
[119] In this context, see the texts that appeared in the last edition of *Ligne Rouge* in November 1986.

its criticism – its members were arrested and given lengthy prison sentences, and its journal, *Ligne Rouge*, ceased publication.

Ligne Rouge published only two RAF texts, although it reproduced many important texts of the BR and the Spanish GRAPO, and even devoted two special editions to BR documents. These were published despite basic differences of opinion between the RAF and the BR, and at a time when GRAPO was one of the leading European opponents of RAF's doctrine. Why then did the CCC fail to seek an alliance with the BR-PCC, an organization it admired on both ideological and organizational grounds? The answer should be sought at the organizational rather than the ideological level.

CHAPTER 7
ITALY – RADICAL RIGHT-WING ORGANIZATIONS

I. THE IDEOLOGICAL ROOTS OF RADICAL RIGHT-WING
    TERRORIST ORGANIZATIONS

Julius Evola, the main Italian radical right-wing ideologue, began his career before the Second World War, but was especially influential after the war in Italy and elsewhere in Europe.[1] Almirante, leader of the neo-fascist Italian Social Movement (Movimento Sociale Italiano – MSI), described Evola as 'our Marcuse, only better'.[2] In his book 'Revolt Against the Modern World', Evola drew on the teachings of Plato and Nietzsche to argue that progress had failed to change certain axioms about the individual and society, such as hierarchy, caste, monarchy, race, myth, religion, and ritual. Evola called these axioms 'spiritual virility' (*viriltà spirituale*). He admired Hitler far more than Mussolini, and taught for a while in Nazi Germany. Although officially supporting fascism in Italy, he criticized it for its inability to modify the 'Italian character'.[3]

Evola rejected Nazi theories about Jews, (which he termed a 'demagogic fallacy') and biological theories of race; in his 'Synthesis of the Doctrine of Race' (Sintesi di dottrina della Razza) he claimed that racism in the spiritual – rather than the biological – sense, based on Nietzsche's teachings, could be a positive force. Although Evola did not blame Jews for all the world's evil, he regarded over-representation of Jews in political, economic and intellectual life in the West as problematic. Evola also believed that Jews were intrinsically antagonistic towards the Aryan ideals of faith, loyalty, courage, devotion, and stability. Evola steadfastly advocated the inferiority of certain races, as witnessed by his comments on the Ethiopians who fell under the fascist yoke.

After the war, Evola argued that the function of the Right was to trigger a conservative counter-revolution, with two major objectives: politically, to defeat the Italian 'agents' of American capitalism (the Democrazia Cristiana) and Russian Marxism (the Partito Comunista Italiano); ideologically, to form a

---

[1] For a bibliography on Evola, see Fondazione Julius Evola at <http://www.fondazione-evola.it> and Bibliografia sulle stragi di stato e il neofascismo in Italia at <http://www.bfs.it/stragi.html#m>.

[2] Quoted in Giorgio Galli, *La Crisi Italiana e la Destra Internazionale* (Torino: Arnaldo Mondadori Editore, 1977), p. 20.

[3] This survey of Evola is largely based on Richard Drake's 'Julius Evola and the Ideological Origins of the Radical Right in Contemporary Italy', in Peter Merkl (ed.), *Political Violence and Terror. Motifs and Motivations* (Berkeley: University of California Press, 1986), pp. 61-89. See also Ferraresi's important article 'Da Evola a Freda. La dottrina della destra radicale fino al 1977', in Franco Ferraresi (ed.), *La Destra Radicale* (Milano: Feltrinelli, 1984), pp. 54-118.

counter-hegemony, led by people capable of resisting all the ideologies that had sprung out of the French Revolution, from liberalism to bolshevism – an elite of 'reactionary supermen' to restore the world that fascism had destroyed.

Evola emphasized that this revolution should not be predicated on the bourgeois socio-political system but rather on 'a general view of the world and the state ... on superior values and interests that override economic or class considerations'.[4] Ironically, Evola was opposed to nationalism. On the other hand, he admired the Waffen-SS units set up to fight Russia. He called for a new, supranational fighting spirit in the struggle against American and Soviet occupation of Europe. This, he believed, could be accomplished through international cooperation among reactionary European elites. Evola was encouraged by the establishment of Euro-fascist groups and urged them to challenge the Left and Center in a bid to seize control through revolutionary struggle.[5] He also advocated that the ensuing war – which was to be a total war – be conducted on enemy territory.

During the 1950s Evola saw communism as the most immediate threat to the traditional world. Consequently, contrary to his previous doctrine, he adopted a pro-Western stance. Although both East and the West were portrayed as two jaws of the vise that was holding Europe in its grip, in the short term, the lesser of the two evils was to be preferred. In concrete terms, this meant that Europe had to accept US and Atlantic tutelage.[6] A constant in Evola thinking was the need to use the national movement in its anti-subversive [i.e., anti-communist] capacity in order to protect the country, while simultaneously supporting its 'healthy organs' (the army, police and security services).[7]

Another Italian right-wing ideologue, Adriano Romualdi, attempted to translate Evola's ideas, particularly his 'pro-Western' position, into political-strategic terms. 'If, for us, the West does not exist as "freedom", at least it exists as a "bloc", a joint European-American front that is capable of preventing little Europe from being sucked into the vast Soviet *lebensraum*', wrote Romualdi.[8] The subject of Europe represented a major concern for Romualdi and the Italian radical right. According to Romualdi, Europe should be rebuilt as a 'new order', the antithesis of the caricature projected by the institutions of Brussels. A united Europe was unthinkable without the revival of fascism, which had demonstrated, before the Second World War, that only the 'International of Nationalists ... international brigades of

---

[4]   See Drake, *Julius Evola and the Ideological Origins of the Radical Right in Contemporary Italy*, p. 73.
[5]   He referred to New Order (Ordine Nuovo) and Revolutionary Action Groups (Fasci d'Azione Rivoluzionaria) in Italy, the British National Party and the National Socialist Movement in Britain, the National Movement (Movimento Nacional) in Spain, the New European Order (Ordre Européen Nouveau) in France, among others.
[6]   These ideas appeared in his book, *Men Among Ruins* (*Gli uomini e le rovine*), published in 1953.
[7]   See Ferraresi, 'Da Evola a Freda,' p. 28.
[8]   Ibid., p. 30. Cited from an article written by Romualdi in 1970 in Ordine Nuovo.

German, French, Danish, Slav, and Arab warriors fighting for civilization', along the lines of the Waffen-SS units, was capable of hoisting Europe's flag.[9]

In January 1970, a few years before his death, Evola became pessimistic about the political situation in Italy. 'Polemics and debates no longer have a place. The time has come to destroy everything.' He recommended 'refraining from terrorism if it has little chance of succeeding'. This view evolved into what later became known as the 'tension strategy' of the radical right, a policy that advocated indiscriminate attacks against civilian targets.[10]

II.   TYPOLOGICAL DEFINITION

The terminology used to describe right-wing terrorism often appears vague and inconsistent (neo-Nazism, neo-fascism, right-wing extremism or radicalism, etc.).[11] Ferraresi coined the term 'the radical right' to denote the authoritarian, anti-egalitarian, anti- or a-rational cultures that occasionally surfaced during the twentieth century, particularly during periods of reform. This book uses the term 'radical right' to describe right-wing organizations which tend towards physical, as well as political, violence.[12]

The four movements studied in this chapter belonged to the camp which Ferraresi called the 'subversive right', a camp that planned to undermine the democratic regime of post-Second World War Italy through the use of non-random violence.[13]

---

9   Ibid., p. 31.

10   See Drake, 'Julius Evola and the Ideological Origins of the Radical Right in Contemporary Italy', p. 79.

11   See Ferraresi (ed.), La Destra Radicale, p. 12.

12   On right-wing radical groups see, besides the basic works by Ferraresi and Galli, some new books: A. Baldoni and S. Provvisionato, La notte piu lunga della Repubblica. Sinistra e destra. Ideologie, estremismi, lotta armata (1968-1989) (Rome: Serarcangeli Editore, 1989); G. Bianconi, A mano armata. Vita violenta di Giusva Fioravanti, terrorista neo fascista quasi per caso (Milan: Baldini and Castoldi, 1992); R. Chiarini, Destra italiana. Dall'Unità d'Italia a Alleanza Nazionale (Venice: Marsilio, 1995); G. Cingolani, La destra in armi. Neofascisti italiani tra ribellismo ed eversione (1977-1982) (Rome: Editori riuniti, 1996); Piero Corsini, Storia di Valerio Fioravanti e Francesca Mambro (Napoli: Tullio Pironti editore, 1999); Franco Ferraresi, Minacce alla democrazia. La destra radicale e la strategia della tensione in Italia nel dopoguerra (1945-1984) (Milan: Feltrinelli, 1995); Francesca Mambro, Il bacio sul muro (Sperling & Kupfer, 2000).

13   See Ferraresi, 'Da Evola a Freda,' p. 54. Most of the updated information on the trials concerning right-wing terrorist attacks was published in leftist books and websites. See for example, two chapters of the parliamentary commission report on Italian terrorism: Il Terrorismo, le Stragi e il Contesto Storico-Politico [Relazione Pellegrino]: Capitolo V: L'estremismo di destra nella prima meta' degli anni settanta and Capitolo IX: L'eversione di destra dopo il 1974, at <http://www.clarence.com/contents/societa/memoria>. But as noted on one of these websites, the Pellegrino report should be read not as an ultimate court decision, but rather as a historical-political analysis, subject to changes and updates.

(1)   The New Order (Ordine Nuovo – ON) defined itself as a revolutionary organization, but it did not openly espouse armed struggle or terrorism, arguing that its role was to protect Italy against left-wing subversion.[14] It was a movement that used a global national/revolutionary strategy in order to gain power.[15] The organization had a sound theoretical platform and a reasonably solid infrastructure, variously estimated at 2,500 to 10,000 members, with a large nucleus in the Venetto region.

(2)   The National Vanguard (Avanguardia Nazionale – AN) was smaller than the ON, had a markedly terrorist bias, and meager cultural/ideological performance. It advocated a hierarchical society led by an elitist avant-garde, based on nationalist and racist principles.[16]

(3)   The Third Position (Terza Posizione – TP) and the Revolutionary Armed Nuclei (Nuclei Armati Rivoluzionari – NAR) both belonged to a group of terrorist organizations on the radical right which adopted the radical left's strategy of 'armed spontaneity'. Their principles strongly resembled those of the radical left-wing Autonomy groups. They were right-wing anarchist organizations disdaining ideology.[17]

III.   THE EVOLUTION OF IDEOLOGY AND STRATEGY OF RIGHT-
        WING TERRORIST ORGANIZATIONS

Right-wing terrorist activity in Italy began towards the end of the 1960s and ended in 1981-82, six or seven years before the radical left was effectively liquidated in Italy.[18]

---

[14]   Ibid., pp. 62-66.

[15]   See Rosario Minna, 'Il Terrorismo di Destra,' in Donatella della Porta (ed.), *Terrorismi in Italia* (Bologna: Societa Editrice Il Mulino, 1984), pp. 32-34.

[16]   See Ferraresi, 'Da Evola a Freda,' pp. 66-71.

[17]   Ibid., pp. 75, 83-85. Right-wing anarchism as defined by Evola differed from Western (French) and Russian anarchism in its wish to rebuild a new world on the ruins of the old, bourgeois order. According to Ferraresi, Evola was closer to German nihilism. See Ferraresi (ed.), La Destra Radicale, p. 30.

[18]   Ferraresi, the first to undertake a serious and comprehensive study of radical right-wing terrorist organizations in Italy, divided them into five periods: from the end of Second World War to the establishment of the National Front; the National Front period – the tension strategy; the period of ON and AN; crisis and change – the mid-1970s; armed spontaneity post-1977. Ferraresi based his study mainly on ideological documents published by various right-wing groups, journalistic material and legal material available to researchers. At the time, the trials of right-wing terrorists were in full swing, and much of the material was classified.

1.   From the 'tension strategy' to crisis and change

Italian fascists who had survived the Second World War lost no time in organizing politically in the new Italy which had joined the Allied forces in 1943. As early as 1946 they established the first neo-fascist party in Europe, which attracted the most violent remnants of the Italian Social Republic in Salo. These elements switched allegiances frequently, depending on internal politics and on the degree of MSI antagonism towards the democratic regime in Italy.[19] Their attitude to the MSI was similar to the radical left's attitude to the PCI.

Leaders of the ON and AN have been at the forefront of violent neo-fascist activity in Italy. Both organizations played a major role in the tension strategy espoused by the National Front movement. The AN was rebuilt in 1968 with the aim of establishing a new political order that would counteract the 'materialism and mass-orientation' of the democratic regime by destroying the parties and parliament. The extremism of the radical right was fuelled by fear that the government was about to fall into the hands of the 'lower classes'. The consolidation of left-wing parties in parliament, the incorporation of socialists into the DC government, the success of the workers' strikes of autumn 1969, and the escalation of violent radical left-wing activity all contributed to this feeling.[20] Indeed, one of the main themes in documents of the radical right was the fear of a communist takeover. Communism was blamed for instigating a total, revolutionary third world war, which although usually covert and subversive, sometimes erupted into violence. It was therefore deemed imperative to train professionals to carry out counter-terrorist acts.

The state was not regarded as the enemy of the radical right, but rather as an institution that should be strengthened through the elimination of disruptive elements. It followed that cooperation with 'healthy forces' within the army and security services was encouraged. Before the security services could set about building up a strong state, it was first necessary to instill the wish for order and peace among the public. This could be accomplished through terrorism, which would raise the level of political and social tension and sow the seeds of fear among the public.

It was well-known that the Italian radical right courted officials in the army and secret services – conservatives who feared the rise of the PCI, the government coalition with the socialists, as well as international events such as the success of the National Liberation Front (Front de Libération Nationale – FLN) in Algeria, or the Vietcong in Vietnam, and the rise of guerrilla movements worldwide. As

---

[19]   For details, see Ferraresi, 'Da Evola a Freda,' pp. 55-57. See also Relazione Pellegrino: Capitolo V: L'estremismo di destra nella prima meta' degli anni settanta and Capitolo IX: L'eversione di destra dopo il 1974.

[20]   Ibid., pp. 57-62.

early as the late 1950s, Gen. De Lorenzo, commander of the Carabinieri (Italian military police) and former chief of military intelligence, was accused of planning a coup. Army circles apparently offered the ON and AN financial assistance in order to exploit them as useful allies in case the government fell.[21]

The ON, which was set up in 1956 under Pino Rauti, lasted in its original form till 1969.[22] It later changed its name to the Political Movement for the New Order (Movimento Politico per un Ordine Nuovo – MPON) led by Clemente Graziani, and defined itself as a revolutionary movement fighting to topple the corrupt Italian regime and to free Europe of Russian and US colonialism. The ON was opposed to nationalism, or the 'naturalist worship of the homeland'. Graziani argued that although his revolutionary movement advocated non-violence, the violence of the system forced him to use violence in self-defense. The first attack for which the organization took responsibility was carried out in May 1972, and caused three deaths. Between 1974 and 1979, it carried out a total of 25 attacks.[23] Ferraresi pointed out that the ON played down its antisemitic ideology in order to project a more moderate image. The ON operated in a semi-clandestine manner until 1973, when it was banned.[24]

The AN, founded by Stefano Delle Chiaie in 1960, disbanded in 1965, only to be resuscitated in 1970 by elements affiliated with the MSI or ON. The organization, one of the most violent towards its radical left rivals (imitating the fascist squadrismo of the 1920s), was responsible for terrorist acts in the late 1960s and early 1970s. Cells sometimes used pseudonyms in order to disguise their political affiliations. Despite the serious charges brought against members of the AN, it was only outlawed in 1976 for having revived a fascist party. The AN was more active than the ON in southern Italy, and participated in the farmers' riots in Reggio-Calabria in April 1974 in a bid to extend its influence in the region, traditionally a radical right stronghold.[25] The AN leaders went underground in 1970 after the first massive attacks. Even before it was banned, some activists rejoined the MSI, while loyalists set up a separate group called the Black Order (Ordine Nero).

The Black Order was set up by members of the ON, the AN, and other radical right-wing groups, but was banned in November 1973. Between 1974-75, the Black Order was responsible for 21 attacks. It was a rather enigmatic organiza-

---

21   See Marco Rimanelli, 'Italian Terrorism and Society, 1940s – 1980s: Roots, Ideologies, Evolution, and International Connections', Terrorism, Vol. 12 (1989), pp. 263-64, and Robert C. Meade, Red Brigades: The Story of Italian Terrorism (London: Macmillan, 1990), pp. 34-35.

22   Rauti, a founder of MSI, was responsible for setting up various right-wing organizations and movements. He wooed or shunned the MSI depending on the extremism of its political line. In the late 1980s, he served as secretary-general of the party. He was accused and acquitted of the bombing in Milan's Fontana Square in 1969, considered the first massacre perpetrated by the far right.

23   See Terrorisme et Violence Politique, No. 3 (Oct. 1991), p. 22.

24   See Ferraresi, 'Da Evola a Freda,' p. 65.

25   See Minna, 'Il Terrorismo di Destra,' pp. 35-39 and 66-71.

tion, serving as a front for the illegal activities of legal organizations or, as many researchers believed, for elements collaborating with extremist elements in the Italian military and political establishment. During this period, most attacks were carried out in city squares or trains in northern Italy (Milan, Bologna, Brescia).

The tension strategy reached a peak in 1974 after its architects drew encouragement from the right-wing military coup in Chile in September 1973. Most of the attacks during this period remain unsolved to this day.[26] As right-wing terror escalated, a significant change took place in government policy towards right-wing organizations and elements suspected of terrorist acts. The organizations were banned and their leaders were forced to flee the country, mainly to countries with right-wing regimes, such as Spain, Greece, and Latin American states. The special contacts between these organizations and government officials who exploited the radical right for their own purposes also ceased.[27]

In September 1975 ON and AN leaders met secretly and decided to merge the organizations and set up new cells throughout Italy. Like the BR, the judiciary became their prime target (it was during this period that the BR kidnapped Judge Sossi). The new plan was to attack the state as part of a strategy of self-defense, and to wrest the terrorist monopoly from the BR. The murder of the judge trying ON terrorists, the robbery of a large arms depot and of a safe in the Ministry of Labor, indicated a firm commitment to armed struggle.[28] However, the successful attacks of July 1976 were the last to be carried out by the joint organization. Many terrorists, including Sossi's murderers, were arrested in the ensuing months and the AN, which was supposed to act as a legal front for the new cadres, was also outlawed.[29]

2. 'Armed spontaneity' after 1977[30]

The radical right's assessment of domestic and international events in the mid-1970s revealed a significant change in the Italian political map. The MSI, the legal right-wing party, had failed in its attempt to win respectability and enlist popular support. On the contrary, public opinion swung towards the left, as reflected in the election results when the PCI joined the democrats to form a national coalition.

---

[26] Ibid., pp. /1-72.

[27] Galli, a pioneer in research into the radical right in Italy, called these officials 'the invisible government', a powerful pressure group which was interested in preventing the PCI from rising to power, squashing pressure from the revolutionary left, and undermining the pro-Arab policy of the ruling DC party. Only the most extreme elements in this 'invisible government' cooperated with or exploited the radical right. See Galli, La Crisi Italiana e la Destra Internazionale, pp. 32-34.

[28] Judge V. Occorsio took part in the trial against ON and was murdered on 10 July 1976. See Vittorio Boraccetti, Eversione di destra, terrorismo, stragi (Milan: Franco Angeli, 1986), pp. 182-83.

[29] See Ferraresi, 'Da Evola a Freda,' pp. 72-74.

[30] This section is based mainly on Ferraresi (ed.), La Destra Radicale, pp. 32-41, and 'Da Evola a Freda,' pp. 74-96.

Moreover, attempts to organize coups with the assistance of the military not only proved abortive, but also encouraged the security forces, and especially the judiciary, to step up activities against subversive elements on the radical right.[31]

1977 was a peak year for the BR. It was a year during which 'new revolutionary issues' surfaced and violent confrontation between the autonomous elements and the regime spread.[32] Ironically, the radical right's reading of the political map resembled that of radical left. Likewise, it saw the overthrow of the bourgeois régime as the immediate strategic goal.[33] The ideological basis for this assessment were two texts, written by Evola and by Franco Giorgio Freda.[34]

Evola, in 'Riding the Tiger', spoke of the irredeemable bankruptcy of contemporary society. Evola coined the term *apoliteia*, to designate the abandonment of political activity in order to focus on the inner self. The violent radical right-wing elements, however, interpreted this term as meaning disaffection with conventional politics and a preference for political involvement of the 'heroic' type, namely a 'holy war' as a tool for spiritual self-realization.[35]

Freda proposed the second option in a document entitled 'The Disintegration of the System', considered faithful to Evola's principles.[36] Freda's starting point was the need for an all-out offensive against the concept of Europe and the political/spiritual heritage of the West:

> The neo-fascist youth are shouting: Europe-fascism-revolution! without even bothering to consider whether there is such a thing as European cultural homogeneity. There is no connection between us and a democratic, Jacobean Europe, a Europe of businessmen, a Europe of plutocratic colonialism … with Jewish Europe, we have a score to settle. Europe is a whore who had slept around shamelessly and had caught all the ideological infections … Jacobeanism, Masonism, Judaism, Zionism, Liberalism, and Marxism.[37]

---

[31] This was a reference to the National Front's attempted coup, and Prince Junio Valerio Borghese's abortive coup, known as 'Rosa dei Venti'.

[32] In this context, see the subsection 'Strategy of Liquidation (1977-78)' in Chapter 4.

[33] Freda argued that it was too late for an operation, blood should be allowed to flow and the body [bourgeois society] buried. See the French translation, Giorgio Freda, 'La désintégration du système', Totalité, Supplement No. 9, p. 32.

[34] Freda was the most radical ideologue and leader of the Italian national/revolutionary camp, Evola's successor and interpreter, and the founder of Ar publications.

[35] 'Riding the Tiger' (Cavalcare la tigre) was published in 1961.

[36] 'The Disintegration of the System' (La Disintegrazione del sistema) was presented by Freda as an ideological document at a meeting of the executive of the Revolutionary European Front (Front révolutionnaire européen) on 17 August 1969. The front was an umbrella organization for European nationalist/revolutionary organizations.

[37] Quoted by Freda, La désintégration du système, pp. 17-8.

If liberal, democratic Europe, the product of the French Revolution, did not meet Freda's ideal, what did?

> The Latin American guerrilla … identifies more with our world view than does the Spaniard who is besotted with priests and the United States; the Spartan, heroic Vietnamese warriors are closer to our worldview than are the Italians, the French or the West Germans; the Palestinian terrorist is closer to our avenging spirit than is the English (European?) yid…[38]

Freda proposed joining forces with the radical left in order to destroy the bourgeois order. This theoretical platform formed the background to the activity of radical right-wing groups after 1977.

Groups that advocated armed spontaneity shunned ideology and despised hierarchical structures. At the organizational-strategic level, this was translated into small loosely connected groups. The two main groups of this kind were the NAR and the TP.[39]

The NAR, founded in October 1977, was the most active of all radical right organizations, carrying out no less than 119 attacks between 1977 and 1982. It called itself Black Autonomy after Workers Autonomy and attacked similar targets: politicians, judges, and others perceived as traitors. Its objectives were usually arbitrary, and there was a conspicuous lack of organizational-strategic planning. The NAR published only short leaflets after attacks, and no ideological tracts. Despite a proposed cease-fire with the radical left in January 1979 it attacked an Autonomy radio station wounding five broadcasters.[40]

The TP was set up by members of the Students' Struggle (Lotta Studentesca) and bore Freda's ideological imprint. Its leaders were inspired by Autonomy and about a third of its activists had formerly belonged to radical left-wing organizations. Although TP had cells nationwide, in 1979, at its apogee, it was mainly based in Rome.[41] The TP was a nationalist/revolutionary movement that opposed the two ideological blocs, and the right-centre-left coalition ('not right, not left, but a third position'). It preached solidarity with all national and ethnic liberation movements, and opposed all representatives of the ruling system (parties, syndicates, Marxism, Zionism, multinational corporations). Its leaders fluctuated

---

[38] Ibid., pp. 16-17. The original text is far more crude than the author's translation.
[39] A third group, We Shall Build Action (Costruiamo l'Azione), assembled around the publication of the same name. It acted chiefly as a liaison cell with Autonomy groups in Rome, as a logistic rearguard, and as the mouthpiece of 'armed propaganda'.
[40] See Terrorisme et Violence Politique, No. 3 (Oct. 1991), p. 24.
[41] Ibid., p. 23.

between spontaneous versus organized struggle. They modeled themselves on the Romanian fascists, organized via a network of secret cells and legions.[42]

The fluidity of the radical right movement in Italy allowed activists to switch allegiances at will. This changed in the second half of 1979, with the sweeping arrests of many leaders on the radical right – a development that led to the radicalization of terrorist activity. Armed robbery or attacks against law officials, particularly police officers, became commonplace. The security forces continued to crack down on the terrorists, and by the end of the year, managed to paralyze both NAR and a third activist group, Costruiamo l'azione. Surviving members joined the TP in June 1980 and murdered the officiate judge in Rome, in addition to a number of suspected collaborator'.[43] The massacre at Bologna railway station in August 1980 led to a new wave of arrests, which effectively signaled the organization's demise. The TP leaders were charged with perpetrating the deadliest terrorist attack in Italian history, and of acting as a legal front for the NAR. However, after spending several years in jail, they were acquitted for lack of sufficient evidence.

Since the 1970s dozens of right-wing activists in Italy were tried for perpetrating large-scale terrorist attacks. Despite the heavy sentences handed down by the lower courts, the accused were ultimately released for lack of sufficient evidence. According to Haut, the true perpetrators of the Bologna train station massacre were never found. Even worse, innocent people and groups were incriminated.[44] In 1991 Italian president Cossiga declared that the theory that fascists were responsible had been discredited. Haut also pointed out that in a country in which the BR hard-core leaders had repented, no terrorist would ever admit to responsibility for a serious terrorist attack. French researchers hazarded a very cautious assessment that the Bologna operation was the work of marginal 'psychopaths' in the extremist movements, part of a power game that smacked of politics and corruption.[45]

3.   Cooperation with Palestinian organizations

There is no evidence of any real cooperation between Italian radical right-wing and Palestinian organizations during the period in question and no new data on

---

[42] The Italian nationalists/revolutionaries were strongly influenced, both ideologically and organizationally, by the doctrine of Codreanu, leader of the Romanian fascist organization, the Iron Guard, before the Second World War. See Ferraresi, 'Da Evola a Freda,' p. 84.

[43] Justice Mario Armato was murdered on 23 June 1980.

[44] Raufer and Haut published a file on the subject of the riddle of the fascist attacks in Italy. See Terrorisme et Violence Politique, No. 3 (Oct. 1991), pp. 13-38.

[45] Ibid., p. 34. The terrorist attack in the Bologna railway station on 2 August 1980, caused by the explosion of a suitcase bomb, left 85 dead and about 200 injured. This was the most lethal attack in the history of Italian terror and members of the radical right were deemed responsible.

this subject has surfaced since the beginning of the 1980s to day. Only one serious reference to such cooperation was documented – Freda's purchase of timing devices in 1969 for an unidentified Palestinian organization.[46] Media rumors that radical right-wing activists trained in Palestinian camps in the Middle East were never substantiated. What was proven, however, was that three NAR members trained in Christian Phalangist camps in Lebanon and even participated in anti-Palestinian activities.[47]

On the other hand, almost all right-wing nationalist/revolutionary organizations expressed solidarity with the Palestinian struggle, as indicated in the letters of three of their political/ideological leaders: Freda, Claudio Mutti and Carlo Terraciano, all active to this day in the political and media affairs of the nationalists/revolutionaries in Europe.[48] Their activities centered on the Ar publishing house set up by Freda.[49] Terraciano notes that as early as 1963 the group had published a manifesto against the 'holocaust the Zionists were wreaking against the Arabs in Palestine', and in 1969 organized the first demonstration in Italy in support of the 'Palestinian nationalist/popular struggle against the Zionists'.[50] Similar diatribes appeared in the monthly *Terza Posizione*. Mutti was responsible for setting up a fascist organization called The Peoples' Struggle Organization (Organisazione di Liberazione del Popolo – OLP) in 1972, as well as chairing the Italy-Libya Friendship Organization.[51] The few texts available for this research indicated support for the Palestinian struggle, woven with crude antisemitic expressions.

---

[46] Interestingly, the judges trying him for this offence were the same who accused him of perpetrating the attack against the Milan bank in December 1969. Unable to prove that the timing devices were used in the attack (Freda himself argued that they were intended for an Arab group), the judges had no choice but to acquit him. See Revue d'Histoire du Fascisme, No. 1 (1974), p. 12. In December 1974 an ON leaflet was circulated, demanding Freda's release. The leaflet quoted the resolutions of the 'First Secret Conference of the Organization', which attacked Zionism and the 'Chosen People' for its crimes. According to the leaflet, Freda was arrested for supplying the 'Palestinian Resistance' with timing devices. The leaflet ended with the call: 'We shall turn Italy into our own Palestine'.

[47] See L'Espresso of 13 January 1985.

[48] Mutti, former lecturer at Bologna University, published a series of books and articles on Islam, and ended up converting to Islam himself. He was one of the most rabidly antisemitic and pro-Palestinian figures on the Italian right. Carlo Terraciano, also a member of Freda's group, was actively involved in Italian nationalist/revolutionary publications to this day.

[49] The publishing house, Le Edizioni di Ar, was set up in 1964. A number of radical right-wing intellectuals, who called themselves the 'Ar group', were active within its framework.

[50] The text, entitled 'The Enemy of Man', included Palestinian battle songs, and was written by Freda at a time when the Italian right backed Israel, as Terraciano pointed out. See Carlo Terraciano, 'Nel fiume della storia', in Risguardo, rassegna periodica di cultura, IV (1984), Special edition to mark the twentieth anniversary of Ar publications (Brindisi: Edizioni di Ar), p. 179. The demonstration was a reference to the conference on behalf of 'the Palestinian Resistance' organized by Freda in March 1969 in Padua.

[51] See Xavier Raufer and Francois Haut, 'Le terrorisme noir en Italie', Terrorisme et Violence Politique, No. 3 (Oct. 1991), p. 26.

4.   International and regional factors

In a famous speech that was to become the manifesto of the national-ist/revolutionary camp, Freda proposed a foreign policy that would influence the strategic positions of the radical right: Italian withdrawal from NATO, its dissociation from 'supranational neo-capitalist structures', the alliance of the national state with the anti-imperialist states and international support for movements fighting Western and socialist democracies.[52] Terraciano went on to clarify the international outlook of these movements, all of which were based on Freda's doctrines.[53] According to this view, the principal global agents of control were Christianity, capitalism and state capitalism, which worked together as part of 'a global system of exploitation and control'.

Christianity, particularly the Catholic Church, was regarded as rich and pow-erful; capitalism, especially financial neo-capitalism in post-modern society, expressed its global control strategy through supranational, plutocratic govern-ance; state capitalism as expressed through Marxism, under the influence of Slavic expansionism and Jewish cosmopolitanism, had become a subversive element in European and national cultures, a tool in the hands of Soviet imperial-ism, and a fifth column in the nations it wished to control. The common denominator of all three agents of control could be traced to be monotheistic-messianic philosophy of Judaism.

According to Terraciano, the confrontation zones between the two imperialist blocs – such as the Middle East, Afghanistan, and Iraq-Iran – served as playing fields in which they could try out their modern weaponry at the expense of the smaller and weaker nations. The subservient nations had no option but to form alliances with stronger nations, sometimes even serving as colonial agents (e.g., Italian involvement in Lebanon on behalf of the US, and Cuba's involvement in Angola on behalf of the USSR). Although the imperialist blocs supported each other in turn, the fate of the world was always decided in the banks and syna-gogues of New York and Tel Aviv.

Nationalist/revolutionary forces were interested in *lebensraum* to the east, in European and Eurasian integration.[54] The main enemy was America. The nation-

---

[52] See Freda, 'La désintégration du système,' p. 40. Freda's style and statements in favor of Chinese communism earned him the title of 'Nazi-Maoist'.

[53] See Terraciano, Nel fiume della storia.

[54] The same interest was shared by the Soviet satellites, especially after the demise of Soviet Marxism. This text was published in 1985, at the beginning of Gorbachev's glasnost policy. However, the geopolitical theories of the nationalist/revolutionary right were advanced in the 1960s by Jean Thiriart in his book Un empire de 400 millions d'hommes: Europe and were a continuation of the German national-Bolshevik ideologies of the 1920s.

alists/revolutionaries were vehemently opposed to 'American culture, consumerism, bourgeois democracy and American economic colonialism'.

'The nation of Europe' would support Arab-Muslim cultural unification within the context of Mediterranean and Afro-Asian cooperation. The Mediterranean basin, considered of vital strategic importance to neighboring states, would be closed to imperialist fleets. Within this scheme Zionism was perceived as a disruptive factor in the Mediterranean basin and the Middle East, rather than representing an eastern 'shield' for the West.

IV.   ANALYSIS OF RESEARCH ASSUMPTIONS

One might have expected some form of practical cooperation or close ties between the Italian radical right and Palestinian terrorist organizations. However, apart from a general ideological and political solidarity towards the Palestinians, a coalition between the two never materialized.

A theme common to all radical right-wing organizations was the threat represented by the enemy, whatever its form. During the transition to terrorism in the late 1960s, thinkers on the radical right believed that communism was planning a third world war, even if this sometimes took the form of a psychological, cultural or political war.[55] Terraciano described it as 'a war of blood against gold, a war without rules or restraints, a war without quarter which would tolerate no neutrality, a war of the people'.[56] For the more intellectual ideologues of Evola's ilk, the cultural-spiritual threat symbolized by modern society and its dominant ideology was an existential threat that could harm mankind. To ward off this threat, a global counter-recruitment strategy was essential.

1.   Influence of the variables at the international and regional level

As noted previously, two of Evola's books had a profound influence on the strategy of radical right-wing organizations: 'Men Among Ruins' (Gli uomini e le rovine) and 'Riding the Tiger' (Cavalcare la tigre).[57] In the first, Evola asserted that the Cold War could be exploited to curb the 'sovietization' of the West. It was this conviction that gave birth to the ON.[58] Eight years later, in 'Riding the Tiger', Evola admitted that nothing in bourgeois society supported this convic-

---

[55]   Ferraresi pointed out that the fear of the revolutionary offensive made members of the far right paranoid. See Ferraresi, 'Da Evola a Freda,' p. 58.

[56]   Quoted from Carlo Terraciano, 'Adriano Romualdi: anima delle rivoluzione, rivoluzione dell'anima' in Risguardo, rassegna periodica di cultura, p. 18.

[57]   See Francesco Ingravalle, 'Le edizioni di Ar e l'estrema destra', p. 102.

[58]   'Gli uomini e le rovine' was published in 1953.

tion, and that it was essential therefore to aim at the swift destruction of bourgeois society.[59]

The ON and the AN, which functioned as political organizations from the mid-1950s, and as terrorist organizations from 1969 to 1974, felt that bipolar tension called for a strategy that would build up the 'healthy forces' of the state, and for an alliance with right-wing elements within the democratic regime that wished to stop the spread of communism.[60] (See Hypothesis 1).

Those influenced by 'Riding the Tiger' and by Freda's writings doubted the existence of bipolarity. On the contrary, they believed that cooperation existed between the two superpowers, also reflected in an aggressive Italian policy towards the subversive radical right.

There was a certain symmetry between the radical right and the radical left: the more the radical right believed in classical bipolarity, in the aggressive intentions of the USSR, the closer it drew to the ruling democratic establishment and to the Western worldview; the more the radical left viewed bipolar tension as an US imperialist plot against the communist bloc and the revolutionary forces in the world, the closer it drew to the USSR, even to the point of tactical cooperation.

Radical right-wing organizations therefore considered a priority cooperation with extremist elements within the security and military establishments in their countries, and with the West, in general, in order to prevent a communist takeover of Italy and Europe. Under such conditions, an alliance with revolutionary forces of the Third World, such as Palestinian organizations, was untenable. When, however, the radical right felt that all hopes of bringing about change through a coalition with forces within the establishment were dashed, they turned to Third World revolutionary forces and the radical left in their own countries. This trend was helped by Freda's admiration of Mao and the Chinese revolution.[61] But right-wing revolutionary organizations failed in their attempts to enter a dialogue with

---

[59]   'Riding the Tiger' was published in 1961. It was this perception that gave rise to the Ar collective.

[60]   Evola argued that at the spiritual level, there was no practical difference between the democratic West and the communist East. The 'West' did not represent a loftier ideal, and its basic values were no less destructive than Marxism and communism. However, it did allow a certain material latitude, which the communist regime did not. This perspective alone justified an anti-Soviet and anti-communist position, on purely physical grounds. See Julius Evola, Chevaucher le tigre (Paris: Editions de la Maisnie, 1982), pp. 217-18.

[61]   Freda saw Chinese communism as 'the triumph of the equal distribution of tasks in society, of discipline over bourgeois laxity, of totalitarian order over individualistic disarray, the victory of the political soldier (poor but strong) over the commercial and bureaucratic oligarchies in the West (including Russia)'. See Ardenghi's analysis of Freda's text 'Two Letters Against the Current' (1972) in Flavio Ardenghi, 'Le edizioni di Ar e l'estrema destra' in Risguardo. rassegna periodica di cultura, p. 95.

the radical left in Italy. Like their left-wing counterparts, when the strategic turning point came, it was too late – the organizations had virtually been annihilated by the security forces.

Since the nationalist/revolutionary forces regarded Israel and international Zionism as dominating the whole world, solidarity with the Palestinian people was a fundamental tenet of their ideology.

> Only unity on the Arab front, together with action by the European and Latin American revolutionary vanguards, can succeed in vanquishing imperialism and Zionism. Therefore, it is necessary to support 'Third Force' movements (the Montoneros, the IRA, the PFLP, etc.) and anti-imperialist forces such as the PLO.[62]

This explains why the TP instantly supported the Islamic revolution in Iran which, as well as being anti-imperialist and anti-Zionist, was perceived as a religious struggle on behalf of an ancient culture and tradition.[63]

2. Influence of the variables at the organizational level

The nationalist/revolutionary camp and the Palestinian terrorist organizations had a similar perception of the forces operating in the international arena, and of the struggle against US imperialism in the Middle East. This was expressed by verbal solidarity, at least by the Italian organizations towards their Palestinian counterparts. Moreover, some right-wing ideologues felt enormous respect for Islam. Ferraresi emphasized Evola's dogma of the 'superior man', which included Eastern concepts such as *jihad* (holy war) and 'the heroic path' (from Aryan mythology), both embodied in Himmler's 'elite units'.[64] The Islamic influence on the nationalist/revolutionary camp intensified after Freda became its guru and Mutti converted to Islam.[65] Both were fond of repeating how the Mufti of Jerusalem, Haj Amin al-Husseini, supported the Nazi regime, how the Italian fascists assisted the Palestinian rebels during the Arab revolt, and how the Waffen-SS units drew thousands of Muslim recruits.[66] Veneration for the Muslim warrior could also be seen in Terraciano's rhetoric:

---

[62] Quoted in the monthly *Terza Posizione* of January 1980.

[63] Ibid., January and March 1980.

[64] Ferraresi (ed.), La Destra Radicale, p. 25.

[65] Mutti published Qadaffi's 'Green Book' and served as head of the Italy-Libya Friendship Association.

[66] To prove the destructive influence of modern science on the Christian West, Mutti quoted a Muslim researcher, Hussein Nasser, who argued that 'Christianity was a religion without a holy law'. See Mutti's notes to Freda's article in Freda, La désintégration du système, p. 50, and also Claudio Mutti, 'Sombart, gli Ebrei e il capitalismo', in Risguardo. rassegna periodica di cultura, p. 19.

He who storms the enemy in a booby-trapped truck with a smile on his lips and his eyes fixed on eternity, is invincible. He who steps into a minefield with the symbolic key of the martyrs' paradise around his neck, is likewise invincible. Nay, he is victorious from the start... This is what we aspire to in our homeland...[67]

In addition, antisemitism was a basic element of radical right ideology. Ar publishing house, set up in 1964, developed the theme of 'Pluto-Jewish' power, and published classical antisemitic works such as 'The Protocols of the Elders of Zion', Evola's texts on race, and books which set out to prove that capital was inextricably linked to 'Hebraism'.[68] Italian governments were portrayed as Judas Iscariots, the lackeys of imperialism and Zionism. Right-wing ideology was also rife with anarchistic-nihilistic themes. One of Evola's favorite themes in 'Riding the Tiger' was 'right-wing anarchism' as a means of countervailing the beatnik phenomenon. TP strategy embraced anarchism alongside organized activity, believing in action for its own sake as a means of creating the 'new man' who would stir the masses to rebel.[69] In this respect, the NAR and the TP resembled the anarcho-communist RAF and AD.

3.   Influence of the variables at the decision-maker level

The antisemitism of right wing ideologues was deep-seated and personal. Freda, Mutti and Terraciano, for example, labeled any idea or phenomenon they considered negative as Jewish. The Jewish origins of Marx, Freud, Marcuse or Lukacz were always highlighted, the US was dubbed the 'American *Judenland*', and the Vietnamese people was described as waging an 'anti-plutocratic struggle against Judeo-American strategy'.[70] Holocaust denial played its part too. Romualdi considered the number of six million Jews who perished in the Holocaust as 'grossly inflated'. Finally, the Palestinian/Islamic warrior represented the salutary antithesis of the 'domineering and corrupt Yid'.[71]

4.   Reasons for lack of cooperation with Palestinian organizations

The ON and AN, active during the period when Italy was defending itself against the 'red threat', were prepared to go to any lengths to avert the danger of a

---

[67] See Terraciano, Adriano Romualdi: anima delle rivoluzione, rivoluzione dell'anima, p. 19.

[68] Thus for example, it published the works of W. Sombard 'The Jews and Economic Life' and 'The Metaphysics of Capitalism'. Mutti was actively involved in the publication of antisemitic articles and edited antisemitic books written by others. See also Ferraresi (ed.), La Destra Radicale, p. 36.

[69] See Boraccetti, Eversione di destra, terrorismo, stragi, pp. 188, 210, 218.

[70] Quoted in Ferraresi (ed.), La Destra Radicale, p. 49.

[71] Ibid., p. 51.

communist takeover of Italy; however neither perpetrated any attacks against Soviet or other Eastern bloc targets. Similarly, the NAR and the TP, which felt threatened primarily by the US and Western culture, supported Third World national liberation movements and were prepared to reach an understanding with radical left-wing organizations and copy their modus operandi, refrained from lethal attacks against US or NATO targets.

These organizations were preoccupied with the internal struggle within Italy. During the tension strategy period, the radical right campaigned against communists, socialists, and the growing radical left-wing organizations. Generally, attempts were made to ensure the participation of the security forces. Large-scale attacks were perpetrated in order to generate tension and insecurity, in the hope of triggering a radical right-wing coup. During the period of armed spontaneity, almost all attacks were directed against the security forces and the judiciary that led the campaign against the right-wing, and occasionally also against left-wing elements. These domestic concerns precluded a common meeting ground with the Palestinians.

Furthermore, just when the nationalist/revolutionary right-wing organizations were ideologically most sympathetic towards the Palestinian/Islamic cause (1979-82), the PLO/Fatah and the PFLP began to cooperate closely with radical left-wing organizations, especially the BR. 1978-79 were the years in which large weapons consignments left Lebanon en route to left-wing organizations in Italy and in 1981 Gen. Dozier was kidnapped in order to mark the BR's entry into the world of international terror. Moreover, there is no evidence of Palestinian readiness to cooperate with Italian radical right-wing organizations. On the contrary, when armed spontaneity was at its height, NAR members took refuge with the Christian Phalanges in Lebanon, probably participating in activities against the Palestinians in Lebanon.

Although all the aforementioned right-wing organizations supported European unification under the flag of nationalist/revolutionary ideology and considered the nation state as antagonistic towards ethnic freedom, much of their ideology was imbued with the spirit of Italian nationalism, harnessed against Soviet and US imperialism. Francesco Ingravalle, one of the few major militants on the radical right capable of analyzing right-wing extremism with detachment, suggested that many activists interpreted Freda's new ideology erroneously in the light of old, nationalist concepts.[72] As noted previously, nationalism is not particularly conducive to cooperation with other organizations. Ingravalle also took the far right activists to task for their failure to accept the pro-Palestinian positions of the Ar ideologues. He pointed out that the pro-Palestinian texts were published at a time in which the entire right-wing in Italy supported Israel and was plagued by

---

[72]   Ingravalle, Le edizioni di Ar e l'estrema destra, p. 104.

narrow-mindedness. He further castigated it for greeting his tract on Zionism with apathy, despite the fact that it contained a topical section on 'Israeli concentration camps in Palestine'.[73]

It is interesting to explore why antisemitic and anti-Zionist leanings, however extreme, were not sufficient for the radical right-wing organizations to carry out terror operations against Jewish or Israeli targets.

Galli pointed out that during the 1930s, the European radical right was, by definition, antisemitic and pro-Arab. With the establishment of Israel and the decolonization of the Arab world, the situation changed. Against the background of the Algerian War the new European-nationalist right and military circles cooperated with Israel, while the movement for Arab revival drew closer to the USSR. In the mid-1960s, after De Gaulle brought the Algerian war to an end, loyalties switched yet again, and Israel drew closer to the US and to what Galli called the 'invisible government'. Thus, at the end of the 1960s, antisemitic and pro-Arab feelings existed in radical right-wing circles, alongside the belief that Israel was the West's bulwark against the Russo-Arab alliance. The situation was exacerbated after the Yom Kippur War by the failure of European left-wing parties to translate their verbal support of Israel into action, leaving it dependent exclusively on the US. The radical right continued to be divided on the subject of Zionism and Israel. Although the more extremist camp identified Israel with the traditional plutocratic enemy, a large portion of the new right considered it the West's defense on the front line. Galli's description shed some light on Ingra-valle's remarks above.[74]

The European radical right drew closer to the Arab world and became increas-ingly anti-Israel during the 1980s. A late 1988 edition of *La Contea*, a monthly publication of the MSI's radical stream, featured a long article endorsing recon-ciliation between the Italian neo-fascist camp and the PLO.[75] In an interview to this newspaper, the PLO representative in Italy thanked the MSI for recognizing the Palestinian declaration of independence a year after the onset of the intifada. 'Today', he said 'you can criticize Israeli aggression without being accused of antisemitism, because all political forces are opposed to Israel's policy in the territories'.[76] It is no coincidence that in the same issue, Israel was accused of shooting down an Italian military plane in 1972 in order to 'punish' Italy, as it were, for its pro-Arab policy, and that another article nostalgically reviewed the ties of the mufti of Jerusalem with the fascist regime of the 1930s.

---

[73] Ibid., p. 103.
[74] Galli, La Crisi Italiana e la Destra Internazionale, pp. 96-100.
[75] See *La Contea*, No. 39-40, November-December 1988. The editor of the journal was none other than Rauti, one of the most fanatical and antisemitic leaders of the Italian right.
[76] Ibid.

In this context, it is important to stress that Mussolini's fascist regime was ambivalent towards the Jews and Judaism, and that antisemitism was not a sine qua non of its original fascist ideology. Two leading researchers, Renzo de Felice and Meir Michaelis, concluded that 1938 was a turning point as far as anti-Jewish policy and racist legislation was concerned, and that this was triggered mainly by the political pressures of the Rome-Berlin axis.[77] Nonetheless, even during the fascist Salo republic under German occupation, the Italian regime tried – albeit unsuccessfully – to prevent the implementation of the 'final solution' on the Jews of Italy. The disparity between the Germans and the Italians on racist issues was particularly evident in their policy towards the Jews in occupied countries. The Italian army refrained from harming Jews in the countries it overran, at least until Italy surrendered to the Allies in September 1943.[78]

Even neo-fascists who defended Mussolini's racist policy, such as Evola and Rauti, did so without much conviction, and even made a point of differentiating between the German and Italian approaches to the Jewish question, as stated above in the analysis of Evola's ideology.[79] Therefore, it is clear that the antisemitism that was expressed in Italian radical right-wing publications was not translated into action, *inter alia*, because Italian fascism and the Italian people harbored a traditionally benign attitude towards the Jews.

Mutti, one of the most antisemitic nationalist/revolutionary thinkers, described the inability of antisemitism and anti-Zionism to generate a radical right-wing-Palestinian coalition. At the end of an article on Jewish control of the world economy, Mutti stated:

> It is naïve to think that the decline of capitalism can be arrested through the adoption of anti-Jewish measures, however moderate. The persecutions the Jews allegedly suffered have a superficial effect and do not get to the root of the evil – an evil whose true source lies in the anti-traditional spirit of negation.

As an antidote to the negative influence of the 'Jewish spirit', Mutti proposed 'extensive study and a return to tradition'.[80]

---

[77] In this context, see Renzo De Felice (3rd ed.), Storia degli ebrei italiani sotto il fascismo (Torino: Arnaldo Mondadori Editore, 1977) and Meir Michaelis, Mussolini and the Jews: German-Italian Relations and the Jewish Question in Italy, 1922-1945 (Oxford: Published for the Institute of Jewish Affairs, London by the Clarendon Press, 1978).

[78] See Michaelis, Mussolini and the Jews, pp. 346 and 458. Carpi researched how the Italian army saved the lives of the Jews of southern France and Tunisia in the Second World War. See Daniel Carpi, *Between Mussolini and Hitler: The Jews and the Italian Authorities in France and Tunisia* (The Tauber Institute for the Study of European Jewry, Series 17, Hanover, N.H.: University Press of New England, 1994).

[79] Michaelis, Mussolini and the Jews, p. 454.

[80] Mutti, Sombart, gli Ebrei e il capitalismo, pp. 214-15.

CHAPTER 8
SPAIN – THE ETA

I.   HISTORICAL BACKGROUND[1]

The Basque country, which straddles the Pyrenees, consists of seven regions – four in northwest Spain (Navarra, Vizcaya, Guipuzcoa, and Alava) covering some 20,000 sq. km., and three in southeast France (Soule, Basse-Navarre, and Labourde). Eighty-five percent of the Basque country is Spanish and accommodates some 90% of the total Basque population. Of the 2.3 million inhabitants on the Spanish side, about 65% are Basques by birth. The bi-national character of the Basque country has weakened Basque national consciousness; at the same time, France has served as a refuge for Basque Homeland and Freedom (Euskadi ta Askatasuna – ETA) militants pursued by the Spanish government.[2] The Spanish Basque regions enjoyed political and administrative autonomy from the seventh century, through a series of laws known as *fueros* (privileges), zealously safeguarded by the Basque people until the nineteenth century. The long and bloody wars with Spain have left their mark on the collective memory of the Basque people.[3]

From the early twentieth century the Basque country underwent a process of industrialization, particularly in its coastal towns that drew workers from other regions, thereby aggravating the problem of Basque nationalism. The Spanish Civil War (1936-39), which for the Basques was largely a war for greater political and cultural autonomy, led to much bloodshed. The scars it left were etched even deeper by Gen. Franco, who forbade the study of the Basque language (Euskera) and suppressed any attempt at national or political organization. Ironically, it was Franco's economic development policy that helped turn the Basque country into an industrialized zone whose population enjoyed the highest standard of living in Spain.

---

[1]   This chapter is based on Robert Clark, *The Basque Insurgents. ETA, 1952-1980* (Madison, Wisconsin: University of Wisconsin Press, 1984); R. Moxon-Browne, 'Spain and the ETA', *Conflict Studies* No. 201 (1988); and Michel Wievorka, *The Making of Terrorism* (Chicago: The University of Chicago Press, 1993).

[2]   See Moxon-Browne, 'Spain and the ETA,' p. 1.

[3]   Gurutz Bereciartu Jauregui, *Ideologia e estrategia de ETA. Un análisis de su evolución entre 1959 y 1968* (2nd edn.) (Madrid: Siglo XXI de España, Editores S.A. 1985).

1.   The establishment of the ETA

In the early 1950s the Spanish Republican forces, including the Basque Nationalist Party (Partido Nacionalista Vasco – PNV) leadership, which joined the
Republican government-in-exile in France, abandoned hopes of changing the
dictatorial Franco regime that was supported by the victorious allied forces. The
PNV, like other opposition parties in exile (the socialists and communists), set
about organizing active resistance to the dictatorship.

The PNV youth section (Euzko Gaztedi – EGI), participated in this underground movement – mainly by disseminating propaganda. Concurrently, a small
group of nationalist students formed a group called Ekin (Action), which focused
mainly on cultural activities and the promotion of the Basque language. EGI and
Ekin began to cooperate, and between 1957-58 they tried to persuade the PNV
leadership in France to adopt a policy of direct action. However, the PNV was
unable to accept two of Ekin's ideological tenets, namely that the language of the
future Basque state should be Basque, and that the reinstatement of the Republican parties was not a precondition for Basque independence.

A new organization named Euskadi ta Askatasuna (ETA) was subsequently
set up on 31 July 1959. From 1959 to 1962 the ETA distanced itself from the
PNV, and eventually established a military arm. The ETA aimed to accomplish
something the war generation had been unable to do, namely to renew the
national struggle. This represented a strategic rather than an ideological break
with historical nationalism. Therefore, the ETA did not see itself as merely a
political organization, but rather as a liberation movement.[4] In July 1961 an
abortive attempt to derail trains carrying Franco supporters to anti-Basque
demonstrations, and a spate of strikes in Spain and in the Basque country led to
heavy clampdowns and arrests. Some ETA leaders moved to France where they
set up secret cells.

II.   TYPOLOGICAL DEFINITION

The architect of Basque nationalism was Sabino Arana who was born in 1865. He
established the Basque Nationalist Party (Partido Nacional Vasco – PNV), named
the divided Basque country Euskadi and designed its flag. He was responsible for
consolidating Basque nationalist ideology, based on the following tenets: the need
for national unity; adherence to the Catholic faith; adoption of non-violent means;

---

[4]   Ibid., p. 82.

and, in particular, the centrality of the Basque language.[5] Arana identified the source of the Basque problem as the Spanish occupation and domination, and stressed 'the doctrinaire contradiction between the Basque and Spanish cultures – as represented by language – and races'. Arana completely ignored the role of class in Basque society, social/economic changes in the second half of the nineteenth century and the early twentieth century, and the pro-integration activities of the Basque bourgeoisie.[6]

Another nationalist ideologue, Eli Gallastegui, openly supported the Moroccans in their revolt against the Spanish conqueror and suggested that Moroccan independence might further Basque independence. He compared between the oppression of Morocco and Euskadi by Spain, on the one hand, and the oppression of Ireland and India by Britain, on the other. He therefore called on Morocco and Euskadi to unite against Spain, and for all four countries to work together in the struggle against colonialism.[7]

III.   THE REVOLUTIONARY STRUGGLE (1963-65)[8]

The Third World national liberation struggles, especially the revolutionary struggles of Algeria and Cuba, made a deep impression on Basque youth during this period. Initially, ETA leaders naively failed to distinguish between independence movements as different as the Jewish National Military Organization (Irgun Zvai Leumi – IZL) in British mandate in Palestine and the Algerian National Liberation Front (Front de Libération Nationale – FLN).[9] The ETA valued its independent status but maintained a pragmatic approach to alliances with other organizations.[10]

During this period, the Basque nationalists rejected the Spanish Communist Party or, more accurately, communism in general. This aversion stemmed from peasant tradition, the religious character of the Basque people and the PNV, and

---

[5]   See Moxon-Browne, *Spain and the ETA*, p. 2.
[6]   See Jauregui, *Ideologia e estrategia de ETA*, pp. 24-31
[7]   Ibid., pp. 30-31.
[8]   According to Guell, ETA's early years (1959-63) in which it was trying to forge its own identity, were marked by violent activity and no clear strategy. Guell divided ETA activity into three main periods: the revolutionary struggle (1963-65); the 'activity-suppression-activity' spiral (1965-74); the negotiations period (1974-87) which was given particular emphasis from 1977 on. See Pedro Ibarra Guell, *La evolución estratégica de ETA*, (Donostia: Kriselu, 1987), p. 57.
[9]   See José Mari Garmendia, *Historia de ETA* (2 vols.) (San Sebastián: Haranburu, Editor S.A. 1983) p. 17, and Guell, *La evolución estratégica de ETA*, p. 63.
[10] Ibid., p. 20. It is not clear if by alliances they meant only internal alliances or alliances with other liberation movements.

from the ties between the nationalist party and the US during the Second World War. Until 1963 the ETA rejected all socialist models, although those trained by ETA were required to study Marxist writings.[11] Three distinct factions can be discerned within the ETA of the early 1960s:[12]

(1) The ethno-linguistic or cultural faction regarded language as the main, perhaps the only, element of nationality. It called for a broad national front embracing all Basques, irrespective of class in order to establish an independent country with Basque as the official language.[13]

(2) The Espaniolista faction was influenced by the Marxism of the European New Left in the early 1960s. The liberation of Basque workers was perceived as contingent on an alliance with their Spanish counterparts against the Spanish, British and US oligarchy. The Espaniolistas advocated social revolution, and feared that armed struggle could harm it.[14]

(3) The Tercermundistas (pro-Third World) faction was influenced by anti-colonialist struggles in the Third World, especially in Algeria, Cuba and Vietnam, and by the writings of Frantz Fanon.[15] They saw Euskadi 'as a Spanish colony, and called for a revolutionary war including armed struggle by urban guerrillas against non-Basques and against the Basque bourgeoisie.[16] This faction was deeply influenced by the ideology developed by Krutwig in his book 'Vasconia,' which in turn was largely inspired by the Algerian experience.[17]

1964 was a key year in the history of the Basque people, for three reasons: firstly Basque language, literature and culture was experiencing a revival; secondly,

---

[11] During this period, ETA saw the Euskadi as belonging to the democratic European nations, and the rest of Spain (apart from Catalonia) as belonging to the Third World. See Jauregui, *Ideologia e estrategia de ETA*, pp. 93-109 and Garmendia, *Historia de* ETA (I), p. 55.

[12] See Robert Clark, *The Basque Insurgents*, pp. 32-35.

[13] The leader of this faction was José Luis Alvarez Enparanza – 'Taxillardegi'.

[14] The most striking personality of this faction (also known as the Trotskyists) was Paco Iturrioz, head of the Political Bureau in the mid-1960s.

[15] Peter Janke added the influence of the Israeli national liberation struggle. See Peter Janke, 'Spanish Separatism. ETA's Threat to Basque Democracy,' *Conflict Studies* (1980), p. 4.

[16] The ideologue of this faction was Sagredo Federico Krutwig, whose mother was Basque and whose father was a German industrialist from Bilbao.

[17] For the first time the organization systematically outlined the principles of revolutionary war in a pamphlet entitled 'The uprising in the Basque country', published in early 1964. See *La insurrección en Euskadi*, as quoted in Garmendia, *Historia de ETA (I)*, pp. 103-107.

after a three-decade hiatus, nationalism once again flourished at grass roots level; and finally, the ETA was sufficiently organized, for the first time, to directly influence large sections of the population.[18] The ideological changes taking place within the ETA received an official stamp of approval at annual conferences. The first such event, in May 1962, declared the ETA 'a Basque revolutionary national liberation movement'. ETA's anti-colonialist analysis drew parallels between Euskadi and Algeria and Vietnam, and between the ETA, with its several dozen militants, and the FLN or the Vietcong, movements that enjoyed much broader popular support. The analysis completely disregarded the fact that in socio-economic terms the Basque country bore no resemblance to Third World countries.

IV.   THE ACTIVITY-SUPPRESSION-ACTIVITY SPIRAL (1965-74)

The concept of revolutionary war on the Algerian model, as developed in 1962 by Krutwig, was superseded at ETA's fourth conference in 1965 by the 'spiral' strategy. This advanced terrorist attacks in order to provoke brutal repression by the government and thereby rally the people around the ETA. At the fifth conference, in December 1966, the Marxist Espaniolista faction was expelled from the organization, and four fronts (military, cultural, political, and economic) were created as part of a plan to unite workers, peasants, and the middle class (the middle class was later excluded).[19]

In 1968 the ETA carried out its first murder, of a police officer in the Guardia Civil. In the same year, a senior police officer considered responsible for the interrogation and torture of ETA members was murdered. Dozens of militants were subsequently arrested and a provisional state of emergency was declared. Several ETA leaders were jailed, while others fled to France. Within three years, two generations of ETA leaders disappeared or were banished. They were replaced by new leaders who were prepared to review ETA ideology, operational principles and organizational structure.[20] Those implicated in the 1968 murder of the police officer stood trial in 1969 in Burgos. The trials attracted far more publicity than ETA's own propaganda: solidarity movements mushroomed in Europe and worldwide, and many youngsters joined the ETA's depleted ranks.

Although the ETA became weaker during this period, it identified more closely with the working class and participated in mass strikes. The ideological

---

[18]   Jauregui, *Ideologia e estrategia de ETA*, p. 273.
[19]   See Wievorka, *The Making of Terrorism*, p. 152.
[20]   See Clark, *The Basque Insurgents. ETA*, pp. 51-52.

struggle between the two main factions erupted at the sixth conference in August 1970: the Marxist faction, which rejected the focus on nationalism; and the patriotic nationalist faction, which viewed the Basque country as a Spanish colony, and emphasized military action. This fight continued to weaken the organization throughout the 1970s.[21]

The ETA-VI, the stronger, Marxist faction, heir to the sixth conference, controlled the organization, enjoyed the support of most rank-and-file members in Spain, including those who stood trial in Burgos.[22] The ETA-VI disbanded in late 1972, after the second session of the sixth conference, and joined the Trotskyist Revolutionary Communist League (LCR). It had failed to meet demands by other Basque groups to set up a common front, and was accused of Espaniolism, namely an alliance with Spanish leftist counterparts. This effectively marked ETA-VI's end.

The ETA-V, which was inspired by ideological decisions adopted at the fifth conference, enjoyed a strong leadership, and advocated ethnicity, rather than class struggle, as a basis for action.[23] Although some of the principles of Third World struggle were abandoned in the early 1970s, the ETA-V maintained that Euskadi was a Spanish colony.[24] The ETA-V defined itself as a socialist organization, based on the Leninist model, one in which the revolutionary vanguard working-class masses happened to be Basques. With the demise of the ETA-VI, the revitalized ETA-V faction readopted the name ETA. It immediately launched an intensive campaign, which included the kidnapping of business leaders, bank robberies, and attacks against Spanish targets and the property of Basque right-wingers.

It was during this period that the ETA broadened its international ties, signing declarations of solidarity with Fatah, the Kurdish Democratic Party (KDP), the IRA and the Breton Liberation Front (Front de Libération Breton – FLB). Alongside its military wing, the ETA developed a 'work front' and a 'cultural

---

21   See Wievorka, *The Making of Terrorism*, p. 154.
22   The prisoners on trial in Burgos attacked the conservative Basque nationalists and bourgeoisie in a letter, and rejected the idea of a confrontation between Euskadi, and Spain/France. It was perhaps this letter that influenced the ETA-VI to abandon the ethnic/nationalist line in favor of closer cooperation with the working class.
23   Prominent among them was Eustaquio Mendizabal Benito, alias 'Txikia', who participated in the kidnapping of the German consul in Bolivia. Its activist policy was well suited to the spirit of the times on the international front. The Tupamaros in Uruguay were at the height of their activity, and the Black September attack on the Israeli athletes in Munich took place around that time (September 1972).
24   The faction's primary text was *Toward a Basque Revolutionary Strategy*, by José Luis Zalbide. It called for an armed struggle against the agents of colonialism and imperialism, in order to cause the collapse of the Spanish administration.

front'. By late 1973, the organization had some 50-60 members belonging to cells of 5-6 activists.[25] Its terrorist activity peaked on 20 December 1973, when Spanish prime minister Admiral Luis Carrero Blanco, was murdered by a car bomb.[26]

The ETA leadership believed that military action had to be combined with political activity among the masses. The work front found the growing autonomy and importance of the military front intolerable. The military front, for its part, was critical of these views, and succeeded in imposing a quasi-military hierarchy on the entire organization.[27] In the autumn of 1974, the rift between factions, namely the ETA political-military (ETA político-militar – ETAp-m) and the ETA military (ETA militar – ETAm) became irreversible. The immediate cause of the rift was the attack on a Madrid café that caused many casualties, for which the organization long refused to take responsibility. The leader of the ETAp-m, Bergartze, tried to unite the two rival factions, but the rift grew during 1975-76, until Bergartze himself was killed, apparently by political rivals.

V.   THE ETA ACTIVITY AND NEGOTIATIONS (1974-90)

The new phase, which began in the summer of 1974 after the split with the ETAp-m, lasted until the end of the 1980s. By then, the ETA's sole objective was to compel the Spanish government to negotiate over the so-called 'KAS alternative' (Koordinadora Abertzale Sozialista – Socialist Patriotic Coordination). This was a set of demands devised by the organization to ensure the Basque people's right to self-determination, and finally, full independence. To obtain this objective, the ETA had developed a number of front organizations (syndicates, a youth organization, a women's organization, a political party) and a national unity party (Herri Batasuna – HB), ostensibly to coordinate political and military activity among the masses. The ETA focused all its activities on military achievements, channeling the political struggle first through KAS and later through the HB. The establishment of the HB in April 1978 and its outstanding success in the March 1979 elections, together with the overwhelming Basque vote against the new

---

[25] After the charismatic leader Mendizabal was killed in action, a new collective leadership took control.

[26] Reinares, like many others, viewed this assassination as the catalyst for the change of regime in Spain, from authoritarianism to liberal democracy. Thus, terrorism left its mark at the beginning of the transition period, a legacy from the dictatorship. See Fernando Reinares, 'The Dynamics of Terrorism during the Transition to Democracy in Spain', in Paul Wilkinson and A.M. Stewart (eds.), *Contemporary Research on Terrorism* (Aberdeen: The University Press, 1987), p. 121.

[27] See Fernando Reinares, 'The Dynamics of Terrorism during the Transition to Democracy in Spain,' p. 123 and Jauregui, *Ideologia e estrategia de ETA*, p. 470.

constitution of December 1978, strengthened the ETA politically, and helped it recover from the decline it had experienced in early 1978.[28]

Despite the Spanish transition to a democratic regime between 1976-77 and the gesture towards the Basque region, which ultimately led to Basque autonomy, some Basque parties, including the ETA, were dissatisfied with the nature and pace of reform. The armed struggle therefore continued unabated; against all political logic, it even escalated because ETA leaders feared that democracy would render the organization superfluous.[29]

This period was marred by tension surrounding the results of negotiations on Basque autonomy and amnesty for ETA prisoners. An internal struggle ensued over leadership, organizational changes and an attempt to set up a front organization to engage in the democratic process. The ETAp-m, at its seventh conference held in October 1976, finally decided to break with the ETA-m and to establish the Revolutionary Basque Party (Euskal Iraultzako Alderdia – EIA). However, the opposition of extremist elements within the organization, attacks against members of the Guardia Civil and the kidnapping of a famous Basque industrialist, undermined the legitimacy of the ETAp-m.

Violence escalated during 1978-79 after the liquidation of several, more moderate leaders. Most of the Basque supporters and parties accepted the autonomy compromise proposals, driving an even deeper wedge between mainstream and ETA extremists. The escalation in terrorist activity compelled the Spanish government to take stronger action against the ETA.[30]

Terrorist activity peaked in 1980, with a death toll of more than 80, including police officers and the Guardia Civil. The ETA specifically targeted tourist resorts in an attempt to damage the economy. In 1982 the ETAp-m resumed its terrorist activity after a year's cease-fire, on the grounds that the situation of the Basque country had deteriorated. In addition to targeting the police and military, the ETAm opened a new front – against the nuclear power station that was to be built in the Basque region. It was in the context of this campaign that the ETA, for the first time, murdered working-class individuals.[31]

During Franco's long rule, the French government had refused to cooperate with Spain in its fight against Basque militants seeking asylum in France. There were several reasons for this: the dictatorial character of the Franco regime; French annoyance with the Spanish government for helping members of the French terrorist Secret Army Organization (Organisation Armée Secrete – OAS)

---

[28]   See Guell, *La evolución estratégica de ETA*, pp. 99-124.
[29]   See Reinares, 'The Dynamics of Terrorism during the Transition to Democracy in Spain,' p. 125.
[30]   See Clark, 'The Basque Insurgents. ETA,' pp. 89-111.
[31]   See Moxon-Browne, 'Spain and the ETA,' pp. 8-9.

and other French right-wing extremists who had fled to Spain after the events in Algeria in 1958; and its fear of antagonizing the Basque nationalists in French Basque country. President Mitterand's rise to power did not improve the situation. The situation only began to change in 1983 when a socialist party took office in Spain, and terrorism escalated in France. The French even deported some ETA leaders to Central America, Algeria and other African countries, and attempted to extradite to Spain a number of militants suspected of terrorist activity.[32]

It was around the same time that an anti-Basque terrorist organization called the Anti-Terrorist Liberation Groups (Grupos Antiterroristas de Liberación – GAL) emerged. According to some sources, the GAL was paid by the Spanish government and hired mainly French or North African thugs to kill or injure ETA militants, particularly in France. The arrest and trial of a number of GAL militants in France sparked a serious diplomatic crisis between the two countries.

The aggressive policy of France towards the Basque exiles in France, on the one hand, and Spain's new policy of social integration for ETA members who abandoned the armed struggle, created a more suitable climate for negotiations between the ETA and the Spanish government. The negotiations, which were backed by the Basque political parties, vacillated and were stalled for long periods of time. The ETA stepped up its activities in the Basque country in 1986-87 by a Madrid-based cell, known as the Spanish Commando. Until the arrest of its members this cell was notorious for carrying out car bomb attacks against the Guardia Civil. In the late 1980s, Barcelona became the focus of some terrorist operations. As the 1992 Olympics approached, there was a growing fear that the ETA would try to exploit this international event to carry out ostentatious terrorist attacks.[33]

It was only in 1986, when both parties believed the other was weak and willing to speak from a position of inferiority that negotiations got under way. Since the ETA leadership refused to consider any solution other than full independence, the hawkish elements, which opposed further contacts, triumphed.[34] ETA's continued policy of terrorist activity and stubborn negotiations with the Spanish administration continues to this day.

1.   Cooperation with Palestinian organizations

Very little data exists concerning ties between the various ETA factions and Palestinian terrorist organizations. Clark referred to a joint ETA-Fatah statement

---

[32]   Ibid., pp. 13-15.
[33]   See Edgar O'Ballance, *Terrorism in the 1980s* (London: Arms and Armour, 1989), p. 89.
[34]   After the charismatic and more moderate leader 'Txomin' disappeared from the scene in a rather mysterious accident in Algeria.

signed in February 1972 but provided no details concerning its content or implications.[35] During this period, the ETA sought to expand its foreign ties, and signed joint communiqués with the KDP, the IRA and the FLB. Clark claimed that the ETAm faction was influenced in its terrorist activity by the Black September strategy and the attack at the Munich Olympics.[36]

Evidence of real cooperation emerged when four ETA militants were arrested by the Dutch authorities in May 1980 at Amsterdam airport, returning to Spain after training assignment in a PFLP camp in South Yemen. Together with eight other ETA members and a number of Palestinians, the ETA militants had spent about four months there studying urban guerrilla tactics.[37] Interestingly, ETA's leader declared in September 1979 that 'we see ourselves as an integral part of the Palestinian struggle. We have a common enemy'.[38]

Basque terrorists were known to have trained in Lebanon and Libya. More significant by far were ETA ties with Algeria, which became more practical following the FLN rise to power: ETA activists were trained in Algeria and outlawed members were granted asylum there in the early 1980s. Algeria officially agreed to accept some ETA leaders expelled from France; Algeria also served as mediator in negotiations between the ETA and the Spanish government.[39]

According to an official Spanish document from 1979, during the 1970s the ETA maintained ties with many terrorist organizations, including Palestinians ones (only in one case is the BSO mentioned specifically), but there were no details about these contacts.[40] Attached to this report was the 1972 statement signed by the ETA, Fatah and the PDK. In addition to phrases of solidarity, the document mentioned a proposal for mutual aid between liberation organizations worldwide to include 'exchange of information on revolutionary experiences, military cooperation, etc.' Nothing is known about the implementation of this proposal.[41]

---

[35] See Clark, 'The Basque Insurgents,' p. 69.

[36] Ibid., p. 80.

[37] See Mickolus, *ITERATE* database, incident 80052302, 23 May 1980.

[38] See Guy Bechor, *A PLO Lexicon* (in Hebrew), (Israeli Ministry of Defense Publication, 1991), p. 53.

[39] Janke reported that in the early 1960s, ETA had already established ties with the Algerian government and that two ETA leaders traveled to Algeria in order to organize military action and training for their militants. According to Clark, about 20 ETA members were trained in Algeria in late 1976. See Janke, 'Spanish Separatism,' p. 7, and Clark, *The Basque Insurgents. ETA*, p. 234.

[40] See the report *La organisacion revolucionaria y terrorista ETA* (Madrid, Ministry of Defense, April 1979). Parts of this document were provided to the author by a Spanish journalist. It seems that most of the information mentioned by Clark and others were based on this report, including the subject of close ties with Algeria.

[41] Ibid., Annex 43. The statement was published during the fifteenth congress of Kurdish students in Europe, which took place in Bucharest, Rumania, on 19 February 1972. This is probably the statement to which Clark referred.

Given that ETA maintained close relations with the Algerian government and its leaders spent many years in Algeria one might have expected closer ties with Palestinian terrorist organizations operating in Algeria since 1964. In reality, however, such ties never evolved.

VI.   ANALYSIS OF RESEARCH ASSUMPTIONS

1.   Influence of the variables at the organizational level

ETA's reluctance to form alliances was primarily due to the strongly nationalist character of the organization.[42] From the outset, the ETA attracted two types of militants: those who lived and fought in the Basque country and in Spain; and those who fled to other countries, particularly to the neighboring French Basque region. As the armed struggle and the confrontation with the security forces persisted, an increasing number of militants were forced to flee. Naturally, those who lived in France, and later Algeria, were more open to revolutionary influences in Europe and elsewhere. As the ideological rift within ETA between Marxist and nationalist elements evolved, the exiles were invariably influenced by Marxism. Those who remained in Spain were more concerned by domestic issues, by the more conspicuous trappings of Basque nationalism – the Basque language, the revival of Basque culture, the symbols of the Spanish regime – and less interested in global revolutionary struggles.

It is noteworthy that the ETA did not cooperate with other left-wing revolutionary organizations (such as GRAPO), or even other separatist movements in Spain. Between 1974-87, the ETA was at the forefront of the armed struggle in Spain.[43] Relations with the anti-capitalist autonomous commando units were either hostile or non-existent.[44] Even the Basque anti-nuclear movement distinguished itself from similar movements worldwide by continuously emphasizing

---

[42] The ETA was deeply rooted in the Basque country and its long historical tradition. One can even pinpoint the geographical area where many of its leaders and militants grew up and which served as the cradle of ETA activities for many years – the rather isolated mountainous region of Goierri. See Clark, *The Basque Insurgents*, p. 203 and Wievorka, *The Making of Terrorism*, p. 180.

[43] See Wievorka, *The Making of Terrorism*, p. 169.

[44] In an interview with a Spanish journal in 1988, ETAm leaders were questioned about their attitude towards the Catalan separatist nationalist organization, Tierra Llure, and towards 'The guerrilla army of the Galician people', a separatist organization in the region of Galicia, eastern Spain. Their answer was extremely succinct: 'In general, ETA agrees with the way these organizations analyze the situation in the provinces where they are struggling, and wishes them success, but there is no organizational link with them.' The interview was granted to *Diario 16* on 21 February 1988, and was quoted in *Il Bollettino*, No. 37-38, Sept. 1989, p. 44.

its Basque character. At the most, it saw itself as a pan-Spanish movement, rather than a pan-European one. The ETA, which spearheaded violent protests against the proposed construction of a nuclear power plant in the Basque country, was even reluctant to admit independent Basque anti-nuclear groups into the broader political front organizations.[45] To ETA's credit, it was the only European organization in the early 1980s that managed to thwart the construction of a nuclear power station.[46]

Perhaps ETA's self-sufficiency can best be summarized by Wievorka's comment that the political power struggle against Franco's regime never spilled over the borders of the Basque country, with the exception of some small, short-lived organizations.[47] ETA's sixteen-year struggle against Franco's dictatorship served to strengthen its nationalist character, and set it apart from other national and revolutionary movements in Western Europe.

Nonetheless, the ETA was more than just a nationalist, separatist movement, as it also adopted modern revolutionary ideology. The Palestinian organizations belonged to the same camp as the revolutionary Third World liberation movements, which inspired the Tercermundista ideology of the ETA. Why then, did exposure to these ideologies fail to lead to greater cooperation or solidarity with the Palestinians organizations? One reason was bad timing. ETA's Third World, anti-colonialist ideology had already been superseded in 1965 by the 'spiral strategy' adopted at the fourth conference. In 1968, the ETA abandoned its perception of Euskadi as a Spanish colony and in 1970 the sixth conference formally endorsed the anti-imperialist propositions.[48] The Palestinian organizations, however, only emerged on the international stage after the Six Day War, at a time when the Third World phase of the ETA was drawing to a close.

Equally important was ETA's admiration for the Zionist militants of the IZL. Garmendia pointed out that in the early years, ETA's esteem for liberation and revolutionary movements around the world was somewhat simplistic – it failed to discriminate between organizations as different as the IZL and the Algerian FLN, for example.[49] Indeed, the 1964 booklet 'The Uprising in the Basque Country' suggested that the victory of small commandos of Zionists against the British

---

[45]   See Wievorka, *The Making of Terrorism*, p. 174 and Guell, *La evolución estratégica de ETA*, p. 165.

[46]   ETA 'persuaded' the companies that built the power station at Lemoniz to abandon the project after militants murdered the chief engineer in 1981 and the project director in 1982.

[47]   See Wievorka, *The Making of Terrorism*, p. 177.

[48]   These changes were proposed in the booklet *Hacia una estrategia revolucionaria vasca*, written in jail by José Luis Zalbide under the pseudonym of K. de Zunbeltz. See Jauregui, *Ideologia e estrategia de ETA*, p. 417.

[49]   See Garmendia, *Historia de ETA (I)*, p. 17.

army inspired hope for the ETA.[50] Although the document referred to the Algerian and Vietnamese national liberation struggles, there was no mention of the Palestinians.

Certain Basque militants appeared to identify somewhat with problems facing the Jewish people. In the early 1960s, for example, ETA militants in Caracas proposed the formation of a mass movement to bring about a 'return to the homeland' for the many Basque emigrants in Latin America, based on the Zionist model.[51] Similarly, until the late 1960s, the revival of the Basque language was a major tenet of ETA ideology. The revival of the Hebrew language in Palestine provided an example, and encouraged them to set up special schools for the study of Basque.[52]

The differences between nationalist and Marxist elements within ETA resulted in a protracted ideological struggle. The growing rift between the two factions culminated at the sixth conference in 1970, when the majority Marxist-Leninist ETA-VI faction began the process of abandoning the armed struggle and transforming itself into a left-wing political movement. During 1972-73, the leadership abroad was influenced by French Trotskyists, who had gained credibility after the events of May 1968 and by Maoist doctrines.[53] Like Trotskyist and Maoist movements everywhere, ETA's thriving Marxist-Leninist faction focused on the political struggle and was unwilling to cooperate with terrorist organizations in Spain or elsewhere.

The nationalist faction also abandoned the armed struggle in order to 'keep a clean image'. After acknowledging that Euskadi was a developed and industrialized West European country rather than a Third World colony, the nationalist faction embraced the class struggle and joined the powerful Basque workers' movement. This trend, which began in the late 1960s and intensified in 1970, resulted in the establishment in 1974 of a broad political movement – the KAS Alternative.[54] This transition to the political arena compelled the ETA to distance itself from international terrorist organizations. Nevertheless, there were several isolated cases of cooperation with Palestinian organizations. Why did the ETA agree to cooperate in these cases?

---

[50] See *La insurrección en Euskadi*, published in early 1964 and quoted in Garmendia, *Historia de ETA (I)*, p. 109. On the subject of the influence of the Jewish struggle for independence, see also Guell, *La evolución estratégica de ETA*, p. 64 and Janke, 'Spanish Separatism,' p. 4.

[51] See Jauregui, *Ideologia e estrategia de ETA*, p. 143.

[52] In the 1980s, there were reports in Israeli newspapers about Basques (not necessarily connected with specific nationalist circles) who wished to learn from Israel's experience in developing and studying an ancient language.

[53] Garmendia, *Historia de ETA (I)*, pp. 137-38.

[54] See Jauregui, *Ideologia e estrategia de ETA*, p. 297 and Guell, *La evolución estratégica de ETA*, pp. 78-81.

It should be stressed that the joint communiqué with Fatah and the PDK was merely an expression of solidarity. At the time, the ETA was divided between the Marxist ETA-VI and the nationalist ETA-V. The latter was further divided between the military and the political-military wings, with the military ultimately gaining the upper hand. The military wing, which was inclined towards anarchism, did not debate political issues, only structural ones. It was this group that planned the murder of Admiral Carrero Blanco, Franco's designated heir.[55] This tendency towards anarchism and terrorism probably explains the willingness to align itself with Fatah.

It is more difficult to explain why a relatively large number of ETA militants trained in PFLP camps in southern Yemen in 1979-80. This was all the more surprising given the establishment of the HB front party and its impressive results in the March 1979 elections. However, it was in these elections that most Basque nationalist parties and movements agreed to accept autonomy, thereby damaging ETA's claim to represent the only nationalist solution.

According to Wievorka, the ETA's transformation into a terrorist organization was due to two factors: important developments within the Basque country in the wake of Spanish democracy; the difficulty of a single symbolic enemy; and the weakening of the social struggles – or what he called a process of inversion.[56] In early 1979, the ETA declared open war against the Spanish armed forces and stepped up activity against senior army officers. ETA leaders may therefore have sensed a need to improve the combat capabilities of their militants. Furthermore, ETA relations with France – a former ETA refuge and training ground – had worsened, and terror against French interests in Spain had increased. The pro-Palestinian declaration by ETA's leader in September 1979 ('we see ourselves an integral part of the Palestinian struggle') should be viewed in the context of the agreement concerning the training of ETA militants in PFLP camps.

2.   Influence of the variables at the international and regional level

International issues rarely figured in ETA documents. It was only in the late 1960s that the ETA began to express concern over Western imperialism, and even then mainly Spanish imperialism. A document from 1969 stated:

> If the Spanish people succeeds in launching a national liberation struggle against imperialism, the struggle will definitely be anti-American. The Basque people's national liberation struggle, however, is directed against Spanish (and French) imperialism. We [ETA] know that the Americans are behind Spanish imperialism,

---

[55]   See Garmendia, *Historia de ETA (II)*, pp. 141-75.
[56]   See Wievorka, *The Making of Terrorism*, pp. 168-69.

but they are still only behind, not in front [of the camp]. Possibly, the collapse of the Spanish state would lead to its conquest by the USA, as happened with Vietnam. In such a case, the Basque people would have to fight American imperialism directly. The Basque people must fight against Spanish (and French) imperialism... The confrontation between the Basque people and American imperialism is secondary.[57]

The fact that there were no US forces in the Basque country, unlike other regions in Spain and Western Europe, lessened potential friction with 'American imperialism'. On one occasion ETA militant even posited that America had failed to install bases in the Basque country because it was afraid of the ETA.[58]

Similarly, the examined ETA documents contained no references to the USSR and the communist bloc, nor to the bipolar struggle between the superpowers and the ideological blocs.[59] On the regional level, only relations between Spain and France were relevant to the ETA struggle. Since one of the Basque regions (referred to as Euskadi Nord by the organization), was located within French territory, French imperialism was condemned.[60] However, as long as France served as the main asylum for ETA militants, and as long as the authorities turned a blind eye to ETA's operations, the organization refrained from attacking French targets. It not only failed to help, but even thwarted the activities of the French radical Basque organization Those of the North (Iparretarrak – IK).[61] From 1979, however, the attitude of the French authorities changed, and in the wake of the 1984 agreements between France and Spain to fight Basque terror, the ETA began to attack French targets, especially in Spain.[62]

Possibly, the ETA indifference towards the situation in the Middle East was due to the political and diplomatic rift between Spain and Israel.[63] It is noteworthy

---

[57]   Quoted in Garmendia, *Historia de ETA (II)*, p. 309.

[58]   Quoted in Wievorka, *The Making of Terrorism*, p. 203.

[59]   NATO too barely figured in ETA's ideological literature. Guell noted that these issues were of secondary importance to the ETA. He referred to a leaflet in which ETA asked its sympathizers to vote in the referendum against Spain's joining NATO. See Guell, *La evolución estratégica de ETA*, p. 156.

[60]   The journal *Zutik 67* pointed out that this position was reasserted by the platform that was approved in 1976.

[61]   This was confirmed to the author by members of the French prosecution dealing with cases against IK.

[62]   Thus, for example, in 1979 ETA threatened to attack French tourists in Spain, and bombed the Basque offices of Renault and Citroën. In 1984, after France began to expel some of its leaders, the ETA torched cars of French tourists and renewed its attacks against Renault. At the time, GRAPO supported ETA's struggle against French interests in Spain. Similar attacks took place in 1986.

[63]   At first, the newly independent State of Israel did not recognize Franco's regime, and later Spain refused to establish diplomatic ties with it until 1986. This also accounted for the lack of Spanish

that ETA's reluctance to enter into international alliances was true not only in respect to Palestinian organizations, but other revolutionary organizations too. Although the 1980s trials of Italian terrorists 'revealed' that the ETA sought ties with the BR, it only actually established contact with PL, Italy's second most important terrorist organization (see Chapter 4).

The ETA maintained ties with other nationalist organizations, in the framework of European 'oppressed' minorities, like the Bretons in France, the Flemish in Belgium or the Polisario in Morocco.[64] The main cooperation however, was with the IRA.[65] Contacts between the two organizations, led to mutual declarations of solidarity, and an attempt to organize a union of European separatist organizations.[66] There was, however, little evidence of actual cooperation.

With the exception of its attacks against French targets, which apparently produced no fatalities, the ETA was responsible for very few international terror attacks: the kidnapping of the German consul in San Sebastian in December 1970, perpetrated in order to obtain the release of ETA jailed militants; the kidnapping in February 1981 of the consuls of Salvador, Austria, and Uruguay; and occasional bomb attacks against branch offices of multinational and US corporations in the Basque country. Finally, in the 1980s, the ETA carried out sporadic attacks against Spanish interests in Europe.

VII. SUMMARY

The ETA's highly nationalist character, its determination to retain its independence in all spheres and its separatist aspirations precluded the formation of a meaningful coalition with any other terrorist organizations. The 1976 platform of the KAS Alternative contained a general declaration about 'the maintenance of mutual relations based on international solidarity but free of any dominance'.[67] This lukewarm attitude towards international cooperation was characteristic of the

---

involvement in Middle Eastern affairs and the absence of any official Israeli presence in Spain until the mid-1980s.

[64]   See the report *La organisacion revolucionaria y terrorista ETA*, pp. 10/1-10/5.

[65]   This cooperation attained a peak in 1973, when ETA militants trained in Northern Ireland, IRA specialists in explosives came to the Basque country and the two organizations published a common statement in September attacking the European Common Market, NATO, and the 'capitalist states'. The statement closed with general slogans about a 'European society of united free peoples without classes, an united socialist Europe'. Ibid., and Annex 45.

[66]   The attempt resulted in the publication of the Brest Charter, signed in 1974 by ETA V, and Corsican and Occitan nationalists in France. The statement called, again, in very general terms to 'solidarity of all the oppressed peoples'. Ibid., Annex 46.

[67]   Quoted in Guell, *La evolución estratégica de ETA*, p. 112.

ETA throughout its existence. More specifically, the lack of contacts with Palestinian organizations was probably influenced by the ETA's sensitivity, during its formative years, to the Jewish people's struggle for independence.

CHAPTER 9
THE PALESTINIAN TERRORIST ORGANIZATIONS

I.   HISTORICAL BACKGROUND[1]

1.   Fatah

The Palestine National Liberation Movement (Harakat al-Tahrir al-Watani al-Filastini – Fatah) is the oldest and most important of the many Palestinian terrorist organizations that emerged from the mid-1960s. It dominates the institutions of the Palestinian Liberation Organization (PLO) and therefore represents the Palestinian national movement.[2] Fatah was founded by Palestinian students from Gaza, mostly studying at Cairo University, who set up the Union of Palestinian Students in Egypt in late 1952. The Palestinian students, led by Yasser Arafat, were affiliated with the Muslim Brothers (MB) in Egypt, then in its prime, and by far the most active organization on the Cairo campus.[3] The ideology of the Palestinian national movement, as symbolized by Abd al-Kader al-Husayni, and the MB both struck a chord among disenchanted Palestinian youth who had suffered exile and persecution in Egypt, only to realize that the Arab regimes were unable or unwilling to assist the Palestinians against the Jewish state.[4] According to Bechor, 'the essence of Fatah was Palestinian activism by the "generation of vengeance" in contrast to the perceived apathy of the previous generation, scornfully dubbed "the generation of defeat".'[5]

Palestinian activists were increasingly influenced by the struggle of the Algerian National Liberation Front (Front de Libération Nationale – FLN) against the French, and by the revolutionary philosopher Franz Fanon, who not only laid the ideological groundwork for the FLN, but had a major impact on all Third World liberation movements. Fanon's influence was reflected in the third Fatah leaflet,

---

[1]   The most comprehensive work on the Palestinian armed struggle is that by Yazid Sayigh, *Armed Struggle and the Search for State: The Palestinian National Movement, 1949-1993* (New York: Oxford University Press, 1997).

[2]   The historical and ideological background on Fatah is based mainly on Ehud Ya'ari, *Fatah* (in Hebrew), (Tel Aviv: A. Levine-Epstein, 1970). See also Sayigh, *Armed Struggle and the Search for State*, pp. 80-92.

[3]   The liquidation of the MB by the Egyptian regime explained Arafat's subsequent hostility towards Egyptian premier Gamal Abdul Nasser.

[4]   Abd al-Kader al-Husayni, a member of one of the two most famous Palestinian families, led Palestinian military forces against the Israelis during the 1948 War and died in the battle for Jerusalem.

[5]   See Guy Bechor, *Lexicon of the PLO* (Tel Aviv: Israeli Ministry of Defense, 1991), p. 276.

entitled 'Revolution and Violence, the Path to Victory', which was little more than a collection of quotations from Fanon's book 'The Wretched of the Earth'.

In the late 1950s, upon completion of their studies, most of the Palestinian students left Egypt for the Gulf States (Kuwait, Qatar and the United Arab Emirates) in search of a more favorable political climate. From there, Fatah transferred some of its activities to Beirut and launched its own journal, *Filastin-una* (Our Palestine). In contrast to the Nasser-inspired trend towards Pan-Arabism, Fatah advocated an independent Palestinian struggle against Israel that would evolve into a general confrontation between the Arab nations and Israel. It called for a revolutionary approach:

> An armed Palestinian revolution is the only way to liberate our homeland. In the initial stages at least, the revolution must be conducted by the Palestinian masses, independently of party and state. Although the active support of the Arab world is essential for the success of the operation, the Palestinian people shall retain its discretionary powers and primacy... Only the idea of the armed struggle can bridge ideological differences and accelerate the process of unification.[6]

From 1959-64 Fatah relied on this simple, nationalist ideology, eschewing a clearly defined social doctrine (similar to the FLN in its early stages). Fatah set about building an infrastructure based on secret cells in the West Bank and Gaza, Jordan, Syria and Lebanon, in the large cities and refugee camps. Arafat's deputy, Salah Khalaf (Abu Iyad), defined this stage as the 'training of cadres'.[7]

In the Arab world, dominated by Egypt and Nasser's pan-Arabism, only two states actively assisted Fatah in the early 1960s, namely Algeria and Syria. Earlier ties with the FLN enhanced Fatah's status among other revolutionary organizations worldwide, including those within Europe, despite the bourgeois, Islamic background of many of the Palestinian leaders.[8] In January 1964 Egyptian President Nasser organized the first Arab summit. The only far-reaching resolution adopted at the summit was that the Palestinian people should play a part in liberating their country and in achieving self-determination. This led to the creation of the PLO, initially headed by veteran diplomat Ahmed Shukayri, a pawn of Nasser's.

---

[6]   See Abu-Iyad, *Lelo Moledet. Sihot 'im Erik Rulo* [Stateless: Conversations with Eric Rouleau] (Jerusalem: Mifras Publications, 1983), p. 66 and also Sayigh, *Armed Struggle and the Search for State*, p. 89.

[7]   See Abu Iyad, *Stateless*, p. 67.

[8]   Algeria mediated in the talks between Fatah and the People's Republic of China in 1962 and Algiers was chosen as the venue of Arafat's first meeting with Che Guevara. See Sayigh, *Armed Struggle and the Search for State*, pp. 102-103.

By late 1964, Fatah was ready to launch a military offensive against Israel, helped by the Syrian military brass, whose ongoing conflict with Israel had been exacerbated by skirmishes over water sources. The Fatah 'hotheads' believed that despite Israel's military superiority, a guerrilla war was the only way to unite the Palestinian people into a popular movement, and raise awareness worldwide of the Palestinian problem.[9] From early 1965 to the Six Day War in June 1967, Fatah pursued a policy of border attacks against Israel, particularly along the Lebanese and Jordanian borders. Criticism of these activities by Arab governments and public opinion in the Arab world persuaded Fatah leaders to adopt a new approach known as 'the entanglement theory'. This was based on the idea of using sabotage to force Israel to retaliate, which, in turn, would force the Arabs to step up their military readiness. This cycle of action-retaliation-reaction, it was believed, would lead to a gradual escalation of tension on the borders, and eventually war.[10] The Syrian offensive against Israel, with Fatah's help, did indeed trigger such a war, but with disastrous consequences for Arab armies and governments alike.

During this period, Fatah saw itself as a movement transcending nation, class or party. The supreme goal of the 'Palestinian revolution' was the return to Palestine, and the only way envisaged was armed struggle. To this end, all ideological-social dissent had to be abandoned; any commitment to a particular social orientation within the armed struggle detracted from the effectiveness of the struggle. PLO leaders believed that the Algerian, Cuban, Chinese, Vietnamese, and Latin American revolutions could, with suitable adaptations, all serve as models for the Palestinian revolution.[11]

2.   The PFLP

The Popular Front for the Liberation of Palestine (al-Jabha al-Sha'biyya li-Tahrir Filastin – PFLP), set up in December 1967, grew out of an older and established Middle East movement, namely the clandestine Arab Nationalists' Movement (Harakat al-Qawmiyyin al-'Arab – ANM), founded in Beirut in 1949 by George Habash, a Christian Palestinian. The ANM advocated Arab unity as a prerequisite for the liberation of Palestine. Initially it espoused a reactionary and rather conservative Arab nationalism, and was influenced by fascist ideas, also expressed in ANM invectives against the 'Jewish threat' and the identification of

---

[9] See Sayigh, *Armed Struggle and the Search for State*, p. 106.
[10] Egyptian criticism of and action against planned guerrilla attacks from Gaza Strip led Fatah to state that it sought 'the conscious entanglement of the Arab masses as a whole and not of the Arab rulers and states as such in the conflict with Israel'. Ibid., pp. 119-20.
[11] On Fatah ideology see Sayigh, *Armed Struggle and the Search for State*, pp. 87-92.

Zionism with Judaism. As a result of its subversive activities it was banned in a number of Arab states.[12] Despite prolific activity and Egyptian backing, the movement made political headway in only one country – South Yemen. Although the South Yemen branch of the ANM peremptorily discarded Habash's authority after coming to power in the wake of the struggle for independence of that country, it was thanks to him that this small and impoverished country became a center of Palestinian terror.[13]

The PFLP represented the amalgamation of three smaller organizations:

(1) The Young Avengers (Shabab al-Tha'r), the Palestinian military branch of the ANM, set up in 1964 that already carried out terrorist attacks through the borders against Israel in November of that year.

(2) The Heroes of the Return (Abtal al-Awda), set up in Lebanon in late 1966 by several of Ahmed Shukayri's opponents in the PLO, and some members of the Young Avengers.

(3) The Palestinian Liberation Front (Jabhat al-Tahrir al-Filastinyya – PLF), set up in the early 1960s by Ahmed Jibril and Ali Bashnak, Palestinian officers in the Syrian army. PLF assets included extensive military experience, bases in Syria, and a network of operatives in the West Bank.

Habash provided the embryonic organization with Egyptian aid, an organizational infrastructure, sophisticated propaganda, and a network of cells in the West Bank and Gaza.

The PFLP was created by the ANM to counter Fatah, which had won considerable support amongst the Arab and Palestinian masses, largely due to its doctrine of armed struggle against Israel. Fatah's acts of sabotage forced the ANM militants back into the Palestinian camp where they had begun their career.[14] After the Six Day War, the PFLP, influenced by national liberation movements worldwide, adopted a Marxist-Leninist ideology.

According to the PFLP, it was essential that the Palestinians and ANM establish alliances with all revolutionary forces worldwide, in order to defeat the technological superiority of the enemy. Only through alliance with the liberation movements of Vietnam, Cuba, North Korea, Asia, Africa, and Latin America, as well as revolutionary forces in Europe and America, could the Palestinian and

---

[12] See Rex Brynen, *Sanctuary and Survival: The PLO in Lebanon* (Boulder, Co.: Westview Press, 1990), p. 41 and Sayigh, *Armed Struggle and the Search for State*, p. 72.
[13] For a good background on ANM, ibid., pp. 71-80.
[14] See Bechor, *Lexicon of the PLO*, pp. 123-24.

Arab national liberation movements resist Zionism and the imperialist camp.[15] The PFLP also advocated war against the Arab bourgeoisie, 'the objective ally of Zionism and imperialism', accused of using the Palestinian problem in order to distract the Arab masses from their own interests.[16]

II. TYPOLOGICAL DEFINITION

1. Fatah

The sole aim of Fatah was the liberation of Palestine from what it saw as colonial occupation, and the establishment of an independent Palestinian state. After gaining control of the PLO, Fatah expanded the concept of national liberation into that of a Palestinian revolution, which would not only lead to the liberation of Palestine but to the liberation of the entire world from imperialism.[17]

2. The PFLP

The aim of the PFLP, apart from the liberation of Palestine, was to foster Arab unity and bring about revolution throughout the Arab world. The prolonged struggle for liberation was regarded as a catalyst for radical change in the reactionary Arab world. These multiple goals were associated with a multiplicity of adversaries: Israel, world Zionism, US-led global imperialism, and last but not least, the Arab reactionary regimes.[18] The ideological tool for this struggle was Marxism-Leninism, originally the Chinese version, and later the Soviet manifestation. However, PFLP activities during this period did not truly reflect a Marxist-Leninist ideology.[19]

---

[15] See 'The Military Thinking of the Front' in Elyakim Rubinstein (ed.), *Compilation of Documents of the PFLP, DFLP and ALF – Texts for the Seminar of Dr. Yehoshafat Harkabi* (Jerusalem: Hebrew University, 1971, in Hebrew), pp. 3-69.

[16] For a detailed discussion of the PFLP ideology, see Harold Cubert, *The PFLP's Changing Role in the Middle East* (London: Frank Cass, 1997), pp. 98-112 and Matti Steinberg, 'The World-view of Habash's 'Popular Front'', *The Jerusalem Quarterly*, No. 47, (Summer 1988), pp. 3-26.

[17] This last version was adopted at the PNC's Seventh Congress (30 May-4 June 1970). Arafat expressed this when he said that 'Palestinian liberation struggle links up with all other liberation struggles in the world to form a united struggle for the liberation of man and country'. Quoted in an interview to the Lebanese newspaper *Al-Yum*', 24 June 1969.

[18] On this subject, see Steinberg's exhaustive article 'The Worldview of Habash's 'Popular Front'.

[19] According to Wievorka, the PFLP used Marxism-Leninism largely as a strategy to keep a high level of mobilization among its militants, rather than as a tool for ideological and political activation of the masses. See Michel Wievorka, *The Making of Terrorism* (Chicago, Il.: The University of Chicago Press, 1993), p. 234

III.   THE 'GOLDEN AGE' OF PALESTINIAN TERROR (1968-80)

1.   The period of consolidation (1968-70)

The 'golden age' of Palestinian international terror opened on 23 July 1968, when a PFLP commando unit hijacked an El Al plane en route from Rome to Lod and diverted it to Algeria. Although the immediate goal of this spectacular action was to enhance the status of the PFLP within the Palestinian world, the motives were far more complex, and related to the consequences for the Arab nations and the embryonic Palestinian national movement of the Six Day War.

Fatah was the first Arab/Palestinian organization to recover from the shock of the 1967 defeat. Its leaders decided that conditions were ripe for a major guerrilla war against Israel, and for transferring its headquarters to the occupied territories. After reaching a certain peak in late September 1967, the guerrilla activities initiated by Fatah – mainly infiltrations of hundreds of terrorists across the Jordanian border – declined due to the efficacy of the Israeli security forces. By early 1968, the dream of leading 'a national liberation war' in the West Bank and Gaza evaporated.

The failure of the guerrilla war can be attributed to a number of causes. Firstly, Fatah leaders did not take into account the topographical differences between Vietnam, Algeria and Israel, or the fact that they were fighting different enemies; Secondly, Fatah failed to accurately predict the behavior of the local population, led by a coalition of traditional village dignitaries, and urban business-owners, seeking to profit from the economic prosperity ushered in by the Israeli occupation.[20] Finally, the Israeli security services and the IDF took swift and resolute action against the terrorists.

Nonetheless, Fatah emerged from the fray politically strengthened, the only element in the Arab world that dared to confront Israel. Its status soared far beyond that of the PLO, which was identified with the established Arab regimes. Under pressure from Arab governments, Shukeyri resigned from the PLO leadership and in July 1968 Fatah joined the organization. In less than a year, with the assistance of various Arab nations, Fatah rose to the top of the PLO. Arafat's appointment as chairman of the PLO Executive Committee in February 1969 granted Fatah virtual control of the Palestinian umbrella organization.[21]

---

[20]   Jabber claimed that the main reason for lack of cooperation among the West Bank population was the belief that a general revolt would give Israel the excuse for deporting it to Jordan; he admitted that Fatah's warfare did not resemble traditional guerrilla, or national liberation warfare. See Fuad Jabber, 'The Arab Regimes and the Palestinian Revolution, 1967-71', *Journal of Palestine Studies*, Vol. 2, No. 2, (1973), p. 81.

[21]   See Arieh Yodfat and Yuval Arnon-Ohanna, *PLO. Strategy and Politics* (London: Croom Helm, 1981), p. 24.

In early 1968 the residual cells of Fatah and other small organizations were forced to withdraw from the West Bank and relocate to Jordanian territory. The various organizations began to restructure in preparation for a new phase in their activity – cross-border attacks. In January 1968 Fatah convened a conference of all terrorist organizations in Cairo in an effort to coordinate activities. The only organization that failed to attend was the PFLP, which claimed that the PLO, not Fatah, should be sponsoring a conference of this kind.

The battle of Karameh on 21 March 1968 signified, according to Fatah mythology, a turning point in the military struggle against Israel.[22] Despite heavy losses (about 120 dead) and the destruction of its command, the Fatah leadership considered this an outstanding victory. The battle became the symbol of 'honor' (*karameh*) in the Arab world, and enhanced the status of Fatah among the Palestinians and in the West. Fatah accused the PFLP of shirking its duty by evacuating its forces from the village.[23] Cobban identified this event as one that turned the PFLP into the main opposition group within the PLO, which had begun to come under Arafat's influence.[24]

It was the need to atone for the Karameh fiasco and to keep abreast of other organizations that stoked the PFLP decision to carry out a sensational terrorist act. The decision to attack Israeli and Western targets outside Israel and even beyond the Middle East was in line with the PFLP ideological and strategic thinking, as reflected in the document entitled 'The Military Thinking of the Front'. Two other factors contributed to the decision on hijacking: pressure by extremists within the organization; and the erosion of the organization in the occupied territories by the Israeli security forces.[25] Another motive for some of the hijacking operations was the wish to free PFLP terrorists imprisoned or arrested during previous PFLP operations in Western countries. Since Western governments invariably submitted to the terrorists' demands for fear of antagonizing the terrorist organizations or Arab governments, a vicious cycle was soon established. Wadi Haddad, one of the founders of the ANM, reportedly convinced PFLP leaders that the organization had

---

[22] A reference to the IDF raid on the Fatah command of cross-border activities against Israel, situated in the village of Karameh in Jordan. The IDF suffered relatively heavy losses because the Jordanian army, which had been alerted of the imminent raid, warned the local Fatah forces, and dispatched an artillery unit to help them, a development the IDF failed to anticipate.

[23] This accusation was subsequently corroborated by a commission of inquiry which ruled, however, that such behavior was admissible in guerrilla warfare. Fatah, unconvinced, retaliated by revoking the month-old agreement on the gradual merger of the two organizations.

[24] See Cobban, *The Palestinian Liberation Organization. People, Power and Politics* (Cambridge: Cambridge University Press, 1984), pp. 144-46.

[25] A PFLP member claimed that the first three hijacking operations were perpetrated in order to satisfy the more extremist youth. See Ariel Merari and Elad Shlomi, *Paha' Hul: Teror Palestinai be-Hutz la-Aretz* [Palestinian Terror Abroad] (Tel Aviv: United Kibbutz and Jaffee Center for Strategic Studies publication, 1986), pp. 30-31. In the event, the leadership's assessment that a hijacking operation would attract Palestinian youth to the organization, proved correct.

to 'hit the Israeli army in a qualitative way, not a quantitative way', to hit the Israelis 'at the painful joints'. This could be done by spectacular operations which would focus world attention on the problem of Palestine. 'We must be a constant irritation', he said, a bug under the skin of the developed world.' This approach apparently 'electrified' the young PFLP militants.[26]

The hijacking of an El Al plane to Algiers in July 1968, and the hijacking of four Western planes to a desert field in Jordan in September 1970 were swiftly followed by a relentless clampdown on Palestinian terrorist organizations in Jordan. In sum, the PFLP carried out about 15 international terror operations, ranging from hijackings to attacks against Israeli embassies or American and Western targets.[27]

Fatah and the left-wing branch of the PFLP itself criticized the sensational hijacking operations of the PFLP. According to Weisband and Roguly, Fatah propaganda condemned international acts of violence. Dissenters within the PFLP criticized the 'romanticization of terrorist violence', claiming that it ran counter to the right of the masses to participate in the armed struggle.[28]

The Palestinian terrorist organizations subsequently adopted a strategic decision to secure 'safe areas' in the confrontation states (i.e. those neighboring Israel), to serve as springboards for action against Israel. Jordan seemed a natural choice since it shared a long border with Israel and approximately half of its population was of Palestinian origin. Conflict inevitably brewed between the Palestinian terrorists and the Hashemite government, starting with major clashes in November 1968 and ending with the expulsion of Palestinian forces in July 1971, after the civil war of September 1970.[29]

---

[26]   See the testimony of Abu Sharif in Bassam Abu-Sharif and Uzi Mahnaimi, *Tried by Fire. The Searing True Story of Two Men at the Heart of the Struggle between the Arabs and the Jews* (London: Warner Books, 1995), pp. 59-60.

[27]   In early September 1970 the PFLP hijacked four planes: one Pan-Am plane was diverted to Cairo and blown up, while the other three (TWA, Swissair, and BOAC) were diverted to Dawson airport in Jordan. There, they were blown up in front of TV cameras, amidst tense negotiations for the release of the passengers (including some Israelis) in exchange for the release of PFLP activists incarcerated in Europe. On the day of these hijacks, there was an abortive attempt to hijack an El Al plane, flying from Amsterdam to New York. In the course of this operation, one of the terrorists, Patrick Arguelo, a member of the Nicaraguan Sandinistas, was killed. The other terrorist, Leila Khaled, was arrested and handed over to the British authorities when the plane landed in London. Apparently, this Palestinian hijacking operation was the first one in which a foreign terrorist organization participated.

[28]   Fatah even sent a condolence letter to the victims of the Swissair disaster on 23 February 1970, stating that those connected with such attacks 'did not belong to the Palestinian revolution'. The Swiss plane was blown up by Ahmed Jibril's PFLP-GC. See Edward Weisband and Damir Roguly, 'Palestinian Terrorism: Violence, Verbal Strategy, and Legitimacy', in Yonah Alexander (ed.), *International Terrorism. National, Regional and Global Perspectives* (New York: Praeger Publishers, 1976), pp. 284-85.

[29]   See Jabber, 'The Arab Regimes and the Palestinian Revolution,' pp. 87-91.

The acceptance by Egypt and Jordan of the Rogers peace plan in June 1970 was the last straw for the Palestinian organizations. Left-wing groups, namely the PFLP and the Democratic Front for the Liberation of Palestine (DFLP), believed they could foil the peace plan by carrying out their Arab revolutionary strategy in Jordan. Fatah, for its part, preferred to wait. This characteristic lack of unity and discipline among the organizations ultimately enabled the Hashemite regime to destroy them.

In February 1969 the left-wing faction, led by Na'if Hawatmeh, had left the PFLP to set up the DFLP.[30] The DFLP adopted a purer Marxist-Leninist doctrine, established ties with other left-wing organizations and Arab communist parties, and based itself more on the Vietnamese and Cuban models than on the Soviet one (this was to change in subsequent years). Hawatmeh, who was more committed to left-wing ideology than Arab nationalism, was the first to advocate 'a democratic state' in Palestine.[31] Since his interpretation of Marxist-Leninism stressed the need for action by the masses under the guidance of a communist party, the DFLP condemned international terror as the act of individuals that did not further the revolution.

Several months before Hawatmeh's resignation, Ahmed Jibril, leader of the PFLP's right-wing branch and formerly head of the PLF before its merger with Habash's group, also resigned to set up the PFLP – General Command (PFLP-GC). This organization has been intermittently active in international terror, with Syrian and later Iranian assistance.

2. The rise of the Black September Organization (September 1970-October 1973)

The Jordanian massacre of Palestinians in September 1970 had two important consequences. Firstly, the headquarters and military units of all Palestinian organizations were transferred to Lebanon. Secondly, inspired by anger and a desire for revenge a process of radicalization took hold of Palestinians of all classes. These events also pushed Fatah towards international terror and led to the establishment of the Black September Organization (BSO), the most radical terrorist group active until the Yom Kippur War.

Merari and El'ad called this period a 'total war to restore lost honor', conducted by Fatah against its archenemies – Jordan and Israel. In this war, Fatah adopted elements of the PFLP global terror strategy, as witnessed by some

---

[30] Hawatmeh, of Jordanian origin, tried to take over the organization during the months that George Habash was imprisoned in Damascus, following a disagreement with the Syrian regime. Upon his return to Lebanon, Habash reasserted his control, and Hawatmeh, as stated, resigned.

[31] See Yodfat and Arnon-Ohanna, *PLO. Strategy and Politics*, pp. 26-7.

[anonymous] statements by BSO leaders that paraphrased PFLP concepts. But there was a fundamental difference between the way Habash and Abu Iyad each perceived international terror: Habash saw it as part of the armed struggle, Abu Iyad considered it primarily a substitute for military or political activity. For the latter terrorism 'was not a free choice between various options, but a direct consequence of the lack of alternatives ... and pressure by extremist elements who, against the majority opinion, insisted on an escalation of the struggle'.[32] According to Sayigh, 'the two years foray into international terrorism' was intended to disguise Fatah's predicament from external enemies and regain the strategic initiative, as well as to contain internal dissent and rebuild military strength.[33]

The BSO, which relied on Fatah's security apparatus, was set up at the Fatah general congress in Damascus in August-September 1970.[34] In order to safeguard the international image of Fatah and the political interests of the PLO, the connection between the BSO and its mentors was kept secret. Although Abu Iyad headed the organization, the BSO refrained from publishing statements, and the identity of its leaders remained concealed.[35] Researchers sympathetic to Fatah tried to downplay its responsibility for BSO activities, arguing that information on the subject was disseminated mainly by Israeli sources.[36]

Abu Iyad's book, 'Stateless', lent support to the theory that BSO was none other than Fatah itself. Abu Iyad frequently referred to his personal involvement in the BSO and dropped transparent hints to this effect.[37] A comparison of the PFLP and BSO (Fatah) international terrorist attacks during two periods, July 1968-September 1970 and September 1970-October 1973, showed that the PFLP

---

[32] See Merari and Elad, *Palestinian Terror Abroad*, p. 33.

[33] See Sayigh, *Armed Struggle and the Search for State*, p. 684.

[34] Ibid., pp. 53-63.

[35] See Weisband and Roguly, *Palestinian Terrorism: Violence, Verbal Strategy, and Legitimacy*, pp. 190-91.

[36] Muhammad Oudeh (Abu Da'ud), a Fatah leader arrested for terrorism in Jordan, declared on Jordanian television in February 1973 that 'there was no such thing as the BSO organization. Fatah simply used the name in order to cover its tracks'. Cobban tried to exonerate Fatah by describing how the Fatah leadership, immediately after the massacre of the Israeli athletes in Munich, decided to put an end to the 'flirtation' of some of its members with the BSO. See Cobban, *The Palestinian Liberation Organization*, pp. 54-55. Cobban, however, failed to explain why BSO continued its attacks until after the Yom Kippur War, or why in October 1974, a new cell in Morocco was caught planning to assassinate King Hussein during the Rabat Conference (no less than Abu Iyad was accused of organizing the attempted assassination).

[37] 'Black September was not a terrorist organization', wrote Abu Iyad, 'but was rather an auxiliary unit of the resistance movement, at a time when the latter was unable to fully realize its military and political potential. The members of the organization always denied any ties between their organization and Fatah or the PLO. I myself am personally acquainted with many of them, and can state with conviction that most of them belong to various Fedayeen organizations'. See Iyad, *Stateless*, pp. 146-47.

was responsible for most of them in the former period, and the BSO in the latter. This may well be because PFLP terrorists preferred to participate in BSO operations rather than acting independently, as Arab sources claimed at the time.[38] The official history of the PLO armed struggle later confirmed that the BSO was actually a covert terrorist arm of Fatah.[39]

3. From the Yom Kippur War to the Lebanese Civil War (October 1973-October 1976)

The Yom Kippur War dramatically altered the strategic balance of powers in the Middle East. Despite Israel's military victory in the face of tremendous odds, the war was perceived as a victory by the Arab states, particularly Egypt, and undermined the morale of the Israeli public. The war also consolidated Arab political and economic strength due to the use of the oil weapon against the West. But the war also had strengthened the desire of Israelis and Arabs, particular Egypt, to reach a peaceful political settlement, and American resolve to exert pressure in favor of such a settlement.

Palestinian forces played little part in this war, despite Abu Iyad's inflated description of strategic coordination with President Sadat, 'heroic' warfare in the Suez area and behind the Israeli lines in the Golan, and guerrilla activities in South Lebanon. The Palestinians hoped to benefit from the diplomatic initiative following the war; given the initial Arab euphoria in late 1973, this aim did not seem unrealistic.[40]

The Yom Kippur War had a strong impact on the mainstream leadership of the PLO. Fatah began to develop a strategy aimed at obtaining recognition of the Palestinians by the Arab states and the international community, as a preliminary stage for PLO participation in negotiations. At the Palestinian National Council (PNC) convention in Cairo in June 1974, Fatah called for the establishment of a national authority in all parts of liberated Palestinian land. This was meant to convey a more moderate image of the PLO to the world, so that it could participate in negotiations for less than Palestine, if Israel agreed to withdraw from some of the territories.[41] Fatah's central committee stated that the military and

---

[38] Proof can be found in the hijacking of the Sabena plane to Ben Gurion airport on 8 May 1972 by a PFLP commando that claimed it was affiliated with BSO. On this subject, see the Egyptian *Al-Jumhuriyya* of 30 September 1972. In the same article, a member of BSO who took part in the planned assassination of the Jordanian prime minister in Cairo stated: 'We all belonged to Fatah – no-one will cut himself off from his mother'.

[39] See Sayigh, *Armed Struggle and the Search for State*, pp. 307-11.

[40] See Cobban, *The Palestinian Liberation Organization*, p. 57, and Sayigh, *Armed Struggle and the Search for State*, pp. 329-32, 343.

[41] See Merari and Elad, *Palestinian Terror Abroad*, pp. 43-44.

political struggles should both continue, but as the Middle East was a region of primary global importance, 'external factors were determinant in the course of the Palestine conflict and encouraged a move away from the direct strategy of constant war to liberate the whole of Palestine, towards an indirect strategy or "policy of phases".'[42]

Alongside these strategic changes, pressure to renounce international terror also grew. Although the constituent organizations of the PLO were divided on political issues, and those opposing a political solution had formed a 'rejection front', all organizations under the PLO umbrella, including the PFLP, agreed that international terror was no longer appropriate. The rejection front included the PFLP, the PFLP-GC, the PSF and the pro-Iraqi Arab Liberation Front (ALF). Both Fatah's moderate stream and the DFLP, were opposed to international terror, the former for pragmatic reasons (to safeguard its international image) and the latter for ideological reasons. Merari and El'ad claimed that the PFLP, the pioneer of Palestinian international terror, revoked its stand at some unknown date and that George Habash apparently informed journalists as early as March 1972 that the countries of the socialist bloc did not support this kind of action.[43]

The debate on whether to renounce international terror centered mainly around hijackings, which had tarnished the Palestinians' image. Even states sympathetic to the communist bloc feared the hijacking epidemic would spread to their countries. Habash, questioned about the hijacking of a Japanese plane in July 1973, denied PFLP involvement and stressed that the incorrect application of Marxist-Leninist principles could harm the revolution. He immediately qualified this, however, by saying that the Palestinians had a legitimate right to attack enemy targets abroad, since the enemy was dependent on the world Zionist movement.[44] The PFLP spokesperson, Bassem Abu Sharif, stated in early 1974 that the 'change of heart' was simply 'a tactical change, not a total cessation of activities... Hijacking has outlived its usefulness. Our methods have changed.'[45]

The dismissal of Wadi Haddad, PFLP head of the Special Apparatus responsible for international terror activities by veteran comrade-in-arms Habash, provides some insight into the issue of cooperation between various terrorist organizations during this period. According to Merari and El'ad, Haddad's expulsion from the PFLP occurred in 1974, though a number of sources quoted

---

[42] See Sayigh, *Armed Struggle and the Search for State*, p. 334-5.
[43] See Merari and Elad, *Palestinian Terror Abroad*, pp. 44-54.
[44] Actually, the Japanese plane was hijacked by a PFLP commando unit in coordination with the Japanese Red Army. The interview with Habash appeared in the Lebanese *Al-Ahbar* on 4 August 1975 and is quoted in *Journal of Palestine Studies*, Vol. 3, No. 2 (1973), pp. 194-98.
[45] Quoted in Merari and Elad, *Palestinian Terror Abroad*, p. 45.

1972.[46] Activities involving cooperation with the Japanese Red Army (JRA) and those of the Muhammad Budyah Commando unit in Europe were attributed to the PFLP in 1973-74 but may have been carried out by the Haddad faction, without Habash's approval. The PFLP announced Haddad's expulsion from the organization in November 1977, after the hijacking of the Lufthansa plane to Mogadishu. The organization stated that Haddad had already been expelled in 1976 because of disagreements between Habash and Haddad over hijacking operations.[47]

Some observers suggested that Haddad's expulsion was contrived with Habash's connivance merely to allow the PFLP to present a 'clean' political slate. Sayigh described in detail the disagreements within the PFLP concerning the 'external operations', mainly under the pressure of Soviet leaders. He reported that the PFLP third general conference expelled Haddad in March 1972, that the official account of this decision was published nine years later but that Haddad 'did not abandon the PFLP entirely, however, keeping close ties with his old friend Habash and channeling funds to the PFLP over the next three years'.[48] It was not surprising therefore, that Sayigh's account of the Entebbe operation claims: 'When Israeli commandos freed the hostages and killed the hijackers the PFLP described their leader, Fayiz Jabir, as the head of its Special Operations branch, although the operation had, in fact, been conducted by Wadi Haddad'.[49]

The Lebanese Civil War began in April 1975, reaching a peak in September-October 1976 when Palestinian forces intervened alongside left-wing Lebanese forces to combat the Syrian army. It was around this time too that the Fatah – Revolutionary Council (Abu Nidal Organization – ANO) began to attack Syrian targets. Heavy Palestinian involvement in the Lebanese Civil war left the Palestinians with few resources for international terror activities, which subsequently declined dramatically over the next two years.[50] In the period under review, the Palestinian organizations perpetrated a total of 32 international terror operations. Eleven of these were carried out by the PFLP (one with the help of the notorious Carlos, and two with the help of the JRA) and three including the hijacking of an Air France plane to Entebbe by the Haddad Special Apparatus.[51]

---

[46] Ibid., p. 59. According to Merari and Elad, the Haddad faction began to operate as an independent faction from the attack against OPEC headquarters in Vienna on 21 December 1975.

[47] See Edward Mickolus, *Transnational Terrorism: A Chronology of Events, 1968-1979* (London: Aldwych Press, 1980), pp. 748-49.

[48] See Sayigh, *Armed Struggle and the Search for State*, p. 304-305.

[49] Ibid., p. 395.

[50] See also Dennis Pluchinsky, 'Political Terrorism in Western Europe: Some Themes and Variations', in Yonah Alexander and Kenneth Meyers (eds.), *Terrorism in Europe* (London: Croom Helm, 1982), p. 54.

[51] The National Arab Youth Organization, sponsored by the Libyan regime, carried out six attacks; Fatah carried out only two attacks, including the last in a series of BSO attacks – the attempted assassination of King Hussein at the Rabat Conference in October 1974.

4.   October 1976-late 1980

From October 1976 until President Sadat's historic visit to Jerusalem in October 1977, virtually the only Palestinian organization active in international terror was the ANO, which carried out seven attacks against Syrian and Jordanian targets. The Syrian targets were selected to protest Syrian enmity with Iraq's Ba'ath regime, and the Jordanian targets because of Abu Nidal's hatred of the Hashemite regime. No Israeli targets were attacked. The Haddad faction attempted only one operation, namely the hijacking of a Lufthansa plane to Mogadishu. After Haddad's death in March 1978 following a lengthy illness, the faction split into two smaller independent organizations: the Fifteen May Arab Organization headed by Muhammad Hussein al-'Omari (Abu Ibrahim) and the Popular Front for the Liberation of Palestine – Special Command (PFLP-SC) under Salim Abu Salem (Abu Muhammad).[52]

Sadat's visit to Jerusalem and the Camp David accords of March 1979 were perceived throughout the Arab world as a betrayal of the Palestinian cause. The peace process led to a wave of threats and attacks against Egyptian targets, for which no organization or state dared accept responsibility.[53]

As early as December 1977 the Arab Steadfastness Front, which included the PLO, Syria, Iraq, Libya, Algeria and South Yemen, had began an organized protest against the Egypt-Israel negotiations.[54] The PNC was convened in January 1979 to consider a response to the 'serious threat of the US-inspired Camp David accords for the Palestinian cause and the Arab liberation movement'.[55] But, as usual in the Arab world, this show of unity did not last long. Iraq exploited Egyptian isolation to assume a leading role in the Arab world, toned down its anti-Egypt position during the second Baghdad conference in March 1979, and set up a new Iraqi-Jordanian-Saudi axis. Although Arab opposition to Camp David worked in favor of the Palestinian organizations, it led to deep polarization between the Iraq-Jordan-Saudi Arabia axis, and the Syria-Libya axis. The situation within the Arab world deteriorated further after Khomeini's rise to power in Iran and after the Iraq attack on Iran in September 1980, when Syria and Libya both dissociated themselves from the Iraqi initiative and offered military help to Iran.[56]

---

[52]   See Bechor, *Lexicon of the PLO*, pp. 50-51.
[53]   See Merari and Elad, *Palestinian Terror Abroad*, pp. 47-8.
[54]   For the platform of the 'Steadfastness Front', see Yehuda Lukacs (ed.), *The Israeli-Palestinian Conflict: A Documentary Record* (Cambridge: Cambridge University Press, 1992), pp. 335-39.
[55]   Ibid., pp. 339-44.
[56]   See Alan R Taylor, 'The PLO in Inter-Arab Politics', *Journal of Palestine Studies*, Vol. 2, No. 2 (1982), pp. 79-80.

Fatah became embroiled in a war of terror not against Egypt or Israel, but against the 'allies' of the Steadfastness Front – Iraq and Syria – the former for its support of the ANO and its attacks against moderate PLO figures, and the latter for its support of the 'other side' in the Lebanese Civil War.[57] The internal fighting reached new heights, when Fatah militia in Lebanon attacked and killed opposition elements.[58] Of the 44 operations in this period, seven were directed at Egyptian targets (immediately after Sadat's visit to Jerusalem), seven at PLO representatives throughout the world, and four at Iraqi diplomats or targets. Fatah topped the list with ten attacks (mostly against Iraqi targets or reprisals against the ANO for attacking Fatah activists, and possibly two attacks against Jewish targets in Western Europe). The ANO carried out 12 attacks, mostly against PLO targets, but also against Israeli and Jewish targets. Meanwhile, the PFLP carried out three attacks. The Haddad faction effectively ceased to exist.

5.   Cooperation with European terrorist organizations

As noted in Chapter 3, cooperation between European and Palestinian terrorist organizations had already began in 1968-69, when the PFLP was entering the field of international terror. Interestingly, Fatah, which only resorted to international terror towards the end of 1971, had established ties with European organizations in 1969. In August-September 1969, the Arab media began to report that a group of 50 (according to some, 145) youngsters and students from West Germany, France, Italy, Britain and Holland, among others, were training in Fatah camps in Jordan.[59] There was considerable controversy concerning their numbers, origins, and purpose. While some supposedly received military training, others assisted the Palestinians in the refugee camps or carried out propaganda activities on the Palestinians' behalf. There were even reports in the Arab press of a French youth falling in battle against 'the Zionist enemy'. Nonetheless, there is no evidence of any institutionalized cooperation with European terrorist organizations.[60]

---

[57] The reciprocal attacks began after the murder of PLO representative Sa'id Hamami, in London in January 1978 by 'Black June', an alias for the ANO. ANO also carried out a series of attacks for the Iraqis against the rival Ba'ath regime in Syria. See Pluchinsky, Political Terrorism in Western Europe, p. 54.

[58] For details of this stormy period see Sayigh, *Armed Struggle and the Search for State*, pp. 441-46.

[59] See the Jordanian daily *Al-Dara'a* of 16 August 1969, and the Egyptian daily *Al-Ahram* of 3 August 1969.

[60] The author found no data on this subject among Palestinian or Arab media cited in the daily bulletins on 'hostile terrorist acts' of the IDF intelligence branch from 1969-72, which he consulted at the Dayan Center for Middle Eastern and African Studies at the Tel Aviv University.

From the outset, the Palestinian terrorist organizations, particularly Fatah, were extremely reserved about their international terrorist activities. While they boasted about domestic operations or border attacks, so much so that sometimes two or three organizations claimed responsibility for the same attack, they were reluctant to claim responsibility for operations overseas. Even the PFLP ceased boasting about its hijackings or lethal attacks in Europe, preferring to use aliases after 1970.[61] This practice became particularly widespread after the emergence of the BSO, which served as a convenient cover for both Fatah and the PFLP (see above).[62]

6.   The reasons for cooperation with European organizations

Barely a year after the Six Day War, and despite the failure of their guerrilla campaign in the West Bank, Palestinian organizations were aware of growing sympathy towards them, not only among the Arabs, but also among revolutionary movements in general, particularly in West Europe. The Palestinian problem gradually came to assume a central place in radical left-wing rhetoric, and was heatedly debated during the French students' revolt of May 1968.[63] Fatah and the PFLP lost no time in exploiting this shift to step up propaganda activities and contacts among left-wing circles. PFLP propagandists asserted that they 'did great damage to Israel', 'winning hearts and minds' and 'turning opinion around in countries that had previously been friendly towards the Jewish state.'[64]

The Palestinian national poet, Mahmud Darwish, expressed the same sentiment:

> A few years ago [we] were supposed to receive food and clothes parcels ... and behave like good children. Our role was that of refugee... When we changed our role, the world also changed its attitude towards us. We exchanged a mentality of pride and individual heroism for one of collective, organized, revolutionary action with clear and just goals... In the global consciousness, the torch has passed from Vietnam to us. Can we meet the challenge?[65]

---

[61]   Thus, for example, the PFLP commandos that kidnapped the Lufthansa plane in New Delhi in order to liberate Sirhan Sirhan, Robert Kennedy's assassin, called itself 'the Organization of the Victims of the Zionist Occupation' or 'the Organization of Resistance to the Zionist Occupation'.

[62]   This happened with the hijacking of the Sabena plane to Ben Gurion airport by the PFLP in 1972.

[63]   The author can personally testify to the stormy debates that took place in the Sorbonne court during the students' revolt, on the then new and controversial issue of support for the Palestinian cause, unlike support for Vietnam, which was universally approved by the students.

[64]   See Abu-Sharif and Mahnaimi, *Tried by Fire*, p. 97.

[65]   Quoted from an article in *Shu'un Filastiniyya* of September 1973, *Journal of Palestine Studies*, Vol. 3, No. 1, p. 168.

During the 'decade of terror' 1968-1980, cooperation between Palestinian and European terrorists emerged as follows:

1968-70: Palestinian organizations cooperated only with the German Baader-Meinhof Gang (RAF), and West-Berlin Tupamaros (M2J). This consisted mostly of providing safe havens for fugitives, and training Germans in Palestinian camps in Jordan, under full Palestinian control until August 1970. Fatah refrained from international terrorism while the PFLP appeared self-sufficient, with no need of foreign assistance.[66]

1971-73: Cooperation with German organizations, especially the RAF, continued, but once again the Palestinians did most of the giving. While the Germans mostly paid lip service to solidarity with the Palestinians, the BSO actually demanded the release of jailed RAF leaders during two of its major hostage-taking operations (at the Munich Olympics in September 1972, and of Western diplomats in Khartoum in March 1973). During this period there were also a few abortive contacts with ETA.

1974-77: Palestinian-German cooperation broadened to include the RZ, as well as the RAF and M2J. On the Palestinian side, the PFLP and the Haddad faction, particularly the latter, were the most active. By now the Germans were more forthcoming. They participated in a number of major PFLP operations, such as the attack on OPEC headquarters, the attempted hijacking of an El Al plane in Kenya, and the hijacking of Air France plane to Entebbe. Meanwhile the Palestinians provided financial assistance, training, and a safe haven for fugitives or prisoners released during negotiations. In the last PFLP operation – the hijacking of the Lufthansa plane to Mogadishu – the PFLP terrorists also bargained for the release of jailed RAF leaders.

1978-80: Fatah reappeared on the international scene, cooperating primarily with the Italian BR. However, Fatah's hopes that the BR would attack Israeli targets in exchange for supplying it with weapons were disappointed. The PFLP also cooperated with smaller organizations and autonomy groups on the Italian radical left. Finally, during this period, both the PFLP and Fatah helped ETA, the PFLP by training ETA activists, and Fatah by providing weapons. Fatah also planned to help the IRA via the BR.

---

[66] The first known case of assistance by a foreign terrorist in a PFLP operation was the involvement of a member of the Sandinista FSLN in the attempted hijacking of an El Al plane on 7 September 1970.

7.   International and regional factors

After the Six Day War, Fatah was in a strong position compared to that of the defeated Arab states. According to the Fatah leadership, the Palestinian revolution would act as a revolutionary trigger for all peoples of the region; the obstacle was the strategic alliance between imperialist interests and Zionist ambitions against the Arab nation. It was global imperialism that provided Israel with the weapons and financial aid that enabled it to attack the Arab nations. The Palestinian struggle was viewed as part of a historical process of liberation from colonialism and imperialism, similar to the struggle of the Vietnamese people and other nations in Asia, Africa, and America.[67]

After establishing ties with the People's Republic of China in 1964, Fatah became influenced by the doctrines of Mao and the Vietnamese Gen. Giap. Maoism continued to influence the Fatah leadership even after the establishment of ties with the USSR in 1968. While the USSR supported a political solution, recognized Israel, and failed to approve the establishment of an independent Palestinian state, China supported Palestinian claims, and even supplied Fatah with weapons.[68] Abu Iyad declared:

> [he] felt a great affinity with Mao, whose moral sense ... is closer to the spirit of Islam, than is Lenin's grim materialism. What has especially captured my imagination is the 'Long March'. In my mind's eye I see the Palestinians armed with weapons returning to their land in order to expel those who have stolen it from them.[69]

Although Fatah did not advocate a left-wing ideology, most of its sympathizers came from left-wing movements or communist states.[70] The fact that certain radical left-wing elements in Germany, particularly the founders of the RAF, believed that the Third World liberation movements had a key role to play in the anti-imperialist revolution, and were admirers of Mao, explained the sympathy between them and Fatah. As pointed out in Chapter 3, Fatah established a broad infrastructure among Palestinian students in West Germany, and by 1968 German students and youths were visiting Palestinian refugee camps. Fatah leadership

---

[67] On this subject, see the communiqué published by the Fatah Central Committee on 1 January 1969, and 'From the Palestinian Revolution to the Arab Revolution,' of 1970, in Khadder and Naim Bichara (eds.), *Testi della revoluzione Palestinese. 1968-1975* (Verona: Bertoni Editore 1975), pp. 200-8. See also Olivier Carré, *L'Ideologie palestinienne de resistance. Analyse de textes:1964-1970* (Armand Colin(, pp. 59, 61, and 71.

[68] See Yodfat and Arnon-Ohanna, *PLO. Strategy and Politics*, p. 45.

[69] See Abu Iyad, *Stateless*, p. 65.

[70] See Yodfat and Arnon-Ohanna, *PLO. Strategy and Politics*, p. 25.

presumably took the overtures of the German radical Left to mean that it, Fatah, had achieved a high status within the Arab world and the world in general, comparable perhaps to that of the Vietcong. Flattered by the approaches of the German Left, it promptly agreed to train several dozen German activists in its camps, without even consulting the Jordanian authorities. The antisemitic opinions entertained by some left-wing Germans further endeared them to the Palestinian organizations.

The PFLP, on the other hand, espoused a supposedly Marxist-Leninist ideology, emphasizing the struggle against Zionism, imperialism (especially American imperialism) and Arab reactionary forces. The PFLP saw itself as part of a global social and political revolution and viewed the struggle against Zionism not only as a national struggle, but also as a class struggle.[71] The PFLP eschewed the Soviet political line in favor of the teachings of Fidel Castro and Mao. The Cuban model was adopted because of its success in turning a group of petit bourgeois into a successful communist party. According to the PFLP, world Zionism, both a religion and a racist ideology, wished to extend its pro-Israel alliances, and therefore represented a threat to the Palestinian people. World imperialism also had an interest in strengthening Israel, an ally of imperialism, but also an imperialist and expansionist state in itself.[72]

The PFLP ideology and its decision of July 1968 to extend the struggle to the international arena, favored cooperation with global revolutionary forces, particularly those with Marxist-Leninist leanings. Since, however, the PFLP's Marxism-Leninism was not of the orthodox Soviet kind, ideological purity was not a major concern in its choice of allies. As with Fatah, the Chinese and Cuban influence encouraged rapprochement with German radical left-wing organizations.

Although the training of foreign terrorists was undertaken mainly by Fatah, some foreigners, including Germans, were trained in PFLP camps in Jordan and South Yemen. The PFLP, faithful to its global view of the revolution and its place within the international revolutionary movement, recruited foreign revolutionaries at a very early stage (for example, in the attempted hijacking of the El Al plane in September 1970). 'My liberation strategy is [essentially] a Palestinian-Arabic liberation strategy but one that includes our global allies, until our camp is in a

---

[71] Ibid., pp. 25-26. See also the PFLP platform in Walter Laqueur and Yonah Alexander (eds.) *The Terrorism Reader* (New York: Nal Penguin, 1987), pp. 145-49 and the document 'The Political and Organizational Strategy' in Rubinstein, *Compilation of Documents of the PFLP, DFLP and ALF*, pp. 37-8.

[72] Ibid. See also Carre, *L'Ideologie palestinienne de resistance*, pp. 59-61, 72 and Habash's text of February 1969, entitled 'The Enemy of the Revolution' in Khadder and Bichara, *Testi della revoluzione Palestinese*, pp. 238-48.

position to confront the enemy', stated Habash in a press interview in September 1969.[73] German terrorist organizations, particularly the RAF, were undergoing a restructuring process and consolidation. In Italy, the BR was trying to extend its appeal to the working class and it focused on domestic terror, while the Italian radical right was busy trying to curb the Italian left. France had no organized terrorist organization to speak of. Thus, the small German left-wing organizations were the only serious European partners as far as the Palestinian organizations were concerned.

Macintyre pointed out that just as the Six Day War pushed the PLO to the center of the political arena in the Arab world, the civil war in Jordan pushed the PLO into the international arena.[74] The subsequent entrenchment of the Palestinians' main fighting force in Lebanon, of all Israel's neighbors the weakest and the most open to the West, also facilitated the spread of Palestinian propaganda throughout the world.[75]

From the second half of 1970 to late 1971, the PLO had to contend with two disastrous developments: the first was the wholesale massacre of Palestinians in Jordan, while the Arab states failed to intervene; the second was the Egyptian rapprochement with the US and newly elected President Sadat's willingness to make concessions in exchange for the Israeli withdrawal from the occupied Egyptian territories. Developments in Syria too, such as the advent of Hafez Asad, who was opposed to the pro-Palestinian policy of his predecessor Saleh Jadid, worked against the Palestinian organizations.[76]

The establishment of the BSO was the principal expression of the Palestinians' new policy. After the BSO murder of the Jordanian prime minister in November 1971, the Hashemite regime unleashed an all-out war against Fatah, the only Palestinian organization still considered a bona fide resistance organization.[77]

On the international level, the Soviet attitude towards the PLO and the Palestinian cause gradually changed. As the status of the Palestinians in the Arab world grew, and in order to neutralize Chinese influence in the region, the USSR decided to strengthen ties with the PLO. Between February 1970 and July 1972, Arafat visited Moscow no less than three times, and the USSR began to offer military assistance, albeit limited, to the PLO. Although the Soviets opposed

---

[73] Quoted in the Lebanese *Al-Jaridah*, 1 September 1969.

[74] Ronald R. Macintyre, 'The Palestine Liberation Organization. Tactics, Strategies and Options towards the Geneva Peace Conference', *Journal of Palestine Studies*, Vol. 4, No. 4, 1975, pp. 75-77.

[75] On the Palestinian entrenchment in Lebanon and Syria's role in this process, see Jabber, 'The Arab Regimes and the Palestinian Revolution,' pp. 82-85 and Yodfat and Arnon-Ohanna, *PLO. Strategy and Politics*, pp. 31-33.

[76] See Jabber, 'The Arab Regimes and the Palestinian Revolution,' pp. 96-97.

[77] Ibid., p. 100.

hijackings, their reaction toward the BSO operation at the Munich Olympics and other terrorist acts was, if anything, mild.[78]

The leaders of the Palestinian organizations were forced to reassess their strategy in order to find a way out of the political and military morass. As Arafat asserted: 'The Americans have decided to destroy the Palestinian revolution. They have set up an American committee ... and a committee alongside Golda Meir's office, for this purpose.'[79] Habash saw the events of September 1970 as a plot to exploit the shifting balance of power in the Arab world and to eliminate the Palestinian problem.[80]

According to Fatah, the Zionist-imperialist plot to foil the Palestinian revolution had capitalized on 'several of the resistance's excesses' in order to persuade reactionary circles in the Arab world to support the American political initiative, which aimed at turning the West Bank into an 'investment zone for American, British and German capital'.[81] American imperialism, Fatah alleged, tried hard to squash the Palestinian revolution in July 1971 in Jordan and subsequently in Lebanon. The Palestinians therefore had to strengthen ties with the Arab liberation movement and 'all progressive and anti-imperialist forces'.[82]

The PFLP position was even more extreme. It anticipated an imperialist plot to destroy the Palestinian forces in Lebanon, similar to the destruction of Palestinian forces in Jordan:

> Our alliance strategy must ensure the Palestinian movement the place that behoves it in the international struggle... More specifically, the left-wing forces of the resistance movement must establish close ties with the progressive forces – the workers and students – of the Western bourgeois states. They must strengthen international solidarity in the knowledge that the sole expression of this solidarity is the support these movements can offer in the form of materials, propaganda and experience.[83]

---

[78] See Yodfat and Arnon-Ohanna, *PLO. Strategy and Politics*, pp. 87-90.

[79] See Arafat's interview to *Filastin al-Thawra* of 1 August 1973, quoted in *Journal of Palestine Studies*, Vol. 3, No. 2, pp. 192-93.

[80] See Habash's interview to the Egyptian *Al-Anbar* on 4 August 1973. Ibid., pp. 194-98.

[81] Fatah's position was described in the PLO political platform of January 1973. For the full text as approved by the eleventh PNC, see Khadder and Bichara, *Testi della revoluzione Palestinese*, pp. 155-64.

[82] This is apparently an allusion to the rapprochement between Fatah and PFLP positions on issues relating to international terrorism.

[83] See the text of the report presented by the PFLP leadership at its third conference in March 1972 as quoted in Khadder and Bichara, *Testi della revoluzione Palestinese*, pp. 249-67. On the same subject, see 'The Political and Organizational Strategy' in Rubinstein, *Compilation of Documents of the PFLP, DFLP and ALF*, pp. 63-68.

The PFLP also called on the resistance movement to step up activity among Palestinian youths who had emigrated to Western Europe and America.[84]

The evolution of PLO and PFLP strategy from late 1971 explained the closer cooperation with European terrorist organizations in 1972-73. In practice, because of the peculiar situation in France and Italy, cooperation only intensified with the German organizations.

In the author's opinion, the Palestinian 'flirtation' with West German terrorist organizations was bound up with PLO/Fatah ties with East Germany. Between October 1970 and July 1973, Arafat visited East Germany three times.[85] On the first visit, East Germany declared full support for the Palestinian revolution. On the second visit, in early 1973, the PLO and East Germany called for a strategic alliance between the Palestinian revolutionary camp and the socialist camp. On the third visit, in late July 1973, it was agreed to open a PLO office in East Berlin, the first of its kind in Eastern Europe.[86] This alliance between the PLO/Fatah and East Germany, orchestrated behind-the-scenes by the USSR, was evidently a factor in Fatah's decision to support the enemies of the West German regime and fight for the release of their jailed leaders.[87]

After a short period of unity between 1971-73, Fatah and the PFLP parted ways. Although the acceptance of the political option did not alleviate fears about Sadat's role in the peace process, Fatah stood by its decision to renounce international terror. Growing international support for the PLO, and the special observer

---

[84] This would seem to be an allusion to the role of Palestinians living abroad in liaising directly with local terrorist organizations. Note that during this period, the PFLP used to recruit local left-wing youngsters and students (in France, Switzerland, Holland, etc.), who were sent to Israel as part of terrorist cells.

[85] This section is based mainly on an article that appeared in *Filastin al-Thawra* of 15 August 1973, quoted in *Journal of Palestine Studies*, Vol. 3, No. 1 (1973), pp. 166-67.

[86] The Fatah journal wrote on the occasion: 'The revolution in the Middle East protects the global forces of progress and freedom against the forces of oppression and subjugation... The Socialist bloc countries support the revolutionary forces in the Middle East. Therefore, imperialism is incapable of putting down the revolutionary forces on a piecemeal basis'. The journal praised the East German government for opening its doors to Palestinian students expelled from West Germany after BSO Munich operation, and for offering political, military and economic aid to the Palestinian revolution.

[87] See C. John Reppert, 'The Soviets and The PLO: The Convenience of Politics', in Augustus Richard Norton and H. Martin Greenberg (eds.), *The International Relations of the Palestine Liberation Organization* (Southern Illinois University Press, 1989), p. 113. In this context Reppert pointed out that the Soviets claimed they supported Arafat and the PLO as a moderate alternative to BSO! Even more outrageous, according to Reppert, was the East German decision to permit the opening of a PLO office after the Munich massacre. Note that East Germany was itself keen to receive international recognition from as many states and international movements as possible, and felt that ties with the PLO would further its interests in the Arab world. The PLO benefited from East Germany's military assistance and intelligence training for many years. See Yonah Alexander and Joshua Sinai, *Terrorism: the PLO Connection* (New York: Crane Rusack, 1989), pp. 127-9.

status bestowed on it by the UN, after Arafat's appearance before the General Assembly in November 1974 helped it move in this direction.

Fatah's growing confidence in its political strength was evident in the program presented at the PNC of 12 June 1974. This described the Palestinian revolution as a powerful and dominant force after the [Yom Kippur] war, particularly after the PFLP expanded its base in the occupied territories, and the PLO achieved international recognition as the Palestinian sole legitimate representative.[88] The PLO, continued the statement, aspired to strengthen solidarity with the socialist states and the progressive forces of liberation throughout the world.

Ties with the USSR intensified after the Yom Kippur War, and in July 1974 a PLO office opened in Moscow. The Soviet leadership saw the PLO as an important element in the superpowers rivalry in the Middle East, particularly after the expulsion of the Soviets from Egypt in 1972, and the Egypt-US rapprochement. The PLO/Fatah saw the American political process as a new plot, and believed that the USSR had a major role to play in neutralizing it.[89] Soviet support for the PLO was undeniably a factor in its decision to refrain from international terror, since the USSR was highly critical of 'Habash's irresponsible and extremist actions … and his hodge-podge of Maoist demagoguery and would-be revolutionary activism'.[90]

Following the Yom Kippur War, the PFLP believed that American imperialism sought to contain the negative effects of war as swiftly as possible. It saw that the USSR, Europe and the non-aligned countries were also interested in détente. The PFLP did not believe the USSR capable of helping it achieve its ultimate goal – the elimination of Israel and the establishment of a democratic Palestinian state in its stead.[91] Behind the Geneva conference, Habash perceived a plot to destroy the Palestinian resistance movement, both militarily and politically. Therefore, it rejected any form of participation.[92] Furthermore, when the PLO began to prepare to join the Geneva conference in September 1974, the PFLP announced its resignation from the PLO executive.[93]

Thus the PFLP launched a new international terror offensive, this time with the help of foreign agents, such as 'Carlos' and his Western European and South American contacts, and members of German organizations, especially of the RZ.

---

[88] See *Journal of Palestine Studies*, Vol. 3, No. 4 (1974), pp. 224-26.

[89] See article in *Filastin al-Thawra*, 30 July 1974, quoted in *Journal of Palestine Studies*, Vol. 4, No. 1, (1974), pp. 167-68.

[90] Ibid., pp. 168-69. The article on Soviet-PFLP relations appeared in the Lebanese *Al-Nahar* of 14 August, 1974.

[91] See interview with Habash in *Journal of Palestine Studies*, Vol. 3, No. 3 (1974), pp. 201-205.

[92] From an interview to the Beirut *Al-Hadaf* of 3 August, 1974, in *Journal of Palestine Studies*, Vol. 4, No. 1 (1975), p. 201.

[93] For the full text, see *Journal of Palestine Studies*, Vol. 4, No. 2 (1975), pp. 165-71.

This prolonged campaign, designed primarily to disrupt the peace process and US-Soviet agreements concerning the region, was also directed against Egypt and Jordan, which were party to the peace process. The outbreak of the Lebanese Civil War, and the heavy losses suffered by the Palestinians at the hands of the Christian, and later Syrian, forces, lent additional fuel to the PFLP offensive.

As explained above, the crisis between the PFLP leadership and the Haddad faction occurred either after the attempted hijacking of an El Al plane in Nairobi in January 1976, or after the hijacking of Air France plane to Entebbe in June of that year. It is unlikely that this crisis had any real bearing on Palestinian-German cooperation, for several reasons. After Entebbe, the faction carried out only one operation (in October 1977) with the assistance of German terrorists, and the help was logistical rather than operational. As for the Germans, they hardly cared which organization they were working for; ultimately, they were recruited and coordinated by the Haddad faction, to which they owed direct allegiance. Since the split became public only in November 1977, after the Mogadishu operation, the German terrorists were not even aware of the faction's 'legal' status. This might also have been the cause for the PFLP, which, from 1971 on used aliases (BSO, Muhammad Budyah commandos, etc.), and denied participation in international terror, even when evidence revealed otherwise. The fact that the PFLP only announced Haddad's expulsion after the failure of the third hijacking operation apparently indicates that his leadership status was sufficiently strong to prevent this happening earlier.[94]

In October 1977 political coordination between the USSR and the PLO finally seemed to be yielding results: a joint American-Soviet communiqué urged the resumption of the Geneva talks, with emphasis on the Palestinian problem. For the first time the US began to mention, albeit vaguely, Palestinian rights in the negotiations. However, the negotiations were dramatically altered by Sadat's visit to Jerusalem in November of that year. Following the Camp David accords of 17 September 1978, the PLO executive held an emergency session in which it threatened all those who supported the 'Camp David plot'.[95] Fatah had already tried to escalate regional tension in March 1978, by attacking a civilian bus in Israel. (Israel had retaliated by bombing South Lebanon). Despite anger at Egypt, the Palestinians were unable to halt the progress of the negotiations.

On the operational front, the PFLP was licking its wounds after botching a number of operations. Following the expulsion of the Haddad faction, and Haddad's death, the organization split once again, as leaders fought over the

---

[94] Alternatively, the delay in announcing his expulsion may have been due to Haddad's poor health (only five months later, in March 1978, he died of leukemia). Finally, his expulsion may simply have been a tactical ploy to be used in extremis in order to safeguard the organization's political interests and public image of the organization.

[95] See Reppert, *The Soviets and The PLO*, pp. 117-18.

succession. These internal squabbles left little room for terrorist action. Indeed, the PFLP carried out only one attack in that period – the Orly Airport operation in Paris, in which the passengers of an El Al plane were taken hostage. The PFLP was not the only organization in a state of disarray: its German allies, with which it had collaborated in 1975-76, were also on the verge of collapse. The RAF was devastated by its leaders' suicide in Stammheim prison in October 1977. Moreover, a number of RAF and RZ terrorists were arrested or killed in the Nairobi and Entebbe operations, while the international division of the RZ simply ceased to exist. The only act of international cooperation of any significance was the training of ETA terrorists in Palestinian camps in South Yemen in 1980. It is not clear if this help was provided by the PFLP or by an offshoot of the Haddad faction. The PFLP leadership apparently felt a need to abide by public declarations that the organization had renounced international terror.

In view of the above, the special relationship between Fatah and the BR, especially the large weapons consignments from Fatah to the BR, is somewhat difficult to explain. Some sources claimed that the initiative came from Fatah's 'Marxist Division', which opposed the rapprochement between Fatah and Western Europe.[96] However, even if differences existed between leftist, mainly pro-Syrian, elements and the more rightist wing in Fatah, the chief negotiator with the BR was Abu Iyad, close to the Islamic and right-wing circles within the organization, and the agreement that resulted from the negotiations was approved by Arafat himself. After Sadat's visit to Jerusalem, Fatah joined the Steadfastness Front as an equal partner. Its desire for West European recognition evidently did not prevent it from resuming its international terrorist activities.

The agreement with the BR conformed to Fatah's anti-Sadat and anti-peace strategy. The Fatah leadership apparently believed that following the kidnapping and murder of Aldo Moro, the BR was on the verge of a military breakthrough in the war against the Italian regime, and could be an important ally in the struggle against the US-brokered peace process supported by the Italians and the Europeans. At that time, Italy was beginning to play an increasingly important role in the eastern Mediterranean, and had sent units to the US-led peacekeeping force in Sinai. BR leader Moretti's promise to attack Israeli targets in Italy was a further incentive for arming the BR, and through it other organizations able to help the PLO. Following the RAF collapse the previous year, the BR was the only European terrorist organizations that met the criteria for partnership in Fatah's coalition against the US and its allies in the Middle East.

Military support for the BR aside, Fatah continued to foster an image of respectability in the international arena, by steering clear of international terror, or

---

[96] On the leftist influence inside Fatah, see Sayigh, *Armed Struggle and the Search for State*, pp. 492-4.

aid to European terrorist organizations. In line with this policy, Arafat was quick to denounce the murder of Aldo Moro. Although the PNC statement of January 1979 expressed solidarity with all national liberation movements in the world (particularly Zimbabwe, Namibia and South Africa); calls for solidarity 'with the revolutionary forces of the world' of the kind that appeared in its documents from 1972-73, were conspicuously absent.

After the election of President Reagan in late 1980, the PLO/Fatah became increasingly concerned that the US might tougher its stand against Palestinian terrorist organizations. Therefore, they felt an even greater need to avoid antagonizing Western Europe.[97] Fatah's political platform, presented at its fourth conference in May 1980, emphasized the need 'to intensify political activity in Western Europe ... and obtain the support of the democratic and progressive forces in these countries, and to safeguard and sustain the political fruits that had been reaped in the international arena'.[98] Thus, by the end of the 1970s, there was a growing tendency within the PLO/Fatah, and also within the PFLP, to renounce international terror in favor of military and territorial consolidation in Lebanon, particularly South Lebanon, as a springboard for activities against Israel.

IV.   THE LEBANESE WAR AND THE STRATEGIC TURNING POINT (1981-84)

For the year and a half preceding the Lebanese War, Fatah and the PFLP both focused on strengthening their military infrastructure in Lebanon. Following heavy shooting by the Palestinians and Israeli retaliatory action, the ceasefire with Israel, obtained with Saudi Arabian support, was interpreted by them as a victory for the Palestinian forces.

Fatah and the PFLP were significantly weakened by the Lebanese War, especially their forced evacuation from Lebanon (first from the Beirut area by the Israeli forces, and later from the Tripoli area, by their Syrian 'brothers' and their Palestinian allies). The Palestinian organizations were forced to relocate to Tunis, Algeria, the Yemen, and Iraq, far from the center of action. More importantly, in being driven out from South Lebanon they not only lost their stronghold, but also the freedom of action that had enabled them to conduct a war of attrition against

---

[97]   In an interview given by Faruq al-Qaddumi, head of the PLO political branch, to the Lebanese weekly *Monday Morning* on 23 November 1980, he pointed out that Reagan had called the PLO a terrorist organization before the elections, and stated that in his opinion, Reagan's Middle East policy would lead to an escalation of tension and to war in the region. Quoted in *Journal of Palestine Studies*, Vol. 10, No. 2 (38) (1981), pp. 117-20.

[98]   For full text of the platform, see Lukacs, *The Israeli-Palestinian Conflict: A Documentary Record*, pp. 345-49.

Israel's northern settlements, including lethal attacks by sea. To make matters worse, internal rifts within the organizations deepened, as Syria became the driving force behind organized opposition to Arafat's political line. As well as its traditional Palestinian allies (Jibril's PFLP-GC and the pro-Syrian 'Sa'ika' organization), Syria drew rebels from within Fatah itself, led by of Sa'id Musa Mahmud Marjad (Abu Musa), a senior officer and member of Fatah's Revolutionary Council.

From the outbreak of the war until the expulsion of Fatah forces from the Tripoli area in northern Lebanon, the ANO was virtually the only Palestinian organization to carry out international terrorist attacks, mainly against Fatah and Jordanian targets and some Jewish targets.[99] Although Fatah suddenly resumed attacks against Israeli targets in late 1983, these did not represent a significant departure from its policy.[100] As for the PFLP, from January 1981, it refrained from carrying out acts of international terror.

1.   Cooperation with European organizations

Of all European terrorist organizations, only the French AD expressed active solidarity with the Palestinian struggle by launching a series of attacks about a month after the outbreak of the Lebanese War. This campaign had been inspired by an ideological alliance with the Lebanese FARL, whose ideology resembled that of the PFLP. However, Chapter 5 demonstrated that AD had its own reasons for acting as it did during that period.

The RAF was at an operational low during the Lebanese War, as its leaders themselves admitted. As it began to recover, it moved clearly toward Euro-terrorism, abandoning the Third World arena, and ties with the Palestinians. As for the BR, it was just emerging from a series of internal crises and botched operations, and was hardly able to turn its attention to international terror. Its only operation during the period, the murder of Leamon Hunt in February 1984, was carried out with the FARL in a singular, limited act of cooperation.

2.   International and regional factors

The expulsion of the PLO from South Lebanon pushed it to adopt the 'Jordanian option', a choice that had aroused stormy debates before the war. This involved transferring the center of operations from Lebanon and Syria, to the West Bank,

---

[99] For example the attacks against Jordanian and Kuwaiti targets, the murder of 'Assam Sirtawi, a PLO leader, or the attack against the Great Synagogue of Rome on 9 October 1982. As explained earlier, ANO gave priority to attacks on its Arab enemies.

[100] These were the attacks against the Israeli representative in Malta, and the ambassador in Greece.

Gaza and Jordan, from where it could implement 'a policy of diplomacy'.[101] This development, combined with Syria's behavior during the Lebanese War, pushed the PLO toward a rapprochement with Egypt, which had tried to help during the evacuation of Palestinian forces from Beirut. PNC resolutions adopted in Amman subsequently placed the aspirations of the Palestinian population in the Israeli-occupied territories at the top of the PLO agenda.

The Lebanese War also convinced the PLO/Fatah that it could not defeat Israel on the battlefield, and that the US did in fact have a central role to play in the politics of the entire Middle East. Possibly for the first time, the PLO understood the dependence of Arab states on the US, and its paralyzing effect on them. Despite their beleaguered situation in Beirut, the PLO forces had received no practical help – other than propaganda – from the USSR, and the US, acting on Israel's behalf, had been the only mediator in the evacuation. During the siege of Beirut, the PLO had conducted intensive debates on the ability of its 'strategic allies' to stop the Israelis, the validity of its alliance with the Soviets, and the soundness of its past policy towards the Soviets. It is not therefore surprising that a slow but steady process of political dialogue with the American administration was set in motion.[102]

Only Fatah adopted the new strategy. Syrian pressure, and loyalty to the idea of the liberation of the whole of Palestine, caused the PFLP to boycott the PNC in Amman, marking the end of the short-lived consensus within the PLO after the Lebanese War. The PFLP clung to its own assessment of the US role in international politics following President Reagan's election. It condemned

> US-led imperialism for stepping up the arms race and heightening international tension, thereby threatening to bring back the specter of the Cold War; for the deployment of missiles in Western Europe, the expansion of its fleet in the Mediterranean and the Persian Gulf, *inter alia*, and the establishment of military bases in Egypt, Oman, Saudi Arabia, and East Africa.

The PFLP also supported guerrilla organizations in Oman, Bahrain and Saudi Arabia, and condemned the Iraqi attack on Iran.[103]

---

[101] Considerable support was elicited for the Jordanian option at the sixteenth PNC that took place in Algiers in April 1983, which overwhelmingly accepted the idea of a Palestinian state confederated with Jordan. A similar resolution was passed at the seventeenth PNC, which took place, for the first time, in Amman, in November 1984. This section on the PLO's new strategy is based on Rashid Khalidi, 'The Palestinian Dilemma: PLO policy after Lebanon', *Journal of Palestine Studies* Vol. 15, No. 1 (57) (1985), pp. 88-103 and Ibrahim Abu-Lughod, 'Flexible Militancy: A Report on the Sixteenth Session of the Palestine National Council, Algiers, February 14-22, 1983', *Journal of Palestine Studies*, Vol. 12, No. 4 (48) (1983), pp. 25-40.

[102] See Reppert, *The Soviets and The PLO*, p. 123 and Abu-Lughod, *Flexible Militancy: A Report on the Sixteenth Session of the Palestine National Council*, pp. 28-33.

[103] For the resolutions of the fourth PFLP conference of April 1981, see *Journal of Palestine Studies*, Vol. 11, No. 4 (40) (1981), pp. 189-93.

Fatah's policy at the time was summarized by Abu Iyad, who stated that the PLO was opposed to terrorism, hijackings, and murders, but supported armed action in the occupied territories.[104] Habash, for his part, claimed that what had changed after the evacuation from Beirut was the willingness of the PLO dominant right-wing element to accept American conditions, in the hope of receiving recognition from it. The PFLP on the other hand, saw itself as part of the global revolutionary current, led by its ally, the USSR. In short, the PFLP remained loyal to its historical and strategic revolutionary alliances, while the right-wing element, it claimed, had gone over to the enemy camp. The PFLP still considered Lebanon – with the help of Syria and the Lebanese national forces – an important strategic arena in the struggle against Israel.[105]

V.   THE POLITICAL PATH (1985-90)

The seventeenth PNC granted Arafat carte blanche to conduct negotiations with King Hussein of Jordan on the establishment of a Palestinian state, thereby indicating that the PLO was willing to accept a political solution based on partition.[106] The Hussein-Arafat agreement was reached in mid-February 1985, although Arafat argued that military pressure should still be applied on Israel within the occupied territories and Lebanon, in order to strengthen the PLO position in these negotiations.[107] Hopes of furthering the political process through a Palestinian-Jordanian alliance soon foundered, as Syria moved toward rapprochement with Jordan, effectively invalidating the Hussein-Arafat agreement. The failure of the Jordanian option was compounded by failures in the armed struggle against Israel, both within the territories and in abortive attempts to infiltrate terrorist cells into Israel via the sea.

Pressure to renew terrorist activity was intensified by the political morass engulfing the PLO/Fatah, and by the fact that opposition groups, particularly the ANO, were using international terrorism.[108] Fatah attacks in September 1985 in Larnaca and Barcelona, and, more so, the hijacking of the Achilles Lauro ship by Abu Abbas's PLF, an organization close to Fatah and financed by it, signaled a

---

[104] See interview to the British weekly *New Statesman*, published in *Journal of Palestine Studies*, Vol. 14, No. 2 (54) (1985) pp. 219-21. A similar declaration was made by Khalil Al-Wazir (Abu Jihad). Ibid., pp. 3-7.

[105] See Habash's interview, *Journal of Palestine Studies*, Vol. 19, No. 4 (56) (1985), pp. 3-14.

[106] See Hana Siniora's report on the seventeenth PNC in *New Outlook*, Dec. 1984-Jan. 1985, quoted in *Journal of Palestine Studies*, Vol. 14, No. 3 (55) (1985), pp. 168-70.

[107] See Arafat's interviews to the Egyptian daily *Al-Ahram* of 21 February 1985 and to *Al-Hawadith* of 1 March 1985. Ibid., pp. 151-56.

[108] On the subject of PLO/Fatah terrorist policy in 1985-87, see the excellent review in *InTer* (1987), pp. 21-32.

dramatic return to the BSO-style terrorism.[109] At the same time, Fatah launched an offensive against Syrian targets in Lebanon, to retaliate against Syrian support for ANO terrorist attacks against members of the PLO. Although the members of several Fatah cells were arrested in 1986 and 1987, the new onslaught only subsided in 1987.[110]

Pressure by Egypt and Jordan, and the strong stand taken by the US and Western Europe against international terror, ultimately persuaded Arafat to renounce the use of international terror. In November 1985 in Cairo, he publicly committed himself to this position.[111]

The event that had the greatest impact on Palestinian, and particularly Fatah policy, was the outbreak of the intifada (Palestinian uprising in the West Bank and Gaza) in December 1987. Its political impact in Israel and the Arab world, as well as renewed efforts by the American administration to revive the peace process, confirmed to the leaders of the PLO that international terrorism could harm their long-term political and strategic interests.[112] The proceedings of Fatah fifth conference stated that the 'intifada has occasioned a deep rift within the Zionist entity, directed world attention to the justice of the Palestinian cause, and imposed a new political reality, with repercussions at the Palestinian, Arab and international level.'[113] In a declaration published in May 1989, Arafat declared that the paragraphs in the Palestinian Charter calling for the destruction of Israel were 'null and void' (*caduc*), and that the PLO advocated a two-state solution.[114] This apparent moderation of its political position and the abandonment of international terror made political dialogue with the American administration possible and led to the Madrid conference in October 1991 and the peace accords with Israel.[115]

---

[109] On 25 September 1985 three Israelis were killed in a yacht anchored in the port of Larnaca, Cyprus, by a commando unit belonging to Force-17, Fatah's security unit. On 5 October 1985, two Israeli marines were killed in Barcelona, Spain, again by a Force-17 cell. The hijacking of the Achilles Lauro on 7 October 1985 in the port of Alexandria, Egypt, was meant to be an anti-Israel operation, but a disabled American Jewish passenger was killed on deck. According to researchers, Abu Abbas, the leader of the PLF, could not have carried out the hijacking without Arafat's consent.

[110] A Fatah cell was arrested in July 1986 in Morocco, and militants of the organization were expelled in April 1986 from Paris and Stockholm, after the discovery of an extensive terrorist infrastructure and plans to carry out attacks.

[111] For Arafat's declaration on terror delivered in Cairo on 7 November 1985, see Lukacs, *The Israeli-Palestinian Conflict: A Documentary Record*, pp. 370-71.

[112] Neither the attack against three Fatah activists in Cyprus in February 1988 nor the assassination of Khalil al-Wazir in Tunis in April of that year, triggered a retaliatory response, despite the fact that Israel was accused to be behind these incidents.

[113] For proceedings of the conference, held on 8 August 1988, see *Journal of Palestine Studies*, Vol. 19, No. 1 (73) (1988), pp. 134-39.

[114] See Arafat's interview with the French TV1 network, as quoted in *Journal of Palestine Studies*, Vol. 19, No. 2 (74) (1990), pp. 144-46.

[115] Khalidi, in analyzing the resolutions of the nineteenth PNC of November 1988 declaring the establishment of an independent Palestinian state, emphasized that for the first time in the history of

Surprisingly, throughout this lengthy period the PFLP also refrained from international terror, despite pressure on Fatah to adopt a more radical position, and attempts to sabotage both the agreement with Jordan and the dialogue with the US. After boycotting the seventeenth PNC in Amman in November 1984, the PFLP returned to the fold at the eighteenth PNC in April 1987, due to the PLO disaffection with Jordan, the rift with Morocco, and tension with Egypt.[116] The PFLP, together with Na'if Hawatmeh's DFLP, tried hard to persuade Arafat to condemn the peace accords between Egypt and Israel, with only partial success. The PFLP strongly opposed the resolutions adopted by the nineteenth PNC and has since been steadily and actively opposed to all of Arafat's involvement in the peace process.

The only official decision relating to international terror was adopted at the fourth PFLP conference in February 1981. In principle the PFLP did not oppose terrorist activities abroad, provided they were chosen 'with great care and circumspection', as Habash put it. In other words, it sanctioned international terror attacks against Israeli targets.[117] Although the PFLP rejected Arafat's 1985 'Cairo declaration' it did not carry out any terrorist attacks during this period.

1.   Cooperation with European organizations

The three European radical left-wing organizations that were active during this period, namely the RAF, BR and AD, focused almost exclusively on European or domestic issues, and had little time for the Palestinians. It should also be noted that between 1986-88 these three organizations were almost totally liquidated by the security forces in their respective countries.

Nonetheless, the intifada kindled the imagination of the BR and the RAF leaders; the BR-PCC even considered setting up a coalition with those Palestinian organizations 'responsible for the revolutionary situation' in the Israeli-occupied territories.[118] The BR was unable, however, to persuade the RAF leadership of the need to take concrete steps in this direction. By the time it was ready to establish a Euro-terrorist coalition with the RAF in November 1988, the two organizations were expunged from the European map of terror.

---

the PNC, the proceedings made absolutely no reference to the 'Palestinian Charter' or the 'armed struggle' that was so central to the organization's ideology. Nor did it demand that its forces in Lebanon be allowed freedom of action against Israel. Instead, it announced renunciation of terrorism in all forms. Khalidi pointed out that these two themes still appeared in the proceedings of the eighteenth PNC of April 1987. See Rashid Khalidi, 'The Resolutions of the 19th Palestine National Council', *Journal of Palestine Studies*, Vol. 19, No. 2 (74) (1990), pp. 35-39.

[116] On the subject of the eighteenth PNC, see report by the KUNA news agency, of 26 April, 1987, quoted in *Journal of Palestine Studies*, Vol. 16, No. 4 (64) (1987), pp. 152-54.

[117] See Steinberg, The Worldview of Habash's 'Popular Front', pp. 23-24.

[118] See Yonah Alexander and A. Dennis Pluchinsky (eds.), *Europe's Red Terrorists: The Fighting Communist Organizations* (London: Frank Cass, 1992), p. 229.

Despite the terrorist interlude of 1985-86 following Fatah's change of heart, the overall trend remained constant, with the US continuing to play a major role in the area. As the Soviet economic and political situation weakened, and the USSR sank further into the Afghan quagmire, the Americans were increasingly seen as the only power capable of furthering peace and meeting at least some of the Palestinians' demands. Palestinian rhetoric concerning the US was modified accordingly. In the 1970s and early 1980s, PLO leaders portrayed the US as the war mongering leader of the imperialist camp, conspiring against the Palestinian people and the Arab nation; now they began to appeal to the American administration to recognize the legitimate rights of the Palestinian people and to give the Palestinians the go-ahead to convene an international conference.[119]

Reagan's tough stand against terrorist organizations and their Arab sponsors began with the interception of an Egyptian plane carrying Abu Abbas after the Achilles Lauro attack, and continued with the air strike over Libya in April 1986 following a spate of anti-American terrorist attacks in Western Europe. In the spring of 1986, Europe, too, tightened its counter-terrorist policy after the capture of Syrian-sponsored terrorists sent to carry out acts of sabotage against Britain and West Germany. Diplomatic ties between Britain and Syria were subsequently severed, and economic sanctions were imposed on Syria by the EC.[120] These measures significantly curbed terrorist activities by Syrian and Libyan-sponsored organizations, particularly the ANO, resulting in a sharp drop in attacks by the more radical Palestinian organizations in 1987-88.

The USSR was greatly embarrassed by the Palestinians' forays into international terror in 1985-86. It condemned the Achilles Lauro hijacking unequivocally. Its anti-terrorist stand was hardened by the kidnapping of four Soviet diplomats (one of whom was assassinated) by radical Sunnis in Beirut. The Soviets also realized that while the PLO was wooing 'the leading imperialist power,' it could no longer serve Soviet objectives in the Third World. Therefore, they adopted a far more pragmatic approach, including negotiations for the resumption of relations with Israel. These negotiations resulted in renewed ties between Russia and Israel in 1989, which, in turn, led to a huge influx of Jewish immigrants from the USSR, much to the Palestinians' dismay.

The political response of Western Europe, particularly France, Italy and Greece, to the siege of Beirut encouraged the PLO to continue its policy of rapprochement with the West. The Achilles Lauro affair taught the PLO leadership a lesson. In March 1986 the PLO executive committee committed itself to

---

[119] Thus, for example, a communiqué published by the PLO Central Committee on 16 October 1989 no longer mentioned 'the conspiracies of American imperialism', but 'elements in the administration who support Shamir and his policy'. See *Journal of Palestine Studies*, Vol. 19, No. 2 (74) (1990), pp. 154-59.

[120] See 'Palestinian International Terrorism in 1986,' in *InTer 86*, p. 49.

strengthening the alliance with Europe.[121] Fatah was therefore naturally reluctant to jeopardize the situation by attacking Western targets or carrying out overt terrorist activities in Western Europe. The hijacking of the Achilles Lauro was a lapse that may have resulted from faulty planning.[122]

On the regional level, countries that had traditionally influenced Palestinian policies were still an important factor in strategic and tactical considerations. Syria was still spearheading opposition to Fatah from inside the PLO, in an attempt to sabotage any political process that did not suit its interests. After the Hussein-Arafat agreement of February 1985, Syria made friendly overtures to Jordan in an attempt to undermine the agreement. Syria, with the help of the PFLP and the DFLP, campaigned against the PLO rapprochement with Egypt, with partial success, as the eighteenth PNC of April 1987 testified. Jordan, for its part, tried to preserve its pivotal role in finding a solution for the Palestinian problem, and the Hussein-Arafat agreement appeared to be a step in the right direction. After the annulment of the agreement, Jordan sought in 1987-88 to join the political process over the heads of the Palestinians, and almost succeeded in reaching an agreement with Israel to this effect. Despite this 'betrayal', the PLO refrained from attacking Jordan, in order not to tarnish its international image, which made dialogue with the American administration possible. Egypt gradually returned to the picture, and managed to elicit PLO support by acting as its representative before the US. Towards the end of the decade, after a brief period of unity, rifts between the Fatah-led moderates, supported by Egypt and Jordan, and the PFLP-led radical opposition, supported by Syria, once again beset the Palestinians.[123]

VI.   ANALYSIS OF RESEARCH ASSUMPTIONS

For many years, Palestinian organizations considered the unholy alliance between Israel, world Zionism and imperialism (usually American imperialism) as their greatest enemy. The PFLP went even further, including the reactionary Arab states in the enemy camp, as the objective allies of Israel and imperialism. Thus, both Fatah and the PFLP saw the enemies of the Palestinian revolution as a constant threat to their existence, and felt a need for strong, reliable allies capable of challenging the enemy's superior forces. Typically, they showed a large degree of flexibility and pragmatism in choosing their allies, although the PFLP remained consistent with its ideology.

---

[121] For full text, see Lukacs, *The Israeli-Palestinian Conflict: A Documentary Record*, pp. 384-85.

[122] Note how the planners correctly predicted the Italian government's rather ineffectual response (in contrast to America's hard-line response). The Italian government was afraid to arrest Abu Abbas while his plane was stranded in Italy, and only agreed to try the hijackers under US pressure.

[123] See 'Mainstream PLO International Terrorist Activity in 1987,' in *InTer 1987*, pp. 21-25.

1.   Influence of international and regional factors

As previously noted, Palestinian terrorist organizations perceived a sharp division between the Western imperialist camp (including Zionism and Israel), and the progressive revolutionary camp, including the socialist bloc, the Third World, the national liberation movements, and revolutionary movements in the West. The PFLP landed itself in a serious ideological and 'methodological' quandary, by including the reactionary Arab states and regimes in the imperialist camp. Attempts to balance its revolutionary commitments against its Palestinian or pan-Arab commitments (and against its financial interests) were not always congruent with its declared ideology.[124]

Palestinian organizations were aware of both dangers and opportunities arising from bipolar tension. Ironically, they were more worried about détente, fearing that it would be achieved at their expense.[125] There is no indication that bipolar tension strengthened the desire for an alliance with European terrorist organizations (Hypothesis 1). Although the PFLP expressed concern at Reagan's hard line, and at the possible deployment of medium-range nuclear missiles in Western Europe, it made no attempt to set up a coalition in the early 1980s, when Reagan came to power. On the other hand, the rift between the USSR and China, and the emergence of new revolutionary foci in Algeria, Cuba, Vietnam and Africa, did encourage the Palestinian terrorist organizations to form alliances with European terrorist organizations, especially those which upheld the primacy of the Third World in the global revolutionary struggle, such as the RAF (Hypothesis 2). Both Fatah and the PFLP felt closer to the Chinese and Cuban doctrines, or to the Algerian and Vietnamese revolutionary models, than to the USSR or orthodox Marxist-Leninist movements. Both organizations identified with the national liberation movements, and with all revolutionary movements and organizations throughout the world. The PFLP statement on the hijacking of the El Al plane to Algiers in July 1968 concluded that the 'the Palestinians are simply one of various revolutionary foci in the Third World'.[126] In the early years, the PFLP favored China, Vietnam and Cuba as its main allies, and criticized the USSR for its stand on the Palestinian issue. From the mid-1970s, it began to suspect China of 'collusion with imperialism', suspicions that were soon corroborated by

---

[124]   On the contradictions between PFLP ideology and praxis, see Steinberg, 'The Worldview of Habash's "Popular Front"', pp. 9-12.

[125]   Macintyre pointed out that the greatest danger to the PLO since its establishment in 1964 was the Geneva peace conference, since its discussions were based on UN Resolution 242, which related to the Palestinian problem as a refugee problem only. Macintyre, *The Palestine Liberation Organization. Tactics, Strategies and Options*, p. 65.

[126]   See Sayigh's, *Armed Struggle and the Search for State*, p. 213.

China's support for the Camp David accords, and for Sadat himself, to the Palestinians' consternation.[127]

One of the reasons for Palestinian cooperation with German terrorist organizations, especially the RAF, until the mid-1970s, was the fact that the Germans supported national liberation movements and shared a common strategic outlook. From the mid-1970s, however, Fatah and the PFLP relied almost exclusively on their strategic alliance with the USSR (as well, of course, as their alliances with various Arab states). After the Lebanese War, however, the strategic paths of Fatah and the PFLP parted: while Fatah drew nearer to the West and reached an understanding with the US over the political process, the PFLP continued to rely on the USSR, albeit with lower expectations at the strategic level (and closer ties with Syria).

From the early 1980s on, the strategy of the European organizations also changed, as they focused increasingly on domestic problems, NATO and the American nuclear presence in Europe. This change of strategic perception led to an estrangement between the Palestinian and European organizations, and to greater unity and cooperation within the European camp, as described in previous chapters. Although the outbreak of the intifada in December 1987 awakened a glimmer of hope that a new revolutionary focus was emerging which the European organizations could emulate, exploit, and perhaps even join, the European organizations were barely viable at the time, and a few months later were completely extinct. The Palestinians understood that the main contribution of the intifada was political, and that it should not be tarnished by acts of international terror. Therefore, even supposing the European terrorist organizations had still been active the intifada would not have made an alliance with them any more likely.

Regional wars, armed conflicts between Palestinian organizations and Arab host states, and other regional tensions also encouraged the formation of coalitions by Fatah and the PFLP, particularly during the 1970s (Hypothesis 3).

The PFLP's entry into the field of international terror (with sporadic assistance by European and South American terrorists) was triggered by military defeats in the guerrilla war in the West Bank, and tension with Fatah in the wake of the 'Battle of Karameh'.[128] The bloody events of September 1970 in Jordan no doubt contributed to the upsurge in Palestinian international terror and accentuated the need for allies in the struggle against the Jordanian regime which, they believed, was backed by American imperialism in its attempt to put down the Palestinian revolution.

---

[127] See Steinberg, 'The Worldview of Habash's "Popular Front"', p. 20.

[128] Note that internal factors also influenced the strategic decision, as explained above.

The aftermath of the Yom Kippur War affected Fatah and PFLP in opposite ways. While it strengthened Fatah resolve to reach a political solution and renounce international terror, it intensified the PFLP opposition to the political process. The Lebanese Civil War merely enhanced this trend, and was the driving force behind the PFLP policy from 1975-77, its most productive period in terms of European cooperation. Why, then, did the Lebanese War of 1982 fail to elicit a similar response? The answer can be found in two new developments: the need to preserve sympathy of most West European nations, and the increasingly dominant role of the EC in shaping regional policy; and a growing awareness that the Israeli-Palestinian conflict could be resolved only at the global level, and that since only the US could 'deliver the goods', international terror should be abandoned as the Americans stipulated.

There is no evidence that Palestinian collaboration with European terrorist organizations was inspired by European-Israeli counter-terrorist cooperation (Hypothesis 4). Although Palestinian organizations were aware of security cooperation in Western Europe, they realized, probably around the mid-1970s, that the main target of security services were national terrorist organizations, and that the Palestinians, were targeted inasmuch as they cooperated with these organizations.

2.   Influence of the variables at the organizational level

A.   Ideological variables

Solidarity between the Palestinian organizations and the European radical left-wing organizations was generally predicated on affiliation to the same revolutionary anti-imperialist camp. This camp embraced national liberation movements (such as Fatah and the PFLP) as well as revolutionary movements in the fighting for social change (such as the European terrorist organization). These were united by a common goal – to bring about revolution – each in its own way.

This common ideology persisted until after the Lebanese War, when Fatah embraced the political process, sought the help of the US and strengthened its political ties with West European governments.[129] Indeed, from the mid-1980s on, after the Hussein-Arafat agreement, and even more so after the PNC resolutions of 1988-89, radical left-wing publications began to accuse the PLO/Fatah leadership of betraying the Palestinian cause and the goals of the revolution. From that time on, the radical left published the PFLP's views only. These were

---

[129] On the price the PLO paid for dialoguing with the US, see Nasser Aruri, 'The United States and Palestine: Reagan's Legacy to Bush', *Journal of Palestine Studies*, Vol. 18, No. 3 (71) (1989), p. 16.

portrayed as courageous revolutionary doctrines, in contrast to Arafat's capitulation.[130]

Solidarity with the Basque ETA was likewise based on the principle of a common revolutionary goal, although the Basques renounced their Third World strategy early on. Nonetheless, ETA continued to see itself as belonging to the anti-imperialist revolutionary camp in the broader sense of the term. However, there are no documented expressions of Palestinian solidarity with the Basque cause. Conversely, there were some Basque expressions of solidarity with the Palestinian cause, albeit few and far between.

Palestinian organizations played a significant role in introducing antisemitic motifs into the anti-Zionist ideology of the radical left. Bernard Lewis attributed the radicalization of antisemitic attitudes in the Arab world to the 1956 Sinai campaign and the 1967 Six Day War. After these wars, the Arabs and Palestinians had to justify their ignominious defeat by 'little' Israel and the cowardly Jews, as they had so far been depicted in the Arab media. Since there was no rational explanation for this defeat, they had to look beyond the bounds of reason. Hence the growth of Arab antisemitic literature.[131]

Wistrich pointed out that the Arabs in general, and the Palestinian leadership in particular, failed to understand the full dimensions of the Holocaust, and played down the fact that several Arab leaders, especially the Mufti of Jerusalem, Haj Amin Al-Husseini, had collaborated with the Nazis. Rather, they trivialized the Holocaust by portraying it as simply a political weapon used by Zionists to further their aims, and by claiming that the 'holocaust' perpetrated by Israel against the Palestinian people was more terrible than the one perpetrated by the Germans against the Jews.[132]

Rabinovich also saw the Six Day War as the turning point in the Israeli-Arab conflict, and its antisemitic manifestations in the Arab world. This growth of anti-Jewish sentiment had turned the Arab states into the potential allies of antisemitic groups throughout the world. Indeed, cooperation between the Palestinian terrorist organizations and antisemitic individuals and groups existed, as was seen in earlier chapters.[133]

---

[130] In 1989, *Il Bollettino* dedicated a special edition to an interview with Habash on the intifada. Throughout the interview, Habash never mentioned Fatah's key role in leading the uprising.

[131] Lewis traced the roots of modern antisemitism in the Muslim and Arab world back to the nineteenth and twentieth century Christian empires, whose influence spread to the Ottoman Empire. See Bernard Lewis, 'Antisemitism in the Arab and Islamic World', in Yehuda Bauer (ed.), *Present-Day Antisemitism* (Jerusalem: The Vidal Sassoon International Center for the Study of Antisemitism, The Hebrew University of Jerusalem 1988), pp. 61-66.

[132] See Robert Wistrich, 'Anti-Zionism as an Expression of Antisemitism in Recent Years', in Bauer (ed.), *Present-Day Antisemitism*, p. 179.

[133] See Itamar Rabinovich, 'Antisemitism in the Muslim and Arab World', in Bauer (ed.), *Present-Day Antisemitism*, pp. 261-62.

Horchem described how in the summer of 1967, immediately following the Six Day War, a Hilfskorps Arabien was set up by the German 'Association of Young Patriots' to help the Palestinians (Fatah) in their struggle against Israel.[134] This was less successful than the Freikorps Adolf Hitler, set up by the East German refugee Udo Albrecht, who had spent some 17 years in jail. Albrecht, together with ten of his followers, fought alongside the BSO in 1970 against King Hussein's forces, and in 1975-76, was still trying to recruit mercenaries for Fatah. Another German antisemitic group, with which Abu Iyad cooperated, was led by Karl Heinz Hoffman, 15 of whose members trained in Fatah camps in Lebanon in 1979-80.[135]

It is strange, to say the least, that Fatah, and Abu Iyad in particular, continued to cooperate with radical right-wing organizations even though this harmed their image among sympathetic left-wing organizations. Evidently the Fatah top brass, ideologically close to the Muslim Brothers and other religious fundamentalist organizations, felt a special rapport with certain neo-Nazi groups. In his book 'Stateless', Abu Iyad alleged that the Palestinian leader, Haj Amin Al-Hussayni, cooperated with the Nazi regime in Germany for tactical reasons only, not because he himself was a Nazi sympathizer. One wonders what weighty tactical consideration induced Fatah to cooperate with eccentrics such as the Hoffman group, other than identification with their antisemitic ideology.

The expressions of solidarity, which the Italian far right showed the Palestinians, were not answered in kind. Despite claims by Fatah and PFLP that they belonged to the same anti-imperialist and anti-American camp, they were extremely wary of expressing solidarity with Italian right-wing organizations, not because the Palestinians were displeased with the support these groups offered, or with their antisemitic ideology. On the contrary, several years later, a grand reconciliation took place between the PLO representative in Italy and the extremist faction of the neo-fascist party, the MSI. The Palestinian organizations were simply not prepared to pay the political price for overt solidarity with the Italian far right – alienation of the Italian radical left, the Italian government, and the progressive groups in Western Europe.

Inconsistencies and contradictions appeared when analyzing the importance of ideology in the formation of coalitions by the two Palestinian organizations. Fatah was basically a nationalist organization, despite its revolutionary pretensions, particularly in the early years of its armed struggle. Unlike the ETA, however, Fatah had no defined social ideology, and preferred to postpone ideological

---

[134] See Horchem, *Terrorism in Germany: 1985*, pp. 154-56.
[135] The only documented terrorist attack carried out by Hoffman's group for the Palestinians or in cooperation with them was the murder of the Jewish publisher Lewin and his partner Puschke on 19 December 1980 by Uwe Bemrendt. After the murder, Bemrendt found refuge in a Fatah camp, later returning to Germany where he committed suicide.

decisions until after it had achieved its strategic goal – the liberation of Palestine. Nevertheless, one would have expected Fatah, as a nationalist organization, to confirm Hypothesis 8 concerning the reluctance of nationalist organizations to cooperate with other organizations (see the chapter on ETA). However, this was not the case. For a long time, Fatah allowed terrorists from other countries – including Third World countries – to train in its camps and offered them sanctuary in times of trouble. After the events of September 1970 in Jordan and after the Camp David accords, Fatah went even further, and cooperated far more actively with revolutionary organizations in Western Europe, albeit for shorter periods of time.

One explanation for this apparent anomaly could be Fatah's overwhelming need to obtain international recognition of the Palestinians, not as refugees but as a people with the right to struggle against Israel. The shift in the European radical left's attitude towards Israel and the Palestinians after the Six Day War, gave the Palestinian organizations a historic opportunity to strengthen its national and international image, and enhance its status within the demoralized Arab world.

The transfer of the revolutionary torch from the Vietnamese to the Palestinian people posed a new challenge for the Palestinian organizations The influx of young European revolutionaries into Palestinian camps, their eagerness to be trained by Palestinian guerrillas, their admiration for their achievements in the battlefield, left Fatah with little choice.[136] Fatah was induced into helping these organizations, at least until 1974, when no political assets were at stake.[137]

The PFLP policy of forming ties with other revolutionary organizations was far more understandable; it was consistent with Marxist-Leninist ideology, and with the Chinese and Cuban revolutionary models. It also conformed to the strategy of launching surprise attacks against Zionist targets throughout the world – a strategy that relied on cooperation with foreign revolutionaries. For the PFLP, particularly the Haddad faction, mere cooperation with the radical left was not enough. Aware of its leaders' reservations, it preferred to recruit activists with radical left-wing, preferably anarchist, leanings, and deploy them directly as 'ideological mercenaries'.[138]

---

[136] 'Despite the label "terrorist" that many tried to hang round our necks, everywhere we found young people who were sympathetic, and eager to learn more about our cause', wrote Abu-Sharif in his memoirs. See Abu-Sharif and Mahnaimi, *Tried by Fire*, p. 97.

[137] See, for example, the atypical RAF document *The Black September Operation in Munich, the Strategy of the Anti-Imperialist Struggle*, (1972).

[138] The PFLP splinter groups, such as Ahmed Jibril's PFLP-GC and Abu-Ibrahim's 15 May faction, used to recruit criminal mercenaries or ordinary passengers who did not know their true role. Abu-Sharif described this process: 'Many of these dissatisfied youths were active, as students, in their university unions. Thousands were members of anti-capitalist parties. Many wanted to do something more concrete than just "show solidarity" with a given cause … virtually all saw the Palestinian liberation movement as the number one revolutionary cause in the world at the time.

B.   Influence of the variables at the organizational level

As seen in Chapter 2, Fatah and the PFLP fit the definition of non-state nations (NSNs).[139] This status became institutionalized immediately after the Six Day War, due to the military weakness of the Arab nations, and the subversion of the governing regimes there. From 1969-70 both Fatah and the PFLP enjoyed considerable freedom of action as the vanguard of the anti-Israel struggle (Hypothesis 9). Changes in the regional balance of power, the attenuation of the conflict between the conservative and progressive Arab states, and the growing intervention of the oil-rich countries in the Israeli-Arab conflict, enabled the PLO to maximize its tactical options. The freedom to carry out cross-border attacks and develop a revolutionary policy was contingent on the weakness of the Arab states, and triggered a confrontation between the Palestinians (particularly the PFLP), and the Arab (particularly the Hashemite) regimes.[140]

Fatah and the PFLP subsequently agreed to strengthen ties with West European revolutionary organizations and to open their camps in Jordan (and later in Lebanon) to those interested in receiving military training. Their publications of this period are replete with expressions of solidarity with revolutionary organizations around the world. Any manifestation of solidarity with the Palestinian struggle, whether ideological or practical, was eagerly welcomed. Nevertheless, a certain amount of political caution was retained, and the European terrorist organizations were never mentioned by name, but were rather vaguely referred to as 'revolutionary forces in the Western capitalist states'. Even the Marxist-Leninist PFLP did not dare publicly identify with these organizations. In effect, the PFLP, in line with its NSN status, showed the same degree of prudence *vis-à-vis* its enemies in the reactionary Arab states.[141] This policy intensified over the years, especially after the Six Day War and was facilitated by the widespread use

---

They saw it as a cause to which they should give help, and from which they could receive help. Haddad's spectaculars proved that a relatively small number of committees and well-organized people could kick the West up the backside, and get away with it. This was a magnet to these fledgling Che Guevaras.' See Abu-Sharif and Mahnaimi, *Tried by Fire*, p. 65.

[139] See Judy S. Bertelsen, 'The Palestinian Arabs', in Judy S. Bertelsen (ed.) *Non-state Nations in International Politics. Comparative System Analysis* (New York: Praeger Publishers, 1977), pp. 19-22.

[140] Macintyre called this period 'the freedom to self-destruction'. See Macintyre, *The Palestine Liberation Organization. Tactics, Strategies and Options*, pp. 73-74.

[141] Thus, for example, in late May 1969, the PFLP attacked the oil pipe Tapeline, causing Saudi Arabia (as well as Jordan and Lebanon) serious economic harm. But several days after the PFLP spokesperson declared that this was 'one of the most important strategic blows struck by the armed Palestinian struggle ... against American imperialist interests', the organization denied involvement in the attack, for fear of losing the financial aid it received from Saudi Arabia via the PLO. See the Lebanese *Al-Nahar* of 1 and 7 June 1969.

of aliases by Palestinian terrorist groups operating abroad. This enabled PFLP leaders to publicly renounce terror, while the facts spoke otherwise.[142]

VII. SUMMARY

There is no evidence of any public Palestinian support for a European or Western terrorist organization. On the contrary, when questioned, Palestinian leaders were quick to deny any links with European organizations. Arafat, for example, emphatically denied any ties with the BR following the murder of Aldo Moro, although several months later, Fatah supplied the BR with large amounts of weapons.

After 1970 the Palestinians learnt the hard way that the national interests of their host countries or sponsor states were not to be trifled with, and that they had to tread a delicate tightrope between courting Western support and continuing their revolutionary strategy.[143]

Growing international recognition of the Palestinian cause after the Yom Kippur War forced the Palestinian organizations, particularly Fatah, to justify their roles as political actors on the international scene. The years 1974-75 were characterized by growing Soviet support for the Palestinians' national demands, Italian and Japanese recognition of Palestinian rights, Indian recognition of the PLO diplomatic status, and the appearance of Arafat before the UN General Assembly. Fatah cultivated a moderate image, and apart from brief lapses occasioned by the Camp David accords and the Lebanese War, renounced international terror and cut off all ties with European terrorist organizations. Likewise, the PFLP effectively abandoned international terror, with a few exceptions (attempted operations and even ties with local terrorist organizations).[144]

---

[142] In March 1972 Habash had claimed in a press conference that since the friendly socialist states showed no understanding for hijackings, the PFLP had decided to renounce such operations. After a plane in which Habash himself was supposed to fly was intercepted by the Israeli air force, Habash declared that world public opinion was not prepared to understand the special cause of the Palestinian people, whose victory would be assured by all means. See Merari and Elad, *Palestinian Terror Abroad*, pp. 44-45.

[143] See Macintryre, *The Palestine Liberation Organization. Tactics, Strategies and Options*, pp. 75-76.

[144] Thus, for example, in 1989 a local makeshift terrorist organization called 'Apple' was discovered in Denmark. This organization had ties with the PFLP in the 1970s and 1980s, and donated money to the PFLP from the proceeds of an armed robbery it had carried out in Denmark. It is noteworthy that the Danish comrades were under the illusion that they were still working for the Haddad faction. See '"Réseau Apple": un groupe maoïste européen au service du FPLP, 1968-88', *Terrorisme et Violence Politique*, No. 5, May 1992.

Nonetheless, Palestinian organizations still enjoyed freedom of action in Lebanon, where their camps formed an extra-territorial enclave. The Lebanese Civil War merely extended their sphere of influence and areas of control in this fragmented country, enabling them to attract and train terrorists from many other countries, until the outbreak of the Lebanese War in 1982. The vast majority of trainees came from the Third World. Barely any evidence was found by the IDF in these camps concerning European trainees. PFLP camps in South Yemen, approved of by the ANM influenced revolutionary regime, did train terrorists from West Germany, Spain, Holland and elsewhere. Evidently these camps were closed down following their discovery in the early 1980s, possibly as a consequence of the Lebanese War.[145]

In conclusion, the status of Fatah and the PFLP as international actors of NSN stature had a definitive bearing on their international terror policy, in general, and on their ties with Western terrorist organizations, in particular. Fatah, the foremost and most moderate organization within the PLO, was particularly sensitive to the international climate, as its ties with West European countries intensified after the Yom Kippur War. The PFLP took a little longer to decide to renounce its ties with West European terrorist organizations.

A striking feature of Palestinian terrorism was the geographical distance of such activity from the Middle East. Although Western Europe served as a vital springboard for attacks against Israel, both Fatah and the PFLP were also active in Asia, Africa, and especially Latin America, with its substantial Arab and Palestinian communities. Both Palestinian organizations had ties with terrorist and revolutionary organizations in Latin America, and were extremely active in the subcontinent in the early 1980s.[146]

All ties with foreign terrorist organization were bilateral. The formation of ties with each of the European organizations was complex and sensitive, a lengthy and tortuous process by which agreements and understandings were reached and implemented. This may explain why the Palestinian-European coalitions, unlike their Euro-terrorist counterparts, never attempted to broaden their scope. The leaders were aware clearly of the obstacles to reach a broader consensus, and the price each party had to pay in ideological, political, and security terms. Multina-

---

[145] In August 1995 Radio San'a announced that the Yemenite authorities had arrested the German terrorist Johannes Weinrich, an important member of the Carlos group in the 1970s and 1980s, and had extradited him to Germany. Subsequent broadcasts stated that the German terrorist enjoyed the protection of the Aden authorities even after the unification of South and North Yemen in 1990, and that Carlos too visited the country freely up till 1992 when the Yemenite authorities banned him.

[146] In the early 1970s the PFLP created a substantial infrastructure in South America, which recruited terrorists such as Carlos and the Ecuadorian Bouvier, who participated and was killed in the Entebbe operation. On the Palestinian organizations' ties with Latin America, see Alexander and Sinai, *Terrorism: the PLO Connection*, pp. 170-75.

tional contacts did take place, however, although on an ad hoc rather than on an institutionalized basis. Moreover, these contacts were far more helpful in building bilateral than multinational ties.[147]

---

[147] For example, the Italian BR's cooperation in the attempt to deliver Fatah arms consignments to the IRA and ETA was more in the nature of a one-time favour to the Palestinians, than a multilateral agreement with deeper implications.

CHAPTER 10
TESTING THE HYPOTHESES

The basic thesis of this research – the tendency of terrorist organizations to cooperate and ally when they feel threatened – was clearly corroborated, by analysis of their texts and behavior.

However, the left-wing organizations discussed in this book expressed their awareness of the threat of imperialism more explicitly; they considered Western imperialism, and more specifically the US, to be inherently aggressive and exploitive. The liberation movements of the Third World and the revolutionary movements in the West were generally depicted as weaker forces trying to free themselves from the yoke of imperialism, capitalism and colonialism. Therefore, international solidarity between these forces was presented as a natural character-istic of the world revolutionary movement.

Left-wing organizations also viewed imperialism as developing belligerent policies in times of internal or international crisis: during economical and social predicaments in the imperialist system or in one of its leading members; as a result of victories by revolutionary or progressive forces on one of the fronts; or as a result of tension with the Soviet imperialist bloc leading to imperialist warfare or even a third world war.

The picture that emerges of the right-wing organizations is more complex. Until the mid-1960s most of these organizations cooperated with the political establishment in the western democratic countries, or at least refrained from acting against it because they feared Soviet overtaking on Western Europe. The leftist revolutionary wave at the end of that decade only intensified perceptions of communist threat. In Italy, for instance, the radical right adopted a strategy of terrorism in order to permit conservative or right-wing elements to take power. However, when the Italian government decided to wage an all-out war against the right-wing terrorist organizations, the nationalist/revolutionary groups turned against it. They were even ready to cooperate with the radical left, albeit on a limited scale, to destroy the democratic regime.

This was also true for other countries such as West Germany and France, where the right-wing terrorist groups never achieved the same size or level of violence. In West Germany, right-wing terrorist groups emerged at the end of the 1970s: the German Action (Deutsche Aktion – DA) and the Hoffmann Military Sport Group (Hoffmann Wehrsportgruppe – HW).[1] DA leader Manfred Roeder

---

[1]   The two groups were responsible for a number of terrorist and arson attacks and desecrations of Jewish cemeteries. A former member of the HW perpetrated the most lethal attack in the history

argued that it was necessary to build an 'anti-imperialist and radical-democratic' country on German soil using the tactics of the radical left.[2]

Taguieff argued that the perception of the American imperialism and its vanguard, 'world Zionism', as common enemies of the radical right and left was characteristic of all right-wing radical movements in Europe, mainly those in France, Italy and Germany.[3] This perception also developed in the radical right-wing movements active in Eastern Europe after the fall of the communist regimes.

In the case of the nationalistic organizations the threat was much more focused: ETA's enemies were the Spanish and French imperialism. The US imperialism was in the background, but there was no intention to fight it as long as it did not represent a direct danger to the Basque national movement. The struggle concentrated against the Spanish imperialism; it turns against the French imperialism only when its security authorities acted against ETA militants living on French territory. Therefore, from the outset the international cooperation of the nationalist organizations was limited, as all efforts were focused on the country from which it wanted to secede, and not some artificial enemy camp threatening all the liberation and revolutionary movements. Clearly, there were also other reasons, as seen in Chapter 8.

The same was true about the Irish Republican Army (IRA), the most important European nationalistic organization. The direct and immediate enemy was the United Kingdom and its 'occupation army' in Northern Ireland. In the case of IRA there was another important strategic factor: the vital support from the Irish community in the US. In order to insure the flow of financial support, and in the past also arms, from the US, it was imperative not to upset the American administration and the generous donors from the Irish community.[4] Even Gerry Adams, the leftist Sinn Fein leader (the political wing of the IRA), presented the socialist

---

of modern German terrorism: On 28 September 1980, at the Oktoberfest in Munich, a 24lb bomb killed 12 people, including the bomber, and injured 312. A neo-Nazi group initially suspected to be the Wehrsportgruppe Hoffmann, claimed responsibility, although it was later discovered that the bomber had left the paramilitary group prior to the attack. See Reginald M. Rushton, 'Right-wing Extremism in the Federal Republic of Germany 1973-1995' at *Shofar FTP Archive File*, <http://www.nizkor.org/ftp.cgi/people/f/floth.joachim/rushton-report>.

[2] Ibid.

[3] See Pierre Taguieff, 'Sur un heritage tardif de l'Action Française: voyage aux origines du retournement "antisioniste" de l'antisemitisme "prosioniste"', *Cahiers Bernard Lazare*, 1998-99, Jan. 1983, pp. 17-18.

[4] On the subject of financial support of the US Irish community to IRA, see J. Bowyer Bell, *The Secret Army: A History of the IRA. 1916-1979* (4th edn.) (Dublin: Poolberg, 1990), p. 248. Financial support of the American Irish community to the IRA dwindled after 1979 when the organization assassinated Lord Mountbatten, the British military leader of the Second World War.

and anti-colonialist ideologies of the organization as directed against the British imperialism and not against the Western bloc and the US.[5]

I.   THE VARIABLES AT THE INTERNATIONAL AND REGIONAL LEVEL

Hypothesis 1

This hypothesis, regarding the influence of tension within the bipolar system, must be examined through the prism of the different definitions given to this concept by different organizations. As explained earlier, the definition of bipolarity was influenced by the basic ideology, the evaluation of major international events and the influence of internal and regional events on the standing of the organization in its country. Three kinds of bipolarity can be discerned:

(1)   The classical bipolarity – the conflict between the Western democratic bloc led by the US and the communist camp led by the USSR – was only viewed as a direct threat by radical left-wing organizations such as the RAF, AD and BR during Reagan's presidency. This stemmed form the increased military, economic and political, and not least moral strength of the West, after the fading of the 'Vietnam syndrome' and Reagan's aggressive policies against the communist bloc and international terrorism, viewed as a weapon in the hand of the Soviets. In a sense, the Reagan Doctrine against international terrorist organizations and guerrilla movements in the Third World can be viewed as a reaction to the 'international revolutionary solidarity', which, in Reagan's view, tended naturally to a strategic alliance with the USSR.[6]

This approach necessitated a gradual change in the basic ideological assumptions of the BR and AD, which had until then accused the USSR of 'social imperialism'. This process began in the Italian organization in 1981 and was completed by 1986-87, not without splits and internal crisis. As for the anarcho-communist AD, the switch in its stand *vis-à-vis* the USSR was quick and produced no major intellectual or ideological predicament. The situation differed in the case of the RAF, which led the pro-USSR gear and

---

[5]   See in this context the declarations of Gerry Adams, the Sinn Fein leader, in which he condemned the terrorist activity of the BR, AD and RAF in Gerry Adams, *The Politics of Irish Freedom* (Belfast, Brandon, 1986), pp. 128-36.

[6]   In a well-known article, US State Department Secretary George Schultz presented international terrorism as a major strategic threat against democratic countries. See George Shultz, 'New Realities and New Ways of Thinking', *Foreign Affairs*, No. 3 (1985), pp. 705-21. See also Stephen Walt, *The Origins of Alliances* (Ithaca and London: Cornell University Press, 1987), p. 34.

was accused by other European organizations of ideological sclerosis and even of serving Soviet interests. Indeed, after the fall of the communist regime in East Germany, documents of the security service Stasi provided evidence of the close relationship between RAF militants and the Soviet bloc.[7]

(2) The bipolarity concept as a conflict between the capitalist imperialist camp and the national liberation movements and the revolutionary ones, was part and parcel of the ideology of those organizations which believed in the vital role of the Third World movements in the victory of world revolution. During the 1970s, the RAF spearheaded this concept, which led it to express verbal and practical solidarity first with the Vietnamese, and later, with the Palestinian peoples. The AD also supported this stance during its first years of activity (1980-82), which explains, to a certain degree, its anti-Israeli and antisemitic activity, as a token of solidarity with the Palestinian people.

(3) A third group believed bipolarity to be a conflict between Western imperialism and a world revolutionary camp in which the Western movements had a leading role. The BR was the leading supporter of this view during the 1970s. The German RZ and M2J came close to it.[8] Generally speaking, these groups preferred to wage a revolutionary armed struggle against the regime and its targets in their own countries and were therefore less interested in international coalitions. The BR-UCC faction, which split from the BR in 1985, continued on this path until 1987, when it was eliminated by the security services.

Among the radical right-wing Italian organizations there was also disagreement as to the concept of bipolarity. When they believed that tension between the Western and Eastern blocs could lead to a Soviet take-over of Italy, they readily entered into a coalition with the most conservative anti-communist forces in the Italian establishment. Such was the case of the AN and ON during the first half of the 1970s. When, as a consequence of an ideological change the US was regarded by the NAR and TP as the main enemy, they attempted, albeit a limited way, to cooperate with Palestinian and other national liberation movements.

---

[7]   Inge Viett, one of the main militants of M2J made contact with the Stasi in 1980 and arranged the 'retreat' of eight activists in East Germany. She herself retired to Dresden in 1982 and was arrested in 1990 after the reunification of Germany. See also the declaration of the former Stasi chief, E. Mielke, about the asylum given in East Germany to RAF militants in the 1980s, *Reuters*, 30 Aug. 1992.

[8]   As explained in Chapter 3, the international branch of the RZ acted mostly as an operational arm of the PFLP, and not a real component of the parent organization.

The nationalistic organizations, ETA and IRA, were not bothered by the large imperialist camp, neither did they consider the global scene in terms of clashing blocs, although no doubt that they were aware of the real international situation. During a short period of time, the ETA identified with Third World liberation movements, but the solidarity it expressed did not ripen in a true coalition with any other organization, besides the long and intense relationship with the Algerian revolutionary regime.

The Palestinians estimated that the tension in the bipolar system rather served their interests, because the USSR and its satellites needed allies in the Middle East and conflict in the region helped Soviet strategic penetration into the Arab world. They also understood that détente and compromise between the two superpowers could be achieved at the expense of Palestinian vital interests. In this sense, their approach differed from that of the radical left-wing organizations. Some BR leaders even judged that Fatah provided them weapons as a service to the Soviets, which were interested to weaken the democratic regimes in key Western countries.[9]

Therefore, perceived threats deriving from bipolar tension were insufficient cause for organizations to cooperate. In order to strive to a coalition the organizations in question needed to share evaluations regarding the kind of bipolarity, the degree of tension, and its direct threat to the organization itself.

Hypothesis 2

The rift between ideologically similar powers, in this case the USSR and communist China, and the emergence of new revolutionary and ideological foci, influenced mainly those organizations which regarded the Third World liberation movements as the vanguard of world revolution, and which felt threatened when the tension between this camp and the Western imperialist camp grew. Fatah and the PFLP belonged to this group, as they identified strongly with the liberation movements, and considered themselves disciples of the Maoist, Cuban or Algerian strategy. During the 1970s the RAF aligned itself clearly with this camp and found common ground with the Palestinians, which led to mutual support. From the beginning of the 1980s, the RAF passed to the camp of those organizations that believed in the central role of the revolutionary movements in the West and as a result the cooperation with the Palestinian comrades diminished considerably.

---

[9] See the indictment by Judge Imposimato in the trial against BR militants, Tribunale di Roma. Ordinanza di rinvio a giudizio. Il Giudice Istruttore Dott. Ferdinando Imposimato. Ordinanza-Sentenza n. 54/80 AGI contro Arreni Renato + 50. Estrato relativo a 'Collegamenti delle BR con l'estero' (16072/79 RGPM), p. 242.

The situation was somewhat different for the French AD, which began its terrorist activity during a period when radical leftist circles considered China an objective ally of American imperialism. However, the Maoist past of several of its leaders and the direct contact with 'representatives' of the Third World – the Algerian militants of the organization and the immigrants' community in France – draw it closer to this camp and influenced its strategy in its initial years.

Paradoxically, the Italian radical right-wing organizations of the nationalist/ revolutionary kind felt closer to the Third World and Maoism than the leftist BR. Perhaps this is the reason that expressions of solidarity with the Palestinians figured more frequently in the few right-wing documents than in the long BR manifestos. It is noteworthy that the nationalist organizations, namely the ETA and IRA, paid only lip service to solidarity with other liberation movements, rarely mentioned it and almost never implemented it.

Hypothesis 3

Regional wars and tensions perceived as a threat to a terrorist organization or to the same ideological camp encouraged it to seek allies and to reinforce cooperation with other organizations. However, as in the case of bipolar tension, the organization assessed such cooperation first and foremost in light of its own strategy and interests.

Terrorist organizations were primarily influenced by the policies of their own governments during regional conflicts and violent international events. For example, the radical Italian groups, of the left and right alike, adopted strategies concerning the Middle East which contradicted the policy of the Italian government. Italian military intervention on behalf of the US or NATO, and Italian involvement in the Middle Eastern peacekeeping forces (in Sinai after the Israeli-Egyptian agreement and in Lebanon after the Lebanon War), provoked counteractions by the radical leftist terrorists. The murder of Leamon Hunt, for example, was intended to disrupt the Italian government policy and to indicate support for the Palestinians and the Lebanese Left.

The RAF, RZ and M2J were deeply influenced by the American military presence on West Germany soil and what they saw as direct German support to the destruction of the Vietnamese people by the US. This led to many terrorist attacks against US targets in West Germany. Assistance to the Palestinians was granted against the background of the military clampdown on their forces in Jordan by the Hashemite regime during the events of 1971-72, or by the Syrians and the Christians during the civil war in Lebanon in the mid-1970s. The Euro-terrorist strategy was adopted first by the RAF, then by the AD, and finally by the BR-PCC, in response to the deployment of US nuclear missiles on European soil and the European rearmament effort against the communist bloc, promoted by

President Reagan. The RAF-AD coalition tightened as a reaction to the political/military/economic axis between France and West Germany, perceived as the dominant forces behind the aggressive policy of NATO and the EC.

By contrast, the nationalistic organizations showed little interest in regional conflicts, even when these occurred close to their territory. The central matter for them was the struggle against the occupying power – Spain in the case of ETA, Britain in the case of the IRA. The ETA used terrorism against French interests when it felt threatened by its government, but did not act against France during its military interventions in Chad, Libya or Black Africa. In the case of the IRA, since there was no other enemy besides Britain, the Irish organization did not attack targets of other countries. On rare occasions the IRA did target British interests in Europe, mainly military bases in West Germany, but always took care not to hurt American or local targets.[10]

It is obvious that the Palestinian organizations were directly influenced by violent events in the Middle East. For instance, Fatah's failure to wage guerrilla warfare in the West Bank pushed the PFLP to initiate a new front of international terrorism. Likewise, the bloody events of September 1970 in Jordan influenced Fatah's terrorist strategy, while the results of the Yom Kippur War led to the dismantling of Black September and a review of the strategy concerning a possible political solution of the conflict. It is noteworthy that after the peaks of 1975-77, international terrorism by both Fatah and the PFLP diminished considerably due to growing pressure from Western Europe and the Reagan administration, and the damaging consequences of the civil war in Lebanon.

Hypothesis 4

International and regional cooperation between security forces against terrorist organizations encouraged their tendency to form coalitions, although this was not always reflected in their documents. In many cases terrorist organizations

---

[10] There were 53 acts of IRA terrorism during 1970-90, in places as diverse as Washington DC and Kinshasa, Zaire. However, the overwhelming majority of these acts occurred in Western Europe. In a detailed analysis of the period 1968-83, Michael McKinley concluded that Irish Republican terrorists either did not intend, or perhaps were unable, to extend the conflict beyond the borders of Northern Ireland under 'normal' circumstances. His view, at least to the end of 1983, is that out-of-theatre operations were abnormal. It seems that the IRA chose to conduct operations in Europe because it combined opportunities not available elsewhere with considerably less pressure from the security forces. The non-UK target breakdown for 1970-90 reveals that 39 were military, 13 involved official facilities or personnel (all pre-1982), and one incident where a Belgian police officer was shot. There were no incidents where civilian targets were deliberately struck. See 'Irish Nationalist Terrorism Outside Ireland: Out-of-Theatre Operations 1972-1993', *Commentary* No. 40, A Canadian Security Intelligence Service publication, Feb. 1994.

preferred to describe their struggle as a war against the 'imperialist military machine' rather than against the police or security services.

The 1978 decision of BR leaders to enter a coalition with Fatah was adopted against the background of growing cooperation between European security agencies and the suicide of imprisoned RAF leaders. Given that the BR was at the height of its operational strength and had threatened the Italian regime by kidnapping and murdering Aldo Moro, this decision proves how insecure its leaders felt in face of the regional coordination of European police and intelligence forces against terrorist organizations.[11] One of the AD last terrorist attacks which targeted the Interpol headquarters in Paris, the symbol of international police cooperation, was also a token of solidarity with other terrorist organizations.

The nationalistic organizations did not bother much about the international police cooperation, as they were far less active abroad. It would have seemed natural for the ETA to look for an ally in France in the fight against the French imperialism. However, there was no such organization active in France until 1980 and the Basque organization itself enjoyed a great deal of leniency from the French authorities. This official approach towards ETA changed in 1984-85 but did not lead to any coalition with the AD, although some of its leaders had links with Spanish anarchist groups. It seems that the basic nature of the two organizations, the separatism of the ETA and the AD Euro-terrorism strategy was not conducive to such a coalition.

The relationship between the Palestinians and the European authorities and the international cooperation against the extensive Palestinian terrorist activity on the continent were influenced by two major factors: the need for political and diplomatic recognition by the Europeans; and the critical importance of terrorist activity against Israeli targets on the continent and of European territory as a basis for attacks against Israel itself. Therefore, the Palestinians, primarily Fatah, had to pursue a subtle and intricate policy *vis-à-vis* the European countries where they acted. As a result, the Palestinian organizations reached agreements with several European countries committing themselves to refrain from terrorist activity on their territories.[12] In spite of such agreements and the alertness of the European

---

[11]   In fact, the Italian authorities found an original solution to the problem of internal terrorism: they promulgated laws which encouraged members of these organizations to renounce the armed struggle in exchange for lesser penalties or even freedom (the so called *pentiti* – repentant – laws).

[12]   During the 1980s Palestinian and also Shi'a groups, obtained informal concessions from the French government. See Brynjar Lia and Ashild Kjok, *Islamist insurgencies, Diasporic Support Networks, and their Host States: The Case of the Algerian GIA in Europe 1993-2000*, Norwegian Defense Research Establishment, FFI Rapport – 2001/03789, p. 46. It is worth noting the affair of two Soviet anti-aircraft SA-7 missiles seized by the Italian police in Ortona. The PFLP argued in a letter to the Italian government that the missiles were owned by the organization, and were not intended for use in Italy. See note 36 in Chapter 4.

security authorities towards the Palestinian organizations, terrorist activity continued undeterred by the coordinated international effort to thwart the attacks.[13]

II.   THE VARIABLES AT THE ORGANIZATIONAL LEVEL

Hypothesis 5

The main hypothesis at the organizational level was that terrorist organizations form a coalition only if they share a joint ideological basis. This research indicates that cooperation at all levels, and, by extension, the establishment of coalitions cannot take place without the existence of a minimal ideological common denominator. It should be noted that a terrorist organization may share different ideological bases with different organizations and that these may change over time.

The coalition between the RAF and the Palestinian organizations was based on the shared assumption that revolutionary national liberation movements, in concert with revolutionary organizations in capitalist states, would bring about world revolution. The RAF drew inspiration from the neo-Marxist theorists who influenced German students in the protest movements, while Fatah drew inspiration from Fanon's premise that revolutionary organizations in the West should atone for their colonialist past by helping national liberation movements. The PFLP, for its part, supported Marxism-Leninism and felt a natural solidarity with the revolutionary movements influenced by the doctrines of Mao, Giap, and Castro. Nonetheless, as soon as international circumstances changed, the RAF leaders abandoned cooperation with the Palestinian organizations, to build the Western European Guerilla Front, in the belief that only such a front could fight American imperialism, NATO, and their European lackeys.

The attitude of the two BR factions (the BR-PCC and BR-UCC) towards Euro-terrorism and a united West European front is further proof that an ideological common denominator is a minimal prerequisite for dialogue and practical cooperation. The BR-PCC focused on the abstract concept of 'proletarian internationalism' formulated by its founders, and tried to imbue it with a concrete dimension. It undertook considerable effort, ideological experimentation, and internal and external compromises before it was ready to publish a joint strategic communiqué with the RAF. The BR-UCC, for its part, was not prepared to

---

[13]   The agreement between Fatah and the BR and the transfer of weapons to the Italian organization occurred after Yasser Arafat publicly condemned Moro's assassination and even claimed that he had tried to obtain the liberation of the Italian politician.

renounce its ideological principles, internal struggle, or socio-economic crusade on behalf of the working class, for the sake of internationalism. On the contrary, it believed that it would take many years until it found a common denominator with a potential ally, one that espoused the same, pure Marxist-Leninist principles.

Solidarity between the Italian right-wing revolutionary organizations and the Palestinian organizations was based on a number of contradictory ideological considerations: solidarity with Third World liberation movements opposed to American imperialism; antisemitism; and an admiration for certain aspects of Islam, fueled by historical memories of cooperation between the Italian Fascist and Palestinian national movements. The radical right-wing organizations outside the revolutionary/nationalist stream, however, saw Israel as a bastion against Soviet expansionism in the Middle East, and were not prepared to cooperate with the Palestinians.

The nationalist organizations, on the whole, did not share any common ideology with the Palestinian organizations. Their ideological compatibility was predicated on ethnic solidarity. Thus, for example, ETA's ties were mostly with organizations with a Celtic background, such as the IRA and the Breton secessionist organizations in France.[14]

As stated at the beginning of this book, and as demonstrated throughout it, some ideologies lend themselves to coalitions between terrorist organizations, while others inhibit them.

Hypothesis 6

This hypothesis showed how anarchist or anarcho-communist organizations, more than others, tend towards coalitions and cooperation, even in the sensitive field of operational cooperation. Indeed, the members of the largest and most efficient coalition – the RAF and AD – were both anarcho-communist organizations. And when the BR-PCC faction decided to establish a coalition with the RAF, it had already strayed from its Marxist-Leninist ideology, and started to adopt more anarchist tactics. Likewise, ETA's cooperation with the Palestinians (in 1972, and 1979-80) occurred as its anarchist leanings intensified, as reflected in a steep rise in the number of murderous attacks it carried out.

The same was true of the Italian radical right-wing organizations. As their anarchist and nihilist elements prevailed and the splits produced smaller factions, the strategy of armed spontaneity gained ground, and so did the tendency to view Third World national liberation movements and even Italian radical left-wing

---

[14]   On IRA's 'Celtic Conspiracy', see Sean MacStiofain, *Revolutionary in Ireland* (Edinburgh: Gordon Cremonesi, 1975), p. 53. See also the 'Brest Charter', signed in 1974 by ETA V, and Corsican and Occitan nationalists in France.

organizations as 'objective' allies. However, despite attempts at dialogue and tactical coordination with several radical left-wing elements, particularly within the autonomy movements, the Italian radical right never expressed any verbal solidarity with the Palestinians or the IRA, for example.

The Wadi Haddad faction, particularly when it split from the PFLP, may be considered an anarchist organization inasmuch as, unlike the parent organization, it lacked a coherent ideology, a broad activist base and hierarchical institutions. Like the nineteenth century Russian anarchist organizations, action became the only way for it to deliver its ideological message. The Wadi Haddad faction therefore had a common language with the more anarchist elements of the RAF, RZ, and MJ2, and recruited members of diverse ethnic origins. These trends were even more noticeable among the offshoots of the Wadi Haddad faction. Thus, for example, the Fifteen May Organization, which was active in the early 1980s, used suitcases packed with explosives as its main modus operandi in order to bring down civilian planes.[15]

Hypothesis 7

The historical evolution of the BR confirms the hypothesis that radical left-wing revolutionary organizations whose main aim is to overthrow the governments in their countries, tend not to form alliances with other organizations. When the BR emerged, most of its members, out of solidarity with the working class, left the world of academia and politics to work in the large factories in northern Italy. There they joined the autonomous trade unions, or fought against the trade unions controlled by the despised parties on the left (PCI) and right (MSI).

As terrorist violence escalated in the mid-1970s BR activists went underground, gradually loosing contact with the working class, which they professed to defend. As the threat to their leaders' lives became more tangible, the BR, like the RAF before them, approached the large Palestinian organizations for help. However, the BR leadership was not yet ready to abandon its main agenda – spearheading the socio-political revolution for the working class.

The gradual devolution of BR organizational structures in the early 1980s and the shrinking of its social base led to ideological splits, and caused the BR-PCC to choose international struggle as its strategy. However, despite constant calls for international solidarity and cooperation, it was only after much soul-searching, that the BR-PCC finally formed a coalition with the RAF. Years of indoctrination concerning its role as vanguard of the working class undoubtedly caused the BR-PCC, like its parent organization, to be wary of joining an international coalition.

---

[15]   See Guy Bechor, *Lexicon of the PLO* (Tel Aviv: Ministry of Defense Publishing House, 1991), p. 51.

The BR-UCC, which stuck more to the original BR ideology, was not inclined to seek partners outside Italy. Instead, it stressed the importance of promoting social and economic issues closest to the interests of the working class. The organization vetoed coalitions with organizations that did not espouse Marxist-Leninist ideology, preferring to wait until other organizations realized the error of their ways, and embraced the 'correct' ideological path.

The Italian radical right focused on seizing power or undermining the existing regime. Irrespective of the type of strategy it used at various periods, it never resorted to international terror.

ETA, the Basque nationalist separatist movement, cooperated minimally with other terrorist organizations. Its attempts, from the early 1970s, to win working class support in the Basque country, were among the factors that influenced its tendency to avoid international ties and cooperation with other terrorist organizations.

Hypothesis 8

The behavior of ETA corroborated the hypothesis that nationalist terrorist organizations are less likely to form international coalitions with other groups. Its separatism and distrust of other revolutionary groups, both at home and abroad, alienated it from those that sought alliances as a means of consolidating their national/international standing. Although ETA had sporadic contacts and cooperated with other organizations (the PFLP, and the Italian PL, for example), these usually happened at times of extreme weakness.

Although IRA leaders were sympathetic towards other nationalist struggles (the Welsh in Britain, the Bretons in France, and the Cypriots and Kenyans against Britain), this sympathy was limited to lukewarm political ties or mutual aid between IRA and Cypriot EOKA prisoners being held in British jails. Although Vietcong and Cuban guerrillas fired the imagination of Irish leaders, the sole expression of their admiration for revolutionary national liberation movements was graffiti they painted on the walls of Belfast in support of the South African ANC, or the PLO fighters deported from Beirut.[16] According to MacStiofain, IRA leader in the early 1970s, the organization's main goal was to bring about a 'true republic, the Irish republic, without the British, without partition, and without a neo-colonialist compromise'.[17] Although Gerry Adams, IRA leader from the late 1970s to this day, called for the establishment of an anti-imperialist

---

[16] Adams points to the slogans on Belfast's walls as 'proof of the strength of anti-imperialist feeling and international instincts.' See Adams, *The Politics of Irish Freedom*, p. 131.

[17] See MacStiofain, *Revolutionary in Ireland*, p. 161.

movement, what he really meant was a movement uniting all social classes in Northern Ireland.[18]

While both Fatah and the PFLP are classified in this book as nationalist organizations, their struggle had an internationalist aspect too. Fatah's affiliation with the anti-imperialist Third World movement was far more concrete and enduring than ETA's brief flirtation with the idea of *tercermundismo*. Although PFLP support for pan-Arabism and a Palestinian social revolution based on Marxist-Leninist principles never materialized, it strengthened its solidarity with revolutionary organizations and movements.

Hypothesis 9

The hypothesis that NSNs (non-state nations) tend to act as independent political entities when cooperating or allying with other terrorist organizations, especially on the level of international policy, was corroborated by the policies of Fatah and the PFLP after the Six Day War.

The relatively close cooperation between the Palestinians and other terrorist organizations, some of whose members had trained in their camps in Jordan and Lebanon, was prompted mainly by NSN considerations. The Palestinian desire for international recognition drove them to seek allies, even among non-governmental and marginal elements in Western states. For Fatah and the PFLP, such recognition was a significant achievement, given their difficult situation before the Six Day War. As it turned out, the Fatah and PFLP leaders were right. Their enhanced status among the revolutionary movements enabled them to replace the Vietcong in the consciousness of the communists, Third World and left-wing organizations in Western capitalist countries.

After the Yom Kippur War, this policy changed. Fatah jumped on the political bandwagon by abandoning international terror (except within Israel and the occupied territories), i.e., limiting or freezing contacts with terrorist organizations in the West. The PFLP, however, Fatah's opponent within the PLO, felt fewer obligations as an NSN and stepped up its use of international terror and cooperation with international terrorist groups in order to undermine the peace negotiations prior to the Geneva conference, especially after the outbreak of civil war in Lebanon. The situation balanced out again after Sadat's visit to Jerusalem in November 1977, when Fatah decided to resume international terror albeit temporarily and strengthen its ties with the Italian BR.

International pressure on the PFLP, particularly by the USSR and Fatah's entrenchment in South Lebanon also influenced the dwindling cooperation between Palestinian and European organizations. From the early 1980s, the

---

[18]   See Adams, *The Politics of Irish Freedom*, p. 135.

leaders of both organizations appeared as potential 'heads of state' – Fatah courted the West and moderate Arab states, while the PFLP sought links with the USSR and the communist bloc. Fatah's eagerness to draw closer to the US after the Lebanese War, and the tough measures adopted by the US against terror sponsor states (Libya and Syria), which undoubtedly deterred the PFLP, strengthened the trend to refrain from international terror, or at least to avoid being caught collaborating with terrorist organizations in Europe – the main field of PLO political action.

Even during periods of close cooperation between the Palestinian and European organizations in the 1970s, the Palestinians used fictitious names and sought to deny evidence of such cooperation exposed following failed terrorist attacks. Neither organization, and especially Fatah, referred publicly to solidarity or cooperation with 'outlawed' terrorist organizations, as distinct from national liberation movements, such as the Vietcong or the South African ANC, in order to preserve their international image, and maintain political dialogue with West European countries.

Hypothesis 10

No significant dependency between the donor and the recipient organization was found, although the power relationship between the different pairs of organizations was generally unequal in terms of size and available resources.

In the RAF-Palestinian dyad, Fatah and the PFLP enjoyed a clear advantage over the smaller German organization; during the period of cooperation between them (1970-77), most of the help came from the Palestinian side. In the 1980s the tables were turned, with the RAF mostly supporting the Palestinian organizations. However, this support was largely symbolic, restricted to references to Palestinian 'martyrs' when the RAF claimed responsibility for attacks in Germany. There were certainly no signs of ideological or strategic dependency on the Palestinian organizations. On the contrary, towards the end of the 1970s, when the RAF leadership realized that the Third World revolutionary movements had lost their momentum, it switched its strategy in favor of a European terrorist front directed against NATO and the American nuclear presence in Europe. This explains why the RAF restricted itself to verbal expressions of solidarity with the Palestinian organizations during the second period of its activity (1980-90).

In the case of the RZ-PFLP dyad, the asymmetry is even more striking, and the RZ, unlike the RAF, was the donor organization. Not only was the help offered by the RZ to the PFLP of the most important and sensitive kind (operational assistance), it even used a modus operandi that it was reluctant to use in its own strategy in Germany. This would seem to support the premise that the RZ was actually 'hiring out its services' to the PFLP, in exchange for generous material aid and perhaps also in approval of its adventurous and anarchical spirit. Any other thesis would fail to explain the disproportionate RZ support for the PFLP.

Cooperation between the BR and Fatah was more or less evenly balanced, as reflected in their agreement that the Palestinians could use some of the weapons supplied to the BR for their own purposes. In practice, the BR used all the weapons itself, and even distributed some to other Italian organizations without consulting with the Palestinians or offering any compensation. Furthermore, the BR refused the Palestinians' request to attack Israeli targets, and the stronger Palestinian side had far more to lose, politically, over this large arms deal than the BR. Indeed, once the case reached the Italian courts, injunctions were issued against Yasser Arafat and Abu Iyad.

In considering the AD-Palestinian duo, it should be noted that AD attacks against Israeli and Jewish targets were partly motivated by solidarity with the Palestinians (as well as internal reasons), yet it received no material help in return. Likewise, the Palestinians never rewarded the Italian radical right-wing organizations, Terza Posizione and NAR, for their support of the Palestinian cause, although this was restricted to the ideological and propaganda level. In the case of ETA, the opposite was true: Palestinian organizations helped train ETA activists, and may even have supplied them with weapons. It would appear, however, that ETA did not repay them other than by publishing a statement in support of the Palestinian struggle.

What is striking about the RAF-AD coalition, the only true coalition frame-work that existed during the period in question, is that although the two parties were unequal in strength (the RAF being experienced with considerable resources at its disposal, while the AD was small, divided and unstructured), their opera-tional contribution to the joint strategy was virtually equal. Moreover, the AD was not beholden to the stronger organization. When it realized that the only joint attack perpetrated by the two organizations, in which an American serviceman was murdered, could tarnish its 'revolutionary' image, it abandoned the common front, without a public announcement or concern for the RAF's reaction. AD leaders may also have been prompted by their wish to intensify their struggle on behalf of the working class.

Hypothesis 11

This hypothesis claimed that a coalition between more than two terrorist organi-zations is viable only when they share geographical proximity, an ideological affinity and a common strategic goal. Although the Palestinian organizations cooperated or had ties with many organizations, including some outside Europe, they were evidently not interested in setting up a broad-based, institutionalized coalition.[19] The only evidence of an attempt at multilateral cooperation was when Fatah asked the BR to transfer some weapons to the IRA and ETA. According to most sources, including the BR leader himself, no weapons were actually transferred to the nationalist organizations, and no significant ties existed between the BR and these organizations.

The only serious attempt to set up a multilateral coalition – the West European Guerrilla Front – was sponsored by the RAF. This ultimately failed despite lofty calls for revolutionary proletarian solidarity by each of the member organizations. The Spanish GRAPO and the Portuguese FP-25 were never considered possible candidates for membership of the front. Geographical distance and differing socio-political conditions apparently account for the lack of contact and under-standing between them and other European organizations. GRAPO eventually became the staunchest opponent of the West European Guerrilla Front, and even published a tract denouncing its proposed strategy.[20]

This leaves four organizations that were geographically close, and could, in theory, have joined the West European Guerrilla Front. The Belgian CCC rejected the front on ideological grounds, despite the unrelenting efforts of their leader, Pierre Carette, on behalf of the AD leaders and RAF prisoners. Despite the help it offered the RAF and AD (explosives and printed propaganda), the CCC made a point of disclaiming membership of the coalition. And at the revolutionary conference held in Frankfurt in 1986, the Belgians were the most vehement opponents of the RAF's proposed strategy.

The three organizations – the RAF, AD, and BR-PCC – seemed natural candi-dates for constituting the Euro-terrorist nucleus, but even they failed in this task. For a start, the ideological differences between the BR-PCC and the RAF held back the BR-PCC from joining the coalition, despite the fact that the idea of the West European Guerrilla Front had been conceived by both organizations before 1984.[21] When, at last, the differences – particularly regarding the front's position on the USSR and the communist bloc – were ironed out, the two organizations could not agree on common targets of their terror campaign, as reflected in the document describing the dialogue that led to the publication of the joint commu-niqué in September 1988. When these strategic differences were finally resolved, the coalition was no longer viable: the AD had quietly dropped out of the coalition and was subsequently liquidated; the BR-PCC faced a similar fate; and the RAF had become significantly worn. It can be inferred from the above that ideological affinity and geographical proximity are not sufficient per se for the

---

[19]   See Y. Alexander and J. Sinai, *Terrorism: The PLO Connection* (N.Y.: Crane and Russack, 1989). pp. 166-90.
[20]   The document was published in March 1987 under the title 'Texts for Debating the European Revolutionary Movement.' See Pluchinsky, *Europe's Red Terrorists*, p. 43.
[21]   Ibid., p. 42.

establishment of a multilateral coalition. A consensus regarding the coalition's proposed strategic policy is clearly vital.

Hypothesis 12

This hypothesis told of racist and antisemitic preconceptions as influential factors predisposing some terrorist leaders, at both ends of the political spectrum, to espouse a policy of cooperation with Palestinian organizations and/or to carry out attacks against Israeli and Jewish targets. This trend was particularly evident in the case of the RAF and RZ, whose antisemitic leaders attempted to legitimize their anti-Jewish attacks by cloaking their views in an ideological garb, and introducing antisemitic themes into their ideological and strategic tracts. A good example of this trend is the RAF document expressing support for Black September's attack on Israeli athletes at the Munich Olympics. Even the die-hard terrorist Hans Joachim Klein was shocked when he heard that his RZ comrades had decided to separate the Jewish passengers from the non-Jewish ones, after the hijacking of the Air France plane to Entebbe. For him, this act was reminiscent of Nazi 'selections' in Auschwitz, and no ideological rationalization could persuade him of the justice of this act.

Similarly, the AD attempted to justify a series of anti-Israeli and anti-Jewish attacks in 1982 by comparing IDF actions against Palestinian units in Lebanon to Nazi and fascist actions, and by setting up 'Jewish combatant units' to fight 'the Zionist state' and the interests of the Zionist-Jewish lobby in France. Although Max Frerot's attack against Bank Leumi in Paris in 1985 was carried out in the name of a Lebanese suicide bomber, Frerot's antisemitism evidently motivated it.

The Italian organizations steered clear of the cheap and brutal brand of antisemitism espoused by their German and French counterparts. The BR, with its solid ideological base, avoided   antisemitism in explaining its pro-Palestinian strategy or in justifying its political and strategic opposition to Israeli policy in the Middle East.

Even when antisemitism was a basic component of the pro-Palestinian or pro-Islamic attitudes of Italian radical right-wing organizations, it never translated into physical attacks against local Jews or Israeli targets. One wonders whether the different policies of the three organizations were culturally determined – as were the different policies of their respective countries towards Jews during the Second World War.

As indicated in Chapter 2 the Palestinian organizations understood full well the advantages of using antisemitic images in their propaganda. They, thereby, helped implant antisemitic motives into the ideologies of the European radical left-wing organizations. It suited them to dialogue and cooperate with German radical left-wing organizations and recruit them in order to attack Zionists and

Jews. For the same reasons, Fatah had no compunctions in cooperating with the neo-Nazi Hoffmann Military Sports Group (Hoffmann Wehrsportgruppe – HW) or allowing members of the group to train in Fatah camps in Lebanon, even though it was simultaneously fostering close ties with the communist bloc and with revolutionary left-wing movements throughout the world.

III.   SUMMARY

This study of international coalitions between terrorist organizations was sparked by concern among many researchers, policy-makers, and the public in general, that a coalition between terrorist organizations might destabilize the international system. The lack of research on this issue presented a serious but stimulating challenge, and required a major commitment on both the theoretical and empirical levels.

The basic hypothesis was that terrorist organizations are prepared to cooperate or set up coalitions with organizations in other countries when they feel threatened. The main questions addressed were: what kind of threat determines one terrorist organization to cooperate with others, and what are the conditions that allow such cooperation to mature?

Evidence suggests that the kind of threats that encouraged cooperation or the formation of coalitions were usually threats at the international level. Tension within the bipolar system, armed conflicts, regional tension, and international cooperation between security forces were the main factors predisposing terrorist organizations to unite. Internal factors also played a part – sometimes internal weakness, whether intrinsic or due to crackdowns by the security forces, estrangement from the community or class the organization purported to represent – or even a conscious decision to chose an international strategy suited to the conditions of the moment.

And yet, although all the terrorist organizations in the study saw significant threats to their activities and sometimes even to their very existence, only one true coalition, namely that between the RAF and AD, was ever set up, and even this barely survived for two years. The coalition between the German RAF and RZ and the Palestinian organizations turned out to be problematic – and was more in the nature of the German organizations 'volunteering' to join the ranks of the PFLP. The AD recruitment to the pro-Palestinian, anti-Israel terrorist campaign for a single season (the summer of 1982) was inspired by internal pressures rather than by an understanding with a Palestinian organization. Cooperation between the BR and Fatah lasted only about a year, was limited to logistical aid, and mainly served the interest of the Italian organization.

What factors limited the influence of the independent variables that incline terrorist organizations towards the establishment of a coalition?

As far as the variables at the international and regional level are concerned, a perceived threat was not sufficient reason for terrorist organizations to form a coalition. Also necessary was a similar perception of what constituted this threat. For example, although all the organizations (except for nationalist ones) referred to the dangers arising from tension in the bipolar system, each organization interpreted this differently. Only after a consensus was achieved – in a relatively short space of time in the case of the RAF and AD, and only after long deliberations in the case of the RAF and BR-PCC – was it possible to establish a coalition.

Similarly, the perception of the terrorist organizations of regional tension and armed conflict varied from one organization to the other. European terrorist organizations consistently opposed the strategy and policy of their respective countries towards different parts of the world, and cooperated with those revolutionary organizations that were regarded as the victims of this policy or strategy. Thus, the German organizations carried out numerous attacks against American targets in West Germany because their government supported the American armed forces that were stationed in Germany and participated in the Vietnam War. The BR favored cooperation with the Palestinian organizations after the Italian government decided, in the early 1980s, on strategic intervention in the Middle East via NATO. Even the sympathetic policy of the Italian government towards the PLO at the time was considered by the BR as a ruse by the imperialist camp, and triggered the wrath of the Italian revolutionary camp. Likewise, the Bonn-Paris axis within the European Community was largely responsible for the establishment of the RAF-AD coalition, which acted as a kind of Euro-terrorist counter-axis.

The rift within the communist bloc between the USSR and the People's Republic of China affected the European terrorist organizations differently, depending on their situation at the time. Its main consequence, however, was the emergence of new revolutionary foci (Cuba, Vietnam, Algeria and Palestine) to which the terrorist organizations were drawn. From 1972, after its rapprochement with the US, and especially in the 1980s, when it made moves towards the free market economy, China gradually began to lose its appeal among the revolutionaries.

The effect of the threat represented by the internal and external security forces was clearly demonstrated in two cases. The threat of life imprisonment which the entire RAF leadership faced in the autumn of 1972 led to the publication of an unusual document expressing wholehearted support for the Black September attack at the Munich Olympics, in the hope that the Palestinian organization would help obtain the release of the RAF prisoners. Similarly, the BR leadership, traumatized by the suicide of the imprisoned RAF leaders in the autumn of 1977, published a eulogy of the 'heroic Palestinian people' in its RDS of March 1978, evidently also in the hope that the Palestinian organizations would stand by it in times of trouble. In the first case, the gradual decline of the RAF during the two or three years following publication of the document prevented closer cooperation between the two organizations. In the second case, a cooperation agreement was indeed drawn up between the BR and Fatah.

In practice, the international perspective and strategy of a terrorist organization is determined by its ideology. Without a minimal common ideological denominator, cooperation – let alone a coalition – cannot exist between two terrorist organizations. As seen, certain ideologies are more likely to inhibit cooperation and mutual help. Nationalism falls into this category. The ETA, IRA and organizations on the far right were reluctant to cooperate with other organizations or with each other.

Another ideology that inhibits the formation of coalitions is orthodox Marxism-Leninism, which stresses the centrality of the working-class party, the need to work among the masses, and the importance of focusing on the internal struggle against the capitalist regime and the bourgeois class. This ideology undoubtedly influenced BR strategy for many years, despite its adoption of terror in defiance of Marxist-Leninist dogma, and its subsequent alienation from the working class. Since the main goal of the BR and its various splinter groups was the destabilization of the Italian government and the victory of the working class, it tended to shun from the international arena. It was only in the 1980s, following internal developments that the BR-PCC faction deviated from its historical path and decided, at long last, to join the international struggle.

Walt remarked that Marxist-Leninist ideology leads to schisms in countries that adopt it, because of each country's desire to spearhead the movement and determine its ideology.[22] A similar process took place with the terrorist organizations that claimed to be the true heirs of Marxism-Leninism. Each group or faction within the organization tried to influence the ideological line of the organization, which led to schisms and rifts over time. The same can be said of the radical right-wing organizations, which also found it hard to unite around a single leader.

In view of the above, terrorist organizations may find it hard to express solidarity with foreign organizations that developed under different conditions, and embody different aspects of the same ideology, or even with currents that are opposed to its ideological outlook. The RAF, for example, stated that 'solidarity is not a reflex action, as anyone who has ever acted out of solidarity will know'.[23]

---

[22]   See Walt, *The Origins of Alliances*, p. 280.
[23]   Quoted from a document entitled, 'The Black September Operation in Munich, The Strategy of the Anti-Imperialist Struggle.' See *Texte der RAF*, p. 425.

The ideological document, *Guerrilla, Resistance and Anti-Imperialism* (May 1982) stated: 'Although dialogue between anti-imperialist groups began in 1979, the same [ideological] constraints prevent the establishment of a joint action front, which should, by rights, have emerged long ago.'[24]

Conversely, it is far easier for anarchist or anarcho-communist organizations to cooperate with other organizations since they do not suffer from the same ideological rigidity, the clear-cut perception of strategic goals, the same internal hierarchy whose purpose is to preserve ideological purity and adherence to current strategy. It is not, therefore, not surprising that the only true coalition to emerge was one between two anarcho-communist organizations, namely the RAF and AD, and that the AD adapted itself to the RAF's ideological line. The anarchist nature of the AD enabled for its leaders to abandon their defunct anti-Israel and anti-Jewish strategy and to join the RAF-sponsored West European Guerrilla Front.

Ideological, political and propaganda support for Palestinian terrorist organizations by a number of radical European left-wing organizations (the RZ, RAF and AD) and the pro-Palestinian position of the radical right-wing terrorist organizations resulted from infiltration of antisemitic ideology into those revolutionary movements, as well as the racist and antisemitic preconceptions of some of their leaders. The combination of anarcho-communist ideology and antisemitism strengthened the tendency of European organizations to cooperate with national liberation movements, especially Palestinian terrorist organizations.

But are ideological factors most significant for the formation of coalitions between terrorist organizations, or are material interests and political considerations equally, or even more, important? In many cases it would appear that terrorist organizations are prepared to make ideological compromises for the sake of material or political expediency. The BR-PCC, for example, advocated support for the Palestinian organizations, irrespective of their ideology, in order to further global strategic goals and undermine imperialism in the Middle East. The BR – the most ideological organization discussed in this study – was closer to Fatah, a nationalistic movement, than to its Palestinian Marxist-Leninist counterpart, the PFLP. Similarly, the BR-PCC was prepared to abandon the Kurdish nationalist movement when the Islamic regime in Iran was in danger, in order to avoid weakening the Iranian struggle against imperialism.

Likewise, the attitude of ETA towards the French Basque nationalist organization, Itapparak, was guided by political and operational, rather than ideological considerations. For years, the Spanish Basque organization tried to prevent the development of a strong Basque secessionist movement in France despite its claim on this territory in order not to incite the French government.

---

[24] Taken from *Notes et Etudes*, No. 5 (May 1988), p. 75.

Even in coalitions between organizations that were ideologically very close, political considerations sometimes took precedence over ideological ones. With reference to its coalition with the AD, RAF leaders declared that ideological differences could be tolerated as long as they did not turn into political differences.[25] Similarly, the Belgian CCC provided the RAF and AD (and probably other organizations, too) with logistical support (explosives, stolen documents and propaganda), without renouncing its rigid ideological stand.

The Palestinian terrorist organizations made a significant contribution to international terror and to international cooperation in the field of terror. This was due to a rare combination of independent variables that favored coalitions in general, and a number of variables that were peculiar to the Palestinian organizations: an ideology that preached world revolution and the need for unity in the anti-imperialist revolutionary camp; the weakness of the Palestinian organizations in their struggle against Israel; anarchist influences, in particular within the PFLP factions; a special brand of Marxism-Leninism developed by the PFLP, that called for the use of international terror as a central strategy in the war against Israel and Zionism; the NSN status of the two organizations, particularly Fatah, and their territorial hold in Jordan and, subsequently, Lebanon; and above all, support by Arab states, which allowed the Palestinian organizations a certain freedom of action, and protected them from reprisals, thereby enabling them to survive over long periods of time.

The above was particularly true from the 1970s to the 1982 Lebanese War. The consolidation of the Palestinian organizations as NSNs (which, although restricting their use of international terror, gave them greater freedom to use guerrilla tactics along Israel's borders), and especially their decision to adopt the diplomatic option after the Lebanese War, significantly reduced their need for international cooperation with other terrorist organizations. This was especially evident when it came to cooperation with European terrorist organizations, an area in which the PLO had been quite successful. Reinforcing this trend was the fact that, from the mid-1980s, following changes in the international arena, sponsor states were no longer as able or as willing to help and defend Palestinian international terror activities.

A common ideological denominator predisposed the Palestinian organizations – particularly the PFLP, but also Fatah, during the Black September period – to help European radical left-wing organizations. A common ideological background of sorts also helped to cement cooperation between Palestinian organizations and radical right-wing organizations (especially the German ones). One should not forget that the PFLP itself was an offshoot of the radical right-

---

[25] Cited from an interview with *Zusammen Kampfen*, 4 September 1985. See Becker, *Terrorism in West Germany*, p. 54.

wing Arab Nationalists movement, and that Fatah inherited the legacy of the Jerusalem mufti, Hajj Amin Al-Husseini, who had allied with the Nazi Germany, and cooperated with the Italian Fascist regime before the Second World War. In practice, the antisemitic attitude of the Palestinian organizations was, in itself, a sufficient basis for cooperation with these organizations.

Nonetheless, political considerations also played a decisive part in the attitude of Fatah and the PFLP towards European terrorist organizations. The Palestinian organizations never forgot their political interests and image among the West European nations, the moderate Arab states, or the USSR and the communist bloc, or even world public opinion and the media. This explains their concern to conceal their ties with European terrorist organizations, their use of aliases in joint operations, or in operations designed to obtain the release of arrested comrades, and their leaders' vehement denials of cooperation with European revolutionary organizations.

Despite the extreme caution of the two large Palestinian organizations – understandable, given their NSN status and their international commitments to countries that granted the PLO diplomatic or political status – all researchers agree that the terrorist organizations that most helped the European and other terrorist organizations, at least until the 1982 Lebanese War, were the Fatah and PFLP. This help came mainly in the form of weapons (as in the case of Italian leftist groups) and the granting of safe haven to terrorists, but also, and principally, in the training of terrorists for guerrilla and terror warfare.

The Palestinians were able to offer this help because of the support they themselves received from Arab states. The Palestinian training camps open to members of the German radical left-wing organizations (from the RAF and RZ to the West-Berlin Tupamaros), the ETA, and German radical right-wing organizations, among others, were situated in Jordan, Lebanon and South Yemen. Although the Palestinian organizations were accorded a special status in Jordan (until September 1970) and Lebanon (until 1982), they also owed their status to the political support they received from Egypt, Syria, Iraq and Libya, all of which had their own reasons for wishing to boost Palestinian military power in Israel's weaker Arab neighbors.[26] This was particularly evident in the Syrian military hold on Lebanon, especially after the civil war. The South Yemen government did not even have the pretext of internal weakness to justify the freedom of action it granted the PFLP and its various factions for many years, but rather based its policy on an ideological identification with the movement from which it, too, had sprung.

---

[26] Thus, Egypt stood behind the Cairo Agreement of November 1969, which determined the PLO status in South Lebanon. See Bechor, *Lexicon of the PLO*, p. 182.

A number of incidents serve as reminder of the efforts to encourage coopera-tion with European terrorist organizations. Cairo's forgiveness of the members of Black September after the assassination of the Jordanian prime minister, Wasfi al-Tal, the enthusiastic reception in Damascus of the murderers of the Israeli Olympic athletes after their release following the hijacking of a Lufthansa plane, or the sanctuary granted to members of M2J in South Yemen, after their release following the abduction of a German politician.[27] The expulsion of the Palestinian organizations from Jordan, the ousting by the IDF of some of these organizations from Lebanon and the continued tough stance of the US towards Arab states sponsoring international terror (primarily Libya and Syria) went a long way towards restricting the scope of international terror activities by Fatah and the PFLP, as well as their cooperation with terrorist organizations particularly in Europe. It was certainly not by chance that from the early 1980s, media reports about foreign terrorists training in South Yemen ceased.[28]

Although the smaller Palestinian organizations are beyond the scope of this study, evidence suggests only isolated cases of international cooperation by the more active of these organizations, such as Fatah-Revolutionary Council, led by Sabri al-Banna, and the PFLP-General Command, led by Ahmed Jibril. Why, one wonders, did these organizations, which were very active in Europe, not try harder to cooperate with European terrorist organizations? Based on partial data only, it appears that these two organizations working in close cooperation with Arab regimes did not feel the need for support by European terrorists. Throughout the period in question, Ahmed Jibril served the goals of the Syrian regime in the Palestinian camp. Sabri al-Banna's (Abu Nidal's) organization cooperated with several Arab regimes (Iraq, Syria and Libya) on which he relied to further the ideology and goals of his organization.

It is worth noting, in this context, that the RAF, the longest-surviving Euro-pean terrorist organization (it lasted for 22 years), the most heavily involved in international cooperation, and the only one to form a real coalition, was supported by East Germany.[29] The RAF investment in, and loyalty to, the Euro-terrorist strategy of the West European Guerrilla Front, and its attempt to win other organizations over to this strategy, and to present the USSR as an ally in the

---

[27]   The international terrorist Carlos was extradited to France from Sudan only in 1993, evidently with Syria agreement, while Yemen extradited Weinrich, a senior RAF terrorist, only in 1995, in order to obtain economic concessions from Germany.

[28]   In contrast, in Lebanon the Hizballah, with Syrian approval, took over from the Palestinian organiza-tions as the main provider of training for foreign terrorists from radical Islamic organizations.

[29]   Although the only certain fact is that nine RAF members (a third of the core leadership) were granted sanctuary in East Germany (suspicions concerning their participation in terror activities there have not yet been corroborated), this in itself amounted to substantial support for an or-ganization of that size.

struggle against American imperialism and NATO, led other revolutionary organizations to suspect that it served the goals of the communist bloc. The fact that South Yemen, whose security services were trained by East German intelligence services, effectively acted as a sponsor state for members of all the German terrorist organizations in the 1970s, allowing them to train and prepare there for their most lethal attacks, also supports this thesis.[30]

The rise of radical right-wing terrorist organizations in Europe was also made possible by the support they received from radical right-wing governments. For example, after the Second World War, Franco's Spain provided asylum to thousands of Nazis and fascists from various countries. These included members of the French right-wing terrorist organization, the Armed Secret Organization (Organisation Armée Secrète – OAS), in the 1960s, and Italian neo-fascists, who were accused of perpetrating large-scale terrorist attacks in Italy in the first half of the 1970s. Under the right-wing colonels' regime Greece sheltered Italian neo-fascists, and may even have helped a number of violent radical right-wing organizations in Western Europe.

Testimonies of German and Italian terrorists indicate that when they went underground, they became totally isolated from the political and social reality of their respective countries, and were unable to form an accurate assessment of their own strength, nor that of their sister organizations or movements.

The BR leaders, for example, were extremely suspicious of RAF ties with intelligence services in the communist bloc, and suspected the RAF of serving Soviet interests. Members of the RAF doubted the discretion and professionalism of their French colleagues, and therefore did not apprise them of their operational plans. When Mario Moretti, the BR leader, met with the Fatah leadership, he apparently knew nothing about Fatah's structure, or who the leaders, with whom he had agreed to cooperate, were representing. Likewise, top-ranking BR activists were unable to say for sure which Palestinian organization had provided them with arms or ammunition. Although RAF documents praised the positive influence of radical Islamic organizations, they admitted ignorance about them.

Technical difficulties, such as lack of communication channels or intermediaries for setting up initial contacts, greatly restricted the scope of contacts between the RAF and the BR, and between the BR and the Palestinians. Ties between Fatah and the BR were severed because the BR leader, who was virtually the only one to know of these ties, lost a scrap of paper bearing the contact telephone number. Conversely, the good rapport between the RAF and AD, which later developed into a full-fledged coalition, was largely due to the fact that a number

---

[30] For example, preparations for taking over the West German embassy in Stockholm in 1975 were made in Aden, where Siegfried Haag, the RAF leader at the time, had trained.

of senior RAF activists had fled to Paris and received help from their French colleagues there.[31] Also contributing to these ties was the fact that the RAF-AD courier, born in Alsace, was not only a leading AD ideologue and intellectual, but also spoke German, had spent a long period in West Germany, and had helped the RAF.

Given the difficulties of establishing a bilateral coalition, it is hardly surprising that it proved virtually impossible to set up a multilateral, multinational coalition. The Soviet-Cuban attempt in the 1960s to build an international revolutionary camp under the Tricontinental umbrella, soon turned out to be a 'transnational myth'.[32] Even claims that contacts between the representatives of the different terrorist organizations actually existed proved credible, these never had any practical outcome.[33]

Although the RAF succeeded in organizing a large international conference of revolutionary movements in Frankfurt in 1986, most of the participants rejected the strategy proposed by the RAF. This would seem to imply that the factors inhibiting the establishment of a bilateral coalition increase exponentially in the case of multilateral coalitions. The abortive attempt to establish a West European Anti-Imperialist Guerilla Front, despite favorable national and international conditions and the similar ideologies of the constituent organizations, is the best proof of the enormous difficulty of uniting a number of terrorist organizations/movements into a common front.

It would therefore appear that the threat of a broad coalition between revolutionary terrorist organizations on the far left and right, Palestinian national liberation movements and European nationalist organizations, so feared by the democratic governments of the West in the 1970s and 1980s, has not materialized. Although Fatah and the PFLP did cooperate with European terrorist organizations in the 1970s, this cooperation was mainly bilateral and was influenced by opportunistic considerations relating to their NSN status, considerations that in the final analysis prevented cooperation from developing into real coalitions.

Revolutionary left-wing organizations in Western Europe tried to set up a broader anti-imperialist front, and worked hard to establish a common ideological base that would enable them to coordinate a strategic armed struggle. Their

---

[31] Patrizio Peci testified that the encounter between members of the BR and RAF, where the German wife of one of the BR members acted as interpreter, turned into a dialogue of the deaf due to her incompetent interpreting. According to Peci, the ties with the French organizations were closer because a number of BR activists spoke French. See Peci, *Io, l'infame*, p. 104.

[32] See Bowyer Bell, *Contemporary Revolutionary Organizations*, pp. 376-77.

[33] See for example information by Claire Sterling, one of the most important proponents of the 'conspiracy theory', on the international terrorist convention held in the Badawi camp in Lebanon Sterling, *The Terror Network*, p. 98.

attempts ended in resounding failure due to a series of ideological, organizational and technical hitches, turning the process into an obstacle course that most of the organizations were unwilling to navigate.

In view of the above, it is interesting to speculate on why democratic governments, including that of the US, perceived the formation of a broad front of terrorist organizations such a real danger.

During the 1970s, when terrorist organizations with similar ideologies began to proliferate in West Europe, many of these countries were experiencing periods of relative uncertainty. The US itself was licking its wounds after the humiliating military defeat in Vietnam, and was condemned by all the radical terrorist organizations worldwide. The frenzied eruption of Palestinian terror into this fragile arena, in the absence of any moral or political restraints, placed Western governments on the defensive and made them willing to compromise, thereby strengthening the status of the Palestinian and European terrorist organizations. This laid the groundwork for the theory of an international conspiracy backed by the USSR and its satellites and with the help of the radical Arab states against democratic regimes.

In the early 1980s, the Reagan administration launched a comprehensive plan to strengthen the US and the Western bloc against the USSR and the Warsaw Pact, to eradicate the 'Vietnam syndrome', and ultimately curb Soviet expansionism, and usher in an era of international stability through the control of all nuclear weapons and greater détente between the two superpowers. During this period George Shultz, US Secretary of State, described international terror

> as a new international strategy ... an evil weapon which the enemies of freedom were deliberately directing against the democratic states, against the interests, policies, and friends [of those states] ... in order to expel the US from regions in which it had important interests.[34]

Clearly, the West European Anti-Imperialist Guerilla Front, which gave priority to attacking American and NATO targets throughout Western Europe, while sparing all the totalitarian states in the Eastern bloc, was perceived as a Soviet tool.

In hindsight, fears that a broad coalition of revolutionary terrorist and guerilla organizations could undermine the stability of democratic regimes were clearly exaggerated. These fears were largely a psychological and political reaction to a

---

[34] See Shultz, *New Realities and New Ways of Thinking*, p. 717. On the Reagan administration's policy against international terror, see also the speech by Whitehead, the American undersecretary of state, at a convention at the Brookings Institute on 10 December 1986, in P. Whitehead, 'Terrorism: The Challenge and the Response', *Journal of Palestine Studies*, Vol. 16, No. 3(63), Spring 1987, pp. 705-721.

series of terror attacks that took place simultaneously in a number of countries – thereby fulfilling the terrorists' chief aim – the demoralization of the enemy. It would appear, that terrorist organizations succeeded, at least partly, in this goal.

The absence of intelligence necessary for an accurate evaluation of the threat constituted by the terrorist organizations also fuelled fear and suspicion. Lack of information often led to mistaken conclusions. The AD, a small organization, was long considered a faithful and active ally of the Lebanese FARL. The FARL itself was suspected of being responsible for a wave of large-scale attacks that swept Paris in 1985-1986, until it emerged two years later that Iranian-backed Islamists had carried out the attacks. Italian judges were long convinced that a Palestinian organization and/or the RAF had participated in the abduction and murder of Aldo Moro, unable to believe in the ability of the BR to carry out such a daring operation on its own.

In conclusion, the many calls for solidarity and cooperation by terrorist organizations were vague and failed to identify specific goals or plans. This vagueness could have attempted to conceal the confusion, failure, and ideological rigidity which plagued these organizations. Anarchist and anarcho-communist organizations, radical right-wing organizations, and ineffectual revolutionary Marxist-Leninist organizations that failed in their bid to seize power, were evidently most likely to form alliances with similar organizations or with national liberation movements which they perceived as likely to further the goals of a world revolution.

The strategic decision to cooperate or form a coalition with other terrorist organizations resembles the strategic decision to choose terror in the first place, often as a last resort, as suggested by Crenshaw.

This theoretical premise holds true for most of the organizations studied. Fatah decided to help the RAF when it was suffering from strategic weakness following the Black September attacks, and was desperately in need of international recognition. Similarly, the PFLP cooperation with German terrorist organizations and other revolutionary groups peaked in the mid-1970s, when it tried to foil the political settlement – which, it felt, would have disastrous consequences for the Palestinian people – in the wake of the 1973 Yom Kippur War. The RAF and AD, weak at the outset, tended to cooperate with foreign organizations throughout their existence. Nevertheless, it was not by chance that their strategic alliance occurred after the abortive anti-Israel and anti-Jewish terror campaign of the AD, and internal weakening on the part of the RAF.

As further proof of this thesis, certain European terrorist organizations decided to support, or join, the West European Guerrilla Front shortly before their liquidation by the security forces. Although the BR-PCC reached a strategic agreement with the RAF in late 1987, their joint declaration was published only a few months before the entire leadership of the Italian organization was arrested.

Similarly, the international attacks carried out by the BR-UCC and the Belgian CCC (the CCC even coordinated its attack with unidentified 'French revolutionaries') and expressions of willingness to join the Euro-terrorist front, occurred shortly before the liquidation of both organizations by the security forces in their respective countries. Ironically, therefore, a decision by a revolutionary organization to join forces with another organization and advance a qualitative step in the revolutionary struggle, presaged its demise. Under such circumstances, the decision to form a coalition was more in the nature of a swan song than a serious and informed declaration of principles.

Over and above the many ideological and organizational obstacles, technical difficulties also prevented terrorist organizations from cooperating with each other. First was the clandestine nature of the terrorist organization, which hindered the formation of close ties. The lack of ongoing contact with foreign organizations, constant suspicion, and gradual isolation from national and international developments, restricted the ability of the leaders to understand and interpret events correctly and form an accurate assessment of the advantages or otherwise of cooperation with other organizations.

The nature of ties between terrorist organizations makes it hard for them to reach agreements, ensure their implementation, or preserve their spirit. Agreements that do exist are informal, vague, and not binding in the normal sense. There is no bilateral control apparatus to arbitrate in cases of conflict or default by one of the parties, or to ensure the viability and effectiveness of the ties. The fact that even within the terrorist organizations themselves agreements are kept secret means that there is no public pressure to force the leaders to honor their commitments to other parties.

This also helps explain the absence of any significant dependency between donor and recipient organizations. Commitments cannot be made public in order to allege the duplicity of the other party. It follows, therefore, that there is no mechanism for enforcing either side to honor commitments, or indemnify the other party in the case of default. It is therefore easy to see why the BR had no compunctions about reneging on its promise to attack Israeli targets, or using weapons that were intended for the use of Fatah within Italy, or why such behavior elicited no response on the Palestinian side. Similarly, when the AD decided to abandon the joint front with the RAF, it failed to announce its intention publicly, and refused to answer questions posed by a German newspaper editor concerning its relationship with the RAF or the reason for its defection. The editors, for their part, did not see fit to inform their readers of the reason for the crisis between the two organizations.

The greatest threat presented by a coalition between terrorist organizations, in this author's opinion, is when a large, wealthy organization recruits members of another organization through a process of ideological indoctrination and material aid. An example of this kind of coalition was when the PFLP wooed members of the RZ and RAF away from the strategy of their parent organization, to become tools in the hands of the larger organization.[35]

---

[35] A similar process apparently took place among the members of the Italian COLP, a splinter group of the PL, who moved to France and joined AD, where they became among its most dangerous activists.

CHAPTER 11
THE ISLAMIST NETWORKS

The Islamic revival and the expansion of Islamist movements worldwide in the last decades is a complex and debated subject in recent Muslim and Western literature.[1] This last chapter attempts to verify a specific aspect of the Islamist movement, namely the alliances between its various factions and streams. This is based on the theory and analysis of coalitions between ideological and nationalist terrorist organizations of the 1970s and 1980s developed in previous chapters.

This chapter focuses on the World Islamic Front for the Struggle Against Jews and Crusaders (World Islamic Front – WIF), led by the now infamous Osama bin Laden.[2] This movement was chosen because of the proclaimed ambition of its leaders to form an international alliance of Sunni Islamist organizations, groups and Muslim clerics, sharing a common religious/political ideology and a global strategy of Holy War (jihad). Has this goal been achieved, and what are the reasons for the success or the failure of these endeavors?

The tragic events of 11 September 2001 (9/11), the mass attacks on the World Trade Center (WTC) in New York and the Pentagon in Washington DC, as well as the dramatic and rapid international developments which ensued hinder a comprehensive analysis of the Islamist network phenomenon. This chapter

---

[1] See note 26 in the Introduction. According to Paz, Islamic movements are those that employ non-violent means, however subversive, to restore the past—that is to found a single, unified Islamic state (*Khilafah*), whose sole constitution is the Islamic law (*Shari'ah*). Since there is no distinction in Islam between religion and politics, these groups recruit support through political efforts alongside their social-welfare and cultural activities, all of which they call *Da'wah*. In contrast, Islamists direct all their efforts toward fulfilling the duty of Jihad by violence and terror, which often necessitates excommunicating Muslim rivals and the secular parts of Muslim society along with the non-Muslim world. See Reuven Paz, *Tangled Web: International Networking of the Islamist Struggle*. The unpublished manuscript of the book has been kindly provided by the author.

[2] There is today a great bulk of literature on Osama (or Usama) bin Laden (or Ladin) and his organization or network. Unfortunately, most of the books are journalistic or superficial and lack an in-depth academic approach. Hereby the most known books: As'ad Abukhalil, *Osama Bin Laden and the Taliban: Consequences of US Foreign Policy* (New York, London: Seven Stories; Turnaround, 2002); Yonah Alexander and Michael S. Swetnam, *Usama bin Laden's al-Qaeda: Profile of a Terrorist Network* (Ardsley, NY: Transnational Publishers, 2001); Peter L. Bergen, *Holy War, Inc.: Inside the Secret World of Osama bin Laden* (New York: Free Press, 2001); Adam Robinson, *Bin Laden: Behind the Mask of the Terrorist* (Edinburgh: Mainstream, 2001); Yossef Bodansky, *Bin Laden: The Man Who Declared War on America* (Rocklin, CA: Forum, 1999); John K Cooley, *Unholy Wars: Afghanistan, America and International Terrorism* (Sterling, VA: Pluto Press, 1999); Simon Reeve, *The New Jackals: Ramzi Yousef, Osama Bin Laden and the Future of Terrorism* (Boston, MA: Northeastern University Press, 1999).

examines the coalitional trends in the Islamist movements and groups, declared members or close associates of the WIF from its inception in 1998 until 9/11.

I.   HISTORICAL BACKGROUND

According to Kramer, the Islamist forerunners, Sayyid Jamal al-Din 'al-Afghani',[3] the Muslim Brethren, and the Devotees of Islam, advocated jihad against foreigners because they 'saw foreign domination as a symptom of Muslim weakness, and its elimination as the key to Muslim power'. Those who gave priority to direct confrontation sometimes favored alliances with other national-ists, who also opposed foreign rule. The early Islamists also determined that fundamentalist Islam would have a pan-Islamic bent. From the outset, says Kramer, 'fundamentalists scorned the arbitrary boundaries of states,' and used 'the jet, the cassette, the fax, and the computer network ... [to] create a global village of ideas and action – not a hierarchical "Islamintern" but a flat "Islamin-form" countering the effects of geographic distance and sectarian loyalty.'[4]

Sunni Islamist terrorist activities emerged in Egypt in the 1960s and 1970s, mainly focusing on complex domestic issues. The international reach of the Islamist activities can, however, be traced to the Iranian-inspired and successful Hizballah operations against Western, American and French targets in Lebanon in 1983.[5]

---

[3]   Jamal al-Din al-Afghani was born in Asadabad, Iran in 1838. He died in Istanbul in 1897. A philosopher and politician, he promoted the concept of unity of all Muslims against British rule in particular and against global western interests in general. His call for Muslim solidarity influenced Egypt's nationalist movement, Turkey's *Tanzimat* reforms, as well as Iran's constitutional and Islamic revolutions. See Iraj Bashiri, Jamal al-Din al-Afghani, *Bashiri Working Papers on Central Asia and Iran*, 2000, at <http://www.angelfire.com/rnb/bashiri/Afghani/Afghani.html>.

[4]   'In Afghani's anti-imperialist campaign, especially against the British in Egypt, he took all manner of nationalists as allies, including non-Muslims who became some of his most ardent disciples. The Muslim Brethren, who joined the attacks against the British presence in the Suez Canal zone, had many ties to the Egyptian Free Officers who overthrew the monarchy in 1952, but their vision of an Islamic state eventually made them bitter enemies of the new regime. The Devotees of Islam, while thoroughly antiforeign, never collaborated with secular nationalists, whom they deeply distrusted. Whatever their strategies, however, they all worked to redress the gross imbalance of power between Islam and the West... Egypt's Muslim Brethren also looked beyond the horizon... In 1948, they sent their own volunteers to fight the Jews in Palestine.' Cited form Martin Kramer, 'Fundamentalist Islam at Large: The Drive for Power,' Middle East Quarterly, Vol. 3, No. 2 (June 1996), at <http://www.meforum.org/article/304>.

[5]   Hizballah was created in 1982 in Lebanon by Shi'a religious leaders and activists under the direct inspiration of the Iranian Khomeinist revolution and its leader. Using cover names such as 'Islamic Jihad,' 'The Revolutionary Justice Organization' and 'The Islamic Resistance,' Hizbal-lah has carried out a series of high profile attacks against American and Multinational Forces targets in Lebanon and Israeli targets in southern Lebanon: The bombing of the US embassy in Beirut, Lebanon, on 18 April 1983 (63 employees, including the Middle East director of the CIA, were killed and 120 wounded); on 23 October 1983 two suicide-bombers driving trucks crashed

The ideology, strategy and loose organizational framework of Islamists in the 1990s already figured in Hizballah's 1985 covenant:

> We do not constitute an organized and closed party in Lebanon. nor are we a tight political cadre. We are an *umma* [nation] linked to the Muslims of the whole world by the solid doctrinal and religious connection of Islam... This is why whatever touches or strikes the Muslims in Afghanistan, Iraq, the Philippines and elsewhere reverberates throughout the whole Muslim *umma*... Each of us is a fighting soldier... [W]e are an *umma* which fears God only and is by no means ready to tolerate injustice, aggression and humiliation. America, its Atlantic Pact allies, and the Zionist entity in the holy land of Palestine, attacked us and continue to do so without respite.[6]

The success of the 1979 Islamic revolution in Iran gave Sunni Islamic groups a revolutionary Islamic model, despite their many reservations about its content.[7] Efforts by the Iranian regime to export its revolution and to unify the Shi'a and Sunni radical movements met with limited success. It influenced mainly the Lebanese Hizballah, some minor groups and organizations in Shi'a communities in the Gulf area and Iraq, the Palestinian Islamic Jihad (PIJ) group and some violent Sunni organizations in Turkey.[8] In fact, international terrorist activities of the Hizballah and other Iranian-sponsored organizations actually diminished by the middle of the 1990s.[9]

---

into the US Marines and the French paratroopers headquarters in Beirut, killing 241 American and 58 French soldiers and wounding hundreds more; the subsequent bombing of the Israeli Defense Forces (IDF) headquarters in Tyre caused 75 soldiers dead; in April 1984 Hizballah bombed a restaurant near an US Air Force base in Torrejon, Spain, killing 18 servicemen and wounding 83 people; the US embassy in Beirut was again bombed in September 1984, severely damaging the building, killing two US servicemen and seven Lebanese employees and injuring twenty Americans, including the US ambassador; in June 1985 Hizballah terrorists hijacked a TWA flight en route to Rome from Athens and forced the pilot to fly to Beirut (the crewmembers and 145 passengers were held for 17 days during which one of the hostages, a US Navy diver was murdered); in June 1996 Hizballah was involved in the training of Saudi Hizballah militants responsible for a truck-bomb explosion outside the US military Khobar Towers housing facility in Dhahran, Saudi Arabia, killing 19 US military personnel and wounding 515 persons, including 240 US personnel.

[6]   See *An Open Letter. The Hizballah Program*, the website of The International Policy Institute for Counter-Terrorism (ICT), Herzliya, Israel, at <http://www.ict.org.il/Articles/Hiz_letter.htm>.

[7]   See Reuven Paz, *Tangled Web*, p. 7.

[8]   For an in-depth discussion on the ideological roots of the Sunni and Shi'a 'fundamentalism', (today the term Islamism is more accepted in the academia), see Martin Kramer, 'Fundamentalist Islam at Large: The Drive for Power,' Chapter 9 of Martin Kramer's *Arab Awakening and Islamic Revival* (Transaction Publishers, 1996), published in *The Middle East Quarterly*, Vol. III, No. 2 (June 1996), at <http://www.meforum.org/meq/june96/kramer.shtml>.

[9]   This does not include the active involvement of the Hizballah in the fight against Israel: in southern Lebanon, and after the IDF unilateral withdrawal, in Israel itself in support of the Pales-

According to Paz, the Sunni radical groups developed 'a culture of global jihad' which 'reflects the solidarity of variety of movements, groups, and sometimes *ad hoc* groupings or cells, which act under a kind of ideological umbrella of radical interpretations of Islam'.[10] These interpretations stem mainly from developments in the Arab world since the early 1960s: difficulties for both individuals and societies in coping with Western modernization and its values; a relative ignorance of orthodox Islam by the younger generation; the failure of revolutionary movements to attain victory and the failure of Arab nationalism to solve the problems of Arab societies; growing transnational links among different parts of the Muslim world as a result of improved technology, mainly communications; the collapse of the Soviet bloc and communist ideology; and a series of conflicts which seemed to pit Muslims against non-Muslims in Bosnia, Albania, Palestine, Kosovo, Chechnya, the Philippines, Afghanistan, Indonesia and Kashmir.

These factors helped to create a closer solidarity between various scholars, groups, sympathizers and circles of frustrated Islamic elements. This solidarity was primarily based upon deep hatred of a common enemy and a kind of apocalyptic perception of the struggle between divine and Satanic, good and evil, or light and darkness. Global jihad in recent years reflected solidarity based upon narrow-minded interpretations of limited Islamic principles, and perceived confrontation with a Western global conspiracy.[11]

Paz claimed that during the 1990s, developing links between different Sunni Islamist groups were influenced by a Salafiyyah trend, sometimes called neo-Wahhabiyyah, whose main ideological principle was *takfir* – the perception of the secular Muslim society as heretical – and which singled out Muslim secular governments as the target of a permanent jihad.[12]

---

tinian intifada. There is no intention to analyze here the causes of this development. For an analysis of the Iranian sponsored terrorism, see Ely Karmon, 'Why Tehran Starts and Stops Terrorism?' *Middle East Quarterly*, December 1998, Vol. 5, No. 4, pp. 35-44, at <http://www.meforum.org/article/427>.

[10] This citation is taken from the draft article later published by Reuven Paz, 'Middle East Islamism in the European Arena,' *MERIA Journal*, Vol. 6, No. 3 (September 2002), at <http://meria.idc.ac.il/journal/2002/issue3/jv6n3a6.html>.

[11] Ibid.

[12] The influence of the Salafiyyah trend was disseminated in the Arab World during the 1950s by the Saudi religious establishment, in an effort to spread the Wahhabi principles. Its main ideology is based on the Kharijite movement at the early history of Islam, on the writings of Ibn Taymiyyah of the 13-14th centuries and Muhammad Ibn 'Abd al-Wahhab of the eighteenth century. Its organizational principles are those of the Saudi Ikhwan movement (not the Muslim Brotherhood) – a movement of extremists who were sent in the 1920s and 1930s by the Saudis to found settlements on the Saudi borders. See Reuven Paz, *The Heritage of the Sunni Militant Groups. An Islamic Internacionale?* 4 January 2000, at <http://www.ict.org.il/articles/articledet.cfm?articleid=415>.

According to Wiktorowicz, the Salafi movement represented 'a transnational effort for religious purification, connecting members of an "imagined community" through a common approach to Islam,' a movement which enjoys 'a global reach in virtually all countries'. The movement aimed to eradicate all the innovations and deviations which occurred with the passage of time in Islam by returning to the pure form of the creed as practiced by the Prophet Muhammad and his Companions. 'The Afghani experience radicalised Arab Salafi mujahideen who attempted to export the religious justification for war to new contexts and enemies.'[13]

The state in which this effort achieved its greatest success was Egypt, where the Muslim Brotherhood adopted the Salafi/Wahhabi ideas in their more extremist commentaries. Two trends which define themselves in relation to takfir developed:[14]

(1) The Islamic Jihad groups, including the Egyptian Jihad of Sheikh Omar 'Abd al-Rahman, and later the various factions of the Islamic Group (al-Gama'a al-Islamiyya); the different groups of the Palestinian Islamic Jihad, al-Tali'ah al-Islamiyya in Syria; al-Tawhid group in Tripoli, Lebanon; the various Afghan Mujahideen groups (under the ideological guidance of the Palestinian Dr. Abdallah Azzam); and several other small groups in the Arab world and Pakistan.

(2) The Takfir groups, including the Egyptian Jama't al-Muslimin (known also as al-Takfir wal-Hijrah); Egyptian Salafist groups active in Bosnia and later in Albania; and the Jordanian Takfir, which recently developed a large following, composed of several groups of people of different nationalities, mainly Egyptians. According to Paz, the Pakistani Harkat ul-Mujahidin (HuM) and the Committee for the Defense of Legal Rights in Saudi Arabia (CDLR), the political wing of the Saudi Islamist opponents of the Saudi royal regime, also belonged to this trend. The CDLR military wing is probably al-Qaeda al-Sulbah (The Solid Base) of Osama bin Laden, linked ideologically to Abdallah Azzam. The Algerian Armed Islamic Group or Jama'a Islamiyya Musalha (better known by its French name, Groupe Islamique Arme – GIA) can also be regarded as a takfir group.

---

[13] Wiktorowicz analyzes the various trends in the Salafist movement, especially the differences in ideology and strategy between the *jihadi* radical trend and what he considers the reformist trend. He also differentiates between 'nomadic jihad' and 'jihad at home.' See Quintan Wiktorowicz, 'The New Global Threat: Transnational Salafis and Jihad,' *Middle East Policy*, Vol. 8, No. 4 (December 2001), pp. 19, 22.

[14] This paragraph is based on Paz's analysis of the *takfir* and *jihadi* groups in *The Heritage of the Sunni Militant Groups*.

These trends met during the 1980s and mainly the 1990s in the contexts of the war in Afghanistan and the religious/ethnic conflicts in Bosnia, Kosovo and Chechnya. Afghanistan provided the main refuge and meeting place for groups of both currents, well before the Taliban took control of most of the country. A 'brotherhood of the persecuted' developed there among these groups, leading to cooperation and the spread of takfir ideas to the Jihad groups, and the increasing use of the term 'takfir' as interchangeable with 'jihad.' It seems that activists passed quite easily from group to group promoting cooperation between those affiliated with the two trends. Under the influence of the takfir ideology, the Egyptian Jihad group became extremely anti-American, as far as to organize the bombing of the WTC in New York in 1993.[15]

Sunni radical movements and groups flourished as their militants fought alongside Afghani tribes against the Soviets in the 1980s. The victory of the Islamic mujahideen in Afghanistan at the end of the 1980s was perceived by Islamist circles not only as a military victory, but also as a cultural one. It created a broad cadre of seasoned, militant volunteers eager to disseminate fundamental-ist Islamic ideas throughout the Muslim world. The disintegration of the Soviet Union and the collapse of communism left a political and ideological vacuum into which Islamist circles were only too eager to step. It led to the creation of new Muslim states, a new arena of conflict for Islamist circles.

According to Shay and Schweitzer, the radical Islamist elements operated in all Muslim states at different levels of intensity and their struggle against foreign cultures may embrace one or several of the following goals:[16]

(1) The overthrow of secular regimes in Muslim states and their replacement by Islamic theocratic regimes.
(2) Independence for Muslim minorities, and the establishment of independent Islamic states.
(3) The suppression of ethnic/cultural minorities seeking autonomy or inde-pendence in Muslim states.
(4) The neutralization of the influence of foreign – particularly Western – civilizations situated on the fault lines with Islamic culture.

These goals accord with the Islamic basic tenet that the world is divided into two parts which are in perpetual conflict – the world of Islam (*Dar al-Islam*) and the world of heresy (*Dar al-Harb*). The primary concern of Islamists is to reshape the

---

[15] Ibid.
[16] On the subject of the Afghan 'veterans' see Shaul Shay and Yoram Schweitzer, *The Afghan Alumni: Islamic Militants against the Rest of the World*, at <http://www.ict.org.il/articles/articledet.cfm? articleid=140>.

political reality within the Muslim world. Islamic fundamentalism is funneled through dozens of Islamist organizations throughout the Muslim world. In addition, the fundamentalist Islamic regimes in Iran, Afghanistan, and Sudan provide spiritual and material succor to radical Islamic movements. These states work independently and through the radical Islamic movements to export the Islamic revolution to the entire Muslim world, and spearhead the struggle against foreign – particularly Western – civilizations.[17]

Some consider al-Qaeda a direct product of the struggle to eject the Soviet Union from Afghanistan. Veterans of the Afghan campaign shared a powerful life experience, a more global view, and a sense of exaltation. They did not, however, receive a hero's welcome home and were watched with suspicion by the Arab and Muslim regimes, who worried that the religious fervor of the fighters posed an internal political threat. According to Jenkins, 'Isolated at home, they became ready recruits for new campaigns.'[18]

In Europe, meanwhile, for the first time in decades, the issue of Muslim identity arose among the populations of the Balkans (Bosnia, Kosovo and Albania). For the first time, too, the religious and ethnic conflicts in this region presented radical Islam with an opportunity to gain an ideological foothold in these areas.[19]

II.   THE FORMATION OF THE WORLD ISLAMIC FRONT (WIF)

The earliest version of an Islamist terrorist network led by Osama bin Laden was the International Islamic Front, a loose coalition founded in Saudi Arabia in August 1990. This included the Egyptian Jihad and Islamic Group, the Jordanian Mohammad's Army (Jaysh Mohammed), Jammu and Kashmir's Ansar Movement and several other factions, including the Muhajirun.[20]

Ramzi Yusuf, who masterminded the first bombing of the WTC in New York in 1993, claimed to belong to a mysterious Liberation Army Movement (Harakat Jaysh al-Tahrir), an international movement concerned with issues of armed Islamic movements worldwide. He claimed that the movement had groups and military divisions in various countries and one of its objectives was 'to help members of Egypt's Islamic Group, Egypt's Jihad Group, Palestine's Hamas

---

[17] Ibid.

[18] See Brian Michael Jenkins, *Countering al-Qaeda. An Appreciation of the Situation and Suggestions for Strategy*, RAND Publications, at <http://www.rand.org/publications/MR/MR1620/MR1620.pdf>.

[19] Ibid.

[20] See 'International Islamic Front,' *South Asia Terrorism Portal* (SATP) of the Institute for Conflict Management (ICM), India, at <http://www.satp.org/satporgtp/usa/IIF.htm>.

(Islamic Resistance Movement) and Islamic Jihad, and Algeria's Salvation Front (FIS) and armed Islamic movements'. Ramzi was only arrested in 1995 and is also suspected of working with al-Qaeda.[21]

On 22 February 1998 Osama bin Laden announced the creation in Pakistan of the World Islamic Front for the Struggle Against the Jews and Crusaders (WIF), in association with radical groups from Egypt, Pakistan and Bangladesh. Other signatories to the February statement were: Ayman al-Zawahiri, leader of the Egyptian Jihad; Rifai Taha, head of the Egyptian Islamic Group; Mir Hamza, secretary-general of Pakistan's Ulema Society (Jamaat-ul-Ulema-i-Pakistan); Fazlur Rahman Khalil, chief of Harkat-ul-Ansar (HuA) in Pakistan; and Sheikh Abd al-Salam Muhammad Khan, leader of the Jihad movement of Bangladesh.[22] The front reportedly had a supreme council headed by Osama bin Laden.

The establishment of the WIF was accompanied by two Islamic decrees (*fatwas*) by bin Laden and 'The Association of Islamic Clerics in Afghanistan' (Ittihad al-Ulama' fi Afghanistan), declaring a religious war against the US. Bin Laden had assumed the title of sheikh in order to acquire the right to issue such religious rulings.[23]

According to *al-Watan al-'Arabi*, members of the front disagreed over the founding statement, the constituent membership, the authority of the leaders of each group, and the scope of their independent activities. Other Islamist organizations,

---

[21] See Ramzi's interview in London *al-Hayat*, 12 April 1995 (FBIS-TOT-95-012-L). It should be noted that a group calling itself 'The Fifth Battalion of the Liberation Army' took responsibility for the bombing of the WTC in 1993 in a letter sent to the *New York Times*.

[22] In some documents Fazlul Rahman is mistakenly described as the leader of the Jihad Movement in Bangaladesh. According to Indian sources, the Markaz Dawa al Irshad and its militant wing the Lashkar-e-Toiba have also adhered to the WIF. See B. Raman, 'US Bombing of Terrorist Camps in Afghanistan,' *South Asia Analysis Group Papers*, 3 November 1998, at <http://www.subcontinent.com/sapra/terrorism/tr_1998_11_001_s.html>. It must be stressed that although these two groups support bin Laden and his strategy, they did not sign the fatwa or other common documents.

[23] 'In February 1998 Usama bin Laden and his close associate, Ayman al Zawahiri, endorsed a fatwa under the banner of the 'International Islamic Front for Jihad on the Jews and Crusaders'. This fatwa, published in the newspaper, Al-Quds Al-Arabi, on February 23, 1998, stated that Muslims should kill Americans – including civilians – anywhere in the world.
  In May 1998 bin Laden associate Mohammed Atef sent Khaled al Fawwaz a letter discussing the endorsement by bin Laden of a fatwa issued by the Ulema Union of Afghanistan which termed the U.S. army the 'enemies of Islam' and declared jihad against the US and its followers. The fatwa was subsequently published in Al-Quds Al-Arabi. Subsequently, bin Laden issued a statement entitled 'The Nuclear Bomb of Islam', under the banner of the 'International Islamic Front for Fighting the Jews and Crusaders', in which he stated that 'it is the duty of Muslims to prepare as much force as possible to terrorize the enemies of God.' Cited from 'Fact Sheet: Evidence Against Bin Laden Documented,' *USIS* document, 15 December 1999, at <http://usinfo.state.gov/topical/pol/terror/99129502.htm>.

such as the Algerian GIA and the Egyptian Vanguards of Conquest did not join the new front.[24]

The Egyptian Jihad Group – Vanguards of Conquests called on the WIF to recruit new members from other tendencies and to draw up new strategies. A statement signed by its secretary-general Abdallah Mansur, and entitled 'A Step Forward and in the Right Direction,' said:

> The time has come for us to move from hasty thinking based on [emotional] reactions and fighting non-enemies, and hence exhausting almost all our energies, to strategic thinking that takes account of rules of defence and the ability to adapt and develop. Because without that, the outcome is a total freeze [*tajammud*].[25]

The statement cited the need to

> form a higher committee that represents all colors of the fundamentalist movement wishing to join such an alliance in the Arab and Islamic worlds, in addition to drawing up mechanisms for implementing and focusing on these aims while earnestly working to eliminate all psychological barriers among the various *jihad* forces and tendencies in order to close ranks against falsehood and its party [*hizbuh*].[26]

According to one of the leaders of the Egyptian Jihad, Ahmad al-Najjar, only after 1992 did bin Laden attempt to unify the Egyptian Islamic Group and Jihad on the grounds that they shared the same objectives.[27] These efforts were limited, however, by disagreement between the two groups over the religious issue of

---

[24] See *Al-Watan al-'Arabi*, 26 June 1998, cited in Esther Webman, The Polarization and Radicalization of Political Islam, *Middle East Contemporary Survey (MECS), 1998*, The Moshe Dayan Center for Middle Eastern and African Studies, Tel Aviv University, at <http://www.dayan.org/islam98.pdf>, p. 2. Webman's articles on Political Islam in the *Middle East Contemporary Survey (MECS)* for the years 1998-2000, using a wealth of Arab media sources, are a rich resource of information on the Islamist movements in the region.

[25] The Vanguards of Conquest group split in 1993 from the Jihad organization led by al-Zawahiri and was accused of trying to assassinate former Egyptian prime minister 'Atif Sidqi and Interior Minister Hasan al-Alfi. The group merged with another faction breaking away from al-Zawahiri's organization on 17 March 1997, setting up an information office under the name 'Jihad – Vanguards of Conquest.' See London *Al-Sharq al-Awsat*, 26 February 1998.

[26] Ibid. See also Ely Karmon, 'Who's Behind the Bombings? The Terrorist Attack on the American Embassies in Africa', 10 August 1998, at <http://www.ict.org.il/articles/articledet.cfm?Articleid =148>.

[27] Najjar was put on trial with a group of Egyptian Islamists called 'the returnees from Albania case', because they had been extradited from Albania under US pressure. Another defendant in the trial, Shawqi Salama, revealed that significant efforts to bridge the views of the two organizations had also been made by several Sudanese Islamists, particularly the speaker of the Sudanese parliament Hasan al-Turabi. See Webman, *Political Islam at the Close of the Twentieth Century*, p. 13.

'excusing ignorance' (*jahiliya*), and an organizational issue concerning the leadership and the consultative process (*shura*). However, when bin Laden announced the formation of the WIF in 1998 the two groups were prompted to address the issue of merger.[28] Another militant, Sharif Hazza, linked the formation of the front to the period that bin Laden settled in Afghanistan (1996) and used the training camps, with the agreement of the Taliban regime, to become responsible for all the Arabs from various Islamist trends and impose his rules on them. Bin Laden took advantage of this situation to bring all the groups under the umbrella of the new front and thereby settle the leadership issue. He maintained control with some twenty followers, foremost among them al-Zawahiri and Shawqi al-Islambuli, and assumed most of the financial burden. Since international security forces were seeking the leaders of the Islamic Group and the Jihad, they had no choice but to accept these conditions.[29]

According to Arab sources, under the influence of bin Laden, the establishment of the front brought about a rapprochement between the Egyptian Islamic Group, and Jihad groups concerning their objectives and modus operandi. Bin Laden was interested in strengthening relations with Islamist movements everywhere.[30]

The *ad hoc* coalition of the WIF proved to be quite flexible, comprising al-Qaeda as the chief locomotive, some members as religious sponsors or ideological supporters, and others, such as the Egyptians, as strategic, organizational and operational elements.

Towards the end of the millennium, following a wave of arrests of Islamist terrorists worldwide, it became evident that North Africans belonging to various groups which had split from the Algerian FIS and the GIA and the outlawed Tunisian Nahda movement, were beginning to play a key operational role, mainly in Europe and North America.

Cooperation had reportedly existed between these different groups, but prior to the establishment of the WIF there was no mechanism for such cooperation. Moreover, each of these organizations had freedom of action and determined their

---

[28] Ibid. The interrogations of 'the returnees from Albania case' shed light on the modus operandi of the Islamist movements, and highlighted the pivotal role of bin Laden in unifying and financing them. Most revealing was the confession of Ahmad al-Najjar, who was sentenced to life imprisonment at hard labor. His trajectory in the Jihad is typical: after a few years in Egypt as a religious propagator and recruiter for the military wing of the organization, he was sent to Yemen with a forged passport, where he met with al-Zawahiri. After an unsuccessful attempt to assassinate prime minister 'Atif Sidqi in 1993, he left Yemen for Sudan. Following the 1995 bombing of the Egyptian embassy in Pakistan Najjar, along with several other Jihad members, relocated to Albania under the cover of employment in charitable organizations.

[29] Ibid.

[30] Various *Al-Hayat* reports as cited by Webman, *The Polarization and Radicalization of Political Islam*, p. 2.

own objectives independently. Cooperation existed only at the level of 'those who carry arms,' [at the operational level] due to the comradeship developed during the Afghan war. There were no means of cooperation and coordination among 'the people of the call,' the higher organizational level. Significantly, the WIF combined all the organizational levels by establishing a *Shura* (consultative council). According to most assessments, bin Laden led this council and subsequently increased the effectiveness of the WIF.[31]

A Pakistani newspaper commented that until May 1996, the Arabs who had taken refuge in Afghanistan after the end of the Afghan jihad lacked a leader and a clearly conceived agenda. The advent of bin Laden addressed both their problems. The normally fractious Afghan-based Arabs not only found a resourceful leader and a rallying point but also someone who was very clear about his objectives.[32]

The successful formation of the WIF strengthened bin Laden's resolve against the US:

The movement is driving fast and light forward. And I am sure of our victory with Allah's help against America and the Jews... After the Americans entered the Holy Land, many emotions were roused in the Muslim world, more than we have seen before... The co-operation is expanding between general supporters of this religion. From this effort, the International Islamic Front for the Jihad Against Jews and Crusaders was formed.[33]

Bin Laden described the WIF as 'an umbrella to all organizations fighting the jihad against Jews and crusaders' and claimed that the response from Muslim nations had been greater than expected.[34]

Critical to the formation of the coalition and its subsequent terrorist activity was the moral, political and logistical support provided by the Taliban regime in Afghanistan as well as Islamist movements in Pakistan. Further discussion of this aspect of al-Qaeda is beyond the scope of this study.[35]

---

[31] See *International Islamic Front*.

[32] See the Islamabad *The News*, 15 June 1998.

[33] See Usama Bin Ladin: An Interview with ABCNEWS Correspondent John Miller, 28 May 1998, at <http://faculty.smu.edu/jclam/western_religions/miller.html>.

[34] See *Newsweek*, 11 January 1999.

[35] For a detailed account of the Taliban history and their role in the spread of the al-Qaeda network see Ahmed Rashid, *Taliban: Militant Islam, Oil and Fundamentalism in Central Asia* (Yale University Press, 2000); Shaul Shay, *The Endless Jihad ... The Mujahidin, the Taliban and Bin Laden* (Herzliya: The International Policy Institute for Counter-Terrorism, The Interdisciplinary Center Press, 2002). See also Aabha Dixit, 'Soldiers of Islam: Origins, Ideology and Strategy of the Taliban,' *Strategic Analysis* papers of The Institute for Defence Studies and Analyses (IDSA), New Delhi, India, Vol. 20 No. 5 (August 1997), at <http://www.idsa-india.org/an-aug-2.

III.   THE ORGANIZATIONAL STRUCTURE OF THE WIF AND THE
       NETWORK'S ASSOCIATES

1.   The hard core

A.   Al-Qaeda

In 1987 Abdallah Azzam, a Palestinian who had moved to Afghanistan from
Jordan in 1980, wrote: 'Every principle needs a vanguard to carry it forward and
[to] put up with heavy tasks and enormous sacrifices. This vanguard constitutes
the strong foundation (*al qaeda al-sulbah*) for the expected society.'[36] Azzam was
referring here to a mode of activism and a tactic, not about a particular organization. According to Burke, the vanguard is only one of a number of concepts and
tactics borrowed from radical western thinkers ranging from Trotsky and Mao to
Hitler and Heidegger.[37]

       Al-Qaeda (The Base) developed from the civilian and social infrastructure of
Afghan groups, called The Office for Services (Maktab al-Khidamat) that fought
against the Soviet Union invasion in 1980-89. Established by Azzam, it provided
a religious, cultural, and social basis for the Mujahideen struggle.[38] He, and
subsequently bin Laden too, saw the role of al-Qaeda to radicalize and mobilize
those Muslims who had hitherto rejected their message.

       Osama bin Laden became the leader of the group that became known as al-
Qaeda after Azzam's assassination in 1989.[39] Bin Laden and his followers also set

---

html>; Ahmed Rashid, The US, Afghanistan, and Osama bin Laden's Al'Qaeda Network, *Na-
        tional   Strategy   Forum   Review*, Autumn   2001, <http://www.nationalstrategy.com/nsr/
        v11n1Autumn01/110102.htm>; Sumita Kumar, 'The Role of Islamic Parties in Pakistani Poli-
        tics,' *Strategic Analysis* papers of The Institute for Defence Studies and Analyses (IDSA), New
        Delhi, India, May 2001 Vol. 25, No. 2, at <http://www.idsa-india.org/an-may-8.01.htm>.
[36]   Cited in Jason Burke, 'What is al-Qaeda?' *Observer Worldview Extra*, 13 July 2003.
[37]   Ibid.
[38]   In April 1988 Azzam published an article in the magazine *Al-Jihad* – the central organ of the
        Afghan groups, one that he founded and edited – called 'The Solid Base' (Al-Qa'idah al-Sulbah)
        Al-Jihad 41 (April 1988) which laid the groundwork for the new group, Al-Qaeda. Cited from
        Paz, *Tangled Web*, p. 11.
[39]   Osama bin Laden, born 30 July 1957 as the 17th of 20 sons of a Saudi construction magnate of
        Yemeni origin, gained prominence during the Afghan war against the Soviet Union. In 1989,
        when the Afghan war ended, he returned to Saudi Arabia to work in his family's business, the
        Bin Laden Construction Group, although his radical Islamic contacts caused him to run afoul of
        Saudi authorities. In 1991, bin Laden relocated to Sudan with the approval of Sudanese National
        Islamic Front (NIF) leader Hasan al-Turabi. There, in concert with NIF leaders, he built a net-
        work of businesses, including an Islamic bank, an import-export firm, and firms that exported
        agricultural products. An engineer by training, bin Laden also used his family connections in the
        construction business to build roads and airport facilities in Sudan. The businesses in Sudan,
        some of which apparently still operate, enabled him to offer safe haven and employment in

up a small militant group, comprising not more than a dozen men, in Peshawar, the frontier city in western Pakistan. It was here that various Islamists converged and were mobilized around a single project.[40]

Al-Qaeda's hard core consists of the few dozen associates who stayed with bin Laden since the late 1980s. Their numbers were boosted by a number of individual militants who joined bin Laden in Afghanistan. Most were independent Islamists who joined in order to receive safe haven, training and financing. One such was Khaled Sheikh Mohammed, a senior commander, who had been involved in attacks in the Philippines and elsewhere.[41]

A second element of al-Qaeda involves the scores of other militant Islamic groups worldwide linked in some way to bin Laden or his associates but not actually created or run by bin Laden. Tracing the links between various groups and the al-Qaeda core is not easy. Even within individual movements, different factions had different relations with al-Qaeda. For example, the Ansar-ul-Islam group that emerged in Kurdish-controlled northern Iraq in the autumn of 2001 comprised three different factions. While two set off to Afghanistan to meet senior al-Qaeda leaders in the spring of 2001, a third was reluctant to deal with bin Laden. By the end of 2001 Ansar was joined by Arab fighters who had fled the US-led onslaught in Afghanistan

A third element involves numerous young Muslims who share the same ideology and key objectives of al-Qaeda, whether involved in a radical group or not.

Paz remarks that the Jihad movement managed to bring together individuals with vastly different backgrounds. For example, volunteers fighting in Chechnya in the battalion of Arab Afghans commanded by the Jordanian Ibn al-Khattab included citizens from Turkey, Saudi Arabia, Palestine, Yemen, Algeria, Egypt, and elsewhere. Their biographies reveal a pattern of relatively well-educated

---

Sudan to al-Qaeda members, promoting their involvement in radical Islamic movements in their countries of origin (especially Egypt) as well as anti-US terrorism. In the early 1990s, he founded a London-based group, the Advisory and Reform Committee, which distributed literature against the Saudi regime. As a result of bin Laden's opposition to the ruling Al Saud family, his Saudi citizenship was revoked in 1994 and most of his family disavowed him, although some of his brothers reportedly maintained contact with him. In May 1996 following strong US and Egyptian pressure, Sudan expelled him, and he returned to Afghanistan, under protection of the dominant Taliban movement. On 7 June 1999 bin Laden was placed on the FBI's 'Ten Most Wanted List,' and a $5 million reward was offered for his capture. Cited from Kenneth Katzman, 'Al-Qaida (Usama bin Ladin Network),' *Terrorism: Near Eastern Groups and State Sponsors, 2001* (Washington, Library of Congress. Congressional Research Service, September 2001), pp. 13-17.

[40]   Al-Qaeda did not figure in US government reports until 1993. *The Patterns of Global Terrorism* 1993 report claimed that several thousand non-Afghan Muslims fought in the war against the Soviets and the Afghan Communist government during 1979-92 but did not mention the group by name.

[41]   See Burke, *What is al-Qaeda?*

people, some from quite wealthy families, searching for personal fulfillment by fighting in the name of Islam wherever possible.[42]

According to Maha Azzam, the organization initially failed to attract the mainstream of the radical Islamist movements in the Arab world, as most of the groups considered 'that revolutionary Islamist action should be confined within each group's nation-state and that they should not interfere in one another's territory beyond providing moral support.' The tide changed when al-Zawahiri, leader of the Egyptian Jihad, converted to a more internationalist view and joined the al-Qaeda leadership as its theorist while remaining as mentor of Jihad. Al-Zawahiri's premise was that although the enemy of each Islamist group lay within the nation-state, a common enemy would also try to obstruct any radical change on the domestic front. The enemy was identified as 'the amorphous mass accused of being the source of all the ills affecting the Muslim world, especially the US because of its support of Israel and the corrupt dictatorships of the Middle East'.[43]

According to Ahmed Hashim, the work of Muhammad Abdel Salam Al-Farag, the ideologue of the Egyptian Jihad, is critical to understanding bin Laden's outlook. Farag argues that Islamists should focus first on the enemy at home: 'We must begin ... by establishing the rule of God in our nation... [T]he first battle-field for *jihad* is the uprooting of these infidel leaders and replacing them with an Islamic system from which we can build.' Only afterward can the enemy 'who is afar' (in Farag's words) be fought. Bin Laden reversed the order and campaigned primarily against the US, rather than rulers of Islamic states.[44]

This ideology led bin Laden to support Islamic fighters against Serb forces in Bosnia; Russian forces in Chechnya; Indian control over part of Kashmir; and

---

[42]   See the biographies of the Arab 'martyrs' on a Chechen Islamist website linked to Bin Laden's website <http://www.qoqaz.com>. Cited from Paz, *Tangled Web*.

[43]   See Maha Azzam, 'Al-Qaeda: the Misunderstood Wahhabi Connection and the Ideology of Violence,' *Briefing paper No. 1*, The Royal Institute of International Affairs, UK, February 2003, at <http://www.riia.org/pdf/research/mep/Azzaml.pdf>. It is interesting to note that according to the Gama'a 'amir' in the Egyptian Marsa Matruh province, the decision to transform the jihad into a global, not local, war was received already in 1983: to transform the struggle against the local rulers in the Arab world into a jihad against the international infidels (*inter alia* because there was no real possibility to continue the fight under the oppressive regime of president Mubarak). See 'The Reconciliation Initiative of the al-Gama'a al-Islamiyya Organization with the Egyptian Regime' (in Hebrew – Yozmat hapius shel irgun al-Gama'a al-Islamiyya im hamishtar hamitzri), three parts, published by MEMRI, part 1, p. 2.

[44]   However, the situation by the 1990s was far different from when Farag was executed in 1982. In the 1990s the United States established a visible presence in the Arabian Peninsula – the 'land of the two holy mosques'. In this context, Bin Laden, who focuses his anger on the United States as the support of Saudi royal family, sees the enemy at home and the enemy who is afar as intricately linked in a symbiotic relationship. See Ahmed S. Hashim, 'The World According To Usama Bin Laden' *Naval War College Review*, Autumn 2001 at <http://www.nwc.navy.mil/press/Review/2001/Autumn/art1-au1.htm>.

also against secular or pro-Western governments in Egypt, Algeria, Saudi Arabia and Uzbekistan; and against US troops and civilians in the Persian Gulf, Somalia, Yemen, Jordan, and against the US mainland itself.

Membership of the network is estimated to be between 3,000 and 6,000 fighters, all highly dedicated and personally devoted to bin Ladin. The network also contains a large number of non-combatants with a broad range of skills.[45]

B.   The Egyptian Jihad Group (Jamaat-ul-Jihad, Islamic Jihad, New Jihad Group, Vanguards of Conquest, Tala'i' al Fath)

Muhammad Abd-al-Salam succeeded in uniting most Egyptian Jihad groups prior to 1981 in what was known in the media as the Jihad Organization. After his execution, these groups disbanded but a relatively large and cohesive group remained. This evolved into the Islamic Group in Upper Egypt. Other smaller groups which shared the same general ideology were temporarily reunited by Dr. Fadl under the name of the Jihad Group between 1989 and 1992.[46]

The movement is apparently divided into two factions: one led by al-Zawahiri from Afghanistan, and the Vanguards of Conquest led by Ahmad Husayn Ujayza. As noted above, al-Zawahiri is the second-in-command of bin Laden's WIF and al-Qaeda. Like al-Gama'a al-Islamiyya, the Jihad factions regard Sheikh Omar Abd-al Rahman, imprisoned in the US, as their spiritual leader.

The goal of all Jihad factions is to overthrow the government of President Hosni Mubarak and turn Egypt into an Islamic state. They call for an end to Western influence in Muslim countries and show willingness to target Western, particularly American interests.

The Egyptian Jihad group operates in small underground cells and recruits members aged 15-30. They claim responsibility for numerous attacks against Egyptian government officials and institutions, Christian leaders and institutions, and Israeli and Western targets on Egyptian soil. Jihad recruits trained in remote bases in Egypt, Afghanistan, Pakistan, Sudan and elsewhere.[47]

---

[45]   Al-Sharq al-Awsat, 2 September 1998 as cited by Webman, *The Polarization and Radicalization of Political Islam*, p. 8.

[46]   See interview with Ahmad Husayn Ujayzah, 'Egyptian Fundamentalist Leader Who Has Been Sentenced to Death in Absentia,' by Muhammad al-Shafi'i, London *Al-Sharq al-Awsat*, 23 May 2001.

[47]   The original Jihad was responsible for the assassination in 1981 of President Anwar Sadat. The Jihad group specialized in armed attacks against high-level Egyptian government officials including cabinet ministers. It claimed responsibility for the attempted assassinations of Interior Minister Hassan Al-Alfi in August 1993 and Prime Minister Atef Sidky in November 1993. In June 1992, after activists of the Islamic Jihad in Egypt murdered Faraj Fodah, an author who had openly supported Israeli-Egyptian peace, a 'hit list' was revealed that had been prepared by organization activists and which included the names of tens of Egyptians to be killed, including the interior minister, General Moussa; and the journalist Anis Mansour.

From 1993 the group ceased attacks within Egypt but repeatedly threatened to retaliate against the US for its incarceration of Sheikh Omar Abd al-Rahman and for the arrests of its members in Albania, Azerbaijan and the UK. In 1995 the Jihad orchestrated attacks against the Egyptian attaché in Switzerland and the Egyptian embassy in Pakistan, resulting in the deaths of 15 people.[48]

Al-Zawahiri was imprisoned on the charge of involvement in President Anwar Sadat's assassination. He formed his own faction, which included his brother Muhammad, (aka 'the Engineer'), who was extradited by the United Arab Emirates to Egypt in 2000. In addition to opposition to the 'heretical' Egyptian government, this faction began calling for attacks against American and Israeli targets.[49]

C.   The Egyptian Islamic Group (al-Gama'a al-Islamiyya)

The Egyptian Islamic Group emerged during the 1970s mainly in Egyptian jails and later on in some Egyptian universities. The Islamic Group was mainly affected by the militant ideology of the Muslim Brotherhood (MB) leader Sayyid Qutb, executed in 1966 by the Nasserite regime, who paved the way for the establishment of several Islamic militant branches in Egypt and the Arab world.[50]

Following the release of most Islamic prisoners from Egyptian jails by President Sadat after 1971, several militant cells emerged with names such as the Islamic Liberation Party, al-Takfir wal-Hijra (Excommunication and Emigration), Al-Najun min al-Nar (Saved from the Inferno), and Jihad (Holy War), as well as others, including the Islamic Group. Leaders of the different groups evidently maintained some contacts but it is not known whether any overall direction existed.

The organization targeted government officials, including two attempts on the life of President Husni Mubarak, police officers, secular intellectuals, Copts and foreign tourists. In the late 1990s Islamists also began to attack banks in an effort to enforce the Islamic ban on usury. Musical recitals, film shows and video stores deemed morally offensive were also attacked.[51]

---

[48]   See Yoram Schweitzer, 'Osama bin Ladin and the Egyptian Terrorist Groups,' *ICT website*, 25 June 1999, at <http://www.ict.org.il/articles/articledet.cfm?articleid=81>.

[49]   Although al-Zawahiri has appeared on numerous occasions to be bin Laden's deputy, it appears that he is the real leader of al-Qaeda. According to a London militant, 'al-Zawahiri is behind the deep-rooted hatred of the United States and the West in Bin Ladin's heart'. The FBI regards al-Zawahiri as bin Laden's right-hand man and the mastermind of the bombing of the US embassies in Nairobi and Dar el Salam in August 1998.

     See 'Al-Sharq Al-Awsat Publishes Extracts from Al-Jihad Leader Al-Zawahiri's New Book, Parts 1-11 eleven of serialized excerpts from Egyptian Al-Jihad Organization leader Ayman al-Zawahiri's book *Knights Under the Prophet's Banner*, FBIS-NES-2002-0108,' Federation of American Scientists website at <http://www.fas.org/irp/world/para/ayman_bk.html>.

[50]   See the file on the ICT website, at <http://www.ict.org.il/inter_ter/orgdet.cfm?orgid=12>.

[51]   Some militants regard Christians as infidels and therefore appropriate targets for Jihad. Attacks have mainly been concentrated in areas of Upper and Middle Egypt such as Minya, Assiut and Sohag,

A series of indiscriminate bomb blasts in poor neighborhoods of Cairo in June 1993 and the death of a schoolgirl bystander during the attack on Prime Minister Atef Sidki stiffened public opinion against the militants. Attacks on tourist targets barely served to alienate the many Egyptians who earned their livelihood from the tourist industry.

On 17 November 1997 58 tourists and four Egyptians were killed in the southern town of Luxor in the bloodiest attack since the Islamic Group took up arms in 1992. Several weeks later two contradictory statements – one vowing to halt attacks on foreign tourists and a second denying that such a decision had been made – were issued in the name of the Group. The split actually began to surface in July 1998 following a truce called by imprisoned leaders of the Group.[52]

The Islamic Group adopted a historic decision in March 1999 to halt all military operations inside and outside Egypt. This was largely in response to a peace initiative presented by its leaders in July 1997.[53]

2.   The members

A.   Pakistan Scholars/Ulema Society (Jamiat-ul-Ulema-i-Pakistan – JUP)

The Jamiat-ul-Ulema-i-Islam (JUI) was formed prior to the 1947 partition of India. It represents the Deobandi school of Islamic revivalism which emphasizes a puritanical form of Islamic government. In contrast, the modern JUI led by Maulana Fazlur Rahman has had stronger roots in Baluchistan and the North West Frontier Province (NWFP) with a limited constituency in Sindh.[54] It should be stressed that there is much ambiguity concerning the participation of Pakistani groups or individuals to the WIF. The Arab press makes no mention of 'Mir Hamza, secretary-general of Pakistan's Ulema Society (Jamiat-ul-Ulema-i-Pakistan – JUP).[55] Other than signing the WIF constitution and fatwa, there is little evidence of Hamza's activities.[56] As for Maulana Fazlur Rahman, he appears

---

where relatively large communities of Christians exert economic influence. The militants have attacked tourist targets for two main reasons: to shake the confidence of the government and to rid Egypt of Western influences. In an interview with the BBC the Egyptian cleric Sheikh Omar Abdel Rahman, claimed that tourism in Egypt spreads low morals and diseases such as AIDS.

52   Rifa'i Taha, chair of the *shura* council of the Gama'a took responsibility for the attack in Luxor. Taha was among those leaders which later signed the 1998 WIF fatwa. See *The Reconciliation Initiative of the al-Gama'a al-Islamiyya Organization with the Egyptian Regime*, Part 1, p. 3.

53   For a detailed analysis of this strategic decision, see *The Reconciliation Initiative of the al-Gama'a al-Islamiyya Organization with the Egyptian Regime*.

54   For a history of the JUI see Sumita Kumar, 'The Role of Islamic Parties in Pakistani Politics'.

55   In some documents Fazlul Rahman is mistakenly described as the leader of the Jihad Movement in Bangaladesh.

56   According to the Indian researcher B. Rahman, who revised this paragraph, Hamza is from Lashkar-e-Toiba and not from the JUI.

to be the real leader of the JUI. Rahman is described by Indian sources as 'the godfather of the HuM [Harkat-ul-Mujahideen], the Markaz [Dawa Al Irshad] and [its militant wing] Lashkar-e-Toiba of Pakistan'.[57] He is also considered to be the 'godfather of the Taliban and one of the main protectors of bin Laden'.[58]

B.   The Kashmiri Harkat ul-Ansar (HuA)

The Harkat ul-Ansar (HuA), led by Maulana Saadatullah Khan, was formed by the merger of two Pakistani groups, Harkat ul-Jihad al-Islami (Islamic Jihad Movement – HUJI) and Harkat ul-Mujahedeen (Movement of Warriors – HuM). With a pan-Islamic ideology, the group strove to achieve the secession of Jammu and Kashmir from India through violent means and its eventual merger with Pakistan. About 60% of its estimated 1000-strong cadre were Pakistanis and Afghans. The HuA was termed a terrorist organization by the US due to its association with bin Laden in 1997. Hence, the HuA was officially disbanded and regrouped in 1998 as the HuM.

Based in Muzaffarabad, capital of Pakistan-controlled Kashmir, the HuA operated in Kashmir, Myanmar, Tajikistan, Bosnia and Herzegovina. In Kashmir, the group carried out several operations against Indian troops besides attacks on civilian targets. In the process, several of its leaders including the general-secretary and ideologue Masood Azhar, Sajjad Afghani (commander of the HuA in the Indian state of Jammu and Kashmir and Nasarullah Manzoor Langaryal (commander of the former HuM) were captured by Indian security forces. Sajjad Afghani was killed while attempting to escape from jail in 1999. With the near total loss of its senior leadership, the cadre base and Pakistani sponsorship, the HuA appears to have collapsed and is no longer active in the Kashmiri insurgency.[59]

C.   Jihad Movement in Bangladesh

Harkat-ul-Jihad-al-Islam (HJI) is led by Shawkat Osman alias Sheikh Farid. The Bangladeshi militant leader Abdul Salam Muhammad was one of the five

---

[57]   Formed in 1990 in the Kunar province of Afghanistan, the Lashkar-e-Toiba (Army of the Pure – LeT) is the military wing of the Markaz-ud-Dawa-wal-Irshad (MDI), an Islamist organization of the Ahle-Hadith sect in Pakistan. The MDI is based in Muridke near Lahore, Pakistan and is headed by Prof. Hafiz Muhammad Saeed, also the head of the LeT. Its presence in Jammu and Kashmir was first recorded in 1993. See also B. Raman, 'Pakistani Sponsorship Of Terrorism,' *South Asia Analysis Group Papers*, Executive Assessment, 25 February 2000, at <http://www.saag.org/papers2/paper106.html>.

[58]   See B. Raman, 'Rocket Attacks In Islamabad,' *South Asia Analysis Group Papers*, 14 November 1999, at <http://www.saag.org/papers/paper90.html>.

[59]   See *Harkat ul-Ansar*, Institute for Conflict Management (ICM), South Asia Terrorism Portal (SATP), at <http://www.satp.org/satporgtp/countries/india/states/jandk/terrorist_outfits/harkat_ul_ansar_or_harkat_ul_jehad_e_islami.htm>.

signatories of bin Laden's 1998 *fatwa* against the US and the Jews.[60] The organization, which boasts an estimated 15,000 activists, was established with the help of bin Laden in 1992. It runs at least six military training camps in the Chattagong hills. The recruits are mostly students who call themselves the 'Bangladeshi Taliban'.[61]

The HJI, which aims to establish Islamic rule in Bangladesh, has been implicated in several incidents, including the attempted murder of a renowned Bangladeshi poet on 18 January 1999.[62] HJI militants maintain links with terrorist groups in the north-east of India.[63]

D.   The Algerian Islamists

The Front Islamique du Salut movement (FIS) was created in March 1989, when new legislation created the conditions for a more pluralistic political system. In the 1991 national elections in Algeria the FIS won 188 of the 232 seats in the National Assembly; it expected to win control of the parliament and call for an Islamic state. Military leaders decided to confront this threat to the regime by eradicating the FIS. By March 1992, the FIS had been banned by mid-year, leading to isolated outbreaks of violence. Many Islamists subsequently began to organize clandestinely for armed resistance.[64]

The GIA, which brought together Algerian Islamists who had participated or sympathized with the Afghan struggle against the Soviet invasion in the 1980s, was established by Mansour Miliani. Its early leadership was soon dispersed and subsequent leaders resorted increasingly to simple anarchic violence. In late 1993 the GIA announced that its key targets would be foreigners, non-Islamist journalists and intellectuals, civil servants and members of the security forces.[65] The GIA massacred thousands of Algerian civilians thought to support the regime and

---

[60]   No data has been found on Abdul Salam Muhammad.

[61]   See ICM portal at <http://www.satp.org/satporgtp/countries/bangladesh/terroristoutfits/ Huj.htm>. See also <http://www.townhall.com/news/politics/200112/FOR20011206c.shtml>.

[62]   After the assassination of the poet Shamsur Rahman, police arrested 10 HJI activists, who revealed plans to kill 28 prominent intellectuals including the famous feminist writer Taslima Nasreen.

[63]   Reports indicate that the Pakistan Inter-Services Intelligence (ISI) has a hand in the activities of the HJI. The organization has intensified its subversive activities after the Awami League formed the government in June 1996. According to Bangladesh police, a small group called Harkatul Jihad (not synonymous with HJI, unknown by the police), led by Mufti Hannan, is suspected of several bomb attacks in Bangladesh over the last two years. Hannan is believed to have links with the Taliban. See WJHG-TV *News Channel 7*, Panama City Beach, FL, at <http://www. wjhg.com/war/war.htm>.

[64]   See George Joffe, 'Algeria In Crisis,' *Briefing Paper*, No. 48 (June 1998), Middle East Programme, Royal Institute of International Affairs, London.

[65]   Ibid.

oppose their jihad. After a decade of violence, the death toll of the civil war is estimated at 150,000.[66]

In August 1993 the kidnapping of three French consular officials was intended to intimidate foreigners into leaving the country. By mid-December, 23 foreigners had been killed. This new tactic was clearly both a provocation and a warning to Algeria's aid and trade partners, and a reaction from France was not long in coming. Charles Pasqua, French minister of the interior ordered the arrest of 88 people in France with alleged connections to the FIS. With four million Muslims in France, 800,000 of them Algerians, and a French community of 75,000 in Algeria, both countries could bring considerable pressure to bear on each other. By December 1995, 100 foreigners had died in Algeria, many of them French.[67]

The conflict escalated as the GIA hijacked an Air France plane on 26 December 1994. As the incident progressed, three passengers were murdered, 63 were freed, and finally the French Special Forces stormed the aircraft in Marseilles, killing all four Algerian hijackers. Although 170 passengers were rescued, the hijacking greatly internationalized the war. There was also widespread outrage at the evidence that the hijackers had intended to explode the plane over Paris.

The GIA then transferred their campaign to French territory: On 25 July 1995 a bomb exploded in the Paris Metro, killing seven and wounding 17, the first of a series of bombings which had wounded 150 people by October. Ultimately, these attacks appeared to be aimed at diminishing French government support of the Algerian regime.

One of the founders of the GIA, Omar Chikhi, acknowledged that there were many Algerian Afghans in al-Qaeda and that bin Laden offered assistance to the GIA. The GIA leader, Jamal Zetouni, asked Chikhi to meet bin Laden in Sudan As a result, al-Qaeda provided financial assistance and sent many fighters to join the armed action in Algeria. According to Chikhi some were later killed in internecine fighting by Jamal Zetouni and others were arrested.[68]

As a result of the massacres of Algerian civilians, the organization was condemned by many of its former supporters and split in three factions. Even bin Laden decried the massacres of Muslims and chose to support one of the new factions that was founded by Hassan Hattab, former GIA commander and veteran of the Afghan war, namely the Salafi Group for Call and Combat (known in

---

[66] See Jonathan Schanzer, 'Algeria's GSPC And America's 'War On Terror', *Policywatch,* The Washington Institute for Near East Policy, No. 666, 2 October 2002 at <http://www.washington institute.org/watch/Policywatch/policywatch2002/666.htm>.

[67] See Insurgency, 'Legitimacy and Intervention In Algeria,' *Commentary*, A Canadian Security Intelligence Service publication, No. 65 (January 1996), at <http://www.csis-scrs.gc.ca/eng/comment/com65_e.html>.

[68] See interview with Omar Chikhi, last surviving founding member of the GIA, London *Al-Majallah,* 14-20 January 2001.

French as Groupe Salafiste pour la Prédication et le Combat – GSPC, and in Arabic al-Jama'a al-Salafiyya lil-Da'wa wal-Qital). Bin Laden not only provided logistical and financial support for the new movement, but was also rumored to have suggested the name for the new group. The two other factions are: The Islamic Movement for Spreading the Faith and Holy War; and The Faithful to the Oath.[69] The GSPC did not accept a truce achieved between the FIS and the Algerian government in June 1999, while distancing itself from massacres and the targeting of civilians. The group, said to comprise about 700 armed militants, attracted activists of GIA who opposed indiscriminate violence and FIS members who rejected the truce and reportedly received promises of financial assistance from bin Laden in order to activate alternative Algerian networks in Europe.[70]

E.   Palestinians active in the al-Qaeda network

As noted above, the Palestinian Abdallah Azzam, one of the most prominent ideologues of the Afghani mujahideen moved in 1980 from Jordan to Peshawar, Pakistan. From there he influenced many Jordanians of Palestinian origin to join the Afghani jihad in the 1980s against the Soviet occupation, and to either remain there or fight in other places (Bosnia, Albania, Kosovo or Chechnya) during the 1990s.

Palestinian Islamists participated in small terrorist groups in Jordan that were exposed from the 1980s: Jaysh Muhammad (the Army of Muhammad); al-Islah wal-Tahaddi (Reform and Challenge); and Takfir (Repudiation). A small Islamist group called Usbat al-Ansar (the League of Supporters) is active in the Ein el-Hilweh Palestinian refugee camp in South Lebanon. Munir Husein Maqdah, a former prominent commander of the Palestinian Fatah organization in Lebanon, was among the defendants in the millennium bombing plot in Jordan.[71]

F.   Chechnya, the Caucasus and Central Asia

Since 1996 Arab-Afghan veterans became increasingly involved in Chechnya,[72] many collaborating with local Chechen military commanders. An Arab battalion

---

[69] See Wiktorowicz, *The New Global Threat*, pp. 28-29.

[70] See Esther Webman, 'Political Islam at the Close of the Twentieth Century,' *Middle East Contemporary Survey (MECS)* 1999, The Moshe Dayan Center for Middle Eastern and African Studies, Tel Aviv University, at <http://www.dayan.org/islam99.pdf>, p. 18.

[71] See Reuven Paz, 'Palestinian Participation in the Islamist Global Network,' *Policywatch*, The Washington Institute for Near East Policy, No. 453, 14 April 2000, at <http://www.washington institute.org/watch/Policywatch/policywatch2000/453.htm>.

[72] In mid-1991, sensing weakness and confusion within the Kremlin, nationalist leaders within the Chechen Republic began to press demands for independence. A new local government, led by former Soviet Air Force General, Dzhokhar Dudayev, declared Chechen independence in No-

was even formed there under the command of Ibn al-Khattab, a Jordanian veteran of the Afghan war. His group maintained close contacts with bin Laden, but the nature and intensity of these contacts is not clear. The exact ideology of this group is also unknown, but it seems to be part of the growing Wahhabi and Takfiri influence in the Caucasus.

In 1996 an Islamist group was founded under the name of the Islamic Movement of Uzbekistan (IMU). It brought together several small groups of the Central Asian Wahhabi trend and followers of the Muslim Brotherhood under the joint leadership of Mohammad Tahir Farouq (Tohir Yuldashev) as *amir*, Al-Zubair Bin Abd al-Rahim as the religious authority and Juma Namangani as military commander. While viewed as part of the global jihad, its main campaign was against the Uzbek regime. The movement tried to spread its influence in the northern part of Afghanistan, where the population is of Uzbek origin.[73] Its members include individuals who fought in the civil war in Tajikistan between 1992 and 1997 and were trained in Afghanistan or Pakistan. However it is not only Uzbeks who joined the IMU, but young militants from all ethnic groups of Central Asia. It was also joined by Muslim Uighurs in the Chinese province of Xinjiang who were engaged in their own jihad against Beijing.[74] From early 1999, it adopted more violent tactics including bombings and kidnappings.[75]

G.   The Balkan connection

Between 1992 and 1995 some 3,000 Islamic fighters converged to Bosnia from Muslim countries. Many formed a unit called El Mudzahid that was formally part of the Seventh Muslim Brigade within the Third Corps of the Army of Bosnia and Herzegovina (ABiH). The El Mudzahid was disbanded in 1996, under American pressure, and the Seventh Muslim Brigade was disbanded soon afterwards. Some former mujahideen settled in a central Bosnian village, where they sometimes threatened the Stabilization Force in Bosnia and Herzegovina (SFOR) and may have been responsible for crimes against Croat returnees and police. They

---

vember 1991. Shamil Basayev, a Chechen guerrilla commander trained in Afghanistan and Pakistan by the mujahideen, realized that the Chechens would never be able to defend against a full-scale Russian invasion, together with a handful of accomplices he hijacked a passenger plane in the town of Mineralnye Vody demanding that the Russians lift the state of emergency or the plane would be blown up. The invasion was halted when the Russian parliament failed to ratify the decision to invade. After a number of unsuccessful, clandestine attempts to unseat the popular Dudayev, the Russian government, in December 1994, deployed both regular and internal forces to crush Chechnya's self-proclaimed independence.

[73]   See Ahmad Rashid, *Confrontations brew among Islamic Militants in Central Asia,'* 22 November 2000, at <http://www.cacianalyst.org/view_article.php?articleid=113>.

[74]   See Ahmed Rashid, 'CA fears renewed insurgency,' Parts 1 and 2, (Islamabad) *The Nation* 5 April 2001.

[75]   See Reuven Paz, *Tangled Web*, p. 30.

dispersed in 2001 when the new authorities evicted them from properties belonging to returning Serbs. Associates of bin Laden may have been active in Croatia during the war in Bosnia, at a time when several Islamic charitable organizations were operating in the country and weapons from Muslim countries were smuggled through Croatia to Bosnia. While it is highly likely that arms were smuggled through Croatia in this way, the involvement of agents of bin Laden is unproven.[76]

A network run by bin Laden sent units to fight in the Serbian province of Kosovo. Bin Laden is believed to have established an Albanian operation in 1994 after informing the government he headed a wealthy Saudi humanitarian agency which wished to aid Albania. Apparent confirmation of bin Laden's activities came during the murder trial of Claude Kader, a French national who admitted he was a member of bin Laden's Albanian network. Kader claimed that he had visited Albania to recruit and arm fighters for Kosovo.[77] In addition, number of Islamist terrorists were arrested and deported in 1998-99 for plotting to attack the US embassy in Tirana.

H.   Yemen – The Aden-Abyan Islamic Army (AAIA)

The Aden-Abyan Islamic Army reportedly consisted of Yemeni and Egyptian Islamic Jihad members who had received military training and ideological indoctrination in Afghanistan and thereafter joined Yemeni government troops during the 1994 civil war. After the war, some of these militants were integrated in the Yemeni civilian establishment. Others, led by Zayn al-Abidin al-Mihdar (Abu al-Hasan) announced in mid-1998 the formation of the AAIA. The group released a series of communiqués that expressed support for bin Laden, appealed for the overthrow of the Yemeni government and the beginning of operations against US and other Western interests in Yemen. Although it did not belong to bin Laden's WIF, its terminology and objectives were similar: it described the secularist Yemeni regime as infidel and deemed its overthrow a religious duty and it protested the Anglo-US military air strikes against Iraq.[78]

I.   South East Asia

The Islamic Group (Jemaah Islamiyyah – JI) operates from Malaysia to Australia. The JI was founded by Abdullah Sungkar, a long-time Islamist, after meeting bin

---

[76] See 'Bin Laden and the Balkans: The Politics Of Anti-Terrorism,' *ICG Balkans Report* No. 119, 9 November 2001, pp. 3-21.

[77] See *The Charleston Gazette*, 30 November 1998. The newspaper quoted Fatos Klosi, the head of the Albanian intelligence service.

[78] The information on the AAIA is mainly based on Webman, *Political Islam at the Close of the Twentieth Century*, pp. 14-16.

Laden in Afghanistan. Following his death in Indonesia in 1999, spiritual leadership of the group was assumed by his close friend Abu Bakr Bashir (Ba'asyir).

The Malaysian-based leadership termed a shura or consultative council, was headed by Mohammed Iqbal A Rahman (alias Abu Jibril) until his arrest and detention by Malaysian authorities in June 2001. Hambali (alias Nurjaman or Riduan Samuddin), a Malaysian resident of Indonesian nationality, then took over as acting head of the shura.

At least 100 JI members were trained in the use of weapons and explosives in al-Qaeda training camps in Afghanistan from the early 1990s and began planning operations in the late 1990s.

The JI in Singapore reported to the Malaysian shura and was headed by Haji Ibrahim until his arrest in December 2001. He went to Afghanistan for al-Qaeda military training in 1993. Singaporean recruits were trained in Negri Sembilan, Malaysia before being dispatched to Afghanistan for further al-Qaeda training. JI members were also trained in Indonesia and in Mindanao in the Philippines. The al-Qaeda grouping in Kuala Lumpur that supported the 9/11 attacks belonged to the JI.[79]

J.   The emergence of Abu Sayyaf

In late 1969 the Moro National Liberation Front (MNLF) was formed to create an independent Muslim nation in the southern Philippines. The MNLF was supported by Muammar Qaddafi in Libya. By the mid-1970s the MNLF had perhaps 30,000 militants engaging in combat with Philippine Army units and police in the Sulu Archipelago and Mindanao. Initial successes began to fade by late 1975; a cease-fire in 1976 and the establishment of a provisional autonomous, but not independent, Muslim zone in the southern Philippines seemed to signify real gains for the MNLF. In 1977 a leadership split in the MNLF resulted in a breakaway organization that adopted the name of the Moro Islamic Liberation Front (MILF) by 1983. The MILF, though smaller than its predecessor, also had substantial numbers of armed combatants.[80]

In 1991 a radical group opposed to the peace process between the Muslims and the Philippine state left the MNLF to form the Bearer of the Sword (Abu Sayyaf Group – ASG). Its main purpose was to establish an Islamic state in the southern Philippines. The founder of Abu Sayyaf was Abduragak Abubakar Janjalani, who led the group until December 1998, when he was killed by police.

---

[79]   See Jane's Intelligence Review, March 2002, p. 8.
[80]   See Graham J. Turbiville, Jr., 'Bearer of the Sword,' *Military Review*, Command & General Staff College, Fort Leavenworth, Kansas, March-April 2002 English Edition, at <http://www.cgsc. army.mil/milrev/english/MarApr02/turbiville.asp>.

Janjalani developed close ties with other Islamist groups while fighting in the Afghan war. The ASG reportedly trained some 20,000 foreign mujahideen from the Middle East, North Africa and the Philippines. The choice of sensational terrorist actions, like bombings and kidnappings of foreigners, placed Abu Sayyaf's struggle on the international agenda.[81]

By 1990 Janjalani had left Afghanistan and returned to his Basilan Island home in the Philippines. The ASG grew to at least several hundred members and made its presence felt in Basilan, the Sulu Archipelago, and some parts of Mindanao. Following the Afghan war, bin Laden reportedly funneled money and other support to the ASG, although the precise nature of the aid is not known. Bin Laden's brother-in-law, a Saudi financier named Muhammad Jamal Khalifa, was alleged to be one of the principal vectors of funding to the ASG through an Islamic charity in the Philippines. Some sources have linked Khalifa to a key individual, Ramzi Yusuf, who was involved in the 1993 World Trade Center bombing. As the unraveling of the Taliban regime accelerated in mid-November 2001 under the impact of US and Northern Alliance attacks, Moros were reported to be fighting near Kabul with Taliban and al-Qaeda militants.[82]

K.   Al-Qaeda – Hizballah links

According to one of the al-Qaeda activists on trial in the US, bin Laden met in Sudan between 1991 and 1993 with Imad Mughniyah, Hizballah's main terrorist operative. They discussed their common goal of forcing the US to withdraw from the Middle East. The defendant testified that Hizballah provided explosives training for al-Qaeda and the Egyptian Jihad Group and that Iran used Hizballah to supply explosives that were disguised to look like rocks.[83] His testimony adds authority to earlier reports that the Iranian Ministry of Information and Security had called a terrorist conference in Tehran in 1996 that included Mughniyah and a senior aide to bin Laden.[84] According to a founding leader of the Algerian GIA, the group sent two teams to Hizballah camps in South Lebanon for training.[85]

---

[81] See Christos Iacovou, From MNLF to Abu Sayyaf. The Radicalization of Islam in the Philippines, 11 July 2000, at ICT website <http://www.ict.org.il/articles/articledet.cfm?articleid=116>.

[82] Turbiville, Jr., *Bearer of the Sword.*

[83] Ali A. Mohamed, a former Green Beret sergeant and one of six men indicted for the bombings of American embassies in Africa in 1998 confessed in court the first credible, public evidence not only that Mughniyah and bin Laden were collaborating, but that Iran had also been backing them. See Barry Rubin and Judith Colp Rubin (eds.), *Anti-American terrorism and the Middle East. A Documentary Reading* (Oxford University Press, 2002), p, 209.

[84] See Milt Bearden and Larry Johnson, 'A Glimpse at the Alliances of Terror,' *New York Times*, 7 November 2000.

[85] See interview with Omar Chikhi, last surviving founding member of the GIA, London *Al-Majallah,* 14-20 January 2001.

IV.   TYPOLOGICAL DEFINITION

According to Hoffman, one of the distinguishing features of international terrorism during the past 15 years has been the resurgence and proliferation of terrorist groups motivated by a religious imperative. In 1968, for example, none of the 11 identifiable terrorist groups active throughout the world could be classified as religious, that is, having aims and motivations reflecting a salient religious character or influence.[86]

Not until 1980, as a result of the repercussions of the revolution in Iran the previous year, did the first 'modern' religious terrorist groups appear. This form of terrorism, of course, occurred throughout history, although in recent decades it was largely been overshadowed by nationalist/separatist or ideologically motivated terrorism. Twelve years later, Hoffman noted, the number of religious terrorist groups increased nearly six-fold, while the number of ethnic-separatist terrorist groups declined and the number of Marxist-Leninist-Maoist remained unchanged.

Hoffman claimed that the implications of terrorism motivated by a religious imperative for higher levels of lethality was manifest by the violent record of various Shi'a Islamic groups.[87] Admittedly, many 'secular' terrorist groups have a strong religious element: the IRA for instance, and perhaps the PLO. However, the predominant characteristic of these groups is political, as evidenced by their nationalist or irredentist aims. In his seminal study of what he termed 'holy terror,' Rapoport pointed out that the relationship between terrorism and religion was not new; until the nineteenth century 'religion provided the only acceptable justifications for terror'.[88]

According to Rosenfeld, the religion of bin Laden has more in common with movements that arise out of a 'cultic milieu,' i.e. is a parallel religious tradition of disparaged and deviant interpretations and practices that challenge the authority of prevailing religions with rival claims to truth. They adhere to an alternative theology that they regard as more authoritative than the laws, rituals, and interpretations that define their parent religions. By legitimizing violence and terror as a theological imperative, jihadism shares defining features with similar movements in other cultures.[89]

---

[86]   See Bruce Hoffman, 'Terrorism Trends And Prospects,' In Ian O. Lesser, Bruce Hoffman, John Arquilla, David F. Ronfeldt, Michele Zanini, Brian Michael Jenkins, *The New Terrorism*, Rand Report MR-989-AF, p. 11, at <http://www.rand.org/publications/MR/MR989/MR989.chap2.pdf>.

[87]   Although these organizations committed only 8% of all international terrorist incidents since 1982, they are nonetheless responsible for 28% of the total number of deaths.

[88]   See David C. Rapoport, 'Fear and Trembling: Terrorism in Three Religious Traditions,' *American Political Science Review*, Vol. 78, No. 3 (September 1984), p. 659.

[89]   See Jean E. Rosenfeld, 'The 'Religion' of Usamah bin Ladin: Terror as the Hand of God,' at the *Political Research Associates* website <http://www.publiceye.org/frontpage/911/Islam/rosenfeld 2001.htm>.

Wessinger defines the goal of bin Laden and his colleagues as follows: 'to pit the United States against the Muslim world, and in so doing to foment a revolution of fundamentalist Muslims against current Muslim governments (considered apostate) in order to create a unified, "true" Islamic state.' She sees the phenomenon as 'the most dangerous form of apocalypticism in action' and terms it 'revolutionary millennialism'.[90]

V.   COOPERATION BETWEEN THE VARIOUS AL-QAEDA NETWORK MEMBERS PRIOR TO THE FOUNDING OF THE WIF

Al-Qaeda has been linked since 1992 to several acts of international terrorism. Bin Laden himself has been indicted by a US court for involvement in several incidents:[91]

(1) The attempted bombings in December 1992 against 100 US military personnel in Yemen who were supporting UN relief operations in Somalia (Operation Restore Hope).

(2) The provision of weapons to anti-US militias in Somalia. In 1992 and 1993 Mohamed Atef, one of the military leaders of al-Qaeda, frequently traveled to Somalia to organize attacks against US and UN troops stationed in Somalia. On each occasion he reported back to bin Laden at his base in the Riyadh district of Khartoum.

(3) In the spring of 1993, Atef, together with Saif al Adel, another senior member of al-Qaeda, and other activists began to provide military training to Somali tribes for the purpose of fighting the UN forces during Operation Restore Hope.

(4) On 3 and 4 October 1993 al-Qaeda members participated in the attack on US military personnel in Somalia, killing 18.

---

[90] Revolutionary millennial movements also include 'the German Nazis, Nichiren Buddhists involved in Japanese militarism in World War II, Maoist Communists, the Khmer Rouge in Cambodia … and the Euro-American nativist movement in the United States (Neo-Nazis, Identity Christians, Odinists).' See Catherine Wessinger, 'Bin Laden and Revolutionary Millennialism,' *NewOrleans Times-Picayune*, 10 October 2001, at <http://www.mille.org/cmshome/wessladen.html>.

[91] See 'Responsibility For The Terrorist Atrocities In The United States, 11 September 2001 – An Updated Account,' Document of the British Government, 28 November 2003, at <http://www.number-10.gov.uk/output/Page3682.asp>. See also Kenneth Katzman, 'Terrorism: Near Eastern Groups and State Sponsors, 2001,' *CRS Report for Congress*, 10 September 2001, at <http://www.useu.be/Terrorism/TerrorismRptCRS2001.pdf>, pp. 10-11.

(5) Four Saudi nationals involved in the 13 November 1995 bombing of a US military training facility in Riyadh, Saudi Arabia, admitted to being inspired by bin Laden.

(6) Members of al-Qaeda might have aided the Egyptian Islamic Group assassination attempt against Egyptian President Mubarak in Ethiopia in June 1995.[92]

(7) Al-Qaeda is also linked to the 1995 bombing of the Egyptian embassy in Pakistan by the Egyptian Islamic Jihad that killed over 20 Egyptians and Pakistanis.

(8) Members of bin Laden's network plotted to blow up US airliners in the Pacific and separately conspired to kill the Pope.

(9) On 18 December 1995 a car bomb in the town of Zenica, Bosnia, probably targeted the US NATO troops serving in Bosnia-Herzegovina in retaliation for the life sentence given to Sheik Omah Abdel Rahman for his role in the WTC bombing in New York in 1993.

In mid-1996 a meeting of various Muslim leaders convened by bin Laden reached a consensus 'to use force to confront all foreign forces stationed on Islamic land,' and to form a planning committee; a financing, supply, and mobilization committee; and a higher military committee to oversee implementation of the plan.

From 1996, bin Laden's anti-US rhetoric escalated to the point of calling for worldwide attacks on Americans and allies, including civilians.[93]

Bin Laden publicly issued his 'Declaration of War' against the US in August 1996. In November 1996 he pronounced as 'praiseworthy terrorism' the bombings in Riyadh and at Khobar in Saudi Arabia, promising that other attacks would follow.[94] He admitted carrying out attacks on US military personnel in Somalia and Yemen.[95] In an interview broadcast in February 1997, he stated that 'if someone can kill an American soldier, it is better than wasting time on other matters'.[96]

---

[92] See *Patterns of Global Terrorism*, 1997 at <http://www.state.gov/www/global/terrorism/1997 Report/1997index.html>. There is no direct evidence that bin Laden was involved in the February 1993 bombing of the World Trade Center. However, *Patterns of Global Terrorism*, 1999 affirms that bin Laden's network was responsible for plots in Asia believed to be orchestrated by Ramzi Yusuf, who was captured in Pakistan, brought to the US and convicted in November 1997 of masterminding the WTC bombing. The plots in Asia, all of which failed, were: to assassinate the Pope during his late 1994 visit to the Philippines and President Clinton during his visit there in early 1995; to bomb the US and Israeli embassies in Manila in late 1994; and to bomb 12 US trans-Pacific flights.

[93] See Al-Qa'ida (The Base), the *FAS* website at <http://www.fas.org/irp/world/para/ladin.htm>.

[94] See *al-Qa'ida (The Base)* on the website of the Federation of American Scientists, at www.fas.org/irp/world/para/ladin.htm.

[95] See *CIA Fact Sheet – Osama bin Laden* (Unclassified), p. 5, at <http://www.skfriends.com/bin-laden-cia-fact-sheet.htm>.

[96] Ibid.

VI.   TERRORIST ACTIVITY BY AL-QAEDA NETWORK GROUPS: FEBRUARY 1998-SEPTEMBER 2001

In February 1998 bin Laden announced the creation of a new alliance of terrorist organizations, the World Islamic Front for Jihad Against Jews and Crusaders. In May 1998, he stated at a press conference in Afghanistan that the results of his threats would be seen 'in a few weeks'.[97]

From February 1998 Arab and Pakistani media reported that the US authorities were conducting a serious international effort to obtain the extradition of bin Laden from Afghanistan and that special commandos of the CIA and FBI had arrived in Pakistan to arrest him.[98] The permanent representative for the US at the UN, Bill Richardson, visited Afghanistan in April 1998 to hold talks with the Taliban on the issue and the US increased its efforts to obtain bin Laden's arrest after his alleged threats to the US diplomatic missions in Pakistan. When the WIF was presented to a press conference of Muslim journalists in Afghanistan, a reporter maintained that bin Laden and his colleagues could not possibly take on the world's only superpower. Bin Laden contended that the US was vulnerable and could be defeated in war in the same way that the USSR had suffered humiliation at the hands of the Afghan and Arab mujahideen in Afghanistan.

The suicide bombings of the US embassies in Kenya and Tanzania on 7 August 1998, which killed 224 persons (including 12 Americans) in Nairobi and 11 in Dar-es-Salam, can be viewed as the first real operation conducted by the newly formed WIF.[99] An unknown group calling itself the Islamic Army for the Liberation of the Holy Places (al-Jaysh al-Islami li-Tahrir al-Amakin al-Muqaddasa) claimed responsibility for the bombings, referring to the Nairobi attack as Operation Holy Ka'ba and the Dar al-Salam attack as 'Operation al-Aqsa Mosque.' The statements expressed determination to pursue American forces and interests until they withdrew from Muslim lands, particularly the Arabian Peninsula, and ended their support of Israel.[100]

From the latter part of 1993, members of al-Qaeda in Kenya began to discuss the possibility of attacking the US embassy in Nairobi in retaliation for US participation in Operation Restore Hope in Somalia. Ali Mohamed, a US citizen and declared member of al-Qaeda, took photographs and made sketches of the embassy which he presented to bin Laden in Sudan. He also admitted that he had

---

[97] Al-Qa'ida (The Base), the *FAS* website.
[98] See the Rawalpindi *Jang*, 31 March 1998.
[99] For their alleged role in the bombings, 17 alleged members of al-Qaeda were indicted by a US court, including bin Laden. Four of the six in US custody were tried and convicted; three are in custody in Britain.
[100] See Webman, *The Polarization and Radicalization of Political Islam*, p. 4.

trained terrorists for al-Qaeda in Afghanistan in the early 1990s, including many involved in the East African bombings in August 1998. Al-Qaeda and Egyptian Islamic Jihad activists took part in the preparation and the actual attack on the US embassies.[101] Following the bombings, the WIF issued new threats.

A Palestinian from Jordan arrested at the Karachi airport, after arriving from Nairobi on the day of the bombings, revealed that he was part of a cell of Palestinians, Jordanians and Egyptians operated by bin Laden who were responsible for the bombings. Another suspect, arrested in Kenya, was a Yemeni national. All were brought to the US to stand trial in New York.

In late 1999 a series of arrests throughout the US, Europe and the Middle East of Islamist militants belonging to or connected with al-Qaeda foiled a terror campaign called 'the millennium plot'. Several days after the millennium celebrations, President Clinton's national security adviser, Sandy Berger, announced that in the weeks before the New Year, law enforcement had disrupted terrorist cells 'in eight countries and attacks were almost certainly prevented'.[102]

1.   United States

In December 1999 the arrest of the Algerian citizen Ahmed Ressam foiled a plan to bomb the Los Angeles airport. Ressam had lived in Montreal for four years. His home was later identified by Canadian and international police as the Montreal headquarters of a GIA terrorist cell. Ressam trained in Afghanistan in April 1998 at the camps funded and administered by bin Laden. He met there with Abu Zubaida, a senior bin Laden aide in charge of the camps and was later assigned to the European-based cell of the Algerian group. The members of the cell planned to travel separately to Canada to commence an operation in the US before the end of 1999. According to his testimony, Ressam began working out the details of his plan to bomb the Los Angeles airport in the late summer of 1999. During this time, he renewed ties with Mokhtar Haouari, another Algerian refugee in Montreal who expressed interest in attending jihad training in Afghanistan and helped fund Ressam's activities. Haouari also connected Ressam with an associate in New York, Abdelghani Meskini, who was to be his assistant and guide in the US. Ressam maintains, however, that neither Meskini nor Haouari knew of the specific target of Ressam's plan. His arrest led to the discovery of more Algerian terrorists or supporters: Abdelmajid Dahoumane, indicted with

---

[101] See 'Responsibility For The Terrorist Atrocities in The United States,' British Official Document, at www.number-10.gov.uk/output/Page3682.asp.
[102] See 'Other Millennium Attacks,' *Frontline*, PBS, at <http://www.pbs.org/wgbh/pages/frontline/shows/trail/inside/attacks.html>.

Ressam for transporting explosives and timing devices from Canada into the US; Hamid Aich, an Algerian arrested briefly in Ireland, then released; Mohambedou Ould Slahi, a Mauritanian who might link the Algerians directly to bin Laden. Abdelmajid Dahoumane escaped to Afghanistan. He was later caught by Algerian security forces and convicted there on terrorism-related charges.[103]

2.   Jordan

In December 1999, the Jordanian authorities arrested a group of 21 suspected terrorists: 18 Jordanian citizens, an American, an Iraqi, and an Egyptian. According to some sources, the group also included a Yemenite and an Algerian. Some were members of Harakat al-Islah wal-Tahaddi who had come to Jordan from Afghanistan. Seven others were outside of Jordan and were indicted in absentia. Another suspect, a Palestinian named Khalil al-Dik, was extradited to Jordan from Pakistan and was tried separately. The group intended to bomb the Radisson SAS Hotel in Amman on 3 January 2000, and to attack American and Israeli tourists at Mount Nebo and at a site on the Jordan River, purportedly under the guidance of bin Laden. In May 2001 Jordanian authorities detained another 15 suspects connected with this case.

In September 2000 Khadhr Abu Hawshar, the leader of the group, was condemned to death. Abu Hawshar, a veteran of the Afghan war, joined the Jaysh Muhammad (Muhammad's Army). Following his release from a Jordanian prison in 1993, he moved to Yemen, where he joined the Egyptian Jihad. Other defendants sentenced to death in absentia included: Munir al-Maqdah, a Palestinian Fatah commander from the 'Ein al-Hilwa refugee camp in Lebanon; Ra'id Hijjazi, an American citizen considered to be Hawshar's assistant, who was subsequently arrested in October by the Syrian security authorities and handed over to Jordan; and Muhammad Husayn Zayn al-'Abidin, also known as Abu Zubayda, a Palestinian living in Pakistan who was believed to be a key aide to Bin Ladin and coordinator of his 'external operations.'[104] A Jordanian Islamist

---

[103] See 'Inside Ahmed Ressam's Millennium Plot,' *Frontline*, PBS, at <http://www.pbs.org/wgbh/pages/frontline/shows/trail/inside/cron.html> (no date).

[104] Abu Zubayda was arrested in April 2002 in Pakistan and extradited to the US. His capture has been considered a significant achievement in the long battle against the al-Qaeda and its affiliated terrorist cells. He was a key figure in the millennium plot by al-Qaeda cells in Jordan, Canada, and the US. Abu Zubayda instructed Jamal Beghal, the ringleader of a European terror network whose members planned several attacks in France and in Belgium and were detained in September 2001. Beghal, himself, was arrested in Dubai on 28 July 2001. Abu Zubayda is certainly qualified to be seen as 'The' coordinator between al-Qaeda and its affiliated cells. See Yoram Schweitzer, 'The Arrest of Abu Zubayda: An important Achievement with More to Come,' 9 April 2002, at *ICT website*, <http://www.ict.org.il/articles/articledet.cfm?articleid=433>.

living in Britain, 'Umar Abu Qatada, was sentenced in absentia to fifteen years for his alleged role in financing the group.[105]

3.   The Balkans

The US authorities discovered that Ahmed Ressam also had contacts in Bosnia. Among them was Karim Said Atmani, identified as the document forger for the Algerians accused of plotting the bombings. Bosnian authorities discovered that other former mujahideen who had recently lived in the Sarajevo area in the past few years were linked to the same Algerian group or to Khalil al-Dik, on trial in Jordan. A second Bosnian citizen, Hamid Aich (also an Algerian citizen), worked for a charity associated with bin Laden.[106] Bosnian officials believe the former mujahideen – who came from Tunisia, Sudan, Algeria, Afghanistan, Egypt and other Middle Eastern countries – obtained citizenship by marrying Bosnian women, many of them war widows.[107]

Islamist appeals to militants to fight in Kosovo did not gain momentum, as many who offered to join the KLA were rejected, allegedly because of American pressure. The coordinated pursuit by various Western security forces of Islamists in Albania and Bosnia, which led in June 1998 to the capture of three members of the Egyptian Jihad movement, may also have limited Islamist attempts to reach Kosovo.[108]

4.   Chechnya

In August 1999 a group of Chechen and Dagestani separatists led by the hard-line Chechen militia commander Shamil Basayev and the Islamist Ibn al-Khattab

---

[105] See also Esther Webman, 'The Undiminished Threat of Political Islam,' *Middle East Contemporary Survey (MECS) 2000*, The Moshe Dayan Center for Middle Eastern and African Studies, Tel Aviv University, at <http://www.dayan.org/islam2000.pdf>.

[106] In its 26 June 1997 report on the bombing of the Al Khobar building in Riyadh, Saudi Arabia, the *New York Times* noted that those arrested confessed to serving with Bosnian Muslims forces. The terrorists also admitted to ties with bin Laden. According to *the New York Times Magazine* of 6 February 2000, Jordanian intelligence alerted the CIA in 1999 to at least three plots by Bosnia-based Islamic terrorists to attack US targets in Europe.

[107] The Dayton Agreement for Peace in Bosnia and Herzegovina of November 1995, that ended the Bosnia and Croatia war with the Federal Republic of Yugoslavia (1992-1995), ordered all foreign soldiers to leave the country, including those who fought alongside the government army. Many of those who fought in the Bosnian Muslim Army included Islamist radicals from the Arab world, Afghanistan, Pakistan and South East Asia. However, an undisclosed number remained, obtaining Bosnian citizenship as members of the army or by marrying Bosnian women. See Jeffrey Smith, 'Bosnian Village's Terrorist Ties; Links to US Bomb Plot Arouse Concern About Enclave of Islamic Guerrillas,' *The Washington Post,* 11 March 2000.

[108] See Webman, *Political Islam at the Close of the Twentieth Century*, p. 10.

crossed into Dagestan from Chechnya and took control of a number of villages with the stated aim of establishing an independent Islamic republic in the Caucasus region, but were driven back by Russian troops. A spate of bombings in Moscow and Volgodonsk in September 1999 attributed to Chechen separatists claimed the lives of several hundred civilians and prompted Russia to withdraw its recognition of Aslan Maskhadov as the Chechen president and launch military operations against Chechnya in October. According to Russian intelligence reports, financial aid reached the rebels from Saudi Arabia, Kuwait and Qatar and various Islamist groups in Pakistan and Turkey, and Chechen rebels were joined by fighters from a number of Gulf Arab states, as well as Islamists who were trained in Bosnia.[109] Ibn al-Khattab, the leader of the Arab battalion in Chechnya, was accused of receiving $25 million from bin Laden.[110]

5.   Kashmir/Pakistan/India

The first reference by bin Laden to India was made at the press conference in Afghanistan on 26 May 1998. He claimed he would have loved to join the jihad in Kashmir, but the Pakistani authorities would not permit him. Thereafter, he has not referred to India in any of his statements or interviews, although he claimed the right of the Kashmiris to self-determination. In the context of Taliban's interest to keep open the possibility of a rapprochement with India, it is not surprising that the regime denied the report disseminated in September 1999 by an anti-India Pakistani daily that Osama has declared a jihad against India.[111]

A statement issued in Pakistan claimed bin Laden had appointed a military adviser to establish a network in the Indian-ruled Kashmir and that he had 'declared war against the United States and India'. However, Harkat-ul-Mujahideen group leader Fazlur Rehman Khalil told a news conference there was no truth to claims that bin Laden planned to set up a network in Kashmir. 'This is all baseless,' he said, 'Osama has nobody in Kashmir. However, as a Muslim he could express moral support (for Kashmiri Muslim militants) but gives no other support'.[112]

---

[109] Ibid., p. 10-11.

[110] In an exclusive interview to the Islamist Azzam Publications on 27 September 1999, Ibn al-Khattab presented bin Laden as 'our brother in Islam ... a Mujahid fighting with his wealth and himself for the sake of Allah ... well established with the Mujahideen in Afghanistan and other places in the world. But the distance between him and us is very big. As you know, routes and communication between him and us are severed. However, he claimed, bin Laden 'never financed us in the Jihad in Dagestan because the distance between us is too huge and we have no contact whatsoever,' and anyway 'such amounts of money ($25 million) were never spent by the Mujahideen in order to fight the Russian Forces.' See the interview on the *IslamicAwakening.com* website at <http://www.as-sahwah.com/viewarticle.php?Article ID=640>.

[111] See B. Raman, 'Bin Laden, Taliban and India,' *South Asia Analysis Group Papers*, No. 83, 29 September 1999, at <http://www.saag.org/papers/paper83.html>.

[112] See *CNN Asianow*, 30 September 1999.

In December 1999 an Indian airliner was hijacked by the Pakistani group Harakat ul-Mujahidin (HuM), an Islamic militant group based in Kashmir. The hijackers forced the plane to land in Afghanistan and demanded the release of several Islamist activists, among them the group's leader Masoud al-Azhar. One passenger was killed. Through the mediation of the Taliban, the Indian government released three prisoners, including al-Azhar. In addition, other Kashmiri and Pakistani groups stepped up their terrorist campaign against India during this same period. Two of these groups were cosignatories of bin Laden's 'Jihad against the Jews and the Crusaders' *fatwa*. Furthermore, many of the Islamists fighting in Kashmir began to employ suicide attacks since 1999.

In June 2001 at least four Islamist were arrested in India while trying to prepare an attack against the American embassy.

6.   Israel/Palestinian Authority (PA)

In August 2000 the Israeli security service uncovered a Palestinian terrorist ring established in Gaza Strip by bin Laden. Members planned to carry out a series of attacks against Israeli targets, including suicide bombings inside Israel's pre 1967 borders and the launching of anti-tank missiles at settlements in the occupied territories. The terrorist ring was discovered following the arrest of its leader, Nabil Oukal, from the Jebalya refugee camp in the Gaza Strip. Oukal had also tried to recruit two members of the Islamic Movement in Israel. Okal also received help, mostly financial, from Hamas spiritual leader Sheikh Ahmed Yassin. He told his interrogators that he did not inform Hamas of his links with bin Laden and only wanted to receive Hamas cover and help for the organization.[113]

7.   Yemen

In late December 1998 members of the Aden-Abyan Islamic Army in Yemen kidnapped 16 Western hostages (British, Australian, and US tourists), four of which were killed. The trials of 14 and then another eight militants charged with the kidnapping and other subversive activity included four British Muslims and one French Muslim of Algerian extraction.[114] They were charged with associating

---

[113]   The presence of bin Laden cells in Jordan, coupled with Israeli arrests of alleged bin Laden operatives in the West Bank and Gaza Strip suggested that Al-Qaeda might plan acts of terrorism in connection with the Palestinian uprising.

[114]   The group included Muhammad Mustafa Kamil, son of Egyptian Islamist Abu Hamza al-Masri who headed the London-based Supporters of the Shari'a (Ansar al-Shari'a) organization. Some of the defendants confessed that Abu Hamza had sent them to be trained in the Aden-Abyan Islamic Army camps for two months. Upon their return to London, the Islamists were to be sent to Kosovo or Kashmir to carry out jihad.

with armed groups, plotting to blow up British and American targets in Aden, and illegal possession of weapons. The mastermind behind the kidnapping and key defendant, al-Mihdar revealed during the trial that his organization planned to kill American and British citizens in Aden. 'One of our objectives was to expel the Christians and Jews from our land,' he said. The abduction of the tourists aimed to pressure the Christians, the authorities, and the countries from which these tourists came to stop the air strikes against Iraq and end the blockade imposed on the Iraqi people. Mihdar revealed that he had met bin Laden in Afghanistan but claimed he had had no further contact with him since the early 1990s. No operational links between the Yemeni group and bin Laden were found.[115]

Terrorists failed in a planned attack in January 2000 against the American warship USS The Sullivans while it was refueling in Aden, when the assault boat became overloaded with explosives and sank. The attack was part of the millennium plot. However, the same Yemeni cell succeeded on 12 October 2000 in the suicide bombing of the destroyer USS Cole, which severely damaged the ship, killed 17 and injured 39 navy personnel.[116]

Six Yemeni suspects in the bombing were identified by sources close to the investigation as veterans of the anti-Soviet war in Afghanistan in the 1980s. Jamal al-Badawi, the most senior of the six suspects jailed in Yemen told investigators he had received telephone instructions for the 12 October bombing from a man in the United Arab Emirates whom he had previously met in Afghanistan during the war. According to al-Badawi, his contact named Mohammed Omar al-Harazi never admitted to receiving orders and financing for the attack from bin Laden, but only intimated so. Other suspects in the Cole attack were identified as two police officers from Lahej, north of Aden who had provided fake identification and other documents for the suicide bombers.

Yemeni president Ali Aballah Salih identified the detainees as leaders of the Islamic Jihad organization in Yemen. The Cole attack had several parallels with the 1998 bombings of US embassies in Kenya and Tanzania, including the use of TNT, outside explosive specialists, sophisticated electrical detonation devices, and the activation of longstanding local terrorist cells. The strongest clue that bin Laden might have been the ultimate mastermind of the Cole attack was the relationship between Harazi and the suicide truck bomber in the Nairobi attack. The Cole incident spotlighted Yemen as a crossroads of international terrorism, its hinterland serving as a stronghold for Islamic terrorist groups with links to bin Laden.[117]

---

[115] Mihdar was executed on 17 October 2000, a few days after the USS Cole bombing in Aden.

[116] See *Patterns of Global Terrorism 2000*, at <http://www.usis.usemb.se/terror/rpt2000/index. html> and also Investigation (last revised 12 December 2001) at *Yemen gateway*, <http://www. al-bab.com/yemen/cole5.htm>.

[117] See Webman, *The Undiminished Threat of Political Islam*, p. 114-116. Yemeni security captured in November 2003 Mohammed Hamdi al-Ahdal, one of the top al-Qaeda members in Yemen and

8.   United Kingdom

In February-March 2001 the British MI5 uncovered plans by supporters of bin
Laden to use London as a base for a bombing campaign against western targets
and the police arrested the suspected terrorists. Ten Muslims were detained,
including Omar Mahmood Abu Omar, an Islamic cleric who had twice been
convicted for his role in terrorist acts in Jordan and had alleged links to al-Qaeda.
He was later released on bail and disappeared.

9.   Italy

In April 2001 Italian officials announced the arrest in Milan of five North African
men suspected of having ties to bin Laden, and were searching for five others.
The German police also arrested a member of an Islamist cell after raiding eight
sites in Hesse and Bavaria. All those arrests were connected to a planned bombing, probably against the city cathedral and American targets that was averted in
Strasbourg, France, in December 2000.

   The key figures in the Milan affair were Sami Ben Khemais, who was arrested, and Tarek Ma'aroufi, a Tunisian who became a naturalized citizen of
Belgium. Ben Khemais settled in Milan in March 1998, following two years of
training in Afghanistan. Investigators suspect that his function in the terrorist
network was to identify potential candidates from Italy, Germany, Britain and
Belgium for membership in the terror cells, recruit them and dispatch them for
military training and religious instruction in bin Laden's bases in Afghanistan.
The recruits were sent through Geneva and Pakistan to a training base in Khost
across the border in Afghanistan. They were given courses on the handling and
detonation of bombs and explosive charges, surveillance and evasion techniques,
planning of kidnappings and hijackings of individuals, trains, buses and airplanes.

   According to the Italian report, as early as the summer of 2000, Western
European and American intelligence agencies identified two especially noticeable
networks of Islamist terrorists. One was run by a Tunisian named Sayef Alalah
bin Hasin, Ben Khemais' boss. The other network was led by a London-based
Algerian national identified as Haidar Abu Doha, who was nicknamed 'the

---

a suspected mastermind of the suicide bombing of the USS Cole who had evaded arrest despite
heading the Arab state's wanted list for nearly two years. Al-Ahdal has been described as the
main coordinator of al-Qaeda activities in Yemen, ranking second to Qaed Salim Sinan al-
Harethi, bin Laden's top lieutenant in Yemen who was killed in November 2002 in a missile
attack from a CIA-operated Predator drone. Al-Harethi, who was in his mid-40s, was believed to
have coordinated the attack on the Cole. He first met bin Laden in the 1980s during the war
against Soviet occupation in Afghanistan, and the two met again in Sudan, where bin Laden went
in the 1990s. See *USA Today*, 26 November 2003.

doctor.' The two networks were originally established to support the Salafi Group for Call and Combat, a small faction which split from the GIA. However, in the fall of 2000, the two networks affiliated with the Salafi group were ordered to shift their activities from the struggle in Algeria to a new plan inspired and financed by bin Laden, namely the WIF.[118]

10.   Activities of Algerian activists

The US State Department accused the GSPC of planning to disrupt the Paris-Dakar Road Rally in 2000. Italian police arrested several suspects linked to a GSPC cell in Milan on 4 April 2000, while four individuals thought to be members of a GSPC cell in France were arrested in connection with a plot to bomb a Christmas market in eastern France in 2000. The Algerian suspects implicated in the millennium bomb plot are also thought to have ties to the GSPC.[119]

11.   US reaction to al-Qaeda terrorist activity

On 20 August 1998, President Clinton amended Executive Order 12947 to add bin Laden and his key associates to the list of terrorists, thus blocking their US assets – including property and bank accounts – and prohibiting all US financial transactions with them. The US conducted a bombing run with 79 cruise missiles – Operation Infinite Reach – against bin Laden's facilities in Afghanistan on 20 August 1998 without much damage to the al-Qaeda leadership or the organization's infrastructure. The bombings and their aftermath occurred at a difficult time for Clinton. On August 17, he testified to the Office of the Independent Counsel and a grand jury by video conference, acknowledging an extramarital relationship with former White House intern Monica Lewinsky. Later that evening in a national address, Clinton admitted that he had 'misled' the American people about his relationship with Lewinsky. Thus, Clinton had created for himself a serious credibility crisis with the American public.[120]

On 21 October 2000, a former sergeant in the US Army stated in a federal district court in New York City that he had provided information to bin Laden on

---

[118] The degree to which this front was international is reflected in the phone calls made by an aide to Ben Khemais, who was arrested with him during the raid on the Milan apartment. On the night of 30 December 2000, over seven hours, beginning at midnight, he carried on 30 conversations with operatives in Pakistan, Dubai, Germany and Britain, including Haidar Abu Doha. Calls were made to various destinations throughout Italy. See Yossi Melman, 'All roads lead to Milan,' <http://radiobergen.org/terrorism/binladen/binladen_18.htm>.

[119] See Schanzer, *Algeria's GSPC And America's 'War On Terror'*.

[120] See Ryan C. Hendrickson, 'The Clinton Administration's Strikes on Usama Bin Laden: Limits to Power,' from *Contemporary Cases in US Foreign Policy,* ed. Ralph G. Carter. (Washington, D.C.: CQ Press, 2002), pp. 196-216, at <http://www.cqpress.com/context/articles/contemp8.html>.

the US embassy in Kenya in 1993 and 1994 and that Bin Laden had specifically indicated where a bomb could be placed. In November 1998, a federal grand jury indicted bin Laden on 224 counts of conspiracy to commit murder and charged him and his top military commander with orchestrating the bombings of the US embassies. The US also issued a $5 million reward for information leading to bin Laden's arrest. The US, believing that Bin Laden remained in Afghanistan, put pressure on the Taliban to turn him over. Their efforts failed, and bin Laden remained at large throughout the Clinton presidency preparing subsequent terrorist strikes at US and Western targets that culminated on 9/11.

VII. THE INFLUENCE OF INTERNATIONAL AND REGIONAL VARIABLES

The basic premise of this study is that terrorist organizations are eager to form coalitions with other organizations when they feel threatened by internal, regional and international political and strategic conditions and events, other states, or super powers.

The strategy of Salafi jihadis was evidently influenced by Abdallah Azzam who differentiated between two kinds of jihad: the offensive one entails attacks in enemy territory to establish strong borders and harass unbelievers, and is a collective responsibility; the defensive one is waged to protect Muslim territory and populations and is an individual religious obligation.[121]

The defensive jihad compels Muslims situated near the enemy, but if that group alone cannot defeat the enemy then the obligation 'expands to the next closest group of Muslims'. The call for defensive jihad continued after the Soviet defeat at the hands of Afghani tribes, while the Salafi Arab Afghans searched for new venues of combat. According to Wiktorowitcz, 'jihad was thus viewed as an ongoing process of Muslim liberation at a global level', one that he labels 'nomadic jihad'.[122]

The defensive character of the campaign against the US, the Jews and the West was outlined by bin Laden:

The people of Islam had suffered from aggression, iniquity and injustice imposed on them by the Zionist Crusaders alliance and their collaborators; to the extent that the Muslims blood became the cheapest and their wealth as loot in the hands of the enemies. Their blood was spilled in Palestine and Iraq. The horrifying pictures of the massacre of Qana, in Lebanon are still fresh in our memory. Massacres in

---

[121] See Wiktorowicz, *The New Global Threat*, pp. 23-24.
[122] Ibid., p. 24.

Tajakestan, Burma, Cashmere, Assam, Philippine, Fatani, Ogadin, Somalia, Erithria, Chechnia and in Bosnia Herzegovina took place, massacres that send shivers in the body and shake the conscience. All of this and the world watch and hear (sic), and not only didn't respond to these atrocities, but also with a clear conspiracy between the USA and its' allies and under the cover of the iniquitous United Nations, the dispossessed people were even prevented from obtaining arms to defend themselves.[123]

These themes were reiterated in the WIF fatwa of 1998:

The Arabian Peninsula has never – since God made it flat, created its desert, and encircled it with seas – been stormed by any forces like the crusader armies now spreading in it like locusts, consuming its riches and destroying its plantations. All this is happening at a time when nations are attacking Muslims like people fighting over a plate of food… All these crimes and sins committed by the Americans are a clear declaration of war on God, his messenger, and Muslims.[124]

Following the 1998 attacks against the US embassies in Kenya and Tanzania, al-Quds al-Arabi published a *Salafi*-inspired analysis, and bin Laden's WIF issued its own communiqué:

The Muslim Ummah is in a constant state of Jihad, physical, financial and verbal against the terrorist state of America, Israel, Serbia, etc. We can envisage that this is the beginning of much more bloodshed and deaths should the US continue to occupy Muslim land and to oppress Muslims in the Gulf and elsewhere. The Muslims will never rest until their land is liberated from the occupiers and the authority to rule restored to the Muslims from the tyrant, self-appointed, puppet leaders in Muslim countries such as Mubarak of Egypt, Fahd of Arabia, Zirwal of Algeria, Qaddafi of Libya, etc. The struggle will continue against regimes in Muslim countries until al-Khilafah (the Islamic State) is re-established and the law of God dominates the world.[125]

---

[123] See 'Declaration of War Against the Americans Occupying the Land of The Two Holy Places (Expel the Infidels From the Arab Peninsula) A Message From Usama Bin Muhammad Bin in Laden Unto His Muslim Brethren All Over the World Generally and in The Arab Peninsula Specifically,' as it was published in *Al Quds al-Arabi*, 1 August 1996, at <http://www.defend democracy.org/research_topics/research_topics_show.htm?doc_id=185673&attrib_id=7580>.

[124] See Text of Fatwah Urging Jihad Against Americans, published in *Al-Quds al-Arabi* on 23 February 1998, at <http://www.ict.org.il/articles/fatwah.htm>.

[125] Cited in Barry Cooper, 'Unholy Terror: The Origin and Significance of Contemporary, Religion-based Terrorism,' Fraser Institute, Calgary Policy Research Centre, *A Fraser Institute Occasional Paper*, No. 1, March 2002 at <http://collection.nlc-bnc.ca/100/200/300/fraser/studies_in_defense/n01/terrorism.pdf>, p. 34.

Hypothesis 1: Tension within the bipolar system heightens the terrorist organizations' sense of vulnerability vis-à-vis the superpowers, and encourages them to cooperate and form coalitions.

This study shows how the bipolar world and the balance of power between 1970 and 1990 influenced enormously the strategies of the nationalist as well the radical left- and right-wing terrorist organizations. It is interesting to explore whether the theory on coalitions between terrorist organizations can be applied to Islamist networks too.

The crumbling of the Soviet Union and the Warsaw Pact, and the US-led military victory in the Gulf War at the beginning of the 1990s resulted in the primacy of the US as the only global superpower. During the eight years of Clinton's presidency the advent of al-Qaeda under the leadership of bin Laden led to the emergence of a new challenge to the US. Not that this new 'Islamic pole' could present a real military threat to US supremacy, but it appeared primarily to challenge the political stability and the cultural values of the US-led western world.

For more than four decades, superpower rivalry defined international relations. According to John Esposito, the 'threat vacuum' in the aftermath of the fall of the Soviet Union gave rise to a search for new enemies. Some viewed Islam 'as the only ideological alternative to the West that can cut across national boundaries ... politically and culturally at odds with Western society, fear it; [while] others consider it more a basic demographic threat.'[126]

Douglas E. Streusand claimed that 'a new specter is haunting America, one that some Americans consider more sinister than Marxism-Leninism... That specter is Islam.'[127] Washington Post columnist Jim Hoagland described the climate as:

> [an] urge to identify Islam as an inherently anti-democratic force that is America's new global enemy now that the Cold War is over... Indeed, like the Red Menace of the Cold War era, the Green Peril is perceived as a cancer spreading around the globe, undermining the legitimacy of Western values and political systems.[128]

---

[126] See John Esposito, 'Political Islam: Beyond the Green Menace,' originally published in the journal *Current History,* January 1994. Taken verbatim from MSANEWS, at <http://www.arches.uga.edu/~godlas/espo.html>.

[127] See Douglas E. Streusand, 'Abraham's Other Children: Is Islam an Enemy of the West?' *Policy Review* 50 (Fall 1989), cited in Leon T. Hadar 'The "Green Peril": Creating The Islamic Fundamentalist Threat,' *Policy Analysis,* The Cato Institute, No. 177, 27 August 1992, at <http://www.cato.org/pubs/pas/pa-177es.html>.

[128] See Jim Hoagland, 'Washington's Algerian Dilemma,' *The Washington Post,* 6 February 1992, cited in Leon T. Hadar, *The Green Peril.*

The alleged threat from Iran and militant Islam do differ. The struggle between that force and the West is portrayed as a zero-sum game that can end only in the defeat of one of the sides.[129]

On his arrival in Afghanistan in 1996, bin Laden began to develop his conception of the enemy:

> I did not fight against the communist threat while forgetting the peril from the West... I discovered that it was not enough to fight in Afghanistan, but that we had to fight on all fronts against communist or Western oppression. The urgent thing was communism but the next target was America... This is an open war up to the end, until victory.[130]

He and the Afghan guerrillas were aligned at the time with the Americans solely because they perceived themselves fighting a common enemy.

In an interview after 9/11, bin Laden described the clash with the US not as a battle between al-Qaeda and the US but 'a battle of Muslims against the global crusaders.' He boasted that the Soviet Union which at its time 'scared the whole world' was barely remembered today and broke down into many small states while NATO 'tremble[s] of fear' [in front of the Islamic threat].[131]

Bin Laden's 1996 Declaration of War was directed against the American 'occupation' of Saudi Arabia. The ruling Al Sauds were condemned for permitting thus their country to suffer from economic distress and demoralization. The declaration targeted US military personnel stationed in Saudi Arabia. However, that was to change dramatically. The 1998 *fatwa* of the WIF articulated more fully why the US was regarded as an enemy:

> For more than seven years the United States [has been] occupying the lands of Islam in the holiest of its territories, Arabia, plundering its riches, overwhelming its rulers, humiliating its people, threatening its neighbors, and using its bases in the peninsula as a spearhead to fight against the neighboring Islamic peoples...
>
> Despite the immense destruction inflicted on the Iraqi people at the hands of the Crusader-Jewish alliance and in spite of the appalling number of dead, exceeding a million, the Americans nevertheless, in spite of all this, are trying once more to repeat this dreadful slaughter... They come again today to destroy what remains of this people and to humiliate their Muslim neighbours.

---

[129] Leon T. Hadar, *The Green Peril*.

[130] Cited in Hashim, *The World According To Usama Bin Laden*.

[131] Interview to *Al-Jazeera*, October 2001, at *Jihad Unspun* <http://www.jihadunspun.net/Bin LadensNetwork/interviews/aljazeera10-21-2001-1.cfm>.

While the purposes of the Americans in these wars are religious and economic, they also serve the petty state of the Jews, to direct attention from their occupation of Jerusalem and the killing of Muslims in it.

According to Ahmed Hashim, this document is remarkable 'not because it constitutes a declaration of war against America or because it makes no distinction between innocent civilians and military personnel but because … it reaches out to those in the Arab and Islamic worlds who do not share the agenda or language of the Islamic fundamentalists.'[132]

Following the start of the American offensive against al-Qaeda on 8 October 2001, bin Laden launched a verbal onslaught against the US and its allies in the Muslim world, whom he castigated as 'hypocrites.' Bin Laden spoke apocalyptically of the possibility of a war between Muslim and non-Muslim.[133]

The nature of this war became clearer still when President Bush referred to a crusade against a new 'axis of evil.' Thus, according to Paz, began a new global conflict between the US-led Western world and Islam.[134] Ahmad Khomeini, son of Ayatollah Khomeini, summarized the fundamentalist point of view: 'After the fall of Marxism, Islam replaced it, and as long as Islam exists, US hostility exists, and as long as US hostility exists, the struggle exists.'[135]

Al-Zawahiri described this as 'the stage of the global battle, now that the forces of the disbelievers have united against the mujahidin.' He added: 'The battle today cannot be fought on a regional level without taking into account the global hostility towards us.' Al-Zawahiri claimed that the name 'Arab Afghans' was a tendentious description because the mujahideen had never been solely Arab, but came from all parts of the Islamic world, though the Arabs were a distinctive element in this group. 'The seriousness of the presence of Muslim, particularly Arab, young men in the arena of Jihad in Afghanistan consisted of turning the Afghan cause from a local, regional issue into a global Islamic issue in which the entire nation can participate.'[136]

It is worth noting that some of the leaders of the radical Islamist movement became aware of the international constraints on their activity. Karim Zuhadi of the Egyptian Islamic Group revealed that his colleagues concluded that in the difficult international situation created after the first Gulf War, the end of the Cold War, the transformation of Islam into the new enemy pole of the one superpower left (the US), it was imperative to re-examine the relations with the

---

[132] See Hashim, *The World According To Usama Bin Laden*.
[133] Ibid.
[134] Paz, *Tangled Web*, p. 47.
[135] Speech by Ahmad Khomeini, 20 October 1991, in *FBIS*, 21 October 1991, cited again by Kramer.
[136] See al-Zawahiri, *Knights Under the Prophet's Banner*.

Arab regimes which were under tremendous pressure from 'global hegemonic forces' and to seek a new strategy that would preserve the unity of [Islamic] society.[137]

Hypothesis 2: Rifts between ideologically-similar powers and the emergence of new revolutionary and ideological foci create a new type of solidarity, and encourage the formation of coalitions between terrorist organizations which support one of the new ideologies.

According to Esposito, some Islamic organizations engage in terrorism, seeking to topple governments, while others use religious and social services to gain power through legitimate elections. He notes that the world feared that the 1979 Islamic revolution in Iran, led by the charismatic Ayatollah Ruhollah Khomeini, and the creation of an Islamic republic willing to export Islamic revolution to other countries of the Middle East would represent an international Islamic threat, possibly a 'new Comintern' poised to challenge the free world.[138]

The series of terrorist events since the 1979 takeover of the US embassy in Teheran, like the 1981 assassination of Egyptian President Anwar Sadat as well as hostage-takings, hijackings, and attacks on foreign and government installations by groups such as the Egyptian Jihad, Takfir wal Hijra (Excommunication and Flight) and by the Iranian-funded Hizballah in Lebanon helped to promote images in the West of the Islamic world as a fundamentalist, extremist, terrorist religion. Islam was often portrayed as a triple threat: political, civilizational, and demographic.

With the appearance of al-Qaeda, fears of Iran-led revolution were superseded in the mid-1990s by the greater fear of an international pan-Islamic Sunni movement, combining fear of violent revolution and of Algerian-style electoral victories.[139]

The numerous political, socio-economic and sometimes ethnic conflicts between Sunni and Shi'a communities throughout the vast Muslim world, in Pakistan or Iran, Lebanon or Afghanistan, and perhaps more acutely in Iraq, must impact on the behavior of the more radical organizations and also the supportive state players, which can use these conflicts for ideological or tactical reasons to increase the solidarity with allied groups. The existence of two parallel Islamist trends, the revolutionary Iranian Shi'a model as opposed to the radical Sunni Wahhabi or Salafi one and in what measure did it affect the ideology and strategy

---

[137] Cited in *The Reconciliation Initiative of the al-Gama'a al-Islamiyya Organization with the Egyptian Regime, part 1*, p. 6.
[138] See Esposito, *Political Islam: Beyond the Green Menace*.
[139] Ibid.

of the numerous violent groups active in the Muslim world would necessitate in itself an in-depth study.[140]

Hypothesis 3: Regional wars and tensions that are perceived as a threat to terrorist organizations or other organizations belonging to the same ideological camp encourage them to seek allies in order to strengthen their position in the struggle against the common enemy, or in order to help an organization that is under attack in another region.

Throughout bin Laden's public statements and declarations – beginning with his 1996 Declaration of War, his interviews with various Islamic journals and US television networks, and the two *fatwas* published in February 1998 – runs one basic and predominant strategic goal: the expulsion of the American presence, military and civilian, from Saudi Arabia and the whole Gulf region.

After a lengthy analysis of the situation in Saudi Arabia, the 1996 Declaration of War accused the royal regime, aside from all its social and economic misdemeanors, of betraying the Islamic faith: 'The crusaders were permitted to be in the land of the two Holy Places... The land was filled with the military bases of the USA and the allies. The regime became unable to keep control without the help of these bases.'

The declaration was presented as the first step in the work of 'correcting what had happened to the Islamic world in general, and the Land of the two Holy Places in particular.' In his explanation for the Jihad against the US, he stresses that 'we have focused our declaration on striking at the soldiers in the country of The Two Holy Places [which] has in our religion a peculiarity of its own over the other Muslim countries. In our religion, it is not permissible for any non-Muslim to stay in our country'. Praising the explosions in Saudi Arabia against the US military, bin Laden reiterated that they were intended 'to get the American occupation out [of Arabia].'

However, bin Laden and the WIF did not forget the 'crimes' and the perceived wrongs committed against the Muslim nation in other areas: 'the blood spilled in Palestine and Iraq ... the massacre of Qana, in Lebanon ... and the massacres in Tajakestan, Burma, Cashmere, Assam, Philippine, Fatani, Ogadin, Somalia, Erithria, Chechnia and in Bosnia-Herzegovina.' He called, together with the 'brothers in Palestine' upon his 'Muslim Brothers of The World' to help and take part in fighting against the enemy, the Americans and the Israelis.

---

[140] See on this subject the interesting paper by Reuven Paz, 'Hizballah or Hizb al-Shaytan? Recent Jihadi-Salafi Attacks against the Shiite Group,' *PRISM Occasional Papers*, Vol. 2, No. 1 (February 2004), at <http://www.e-prism.org/images/PRISM_no_1_vol_2_Hizbullah_or_Hizb_ al-Shaytan.pdf>.

In a video broadcast on al-Jazeera satellite television in November 2001, bin Laden spoke about the 'crusade' against Chechens and against Bosnia. The Chechens were described as 'a Muslim people who have been attacked by the Russian bear which embraces the Christian Orthodox faith,' annihilated in their entirety and forced 'to flee to the mountains where they were assaulted by snow and poverty and diseases'. This was followed by 'a war of genocide in Bosnia' where during 'several years our brothers have been killed, our women have been raped, and our children have been massacred in the safe havens of the United Nations and with its knowledge and cooperation.'[141]

Indeed, militants of al-Qaeda and affiliated groups were sent or volunteered to fight in every region or country alongside local Muslims, who, according to their view, were occupied, exploited, humiliated by the infidel powers.

Hypothesis 4: International and regional cooperation between security forces against terrorist organizations encourages them to form coalitions.

Al-Qaeda ideologues perceive their enemies as a huge alliance which aims to humiliate and exploit Muslims. 'There exist global conspiracies wishing to deprive it [Jihad] of its fruits and extinguish its lights. We can observe international alliances to smash this Jihad and to prevent its real leadership from continuing to lead this Muslim nation.'[142]

According to Emmanuel Sivan, in 1998 after two decades of failed efforts, fewer and fewer radicals believed they could take power by force.

> The main obstacle has proven to be the stiff and increasingly effective resistance of existing governments... Security services in many Middle East countries cooperate with their counterparts in other Muslim countries (including Turkey and Pakistan) as well as in the West. Perhaps as a result of the widespread anti-terrorist activities, radical Islamic movements have experienced discord and disarray.

Sivan sees in this disarray the seeds of renunciation to the armed struggle, (like the Egyptian Islamic Group or the Algerian FIS and its military arm, the AIS) on the one hand; on the other hand greater fragmentation and internal conflict than anything the radical Islamic movement has known over the last quarter century.[143]

---

[141] See *BBC News*, 3 November 2001.

[142] See Abdullah Azzam, 'Al-Qa'idah al-Sulbah' (The Solid Base), *Al-Jihad*, No. 41, April 1988. Azzam's article was published in Arabic. The English translation was done by Reuven Paz and is cited from Appendix I of *The Tangled Web*.

[143] See Emmanuel Sivan, 'Why Radical Muslims Aren't Taking Over Governments,' *MERIA Journal*, Vol. 2, No. 2, May 1998, at <http://meria.idc.ac.il/journal/1998/issue2/jv2n2a2.html>.

This theme was reiterated in a 1999 Islamist publication which alleged that the US was engaged in an intensive 'witch-hunt against Islamic movement activists all over the world'. Since 1998, it claimed, Muslims were arrested in various countries and extradited for trial in the US. This international witch-hunt was regarded as just one facet of a concerted international strategy to fight the Islamic movement. Other facets included legislation in the US, Britain, France and other western countries to control the political activities of resident or citizen Muslims.[144]

But is cooperation between security and intelligence services in the Middle East and in the international community also leading to more cooperation between militant factions of the al-Qaeda network?

Ayman al-Zawahiri, explained why the Egyptian Jihad Group blew up the Egyptian embassy in Pakistan in November 1995. He claimed that after the campaign to expel the Arab mujahideen from Pakistan began, the Egyptian government 'began to act like a lion, relying on the backing given to it by the United States, which has strong influence on the Pakistani Government.' The Egyptian regime began to pursue the Arabs, but particularly Egyptian nationals, by requesting their arrest or extradition from Pakistan. This 'expansion of the Egyptian Government's anti-fundamentalist campaign in Egypt and the fact that it transferred the battle to areas outside Egypt required a response.' For this reason the JG decided to attack 'a target that would hurt this vile alliance,' firstly the US embassy in Pakistan, and if not possible, another US target in the country, or the Egyptian embassy. After extensive surveillance, it was decided that hitting the US Embassy was beyond the team's capability. 'Hence, it was finally decided to hit the Egyptian Embassy in Islamabad, which was not merely conducting the pursuit campaign against the Arab Afghans in Pakistan but was also playing a serious espionage role against the Arab Afghans.'[145]

The growing awareness of international terrorism as a global phenomenon, and its identification with Islamic transnational militants prompted the international community to seek a joint platform for action. Controversies over the definition of terrorism hindered the adoption of firm resolutions at the Sharm al-Shaykh international conference in March 1996. The bombings in Kenya and Tanzania, however, boosted the need for coordination and cooperation in combating terrorism.[146]

---

[144] See *Crescent International*, 1-15 September 1999. Crescent International is a pro-Iranian radical journal and website published in London.

[145] See Al-Zawahiri, *Knights Under the Prophet's Banner*.

[146] The paragraphs on international cooperation against terrorism in the framework of the Arab League are largely drawn from Webman's *The Polarization and Radicalization of Political Islam*, pp. 10-15.

In January 1998 the interior ministers of 20 Arab states convened in Tunisia and unanimously endorsed the Arab Agreement for Combating Terrorism. They also called up Western countries in which Islamist militants found refuge to cooperate with the Arab countries in order to extradite wanted terrorists.[147] The 43 articles of the agreement laid down guidelines for security coordination between Arab countries for the gathering and exchange of information on terrorist groups, and for the extradition of terrorists. The accord was a particular source of satisfaction for Egypt, the driving force behind the agreement following the failed attempt to assassinate President Mubarak in June 1995, but Islamists criticized it as an act directed against them. Bin Laden reportedly sent a message to the interior ministers' meeting charging that the Arab agreement was 'part of international pressures, especially by the US, to consolidate intelligence and security efforts to combat the growing Islamic movements in the Arab and Muslim worlds.'[148]

Egypt strove to eradicate the Islamist movement through legislation, arrests, trials and executions. It improved security coordination with the UK, reached a security agreement with Pakistan and subsequently with the US and several Arab states. In February 1998 a new group affiliated with the Egyptian Jihad and Islamic group was charged with planning attacks on foreign embassies. In March, the trial resumed of 22 members of the military wing of the Islamic Group, known as 'the returnees from Afghanistan and the Sudan'. The court verdict condemned two main defendants to death (in absentia) and sentenced the others to long prison terms. In May, two brothers accused of the 1997 attack on a tourist bus in Cairo were executed. Forty other condemned terrorists remained on death row. Bin Laden's name was implicated in the interrogations of various defendants, and Egypt considered trying him in absentia for his involvement in the Egyptian embassy bombing in Islamabad in 1995. However, two Egyptian Jihad members extradited by Albania in June denied that either they or bin Laden had any connection with violent attacks in Egypt.[149]

The hunt for Islamist activists intensified in Europe and the US after the bombings in Kenya and Tanzania. The US and Britain also advanced anti-terrorism legislation – the US Freedom from Religious Persecution Act (May 1998) and the establishment of the National Commission on Terrorism to examine national counter-terrorism policies and suggest effective prevention and punishment measures. Britain passed the Criminal Justice (Conspiracy and Terrorism) Act (September 1998). The laws stiffened criteria for granting permits

---

[147] This was a clear reference to the UK, considered a haven for Islamist activists and which had refrained so far from responding to extradition requests by Egypt.

[148] See *Sawt al-Mar'a,* 31 March 1998, as cited in Webman, *The Polarization and Radicalization of Political Islam,* p. 12.

[149] Ibid.

to political asylum-seekers and facilitated the arrest in September of seven Islamists associated with Egyptian Islamist groups and a Saudi, Khalid al-Fawwaz, believed to have links with bin Laden.[150]

Coordination between the security services of the European countries reached a peak prior to the World Cup football games, held in June – July 1998 in France. Suspected Islamist activists were rounded up in Britain, Belgium, France, Germany, Switzerland and Italy as a preventive measure before the games. In Brussels, seven members of an Islamist cell, part of a support network operating in Europe suspected of procuring weapons and false documents for the Algerian GIA, were arrested in March 1998. The detainees — Algerians, Moroccans and a Tunisian — carried Scandinavian passports, indicating that they were senior members of the GIA European network. Another series of arrests was carried out in May 1998, including Islamist activists, mainly of Algerian origin, in France (53), Italy (9), Switzerland (2) and Germany (2) linked with the GIA and receiving instructions from Hasan Hattab, leader of a GIA splinter group. The crackdown targeted followers of Hattab, who allegedly planned to set off bombs at the World Cup games.[151]

Terrorism in Egypt and other Arab countries continued to decline in 1999 due to new preemptive strategies adopted by the police after the attack in Luxor in November 1997 and the implementation of the Arab agreement on combating terrorism. Arab governments continued their crackdown on Islamists; and show trials were conducted in Egypt and Yemen. Islamists themselves were divided over the issues of violence and political participation and paradoxically stimulated a confluence of interests between Arab regimes and the West.[152]

Concerted Arab and international efforts brought the extradition of a number of wanted Islamists, among them 13 Egyptian Jihad members caught in Albania in 1998, reportedly with the help of the CIA. The trial was dubbed 'the returnees from Albania case' and among the defendants were some of the prominent leaders of the Egyptian Jihad and al-Gama'a who were tried in absentia: al-Zawahiri; Muhammad Shawqi al-Islambuli, brother of Sadat's assassin and Gama'a leader who lived in Afghanistan; Yasir Tawfiq Sirri of the Islamic Observatory Center in London and five other Egyptian detainees held by Britain since September

---

[150] In January 1998, the alleged mastermind of the WTC bombing, Ramzi Yousef, who was turned over by Pakistan to the US in February 1995 was tried and sentenced to 240 years in prison. That same month, a Pakistani, Mir Aymal Qazi, who was handed over to the US in 1997 was convicted of killing two CIA employees in Virginia in 1993 and sentenced to death.

[151] A mass trial in Paris of 138 Islamists imprisoned since 1994, accused of belonging to an Islamic network that provided logistical support to the GIA, also began in September 1998. The author has heard from an European judge that the arrests were made possible by the previous coordination between eight senior instruction judges from several countries during an *ad hoc* meeting, the first one of this kind in European juridical history.

[152] See Webman, *Political Islam at the Close of the Twentieth Century*, p. 12.

1998.[153] Nine defendants were sentenced to death, 11 to life imprisonment with hard labor, and 67 to prison terms ranging from one to 15 years. Among those sentenced to death in absentia were al-Zawahiri and his brother Muhammad al-Zawahiri.

The meeting of Arab ministers of interior in Algiers in January 2000 to coordinate measures to combat terrorism adopted a revised version of the 'Arab strategy for combating terrorism' that provided for 'strengthened cooperation between Arab security agencies in combating cross-border crime,' and endorsed an Egyptian initiative to convene a UN-sponsored international conference on combating terrorism.[154]

Many of al-Qaeda's attempts to carry out terrorist attacks in the US, Jordan, Albania and other countries were foiled as a result of joint efforts by intelligence agencies worldwide. Dozens of terrorists trained in Afghanistan and linked to him were arrested in Britain, Germany, Canada, the US, Jordan and Pakistan during 1999 and 2000. The net result of the arrests, the increased surveillance and the cooperation among intelligence services was to weaken al-Qaeda's infrastructure and limit the freedom of movement of its militants.

The war in Chechnya and growing unrest in the other Muslim Central Asian republics and the spate of terrorist activity by ethnic Uighur citizens in the Chinese province of Xingiang, convinced Russia and China to join international efforts to combat terrorism. The Shanghai Five Forum, comprising Russia, China, Kazakhstan, Tajikistan and Kyrgyztan, originally set up in 1996 to resolve border disputes between China and the constituent republics of the former Soviet Union, became the main cooperation and coordination body for this region (Uzbekistan was admitted as full member in June 2001). In a summit held in Dushanbe, Kazakhstan in July 2000, agenda included the growing threat posed by terrorists and separatists trained and armed by the Taliban. The forum discussed coordinated measures to counter this threat, considered the chief source of instability in the region.[155] A dialogue initiated in May 2000 between Russia and the US regarding closer cooperation in counter-terrorism led to an agreement to form a bilateral working group on Afghanistan, while Russia enhanced support to the anti-Taliban Northern Alliance and threatened to carry out preemptive strikes

---

[153] They were part of a larger group of 107 defendants (sixty-three of whom were tried in absentia) tried in a military court in February 1999. All were charged with conspiring to topple the government, membership in an outlawed group, plotting to assassinate state officials and police officers, involvement in terrorist attacks, possession of weapons and explosives, and forging official documents.

[154] See Webman, *The Undiminished Threat of Political Islam*, p.. 14.

[155] See '"Shanghai Five" Nations Sign Joint Statement,' *People's Daily Online*, 6 July 2000. See also John Daly, '"Shanghai Five" expands to combat Islamic radicals,' *Jane's Terrorism & Security Monitor*, 19 July 2001 at <http://www.janes.com/security/international_security/news/jtsm/jtsm010719_1_n.shtml>.

against the Taliban, accused of helping train Islamic militants to fight in Chechnya and Central Asia. Russian-American cooperation on this issue culminated in their co-sponsorship of a UN Security Council resolution on 19 December 2000, imposing additional sanctions on Afghanistan.[156]

VIII.   THE INFLUENCE OF VARIABLES AT THE ORGANIZATIONAL LEVEL

1.   Ideological factors

Hypothesis 5: A coalition between two terrorist organizations exists only when there is some shared ideological base between the two.

Kramer suggested that the insistence not only on power, but on absolute power, 'has tended to make modern Islamists into proto-fascists, obsessed with dragging their compatriots kicking and screaming into paradise.'[157] He traces this ideology to Mawlana Mawdudi's thinking on the need for a 'revolution' to create an Islamic state prepared by a long campaign of persuasion.[158] The Egyptian Muslim Brother Sayyid Qutb borrowed heavily from Mawdudi's vision of an Islamic state, but saw Islam under assault and called on a vanguard of believers to overturn the political order. Qutb thus transformed what had been a tendency toward violence into an explicit logic of revolution. He also placed the anti-imperialism of the early fundamentalists on an ideological footing.[159] According to Kramer, Khomeini also revalidated the anti-Western and anti-American credentials of fundamentalism by designating the US, 'historical heir to unbelief,' as the 'Great Satan.' This posited an absolute conflict between Islam and the West, not just in history but in eschatology.[160]

---

[156]   See Webman, *The Undiminished Threat of Political Islam*, p. 12.

[157]   See Martin Kramer, 'Fundamentalist Islam at Large: The Drive for Power,' *The Middle East Quarterly*, Vol. 3, No. 2 (June 1996), at <http://www.meforum.org/article/304>. Kramer is citing Abdelwahhab El-Affendi, *Who Needs an Islamic State?* (London: Grey Seal, 1991), p. 87.

[158]   Mawlana Abu'l-A'la Mawdudi (1903-79), the founder of Jama'at-i Islami in India and Pakistan. His many writings, translated into every major language spoken by Muslims, provide a panoramic view of the ideal fundamentalist state.

[159]   Sayyid Qutb (1906-66) joined the Muslim Brotherhood (Al-Ikhwan al-Muslimun) in 1950, becoming one of their leading spokesmen. After the movement openly opposed the government of Jamal Abdul Nasser, Qutb essentially spent the rest of his life in jail except for a brief period in 1964-65. He was tried and executed for treason in 1966.

[160]   Kramer citing William O. Beeman, 'Images of the Great Satan: Representations of the United States in the Iranian Revolution,' in Nikki R. Keddie (ed.), *Religion and Politics in Iran* (New Haven, Conn.: Yale University Press, 1983), pp. 191-217.

The younger ideologues, Turabi, Ghannushi, and Fadlallah played down the themes of 'crusaderism' and the 'Great Satan,' substituting them with the more fashionable rhetoric of Third World anti-imperialism and notions of class struggle, more easily understood by the younger generation of disenchanted Muslims. They developed a terminology that referred to Muslims as the 'dispossessed' of 'the South'. Without sacrificing any element of ideological principle, they worked to present Islamist movements as the functional equivalent of the 'reform' movements of the former communist bloc.[161]

According to al-Zawahiri, western forces hostile to Islam, joined by their former enemy Russia, clearly identified Islamic fundamentalism as their enemy, thus leading to 'the universality of the battle'. The tools they enlist to fight Islam, include the UN, the friendly rulers of the Muslim peoples, multinational corporations, the international communications and data exchange systems, international news agencies and satellite media channels, and international relief agencies, which are being used as a cover for espionage, proselytizing, coup planning, and the transfer of weapons.

In the face of this alliance, argues al-Zawahari, a fundamentalist coalition was taking shape.

> It represents a growing power that is rallying under the banner of jihad for the sake of God and operating outside the scope of the new world order ... free of the servitude for the dominating western empire ... [and] ready for revenge against the heads of the world's gathering of infidels, the United States, Russia, and Israel.[162]

Bin Laden clearly presented this conflict between the West and the Muslim world as fundamentally religious and global:

> This war is fundamentally religious. The people of the East are Muslims. They sympathized with Muslims against the people of the West, who are the crusaders.
>
> Those who try to cover this crystal clear fact, which the entire world has admitted, are deceiving the Islamic nation. They are trying to deflect the attention of the Islamic nation from the truth of this conflict.

---

[161] This tendency, says Kramer, has been identified by Keddie, who notes that 'many current spokesmen of the Islamic revival have taken some of their ideas from non-religious third worldism,' an influence so pervasive that 'even a man so apparently separated for most of his life from Western currents of thought as Ayatollah Khomeini echoes third worldism (in fact often leftist third worldism).' See Nikki R. Keddie, 'Islamic Revival as Third Worldism,' in Jean-Pierre Digard, (ed.), *Le cuisinier et le philosophe: Hommage à Maxime Rodinson* (Paris: Maisonneuve et Larose, 1982), pp. 275-81.

[162] See Al-Zawahiri, *Knights Under the Prophet's Banner.*

This fact is proven in the book of God Almighty and in the teachings of our messenger, may God's peace and blessings be upon him. Under no circumstances should we forget this enmity between us and the infidels. For, the enmity is based on creed.[163]

Al-Qaeda therefore preached:

We cannot resist this state of ignorance unless we unite our ranks and adhere to our religion. Without that, the establishment of religion would be a dream or illusion that is possible to achieve or even imagine its achievement. Sheik Ibn Taimia – may Allah have mercy on him – said, 'The interests of Adam's children would not be realized in the present life, in the next, except through assembly, cooperation, and mutual assistance. Cooperation is for achieving their interests and mutual assistance is for overcoming their adversities… Therefore, they unite there will be favourable matters that they do, and corrupting matters to avoid. They will be obedient to the commandment of those goals and avoidant of those immoralities. It is necessary that all Adam's children obey.'[164]

Hypothesis 6: Anarchist or anarcho-communist movements have a greater tendency to enter coalitions with other organizations.

At first glance, it would appear that the concept of anarchism in the sense of the revolutionary European movements of the nineteenth century or the radical leftist groups of the 1970-80s is not relevant to the al-Qaeda network. However, the notion of brotherhood developed by the Muslim Brothers might be reminiscent of the International Brotherhood (or the Alliance of Revolutionary Socialists) that the father of Russian anarchism, Mikhail Bakunin, founded in 1866. The leader of the Egyptian Muslim Brothers, Sayyid Qutb, inserted into his philosophy the anarchists' idea of the revolutionary vanguard, so dear to the leftist radicals in Germany, Italy or France of the 1970s.

In a similar vein, the GIA brought together Algerian Islamists who had been involved in the Afghan mujahideen struggle against the Soviet invasion of Afghanistan in the 1980s. Its early leadership was soon dispersed, however, and subsequent leaders resorted increasingly to simple anarchic violence as an inherent justification of the cause. As such attitudes developed, initial support for

---

[163] Cited from bin Laden's video address broadcast on Al-Jazeera satellite television channel, translated by BBC News, 3 November 2001.

[164] See the *Al-Qaeda Manual* located by the Manchester (England) Metropolitan Police during a search of an al Qaeda member's home. The manual was found in a computer file described as 'the military series' related to the 'Declaration of Jihad'. The manual was translated into English and was introduced at the US embassies in Africa bombing trial in New York.

the movement from within the FIS fell away, particularly after a group of 70 FIS militants were murdered by the organization's leadership in late 1994. As a result, the AIS (the armed militia) turned against the GIA and intense hostility between the two wings of clandestine Islamist opposition to the Algerian regime subsequently intensified.[165]

Hypothesis 7: Radical left-wing or right-wing revolutionary organizations which give strategic priority to the struggle against the régime in a bid to seize power in their country, tend not to enter coalitions with other organizations.

This hypothesis is not relevant to the Islamist organizations, although leftist or right-wing motives can be found in their ideology. Some, like Schurmann, have even claimed that the Taliban, with their mix of Sunni Islam and Maoist 'serve the people' doctrines, are reminiscent of Chinese communist revolutionaries. He suggested that Afghan students were deeply affected by Chinese Maoism which preached an almost missionary moralism to all the poor.[166]

Al-Zawahiri, however, complained about the negative influences of such elements in the Islamist ideology:

The Muslim youths in Afghanistan waged the war to liberate Muslim land under purely Islamic slogans, a very vital matter, for many of the liberation battles in our Muslim world had used composite slogans, that mixed nationalism with Islam and, indeed, sometimes caused Islam to intermingle with leftist, communist slogans. This produced a schism in the thinking of the Muslim young men between their Islamic jihadist ideology that should rest on pure loyalty to God's religion, and its practical implementation. The Palestine issue is the best example of these intermingled slogans and beliefs under the influence of the idea of allying oneself with the devil for the sake of liberating Palestine. They allied themselves with the devil, but lost Palestine.

However, this is a complex subject beyond the scope of this study.

Hypothesis 8. Nationalist organizations, whose main goal is the attainment of independence for the minority they represent, are less likely to set up coalitions with other organizations.

---

[165] See Joffe, *Algeria In Crisis.*

[166] See Franz Schurmann, 'Afghanistan's Taliban Rebels Blend Islam and Maoism,' *Pacific News Service*, 30 September 1996, at <http://www.pacificnews.org/jinn/stories/2.20/960930-afghanis tan.html>.

Observers and Islamists alike hold that the failure of Arab nationalism was one of the main reasons for the rise of Islamism. Gilles Kepel distinguished two phases in the victory of Islamism over nationalism. The first phase, from September 1970, coincided with the death of Nasser and civil war in Jordan and marked the demise of Arab nationalism. The day that Ayatollah Khomeini agreed to return from his exile in Paris, 1 February 1979, marked the second phase that 'opened a huge window of opportunity for an alternative ideology'.[167] Judith Yaphe sees in the loss of faith in Arab nationalism the rising popularity of a radical Islamic theology of social protest, a theology able to shape the tone and terms of political discourse, often with the simple formula, 'Islam is the answer'.[168]

Al-Zawahiri also emphasized the significance of Nasser's death:[169]

> Thus, the myth of the Leader of Arab nationalism who would throw Israel into the sea was destroyed. The death of Abd-al-Nasir was not the death of one person but also the death of his principles, which proved their failure on the ground of reality, and the death of a popular myth that was broken on the sands of Sinai... As soon as some pressure was lifted from the Islamic movement [by president Anouar Sadat], the giant [the Islamic movement] emerged from the bottle and the extensive influence of the Islamists among the masses became clear.

Islamist ideologues and al-Qaeda, in particular, reject completely Arab or Muslim nationalism as a direct threat to the very concept and values of true Islam. A publication close to al-Qaeda explained the conflict between nationalism and Islam:[170]

> Nationalism is a bond between people that is based upon family, clan or tribal ties. Nationalism arises among people when the predominant thought they carry is that of achieving domination... Nationalism cannot unite the people because it is based on quest for leadership. This quest for leadership creates a power struggle between the people and this leads to conflicts among various strata of society... Another drawback of nationalism is that it gives a rise to racism. This is expected if people are allowed to compete with each other on the basis of their race.

By contrast:

---

[167] See Gilles Kepel, 'The Trail of Political Islam', 3 July 2002, at <http://www.opendemocracy.net/debates/article-5-57-421.jsp>.
[168] See Judith S. Yaphe, 'Islamic Radicalism in the Arabian Peninsula: Growing Risks,' *The Strategic Forum*, No. 67, March 1996.
[169] See Al-Zawahiri, *Knights Under the Prophet's Banner*.
[170] See Br. Soadad Doureihi, 'Nationalism.. An Erroneous Concept', *Nida'ul Islam*, July – August 1997, at <http://www.islam.org.au>.

The Muslim Ummah was never confronted with such a dilemma in the past during Islamic rule. They never suffered from disunity, widespread oppression, stagnation in science and technology and certainly not from the internal conflicts that we have witnessed this century like the Iran-Iraq war... The spiritual bond among non-Muslims is a grouping of people based on their 'religious belief' which is not a comprehensive belief covering every aspect of life. An example of a spiritual bond is when people identify with each other on the basis of being a Christian, a Hindu or a Jew. Islam is not classed among these as it is a Deen rather than a religion. The term Deen comprehensively takes on the meaning as 'A complete way of life'. This spiritual bond does not unite people on issues other than matters of belief and worships, hence it is limited and cannot be the basis of any complete unity.

Hassan Tourabi, one of the ideologues of the Islamist movement, considers the first Gulf War 'a blessing in disguise because it turned the Islamist movements into mass movements and radicalized Islam in Saudi Arabia'. Acknowledged the achievements of Arab nationalism but suggested it had run its course. 'And partly they [Arab nationalists] lost their significance because they have failed and people have despaired of their ever achieving their goals.'

However, says Tourabi, Islam did not transcend completely one's allegiances to neighborhood, family and nation 'as long as ... you don't become introverted and you don't become chauvinistically nationalist... As long as one is open to the umma or community of believers then one can possess other loyalties.'[171]

Olivier Roy noted that the important Islamist mass movements like the Muslim Brotherhood, the Algerian FIS, the Turkish Refah party, and the Palestinian Hamas, waged their struggle in a nationalist framework, much like the Iranian regime, and try to be recognized as legitimate political players. Roy categorized them as islamo-nationalists, very different from bin Laden and his allies, described as internationalists and 'de-territorialized', nomads moving from jihad to jihad (Afghanistan, Kashmir, Bosnia) indifferent to their own nationality, or using various ones (Bin Laden lost his Saudi nationality, Ramzi Youssef presents himself as Pakistani by birth and Palestinian by choice, etc.).[172]

2. Structural factors

Hypothesis 9: Organizations that are non-state nations (NSNs) tend to operate as independent political entities, primarily taking into consideration their international policy interests when setting up coalitions.

---

[171] See Hassan Turabi, 'Islam, Democracy, the State and the West;' *Middle East Policy*, Vol. 1, No. 3, 1992, pp. 49-61.

[172] See Olivier Roy, 'Un fondamentalisme sunnite en panne de projet politique,' *Le Monde diplomatique*, October 1998, at <http://www.monde-diplomatique.fr/1998/10/ROY/11134>.

Although the WIF could be considered a large network of terrorist organizations, with a hypothetical ability to take control over state or states, it was not a NSN as defined by Bertelsen: an entity that operated in a manner similar to a nation state but not recognized as such.

As explained above, these organizations rejected nationalism and strove to restore the umma, which designated a people or community; a powerful and sometimes a visionary concept of Islam, the community of the faithful that transcended long established tribal boundaries to create a degree of political unity.

However, if al-Qaeda leaders did not take into consideration the national interests inherent in their terrorist activity and disregarded the consequences of retaliation on their constituencies, they could not ignore the sensitive relations with the host Taliban regime.

The Taliban authorities continued to shelter bin Laden and were not undeterred despite international pressure and sanctions imposed by the UN on the regime in November 1999. However, the Taliban reiterated they had restricted bin Laden's movements and closed his training camps. After the retaliatory strikes on al-Qaeda camps in Afghanistan following the bombings of the US embassies in Kenya and Tanzania, the Taliban forbade bin Laden to give media interviews and this was effective for six months. Bin Laden had reportedly complained in private about the restrictions on his freedom of movement, which had become harsher as external pressure mounted. In the wake of the Palestinian intifada in October 2000, he reportedly sought permission to issue a public statement denouncing the Israeli aggression against the Palestinians on two occasions, only to be refused.[173]

Reports of a planned American military action against bin Laden following the attack on USS Cole circulated by the end of 2000 prompted bin Laden and the Taliban alike to deny any involvement in the incident. The Taliban insisted that bin Laden was under constant surveillance and could not have conducted such an operation from Afghanistan. The Kuwaiti daily *al-Ra'y al-'Am* published a telephone conversation with him in which he denied any links with the perpetrators of the attack or with the suspects apprehended in Kuwait for planning suicide attacks on US military convoys and saying that neither he nor his followers had any intention of attacking US civil or military installations in any Arab country.[174]

Hypothesis 10: In a coalition between a strong organization (the patron) and a weak one (the client), the smaller organization is not significantly dependent on the larger one, and retains freedom to make its own decisions.

---

[173]   See Webman, *The Undiminished Threat of Political Islam*, p. 100.
[174]   See *al-Ra'y al-'Amm*, 13 November 2000, Ibid., p. 116.

As described above, al-Qaeda is not a centralized organization but rather a loose network of quite independent groups or cells.

Most of the proposals for terrorist operations appear to come from the operatives in the field, rather than from the center. Approval from above, however, brings resources that elevate such plans to a deadlier realm. The provision of technical advice, money, documents, and additional manpower to the self-selected terrorists suggests the existence of what Jenkins called 'an underground bureaucracy ... al-Qaeda's middle management.' Some operations seem to receive little central support, but a plan for an attack on the scale of 9/11 would certainly have significant central control and could well have been initiated by al-Qaeda's command.[175]

The millennium plot, for example, demonstrates the decentralization and independent work of the many groups involved. It seems that only the timing and the general framework of the targets were decided, or more probably proposed by al-Qaeda leaders. The implementation of the plot and the single operations were left to the discretionary decision and planning of the involved organizations.

According to Ahmad Ressam, who was not a member of al Qaeda, cells were formed in the camps in Afghanistan dependent, in part, on the timing of the arrival of the trainees, rather than on any cohesive or pre-existing organizational structure. As part of the training, clerics and other authority figures advised the cells of the targets that are deemed valid, including US military installations, US warships, embassies and business interests of the US and Israel. Ressam stated that the cells were independent, but were given lists of the types of targets that were approved according to the doctrine of the international Jihad. He explicitly noted that his own planned attack did not have bin Laden's blessing or his money although bin Laden urged more operations within the US.[176]

In the summer of 2000, two Islamic terrorist networks were becoming very active in Europe: one led by a Tunisian, identified as Seifallah ben Hassine, and the second by an Algerian in London, identified as 'Abu Doha'.[177] Ben Hassine was the external boss of the Italian terrorist cell, led by the Tunisian Essid Sami Ben Khemais, who was himself in direct contact with similar groups in Britain and Belgium. There were many connections between the Italian cell and the Frankfurt cell raided in December 1999 by the German police and a terrorist cell in Spain The two networks supported the activity of the Algerian Salafist Group

---

[175] See Jenkins, *Countering al-Qaeda*, p. 5.
[176] See Bowman, *Some-Time, Part-Time and One-time Terrorism*.
[177] Haydar Abu Doha is in custody in London, where U.S. authorities are seeking his extradition on charges he was a key figure in bin Laden's network and one of the plotters to bomb Los Angeles International Airport on New Year's Eve 1999. Abu Doha also was implicated by U.S. intelligence in the planned attack on the American Embassy in Rome.

for Call and Combat. Ben Khemais claimed in an interview that he didn't knew bin Laden and mainly wanted to help Muslims elsewhere, especially in Chechnya.[178]

The analysis of the juridical documents concerning the 'Milan affair' described above, shows that the Italian cell was not connected directly to the al-Qaeda leadership, but was rather directed from one or two ringleaders resident in London.[179]

Hypothesis 11: Coalitions between terrorist organizations are usually bilateral. A coalition between more than two terrorist organizations is viable only when they are geographically close, and share a common ideology and strategic goal.

From its inception the WIF was intended to be a wide network of Islamist movements and groups acting globally. According to Jenkins, bin Laden and his associates contributed to the unfocused Islamist force 'a sense of vision, mission, and strategy' that 'recast' local conflicts into a single struggle between an authentic Islam and a host of corrupt' regimes that would collapse without the backing of the US. 'By erasing the boundaries between individual countries and their conflicts, al Qaeda could draw upon a much larger reservoir of human resources for the larger battle.'[180]

Paz distinguishes an emerging doctrine of the 'non-territorial Islamic state' which views Muslim communities as a kind of loose-knit Islamic state, though without the territorial and religious mission of reestablishing a Khilafah, an Islamic empire. The interaction in the West between Muslim immigrants from various countries, cultures and ideologies, facilitated the growth of the Khilafah doctrine and promoted solidarity and a shared sense of global threat to Islam and the Muslims. As a result, this new doctrine of brotherhood resulted in a new operational development – the establishment of multinational and multi-organizational terrorist cells among Muslim immigrants in the West, some responsible for planning and carrying out terrorist attacks as much as their leaders in Afghanistan.[181]

---

[178] See Leo Sisti and Maud Beelman, 'Arrested Italian Cell Sheds Light On Bin Laden's European Network,' 3 October 2001, at <http://www.informationwar.org/terrorist_network/bin_laden_european_network.htm>.

[179] The author has had access to the original Italian indictment document, 'Procura della Repubblica Presso il Tribunale Ordinario di Milano, Fermo di indiziato di delitto, N.13016/99 R.G.' by Judge Stefano Dambruoso.

[180] See Jenkins, *Countering al-Qaeda*, p. 4.

[181] See Paz, *Middle East Islamism in the European Arena*, p. 5.

IX.   THE INFLUENCE OF VARIABLES AT THE DECISION-MAKER LEVEL

Hypothesis 12: The personal experiences of revolutionary leaders and racist and antisemitic preconceptions influence their decision to join a coalition against Israel and/or Jews.

Islamic tradition provides the soil on which Islamist antisemitism has taken root. The mentor of Hizballah in Lebanon, Sheik Fadlallah, declared that, 'in the vocabulary of the Qur'an, Islamists have much of what they need to awaken the consciousness of Muslims because the Qur'an speaks about the Jews in a negative way, concerning both their historical conduct and future schemes'.[182]
Wistrich elaborated on this theme:

For Muslim fundamentalists, Jews have come to represent an 'eternal enemy' of Islam from their 'double-dealing' intrigues against the Prophet in seventh-century Arabia to the embattled present, committed as they (supposedly) have always been to destroying the Islamic creed. According to Qutb, Jews invented the modern doctrines of 'atheistic materialism' (communism, psychoanalysis, and sociology) for precisely this purpose. It was the Jews' naturally malevolent disposition, misanthropy, abiding hatred of Muslims (as testified by the Koran) that prompted such actions, but their plots would ultimately fail once the believers returned to the sources of their invincible faith.

However, fundamentalists blended their religious Judeophobias with modern Western twentieth-century motifs of racist and political antisemitism, foremost the *Protocols of the Elders of Zion*, which provides a complete conspiracy theory of history in which satanic Jews relentlessly strive for world domination.[183]
Palestinian loss of territory and loss of the Islamic holy places in Jerusalem during the Six Day War are viewed with a sense of degradation, injustice and anger among Muslims and greatly intensified the demonology of Zionism and the Jews, especially among Muslim fundamentalists. Not by accident, says Wistrich, fundamentalists now pose the conflict in terms of a struggle between Islam and the Jews – 'a battle of culture, civilization and religion. A radical rejection of all things Western and the belief that only Islam was the solution (*Islam huwa al-hal*) henceforth went together with a new vision of the Jewish danger and of Israel as a

---

[182] Cited by Martin Kramer, in *The Salience of Islamic Antisemitism*, a lecture presented at the Institute of Jewish Affairs in London and published in its IJA Reports No. 2 (October 1995).
[183] Robert Wistrich, 'Muslim Anti-Semitism: A Clear and Present Danger,' *American Jewish Committee Publications*, at <http://www.ajc.org/InTheMedia/Publications.asp?did=503&pid=1196>.

total enemy and an existential threat.'[184] Simultaneously, Israel is seen as a surrogate of western neo-colonialism and its continued existence in the heart of Muslim territory a permanent reminder of their inferiority.[185]

It should be remembered that the first terrorist attack in the US by militants of the radical Sunni group under the leadership of the Egyptian Sheik Omar Abdel Rahman was the assassination of the Jewish extremist Rabbi Meir Kahana in New York in 1990. They also prepared attacks against Jewish targets after the WTC bombing on 26 February 1993.[186]

The Algerian GIA attempted to bomb a synagogue in Lyons, France on 24 December 1994, a Jewish school, again in Lyons in September 1995 (injured several people), and a letter bomb was sent to the editor of a Jewish paper in December 1996. It is interesting to note that prior to this wave of bombings the GIA published a virulently antisemitic and anti-Zionist manifesto in Sweden, where it had its headquarters at the time. The manifesto accused the Jews and the Zionists of being responsible for the tragic situation in Algeria.

In his 1998 Declaration of War, bin Laden stated:

I feel still the pain of (the loss) Al Quds [Jerusalem] in my internal organs. That loss is like a burning fire in my intestines... My Muslim Brothers of The World: Your brothers in Palestine and in the land of the two Holy Places [Saudi Arabia] are calling upon your help and asking you to take part in fighting against the enemy your enemy and their enemy the Americans and the Israelis. They are asking you to do whatever you can, with one owns means and ability, to expel the enemy, humiliated and defeated, out of the sanctities of Islam... It should not be hidden from you that the people of Islam had suffered from aggression, iniquity and injustice imposed on them by the Zionist-Crusaders alliance and their collaborators; The people of Islam awakened and realised that they are the main target for the aggression of the Zionist-Crusaders alliance.

---

[184] Ibid.

[185] Magnus Ranstorp, Terrorism in the Name of Religion, Journal of International Affairs, Summer 1996, 50, no. 1, pp. 41-62, at <http://www.lander.edu/atannenbaum/Tannenbaum%20 courses%20folder/POLS%20364%20Terrorism%20course%20folder/ranstorp_terrorism_in_the_ nameof_religion.htm>.

[186] El Sayyid A. Nosair, an American of Egyptian origin killed Kahana on 5 November 1990. Police found in his home a list of Jewish public figures. However he was acquitted by the jury. Nosair was condemned for this murder only after he was arrested for the involvement with the Islamist terrorist group under the leadership of Sheikh Abdel Rahman, responsible for the bombing of the WTC in 1993. The group that bombed the WTC intended, besides waging major terrorist attacks against American targets in New York: to put a large bomb in the NY diamond sector, where many Jews work and live; to attack a Jewish summer camp in the Catskill mountains; to assassinate several prominent Jewish and pro-Israeli personalities (like senator D'Amato) and the Israeli ambassador to the UN, Gad Yaakovi.

Bin Laden, however, paid little attention to the Palestinian issue and has in the past even been criticized for his inactivity in this field.[187] This apparent neglect may have led terrorists connected to bin Laden's network to take an interest in attacking Israeli and Jewish targets, in addition to American ones. As reported above, the Jaysh Muhammad group planned to carry out attacks against Jewish and Israeli tourists in Amman and against visitors to Moses' tomb on Mt. Nebo in December 1999.

It is also noteworthy that since January 2000, the main Islamist website supporting the propaganda war of the radical Chechens intensified its antisemitic messages. 'America's Jewish Secretary of State, Madeline Albright,' was accused of paying little attention to the plight of the innocent Chechens; 'Jewish fascists' controlling the Western media intensify the campaign 'to tarnish the image of Muslims.' The climax of this campaign was attained in March 2000, when the Jews were accused of directly helping the Russian war machine and threatened with retaliation.[188]

The WIF fatwa links the hatred to the US with the one to Israel and the Jews:

> If the Americans' aims behind these wars are religious and economic, the aim is also to serve the Jews' petty state and divert attention from its occupation of Jerusalem and murder of Muslims there. The best proof of this is their eagerness to destroy Iraq, the strongest neighboring Arab state, and their endeavor to fragment all the states of the region such as Iraq, Saudi Arabia, Egypt, and Sudan into paper statelets and through their disunion and weakness to guarantee Israel's survival and the continuation of the brutal crusade occupation of the Peninsula.

X.   SUMMARY

The lack of historical perspective and the necessity to limit the volume of this afterward chapter hinder analysis of the *sui generis* al-Qaeda phenomenon and comparison with the coalitions of leftist, rightist and nationalist terror organizations of the 1970-90s. It appears, however, that some major variables influence similarly the behavior of the two sets of organizations.

The success of the al-Qaeda phenomena in the late 1990s results from a series of strategic victories by Islamic states and new Islamist ideologies over the past

---

[187] See Ely Karmon, 'Terrorism a la Bin Ladin is not a Peace Process Problem,' The Washington Institute for Near East Policy, *Policywatch, Policywatch,* The Washington Institute for Near East Policy, No. 347, October 1998.

[188] See Ely Karmon, 'Radical Islamic Groups and Anti-Jewish Terrorism', in Dina Porat and Roni Stauber (eds.), *Anti-Semitism and Terror* (The Stephen Roth Institute for the Study of Contemporary Anti-Semitism and Racism, Tel Aviv University, 2003), pp. 162-63.

three decades. Also relevant were the backwardness of the ruling regimes in the Muslim and Arab world, and the fear (or short-sightedness) of the rest of the world, particularly the West, to see this phenomenon for what it was.[189]

The victories that boosted the self-confidence of the Islamist leaders and inflated the expectations of the Muslim masses were accompanied by violence and terrorism. A few examples are cited here:

The oil crisis of 1972-73 enhanced the economic, strategic and political power of the regimes in Saudi Arabia and the smaller Gulf states, and those of the more radical Algerian and Libyan regimes *vis-à-vis* the West and practically the entire non-oil producing world.[190] This was the era when Saudi and Libyan money built mosques and so-called Islamic 'cultural' centers in Europe and other countries – institutions which later fell as ripe fruits under the control of more radical Islamist elements, which used them for indoctrination, recruitment, funding and even training. This was also the beginning of the wave of aggressive Islamic religious proselytism and propaganda based on oil-money in new areas of Africa, Asia and even Europe, particularly in Spain and Italy, as well as among the African-American population of the US.

The success of the Iranian Khomeinist revolution was regarded as the first 'military' victory over the US and the Western world, symbolized by the hostage-taking of the American embassy staff and the disastrous US military rescue attempt. The aggressive endeavor of the Ayatollahs' regime to export this revolutionary new Islamist ideology all over the Muslim world had a huge impact on all the radical movements, not only in the Shi'a population but also in most of the Sunni countries.[191] The second real success was the expulsion in 1983 of the US and French peace-keeping forces from Lebanon by the Iranian and Syrian-backed Hizballah, leading to the strategy of mass suicide attacks.[192] The ensuing kidnapping and assassination of Western nationals in Lebanon during the 1980s –

---

[189] See Ely Karmon, 'The War on Terrorism: Who is the Enemy and What is the Coalition?' *ICT* website, 15 October 2001, at <http://www.ict.org.il/articles/articledet.cfm?articleid=397>.

[190] This was evident during the 1970's and the beginning of the 1980's, when Palestinian and Arab terrorism acted almost freely in every corner of the international arena without real punishment. These groups even received a bonus at the UN, with the equation of Zionism with racism.

[191] The Palestinian Islamic Jihad was one of the first Sunni terrorist organizations to be influenced by the Khomeinist revolutionary doctrine.

[192] The attacks targeted the American embassy in Beirut in April 1983 (more than 50 people killed and 90 wounded), and the US Marines and French paratroopers headquarters in Beirut in October of the same year (some 300 soldiers were killed and more than 100 injured). In his audiotape released in February 2003, bin Laden cited the suicide bombings against the headquarters of the US Marines in Beirut, 'which turned the place into hell,' as the first 'American defeat' at the hand of the Islamist radicals.' See p. 5 of the transcript of the cassette as circulated by the Center for Islamic Studies and Research in Pakistan, the main organ of al-Qaeda cited in Reuven Paz, 'Global Jihad and the Sense of Crisis: Al-Qa'Idah's Other Front,' *The Project For The Research Of Islamist Movements* (PRISM), Occasional Papers, Vol. 1 (2003), Number 4 (March 2003).

without any punishment falling upon the Hizballah and its patrons – greatly boosted the self-confidence of Iran and Hizballah. Hizballah and its patron continued to be active in international terrorism during the early 1990s, in Europe, Turkey, the Middle East, South America and Asia.[193]

The victory of the Afghanis and the Arab and Muslim volunteers fighting side by side against the Soviet Union gave an additional boost, both moral and psychological, to the Islamist movements, this time in the larger Sunni world. Again, Saudi and Gulf money supported the Islamic combatants, permitting the temporary removal of subversive elements from their countries of origin. Ironically, the US, using the Afghani conflict in the bipolar contest with the communist bloc, had prepared the stage for the new enemy of the Western democratic world.

The Gulf War, although seen as a great victory for the American-led coalition of the moderate Arab regimes and the beginning of a New World Order, in fact further exacerbated the radicalization of the Islamist movements. The war highlighted the issue of the continued presence of American and Western armed forces on the sacred 'Peninsula of Mohammad,' and the plight of the Iraqi population. The short but significant episode of the shameful retreat of US troops under the UN flag from Somalia in 1993, marked the first direct military intervention of bin Laden's al-Qaeda in the jihad against the Americans through the support to the poor Somali Islamist forces.[194]

Last, but not least, the unilateral Israeli withdrawal from South Lebanon in June 2000 was perceived as a brilliant strategic victory for the small Hizballah guerrilla forces against the powerful IDF. This victory enflamed the hearts of millions of Arabs and Muslims with pride and hope for a rapid destruction of Israel, and played a major role in the outbreak of the second intifada.

The Islamist strategy of continual struggle against the West, the Muslim Soviet republics, and Israel was devised immediately after the Afghani victory in 1988-89. Neither the Gulf War, nor the crumbling of the Soviet empire, nor the peace

---

[193] See Ely Karmon, 'Why Tehran Starts and Stops Terrorism', *The Middle East Quarterly*, December 1998, Vol. 5, No. 4, also at <http://www.meforum org/mcq/dec98/elyk.shtml>.

[194] Following is the plastic description of this event in bin Laden's *Declaration of War*: 'But your most disgraceful case was in Somalia, where after vigorous propaganda about the power of the USA and its post cold war leadership of the new world order you moved tens of thousands of international force, including twenty eight thousands American solders into Somalia. However, when tens of your solders were killed in minor battles and one American pilot was dragged in the streets of Mogadishu, you left the area carrying disappointment, humiliation, defeat and your dead with you. Clinton appeared in front of the whole world threatening and promising revenge, but these threats were merely a preparation for withdrawal. You have been disgraced by Allah and you withdrew; the extent of your impotence and weaknesses became very clear. It was a pleasure for the "heart" of every Muslim and a remedy to the "chests" of believing nations to see you defeated in the three Islamic cities of Beirut, Aden and Mogadishu.'

process between Israelis and the Palestinians had anything to do with the decision to continue the struggle worldwide. Some Palestinian ideologues, such as Abdallah Azzam, were at the forefront of this strategy, but were not at all involved in the struggle for the liberation of Palestine.

A Saudi opposition organization close to al-Qaeda clearly presents a similar evaluation:

> The past two decades witnessed significant shifts in Islamic tendencies. Muslims are becoming more jealous of their identity and are more inclined to view life through Islamic perspective. A plethora of events and circumstances enhanced these changes and gave them a distinct political flavour. Among these events is the jihad in Afghanistan and the defeat of the Soviet Union there. There is also the eruption of the first and second intifada in Palestine, the jihad in Chechnya and the defeat of Israel at the hands of Hizbulla in South Lebanon. There were also more and more significant intellectual, cultural and social changes.[195]

However, it is also obvious that much of the thrust of Islamist ideologues and strategists to act in the framework of a broad alliance derives also from a real perception of threat from internal, regional and international players or events. After the invasion of Afghanistan by the Soviet Union was repelled, the US became the main threat, on the global arena. But for the Chechens the threat is represented by Russia, for the Pakistani and Kashmiris by India, for the Uighurs by China, for the Moros by the Christian Philippine state, etc.

At the same time, virtually all the organizations and groups feel threatened by their own regimes, viewed as inefficient, corrupt, oppressive, collaborators of the 'Zionist Crusaders alliance.' The Wahhabi regime in Saudi Arabia is callously accused in bin Laden's Declaration of War:

> Injustice had affected the people of the industry and agriculture. It affected the people of the rural and urban areas... The situation at the land of the two Holy places became like a huge volcano at the verge of eruption that would destroy the Kufr and the corruption and its' sources.

Just as the Islamists conceive threats and injustices suffered by Muslims everywhere as stemming from the greed of the 'infidel' imperialist powers or the corrupt regimes, they also regard the struggle against the enemy alliance as a legitimate right of the Muslim *umma*.

---

[195] See 'The American Phenomenon and The Bin Laden Phenomenon', published after the September 11 attacks on the US (no date) by The Movement for Islamic Reform in Arabia (MIRA) at their website, <http://www.miraserve.com/pressrev/ARTICLE1.htm.

However, due to 'the imbalance of power' between the Islamist 'armed forces and the enemy forces', bin Laden suggested terrorism as 'a suitable means of fighting' the infidels, 'fast moving light forces that work under complete secrecy'. He threatened the US Defense Secretary:

> Where was this false courage of yours when the explosion in Beirut took place on 1983 CE (1403 A.H). You were turned into scattered pits and pieces at that time; 241 mainly marines solders were killed. And where was this courage of yours when two explosions made you to leave Aden in less than twenty four hours... The explosion at Riyadh and Al Khobar is a warning of this volcanic eruption emerging as a result of the sever oppression, suffering, excessive iniquity, humiliation and poverty.[196]

As noted previously, the Islamists and part of the Arab and Muslim elites see the Muslim world as a whole as a new bloc opposed to the Western democratic one.

Islamists, and bin Laden more than anyone else, are trying to drag the US and the West in an overall campaign against the Muslim world and convince Muslims worldwide that they are indeed the target of Crusaders, rather than the violent fringes of the movement. A Saudi organization close to al-Qaeda asserts that 'bin Laden believes that the final outcome of events is an all-out confrontation with the US' and that America could be easily lured into such confrontation by a bigger attack than that against the embassies in Kenya and Tanzania. He therefore built on the assumption that in the worst case scenario the US will respond to the 9/11 attacks 'more aggressively with vaster capabilities ... by mobilising armies and call upon allies to participate'. In case the US destroyed Afghanistan, the region would be destabilized and many regimes would collapse. Actually, according to this evaluation, bin Laden has always dreamed of a long US ground operation 'with a repeat of the Soviet-Afghan fiasco.' Under 'the great psychological impact of those symbolic buildings collapsing on TV screens ... [t]he readiness, and willingness, of bin Laden supporters to act against America or the local regimes would be many folds bigger than before.'[197]

The same dilemma exists when we evaluate the effect of rifts between ideologically similar powers and the emergence of new revolutionary and ideological foci on new forms of solidarity that encourage the formation of coalitions between terrorist organizations that support one of the new ideologies.

---

[196] Bin Laden refers to the suicide bombing by Hizballah of the Marines headquarters in Beirut in October 1983; the car bomb explosion in November 1995 in the parking lot of the office of the program manager of the Saudi Arabian National Guard in Riyadh, Saudi Arabia, which killed seven persons including US federal and civilian employees, and one US military; and the car bombing in June 1996 of the Khobar Towers, part of a housing complex for military personnel in Dahran, Saudi Arabia. See *Declaration of War*.

[197] See 'The American Phenomenon and The Bin Laden Phenomenon'.

Al-Zawahiri for instance draws a strict distinction between his movement, the Islamic Jihad, and other competing Islamist movements. He condemns the Muslim Brotherhood, the main Islamist movement in the Arab world, for renouncing jihad as a means of establishing the Islamic state and characterizes them as *kuffar* (infidels) because they use democracy to achieve their political goals, thus giving the legislature rights that belong to Allah. He criticizes the Brotherhood for negotiating with the ruling authorities and supporting the election of President Mubarak in 1987. In his memoirs, *Knights under the Banner of the Prophet*, al-Zawahiri considers the Muslim Brotherhood to be a movement that grows organizationally but commits suicide ideologically and politically.[198] By distancing himself from his 'parent movement', the leader of the Egyptian Jihad behaves similarly to the leaders of the German RAF or the Italian Red Brigades *vis-à-vis* the respective reformist or orthodox communist parties.

As the conflict between the Muslim world and the rest of the world, and especially the West, seems to be increasing alongside internal divergences within Islam, these issues call for further study.

Nonetheless, evidence suggests that regional wars, crisis and tensions perceived as a threat to Muslim countries or communities worldwide encouraged Islamist terrorist organizations belonging to the same ideological camp to seek allies in order to strengthen their position in the struggle against the common enemy, or in order to help an organization under attack in another region.

In the 1980s the main thrust of solidarity in the radical Islamist camp was, on the one hand, to support the Iranian regime to enhance its regional status, and on the other hand to sustain the military campaign of Afghan tribes and their allied mujahideen to expel the Soviets from their country. By contrast, the 1990s witnessed enhanced solidarity and cooperation between numerous organizations and individuals, either to support the 'liberation wars' of Muslims in Bosnia, Chechnya, Kashmir, Palestine, the Philippines, or to fight Muslim regimes perceived as oppressing Islamist movements in Algeria, Egypt, Jordan, Indonesia and Saudi Arabia. Some support went to the Taliban regime, which provided the safe haven and training camps so essential to the development of the military (i.e. guerrilla and terrorist) capabilities of Islamist fighters and the forging of a comradeship of arms under the ideological indoctrination of al-Qaeda leadership.

International and regional cooperation between security forces against terrorist organizations clearly provided a strong incentive for Islamist terrorist groups to form coalitions. The authoritarian or absolutist regimes in the Arab and Muslim countries were constantly concerned by the growing influence of radical Islamist movements, even when they were only active on the socio-economic *dawa* level.

---

[198] See Nimrod Raphaeli, 'Radical Islamist Profiles (3): Ayman Muhammad Rabi' Al-Zawahiri: The Making of an Arch Terrorist', *MEMRI Inquiry and Analysis Series,* No. 127, 11 March 2003.

Egypt has been in the forefront of the campaign against Islamism since the Muslim Brotherhood threatened the Nasserite secular regime in the 1950s. The return of Afghan veterans to Egypt at the beginning of the 1990s was accompanied by a spate of terrorist activity, including assassination attempts against the highest echelons of the regime. Algeria suffered a genuine countrywide Islamist rebellion following cancellation of the FIS won elections and the arrest of its leaders. This brought widespread violence, massacres of civilians and the appearance of new terrorist organizations, namely the AIS and the GIA, which later split into smaller factions.

The intensification of Islamist terrorist attacks and the 1998 bombings in Kenya and Tanzania finally convinced Arab governments to achieve a cooperation agreement to combat their respective oppositions, for the first time in the history of the Arab League. Bin Laden, implicated by Egyptian defendants for his involvement in the Egyptian embassy bombing in Islamabad in 1995, reportedly sent a protest message to the Arab interior ministers for bowing to US pressures.

A vicious circle of terrorism and counter-terrorism clearly exists. Islamists attack the regimes, claiming to be under continuous oppression, while governments respond to the terrorist attacks with tougher security measures and heavier penalties for their militants. But if the heavy hand of the authorities led many leaders of movements or terrorist groups (like the Algerian FIS or the Egyptian Jihad and Islamic Group) to proclaim a cease-fire, it convinced the groups affiliated to al-Qaeda to raise the stakes by raising the frequency and lethality of the terrorist attacks. American officials reportedly investigated the likelihood that the embassy attacks in Africa could have been acts of revenge for a raid by security personnel from the US and Albania in June 1998 against an alleged cell of an Islamic terrorist organization and the arrest of two suspected employees of bin Laden by the Americans.

However, the successes of counter-terrorism and enhanced security measures were unable to prevent the deadliest and most daring of all attacks in the history of terrorism, i.e. those that occurred on the morning of 9/11.

These terrible events differed remarkably from all previous attacks related to al-Qaeda, including the foiled millennium plot in terms of the sheer scope of human and material damage, the huge symbolic and political effect, the perfect Machiavellian planning and precise execution, and even the composition of the terrorist teams (14 Saudi citizens from the total of 19, led by an Egyptian). Little is still known about the person or organization that devised this operation. According to a high level FBI official:

> [t]he 9/11 hijackers were not an organization. Nor did they associate themselves
> overtly with al-Qaeda, which sponsored them… What we know of them today does
> not support a theory centered on a traditional terrorist organization, but it does

support a theory of networked radicals supported by al Qaeda. It is also reasonable to conclude that they acted in support of the 1998 fatwa which, in turn has proved to be eloquent evidence of the international jihad.[199]

This is a somewhat nebulous description of those responsible for the worst terrorist attack in history, after more than two years of worldwide investigations.

Al-Zawahiri described the process that brought together militants of many nations and transformed them into a worldwide network: The jihad battles in Afghanistan destroyed the myth of the USSR as a superpower in the minds of the young mujahideen; the jihad was 'a training course of utmost importance to prepare Muslim mujahidin to wage their awaited battle against the superpower that now has sole dominance over the globe, namely, the United States;' and gave young Arabs, Pakistanis, Turks, Muslims from Central and East Asia an opportunity to get acquainted 'through their comradeship-at-arms against the enemies of Islam.'[200]

It is obvious that the ideological bond represented by the common religious and strategic worldview of the many groups and individuals involved in al-Qaeda, as well as the common background and comradeship in the training camps of Afghanistan have forged in great measure the coalitional character of the network. Virtually all observers stress religion, or more exactly the specific brand of Salafi or Jihadi Islam, as the main factor behind the alliance of organizations affiliated to al-Qaeda.

A closer view, however, suggests a more complex picture. Different views on some religious rulings, such as the right to kill civilians or to attack Muslims, or the problem of devising a successful strategy to fight the enemy, can deeply divide these groups, hinder participation in the coalition or provoke splits. This phenomenon, quite obvious in the case of leftist, rightist or nationalist groups, is also present among Islamists and is highlighted in the case of the Egyptian and Algerian organizations. The Egyptian Jihadi groups, the closest associates of bin Laden and probably the most experienced and efficient, are a particular case in point.

In a startling move in February 2000, the Egyptian Jihad announced the dismissal of al-Zawahiri as its leader. His departure was linked to disputes over the issue of a truce with the authorities and the end of violence inside Egypt, announced in 1997.[201] Subsequently, Usama Siddiq Ayyub, one of the Egyptian Jihad leaders living in exile in Germany, and supported by other Jihad leaders within and beyond Egypt called for an end to violent acts at home and abroad in

---

[199] See M.E. Bowman, 'Some-Time, Part-Time and One-time Terrorism,' *INTELLIGENCER: Journal of US Intelligence Studies* (Winter/Spring 2003), Vol. 13, No. 2, pp. 13-18 at <http://www.fas.org/irp/eprint/bowman.pdf>.

[200] See al-Zawahiri, *Knights Under the Prophet's Banner.*

[201] Friction reportedly arose between al-Zawahiri and Sayyid Imam al-Sharif, alias Dr. Fadl, spokesperson of the organization, and between al-Zawahiri and his deputy, Muhammad Makkawi. See *Al-Sharq al-Awsat*, 6, 7 February 2000; Webman, pp. 105-106.

order to focus all efforts on the liberation of the al-Aqsa Mosque in Jerusalem. The initiative represented an extraordinary strategic change in the Jihad group's thinking and al-Zawahiri was unable to accept this initiative because of his strategic alliance with bin Laden.[202] These divergences are probably the background for al-Zawahiri's decision to announce the merger of his faction of Egyptian Jihad with al-Qaeda in June 2001, shortly before the 9/11 attacks.

Similar divisions emerged within the Egyptian Islamic Group. Sheikh Omar Abd al-Rahman, Gama'a's spiritual leader, announced from his prison in the US that he was revoking his support for the cease-fire with the Egyptian authorities declared unilaterally by the movement in 1997.[203] The truce had been opposed all along by the military commander of the Group, Rifa'i Ahmad Taha, who operated closely with bin Laden.[204] Abd al-Rahman's announcement created confusion among the movement's followers and exacerbated an existing split within the Group's two camps.[205] Friction resurfaced after the bombing of the USS Cole in October 2000. Taha issued a statement praising the attack as retaliation for the acts of the Israeli occupation against the Palestinian people. Other leaders, however, disassociated the movement from it.[206]

A meeting of Islamists in Afghanistan in September 2000, attended by bin Laden, Taha and al-Zawahiri, reaffirmed their determination to work for the release of Abd al-Rahman.[207] However, Jamal Ahmad al-Fadl, a bin Laden confidante turned FBI informant, testified that some Egyptian members of al-Qaeda left the organization because it was not ready to do anything to liberate Abd al-Rahman.[208]

---

[202] In August, 11 Jihad members jailed in the Wadi al-Natrun prison in Egypt issued an appeal to the movement leaders inside and outside Egypt to accept the initiative proposed by Usama Ayyub and unify all efforts toward the goal of the liberation of Jerusalem. See *Al-Sharq al-Awsat*, 8 and 13 February 2000.

[203] The truce had been unanimously launched by the Islamic Group original council (shura) established by the founding leaders, jailed in the Tarra prison in Egypt (Sheikh Karam Zuhdi, Sheikh Najih Ibrahim, Sheikh 'Isam Dirballah, Sheikh 'Asim 'Abd al-Majid, Sheikh Usama Hafiz, Sheikh Hamdi 'Abd al-Rahman, Sheikh Fu'ad al-Dawalibi, Sheikh 'Ali al-Sharif and 'Abbud al-Zummar).

[204] Both leaders charged that 'the unilateral truce has not achieved anything, that the state has not reciprocated, and that it will never allow Islamist groups to engage meaningfully in peaceful politics.'

[205] Taha relinquished his role as leader of the Shura Council of the organization abroad. The majority camp led by Mustafa Hamza, head of the Gama'a Shura Council abroad, announced that the decision made by the movement to cease armed operations was still in force. *Al-Sharq al-Awsat*, 25 June 2000, *Al-Hayat*, 15, 22 June, *al-Quds al-'Arabi*, 19 June 2000; Webman, *The Undiminished Threat of Political Islam*,

[206] *Al-Sharq al-Awsat*, 13, 14 November 2000. Webman, *The Undiminished Threat of Political Islam*.

[207] Al-Jazeera Satellite TV, 21 September (BBC Monitoring); *al-Quds al-'Arabi*, 23 September 2000, Webman, *The Undiminished Threat of Political Islam*.

[208] See testimony of Jamal Ahmad al-Fadl in Barry Rubin and Judith Colp Rubin, *Anti-American Terrorism and the Middle East*, p, 171.

One of the leaders of the Egyptian Islamic Group, Isam Darbalah, published a book, 'The Strategy of al-Qa'ida: Mistakes and Dangers,' which outlined sharply 'the wrong arguments and assumptions' of al-Qaeda. These mistaken assumptions included: the existence of a global plan to eradicate Islam and the Islamic movements, irrespective of what al-Qaeda and others were doing toward the US; the affirmation that US interests could never agree with Islamic interests, since enmity was deep-rooted and a clash unavoidable; that concluding peace or negotiating or establishing an alliance with the US was tantamount to treason; that the US, in its conflict with al-Qaeda, could not afford human losses; that the disparity in power between the Islamic *umma* and the US is irrelevant because Islamists fight was based on faith and not on numbers.[209]

According to this text, the strategy of al-Qaeda is founded on a clear misunderstanding of reality, a mistaken evaluation of 'the capabilities of the nation,' and those of 'the opponents'. Darbalah concludes that al-Qaeda strategy cannot achieve its goals and is 'inconsistent with sound logic'. This strategy created numerous enemies and harmed the interests of Islamic countries. In fact, it has contributed greatly 'toward formulating a more negative US strategy toward it and toward the Islamic world' and missed the opportunity 'to benefit from the realities of the international situation'.[210]

Moreover, the flawed al-Qaeda strategy has resulted in the 'collapse of the emergent Islamic state in Afghanistan,' harmed 'the causes of Islamic minorities through the deliberate confusion of movements resisting occupation with terrorism,' allowed 'the achievement of Israeli goals and ambitions,' exposed 'to racial harassment' Islamic communities in Europe and the US, and pushed the US to adopt 'a strategy that responds to the agenda of the Christian right … for the clash of civilizations.'

On the religious and moral grounds Darbalah strongly criticized 'the strange' WIF fatwas calling for the killing of Americans, military and civilians, since they contradict the prevailing interpretation by the majority of Muslim scholars of the

---

[209] Darbalah was a member of the Shura Council of the Egyptian Islamic Group who had been serving a life sentence in the greater jihad case since 1981. See *Al-Sharq al-Awsat*, 6 August 2003. Part one of four part report by Abd-al-Latif al-Minnawi from Cairo: 'New Book For the Egyptian Islamic Group on al-Qa'ida's Mistakes. There Is Not A War Led By the United States Against Islam. Al-Qa'ida's Policies Boosted the Presence of Anti-Islam Currents. The Strange Fatwas That Sanction the Killing of Civilians, Women, and Children Have Nothing to Do With Islam' (FBIS-NES-2003-0809).

[210] Besides its conflict with the US al-Qaeda has entangled itself in conflicts with the Russian Federation by supporting the rebels of Chechnya and Dagestan; India, by supporting the rebels of Kashmir; Europe, by including it under the 'Crusaders;' the Jews; the Philippines, by supporting the Abu Sayyaf group; Australia, by getting involved in the Bali bombing; Kenya and Tanzania, by bombing the US embassies there; The Arab and Islamic countries that were a theatre for al-Qaeda operations, such as Saudi Arabia, Indonesia, and Morocco. Ibid.

Shari'a, which clearly 'prohibits [the] killing [of] civilians and targeting women, children, old people, monks, peasants, hired men, and such people who do not take part in the fighting.'[211]

Paz remarked that 'persistent divisions, conflicts, rivalries, and personal agendas within the global Jihad movement have thus far prevented its terrorist methods from spreading beyond its thousands of militants, activists, sympathizers, and fundraisers,' while the Muslim world at large has never accepted bin Laden as 'the new Islamic Caliph'. And although the consolidation of the neo-Wahhabi and Takfiri ideologies helped increased international cooperation among different Islamist groups, in the whole it does not appear that 'the Islamist *Internationale*' has become a strategic threat.[212]

Rubin also pointed to inherent difficulties in forming Islamist coalitions. One of the problems involved is the competition between spiritual leaders' of the organization, as 'one man's respected cleric may be another man's charlatan or heretic'. Moreover, [since] 'religious doctrine is at the core of their ideology, Sunni and Shi'a Muslim radicals find it difficult – though not always impossible – to cooperate'.[213] These problems are reminiscent of those encountered in ideologically radical groups of the left and right in Europe.

Another major difficulty is the existence of important Islamist mass movements like the Muslim Brotherhood, the Algerian FIS, the Palestinian Hamas which wage their struggle in a nationalist framework. These were termed by Roy islamo-nationalists, in opposition to the internationalists or 'de-territorialized' al-Qaeda associates. Not that these movements are not searching allies and coalitions, but they generally do so in the framework of the local nationalist struggle which aims ultimately to achieve an Islamist state.

Thus the Palestinian Hamas could ally with the Palestinian Islamic Jihad, or with secular movements or groups like the Fatah of the PFLP, or even with the Shia Hizballah in Lebanon, but this coalition's main goal was to support the liberation of whole Palestine, a Palestine under the rule of the Sharia law and an Islamist government. Cooperation with Hizballah does not mean that Hamas was ready to act in favor of Hizballah's goals in Lebanon or attack US and Western targets in the Palestinian territories or abroad.

It is interesting that since the outbreak of the so-called al-Aqsa Intifada, and more so since al-Qaeda's demise in Afghanistan, the Palestinian issue became one of the major unifying motives of the Islamist coalition. Actually, support for the Palestinians and the liberation of the al-Aqsa Mosque in Jerusalem as one of

---

[211] Ibid.
[212] See Paz, *Tangled Web*, p. 45-46.
[213] See Barry Rubin, Islamic Radicalism in the Middle East: A Survey and Balance Sheet,' *MERIA*, Vol. 2, No. 1, May 1998.

the main goals, at least nominally, of the coalition, was a gradual process. Besides the strategic reasons, the pro-Palestinian and anti-Israeli stance of radical Islamists was not so much result of personal antisemitic feelings, but rather the expression of embedded anti-Jewish religious and socio-political outlook of the movements themselves.

The Palestinian problem has been often cited in bin Laden's interviews and documents and his statements in this context were often laden with crude antisemitic conspiracy themes. However, it seems that his use of this particular theme is mainly ideological and propagandistic. In any case, the occupation of Jerusalem by the Jews did not distract bin Laden from his main ambition – the expulsion of the US presence from Saudi Arabia. According to an Arab journalist, bin Laden 'has been criticized in the Arab world for focusing on such places as Afghanistan and Bosnia-Herzegovina, and [he] is therefore starting to concentrate more on the Palestinian issue.'[214]

Immediately after the outbreak of the intifada in October 2000, bin Laden reportedly expressed consternation over the impotence of leaders of Islamist movements, who did not take advantage of the protests by the Arab peoples to support it more vigorously.[215] And before the beginning of the US campaign against al-Qaeda in Afghanistan, al-Zawahiri believed that the 'jihad movement's opportunity to lead the nation toward jihad to liberate Palestine ... doubled'. He accused 'the secular currents' of paying 'lip service to the issue of Palestine' and of accepting to negotiate and recognize Israel's existence.[216]

As a result of the al-Aqsa Intifada, Islamist groups in Central and South East Asia also became more interested in the Palestinian struggle; declarations of support of various Islamist Asian groups stressed the centrality of the issue of Jerusalem.[217] Yet, until the 9/11 attacks they were limited to the sphere of propaganda or fundraising efforts among Muslim communities in the West.[218]

The jailed leader of the Egyptian Islamic Group, Sheikh Abd al-Rahman, called on Muslim clerics to issue a fatwa sanctifying the killing of Jews.[219] A similar call was issued by the Pakistani Islamist movement, Hizb al-Mujahideen, which also announced that a contingent of mujahideen was ready to leave for

---

[214] See Abdel-Bari Atwan, editor of the London *Al-Quds al-Arabi,* cited in Ely Karmon, 'Terrorism a La Bin Laden is not a Peace Process Problem', *Policywatch*, No. 347, October 28, 1998.

[215] *Al-Hayat*, 5 November 2000; Webman, *The Undiminished Threat of Political Islam*, p. 112.

[216] See al-Zawahiri, *Knights Under the Prophet's Banner.*

[217] For example, see: 'Bayan mawqif muaskar al-jihad izaa mu'anat al-muslimin fi filastin' (A Declaration on the position of the Jihad camp toward the suffering of the Muslims in Palestine), published by the Jihad group of Maluku/Indonesia in their web site <http://www.malukujihad. cjb.net> (no date).

[218] See Paz, *Tangled Web*, p. 50.

[219] See CNN, 5 October 2000; Webman, *The Undiminished Threat of Political Islam*, p. 112.

Palestine.[220] Shamil Basayev, leader of the Chechen rebels, declared that a group of 153 Chechen fighters was prepared to be sent to the Middle East, and that Jerusalem was the concern of all Muslims.[221] In November, the Chechen fighting forces issued a 'second Aqsa Declaration,' in which they renewed the pledge to fight the Jews.

Sheikh Omar Bakri Muhammad, leader of the Islamist group Al-Muhajiroun in the UK, who claimed to be associated with the WIF, stated that the Front was recruiting Muslim volunteers from Italy, France and Spain to fight for the liberation of Palestine from Israeli occupation and that 34 mujahideen had already been sent to the Middle East to support the uprising. Bakri added that his organization helped Hamas, the Palestinian Jihad and other Islamist forces by collecting funds, recruiting fighters and sometimes carrying out propaganda for these groups in Europe.[222]

However, only after the demise of al-Qaeda forces in Afghanistan did the organization and affiliated groups began to attack Jewish and Israeli targets, and this because they speculated that backing the Palestinian people and the liberation of Jerusalem would bring them more support from the Arab and Muslim masses.[223] Al-Zawahiri emphasizes that 'the issue of Palestine is the cause that has been firing up the feelings of the Muslim nation from Morocco to Indonesia for the past 50 years. In addition, it is a rallying point for all the Arabs, be they believers or non-believers, good or evil.'[224] It is noteworthy that the first major successful attack after the US army entered Afghanistan was the bombing of the famous synagogue in Djerba, Tunisia.

---

[220] See *Pakistan*, 18 October 2000; ibid.

[221] See *Sawt al-Qoqaz*, 10 October and 24 November 2000; ibid.

[222] See *Il Giornale*, 14 October 2000; ibid.

[223] 11 April 2002: The explosion of a suicide fuel truck erupting at an ancient synagogue on the Tunisian Island of Djerba killed 17 people – 11 German tourists, five Tunisians and a Frenchman; 16 May 2003: five well-orchestrated explosions were carried out by suicide bombers on foot directed at a hotel, a Spanish night club, a Jewish center, a Jewish cemetery and a Jewish-owned Italian restaurant in Casablanca, Morocco. 14 terrorists, divided into five groups, estimated to have participated in the strikes. 41 civilians – three of them French, two Spanish, one Italian and the rest believed to be mostly Moroccan – were killed; 28 November 2002: A Land-rover with three men in it crashed and exploded into the front of a hotel in Mombassa, Kenya, where many Israeli tourists were staying, killing three Israelis and nine Kenyan citizens. At about the same time, two shoulder-fired anti-aircraft missile were fired at but missed an Israeli passenger plane with more than 270 passengers and 10 crew members aboard after takeoff from the airport in Mombassa. 12 December 2003: Suicide bombings of two synagogues in Istanbul, Turkey, killed 25 people.

[224] See al-Zawahiri, *Knights Under the Prophet's Banner.*

CONCLUSION

In conclusion, the many calls for solidarity and cooperation by European and Palestinian terrorist organizations in the 1970s and 1980s were vague and lacked specific goals or plans. This vagueness might have masked the confusion, failure and ideological rigidity plaguing these organizations. Anarchist and anarcho-communist organizations, radical right-wing organizations and ineffectual revolutionary Marxist-Leninist organizations that failed in their bid to seize power were evidently most likely to form alliances with similar organizations or with national liberation movements which they perceived as likely to further the goals of a world revolution.

Over and above the many ideological and organizational obstacles, technical difficulties also prevented terrorist organizations from cooperating with each other. Firstly, the clandestine nature of the terrorist organization hindered the formation of close ties. Given the lack of ongoing contact with foreign organizations, constant suspicion and gradual isolation from national and international developments, terrorist leaders were often unable to either understand and interpret events correctly or to accurately assess the advantages of cooperation with other organizations.

Since the early 1990s fears of lethal conventional and non-conventional terrorist attacks, particularly in the international arena, have escalated.[1] The growth of international terrorism after the 1991 Gulf War was almost entirely due to the activities of radical Islamist organizations. Indeed, some Americans considered this phenomenon 'more sinister than Marxism-Leninism'.[2]

There were growing indications of cooperation between radical Islamist organizations. Hizballah camps in Lebanon accepted members of sister organizations in Algeria, Turkey, and the Philippines, and trained Palestinians from the Hamas and Palestinian Islamic Jihad (PIJ) to perpetrate suicide attacks.[3] In the

---

[1] For a panorama of terrorism in the 1990s, see Bruce Hoffman, *Inside Terrorism*, (London: Victor Gollancz, 1998) and Ely Karmon, 'Trends in Contemporary International Terrorism,' in *Countering Suicide Terrorism – An International Conference* (ICT: Herzliya, 2001), pp. 47-60.

[2] See Douglas E. Streusand, 'Abraham's Other Children: Is Islam an Enemy of the West?' *Policy Review*, No. 50 (Fall 1989), cited in Leon T. Hadar, 'The Green Peril; Creating the Islamic Fundamentalist Threat,' CATO Policy Analysis, No. 177, 27 August 1992, at <http://www.geocities.com/miamivalleyislam/cato.html>.

[3] A total of 415 Hamas militants were deported by Israel to Marj al-Zuhour in Lebanon in December 1992 following a series of terrorist attacks perpetrated by their activists the previous months, the last one killing an Israeli police officer. During their stay in South Lebanon, before the Israeli government was compelled by the Israeli Supreme Court to return them, some of these militants received advanced training by Hizballah specialist, under the sponsorship of the Iranian Revolutionary Guards. On the relationship between Hamas and Hizballah during this period, see

second half of the 1990s Afghanistan and Pakistan became the meeting point for Islamist terrorists from Muslim countries and communities worldwide.[4] Indeed, some of the terrorists involved in the 1993 World Trade Center (WTC) bombing in New York sought asylum there.[5]

As in the past, some countries were still willing to sponsor terrorist and radical organizations, train their members, and provide them with financial and logistical support. Of these, Iran and Syria topped the list. Sudan, with fewer resources and smaller influence came a distant third, at least until the mid-1990s, when it extradited the famous 'Carlos' to France and expelled Osama bin Laden, already regarded as financier of Islamist organizations.[6]

The most significant changes actually took place in the international arena after the Gulf War: the collapse of the communist bloc, the disintegration of the USSR and the appearance of new Muslim independent states in Central Asia; the weakening influence of Marxist-Leninist ideology; the new role of the US as the sole superpower and the victory of the free market economy. All this led to a 'new world order' in which the influence of the democratic camp was dominant. Paradoxically, however, these processes also brought about political, economic, and social instability – conditions that released and strengthened latent nationalistic, religious and ideological forces.

Hisham H. Ahmed, 'From Religious Salvation to Political Transformation: The Rise of Hamas in Palestinian Society,' Palestinian Academic Society for the Study of International Affairs (PASSIA) Research Studies, No. 73 (May 1994), chapter 4, at <http://www.passia.org/publications/research_studies/pub_research_no_73.htm>. For relations in late 1990s, see 'Hamas Divided Against Itself,' Middle East Intelligence Bulletin, Vol. 1, No. 6 (June 1999), at <http://www.meib.org/issues/9906.htm#me2>.

[4] In the mid-1990s Pakistan, under pressure from Algeria, Egypt, Tunisia, expelled some of the thousands of 'Afghans', many of whom were fugitives in their homelands. Islamabad was keen to avoid being branded by the US State Department as a country that sponsors terrorism. See Bruce, *Arab Veterans of Afghanistan.*

[5] Ramzi Ahmed Yousef, who was indicted as a key figure in the bombing of the WTC, was arrested and extradited to the US by Pakistan in February 1995. See US Department of State, *Patterns of Global Terrorism*, 1995 at <http://www.fas.org/irp/threat/terror_95>.

[6] In June 1996 Bahrain exposed an active Bahraini Hizballah cell that was recruited, trained and supported by Iran. Diplomatic relations between Bahrain and Iran were subsequently strained. Kuwaiti Hizballah, a Kuwaiti Shi'a organization possibly linked to Iran, allegedly provided weapons to the Bahraini opposition group in 1996. Kuwaiti Hizballah may also have engaged in activities directed against the US military presence in Kuwait.
    On 25 June 1996 a large fuel truck containing explosives detonated outside the Khobar Towers housing facility of the US military near Dhahran, killing 19 US Air Force personnel and wounding some 500 persons. Several groups, both Shi'a and Sunni, purportedly claimed responsibility for the bombing, including: the 'Brigades of the Martyr Abdallah al-Hudhaifi,' 'Hizballah al-Khalij,' and the 'Islamic Movement for Change.' See *Patterns of Global Terrorism* 1996, at <http://www.state.gov/www/global/terrorism/1996Report/1996index.html>. In June 2001 the US Attorney General John Ashcroft announced a 46-count indictment against 13 Saudis and one Lebanese in the 1996 bombing. He said 'elements of the Iranian government inspired, supported and supervised' members of Saudi Hizballah, the group thought to be primarily responsible for the tragedy. See *AP*, 22 June 2001.

The 1990s witnessed the growth of a new movement, namely the anti-globalization movement, whose protests focused against corporate power: large multinational corporations accused of social injustice as well as mismanagement of natural resources and ecological damage. Campaigns were also waged against multinational economic institutions such as the World Trade Organization (WTO), the World Bank (WB), and the International Monetary Fund (IMF), seen as the spearheads of economic globalization and servants of corporate interests. Protestors claiming to represent those suffering from dire socio-economic conditions in Africa, Latin America, Asia, in addition to parts of Eastern Europe, and the deprived social sectors of industrial countries might join the bandwagon. The more militant activists belong to extremist elements associated with many of the causes, especially environmentalist, animal-rights, and anti-abortion campaigners. This movement therefore represents a breeding ground for radical anarchist and leftist terrorist groups after a long period of eclipse from the international arena, but also for radical right-wing, nationalistic and Islamist groups, which perceive globalization as a direct threat for their respective constituency. The violence witnessed at Seattle (1999), Melbourne and Prague (2000), and lately Davos (2001), could prelude a new trend.[7]

How likely are these forces to cooperate with each other or form coalitions? How likely is the formation of more stable, broader and dangerous coalitions than those analyzed in this book?

The basic hypothesis concerning the need for terrorist organizations to unite against a significant internal or external threat is also true for organizations that are active today in the international arena. They generally feel beleaguered, this time by the sole superpower, the US, often perceived as a supreme imperialist force trying to impose the new world order on all nations and countries, with the help of Western democratic states and the overwhelming forces of globalization. Most of the independent variables used in the research of coalitions in the 1970s and 1980s also apply to contemporary Islamist organizations.

As for the independent variables at the international level, the main change is the disappearance of the classical bipolarity between the democratic and communist blocs. Terrorism subsequently spread through Russia (in Chechnya) and the Muslim states of the Commonwealth of Independent States (CIS) – Kyrgyzstan, Tajikistan, Uzbekistan, etc. – an inconceivable development before the collapse of the USSR. The disappearance of classical bipolarity also enhanced hostility towards the US by radical right-wing organizations, which now feel less threatened by communism and other leftist ideologies. The wave of murderous xenophobic attacks in Germany at the beginning of the 1990s or the bombing of

---

[7] For a discussion on this movement see 'Anti-Globalisation – A Spreading Phenomenon,' *Perspectives*, Report No. 2000/08, A Canadian Security Intelligence Service Publication, 22 August 2000, at <http://www.csis-scrs.gc.ca/eng/miscdocs/200008_e.html>.

the US federal building in Oklahoma City in 1994 clearly signal changes occurring in the radical right-wing organizations' perception of the need to take action against the democratic regimes in their countries. The radical American militias and groups maintain close ideological and political ties with similar organizations in Germany, Britain and Australia, and exploit the freedoms of speech and organization granted by the American constitution to spread neo-Nazi and radical right-wing propaganda.[8]

In the last two decades, a new element has gradually made inroads into the international arena, namely the Islamist pole centered on Iran, Sudan, Afghanistan and Pakistan at least until the events of 11 September 2001 (9/11). These countries permitted the formation of an international network of Islamist terrorist organizations that used their territories to establish headquarters, run international conventions, set up training camps, etc.[9] The ability of these states to offer safe havens, finances, training, military equipment, diplomatic support, and other benefits made seeking their sponsorship a very tempting proposition for the relatively small Islamist groups.'[10]

The tension between the Islamist and the Western democratic poles was affected by important international and regional developments: the struggle of the radical Islamist organizations in Algeria; the war in Bosnia; the insurrection of Muslim Chechen separatists; the US embargo against Iraq and Iran as a consequence of their policies of arming themselves with weapons of mass destruction (WMD) and the bombing of Iraqi targets following the Gulf War; and the peace process between Israel, the Palestinians and its Arab neighbors. These events enhanced cooperation between Islamist organizations and led them to use terrorist strategies against American, Russian, French, Israeli, Jewish and other targets.

The Islamist pole could also have a bearing on the emergence of new revolutionary foci. Algeria, had it not been checked by the military regime after the 1992 elections, could very well have become a revolutionary Islamist centre, as in the 1960s, when it provided an example for Palestinian and other Third World

---

[8] On this subject, see Ely Karmon, *Right-Wing Terrorism on the Rise*, 12 August 1999, at <http://www.ict.org.il/articles/articledet.cfm?articleid=87>.

[9] For example, the 18th convention of the Islamic Group (Al-Jama'ah al-Islamiyyah) of Pakistan was held in Islamabad on 23-25 October 1998 and was attended by delegates from more than 30 Islamist groups and movements, including the Palestinian Hamas. The convention prioritized the key problems of Muslims communities: the liberation of Palestine as the duty of the whole Muslim world and by struggle that 'will be continued as long as needed'; the self-determination of the Muslims of Jammu and Kashmir by the resistance movement there as a target never to be compromised; the freedom of the Muslims in Kosovo. The convention determined the struggle against India, Israel, Serbia and Eritrea as a *Jihad*. See Reuven Paz, 'Islamic Groups: the International Connection,' 3 January 1999, at <http://www.ict.org.il/articles/articledet.cfm?articleid=66>.

[10] See Barry Rubin, 'Islamic Radicalism In The Middle East: A Survey and Balance Sheet,' *MERIA Journal*, Vol. 2, No. 1 (May 1998), at <http://www.biu.ac.il/SOC/besa/meria/journal/1998/issue2/jv2n2a3.html>.

liberation movements. Afghanistan, too, could be defined as a revolutionary hotbed inasmuch as it helped the worldwide expansion of the radical Islamist movements whose members participated in the Muslim tribal warfare against the Soviets. These militants, who subsequently became known as the 'Afghan veterans' or 'alumni', imported radical Islamist doctrine and war tactics to the entire Arab world, the Muslim communities in Europe, the US and elsewhere.

Cooperation between security forces in democratic countries against radical Islamist organizations and radical right-wing European organizations was evident by the establishment and expansion of counter-terrorist units, European legislation against racist propaganda and violence, and growing supervision of financial transfers and activities of seemingly religious institutions. These developments were all perceived by the radical organizations as a direct threat that called for the closing of ranks.

Antisemitism continued to provide a common historical and ideological motive for all radical right-wing movements. Antisemitism also served as a powerful cementing force between radical right-wing organizations and Islamists, as in the 1970s in Italy and Germany. The founders of the Italian revolutionary/nationalist organizations maintained close ties with Iran and admired the Lebanese Hizballah and the Algerian FIS. The Algerian GIA attacked Jewish targets in France, after publishing an antisemitic pamphlet on the lines of the *Protocols of the Elders of Zion*. The likelihood of a concrete alliance between an Islamist organization and a radical right-wing organization is something only the future will tell.

Many Islamist organizations already enjoy non-state nation (NSN) status and are therefore influenced by broader political and strategic considerations. The behavior of the FIS in Algeria – the largest and most popular organization in the political arena – differs from that of the GIA, a more radical organization that resorts to international terror in order to strengthen its status and extend its influence at the expense of the FIS. Hizballah in Lebanon enjoys a quasi extraterritorial status and conducts a 'foreign' policy in its relationship with Iran and Syria.

Of concern today is the fact that the Islamist camp has apparently been able to transcend differences between Sunni and Shi'a Muslims, and between the various streams within the larger sects. Some share a common ethnic base that certainly lends itself to the formation of a coalition, especially in Arab or North African countries. But just how far are these Islamist organizations prepared to cooperate? Are they able to overcome the enormous difficulties encountered by the ideological or nationalistic organizations active in the 1970s and 1980s in the process of cooperation and coalition? How do the new international environment and the conditions of the twenty-first century influence the trend to form new alliances and what today is fashionable to call 'terrorist networks,' using the modern terminology of the Internet?

The question that arises is: did the 1990s create new conditions for the formation of successful terrorist coalitions, as the ones that were responsible for the
unprecedented attacks of 9/11? Will the trends developed during this decade and
after 9/11 persist and threaten the international community? What does the future
hold for the World Islamic Front (WIF) and the network of al-Qaeda?

It should be stressed that documentation relating to the WIF is limited to the
two short fatwas initially published by the organization.[11] Moreover, since the
1998 bombings of the US embassies in Africa, and the demise of al-Qaeda
fighters in Afghanistan, the Pakistani and Bangladeshi elements of the network
remain largely inactive while many North African, Yemeni, Palestinian and Iraqi
groups and individuals, besides the Egyptian ones, became involved in terrorism.
In the spring of 2002 a new name appeared on the affiliated websites and manifestos, Qa'idat al-Jihad (the Jihad base), and WIF virtually disappeared.[12]

After the war in Afghanistan, local or regional groups affiliated with al-Qaeda
were primarily responsible for terrorist operations. These include the Salafi
factions in Algeria and Morocco; Yemeni Islamists; or the Indonesian Jemaah
Islamiyya (in fact, a group led from Indonesia by Abu Bakr Bashir but with
Malaysian, Philippine and Singaporean branches striving to form a new regional
Islamic state).[13] It seems that only the suicide bombings in Saudi Arabia in May
2003 were directly related to al-Qaeda militants.[14]

In spite of threats issued by bin Laden, al-Zawahiri, and other al-Qaeda spokes
persons to hit devastatingly at the heart of the US and the Western world, all
successful terrorist attacks since 9/11 have targeted Muslim countries or Muslim
communities such as Mombassa, Kenya. Interestingly, with the exception of
Saudi Arabia the economies of all these countries or communities (Djerba, Bali,
Casablanca, Istanbul), besides, are heavily dependent on tourism.

In February 2003, just before the US-led war in Iraq, bin Laden distributed
two audiocassettes. One addressed the Iraqi people while the other (at 53 minutes
his longest to date) was directed to Arab governments and clerics. According to
the latter, the 9/11 attacks proved that 'the United States can be targeted on its
soil by focusing on its most prominent points of weakness'. Yet, the main focus

---

[11] Contrary to other researchers, this author does not consider bin Laden's *Declaration of War* a
      fatwa, but rather a message, albeit a strategic message. See for instance Rohan Gunaratna, *Inside
      Al Qaeda. Global Network of Terror* (New York: Columbia University Press, 2002), pp. 28-29.

[12] See Reuven Paz, 'Qa'idat al-Jihad. A New Name on the Road to Palestine,' ICT website, 7 May
      2002, at <http://www.ict.org.il/articles/articledet.cfm?articleid=436>.

[13] Local or regional groups were probably responsible for the bombings in Djerba, Bali, Mombassa,
      Casablanca, or the attack on the French Limburg tanker in Yemeni waters (in an attack reminis-
      cent of the suicide bombing of the USS Cole in 2000, a small boat packed with explosives
      crashed into the French tanker Limburg off the coast of Yemen on 6 October 2002).

[14] See 'Saudis arrest suspects in Riyadh bombings,' ICT website, 28 May 2003, at <http://www.ict.
      org.il/spotlight/det.cfm?id=901>.

of his speech was not the US but the Arab governments and the Islamic clerics that supported them and gave them legitimacy. The conflict with these Arab governments was now presented as eternal and insolvable.[15]

According to Paz, internal conflicts in the Arab and Islamic world, the leadership crisis, the diversity of Islamic movements, and the development of extreme radical views within the Islamist arena, led some Islamist scholars to express reservations concerning Qa'idat al-Jihad's role in the Islamist revolution and the globalization of the Islamist struggle. As the Jihadi-Salafi movement, either Qa'idat al-Jihad or other groups and individuals, had always been based on the Arab element, a crisis of the global Islamist struggle might return them to the Arab fold and signal the decline of the Islamist terrorism of Qa'idat al-Jihad, at least on the global arena, even if it continued to be fed by anti-American and anti-Western views.[16]

The campaign by al-Qaeda terrorists against Arab and Muslim regimes may be explained by a shift in the ideological and strategic thinking of those Islamists who now occupy the vacuum left by bin Laden and his deputy. The targeting of the tourist infrastructures calls to mind the strategy of the Egyptian Jihadi groups in the mid-1990s. One might speculate that this strategy results from the growing influence of al-Zawahiri, bin Laden's deputy.[17]

The significance of a reliable base in Muslim territory is reflected in the return of al-Qaeda to Arab land, and its attempts to destabilize at least one regime and achieve a new safe haven.

Al-Zawahiri explains the importance of the quest for a 'fundamentalist base':[18] '[v]ictory for the Islamic movements against the world alliance cannot be attained unless these movements possess an Islamic base in the heart of the Arab region'. He notes that mobilizing and arming the nation will not yield tangible results until a fundamentalist state is established in the region:

---

[15] Two supporters of bin Laden's developed this critical analysis of Muslim governments in their articles. They present the Arab League and the Muslim Conference as 'two paralyzed associations.' Moreover, Arab Islamic movements are also criticized, and the weak leadership of the Muslim Brotherhood, for instance, was compared with the strong figures of Hassan al-Bana and Sayyid Qutb.

[16] Dr. 'Abd al-'Aziz al-Qari published an article in 23 March 2003 titled 'The crisis of leaderships of the Islamic world' which was circulated on several Islamist web sites. Another article was published on 15 and 22 March 2003 by the Saudi cleric Sheikh Salman bin Fahd al-'Awdah, on his web site *Islamtoday* under the title 'The duty of these times.' See Reuven Paz, 'Global Jihad and the Sense of Crisis: Al-Qa'idah's Other Front,' *Intelligence and Terrorism Information Center at the Center for Special Studies* website, at <http://www.intelligence.org.il/eng/g_j/rp_d_11_03.htm>.

[17] Ayman al-Zawahiri audiocassette, 9 October 2002; September 2003: Parts of the 105-minute tape broadcast by al-Jazeera satellite television showed Bin Laden with al-Zawahiri, who urged supporters to bury Americans in 'the graveyard of Iraq'. Although bin Laden had not appeared on a videocassette for many months, he remained silent but allowed al-Zawahiri to speak.

[18] See al-Zawahiri, *Knights Under the Prophet's Banner*.

The establishment of a Muslim state in the heart of the Islamic world is not an easy or close target. However, it is the hope of the Muslim nation to restore its fallen caliphate and regain its lost glory... We must not despair of the repeated strikes and calamities. We must never lay down our arms no matter how much losses or sacrifices we endure. Let us start again after every strike, even if we had to begin from scratch.

So could Islamists position themselves in such a way to challenge the US and its allies, perhaps by taking control of a Muslim state? Only the following appear vulnerable to such threats and are currently targeted by Islamists:

(1) Pakistan, which has a nuclear arsenal and large radical Islamist movements that control part of the territory;
(2) Indonesia, because of the largest Muslim population, a territory of some 17,000 islands and jungles, political and economical instability, and a small but active Islamist terrorist organization;
(3) Saudi Arabia, led by a corrupt and ineffective regime, with huge oil wealth, has Islamist movements led by Wahabbi ideologues; and last but not least
(4) Iraq, whose internal stability and even integrity is in danger after the US occupation, with the threat of Shi'a radicalism emerging in force after the destruction of the Sunni Ba'athist infrastructure.

Al-Qaeda has chosen to focus its campaign against the US in Iraq and has enlisted all Islamist forces there. It is indeed possible that the future of the balance of power between radical and moderate Islam, between the radical Islamist camp and its Western and Eastern enemies will be decided on the Iraqi battlefront.[19]

The failure of the Islamic regime in Iran to either resolve the huge social and economic problems of the younger population or suppress the opposition of students and the intellectual elites, as well as the backwardness and isolation to which the Taliban regime has brought the Afghani society, both prove that the radical Islamists lack any positive solutions to the challenges of modernization and technology.

---

[19] In October 2003, an audiotape message attributed to bin Laden called on the US to withdraw from Iraq and warned of more suicide attacks within and beyond the US. The message praised the continuing violence against US forces in Iraq and called on young Muslims around the world, and 'especially in the neighboring countries and in Yemen' to go to Iraq to wage jihad or holy war'. Bin Laden threatened to strike ' at the appropriate time and place, to all the states that are taking part in this unjust war, particularly Britain, Spain, Australia, Poland, Japan, and Italy' and also [t]he Islamic world's states that are taking part in this war, particularly the Gulf states, mainly Kuwait, the land base for the Crusader forces, will not be excluded from this.' See 'Bin Laden tape warns US', BBC News, at <http://news.bbc.co.uk/2/hi/middle_east/3203878.stm>

According to Ahmed Hashim, 'Islamic fundamentalists have been very good at highlighting and analyzing the weakness, backwardness, and problems afflicting current Islamic societies, but they were very bad at their proposals for resolving these problems.' Bin Laden and his followers, and many other Islamists 'can cause disorder and conflict with and among the West and its allies in the Islamic world' but it is unlikely they will be able to implement a successful alternative order.[20]

Bowman describes al Qaeda as 'less a large organization than a facilitator, sometimes orchestrator, of Islamic militants around the globe … linked by ideas and goals, not by organizational structure'.[21] The strength of the al-Qaeda network lies in its decentralized and diffuse structure and the loose ideological and organizational bonds to bin Laden and al-Zawahiri.[22]

Al-Qaeda affiliates and sympathizers may bring instability and even wreak havoc in the Muslim world and the world at large, but they fail to present any solutions to the real problems of the Muslim world. It is highly improbable that various ethnic groups with different religious leaders and their own local or regional agendas will ever build sufficient alliances building to give birth to a unified leadership accepted by the majority of Muslims.

However, it is conceivable that in the near future these organizations will acquire WMD and thus threaten large-scale devastation to enemy countries or even within their own countries. The use of such weapons could shake the very foundations of the democratic system and undermine the liberties and barely achieved human rights of modern society.

It is therefore imperative that the international community strive to combat the terrorist activities of radical Islamist movements. Conversely, it is also essential to provide political, social and economical support to Muslim societies to expand the scope of human freedoms, enhance the capacity to guarantee those freedoms through good governance and achieve the higher moral human goals of justice and human dignity, as requested by the UN-sponsored Arab Human Development Report 2003.[23]

---

[20]   See Ahmed S. Hashim, 'The World According To Usama Bin Laden', *Naval War College Review*, Autumn 2001 at <http://www.nwc.navy.mil/press/Review/2001/Autumn/art1-au1.htm>.

[21]   Bowman, *Some-Time, Part-Time and One-time Terrorism*.

[22]   While bin Laden may have been a leading strategic figure he never achieved the standing of a senior Sunni al-Azhar ulema or a Shi'a ayatollah-atma.

[23]   On 20 October 2003 the UN Development Program (UNDP) launched its groundbreaking new Arab Human Development Report. The new report, titled *Arab Human Development Report 2003: Building a Knowledge Society*, focuses on the current state of learning and intellectual inquiry in the Arab world. See <http://www.undp.org/rbas/ahdr/englishpresskit2003.html>.

ABBREVIATIONS

AAIA	Aden-Abyan Islamic Army
ABiH	Army of Bosnia and Herzegovina
AD	Action Directe (Direct Action)
ALF	Arab Liberation Front
AN	Avanguardia Nazionale (National Vanguard)
ANM	Arab Nationalists' Movement (Harakat al-Qawmiyyin al-'Arab)
ANO	Abu Nidal Organization
AO	Autonomia Operaia (Workers' Autonomy)
APO	Ausserparlamentarische Opposition (Extra-parliamentary opposition)
ASG	Abu Sayyaf Group
BI	Brigades Internationales (International Brigades)
BR	Brigate Rosse (Red Brigades)
BR-PCC	Brigate Rosse per la Costruzione del Partito Comunista Combattente (Red Brigades for the Construction of the Communist Combatant Party)
BR-UCC	Brigate Rosse – Unione dei Comunisti Combattenti (Red Brigades – Union of Combatant Communists)
BSO	Black September Organization
CCC	Cellules Combattantes Communistes (Combatant Communist Cells)
CDLR	Committee for the Defense of Legal Rights
CDU	Christlich Demokratischen Union Deutschlands (Christian Democratic Union)
CIA	Central Intelligence Agency
CLFO	Colectif de Liberation de Frédéric Oriach (Frédéric Oriach Liberation Collective)
CLODO	Comité Liquidant ou Détoumant les Ordinateurs (Committee for the Liquidation or Deterrence of Computers)
CoCoRi	Comitati Combattenti Rivoluzionari (Revolutionary Combatant Committees)
COLP	Comunisti Organizzati per la Liberazione Proletaria (Organized Communists for the Proletarian Liberation)
COMECON	Council for Mutual Economic Cooperation
CPM	Colletivo Politico Metropolitano (Urban Political Collective)
DA	Défense Active (Active Defence)
DC	Democrazia Christiana (Christian Democratic Party)
DOCOM	Documentation Communiste (Communist Documentation)
DFLP	Democratic Front for the Liberation of Palestine
DST	Direction de la Surveillance du Territoire (Directorate of Territorial Security – French Security Service)

EGI	Euzko Gaztedi (The PNV youth section)
EIA	Euskal Iraultzako Alderdia (Revolutionary Basque Party)
ERP	Ejercito Revolucionario del Pueblo (People's Revolutionary Army)
ETA	Euzkadi ta Askatasuna (Basque Fatherland and Liberty)
ETAp-m	ETA político-militar (ETA political-military)
ETAm	ETA militar (ETA military)
FARL	Fractions Armées Révolutionnaires Libanaises (Lebanese Armed Revolutionary Fractions)
FATAH	Harakat al-Tahrir al-Watani al-Filastini (The Palestine National Liberation Movement)
FCO	Fighting Communist Organization
FIS	Front Islamique du Salut (Jabha Islamiyya li'l-Inqa – Islamic Salvation Front)
FLB	Front de Libération Breton (Breton Liberation Front)
FLN	Front de Libération Nationale (National Liberation Front)
FNL	Federation of the New Left
FPÖ	Freiheitspartei Österreichs (Freedom Party)
FP-25	Forces Populares 25 de Abril (Popular Forces – 25 April)
GAL	Grupos Antiterroristas de Liberación (Anti-Terrorist Liberation Groups)
GARI	Groupes d'Action Révolutionnaire Internationaliste (Internationalist Revolutionary Action Groups)
GIA	Groupe Islamique Armé (Armed Islamic Group or Jama'a Islamiyya Musalha)
GP-NRP	Gauche Prolétarienne – Nouvelle Résistance Populaire (Proletarian Left – New Popular Resistance)
GP	Gauche Prolétarienne (Proletarian Left)
GRAPO	Grupo Revolucionario Antifascista Primero de Octubre (First of October Anti-Fascist Resistance Group)
GSPC	Groupe Salafiste pour la Prédication et le Combat (Salafi Group for Call and Combat)
Hamas	Harakat al-Muqawamah al-Islamiyya (The Islamic Resistance Movement)
HJI	Harkat-ul-Jihad-al-Islam (Bangaladesh)
HUJI	Harkat-ul-Jihad-al-Islam (Islamic Jihad Movement – India)
HuA	Harkat-ul-Ansar
HuM	Harkat-ul-Mujahideen (Movement of Warriors)
HB	Herri Batasuna (People's Unity)
IDF	Israeli Defence Forces
IK	Iparretarrak (Those from the north)
IRA	Irish Republican Army
IMU	Islamic Movement of Uzbekistan
IZL	Irgun Zvai Leumi (The National Military Organization)
JG	Jihad Group
J&K	Jammu & Kashmir
JI	Jemaah Islamiyyah (Islamic Group)

JRA	Japanese Red Army
JUI	Jamiat-ul-Ulema-i-Islam
JUP	Jamiat-ul-Ulema-i-Pakistan (Pakistan's Ulema Society)
JUSOS	Jungsozialisten (Young Socialists)
KAS	Koordinadora Abertzale Sozialista (Socialist Patriotic Coordination)
KDP	Kurdish Democratic Party
LeT	Lashkar-e-Toiba (Army of the Pure)
MB	Muslim Brothers
MDI	Markaz-ud-Dawa-wal-Irshad
MPON	Movimento Politico per un Ordine Nuovo (Political Movement for the New Order)
M2J	Bewegung 2 Juni (The 2nd of June Movement)
MILF	Moro Islamic Liberation Front
MNLF	Moro National Liberation Front
MSI	Movimento Sociale Italiano (Italian Social Movement)
NAP	Nuclei Armati Proletari (Armed Proletarian Nuclei)
NAPAP	Noyaux Armés pour l'Autonomie Populaire (Armed Cells for Popular Autonomy)
NAR	Nuclei Armati Rivoluzionari (Armed Revolutionary Cells)
NIF	National Islamic Front
N17	Epanastatiki Organosi 17 Noemvri (Revolutionary Organization 17 November)
NSN	Non-state nation
NWFP	North West Frontier Province
OAS	Organisation Armée Secrète (Secret Army Organization)
OLP	Organisazione di Liberazione del Popolo (The Peoples' Struggle Organization)
ON	Ordine Nero (Black Order)
ON	Ordine Nuovo (New Order)
ÖVP	Österreichische Volkspartei (Austrian People's Party)
PA	Palestinian Authority
PCd'I-ml	Partito Communista d'Italia – marxista-leninista (Communist Party of Italy – Marxist-Leninist)
PCF	Parti Communiste Français (French Communist Party)
PCI	Partito Comunista Italiano (Italian Communist Party)
PFLP	The Popular Front for the Liberation of Palestine (al-Jabha al-Sha'biyya li-Tahrir Filasti)
PFLP-GC	The Popular Front for the Liberation of Palestine – General Command
PFLP-SC	The Popular Front for the Liberation of Palestine – Special Command
P-GPM	Partito-Guerriglia del Proletariato Metropolitano (Guerrilla Party of the Metropolitan Proletariat)
PIJ	Palestinian Islamic Jihad
PL	Prima Linea (First Line)
PLF	Palestinian Liberation Front (Jabhat al-Tahrir al-Filastinyya)

PLO	Palestinian Liberation Organization
PNC	Palestine National Council
PNV	Partido Nacionalista Vasco (Basque Nationalist Party)
PSF	Popular Struggle Front

RAF	Rote Armee Fraktion (The Red Army Faction)
RDS	Risoluzione della Direzione Strategica (Resolution of the Strategic Directorate)
RZ	Revolutionare Zellen (The Revolutionary Cells)

SDI	Strategic Defense Initiative
SDS	Sozialisticher Deutscher Studentenbund (Organization of German Socialist Students)
SIM	Stato Imperialista delle Multinazionali (Imperialist State if the Multinationals)
SP	Sinistra Proletaria (Proletarian Left)
SPD	Sozialdemokratische Partei Deutschlands (Social Democratic Party)

| TP | Terza Posizione (Third Position) |
| TW | Tupamaros West-Berlin |

WIF	World Islamic Front for the Struggle Against Jews and Crusaders (Al-Jabhah al-Islamiyyah al-'Alamiyyah li-Qital al-Yahud wal-Salibiyyin)
WMD	Weapons of Mass Destruction
WTC	World Trade Center

BIBLIOGRAPHY

I.   BOOKS

Abukhalil, As'ad, *Osama Bin Laden and the Taliban: Consequences of U.S. Foreign Policy* (New York, London: Seven Stories; Turnaround, 2002).

Abu-Sharif, Bassam and Mahnaimi, Uzi, *Tried by Fire. The Searing True Story of Two Men at the Heart of the Struggle between the Arabs and the Jews* (London: Warner Books, 1995).

Adams, Gerry, *The Politics of Irish Freedom* (Belfast: Brandon, 1986).

Alexander, Yonah (ed.), *International Terrorism. National, Regional and Global Perspectives* (New York: Praeger Publishers, 1976).

—— and Gleason, M. John (eds.), *Behavioural and Quantitative Perspectives on Terrorism* (New York: Pergamon Press, 1981).

—— and Meyers, Kenneth (eds.), *Terrorism in Europe* (London: Croom Helm, 1982).

—— and Sinai, J., *Terrorism: The PLO Connection* (NewYork: Crane and Russack, 1989).

—— and Pluchinsky, A. Dennis (eds.), *Europe's Red Terrorists: The Fighting Communist Organizations* (London: Frank Cass, 1992).

—— and Pluchinsky, Dennis, *European Terrorism. Today and Tomorrow* (Washington: Brassey's, 1992).

—— and Swetnam, S.Michael, *Usama bin Laden's al-Qaida: Profile of a Terrorist Network* (Ardsley, New York: Transnational Publishers, 2001).

Auron, Yair, *We Are All German Jews. Jewish Radicals in France During the Sixties and Seventies* (Tel Aviv: Am Oved Publishers, 1999, in Hebrew).

Aust, Stefan, *The Baader-Meinhof Group: The Inside Story of a Phenomenon* (London: Bodley Head, 1987).

Ayubi, Nazih, *Political Islam: Religion and Politics in the Arab World* (London: Routledge, 1991).

Bauer, Yehuda (ed.), *Present-Day Antisemitism* (Jerusalem: The Vidal Sassoon International Center for the Study of Antisemitism, Hebrew University of Jerusalem, 1988).

Bechor, Guy, *A PLO Lexicon* (Tel Aviv: Israeli Ministry of Defence Publication, 1991, in Hebrew).

Becker, Jillian, *Hitler's Children* (London: Granada Publishing, 1978).

——— , *Terrorism in West Germany. The Struggle for What?* (London: Institute for the Study of Terrorism, 1988).

Bergen L. Peter, *Holy War, Inc.: Inside the Secret World of Osama bin Laden* (New York: Free Press, 2001).

Bertelsen, Judy S. (ed.), *Non-state Nations in International Politics. Comparative System Analysis* (New York: Praeger Publishers, 1977).

Bichara, Khadder and Bichara, Naim (eds.), *Testi della revoluzione Palestinese. 1968-1975* (Verona: Bertoni Editore 1975).

Bodansky, Yossef, *Bin Laden: The Man Who Declared War on America* (Rocklin, CA.: Forum, 1999).

Boraccetti, Vittorio, *Eversione di destra, terrorismo, stragi* (Milan: Franco Angeli, 1986).

Bowyer Bell, J., *The Secret Army: A History of the IRA. 1916-1979* (4th revised edn.) (Dublin: Poolberg, 1990).

Brackett, D.W., *Holy Terror: Armageddon in Tokyo* (New York and Tokyo: Weatherhill, 1996).

Brynen, Rex, *Sanctuary and Survival: The PLO in Lebanon* (Boulder: Westview Press, 1990).

Capanna, Mario, *Formidabili quegli anni* (Milano: Rizzoli, 1988).

Carpi, Daniel, *Between Mussolini and Hitler: The Jews and the Italian Authorities in France and Tunisia* (The Tauber Institute for the Study of European Jewry, Series 17, Hanover, N.H.: University Press of New England, 1994).

Carré, Olivier, *L'Ideologie palestinienne de resistance. Analyse de textes: 1964-1970* (Paris: Armand Colin, 1972(.

Carus, W. Seth, *Bioterrorism and Biocrimes: The Illicit Use of Biological Agents in the 20th Century* (Washington DC: Center for Counterproliferation Research, National Defense University, 1999).

Catanzaro, Raimondo (ed), *The Red Brigades and Left-Wing Terrorism in Italy* (London: Pinter, 1991).

Caute, David, *Sixty-Eight. The Year of the Barricades* (London: Hamish Hamilton, 1988).

Chomsky, Noam and Herman, Edward, *The Washington Connection and Third World Fascism* (Boston: South End Press, 1979).

Clark, Robert, *The Basque Insurgents. ETA, 1952-1980* (Madison, WI: University of Wisconsin Press, 1984).

Cline, Ray and Alexander, Yonah, *The Soviet Connection* (New York: Crane Russak, 1984).

Cobban, Helena, *The Palestinian Liberation Organization. People, Power and Politics* (Cambridge: Cambridge University Press, 1984).

Cooley K. John, *Unholy Wars: Afghanistan, America and International Terrorism* (Sterling, VA.: Pluto Press, 1999).

Crenshaw, Martha, *Terrorism and International Cooperation* (Boulder, CO.: Westview Press, 1989).

—— (ed.), *Terrorism in Context* (State College PA: Penn State University Press, 1995).

Cubert, M. Harold, *The PFLP's Changing Role in the Middle East* (London: Frank Cass, 1997).

Dartnell, Michael, *Action Directe: Ultra-leftist Terrorism in France, 1979-1987* (London: Frank Cass, 1995).

De Felice, Renzo (3d ed.), *Storia degli ebrei italiani sotto il fascismo* (Torino: Arnaldo Mondadori Editore, 1977).

Dekmejian, Hrair R., *Islam in Revolution: Fundamentalism in the Arab World* (New York: Syracuse University Press, 1985).

della Porta, Donatella (ed.), *Terrorismi in Italia* (Bologna: Società Editrice il Mulino, 1984).

—— , *Il Terrorismo di Sinistra* (Bologna: Società Editrice il Mulino, 1990).

El-Affendi, Abdelwahhab, *Who Needs an Islamic State?* (London: Grey Seal, 1991).

Esposito, John L., *The Islamic Threat: Myth or Reality?* (New York: Oxford University Press, 1992).

Falkenrath, Richard, Newman, Robert and Thayer, Bradley, *America's Achilles' Heel* (Cambridge, MA: The MIT Press, 1998).

Ferraresi, Franco (ed.), *La Destra Radicale* (Milano: Feltrinelli, 1984).

Friedman, J., Bladen, C. and Rosen, S. (eds.), *Alliance in International Politics* (Boston: Allyn and Bacon, 1970).

Galli, Giorgio, *La Crisi Italiana e la Destra InterNazionale* (Torino: Arnaldo Mondadori Editore, 1977).

Grosser, Alfred, *L`Allemagne de notre temps (1945-1970)* (Paris: Fayard, 1970).

Guell, Pedro Ibarra, *La evolucion strategica de ETA* (Donostia: Kriselu, 1987).

Gunaratna, Rohan, *Inside Al Qaeda. Global Network of Terror* (New York: Columbia University Press, 2002).

Hamon, Alain and Marchand, Jean-Charles, *Action Directe. Du terrorisme français a l`euroterrorisme* (Paris: Editions du Seuil, 1986).

Higgins, Rosalyn and Flory, Maurice (eds.), *Terrorism and International Law* (London: Routledge, 1997).

Hoffman, Bruce, *Inside Terrorism* (New York: Columbia University Press, 1998).

Holsti, Ole, Hopmann, Terrence and Sullivan, John, *Unity and Disintegration in International Alliances* (New York: University Press of America, 1985).

Jacquard, Roland, *La longue traque d'Action Directe* (Paris: Albin Michel, 1987).

Jauregui, Bereciartu Gurutz, *Ideologia e estrategia de ETA. Analisis de su evolucion entre 1959 y 1968* (sec.ed.) (Madrid: Siglo XXI de Espana Editores, 1985).

Kaplan, David E. and Marshall, Andrew, *The Cult at the End of the World: The Incredible Story of Aum* (London: Hutchinson, 1996).

Kegley Charles W. (ed.), *International Terrorism: Characteristics, Causes, Controls* (New York: St. Martin's Press, 1990).

Kepel, Gilles, *Muslim Extremism in Egypt* (Berkeley: University of California Press, 1985).

Knorr, Klaus, and Verba, Sidney (eds.), *The International System. Theoretical Essays* (Princeton: Princeton University Press, 1967).

Laqueur, Walter, *Terrorism* (London: Weidenfeld and Nicolson, 1977).

——— , *The Age of Terrorism* (Boston: Little, Brown & Co. 1987).

——— , *The New Terrorism: Fanaticism and the Arms of Mass Destruction* (New York and Oxford: Oxford University Press, 1999).

——— and Alexander, Yonah (eds.), *The Terrorism Reader* (new revised edn.) (New York: Nal Penguin Inc., 1987).

Leventhal, Paul and Alexander, Yonah (eds.), *Nuclear Terrorism: Defining the Threat* (Washington, DC: Pergamon-Brassey's, 1986).

Liska, George, *Nations in Alliance: The Limits of Interdependence* (Baltimore: John Hopkins Press, 1962).

Lukacs, Yehuda (ed.), *The Israeli-Palestinian Conflict: A Documentary Record* (Cambridge: Cambridge University Press, 1992).

MacStiofain, Sean, *Revolutionary in Ireland* (Edinburgh: Gordon Cremonesi, 1975).

Mansbach, R. W., Fergusson, Y. H., and Lampert, D. E., *The Web of World Politics. Nonstate Actors in the Global System* (Englewood Cliffs, NJ: Prentice-Hall, 1976).

Marcuse, Herbert, *Five Lectures. Psycoanalysis, Politics, and Utopia* (Boston: Beacon Press, 1970).

Meade, Robert C., *Red Brigades: The Story of Italian Terrorism* (London: Macmillan, 1990).

Merari, Ariel and Shlomi, Elad, *Paha' Hul: Teror Palestinai be-Hutz la-Aretz* [Palestinian Terror Abroad] (Tel Aviv: United Kibbutz and Jaffee Center for Strategic Studies publication, 1986, in Hebrew).

Michaelis, Meir, *Mussolini and the Jews: German-Italian Relations and the Jewish Question in Italy, 1922-1945* (Oxford: Published for the Institute of Jewish Affairs, London, by the Clarendon Press, 1978).

Mickolus, Edward, *Transnational Terrorism: A Chronology of Events, 1968-1979* (London: Aldwych Press, 1980).

——— , *International Terrorism in the 1980s. A Chronology of Events* (Ames: Yowa State University Press, 1989).

Moretti, Mario, *Brigatte Rosse. Una storia italiana. Intervista di Carla Mosca e Rossana Rossanda* (Milano: Edizione Anabasi, 1994).

Morgenthau, Hans, *Politics Among Nations* (New York: Alfred Knopf, 1959).

Norton, Augustus Richard and Greenberg, H. Martin (eds.), *The International Relations of the Palestine Liberation Organization* (Southern Illinois University Press, 1989).

O'Ballance, Edgar, *Terrorism in the 1980s* (London: Arms and Armour, 1989).

Oots, Kent Lane, *A Political Organisation Approach to Transnational Terrorism* (New York: Greenwood Press, 1986).

Osgood, Robert E., *Alliances and American Foreign Policy* (Baltimore: John Hopkins Press, 1968).

Paz, Reuven, *Tangled Web: International Networking of the Islamist Struggle*, forthcoming at The Washington Institute For Near East Policy.

Rashid, Ahmed, *Taliban: Militant Islam, Oil and Fundamentalism in Central Asia* (Yale University Press, 2000).

Reeve, Simon, *The New Jackals: Ramzi Yousef, Osama Bin Laden and the Future of Terrorism* (Boston, MA.: Northeastern University Press, 1999).

Riker, William H., *The Theory of Political Coalitions* (4th edn.) (New Haven and London: Yale University Press, 1968).

Robinson, Adam, *Bin Laden: Behind the Mask of the Terrorist* (Edinburgh: Mainstream, 2001).

Rothstein, Robert, *Alliances and Small Powers* (New York: Columbia University Press, 1968).

Rubenstein, Richard, *Alchemists of Revolution* (London: I.B. Tauris, 1987).

Rubinstein, Elyakim (ed.), *Compilation of Documents of the PFLP, DFLP and ALF – Texts for the Seminar of Dr. Yehoshafat Harkabi* (Jerusalem: Hebrew University, 1971).

Rubin, Barry, *Revolution until Victory? The Politics and History of the PLO* (Cambridge, Mass.: Harvard University Press, 1994).

—— and Judith Colp Rubin (eds.), *Anti-American Terrorism and the Middle East. A Documentary Reading* (Oxford University Press, 2002).

Sayigh, Yazid, *Armed Struggle and the Search for State: The Palestinian National Movement, 1949-1993* (New York: Oxford University Press, 1997).

Schmid, A.P., Jongman, A.J., et. al., *Political Terrorism: A New Guide to Actors, Authors, Concepts, Data-bases, Theories, and Literature* (2nd edn.) (Amsterdam: SWIDOC and New Brunswick, N.J. Transaction Books, 1988).

Segaller, Stephen, *Invisible Armies. Terrorism into the 1990s* (1st American ed.) (New York: Harcourt Brace Jovanovich, 1987).

Shay, Shaul, *The Endless Jihad...The Mujahidin, the Taliban and Bin Laden* (Herzliya: The International Policy Institute for Counter-Terrorism, The Interdisciplinary Center Press, 2002).

Silj, Alessandro, *'Mai più senza fucile!'. Alle origini dei NAP e delle BR* (Firenze: Vallechi Editore, 1977).

Sivan, Emmanuel, *Radical Islam: Medieval Theory and Modern Politics* (New Haven, CT: Yale University Press, 1985).

Steiner, Anne and Debray, Loïc, *La Fraction Armée Rouge. Guérilla urbaine en Europe occidentale* (Paris: Méridiens Klincksieck, 1987).

Sterling, Claire, *The Terror Network: The Secret War of International Terrorism* (New York: Holt, Rinehart and Winston, 1981).

Stohl, Michael (ed.), *The Politics of Terrorism* (3rd edn.) (New York: Marcel Dekker, 1988).

Walt, Stephen, *The Origins of Alliances* (Ithaca and London: Cornell University Press, 1987).

Weisband, Edward and Roguly, Damir, 'Palestinian Terrorism: Violence, Verbal Strategy, and Legitimacy', in Yonah Alexander (ed.), *International Terrorism. National, Regional and Global Perspectives* (New York: Praeger Publishers, 1976).

Wievorka, Michel, *The Making of Terrorism* (Chicago: The University of Chicago Press, 1993).

Wilkinson, Paul, *Political Terrorism* (2nd edn.) (London: Macmillan, 1976).

—— , *Terrorism and the Liberal State* (2nd edn.) (London: Macmillan, 1986).

—— and Stewart, A.M. (eds.), *Contemporary Research on Terrorism* (Aberdeen: The University Press, 1987).

Wright, Joanne, *Terrorist Propaganda. The Red Army Faction and the Provisional IRA, 1968-86* (London: Macmillan, 1991).

Ya'ari, Ehud, *Fatah* (Tel Aviv: A. Levine-Epstein, 1970, in Hebrew).

Yodfat, Arieh and Arnon-Ohanna, Yuval, *PLO. Strategy and Politics* (London: Croom Helm, 1981).

II.   ARTICLES AND CHAPTERS

Abootalebi, Ali, 'Islam, Islamists, And Democracy,' *MERIA Journal*, Vol. 3, No. 1 (1998).

Abu-Lughod, Ibrahim, 'Flexible Militancy: A Report on the Sixteenth Session of the Palestine National Council, Algiers, February 14-22, 1983', *JPS*, Vol. 12, No. 4 (48) (1983).

——, 'Anti-Globalisation – A Spreading Phenomenon,' *Perspectives*, Report No. 2000/08, A Canadian Security Intelligence Service Publication, 22 August 2000, at <http://www.csis-scrs.gc.ca/eng/miscdocs/200008_e.html>.

——, *Arab Human Development Report 2003: Building a Knowledge Society,* United Nations Development Program, at <http://www.undp.org/rbas/ahdr/englishpresskit2003.html>.

Ardenghi, Flavio, 'Le edizioni di Ar e l'estrema destra' in *Risguardo, rassegna periodica di cultura*, IV (1984), Special edition to mark the twentieth anniversary of Ar publications (Brindisi: Edizioni di Ar).

Azzam, Abdullah, 'Al-Qa'idah al-Sulbah' (The Solid Base), *Al-Jihad*, No. 41, April 1988, English excerpts translated by Reuven Paz in *Tangled Web: International Networking of the Islamist Struggle, Appendix I.*

Azzam, Maha, 'Al-Qaeda: the Misunderstood Wahhabi Connection and the Ideology of Violence,' *Briefing Paper*, No. 1, The Royal Institute of International Affairs, UK, February 2003, at <http://www.riia.org/pdf/research/mep/Azzaml.pdf>.

Bashiri, Iraj, 'Jamal al-Din al-Afghani,' *Bashiri Working Papers on Central Asia and Iran*, 2000, at <http://www.angelfire.com/rnb/bashiri/Afghani/Afghani.html>.

Beeman, O. William, 'Images of the Great Satan: Representations of the United States in the Iranian Revolution,' in Nikki R. Keddie, ed., *Religion and Politics in Iran* (New Haven, Conn.: Yale University Press, 1983), pp. 191-217.

Bertelsen, Judy S., 'The Palestinian Arabs', in Judy S. Bertelsen (ed.), *Non-state Nations in International Politics. Comparative System Analysis* (New York: Praeger Publishers, 1977).

———— , 'Bin Laden and the Balkans: The Politics Of Anti-Terrorism,' *ICG Balkans Report* No. 119, 9 November 2001, pp. 3-21.

Bougereau Jean, 'An Interview with Hans Joachim Klein', in Jean Bougereau, *The German Guerrilla: Terror, Reaction and Resistance* (Orkney: Cienfuegos Press, 1981), pp. 7-66.

Bowman, M.E., 'Some-Time, Part-Time and One-time Terrorism,' *Intelligencer: Journal of US Intelligence Studies* (Winter/Spring 2003), Vol. 13, No. 2, pp. 13-18 at <http://www.fas.org/irp/eprint/bowman.pdf>.

Bowyer Bell, J., 'Contemporary Revolutionary Organizations', in R. Keohane and J. S. Nye (eds.), *Transnational Relations and World Politics* (Cambridge, MA: Harvard University Press, 1972).

Caselli G. C. and Della Porta, Donatella, 'La storia delle Brigate rosse: strutture organizzative e strategie d'azione', in Donatella della Porta (ed.) *Terrorismi in Italia* (Bologna: Societa Editrice il Mulino, 1984).

Cooper, Barry, 'Unholy Terror: The Origin and Significance of Contemporary, Religion-based Terrorism,' Fraser Institute, Calgary Policy Research Centre, *A Fraser Institute Occasional Paper*, No. 1, March 2002 at <http://collection.nlc-bnc.ca/100/200/300/fraser/studies_in_defense/n01/terrorism.pdf>.

Cordes, B., 'Euroterrorists Talk about Themselves: A Look at the Literature', in Paul Wilkinson and A.M. Stewart (eds.), *Contemporary Research on Terrorism* (Aberdeen: The University Press, 1987).

Corrado, Raymond R. and Evans, Rebecca, 'Ethnic and Ideological Terrorism in Western Europe' in Michael Stohl (ed.), *The Politics of Terrorism* (3rd edn.) (New York: Marcel Dekker, 1988).

Crenshaw, Martha, 'The Causes of Terrorism', in Charles W. Kegley (ed.), *International Terrorism: Characteristics, Causes, Controls* (New York: St. Martin's Press, 1990).

———— , *Terrorism and International Cooperation*; Martha Crenshaw, 'Is International Terrorism Primarily State-Sponsored? in Charles W. Kegley (ed.), *International Terrorism: Characteristics, Causes, Controls* (New York: St. Martin's Press, 1990).

—— , 'The Logic of Terrorism: Terrorist Behaviour as a Product of Strategic Choice', in Walter Reich (ed.), *Origins of Terrorism: Psychologies, Ideologies, Theologies, States of Mind* (Cambridge: Cambridge University Press, 1990).

—— , 'Current Research on Terrorism: The Academic Perspective', *Studies in Conflict and Terrorism,* Vol. 15 (1992).

Curtis, Michael, 'The Baffling Observer', in Yehuda Bauer (ed.), *Present-Day Antisemitism* (Jerusalem: The Vidal Sassoon International Center for the Study of Antisemitism, Hebrew University of Jerusalem, 1988).

Dixit, Aabha, 'Soldiers of Islam: Origins, Ideology and Strategy of the Taliban,' *Strategic Analysis*, Institute for Defense Studies and Analyses (IDSA), New Delhi, India, August 1997 (Vol. XX No. 5), at <http://www.idsa-india.org/an-aug-2.html>.

Doureihi, Br. Soadad, 'Nationalism. An Erroneous Concept', *Nida'ul Islam*, July-August 1997, at <http://www.islam.org.au>.

Drake, Richard, 'Contemporary Terrorism and the Intellectuals: the Case of Italy', in Paul Wilkinson and A.M. Stewart (eds.), *Contemporary Research on Terrorism* (Aberdeen: The University Press, 1987).

Esposito, John, 'Political Islam: Beyond the Green Menace,' originally published in the journal *Current History,* January 1994. Taken verbatim from MSANEWS, at <http://www.arches.uga.edu/~godlas/espo.html>.

Evola, Julius, *Chevaucher le tigre* (Paris: Editions de la Maisnie, 1982).

Fattah, A. Ezzat, 'Terrorist Activities and Terrorist Targets: A Tentative Typology', in Yonah Alexander and John M. Gleason (eds.), *Behavioural and Quantitative Perspectives on Terrorism* (New York: Pergamon Press, 1981).

Ferraresi, Franco, 'Da Evola a Freda. La dottrina della destra radicale fino al 1977', in Franco Ferraresi, *La Destra Radicale* (Milano: Feltrinelli, 1984).

Fleming, Peter, Stohl, Michael and Schmid, Alex, 'The Theoretical Utility of Typologies of Terrorism: Lessons and Opportunities', in Michael Stohl (ed.), *The Politics of Terrorism* (3rd ed.) (New York: Marcel Dekker, 1988).

Freda, Giorgio, 'La désintégration du système', *Totalité*, Supplement No. 9.

Fritsche, Peter, 'Terrorism in the Federal Republic of Germany and Italy: Legacy of the '68 Movement or "Burden of Fascism"?', *Terrorism and Political Violence*, Vol. 1, No. 4 (1989).

Ganor, Boaz, *Defining Terrorism: Is One Man's Terrorist Another Man's Freedom Fighter?* The Interdisciplinary Center, Herzliya, ICT Papers, Vol. 4, August 1998.

Guetzkow, Harold, 'Isolation and Collaboration: A Partial Theory of International Relations', *Journal of Conflict Resolution,* Vol. 17, No. 1 (1973).

Hadar, Leon T., 'The "Green Peril": Creating The Islamic Fundamentalist Threat,' *Policy Analysis*, The Cato Institute, No. 177, 27 August 1992, at <http://www.cato.org/pubs/pas/pa-177es.html>.

——, 'Hamas Divided Against Itself,' *Middle East Intelligence Bulletin*, Vol. 1, No. 6 (June 1999), at <http://www.meib.org/issues/9906.htm#me2>.

Hasan, Jamal, 'Tainted Islam's diabolical expression in Bangladesh: A Case Study,' *News From Bangladesh*, 14 August 2000, at <http://www.secularislam.org/bangladesh/hasan.htm>.

Hashim, Ahmed S., The World According To Usama Bin Laden', *Naval War College Review*, Autumn 2001 at <http://www.nwc.navy.mil/press/Review/2001/Autumn/art1-au1.htm>.

Healey, Brian and Stein, Arthur, 'The Balance of Power in International History: Theory and Reality', *Journal of Conflict Resolution* Vol. 17, No. 1 (1973).

Hendrickson, Ryan C., 'The Clinton Administration's Strikes on Usama Bin Laden: Limits to Power,' in Ralph G. Carter (ed.), *Contemporary Cases in US Foreign Policy* (Washington, D.C.: CQ Press, 2002), pp. 196-216, at <http://www.cqpress.com/context/articles/contemp8.html>.

Hisham H. Ahmed, 'From Religious Salvation to Political Transformation: The Rise of Hamas in Palestinian Society,' *Research Studies*, Palestinian Academic Society for the Study of International Affairs (PASSIA), No. 73 (May 1994), at <http://www.passia.org/publications/research_studies/pub research_no_73.htm>.

Hoffman, Bruce, 'Terrorism Trends And Prospects,' In Ian O. Lesser, Bruce Hoffman, John Arquilla, David F. Ronfeldt, Michele Zanini, Brian Michael Jenkins, *The new Terrorism*, Rand Report MR-989-AF, at <http://www.rand.org/publications/MR/MR989/MR989.chap2.pdf>.

Horchem, H.J., 'Terrorism in Germany: 1985', in Paul Wilkinson and A.M. Stewart (eds.), *Contemporary Research on Terrorism* (Aberdeen: The University Press, 1987).

Iacovou, Christos, *From MNLF to Abu Sayyaf. The Radicalization of Islam in the Philippines*, 11 July 2000, at <http://www.ict.org.il/articles/articledet.cfm?article id=116>.

Ingravalle, Francesco, 'Le edizioni di Ar e l'estrema destra,' in *Risguardo, rassegna periodica di cultura*, IV (1984), Special edition to mark the twentieth anniversary of Ar publications (Brindisi: Edizioni di Ar).

—— , 'Insurgency, Legitimacy and Intervention In Algeria,' *Commentary*, A Canadian Security Intelligence Service publication, No. 65 (January 1996), at <http://www.csis-scrs.gc.ca/eng/comment /com65_e.html>.

Jabber, Fuad, 'The Arab Regimes and the Palestinian Revolution, 1967-71', *Journal of Palestine Studies*, Vol. II, No. 2 (1973).

Janke, Peter, 'Spanish Separatism. ETA's Threat to Basque Democracy,' *Conflict Studies*, No. 123 (1980).

Jenkins, Brian, *Countering al-Qaeda. An Appreciation of the Situation and Suggestions for Strategy*, RAND Publications, at <http://www.rand.org/publications/MR/MR1620/MR1620.pdf>.

Joffe, George, 'Algeria In Crisis,' *Briefing Paper,* No. 48 (June 1998), Middle East Programme, Royal Institute of International Affairs, London.

Karmon, Ely, *Who's Behind the Bombings? The Terrorist Attack on the American Embassies in Africa*, 10 August 1998, at <http://www.ict.org.il/articles/articledet.cfm?Articleid =148>.

—— , 'Terrorism à la Bin Ladin is not a Peace Process Problem,' *Policywatch*, The Washington Institute for Near East Policy, No. 347, October 1998.

—— , 'Why Tehran Starts and Stops Terrorism', *The Middle East Quarterly*, December 1998, Vol. 5, No. 4, pp. 35-44, at <http://www.meforum.org/meq/dec 98/elyk.shtml>.

—— , *Right-Wing Terrorism on the Rise,* 12 August 1999, at <http://www.ict.org. il/articles/articledet.cfm? articleid=87>.

——, 'Trends in Contemporary International Terrorism,' in *Countering Suicide Terrorism – An International Conference* (ICT: Herzliya, 2001), pp. 47-60.

——, *The War on Terrorism: Who is the Enemy and What is the Coalition?* 15 October 2001, at <http://www.ict.org.il/articles/articledet.cfm?articleid=397>.

——, 'Radical Islamic Groups and Anti-Jewish Terrorism', in Dina Porat and Roni Stauber (eds.), *Anti-Semitism and Terror* (The Stephen Roth Institute for the Study of Contemporary Anti-Semitism and Racism, Tel Aviv University, 2003), pp.150-163.

Katzman, Kenneth, 'Al-Qaed'a (Usama bin Laden Network),' in Kenneth Katzman, *Terrorism: Near Eastern Groups and State Sponsors, 2001* (Washington: Library of Congress, Congressional Research Service, September 2001), at <http://www.useu.be/Terrorism/TerrorismRptCRS2001.pdf>, pp. 10-11.

Keddie, Nikki R., 'Islamic Revival as Third Worldism,' in Jean-Pierre Digard (ed.), *Le cuisinier et le philosophe: Hommage à Maxime Rodinson* (Paris: Maisonneuve et Larose, 1982), pp. 275-81.

Kegley, Charles W. (ed.), 'International Terrorism: Characteristics, Causes, Controls' in Charles W. Kegley (ed.), *International Terrorism: Characteristics, Causes, Controls* (New York: St. Martin's Press, 1990).

Khalidi, Rashid, 'The Palestinian Dilemma: PLO policy after Lebanon', *Journal of Palestine Studies,* Vol. 15, No. 1 (57) (1985).

——, 'The Resolutions of the 19th Palestine National Council', *Journal of Palestine Studies*, Vol. 19, No. 2 (74) (1990).

Kramer, Martin, 'The Salience of Islamic Antisemitism,' *IJA Reports*, No. 2 (October 1995).

——, 'Fundamentalist Islam at Large: The Drive for Power', *Middle East Quarterly*, Vol. III, No. 2, June 1996, at <http://www.meforum.org/meq/june96/kramer.shtml>.

Kumar, Sumita, The Role of Islamic Parties in Pakistani Politics, *Strategic Analysis*, Institute for Defense Studies and Analyses (IDSA), New Delhi, India, May 2001, Vol. 25, No. 2, at <http://www.idsa-india.org/an-may-8.01.htm>.

Lewis, Bernard, 'Antisemitism in the Arab and Islamic World', in Yehuda Bauer (ed.), *Present-Day Antisemitism* (Jerusalem: The Vidal Sassoon International Center for the Study of Antisemitism, The Hebrew University of Jerusalem, 1988).

Liska, George, 'Alignments and Realignments', in J. Friedman, C. Bladen and S. Rosen (eds.), *Alliance in International Politics* (Boston: Allyn and Bacon, 1970).

Macintyre, R. Ronald, 'The Palestine Liberation Organization. Tactics, Strategies and Options towards the Geneva Peace Conference', *Journal of Palestine Studies*, Vol. 4, No. 4 (1975).

Mahler, Horst, *Discovery of God instead of Jewish Hatred*, German Lecture Series on the Final Solution of the Jewish Question, at <http://www.regmeister. net/h_mahler.htm>.

Minna, Rosario, 'Il Terrorismo di Destra,' in Donatella della Porta (ed.) *Terrorismi in Italia* (Bologna: Societa Editrice Il Mulino, 1984).

Morgenthau, J. Hans, 'Alliances', in J. Friedman, C. Bladen and S. Rosen (eds.), *Alliances in International Politics* (Boston: Allyn and Bacon, 1970).

Moxon-Browne, R., 'Spain and the ETA', *Conflict Studies*, No. 201 (1988).

Mutti, Claudio, 'Sombart, gli Ebrei e il capitalismo', in *Risguardo, rassegna periodica di cultura*, IV (1984), Special edition to mark the twentieth anniversary of Ar publications (Brindisi: Edizioni di Ar).

Obote-Odora, Alex, 'Defining International Terrorism,' *E Law – Murdoch University Electronic Journal of Law*, Vol. 6, No 1 (1999), at <http://www. murdoch.edu.au/elaw/issues/v6n1/obote-odora61_ notes.html>.

Paz, Reuven, *Islamic Groups: the International Connection*, 3 January 1999, at <http://www.ict.org.il/articles/articledet.cfm?articleid=66>.

——— , *The Heritage of the Sunni Militant Groups. An Islamic Internacionale?* January 4, 2000, at <http://www.ict.org.il/articles/articledet.cfm?articleid=415>.

——— , 'Palestinian Participation in the Islamist Global Network,' *Policywatch*, The Washington Institute for Near East Policy, No. 453, 14 April 2000, at <http:// www.washingtoninstitute.org/watch/Policywatch/policywatch2000/453.htm>.

——— , *Qa`idat al-Jihad. A New Name on the Road to Palestine*, 7 May 2002, at <http://www.ict.org.il/articles/articledet.cfm?articleid=436>.

——, 'Middle East Islamism in the European Arena,' *MERIA Journal*, Vol. 6, No. 3 (September 2002), at <http://meria.idc.ac.il/journal/2002/issue3/jv6n3a6.html>.

——, *Tangled Web: International Networking of the Islamist Struggle* (unpublished manuscript).

——, 'Global Jihad and the Sense of Crisis: Al-Qa`Idah's Other Front,' *Occasional Papers*, The Project for the Research of Islamist Movements (PRISM), Vol. 1 (2003), No. 4 (March 2003).

——, 'Hizballah or Hizb al-Shaytan? Recent Jihadi-Salafi Attacks against the Shiite Group,' *Occasional Papers*, The Project for the Research of Islamist Movements (PRISM), Vol. 2, No. 1 (February 2004), at <http://www.e-prism. org/images/PRISM_no_1_vol_2_-_Hizbullah_or_Hizb_al-Shaytan.pdf>.

Pilat, J. F., 'Research Note: European Terrorism and the Euromissiles,' *Terrorism*, Vol. 7, No 1 (1984), pp. 63-70.

Pluchinsky, Dennis, 'Political Terrorism in Western Europe: Some Themes and Variations', in Yonah Alexander and Kenneth Meyers (eds.), *Terrorism in Europe* (London: Croom Helm, 1982).

——, 'Academic Research on European Terrorist Developments: Pleas from a Government Terrorism Analyst', *Studies in Conflict and Terrorism*, Vol. 15 (1992).

——, 'Western Europe's Red Terrorists: The Fighting Communist Organisations', in Yonah Alexander and Dennis A. Pluchinsky (eds.), *Europe's Red Terrorists: The Fighting Communist Organizations* (London: Frank Cass, 1992).

——, 'An Organizational and Operational Analysis of Germany's Red Army Faction Terrorist Group (1972-1991)', in Yonah Alexander and Dennis Pluchinsky, *European Terrorism. Today and Tomorrow* (Washington: Brassey's, 1992).

Purver, Ron, *Chemical And Biological Terrorism: The Threat According To The Open Literature*, Canadian Security Intelligence Service documents, June 1995, at <http://www.csis-scrs.gc.ca/eng/miscdocs/tabintre.html>.

Rabinovich, Itamar, 'Antisemitism in the Muslim and Arab World', in Yehuda Bauer (ed.), *Present-Day Antisemitism* (Jerusalem: The Vidal Sassoon International Center for the Study of Antisemitism, Hebrew University of Jerusalem, 1988).

Raman, B., 'US Bombing of Terrorist Camps in Afghanistan,' *South Asia Analysis Group Papers*, 3 November 1998, at <http://www.subcontinent.com/sapra/terrorism/tr199811001s.html>.

——— , 'Rocket Attacks In Islamabad,' *South Asia Analysis Group Papers*, 14 November 1999, at <http://www.saag.org/papers/paper90.html>.

——— , 'Pakistani Sponsorship Of Terrorism,' *South Asia Analysis Group Papers*, 25 February 2000, at <http://www.saag.org/papers2/paper106.html>.

Ranstorp, Magnus. 'Terrorism in the Name of Religion,' *Journal of International Affairs*, Summer 1996, no.1, pp.41-62, at <http://www.lander.edu/atannenbaum/Tannenbaum%20courses%20folder/POLS%20364%2)Terrorism%20course%20folder/ranstorpterrorisminthenameofreligion.htm>.

Raphaeli, Nimrod, 'Radical Islamist Profiles (3): Ayman Muhammad Rabi' Al-Zawahiri: The Making of an Arch Terrorist', *MEMRI Inquiry and Analysis Series*, No. 127, 11 March 2003.

Rapoport, David C., 'Fear and Trembling: Terrorism in Three Religious Traditions,' *American Political Science Review*, Vol. 78, No. 3, September 1984.

Rashid, Ahmed, 'The US, Afghanistan, and Osama bin Laden's Al'Qaeda Network,' *National Strategy Forum Review*, Autumn 2001, at <http://www.nationalstrategy.com/nsr/v11n1Autumn01/110102.htm>.

——— , *Confrontations brew among Islamic Militants in Central Asia,' Central Asia – Caucasus Analyst*, 22 November 2000, at <http://www.cacianalyst.org/view_article.php?articleid=113>.

Raufer, Xavier and Haut, François, 'RAF – Une organisation zéro traces', *Notes et Etudes*, No. 5 (1988).

——— and Haut, Francois, 'Le terrorisme noir en Italie', *Terrorisme et Violence Politique*, No. 3, October 1991.

——— , 'The Red Brigades: Farewell to Arms', *Studies in Conflict and Terrorism*, Vol.16 (1993).

Reinares, Fernando, 'The Dynamics of Terrorism during the Transition to Democracy in Spain'' in Paul Wilkinson and A.M. Stewart (eds.), *Contemporary research on Terrorism* (Aberdeen: The University Press, 1987).

Reppert, C. John, 'The Soviets and The PLO: The Convenience of Politics', in Augustus Richard Norton and H. Martin Greenberg (eds.), *The International Relations of the Palestine Liberation Organization* (Southern Illinois University Press, 1989).

―――― , 'Réseau Apple': un groupe maoïste européen au service du FPLP, 1968-88', *Terrorisme et Violence Politique*, No. 5, Mai 1992.

―――― , 'Responsibility For The Terrorist Atrocities In The United States, 11 September 2001 – An Updated Account,' Document of the British Government, 28 November 2003, at <http://www.number-10.gov.uk/output/Page3682.asp>.

Rimanelli, Marco, 'Italian Terrorism and Society, 1940s – 1980s: Roots, Ideologies, Evolution, and International Connections', *Terrorism*, Vol. 12 (1989), pp. 249-96.

Rosenfeld, Jean E., 'The 'Religion' of Usamah bin Ladin: Terror as the Hand of God,' *Political Research Associates*, at <http://www.publiceye.org/frontpage/911/Islam/Rosenfeld2001.htm>.

Roy, Olivier, 'Un fondamentalisme sunnite en panne de projet politique,' *Le Monde diplomatique*, October 1998, at <http://www.monde-diplomatique.fr/1998/10/ROY/11134>.

Rubin, Barry, 'Islamic Radicalism In The Middle East: A Survey and Balance Sheet,' *MERIA Journal*, Vol. 2, No. 1 (May 1998), at <http://www.biu.ac.il/SOC/besa/meria/journal/1998/issue2/jv2n2a3.html>.

Russett, Bruce, 'Components of an Operational Theory of International Alliance Formation', in J. Friedman, C. Bladen and S. Rosen (eds.), *Alliances in International Politics* (Boston: Allyn and Bacon, 1970).

Schanzer, Jonathan, 'Algeria's GSPC and America's War on Terror,' *Policywatch*, The Washington Institute for Near East Policy, No. 666, 2 October 2002, at <http://www.washingtoninstitute.org/watch/Policywatch/policywatch2002/666.htm>.

Schweitzer, Yoram, *Osama bin Ladin and the Egyptian Terrorist Groups*, 25 June 1999, at <http://www.ict.org.il/articles/articledet.cfm?articleid=81>.

―――― , *The Arrest of Abu Zubayda: An important Achievement with More to Come*, 9 April 2002, at <http://www.ict.org.il/articles/articledet.cfm?articleid=433>.

Shay, Shaul and Schweitzer, Yoram, *The Afghan Alumni: Islamic Militants against the Rest of the World*, at <http://www.ict.org.il/articles/articledet.cfm?articleid=140>.

Shultz, George, 'New Realities and New Ways of Thinking', *Foreign Affairs*, No.3. (1985).

Singer, J. David, 'The Level-of-Analysis Problem in International Relations', in Klaus Knorr and Sidney Verba (eds.), *The International System. Theoretical Essays* (Princeton: Princeton University Press, 1967).

Sivan, Emmanuel, 'Why Radical Muslims Aren't Taking Over Governments,' *MERIA Journal*, Vol. 2, No. 2, May 1998, at <http://meria.idc.ac.il/journal/1998/issue2/jv2n2a2.html>.

Steinberg, Matti, 'The Worldview of Habash's `Popular Front`', *The Jerusalem Quarterly*, No. 47, Summer (1988).

Taylor, R. Alan, 'The PLO in Inter-Arab Politics', *Journal of Palestine Studies*, Vol. 11 (42), No.2 (1982).

Terraciano, Carlo, 'Nel fiume della storia', in *Risguardo, rassegna periodica di cultura*, IV (1984), Special edition to mark the twentieth anniversary of Ar publications (Brindisi: Edizioni di Ar).

―――― , 'Adriano Romualdi: anima delle rivoluzione, rivoluzione dell`anima' in *Risguardo, rassegna periodica di cultura*, IV (1984), Special edition to mark the twentieth anniversary of Ar publications (Brindisi: Edizioni di Ar).

―――― , 'The American Phenomenon and The Bin Laden Phenomenon,' (no date), *The Movement for Islamic Reform in Arabia (MIRA)*, at <http://www.miraserve.com/pressrev/ARTICLE1.htm>.

―――― , 'The Reconciliation Initiative of the al-Gama'a al-Islamiyya Organization with the Egyptian Regime' (in Hebrew: Yozmat hapius shel irgun al-Gama'a al-Islamiyya im hamishtar hamitzri), three parts, *MEMRI*, at <http://www.memri.org.il> (no more available in Hebrew).

Train, Brian R., *The Terror War*, 1993, at <http://www.islandnet.com/~citizenx/TWbody.html>.

Turabi, Hassan, 'Islam, Democracy, the State and the West; ' *Middle East Policy*, Vol. 1, No. 3, 1992, pp. 49-61.

Turbiville, Graham J. Jr., 'Bearer of the Sword,' *Military Review*, Command & General Staff College, Fort Leavenworth, Kansas, March-April 2002 English Edition, at <http://www-cgsc.army.mil/milrev/english/MarApr02/turbiville.asp>.

Verba, Sidney, 'Assumptions of Rationality and Non-Rationality in Models of the International System', in Klaus Knorr, and Sidney Verba (eds.), *The International System. Theoretical Essays* (Princeton: Princeton University Press, 1967).

Ventura, Angelo, 'Il problema delle origini del terrorismo di sinistra,' in Donatella della Porta (ed.), *Terrorismi in Italia* (Bologna: Societa Editrice il Mulino).

Volkov, Shulamit, 'Western Antisemitism Today – An Evaluation', in Yehuda Bauer (ed.), *Present-Day Antisemitism* (Jerusalem: The Vidal Sassoon International Center for the Study of Antisemitism, Hebrew University of Jerusalem, 1988).

Webman, Esther, 'The Polarization and Radicalization of Political Islam,' *Middle East Contemporary Survey (MECS), 1998*, The Moshe Dayan Center for Middle Eastern and African Studies, Tel Aviv University, at <http://www.dayan.org/islam98.pdf>.

―――― , 'Political Islam at the Close of the Twentieth Century,' *Middle East Contemporary Survey (MECS) 1999*, The Moshe Dayan Center for Middle Eastern and African Studies, Tel Aviv University, at <http://www.dayan.org/islam 99.pdf>.

―――― , 'The Undiminished Threat of Political Islam,' *Middle East Contemporary Survey (MECS) 2000*, The Moshe Dayan Center for Middle Eastern and African Studies, Tel Aviv University, at <http://www.dayan.org/islam2000.pdf>.

Wessinger, Catherine, 'Bin Laden and Revolutionary Millennialism,' *New Orleans Times-Picayune*, 10 October 2001, at <http://www.mille.org/cmshome/wessladen.html>.

Wievorka, Michel, 'Les maoistes français et l'hypothèse terroriste', *Esprit*, No. 94, Octobre-Novembre 1984.

Wiktorowicz, Quintan, 'The New Global Threat: Transnational Salafis and Jihad,' *Middle East Policy*, Vol. 8, No. 4 (December 2001).

Wilkinson, Paul, 'The Sources of Terrorism: Terrorists' Ideologies and Beliefs', in Charles W. Kegley (ed.), *International Terrorism: Characteristics, Causes, Controls* (New York: St. Martin's Press, 1990).

Winn, F.T. Gregory, 'Terrorism, Alienation, and German Society', in Yonah Alexander and M. John Gleason (eds.), *Behavioral and Quantitative Perspectives on Terrorism* (New York: Pergamon Press, 1981).

Wistrich, Robert, 'Anti-Zionism as an Expression of Antisemitism in Recent Years', in Yehuda Bauer (ed.), *Present-Day Antisemitism* (Jerusalem: The Vidal Sassoon International Center for the Study of Antisemitism, Hebrew University of Jerusalem, 1988).

——, 'Muslim Anti-Semitism: A Clear and Present Danger,' *American Jewish Committee Publications*, AJC, April 2002 at <http://www.ajc.org/InTheMedia/Publications.asp?did=503&pid=1196>.

Yagil, Limor, *Holocaust Denial in France* (Tel Aviv: Tel Aviv University, The Project for the Study of Antisemitism, 1994).

Yaphe, Judith S., 'Islamic Radicalism in the Arabian Peninsula: Growing Risks,' *The Strategic Forum*, No. 67, March 1996.

III.   MEMOIRS OF TERRORIST LEADERS AND MILITANTS

Abu-Iyad, *Lelo Moledet. Sihot 'im Erik Rulo* [Stateless: Conversations with Eric Rouleau] (Jerusalem: Mifras Publications, 1983, in Hebrew).

Baumann, Michael, *Terror or Love? 'Bommi' Baumann's Own Story of His Life as a West German Urban Guerrilla* (New York: Grove Press 1979).

Curcio, Renato, *A viso aperto. Intervista di Mario Scialoja* (4th edn.) (Milano: Oscar Mondadori, 2000).

Franceschini, Alberto and Buffa, Giustolisi, P., F., *Mara, Renato e io. Storia dei fondadori delle Br* (4th edn.) (Milano: Oscar Mondadori, 2000).

Moretti, Mario, *Brigatte Rosse. Una storia italiana. Intervista di Carla Mosca e Rossana Rossanda* (Milano: Edizione Anabasi, 1994).

IV.   MANIFESTOS, DECLARATIONS, DOCUMENTS AND
      PERIODICALS OF TERRORIST ORGANIZATIONS

1.   Germany

A Brief History of the Red Army Faction, Spring 1994, p. 3, at <http://www.etext.
org/Politics/Arm.The.Spirit/Guerrilla/Europe/Red.Army.Faction/history.of.the.raf>.

A Herstory (sic) of The Revolutionary Cells And Rote Zora – Armed Resistance
in West Germany, at <http://www.etext.org/Politics/Arm.The.Spirit/Guerrilla/
Europe/Rote.Zora/mini-herstory.1988>.

'Action against the expansion of the Frankfurt airport route' (August 1983), and
'The Peace Movement' (December 1983) in *Revolutionarer Zorn* (Revolutionary
Anger).

Armed Struggle in Germany (undated), at <http://burn.ucsd.edu/~ats/MH/armed_
groups.html>.

Bewegung Zwei Juni, Der Blues-Gesammelte Texte (1983), 2 vols.

'Brief History and Critique of the RZ and Rote Zora,' September 2000, *the Dia-
Gruppe of Berlin* (translated by Arm The Spirit from Interim, No. 499, at <http://
burn.ucsd.edu/archives/ats-l/2001.03/msg00028.html>.

'Defense et Vietnam' (Beweisantrage zu Vietnam – 4 May 1976), *Texte der RAF*,
pp. 476-83.

'Guérilla, résistance et front anti-impérialiste' (Guerrilla, Resistance and Anti-
Imperialist Front), *Notes et Etudes*, No. 5 (1988), pp. 69-80.

'Le concept de la guerrilla urbaine' (April 1971), *Notes et Etudes*, No. 5 (1988),
pp. 54-67.

'RAF: We must seek what is new', *Konkret*, August 1992, pp. 4-5 (FBIS document JPRS-TOT-92-040-L of 17 November 1992).

*Rote Armee Fraktion, Widerstand heisst angriff!! Enklarungen, redebeitrage,
flugblatter und briefe. 1977-1988* (Amsterdam: Bibliotheek voor ontspanning en
ontwikkeling, 1988).

Statement Concerning The Attack On The Refugee Administration Centre In Boblingen (undated), at <http://www.etext.org/Politics/Arm.The.Spirit/Guerrilla/ Europe/Revolutionary.Cells/rz-bobl>.

Statement of the RAF (the 1998 disbanding of the Rote Army Faction), March 1998, p. 14, at <http://www.baader-meinhof.com/students/resources/communique/ engrafend.html>.

'The Black September Operation in Munich: The strategy of the anti-imperialist struggle' (Die Aktion des Schawrzen September in Munchen – rafzeitung ende 1972), in *Texte der RAF*, pp 411-47.

'The Other Process, Late April 1976' (konzept a./u. zu einem andern prozess, ende april 76.), in *Texte der RAF*, pp. 27-34.

200 Years Is Not Enough: Revolutionary Cells In The Post-Fordist Era, November 1989, at <http://www.etext.org/Politics/Arm.The.Spirit/Guerrilla/Europe/ Revolutionary.Cells/rz-fordism>.

'Urban Guerrilla and Class Warfare' (Rote Armee Fraktion: Stadtguerilla und Klassenkampf – rafzeitung 1972), *texte der RAF*, pp. 368-410).

2.   Italy

CONTROinformazione.

Private collection of the author of documents and strategic decisions of the Red Brigades, Dec. 1973 – Feb. 1986.

Il Bollettino.

'Contro la guerra imperialista, intensificare la guerra rivoluzionaria, sviluppare l'internazionalismo combattente', *CONTROinformazione*, No. 22, February 1982.

'Crisi, guerra e internazionalismo proletaria', *CONTROinformazione*, No. 22, February 1982.

Classe contro classe: Guerra di classe – RDS no. 1, 1970.

La crisi e lo strumento usato dalla reazione per battere la classe operaia – RDS, dic. 1973.

Risoluzione della Direzione Strategica. Aprile '75.

Portare l'attacco allo stato imperialista delle multinazionali. Disarticolare le strutture della controguerriglia attiva. Giugno 1977.
Risoluzione della Direzione Strategica, febbraio 1978, in Bocca, 1978: 49-112.

Diario di lotta delle fabriche genovesi – Ansaldo Italsider. Ottobre 1978.

Campagna di primavera: cattura, processo, esecuzione del Presidente della Democrazia Cristiana Aldo Moro. No. 6-marzo 1979.

Brigatte Rosse: comunicato no. 21. Costruire ovunque il movimento di resistenza offensiva per il comunismo. Torino, 7 dic. 1979.

Brigatte Rosse – Risoluzione no. 8. Alfa-Romeo – Sabotare il progetto della borghesia di stato. Costruire in fabbrica il potere proletario armato. Gennaio 1980.

Contro la ristrutturazione imperialista costruire nuclei di resistenza in ogni posto di lavoro, in ogno quartiere. Maggio 1980. RDS no. 9.

'L'Ape e il comunista. xx tesi finali,' Dec. 1980, *Docom Montrouge*, France.

Sull'organizzazione. RDS no. 2 (documento provisorio), 1981.

Ospedalieri! Attachiamo la Democrazia Cristiana principale responsabile della ristrutturazione nell'ospedale. Febbraio 1981. (Colonna Walter Alasia).

Riprendere l'offensiva dentro gli ospedali, lavorare tutti, lavorare meno, per il diritto proletario alla salute. Marzo 1981. Risoluzione no. 12.

13 tesi sulla sostanza dell'agire da partito in questa congiuntura. RDS no. 15. Giugno 1981.

La campagna di primavera-estate 1981. Il divenire della guerriglia metropolitana nella congiuntura di transizione alla guerra civile antiimperialista di lunga durata. Brigata delle carceri. Colonna di Napoli. Luglio 1981.

Contro la guerra imperialista, intensificare la guerra rivoluzionaria, svillupare l'internazionalismo combattente. Gruppo di elaborazione '16 Marzo', Novembre 1981. CONTROinformazione, no. 22, Febbraio 1982.

Crisi, guerra e internazionalismo proletario. Brigata di Palmi, Dicembre 1981. in CONTROinformazione, no. 22, Febbraio 1982.

Brigate Rosse per la costruzione del Partito Comunista Combattente. RDS no. 20. Marzo 1985.

Unione dei Comunisti Combattenti. Manifesto e tesi di fondazione. Ottobre 1985.

UCC – Autointervista. Febbraio '86.

BR-PCC – Rivendicazione dell'assalto al furgone postale avvenuto a Roma il 14 febbraio 1987.

BR-UCC – rivendicazione dell'uccisione del gen. Licio Giorgeri, avvenuta a Roma il 20 marzo 1987.

BR-PCC. Developpement de la premiere position, septembre 1984. Ligne Rouge, no. 16, octobre 1985, pp. 3-12.

BR-UCC. Developpement de la seconde position, septembre 1984. Ligne Rouge, no. 16, octobre 1985, pp. 13-22.

Israele, il sionismo, gli ebrei.Gruppo Comunista Internazionalista Autonomo. 1984. Milano.

Considerazioni sulla questione palestinese. Gruppo Comunista Internazionalista Autonomo. 1984. Milano.

3.   France

Pour un projet communiste, Action Directe, March 1982.

Short Collective Biography of Action Directe Prisoners by Joëlle Aubron (a jailed AD militant), July 1996 at <http://www.tao.ca/~solidarity/texts/ad/collbio.html>.

Sur l'imperialisme Americain, Action Directe, April 1982.

Palestine vivra, Palestine vaincra! Septembre 1982. Frederic Oriach.

82, du sommet de Versailles au Liban. Octobre 1982. Action Directe.

'Declaration politique de Marina da Silva et Frederic Oriach,' Nov. 1983. *Ligne Rouge*, no. 2/1984.

'Unite des revolutionnaires en Europe de l'Ouest,' *Cahier Front*, No.2, 16 Nov. 1993, pp. 32-61.

'Une tache revolutionnaire, le combat international.' *L'Internationale*, no. 6, Feb. 1984.

'Frederic Oriach – militant anti-sioniste pro-palestinien – Le sens d'un combat,' *Collectif 'Liberation de F. Oriach,'* June 1984.

'Palestine notre combat,' *Collectif 'Liberation de F. Oriach,'* May 1985.

'Frederic Oriach: La lutte armee, necessite strategique et tactique du combat pour la revolution,' *Ligne Rouge*, No. 17, Nov. 1985. pp.11-24.

Lettre de Max Frerot a Andre Olivier.

Lettres de Frederic Oriach, prisonnier politique a la prison de la Sante a 'L'Internationale' (21.6.1984, 4.7.1984, 22.7.1984).

4.   Belgium

Interview With The CCC Prisoners Collective, published by the Anarchist Black Cross in Gent, Belgium, June 1998 at <http://www.etext.org/Politics/Arm.The. Spirit/Guerrilla/Europe/CCC/ccc.prisoners.interview.june-1998>.

5.   Spain

Documentos de ETA (San Sebastian: Editorial Hordago, 1984).

La organisacion revolucionaria y terrorista ETA (Madrid, Ministry of Defence, April 1979).

6.   Islamists

A Declaration on the Position of the Jihad Camp Toward the Suffering of the Muslims in Palestine (Bayan mawqif muaskar al-jihad izaa mu`anat al-muslimin fi filastin), published by the Jihad group of Maluku/Indonesia at <http://www. malukujihad.cjb.net> (no date).

Al-Zawahiri, Ayman, 'Knights Under the Prophet's Banner,' 2 December 2001, parts 1-11 of serialized excerpts from Egyptian al-Jihad organization leader's book translated by FBIS-NES-2002-0108, at <http://www.fas.org/irp/world/para/ ayman_bk.html>.

An Open Letter. The Hizballah Program, at <http://www.ict.org.il/Articles/ Hizletter.htm>.

'Declaration of War Against the Americans Occupying the Land of The Two Holy Places (Expel the Infidels From the Arab Peninsula) A Message From Usama Bin Muhammad Bin in Laden Unto His Muslim Brethren All Over the World Generally and in The Arab Peninsula Specifically,' *Al Quds al-Arabi*, 1 August 1996, at <http://www.defenddemocracy.org/researchtopics/show.htm?doc_id=185673&attrib_id=7580>.

'Fatwah Urging Jihad Against Americans,' *Al-Quds al-Arabi,* 23 February 1998, at <http://www.ict.org.il/articles/fatwah.htm>.

The *Al-Qaeda Manual* at <http://www.usdoj.gov/ag/trainingmanual.htm>.

V.   INTERNET RESOURCES

AD documents, at <http://www.crosswinds.net/~actiondirecte>.

Arm.The.Spirit website, in the framework of The ETEXT Archive, <http://www.etext.org/Politics/Arm.The.Spirit>.

Centro di Documentazione 'Fausto e Jaio', Centro sociale Leoncavallo, at <http://www.ecn.org/leoncavallo/cdoc/br/index.htm>.

CIA Fact Sheet – Osama bin Laden (Unclassified), at <http://www.skfriends.com/bin-laden-cia-fact-sheet.htm>.

Edizioni di Ar, at <http://www.libreriaar.it/catalogoconnote.htm>.

Euskal Herria Journal, at <http://www.contrast.org/mirrors/ehj/index.html>.

Federation of American Scientists (FAS) website, at <http://www.fas.org/irp/world/para/ladin.htm>.

Il Terrorismo, le Stragi e il Contesto Storico-Politico [Relazione Pellegrino], The Italian Parliamentary Commission Report on Terrorism, at <http://www.clarence.com/contents/societa/memoria>.

Journal of Palestine Studies, at <http://www.ipsjps.org/jps/online.htm>.

La Page d'information sur Action Directe, at <http://www.geocities.com/Capitol Hill/Congress/6781/index.html>.

Misteri d'Italia, at <http://www.misteriditalia.it/terrorismo/brigate-rosse/ index. html>, <http://www.misteriditalia.com/lestragi/index.html>, and <http://www. misteriditalia.com/estremadestra/annisettan>.

Moro punto Doc, at <http://www.apolis.com/moro/index1.htm>.

Nadir, at <http://www.nadir.org/nadir/archiv/PolitischeStroemungen>.

Rote Hilfe, Gottingen, at <http://rafinfo.virtualave.net/quellen.shtml>.

Patterns of Global Terrorism (1996-2001), US Department of State, at <http:// www.state.gov/www/global /terrorism/annual_reports.html>.

South Asia Terrorism Portal (SATP), Institute for Conflict Management (ICM), at <http://www.satp.org>.

The archives of the Institute of Criminology, Paris, at <http://www.u-paris2.fr/ mcc/html/archives/ne/index.htm>.

The International Policy Institute for Counter-Terrorism website (ICT), at <http://www.ict.org.il>.

'Trail of a Terrorist,' *Frontline*, PBS, at <http://www.pbs.org/wgbh/pages/ frontline/shows/trail>.

US Air University's Library Publications on Terrorist and Insurgent Organiza-tions, <http://www.au.af.mil/au/au/bibs/tergps/tgitl.htm#per>.

VI.   ITALIAN JURIDICAL DOCUMENTS

Corte d'Assise di Roma. Pres. Sergio Sarichilli, Filiberto Pagano. 13.10.89 (3/83RPG, 995/81 RGI).

Corte d'Assise di Roma. 32/81 R.G. Agostini. Sergio Luigi + 70.

Ministero dell'Interno. Dipartamento della Pubblica Sicurezza. Raporti interna-zionali dei gruppi terroristici italiani di sinistra (undated).

Procura della Reppublica di Venezia – PM Gabriele Ferrari. Requisitoria del 18/7/83 nel p.p. 179/82 contro Alunni Corrado + 122 (BR). Requisitoria finale.

Procura della Repubblica Presso il Tribunale Ordinario di Milano, Fermo di indiziato di delitto, N.13016/99 R.G., Il Giudice Istruttore Stefano Dambruoso.

Sentenza Ordinanza del Giudice Istruttore presso il Tribunale Civile e Penale di Venezia Carlo Mastelloni contro Alunni Corrado + 77, No. 298/81 AGI.

Tribunale di Padova, Uff. Istr. GI Palombarini. Sentenza-Ordinanza n.183/79 AGI del 4/9/81 contro Del Alisa + 138 (Autonomia Operaia).

Tribunale di Roma. Ordinanza di rinvio a giudizio. Il Giudice Istruttore Dott. Ferdinando Imposimato. Ordinanza-Sentenza n.54/80 AGI contro Arreni Renato + 50. Estrato relativo a 'Collegamenti delle BR con l`estero' (16072/79 RGPM).

Tribunale di Roma. Ordinanza di rinvio a giudizio. Il Giudice Istruttore Dr. Rosario Priore. Ordinanza-Sentenza contro Abbondanza Mauro Agnese + 26, No. 59/80.

Tribunale di Roma. Uff. Istr. GI Francesco Amato. Sentenza- Ordinanza n.995/81A GI del 21/7/83 contro Acanforo Mauro + altri (BR, Autonomia Operaia, Potere Operaio).